WITHDRAWN

Life Skills
for Success

Life Skills for Success

Alka Wadkar

Former Faculty Member, Department of Psychology, University of Pune

$SAGE | TEXTS

www.sagepublishing.com

Los Angeles | London | New Delhi | Singapore | Washington DC | Melbourne

First published in 2016 by

⑤SAGE | TEXTS

SAGE Publications India Pvt Ltd
B1/I-1 Mohan Cooperative Industrial Area
Mathura Road, New Delhi 110 044, India
www.sagepub.in

SAGE Publications Inc
2455 Teller Road
Thousand Oaks, California 91320, USA

SAGE Publications Ltd
1 Oliver's Yard, 55 City Road
London EC1Y 1SP, United Kingdom

SAGE Publications Asia-Pacific Pte Ltd
3 Church Street
#10-04 Samsung Hub
Singapore 049483

Published by Vivek Mehra for SAGE Publications India Pvt Ltd, typeset in Stone Serif 9.5/11.5 pts by Zaza Eunice, Hosur, Tamil Nadu and printed at Saurabh Printers Pvt Ltd, Greater Noida.

Library of Congress Cataloging-in-Publication Data

Name: Wadkar, A. J., author.
Title: Life skills for success / Alka Wadkar.
Description: Thousand Oaks, California : SAGE, [2016] | Includes index.
Identifiers: LCCN 2016003209 | ISBN 9789351507314 (pbk. : alk. paper)
Subjects: LCSH: Life skills. | Social skills. | Success.
Classification: LCC HQ2037 .W33 2016 | DDC 646.7–dc23
    LC record available at http://lccn.loc.gov/2016003209

ISBN: 978-93-515-0731-4 (PB)

The SAGE Team: Amit Kumar, Indrani Dutta, Vandana Gupta, Apeksha Sharma and Rajinder Kaur

To the educators in my family:
My father Late Mr R. R. Aphale
My daughter Aditi Samir—a management teacher
My daughter Dr Prachiti—a psychology teacher

Thank you for choosing a SAGE product!
If you have any comment, observation or feedback,
I would like to personally hear from you.
Please write to me at **contactceo@sagepub.in**

Vivek Mehra, Managing Director and CEO, SAGE India.

Bulk Sales

SAGE India offers special discounts
for bulk institutional purchases.

For queries/orders/inspection copy requests
write to **textbooksales@sagepub.in**

Publishing

Would you like to publish a textbook with SAGE?

Please send your proposal to **publishtextbook@sagepub.in**

Get to know more about SAGE

Be invited to SAGE events, get on our mailing list.

Write today to **marketing@sagepub.in**

BRIEF CONTENTS

DETAILED CONTENTS

PREFACE

In recent years, awareness regarding one's role in improving one's life has increased tremendously. As a consequence, psychology is becoming a very popular field of science as its applications to human life are varied and can improve human achievements and happiness to a substantial extent. Students from various disciplines and also adults are attracted to it and want to know how to utilize their potentialities to the fullest with the help of psychological orientation. This book is an attempt to fulfill their expectations. It is equally useful for parents and housewives. After reading this book, the readers may develop an insight into the salient aspects of self—emotional, cognitive, motivational, value orientation of self, communication styles, and relating to others.

Knowledge about positive outcomes of specific ways of thinking, such as assertiveness and positive and proactive thinking, can be gained while reading this book.

The book is a unique presentation of theories, research, and applications of psychology in a lucid language which is intricately carved. The chapters are organized to understand psychological changes within an individual necessary for leading individually satisfying and socially effective life. The book is divided into four parts.

The first part is regarding enhancing self-understanding. Objectively, evaluating and accepting the self is the starting point of all positive changes. Developing and accepting appropriate and realistic self-esteem is a great achievement. Self-management is the best discipline in life. In Chapters 1 and 2, these issues are discussed in depth to motivate the learner to apply that knowledge to self. Experience of stress is unavoidable in human life. The theoretical discussion and impact of stress are discussed in Chapter 3 along with strategies to overcome the same. The importance of values, ethics, manners, and etiquettes is considered with its influence on human life in Chapter 4.

In the second part, mainly cognitive processes are discussed. Thinking, reasoning, and problems in these processes are also highlighted. Problem-solving and decision-making totally depend on such cognitive processes. Accepting limitations of own thinking and problem-solving is a prerequisite for insight regarding these things. Related issues are discussed at length with various examples and cases. The nature of positive and proactive thinking and assertiveness is explained in this part, and tricks to practice the same are given. Equally important is the chapter about communication in which basic theory and applications intermingle.

The third part is devoted to salient emotions, emotional intelligence, and motivation. Understanding the development of emotions, impact of childhood experiences, and significant emotions, such as love, anger, and fear, is essential for understanding the self and others. They are discussed in depth in a gripping manner.

The last portion of the book is regarding adequately relating to others and minimizing difficulties in relationships, such as empathy, friendship, love, barriers to effective communication, conflict resolution and technics like transactional analysis. Finally, tips regarding leadership and team building for increasing social effectiveness are given.

The intention of this book is to help the reader develop the synergy of intra- and inter-individual potentials. It tries to make every reader aware of the fact that environment, attitudes, and behavior can be changed for better. The only person who can change an individual's life is the individual himself or herself. This book will be the impetus for achieving the same.

ABOUT THE AUTHOR

Alka Wadkar had a bright career throughout her educational endeavors. She has completed her Masters and PhD in psychology with various awards and scholarships. She is associated with various institutes for differently abled individuals, and other educational institutes. She is a trustee of a college of education and is known for free counseling of differently abled students and their parents. She has a rich experience regarding teaching, research, and socially relevant work. She has taught psychology in the Department of Psychology, University of Pune, for approximately 30 years. She has been successfully guiding research students for PhD, MPhil, MEd, and MA for last 25 years.

Dr Wadkar is known for her socially relevant publications. She has written thirteen books and received seven state-level awards for thought-provoking research-based books written for the laymen. She has written five textbooks for different universities.

She has published and presented 75 research papers in regional, national, and international contexts. She has completed five research projects and has been writing articles for encyclopedias, government publications, All India Radio, newspapers, weeklies, monthlies, and yearly publications for the last 30 years.

Dr Wadkar has been a regular faculty for various academic institutes and government organizations for conducting workshops, delivering lectures, and conducting train–the-trainers programs at organizations, such as Academic Staff College, Extramural Board, Yashada (training institute for government officers), Police Training Center, etc. She has contributed substantially to government programs, such as Sarva Shiksha Abhiyan, Aanganwadi, and similar other programs for the welfare of women and children. She has been involved in the evaluation work of different universities for postgraduation and dissertations of MPhil and PhD.

Dr Wadkar has been working for the Government of India and the Government of Maharashtra for various examinations for the last 22 years.

ACKNOWLEDGMENTS

First of all, I would like to express my heartfelt gratitude to Mr Amit Kumar for his efforts in getting this book published. His constant support and encouragement will always be remembered. His benevolent personality is an added impetus to this book.

A special thanks to Ms Indrani Dutta for her valuable academic suggestions and outstanding concern for the book. I owe a special debt to Vandana Gupta, the production editor, for her guidance to make this book a success.

Special thanks is due to the reviewers who have provided their valuable suggestions to make the book what it is today, especially Dr Medha Bhattacharyya from Bengal Institute of Technology, Kolkata.

I would like to proudly mention that my daughter Dr Prachiti discussed various issues and gave substantial support, both academic and technical, for making this book sound and application-oriented. She has contributed to my outlook and perceptions.

I am especially indebted to SAGE Publications, for giving me this golden opportunity and for their invaluable support. I am thankful to all the other unknown friends who have contributed to this book directly or indirectly.

Self-awareness

1 Self-esteem

Objectives

After reading this chapter you will be able to:

1. Understand the significance of self-potentials.
2. Know the importance of accepting one's limitations and accept your limitations.
3. Identify various correlates of self-esteem and evaluate your self-esteem.
4. Know the causes of poor self-esteem.
5. Utilize the ways to enhance your self-esteem.

1.1 UNDERSTANDING SELF

A housewife in the United States was interested in drawing and painting. She used to save money and buy canvas and colors. She used to draw for hours and display the pictures in her bedroom. No one was interested in them and her family members neglected them for years. Once a guest entered her bedroom by mistake and was surprised to see the wonderful art. He insisted that an exhibition should be organized and people should get the opportunity to see those pictures. It was done. Within few days the lady became famous and earned thousands of dollars.

A true story like this creates confusion regarding why that person was not aware of her own potentials, and kept her talent hidden?

The whole science of psychology basically depends on the principle of individual differences. As there are individual differences in appearance, height, and weight, there are also individual differences in abilities, aptitudes, interests, values, and so on. Only the individual can understand his or her own experiences, thoughts, real intentions behind any behavior, and real image of self. Same is true regarding interpersonal relations. Why one wants to maintain a particular interaction, why one wants to get rid of a particular person, why was one feeling annoyed, irritated, or happy at a particular point of time and similar other things are known to the person better than anybody else.

If a question is asked regarding an individual's positive traits or good qualities, it is obviously seen that almost everyone takes time to answer this question. On the contrary, if someone asks about limitations and shortcomings, an immediate response is given. Right from the beginning the whole socialization is done in such a way that the individual is aware of only shortcomings of self. Very few individuals really think about their potentialities.

Potentialities are hidden positive characteristics of an individual. It is the possibility that if enough opportunity is given and the environment is conducive, the individual's performance will be excellent. If the person does not give any justice to it nobody in the world is capable of even sensing their existence. Human intelligence is multidimensional and is a unique combination of intellectual abilities for each individual. Hence, some individuals are capable of solving a particular type of problem while others exceed in a different skill. There are two important things regarding self-understanding. First, the individual is the only person who can understand everything about self, and the second is that the only person who can improve one's life is the individual himself or herself. No one else can do it except the individual.

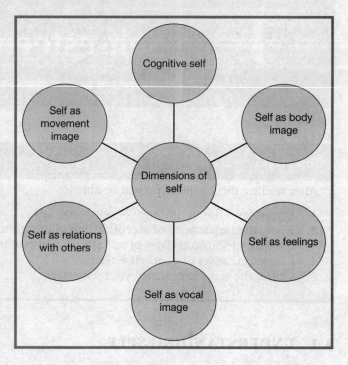

It is necessary to maintain a balance between one's own phenomenological image about oneself and ever-changing environmental dem-ands on the one hand, and flexible and dynamic aspects of human nature on the other. Others are capable of understanding only that much of one's personality which is reveled while interacting with them and the behavior that they can observe. However, one depends on the evaluation done by others when he or she thinks about one's potentials, limitations, and personality pattern. One over-evaluates his or her importance in self-assessment. In such a situation, others' psychological problems are reflected in the individual's understanding about self. Objective evaluation of self should be based on appropriate understanding of every aspect of psychological, cognitive, and behavioral aspects of self. Every individual is motivated toward self-development. There is a need to maintain and enhance whatever one has achieved and all behavior is oriented toward the same. If self-concept of the individual is optimum, he or she will be able to maintain equilibrium or homeostasis in spite of good or bad experiences in daily living. Such a person is capable of understanding own potentials, good qualities, and limitations; takes appropriate decisions; and keeps realistic expectations. Hence, such a person leads a better life—more satisfied and more meaningful. That is why one should try to understand self as objectively as possible. Generally, people think about measurable human qualities, but one should go beyond that and study one's status from every aspect.

Hence, the first most important thing in human life is to understand oneself. Everything depends upon the extent to which any individual understands and accepts self. If not, a lot of psychological energy will be unnecessarily wasted in defending and justifying one's actions and thoughts.

1.1.1 ACCEPTANCE OF REALITY

Sumit always thought sadly about his misfortune that he could not get admission for medicine. Now he is in the second year of BSc in which he is not interested and is getting even more frustrated. He is not a good-looking guy and belongs to a low socioeconomic strata. As a consequence he neither can he enjoy life with his friends and nor is he accepted by good-looking girls as a friend. He always feels sorry for all these things and cannot maintain good self-concept. He thinks that he is not a worthy person and expects that nothing good will happen in his life.

Manav is also facing similar problems. However, he has accepted the facts as they are and is trying to go ahead in the given situation. He is pursuing nursing and getting a lot of knowledge, which is his main interest. He has already started working part-time in a private clinic, and now he is happy and gaining confidence in his field.

A real story of a student is also worth considering. He wanted to go for medicine where he could not get admission. He was getting admission in dentistry but denied that and took admission in Russia to do an MBBS. His economic condition, today, is very poor and his father had to sell their house and agricultural land to collect money. Now they are serving as agricultural laborers. Even after completing two years, there is no possibility of generating more money and he is asking for help and giving appeals in local newspapers to larger public. This is the obvious example of not accepting reality and exploiting others due to this distorted perception.

1.1.2 PROFILE OF SELF

Evaluate yourself objectively on the following dimensions. Indicate position from 1 to 10.

Intellectual life—1   2   3   4   5   6   7   8   9   10
Emotional life
Social life
Family life
Occupational life
Health
General achievements

Such types of exercises are useful to understand whether various dimensions are perceived as being satisfactory by the person concerned.

There are certain things in human life that cannot be changed. No individual can change his or her biological parents, genes, gender, height, and past experiences. Some individuals may not be comfortable with certain things that can never be changed. They think excessively, become upset, and try to modify, hide, or constantly feel awkward about these things. To maintain healthy self-esteem, one has to accept these things as they are. There are some other things that can be changed with great efforts; one can improve one's grades, habits, attitudes, socioeconomic status, and so on. One should be capable of understanding the difference between the two. If the aspects from second category are taken as being from the first category, one may not try to change his or her life at all. Hence, the first thing is to differentiate between what is unchangeable and where should one struggle hard. It requires lot of courage to accept facts and go ahead with whatever is available. Those with positive self-esteem only can do it.

Most of us justify our lack of achievements with the help of unfavorable environment and noncooperation from others. Someone may say that due to my low socioeconomic status I could not go for higher education. The basic question is whether one tries wholeheartedly to change the environment or gives up and forgets about it.

Only those who can change the environment can go ahead, while others may get stagnated.

In a way, it is necessary to change one's self-talk and make it as positive as possible. In this connection, the biography of a very well-known social worker is worth considering. In Maharashtra, Savitribai Phule did some pioneering work about women's education and started a school for girls in Pune approximately more than hundred years ago. People were totally against it and wanted to discourage her. When she used to go to the school, they used to throw cow dung to spoil her clothes. It was every difficult to maintain motivation to continue the noble work. However, she used to be calm and quite while passing through the roads and continued to teach girls. That is why such people are remembered for generations.

1.1.3 UNDERSTANDING ONE'S OWN BEHAVIOR

Ways to understand own behavior

1. Social comparison—Using others to understand oneself

According to Festinger (1954), there is a basic need to evaluate one's opinions and abilities—a need for social comparison. One may get objective evidence to support it; however, sometimes the criteria may be ambiguous. You will be able to compare your height with your friend's height but while comparing your essay with that of your friend's, it is difficult to decide which one is better as there are various views and different dimensions.

The way in which other people generally think, feel, and view the world is social reality. Who is included in an individual's social reality? We generally consider similar individuals who are of the same age, educational background, training related to the comparison, and so on.

2. Knowing our emotions

Similar to social comparison, we also compare our emotional states with others. The way which we label our emotional experiences may depend upon others' emotional experiences and circumstances.

3. Self-perception

Individuals come to know their own attitudes, emotions, and internal states by inferring them from the observations of their own behavior and circumstances in which they occur. When internal cues are weak and ambiguous, the individual is in the same position as the outside observer (Bem, 1972).

Let us take for example case of a college student Anant who is in the third year of his course, and is pursuing commerce. His father criticizes his every activity and is unhappy as Anant could not get admission to engineering on his merit. Though his father could afford to pay, he did not pay capitation fees and asked Anant to join commerce. Since then Anant is very unhappy and thinks that he is good for nothing. He thinks that he will not be able to achieve anything in life. Actually, he is a talented person who sings very well and has won various national competitions of singing and can think of his career in this field. However, he is constantly under the pressure of his father's perception about him who underestimates him in every aspect.

1.1.4 COMPARISON WITH SELF

The principle of individual differences obviously means that no two individuals should be compared. By and large, people are evaluated and compared to others on the basis of some specific achievements, such as, students are compared with reference to grades, housewives are compared with reference to quality of cooking, and so on. However, a particular student who does not get good grades may be a fantastic artist or a cricketer. Comparing any two individuals is unfair. Even siblings have different abilities and aptitudes. Their experiences are also substantially different, their personality, temperament, interest, and every other thing may differ. So, they should not be compared with each other on any grounds. Comparison only leads to dissatisfaction and hostility. Even if a person has achieved a lot, there are always some people ahead and comparison with them may result in a sense of failure. If someone has got an Audi car, he will feel inferior in front of a person who owns a helicopter. The simplest example is that one cannot compare speed of a tiger and that of a penguin. Both have different abilities and capacities. So, if at all one has to compare, two important principles should be followed:

1. Expectations about an individual's achievements must be realistic. The individual's abilities should be taken into consideration and expectations should be based on these facts. For example, if a student having slightly low intellectual power gets 55% of marks, then his or her achievement should be appreciated. On the contrary, 55% marks obtained by a gifted student is actually an underachievement.
2. If at all it is necessary to compare things, then comparison should be done with reference to the prior achievement of the same individual. So, if a student gets even 5% of marks more than the last time, he or she should be happy and others also should encourage and give a positive feedback to him or her. Generally, parents are unnecessarily involved in comparing such achievements with those who get more than 90% of marks.

1.1.5 Johari Window

A very interesting and application-oriented model of self is the Johari window. This particular technic was created by Joseph Luft and Harrington Ingham in 1955. The basic purpose is to enhance self-understanding and understanding relation of an individual with self and others. They have developed different exercises using various adjectives to describe the individual by self and by others.

Self is divided into four sections:

The Johari Window

	Known to self	Not known to self
Known to others	Open	Blind
Not known to others	Hidden	Unknown

The first area, that is, open self, is the awareness area. It consists of the information that one knows about oneself and others also know about the individual. The individual accepts this information and readily shares it with others. As friendship increases this portion increases.

Blind self is the information that others have but the individual does not have. One may not be aware of one's bizarre habits, uncommon dress fashions, and typical verbal and nonverbal communication. Others, however, know these things as they are observing the individual and interpret the things without excessive involvement. If one wants to improve this area of self, one must try to understand how others perceive him or her and what they generally think about his or her behavior. The hidden area marks the information that the individual wants to hide from others. The unpleasant things, shortcomings, or failures and some thoughts that are not socially acceptable are not shared. The last part is unknown self which means that the information in this portion is neither known to the individual nor to others. Unrecognized talents or potentials of the individual, his or her unconscious or semiconscious motives are included in that.

1.2 CONCEPT OF SELF-ESTEEM

The concept of self-esteem is widely used in popular language, psychology, management, and related disciplines. The most frequently cited definition of self-esteem is given by Rosenberg who described it as a favorable or unfavorable attitude toward self. Self-esteem is the judgment that we make about our own worth. It generally rises from the fourth grade, and new dimensions are added in adolescence. Pride and self-confidence are added in adolescence. From childhood, individual differences in self-esteem become increasingly stable and correlated with everyday behavior. Positive self-esteem is related to good adjustment. If the parents are warm and accepting, they expect mature behavior from children, who develop high self-esteem. Excessive parental control is linked to low self-esteem. Indulgent parenting results in unrealistically high self-esteem.

The concept of self-esteem is essentially important from humanistic perspective. Self-esteem is the belief in one's own abilities and being capable of meeting challenges of life and being worthy of leading a happy life.

$$\text{Self-esteem} = \text{self-efficacy} + \text{self-respect}$$

Self-efficacy is the power to produce a positive attitude that affects one's self-esteem; the belief that one can achieve what one wants to. According to a well-known psychologist Bandura, a major source of self-efficacy is the experience of mastery, in which success in one area builds one's confidence to succeed in other areas. If one depends only on others' evaluation of one's abilities, potentialities, and personality, he/she may get a distorted image of self.

Self-respect is a component of self-esteem. Self-respect is the foundation of respect for others. Self-efficacy and self-respect are central themes of definition of self-esteem. Self-concept is the bundle of facts, opinions, beliefs, and perceptions about oneself that are present every moment of every day. Self-esteem affects thinking as well as behavior. It affects perception of the world and one's role and place in it. It affects how others in the world see and treat us. It affects the choices we make—choices about what we will do with our lives and with whom we will be involved. It affects our ability to both give and receive love. In addition, it affects our ability to take action to change things that need to be changed.

Miller has given the basic determinants of identity and self-worth. These are as follows:

1. **The possessions**

The most primitive source of self-worth is related to one's belongings. So, people are interested in accumulating maximum money and commodities to declare their status. It is reported by researchers that in some Western cultures, people have a materialistic perspective. They think that one can compensate for self-doubt and insecurity with a checkbook. Here, the problem is deciding how much money will be sufficient for that, and people may spend their whole life in search of more money.

2. **Educational and professional identity**

Many a time, individuals rely upon their institutional identity for understanding self, as a student of a particular college or university or a doctor working in a particular hospital. Here again, the individual is borrowing ideas from outside to construct his or her self-esteem. If due to some unfair practices that institute loses its credibility, it may directly affect the individual's self-worth.

3. **Internal value system and emotional makeup**

This is the healthiest way to identify oneself with real internal and phenomenological entity. This is a more stable source of maintaining good mental health. People who are in touch with their real identity have a more varied and richer sense of themselves, owing to the importance they attach to their personal lives and activities.

Self-esteem is a value that one places on one's self. Self-esteem is a way in which a person perceives and evaluates himself or herself. A struggle for self-esteem is a major driving force in human life. *A Dictionary of Psychology* (2007) defines it as 'one's attitude toward oneself or one's opinion or evaluation of oneself'. It may be positive, favorable, and high or negative, unfavorable, and low. This is also called as self-evaluation. It is the broader representation of self that includes cognitive and behavioral aspects as well as evaluative and affective ones. It is the importance given to self and related self-regard and self-respect. It is unconditional self-regard. It means that one has to respect and love self as he or she is. It depends on how the person perceives importance given by others to self and realization of his or her own abilities and capacity to shoulder responsibilities.

1.2.1 DIFFERENCES IN SELF-ESTEEM

Cultural differences also affect self-esteem. Asian children have low self-esteem as compared to American children. In the case of India, it becomes obvious that those who are from rural background have lower self-esteem than the urban population. Indian women by and large have low self-esteem as compared to men. Similar differences are seen in cases of caste, creed, and community as well as religion. In short, self-esteem is related to the opportunities one gets, and the positive feedback he or she gets from childhood.

Parents and teachers can have a powerful effect on their teenagers' self-esteem. When they offer encouragement, support, enthusiasm, and commendation for achievements, they enable teens to learn how to take healthy risks, tolerate frustration, and feel proud of their accomplishments.

The distinction between authentic, healthy self-esteem and false, unhealthy self-esteem is also highlighted by many researchers. Authentic self-esteem is not expressed by self-glorification at the expense of others or by the attempt to diminish others so as to elevate oneself. Arrogance, boastfulness, and overestimation of abilities of self are more likely to reflect inadequate self-esteem.

It is assumed that self-esteem is stable across time. Self-esteem is related to personality, behavioral, and cognitive aspects. It is also associated with clinical aspects such as anxiety and depression. The basic idea is that self-esteem is useful as an adaptive and self-protective function. The basic motive for all the acts is to keep oneself in balance with one's self-esteem. If not, then one's self-image is negatively affected. Self-esteem is related to the socioeconomic status, health, and health-related behavior.

Healthy self-esteem depends upon one's ability to assess oneself accurately and still be able to accept oneself and value oneself unconditionally. Self-esteem is basically developed in childhood.

Self-gradually develops out of phenomenological world. Carl Rogers, an influential American psychologist, has also given concepts such as real self and ideal self. If there is any incongruence in the real self (i.e., how the person is in everyday life) and ideal self (i.e., how the person should be), then trouble emerges. To maintain self-esteem the person may need help of distorted perceptions of experiences in a self-serving way. Sometimes people use half-truths to maintain their self-worth and interpret the scenario in a self-oriented style. They select only that part of truth which glorifies their self and neglects the remaining.

1.2.2 Unconditional Positive Regard and a Fully Functioning Person

Self is the central theme of humanistic psychology. One of the pioneering workers, Rogers (1960), was interested in understanding an individual's personal experiences. Many individuals have difficulty in accepting their own positive feelings because of environmental constraints. If unconditional positive regard is not expressed by parents and others, then it leads to poor self-esteem.

In this case, love and affection or praise that the individual gets depends upon the individual's conformity behavior or a particular type of achievement of the individual. This leads to poor self-esteem. Self can be considered as divided into two: the known—that which is thought and the knower—the thinker or I. From the known one can arrive at self-concept, a general term for what one thinks about oneself. Self-concept comprises of various aspects like self-image which is one's perception of what one is. It can be further seen as a combination of:

> **Body image:** One's notion about physical self.
> **Categorical self:** Self labeling with classifying identity terms.
> **Psychological self:** Conception of oneself as thinking being.

Ideal self is what one wants to be.

Unconditional positive regard is accepting, valuing, and being positive toward another person regardless of his or her behavior. If parents express unconditional positive regard, children develop positive self-esteem. One has to realistically acknowledge one's strengths and weaknesses and still accept oneself as a worthy person without reservations and conditions. This is unconditional regard for self.

Rogers has also given the concept of a fully functioning person. It is regarding someone who is open to an experience not very defensive, is aware and sensitive to self and the external world, and has harmonious relation with others. Self-concept is related to the extent to which the person may become a fully functioning individual. Maslow (1954) has given need hierarchy theory to explain human motivation. In this, esteem needs are given as higher order needs and represent an individual's needs to be seen by others and by self as a person of worth. People want to be seen as competent and capable. Hence, self-esteem needs are the needs to achieve, be competent, and gain approval and recognition. A job that is seen as worthwhile by the individual and by others gives an opportunity to maintain self-esteem.

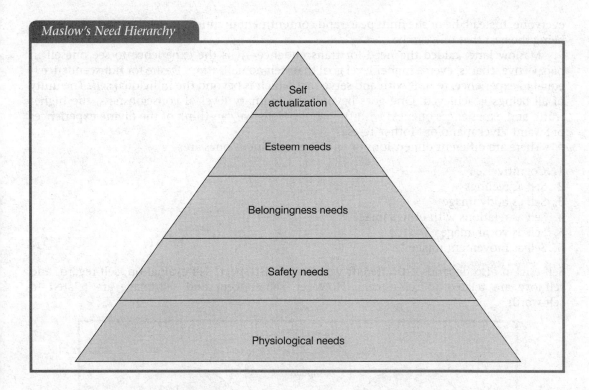

Maslow put forth the view that self-esteem needs must be fulfilled if an individual has to think about higher order needs like that of self-actualization. Self-actualization is described as a motivation to develop one's full potentials as a human being. It is all about being creative, talented, and healthy. According to Maslow those who are near self-actualization show the following characteristics:

1. Self-acceptance and acceptance of others
2. Realistic orientation and democratic values
3. Open to experience vividly, selflessly, with full concentration, and with total absorption
4. Spontaneous, autonomous, and independent
5. Ready to appreciate others with a fresh perspective without any bias
6. Devoted to their goals and trying to be as good as possible in that field
7. Dedicated to some cause outside their field
8. Related to few specially loved ones on a deep emotional plane
9. Capable of resisting conformity and taking independent actions
10. Highly creative
11. Resistant to conformity and capable of transcending the environment rather than just coping with it

It is obvious that those who are striving hard for self-actualization have a strong self-esteem and go even against the society to achieve their goals. Self-actualization is not just excelling in one's work life, but also devoting oneself to higher social goals such as justice and eliminating exploitation. A self-actualized person does not seek fame, glory or love, and approval of everyone. Instead, he or she finds peace and contentment in inner satisfaction that comes with being the best that one can be.

Maslow latter added the need for transcendence—It is the experience to see oneself in perspective, that is, even a higher level goal than self-actualization. Desire for transcendence is equal to experience, to unit with and serve that which is beyond the individual self. The unity of all beings is achieved. One goes beyond the ordinary level of consciousness, the higher truth, and experiences oneness with the whole. Here, we can think of the divine experiences of Swami Vivekanand or Mother Teresa.

There are different dimensions of self. The prominent ones are:

1. Cognitive self
2. Self as feelings
3. Self as body image
4. Self as relations with others image
5. Self as vocal image
6. Self as movement image

Self-esteem also depends on different variables. Self-respect, self-evaluation, self-regard, and self-love are related to self-esteem. However, self-concept and self-image are related to self-worth.

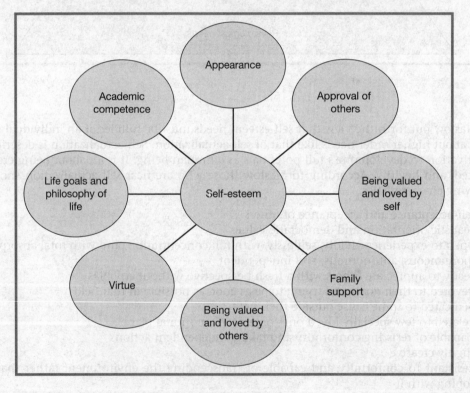

There are various simple exercises to enhance self-understanding. For example, one should rate oneself on various characteristics as shown below.

Careless	−3	−2	−1	0	1	2	3	Careful
Brave	−3	−2	−1	0	1	2	3	Cowardly
Lazy	−3	−2	−1	0	1	2	3	Hard working
Talkative	−3	−2	−1	0	1	2	3	Quite
Affectionate	−3	−2	−1	0	1	2	3	Cold
Thoughtless	−3	−2	−1	0	1	2	3	Thoughtful
Polite	−3	−2	−1	0	1	2	3	Rude
Unsuccessful	−3	−2	−1	0	1	2	3	Successful
Unforgiving	−3	−2	−1	0	1	2	3	Forgiving

If such an evaluation is done twice, once to indicate what one perceives oneself to be and the once to assess what one wants to be, the discrepancy between the two becomes obvious. Once the individual accepts his or her strengths, he will be able to accept the limitations also. It is only after this acceptance that one will be motivated to overcome the limitations. If one does not accept his or her limitations, a lot of defensive reactions may be seen.

If a circle is marked with lines from the center and each line is devoted to one sphere of life, similar understanding can be achieved. Each line should be used to indicate 10 equidistant lines. They will be the indicators of social, spiritual, intellectual, occupational, emotional, and family life, health, and general achievements.

If one has a completely objective view of one's life, achievements, and drawbacks, he or she will be able to mark the position of every dimension of life.

Understanding self includes knowledge of one's personality pattern and its impact on others. For example, in the research done by Eysenck, dimensions of personality are based on two basic dimensions, stability–instability and introversion–extraversion. The sub-dimensions range from anxious to easygoing, and from lively to calm. The detailed understanding of these things leads to clear self-esteem. Improving self-knowledge and self-esteem enhances the quality of life; not only social but also personal.

Coopersmith (1967) gave important characteristics of children and young adults having high, medium, and low self-esteem. High self-esteem individuals have a positive and realistic view of oneself and one's abilities. They are confident, not unduly worried by criticism, and enjoy participating in social activities. They are active, expressive, and academically successful.

People having medium self-esteem are more conformist, less confident of their own worth and more in need of social acceptance.

Low self-esteem individuals are self-conscious, isolated, and reluctant to participate in activities. They constantly underrate themselves and are oversensitive to criticism.

Some recent studies have shown that if self-evaluation of the individuals is low in the area that is important for them, then their general self-esteem is low. If low self-evaluation is in the area which is not so important for the individual, then it does not affect the general self-esteem. One area which is important to children and young adults is appearance.

It was reported in some studies that females have lower self-esteem especially during adolescence; however, it has been proved by some recent studies that the difference between genders is negligible. This remains a controversial question because the impacts of the whole process of socialization, expectations of parents, teachers, and significant adults as well as sex roles in any specific culture are going to affect the self-concepts of both men and women. In almost all cultures these factors have a negative impact on women's self-worth, but a boosting effect on men's self-worth.

1.3   NEGATIVE SELF-ESTEEM

In a drawing competition, Pranoti stood first at the district level. When she was told about it she was surprised and remarked that the examiners must be blind to give her the first prize.

Self-esteem affects behavior of an individual in an organization and other social situations in many important ways. It basically affects the individual's vocational choice.

People who have low self-esteem tend to maintain an external locus of control and believe that their life is almost totally controlled by outside forces and that they bear little personal responsibility for what happens to them. When something goes wrong, they have a tendency to blame the environment, something or someone other than themselves. Even when they succeed, they tend to attribute their success to luck rather than to their own expertise and hard work. They continuously rely on other people to make them feel good about themselves, and therefore, they need an ever-increasing dose of support from others to keep them going. When individuals rely too heavily on validation from external sources, they can lose control over their own lives. They are more likely to participate in self-destructive behaviors. If you do not like yourself, there is no apparent reason to take care of yourself. Therefore, people with low self-esteem are more likely to drink too much, smoke too much, or waste their time unnecessarily.

Negative and low self-esteem is related to:

1. Negative self-talk
2. Self-doubt and being critical of self
3. Being focused on flows, pessimistic, and passive
4. Apologizing and seeking reassurance
5. Fear of failure, no risk-taking
6. Low self-awareness
7. Focus on past
8. Antisocial and loner

Individuals with low self-esteem tend to exhibit poor human-relation skills and may have difficulty developing effective interpersonal skills. Workers with low self-esteem may reduce the efficiency and productivity of a group: They tend to exercise less initiative and hesitate to accept responsibility or make independent decisions, and are less likely to speak up in a group and criticize the group's approach.

Though individual's evaluation regarding oneself fluctuates depending on the ups and downs in daily experiences, there is something more fundamental in self-esteem. In addition, if self-concept is high, ups and downs in daily living make hardly any difference.

There are three faces of low self-esteem:

1. **The impostor:** This individual acts as happy and successful, but is terrified of failure, lives with constant fear that she or he will be found out. This type of person needs constant success to maintain the mask of positive self-esteem which may lead to problems of perfectionism, procrastination, competition, and burn out. Such individuals have self-doubt, inferiority, inadequacy, anxiety, depression, and fear of failure. Their attribution is negative.
2. **The rebel:** This individual acts in a way that the opinions and good will of others do not matter to her or him. She or he shows the 'don't care attitude'. The person lives with constant anger about not feeling 'good enough' and wants to prove that others' criticisms and judgments do not hurt her or him, which may lead to problems such as blaming others excessively, breaking rules, and fighting with authority.

3. **The loser:** This individual acts helpless, is unable to cope with the world, and waits for someone to come to his or her rescue. The individual uses self-pity or indifference as a shield against taking responsibility for changing his or her life. He or she looks constantly at others for love, acceptance, and guidance which can lead to problems such as lack of assertiveness, underachievement, and excessive reliance on others in relationship. No independent decision-making capability is seen him or her.

1.3.1 CONSEQUENCES OF LOW SELF-ESTEEM

Low self-esteem can have detrimental and devastating consequences. These can be listed as follows:

1. Low self-esteem can create anxiety, stress, loneliness, and increased likelihood of depression.
2. It causes problems in relationships.
3. It impairs academic performance and job performance.
4. It can lead to increased vulnerability to drug and alcohol abuse.

These negative consequences reinforce the negative self-image. This results in further deterioration of an individual's self-esteem and increase in self-destructive behavior.

There are many signs of negative self-concept in adolescents. These are:

1. Having no friends or few friends
2. Low academic achievement
3. Devaluation of self and others
4. Rejecting compliments
5. Excessive anger expression
6. Teasing others
7. Being jealous
8. Avoiding new experiences
9. Being arrogant and proud

1.3.2 CAUSES OF LOW SELF-ESTEEM

The causes of low self-esteem are hidden in individual and social interactions that one experiences. Some important aspects are:

1. **Negative self-talk or negative auto-suggestion**

Negative self-talk is regarding one's lack of abilities, knowledge, and confidence regarding various spheres of life. After repeated self-talk of this sort, an individual starts believing that he or she is not capable and, thus, his or her expectations, aspirations, behavior, and every other aspect is molded accordingly.

2. **Environment**

The environment at home and upbringing are the most important factors for developing

Negative self-esteem is associated with
1. Inconsistency and confusion
2. Close mindedness
3. Selfishness
4. External locus of control
5. Jealousy
6. Justifying failure, blaming others
7. Dependence on fate
8. Self-denial and self put down
9. Self-abuse

self-esteem. Parents who have high self-esteem generate good self-confidence and high self-esteem in their children by giving them positive concepts, beliefs, and values. If they themselves have low self–esteem, then they will generate low self-esteem, low self–confidence, and other negative things in children. Poor role models have a detrimental effect on positive self-esteem and self-confidence. Unrealistic and unfair expectations of perfection by parents, teachers, and supervisors are responsible for poor self-esteem. Unnecessary and unfair labeling done by significant adults may hamper the sense of self-worth of any individual. With extreme power of motivation a person can overcome all odds in life; compensate for ill health, handicapping conditions, and environmental pull downs; and achieve fantastic victories.

There are many causes for the lack of self-esteem. Let us review some of them:

Hereditary: This is a main factor for low self-esteem. If the parents are introverts and they never mingle with people for fear of their inability, the chances of children having low esteem are more.

The living conditions: The surrounding in which you live also affects self-esteem. If a child is brought up in a poor environment without giving proper attention to make him or her excel in his or her field or is deprived of doing good activities, it may result in low self-esteem at the adolescent stage.

Lack of proper education: This is another factor affecting the self-esteem. Uneducated children may develop lack of self-esteem as they will face problems in interacting with the educated of their age.

Physiological: Adolescence is a period when major physical changes occur in boys and girls. The sex hormones start functioning in full swing during this period. Many children face problems during this change and are unable to cope with the changes occurring in their body and behavior.

Societal implications: During the adolescent stage of a child, society put many restrictions on their behaviors and attitudes. Girls will be automatically tempted to move away from boys and boys are restricted to mingle with girls during the period. This makes them feel that there are some things to be afraid of. This may automatically lead to fear in a natural interaction.

Fear about future: During the late periods of adolescence, the children may seriously think about their future and in many cases they may get depressed thinking of their future problems. Unemployment, dating problems, insecurity, lack of appropriate financial backgrounds, and many such factors make adolescents afraid of facing the world.

Diseases and other physical ailments: Children may think that they are debris in the world. This thinking process makes them to keep away from others and so they can become agitated.

There are many such reasons for low self-esteem of adolescents. If proper care is not given, low self-esteem may gradually lead to many physical and mental ailments. It is important to bring up the adolescents with high self-esteem.

Those who have low self-esteem have the following characteristics:

1. They are critical in nature, and criticize everyone for something or the other.
2. They are arrogant, and pretend that they know everything. It is difficult to work with them as they want to insult others and want to prove that they are superior.
3. They are close-minded and self-centered.
4. They constantly make excuses and justify their failures.
5. They never accept their responsibility and always blame others.
6. They have fatalistic attitude and always wait for things to happen.

7. They are jealous by nature.
8. They are not willing to accept positive criticism and become defensive.
9. When alone, they feel uncomfortable and bored.
10. Their poor self-esteem leads to the lack of decency.
11. It is difficult for them to get good friends.
12. They give promises they cannot keep.
13. Their behavior is not consistent.
14. Their ego is easily hurt.
15. They are selfish and look down on others.

Actually negative self-esteem is related to self put down, self-doubt, self-abuse, self-denial, self-centeredness, self-deceit, and self-indulgence.

Self-handicapping condition is something like imposing an obstacle to one's successful performance in a particular situation in order to provide an excuse for failure; this is generally seen in individuals with low self-esteem. It is well accepted that women have low self-esteem and they accept the responsibility of failure. They attribute it to their own limitations. If they get success they attribute it to external factors like luck. In India, if a woman gets extraordinary success, then she immediately gives the credit to her teachers, husband, and in-laws. However, a man who gets similar success will, in maximum cases, explain it in terms of his own abilities and efforts.

1.3.3 LOW SELF-ESTEEM CYCLE

Self-talk is intrapersonal communication of an individual. Human mind is active at every moment, especially regarding criticizing and evaluating one's own performance. Whenever the individual faces any new situation or challenge, he or she talks to himself or herself regarding his or her capacities to fulfill the requirements of the task. If the individual has doubts about his or her capabilities he or she will question his or her own future performance.

Negative self-talk can be taken as a starting point, though this cycle keeps on working in such a way that one negative aspect leads to another, and again and again results in the same circular action. Negative self-talk leads to low achievement because the individual has self-doubt and this hidden expectancy of failure results in poor performance. Individuals who have low self-confidence cannot cope with any change in work. This is related to their lack of confidence and not lack of ability. Poor performance results in concentrating on drawbacks and highlighting limitations of self, which in turn are responsible for negative perception of self. As the individual starts underestimating oneself, he or she feels defensive

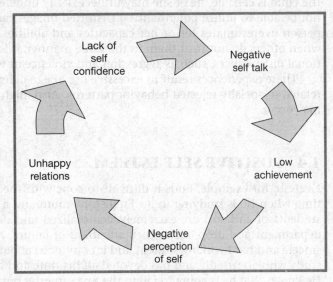

and cannot accept objective criticism by others. This spoils interpersonal relations. All these things taken together are responsible for low self-esteem. Self-esteem influences the way in which stressors affect the individual. People with low self-esteem always need some external experiences to counteract their negative feelings and thoughts. Even when they get success or some positive feedback, their positive feeling is temporary.

If the self-esteem of a person is low, then he or she wants to avoid stressful situations. This vicious circle goes on and on. It is reflected through one's behavior and expressions. Those who have low self-esteem behave in such a way that others also treat them in the same way.

Those who have poor self-esteem treat others as if others are far more superior to them. They assume that their own family, caste, religion, culture, and country are inferior to others. Self-esteem is the basis on which the whole personality depends. One who thinks that he or she is worthless cannot maintain self-respect, and his behavior lacks initiative and spontaneous optimism.

When an individual feels good about self and perceives oneself as a worthy person, his or her motivation and efficiency along with productivity goes up. This also results in better relations with others. Those who have high self-esteem can help others. As they are comfortable with their own selves, they can make others comfortable. However, those who have low self-esteem are not comfortable with self and, hence, cannot make others comfortable too. As they are themselves confused, they cannot help others.

Maslow has stated that everyone has a potential to strive for self-development. Rogers has also put forth the same idea. From that point of view, love and affection given by the parents are extremely important. And if not given, then the child may face problems such as inferiority and low self-esteem. Erikson and others have put forth the view that the development of basic trust that ones' mother is there to support him or her emotionally, essentially, plays an important role in self-development. It is through the interaction with parents that a child learns the socially acceptable behavior along with the development of self-worth.

If the environment is not conducive, then the child may reject himself or herself. Even if the child is capable, he or she may unnecessarily underestimate his or her self. He or she may not be able to utilize potentialities. Distorted images can be of the other sort also, where the person overestimates his or her capacities and abilities. This generates fake confidence, and when others do not treat them in the same manner, it leads to stress and anxiety. Other emotional disturbances, such as aggression and violence or withdrawal, may result from this.

These experiences result in excessive use of ego defense mechanisms. Sometimes, they are related to socially rejected behavior patterns. Also, flight from self and alcohol or drug abuse may occur.

1.4 POSITIVE SELF-ESTEEM

Neetesh, for example, finds it difficult to cope with the academic demands as this is the first time when he is studying in an English-medium and a very well-known university. Usually, students of this sort are extremely demoralized and depressed. They just want to quit the department and drop out as they are afraid of failure. Neetesh, however, knows that he is a sincere and hardworking student and is convinced about his abilities. He, thus, has decided to study wholeheartedly and has devoted all his time and energy for activities related to studies. He knows that he is going to fail in the first semester but has the confidence to make up in the next one. Thus, appropriate self-concept gives a lot of strength to the individual as he or she can objectively evaluate his or her abilities and environmental demands.

Positive self-esteem improves:

1. Personal and professional lives
2. Interpersonal relations
3. Problem-solving
4. Assertiveness
5. Security and honesty
6. Happiness

There is a circular action even in case of positive self-esteem. Positive self-talk and optimism, along with permitting oneself to make mistakes, lead to better achievements. This results in finding new abilities and capabilities of self and positive self-perception. Perceived self-efficacy also increases. In this situation, a person becomes more at ease and free while interacting with others. He or she can accept the objective evaluation of various dimensions of his or her own personality.

1.4.1 POSITIVE SELF-ESTEEM CYCLE

Self-confidence is positively related to high self-esteem. Confident individuals can accept praise freely without feeling awkward. They do not feel the compulsion to return gifts. They neither belittle their selves nor do they talk ill about themselves while talking about the environment.

Positive self-esteem reduces self-doubt, hopelessness, guilt and shame, anxiety, depression, abuse, and being critical about self.

People with positive self-esteem accept others as they are and do not try to correct them. They can express their opinion even if it is different from others and do not feel lonely when alone.

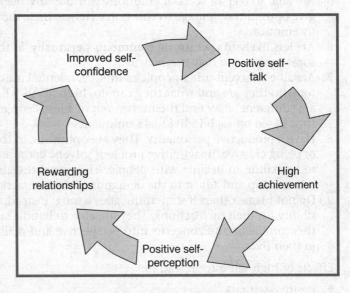

These are people whose self-esteem is high, optimistic, and oriented toward self-development. When the individual has proper self-respect, others also respect him or her. It is proved scientifically that those with high self-esteem also rate others in a positive way, and vice versa. They think that others' perception about them is also high.

There is a well-established relationship between self-esteem and psychological well-being. The presence or absence of negative symptoms, such as anxiety, depression, loneliness, alienation, is related to the self-esteem of the individual. Research has proved a positive relation between self-esteem and health. Self-esteem is also related to self-efficacy, ego strength, hardiness, optimism, and general adjustment. All these things are also proved to be correlated to health.

There is an association between general wellness behavior and self-esteem. Benefits of self-esteem fall in two categories—enhanced initiative and pleasant feelings.

Five types of competences are related to the self-esteem of children:

1. Scholastic competence
2. Behavioral conduct
3. Athletic competence
4. Physical appearance
5. Social acceptance

In adolescence, appearance plays a more important role in self-esteem. Those who give more importance to appearance, and evaluate their appearance as poor, have lower self-esteem.

Researchers have reported that individuals with optimum self-esteem:

1. Tend to maintain an internal locus of control and believe they are largely responsible for what happens to them.
2. Make decisions for their own reasons based on their standards of what is right and wrong.
3. Learn from their mistakes, but are not immobilized by them.
4. Realize that problems are challenges, not obstacles.
5. Are able to feel all sorts of emotions without any negative effect on their behavior. They give optimum weightage to emotions. Hence, their thoughts and behavior are not affected by emotions.
6. Are less likely to take strong comments personally, as they know that these are opinions of some people and may not be true.
7. Are able to accept other people as unique, talented individuals. They learn to accept others for who they are and what they can do. Individuals who cannot tolerate other people who are "different" may find themselves out of a job. People with high self-esteem build mutual trust based on each individual's uniqueness.
8. Have a productive personality. They are optimistic in their approach to life and are capable of being creative, imaginative problem solvers. Because of this, they tend to be leaders and to be skillful in dealing with people. They have the ability to evaluate the dynamics of a relationship and adjust to the demands of the interaction.
9. Do not blame others if something goes wrong; instead, they help others accept the responsibility for their own actions. They are able to handle stress in a productive way by putting their problems and concerns into perspective and maintaining a balance of work and fun in their lives.

Effects of high self-esteem lead to:

1. Positive self-talk
2. Self-confidence
3. Positive perception of self
4. High achievements
5. Good interpersonal relations
6. Feeling competent, secure, valued, empowered, and connected

Individuals with high self-esteem take risks in job selection also. They are attracted to high-status occupations and are likely to choose unconventional or nontraditional jobs. An individual's social and work-related behavior is affected by self-esteem. Employees with low self-esteem are more influenced by others' opinions; however, those with high self-esteem are not. Individuals with low self-esteem set low goals for themselves and are more vulnerable to negative emotional outcomes such as stress, anxiety, and similar other things which lead to poor working conditions. So, it is proved that self-esteem is positively related to achievements and the willingness to put in adequate efforts for the achievement of goals.

It is also reported by researchers that executives who have a clear sense of personal values, goals, and capabilities have lower rate of illness than those who do not have it. They actively interact with new challenges and utilize their inner resources to control the situation. They have unshakable sense of meaningfulness and ability to evaluate the impact of the given situational changes. They experience less stress and depression or negative criticism and enjoy better human relations. Cumulative effects of all these result in improved self-confidence which in turn, again, leads to positive self-talk.

1.4.2 ADVANTAGES OF POSITIVE SELF-WORTH

There are many direct and indirect advantages of high self-esteem.

People with high self-esteem generally have a tendency to increase the credit that they accept for success. This is related to the attribution style of an individual. It is reported that male members have such attribution style where they accept maximum credit of success. Their self-esteem is high. Even if they fail they attribute it to some external factors, not to self.

The advantages of positive self-esteem are obviously seen in every sphere of life.

High self-esteem creates willingness to accept responsibility. It builds optimistic attitudes, leads to better relations and more fulfilling life, and makes the person more sensitive to others' needs. It improves ambitions and motivation, which leads to new challenges and opportunities. People with appropriate self-esteem are assertive. They are more interested in ideas, and have a caring attitude. They are internally driven.

It is also reported by psychologists that high self-esteem is associated with positive thinking and low stress. These people are less vulnerable to drug and alcohol abuse, and can adjust with the environment in a better way.

When the individual feels competent, valued, secured, empowered, and connected to significant others, he or she can achieve better self-esteem.

Self is the central theme of humanistic psychology. One of the pioneering workers, Rogers (1960), was interested in individual's personal experiences. Many individuals have difficulty in accepting their own positive feelings because of environmental constraints.

General experiences of individuals having healthy and poor self-esteem	
Healthy Self-esteem	**Poor Self-esteem**
Being praised	Being harshly criticized
Being listened to	Being yelled at and beaten
Being spoken to respectfully	Being ignored, ridiculed, and teased
Getting attention	Being expected to be perfect all the time
Experiencing success in school and related co-curricular and extra-curricular activities	Experiencing failure in school and related co-curricular and extra-curricular activities

Some crucial past experiences and events which are generally not found in consciousness, become part of one's inner voice. For people with high self-esteem, this inner voice is positive and reassuring. However, for people with low self-esteem, the inner voice is a harsh inner critic, constantly criticizing, punishing, and belittling their own accomplishments.

Comparison between people with high and low self-esteem shows clearly that there are substantial differences and their positions are exactly opposite of each other.

The relation between self-esteem and other self-related issues is also well documented.

Positive Self-esteem	Negative Self-esteem
Self-respect	Self put down
Self-confidence	Self-doubt
Self-worth	Self–abuse
Self-acceptance	Self–denial
Self-love	Self-centeredness
Self-discipline	Self-indulgence
Self-understanding	Distorted self-image
Self-acceptance	Self-defense

It affects not only job performance but response to stressors. When self-esteem is favorable it leads to better performance. One either works up to the level that fits one's self-image or works down the level of self-image. Even in academic achievement, self-esteem is an important factor contributing to success. Same is true in case of organizational success. People with high self-worth always want to go ahead and want to do higher order managerial work. They tend to have confidence in themselves. They know their potentials and capacities and accordingly they can work on as well as overcome their drawbacks.

By and large, it is seen that persons with positive self-esteem talk about ideas, shoulder responsibilities, respect authority, do not blame others, have caring attitude, are sensitive and self-disciplined, can take their own decisions, and are interested in self-development.

1.4.3 DEVELOPING POSITIVE SELF-ESTEEM

Some strategies useful for improving self-esteem are given by psychologists. These include:

1. **Identifying the causes of low self-esteem.** This is critical to improve self-esteem. Is the present low self-esteem a result of lower academic achievement? Is it related to criticism by others? Are poor social relations and poor social adjustment linked with low self-esteem? Answering these questions, one has to recognize which of the areas are responsible for self-esteem problems. These are the areas which need some improvement and attention.
2. **Getting emotional support and social approval.** Emotional support and social approval improve self-esteem. Friends, family members, classmates, or significant people are the actual sources of getting support and approval. If they are warm, sensitive, friendly, and ready to understand and support, then it leads to better self-esteem.
3. **Setting achievable goals.** Achievements enhance self-esteem. Doing well in important areas contributes to the development of self-esteem.
4. **Learning to cope with challenges in life.** Facing problems than avoiding them and developing appropriate strategies to cope with various problems helps to improve the self-esteem of an individual. Coping effectively leads to positive self-image and satisfaction. If one avoids facing the problems, then self-esteem is lowered.

Some more steps to improve self-esteem are:

1. **Rebutting the inner critic**
   Rebutting inner critic can be done by the following methods:

   a. If the inner voice is unfairly harsh, one has to be reassuring. For example, if an individual himself or herself is doubtful about his or her performance even when others praise it, he or she should think about the hard work and improvement as compared to the past achievements.
   b. If the inner voice generalizes unrealistically, generalizing failures may be converted to specific failure in that particular situation. One should think about other success in similar tasks.
   c. Illogical thoughts may result in negative thoughts. One should find out alternative explanations of the same and the possibility that one of them may be true.
   d. Catastrophes should be avoided. If one thinks that he or she is the last person to accomplish a particular thing, and is very unpopular, it will lead to negative effects. One has to be objective and think about some other ways to accomplish a social status, and also accept if he or she thinks that some ways are blocked.

2. **Practicing self-nurturing**
   One should start challenging past negative experiences by nurturing and caring for oneself in ways that show that one is valuable, competent, and deserving. Practicing basic self-care like health care in terms of healthy diet, rest, exercise, and hygiene maintenance helps improving self-esteem. Planning regarding relaxing and having fun is also a must.

   Guided imagery and positive self-talk can help overcome the inner critic that often interferes with personal and professional success.

   Rewarding oneself for accomplishments and forgiving for various mistakes and under-achievement are also useful ways to enhance self-esteem.

3. **Getting help from others**
   As negative past experiences are responsible from low self-esteem, new positive experiences are necessary for modifying it.

   One can ask friends and family members to give feedback about one's positive traits and accomplishments. One can make it a point that there are enough emotional give–and-takes with near and dear ones. Expression of positive emotions helps a lot to regain the confidence that one is wanted and is a valuable person.

   If an individual is suffering from lack of confidence in a particular field, then he or she should try some other activities and accomplish something over there.

Some more steps to improve self-esteem are:

1. Overcome limitations and achieve success according to potentialities in the same field. In India also there are great leaders who were extremely poor and helpless in childhood. With motivation and inner strength, one can achieve success in any area and prove one's metal.
2. Many a time, an individual thinks that conditions cannot be changed and does nothing for their improvement. Like one may think that he or she will not be able to become a successful speaker. However, with efforts and improvement of knowledge one can always do that.

3. Doing something for others which they cannot repay in any way helps to improve self-worth. One can be a volunteer. It builds self-esteem. It gives a sense of gratification. One feels able and that motivates him or her for further work.

4. One should learn to give and receive compliments. Giving sincere compliments and receiving the same graciously and gracefully help in positive interaction and enhance self-worth.

5. Accepting responsibility of one's own decisions and deeds is the most important thing in life. One must stop blaming others for one's problems and become more objective regarding his or her achievements and efforts. As a consequence, the productivity and quality of life improves, which, in turn, improves one's self-esteem. Excuse makes the problem worse and difficult to solve. One is responsible for self, family, work, society, and environment. When an individual accepts more responsibilities, he or she becomes more valuable.

6. One should practice discipline–self-discipline. This enhances not only achievements but enjoyment in life. Even if there are a lot of talents, an individual without self-discipline will not become successful. As a consequence, the person becomes frustrated and this affects his or her business, health, relations with others, and, last but not least, his or her self-esteem. Such persons keep blaming it on luck, others, and environment. They feel helpless. However, self-discipline leads to the proper and critical evaluation of one's conditions and efforts. It is necessary to evaluate whether achievements are on par with potentialities and efforts. This enhances self-esteem.

7. Setting goals gives a direction and a sense of accomplishment when these goals are achieved. Goals give purpose and vision to an individual's life. This gives meaning and fulfillment to human life—a sense of satisfaction and achievement which results in building better self-esteem. Goals should be realistic and achievable. If they are not, then they will cause negative emotions like frustration. Sometimes, parents, teachers, and superiors set very high goals for an individual, and there are many negative consequences—emotional and otherwise—of these for the individual concerned. Realistic goals lead to encouragement, motivation, and high self-esteem.

8. Association with people having high moral character is important; company is associated with one's reputation. Hence, if the company that one keeps is good, then the person will have a high reputation. People with high moral character are involved in positive and socially valued activities. Hence, the person gets a direction as well as motivation and this leads to better self-esteem.

9. Bad company can spoil not only children but also adults. There is every possibility that an individual may get involved in wrong doing and keep the standards low just to keep the peers happy.

10. One has to become internally driven and maintain a strong locus of control. It is of no use if one's self-image depends only on what others say and how others behave. This has been discussed in detail while discussing about proactivity. If an individual's locus of control is external, then his or her happiness, as well as his or her self–image, will depend on others. But when it is internal, the individual will understand his or her self and accept it. Hence, he or she will know what he or she is and what are his or her strengths and weaknesses. One's self-perception, in this case, does not depend on others' reactions and behavior. On the contrary, it depends on his or her self-understanding and maturity. In such a situation, the individual's self-esteem remains high even when he or she is facing states like failure. He knows that still he or she is a worthy human being though others do not think so. Happiness is internal and he or she can get it without depending on others. Happiness is a result of positive self-esteem.

1.4.4 SELF-DEVELOPMENT AND HAPPINESS

As each one is unique, success in case of each one is different. One has to set one's own standards after understanding his or her potentialities and weaknesses. One should compete against oneself. Bitterness is a sign of emotional failure. It paralyzes one's capacity to develop. Emotional maturity is, however, associated with high self-esteem. One may try the following for self-development:

1. Look for the positive in every person and every situation.
2. Resolve to be happy.
3. Set one's own standards judiciously.
4. Develop immunity to negative criticism.
5. Learn to find pleasure in every little thing.
6. Accept ups and downs in life as its natural course.
7. Make the best of every situation.
8. Keep one self constructively occupied.
9. Help those who are less fortunate.
10. Learn to get over things. Do not brood.
11. Forgive self and others. Do not hold guilt and bear grudges.

Giving oneself positive autosuggestions helps a lot. Positive self-talk influences belief system and subconscious mind. As a consequence, it influences one's behavior. It is a self-fulfilling prophecy. When one says to oneself, 'I can do it, I have the power to do it, and I will do it', it affects his or her beliefs, behavior, self-esteem, and possibility to succeed.

Balancing strengths is important; if overexaggeration is done, even strengths may become weaknesses. Any overextended activity becomes a weakness. Hence, any strength should be used with caution.

One's greatest weakness can become one's greatest strength. If one decides to improve and overcome the negative side, then one's weakness may become his or her strength. Extreme anger may take a shape of a socially useful movement.

Having patience creates confidence, decisiveness, and a rational outlook, which in turn leads to success. Constantly devoting time and energy even when one does not get any immediate results is essential for maintaining high motivation and high self-esteem.

Strategies that can be used to improve an adolescent's self-concept include providing praise for accomplishments and efforts, working with the individual to encourage improvement in areas where he or she feels deficient, and refraining from using negative feedback.

It is essential for organizations to create conducive environment to help employees enhance their self-esteem. Many organizations now realize that they need to help build employees' self-esteem and they are doing so by making workers feel valuable, competent, and secure. Organizations should create various opportunities for their employees to develop various potentialities. Employers are empowering their employees to use their creativity and ingenuity to solve problems and make customers happy, which allows workers to develop a sense of personal responsibility.

Psychological success is another measure of performance. It is achieved when the individual's self-concept improves. Self-esteem may increase as one begins to sense personal worth in other ways, for example, through family involvement or through developing competence and confidence in a particular field. Objective career success may become secondary in that case. The achievement of psychological success explains why people who cannot maintain the rate of advancement can be quite happy with their lives.

Self-serving bias is a tendency to perceive oneself favorably. People credit themselves when they succeed but blame others when they fail. This type of attribution style is seen in people whose self-esteem is high. Here, success is attributed to hard work, ability, and good judgment. However, failure is attributed to bad luck, unfair conditions, and impossible odds. An individual explains his or her failure as due to external factors and others' failure as a result of internal factors such as lack of abilities. Here, objective truth does not matter and the person continues to justify his or her views even in case of contrary evidence.

People tend to overrate themselves on nearly any factor that is subjective or socially desirable. They see themselves as better than others. They think that their abilities, leadership, interpersonal skills and everything are superior. Such individuals believe in flattery and neglect any criticism. They overestimate how they will act in a given situation and the extent of accuracy of their judgment. Self-serving bias is strong in people with high self-esteem and low in people with poor self-esteem.

Self-report questionnaires are generally used for evaluation of self-esteem. Statements given are useful for describing oneself. The individual is requested to read each statement carefully and to rate to what extent the statement is applicable to his or her own self. A scale indicating from "strongly agree" to "strongly disagree" is given to the person to indicate the intensity of feeling. Scoring is based on that. Some examples are:

1. I am capable of doing things as well as other people are.
2. I feel I do not have much to be proud of.
3. I sometimes feel that I am useless.
4. On the whole, I am satisfied with myself.

The most popular measures of self-esteem are Rosenberg's self-esteem scale, and Coopersmith's (1967) self-esteem inventory.

Identity crisis has also attracted the attention of researchers as it is detrimental to the development of sound self-esteem. A well-developed identity gives on a sense of one's strengths, weaknesses, and individual uniqueness. A person with a less well-developed identity is not able to define his or her personal strengths and weaknesses, and does not have a well-articulated sense of self.

Being unsure of one's role in life, not knowing the real self, and ambiguity regarding interpersonal relations leads to identity crisis. Erik Erikson coined the term "identity crisis" and believed that it was one of the most important conflicts individuals face during their developmental years.

Erikson described identity as, "A subjective sense as well as an observable quality of personal sameness and continuity, paired with some belief in the sameness and continuity of some shared world image." An identity crisis occurs during the teenage years; it is feelings of identity versus role confusion. Researcher James Marcia (1966, 1976, 1980) argued that identity could be viewed as a structure of beliefs, abilities, and past experiences regarding the self. The less developed this structure is, the more confused individuals seem to be about their own distinctiveness from others and the more they have to rely on external sources to evaluate themselves. Identity is a dynamic structure which involves the adoption of:

1. A sexual orientation
2. A set of values and ideals
3. A vocational direction

To better understand the identity-formation process, Marcia conducted interviews with young people. He asked whether the participants in his study (a) had established a commitment to an occupation and ideology, and (b) had experienced, or were presently experiencing, a decision-making period (adolescent identity crisis). Marcia developed identity framework in terms of four identity statuses.

1. **Foreclosure:** These are people who have made commitments to an occupational future, but have not experienced an identity crisis. They have conformed to the expectations of others such as parents regarding their future. For example, if the parents want their daughter to be a doctor, then she accepts it and never thinks about any other options.
2. **Diffusion:** These young persons are those who have not made any commitment, and there is no identity crisis. It is giving up any attempt to make the commitments needed for developing a clear sense of identity.
3. **Moratorium:** Here, the individual is one who has been actively exploring alternative commitments; however, they are yet to make a decision. Here, an identity crisis takes place.
4. **Achievement:** The individual in this case has experienced an identity crisis and has made commitments necessary for developing a sense of identity.

In western culture as the family system is not very strong and fails to give stable and permanent support to children, adolescents more frequently face identity crisis.

The importance of self-understanding and self-esteem cannot be underestimated for maintaining good mental health. A technique called "self-monitoring" is used to help individuals having psychological problems. It involves recording the aspects of one's own behavior. This is something that nobody else is capable of understanding, for example, something like dysfunctional thoughts or cravings. In this, the individual is asked to keep a record of the negative thoughts that are related to certain issues of his or her life. Self-monitoring itself improves self-understanding.

1.5 SUMMARY

Understanding self is immensely important for the development of personality, good mental health, optimistic, and positive thinking. It also helps in maintaining good interpersonal and intrapersonal relations. The person who understands self, accepts self unconditionally and is comfortable with self, can develop self-confidence and be happy.

One has to be objective about one's good qualities and shortcomings. And thus, instead of being defensive, one will be able to accept oneself as one is and concentrate on overcoming his or her shortcomings. Negative self-esteem is always detrimental to one's performance, happiness, and aspirations. It is necessary for us to find out if our self-esteem is realistic or not. If not, finding out the causes and consequences becomes a must. Even when childhood experiences are responsible for poor self-esteem, it is important to improve one's esteem and image. There are many advantages of realistic self-esteem. Everyone should try to enhance it with the help of various strategies.

QUESTIONS

1. Describe the significance of self-understanding.
2. Discuss the significance and correlates of self-understanding.
3. Explain Johari window and its implications.
4. Elaborate the factors affecting self-esteem.
5. Describe the nature of unconditional positive regard.
6. Discuss the consequences of poor self-esteem.
7. Elucidate the nature of positive self-esteem and its correlates.

APPLICATION ORIENTATION

1. Enumerate various factors that a student should understand about self before taking a decision regarding career choice.
2. Select an unknown person of the same gender. Both of you should write a word to describe each other. Then write another word to describe what the other person must have written for oneself. Then write down three adjectives to predict the other person's qualities and also anticipate what the other person must have written. Now exchange the papers and discuss if there are discrepancies.
3. What do you like the most about your behavior and personality?
4. When do you think your behavior is not congruent with your real intentions?
5. Select a few of your friends and ask them for feedback about you as a person, your strong qualities, and areas where you need to improve yourself.
6. Write down five good qualities of self and five limitations. How many times have the significant adults given a feedback about the same?
7. Discuss an incidence with your friend when you felt extremely inadequate and inferior. What are the causes and how to overcome them?
8. In which sphere of life do you think you have to improve a lot?

SUGGESTED READINGS

Bem, D. J. (1972). Self perception theory. In L. Berkowitz (ed.) *Advances in Experimental Social Psychology* (vol. 6, pp. 1–62). New York: Academic Press. ISBN 978-0-12-015206-3.

Burns, R. B. (1979). *The self-concept in theory, measurement and behavior*. London: Longman.

Coopersmith,S. (1967). *The antecedents of self esteem*. San Francisco W. H Freeman and company.

David Pruitt, M. D. (2000). *Your adolescent emotional, behavioral and cognitive development from early adolescence through the teen years*. New York: Harper Collins.

Feldman, R. S. (2010). *The life span*. New Delhi: Pearson Education.

Festinger, L. (1954). Theory of Social Comparison Processes. *Journal of Human Relations, 7*,117–740.

Hammer, W. D. (2015). *Psychology applied to modern life*, 11th ed. Boston, MA: Cengage Learning.

Hurlock, E. B. (1979). *Developmental psychology*, 4th ed. New Delhi: McGraw-Hill.

Maslow, A. (1954). *Motivation and personality*. New York: Harper. ISBN 0-06-041987-3.

Janasz, S. D., Karen, D., & Schneider, B. (2006). *Interpersonal skills in organizations*, 2nd ed. Boston, MA: McGraw-Hill.

Rogers, C. (1961). *On becoming a person: A therapist's view of psychotherapy*. London: Constable. ISBN 1-84529-057-7.

2 | Motivation

Objectives

After reading this chapter, you will be able to:

1. Define motivation and differentiate between types of motivation.
2. Explain the role of needs and drives in motivation.
3. Describe the importance of incentives in enhancement of motivation.
4. Discuss various theories of motivation.
5. Evaluate implications of research in motivation for teaching and learning processes.

2.1 INTRODUCTION

Mayur met with an accident when he was just 16. Unfortunately, both his legs and left hand were amputated. It was a severe setback in his life and career. However, as he is a motivated person, he patiently went through all sufferings and medical treatment. He continued his education with great efforts. Now Mayur can independently travel with the help of his artificial limbs and manage to do all his daily activities. Today he is teaching in a college and is known as a successful teacher.

This stunning true story is really inspiring. What is the source of Mayur's efforts to overcome the difficulties in his life? What encourages him to struggle so hard?

Hope you know the case of a very well-known scientist Stephen Hawking who is suffering from a completely paralyzing disease called amyotrophic lateral sclerosis and is still doing amazing research. It is a wonderful example of motivation and positive thinking.

There are people who can achieve something substantial in spite of extreme difficulties and odds in their lives. They can be identified as people having very high motivation. The society admires them and helps them to go ahead. A handicapped person who has climbed Himalaya and a very poor student who stood first in board or university examinations are some similar examples. Motivation consists of biological, emotional, social, and cognitive forces that activate and direct behavior.

Motivation has been a very fertile field of research for more than hundred years. Human behavior, aspiration and goals, thinking, and

> Motivation is defined as a driving force or forces responsible for initiation, persistence, direction, and vigor of goal-directed behavior.

feelings cannot be understood without considering the role of motivation in it. Motivation prompts, compels, and energizes an individual to act or behave in a particular way for attending some specific goal.

The word motivation comes from a Latin word meaning to move. Hence, motivation is a study of what helps us move forward with what we do and why we do that. It is the process within that organism which moves it toward some goal. The goal may be to acquire something or to avoid something. Motives are specific forces that energize and direct behavior toward solving a problem or achieving a goal. There are three basic characteristics of motivation: first is the activation or production of behavior, second is persistence or continued efforts and determination regarding the same even in difficult situation, and third is the intensity or greater vigor of responding. Instinct refers to a specific condition that regularly provokes a specific complex response from all the members of a particular species.

We can consider a cycle of deprivation:

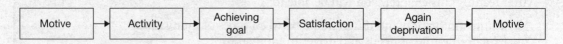

Think of a pet that is hungry, tries to find food, gets it, achieves satisfaction, and is again hungry after some time. This continues and repeats after every few hours.

Motivation affects human learning in four ways:

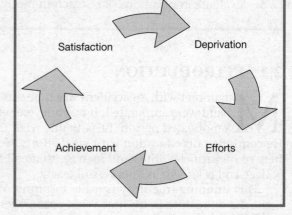

1. It increases the energy and activity levels. It increases the intensity of involvement in a particular activity.
2. It directs the individual to certain goals. It affects the individual's choice and perception that a specific activity is rewarding.
3. It promotes the initiation and persistence of a particular activity even in case of a difficult situation.
4. It affects learning strategies and cognitive processes that the individual uses for that accomplishment. Paying more attention, studying and practicing more, and trying to learn in a more meaningful way are the effects of motivation.

For many decades, the study of motivation was dominated by a focus on biological drives such as hunger and thirst. However, there are many psychological and social factors that are responsible for motivating the individual.

The application of research regarding motivation has enormous scope in socialization of children, teaching and learning, as well as organizational behavior. Reinforcing children by parents and students by teachers for simple achievements is useful for motivating them for better performance. Many theories have been given about motivation, and their application in day-to-day situations for motivating self and others is also well known.

2.2 NATURE AND TYPES

2.2.1 NATURE OF MOTIVATION

Motivation has been a central construct for psychologists, and many theories of learning and development highlight its importance. Learning and motivation both are equally essential for optimum performance. We acquire new skills and knowledge by learning the process. However, without motivation, optimum performance is not possible. In day-to-day life also we can easily notice that better motivated people achieve higher goals. There are four ways in which motivation affects learning and performance:

1. Motivation increases an individual's energy and activity levels. The motivated individual will do that activity intensively and wholeheartedly. On the other hand, if there is no motivation, the work will be done in a haphazard manner and without full concentration.
2. Motivation directs an individual toward certain goals. It affects the choice of the individual and his or her interpretation of whether the results are rewarding.
3. Motivation results in the initiation and persistence of specific activities. The person will begin something on his or her own even in case of difficulties. If that work is stopped because of some problem, the individual will make it a point to start it again as soon as possible.
4. Motivation affects the cognitive processes and learning strategies used by the individual for completing that task. The person will utilize more cognitive efforts for that specific task. If we are interested in a particular subject and have motivation to excel, we pay close attention to the subject matter, make it more meaningful, try to memorize it distinctly, and seek help if there is any problem.

Hamid always wanted to play guitar and aspired to be a known musician in the field form childhood. As his family cannot afford the fees, he works for few hours every day and attends his guitar class late at night.

Success is reported to be a potent motivator. Even a small success motivates individuals for better performance. The teachers, by and large, encourage students' self-motivation.

Aalok is from a very well-to-do family. He attends the best school and coaching classes. Everything that is necessary for studying is made available to him; he is intelligent and has got normal potential to learn. Still his achievement is very poor. He is not interested in studies and does not believe in efforts. Many a time, it is just the lack of motivation that becomes the decisive factor.

2.2.2 TYPES OF MOTIVATION

Motivation is classified in a different way by different researchers such as motivation based on physiological basic needs and that based on sociopsychological needs.

Some examples of such motivations are the need for achievement and the need for affiliation. The need for achievement is a social form of motivation involving a competitive drive to meet the standards of excellence. The need for affiliation is a social form of motivation involving the need to seek and enjoy close and cooperative relationships with others and to adhere and be loyal to a friend. Both these concepts were given long ago by Murray (1938).

Motivation is the drive, energy, or activation required to engage in goal-oriented behaviors. Motivation may be external or internal.

We can take, for example, the pleasure, interest, or enjoyment of playing a musical instrument, painting a picture, or learning for its own sake.

Intrinsic are internally oriented motivations. In this case, the person demonstrates a desire on his or her own to work without any external reward. Here, the student demonstrates the desire to learn on his or her own. There is no need of external inducement, there are no discipline problems. Extrinsic motivation is always there, but if it is in combination of intrinsic motivation, it gives the best results. Intrinsic motivation results in maximum learning and persistence. This is the ideal state. Motivation has to be from within.

Intrinsic motivation is enhanced for activities that are moderately challenging, those that one feels can be worked on well or those that give satisfaction.

2.3   ENHANCING YOUR INTRINSIC MOTIVATION

Think of as many choices as you can, regarding career, leisure time activity, or any other day–to-day issue, and objectively evaluate how you feel about different situations and whether your point of view differs from that of others. This would enhance your autonomy and that, in turn, would increase intrinsic motivation.

If we are relatively free to choose our actions, then it is easier for us to appreciate the reasons for performing them. However, if we are forced to do something, it is more difficult for us to develop and maintain intrinsic motivation.

The other two basic needs of competence and relatedness can also be used as mechanisms for enhancing intrinsic motivation.

In a developing country like India, as the general awareness is less, parents force children and even adolescents to study. Many a time, parents constantly supervise and give suggestions when students are studying. There is no freedom given to children.

Research has proved that it is necessary to avoid rewarding or forcing children to do homework or other desired activities. This may lead to a lack of responsibility. Instead, providing a meaningful rationale for an activity, making it more interesting, empathizing with difficulties, supporting autonomy, and being interested and caring are the keys to raising self-motivated children. It should be remembered that human brain needs some stimulation every now and then. Obviously, knowing something new about studies also has to be pleasurable. Interference of adults is detrimental to the motivation to learn.

The long-term goal of the significant adults and educators as well as that of parents should be to intrinsically motivate the learner. Learning should be self-directed. The learner should be able to initiate and maintain the activity on his or her own.

In the sense, students should enjoy their learning and should be involved in learning. They should learn for getting knowledge, understanding the subject, and relating it to human life. They should not learn only for marks, admissions, and jobs. Research has demonstrated that higher level of intrinsic motivation is related to higher academic achievement.

However, having only external motivation is always better than not having any.

The self-determination theory proposes four different subtypes of extrinsic motivation: external, introjected, identified, and integrated.

1. External motivation occurs when we feel driven by outside forces, performing an activity either to obtain a reward or to avoid punishment. We do something because we have to due to circumstances.
2. Introjected motivation is based on self-control, acting in order to avoid guilt, pressure, and anxiety. We do something because we would feel guilty if we do not.

3. Identified motivation means we do something because we can see why it is important even though we do not enjoy it.
4. Integrated motivation means we do something because we fully subscribe to the values underlying our behavior, which have become a part of ourselves.

On the motivation continuum, identified and integrated motivations are very close to the intrinsic end, which means the more we develop these types of motivation, the less we need to force ourselves to do things. The closer one moves toward identified and intrinsic motivation, the more authentic and fulfilling one's life becomes.

Extrinsic motivation comes from an external source. It may be positive, like a reward such as earning money, getting good grades, making a football team, or negative such as avoiding punishment or the fear of breaking the rules. Competition is generally an extrinsic motivator by desire to win or to beat others.

2.4   FACTORS AFFECTING MOTIVATION

Many factors affect motivation. Some important ones are: anxiety, task difficulty, curiosity and interest, cognitive conflict, and attitude.

1. **Anxiety**

   Some anxiety motivates the students but too much anxiety or complete lack of anxiety leads to deterioration of performance.

   Swarita was extremely upset as she had her examination. She was studying for a month and was completely prepared for the examination academically. However, she was feeling giddy and had trimmers. She could not eat properly and was experiencing uneasiness in stomach. She could not write her paper and left the examination hall without writing anything. This is the best example of test anxiety. In test anxiety, the individual expects failure and loss of status; hence, it has a negative effect on motivation.

   Test anxiety includes:

   1. A test situation that is perceived as difficult, challenging, and threatening.
   2. Students' perception that they are inefficient in handling the task.
   3. Students' focus on undesirable consequences of personal inadequacy.
   4. Strong self-deprecatory preoccupations that interfere with cognitive activity related to the task.
   5. Students' expectation and anticipation of failure and loss of respect by others.

   Test anxiety is seen in children from the age of 7. More than 30 percent students suffer from debilitative test anxiety in school. This leads to academic failure and school dropout. Irrespective of the gender and the socioeconomic status, students suffer from test anxiety if there is a fear of negative self-evaluation, cognitive preoccupation, and less-effective study skills. Correlates of test anxiety are average intelligence, low self-esteem, negative self-talk, more time spent on the task, and irrelevant behavior.

   The relation between anxiety and performance is that of an inverted U.

2. **Task difficulty**

   One important variable affecting motivation is task difficulty. Motivation goes down when task difficulty is very high or very low. If it is medium, motivation is the highest.

3. **Curiosity and interest**

   Curiosity and interest motivate the individuals. They depend on some internal and external factors. It is the conflict regarding what the individual believes to be true and what actually is true. When something unexpected, unpredictable, or novel is seen, individuals are motivated to learn more about it.

4. **Cognitive conflict**

   Learning is motivated by a desire to resolve a cognitive conflict. It is also reported by researchers that a relaxed atmosphere, the freedom to explore, and the acceptance of unusual enhance motivation. Hence, if environment is stimulating, motivation increases.

Along with anxiety, attitude and locus of control also affect motivation. The locus of control is a perception regarding the cause of behavior being external or internal to the individual. Some researchers also have given learned helplessness as related to motivation. Here, the individual feels frustrated and simply gives up after repeated failures. On the other hand, self-efficacy that is an individual's belief in his or her abilities to exert control over his or her life enhances motivation. Attitude toward oneself, toward the task, and toward the teachers may have a direct impact on students' motivation.

For example, Amogh was not interested in economics. However, his teacher of economics Professor Kulkarni taught very well and was a knowledgeable person. He attracted Amogh's attention and gradually motivated him to read more and get good grades in economics. Not only that, Amogh now is seriously thinking of a career in economics.

2.5 NEEDS AND DRIVES

2.5.1 NEEDS

A need is a deprivation that energizes the drive to reduce the deprivation. Needs are general wants or desires. Everyone has to strive for satisfaction of needs if he or she has to improve and prove himself or herself. Basic physiological needs are the need for oxygen, water, and food. These are fundamental needs of survival. Some more biological needs are rest when tired, physiological balance, protection from threats, and sexual satisfaction. Other needs though not essential for survival are important for a sense of well-being. In this, sensory stimulation is most common. Human brain needs some stimulation every now and then. If there is no change in stimulation, we get bored. In a psychological experiment, even if we give monetary rewards to people for being in a condition of sensory deprivation, they are reluctant to do so. The person is supposed to lie down in a tube-like structure without any type of sensory stimulation. Electrodes are fixed to his or her head and instructions are given that he or she is not supposed to sing, count, or think even in mind. If he or she does so, the experimenter can easily understand it through the electrodes. If he or she is capable of being there without any cognitive activity, he or she will receive some monetary reward. It is worth noting that people are not interested in staying in that situation where they can get money by doing nothing. That is because of the sensory deprivation. By this, you must have understood why in vacations we get bored.

There are some other needs of this type which are inherent though they are not physiological. These are general curiosity and the need to find out more about the environment, manipulate it, frame various hypotheses, and test them. You will be able to see those even in young children and in pets. Your dog wants to know more about various places wherever you take it or wants to learn more about your guests. Very young children also want to know more about things lying around and know about their characteristics.

One more need is competence motivation. Every one of us wants to feel competent regarding our everyday routine activities. There are other needs called as sociopsychological needs. These are learned by socialization practices. They are classified into eight categories. The classification is given as follows:

1. **Need for freedom**—It is the urge to remain free and independent.
2. **Need for security**—It includes social, emotional, and economic securities for our well-being.
3. **Need for love and affection**—Everyone irrespective of the age, gender, caste, creed, and community has a strong desire to love and to be loved. Its natural and its intensity as well as expression may differ according to circumstances.
4. **Need to achieve**—We have a strong desire to achieve something or the other depending on our goals and aspirations.
5. **Need for social approval or recognition**—We are motivated to gain recognition, appreciation, and high esteem in eyes of others. Even in the classroom, we want to be the best so that others admire us.
6. **Need for company**—Everybody wants to maintain good relations with fellow beings. We prefer people who are like our own self.
7. **Need for self-assertion**—Self-assertion and the need of power are also very commonly seen in human beings though their intensity and expression may differ according to age, gender and culture.
8. **Need for self-expression and self-actualization**—There is an inherent craving to express our own self and to actualize our own potentials. It gives ultimate satisfaction to the individual.

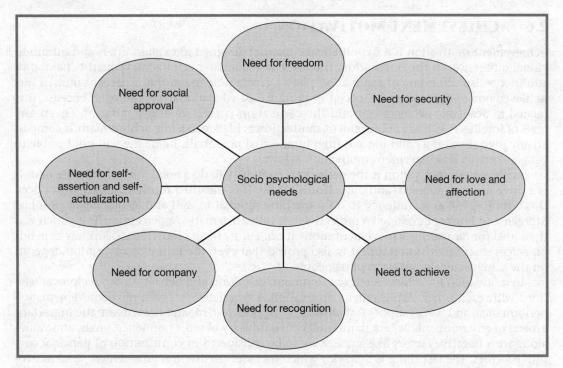

2.5.2 DRIVES

A drive is an internal psychological state that occurs because of a physiological need. A need gives rise to a drive which may be defined as an aroused awareness, a state of heightened tension that increases the general activity level of the individual for getting that particular thing. Activities are directed towards the goal. The strength of a drive depends on the strength of the stimuli generated by related needs.

Psychological needs depend on social learning. These are called as secondary drives. Here, we can consider a cognitive cycle of motivation. The person gets stimulation from outer environment, some memory, or internal stimulation. These things are not related to the physiological conditions of the organism. However, the style of satisfying physiological needs is learned and it becomes a psychological need and motivates us to behave in a particular way. Even when we are feeling full and we still want to eat ice cream is an example of the same. There are extreme individual differences in secondary motivating factors as they are dependent on the socialization of the individual. Some of your friends may be motivated to enjoy life but others may not appreciate the idea of wasting time and prefer studying than anything else.

We keep on working for the whole of our lives to fulfill our secondary drives. Drives are guided by incentives. Awards, rewards, reinforcements, praise, fulfillment of goals, and achievements are incentives. An incentive works as a reinforcing agent as it adds more force to any drive. What will act as an incentive will depend upon age, education, gender, and circumstances. A simple toy or even a chocolate may be useful as an incentive for a young child but may not be equally effective in case of a grown-up person.

2.6 ACHIEVEMENT MOTIVATION

Achievement motivation is a hypothetical construct designed to explain inter- and intraindividual differences in the orientation, intensity, and consistency of achievement behavior. In adulthood also achievement motivation plays a crucial role in various aspects of human life. Achievement motivation is of special importance to educational psychologist because it is related to academic achievement and the correlation is positive and significant. Given any level of intelligence, if the achievement motivation is high, academic achievement is comparatively high. Even if a child has got high intellectual potentials, he or she will not be able to get good grades if achievement motivation is low.

Achievement motivation is the desire to accomplish, to do a good job, or to do the best. It is a drive to excel, succeed, and outperform others. It is a learned motive. Murray introduced this term in 1938 as a tendency to do something difficult as well and as quickly as possible. Morgan and Murray developed a projective test called Thematic Apperception Test which was then used for measuring achievement motivation. Future of any individual definitely depends on achievement motivation, but it is also proved that even the future of any nation depends on the achievement motivation of its people.

In motivation for achievement environment, cognition and behavior have reciprocal relations with each other. Achievement motivation is correlated to academic achievement, job performance, and work output. Task difficulty, support system, and rewards are the important aspects of environment. Beliefs about intellectual capacity of self, confidence, goals, and values along with negative factors like anxiety are to be considered in contribution of personal cognitive factors. The last thing is behavior which includes persistence, engagement, and passive or active goals. All these things interact with each other and decide the degree and nature of motivation. Culture also plays an important role in the expression of achievement motivation. In cultures emphasizing individualism—like American—personal success becomes important. In Asian countries, it is socially, so family becomes more important than personal success.

People with high achievement motivation can take their decisions appropriately and can shoulder more responsibility. Highly motivated individuals select achievable goals and take calculated risks. Individuals work for long hours, delay gratification, and focus on the goals. High achievers attribute their success to their own abilities and efforts and explain failures as being due to external factors. They display original thinking, seek expert advice, and value feedback. They are always interested in positive feedback. It is proved in research that some child-rearing practices are conducive for the development of achievement motivation. Independence training, use of praise, and rewards than punishment for controlling children's behavior are very important in this case. Expectations of parents are equally important. Motivated parents who expect their children to work hard and strive for success will encourage them to do so and praise them for achievement. Parents of children having low achievement motivation expect obedience and good manners. They are aloof or domineering. Willingness to strive for goals depends on children's understanding that they are responsible for their success or failure and their experiences. Mentally creating a picture of success also can help an individual to enhance motivation.

There are gender differences in achievement motivation. Most of the research done indicates that a majority of women have the fear of success. Women are socialized in such a way that they think it is unfeminine to be successful. More women than men attribute failure to a lack of ability. Women easily give up when they are challenged or when there is no encouragement. One more thing is that some tasks are not perceived as having high subjective value by women; hence, they may not be motivated to achieve these.

It is seen that children acquire high need for achievement by observing the behavior of their parents who have high achievement motivation. Researchers have reported that three factors are important in strength of achievement motivation. These are:

1. **Expectation of success**—If a student perceives himself or herself capable of completing a job successfully, he or she will put in extra efforts to do it. The expectation of failure, on the other hand, leads to motive to avoid failure. This results in low motivation.
2. **Positive value of outcome to the person**—The significance of that success for that individual, its relevance to his or her life, and utility in day-to-day life are also related to motivation to pursue the task. Negative value placed on failing leads to poor motivation.
3. **Feeling of personal responsibility for the concerned achievement**—More the individual is involved in the task and the more he or she perceives it as his or her own responsibility, better will be his or her achievement motivation. This is motive to success. Fear of failure or motive to avoid failure is responsible for less achievement-oriented behavior.

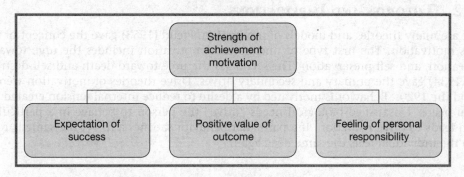

Atkinson and Feather in 1966 gave a theory regarding the determinants of achievement motivation. There are two separate tendencies that are responsible for achievement motivation:

1. Tendency to achieve success, which is determined by:

   a. The motive to success;
   b. Person's estimate of the likelihood to success.

2. The tendency to avoid failure, which is determined by:

   a. The motive to avoid failure;
   b. Person's estimate of likelihood of failure;
   c. Incentive value of failure that is how unpleasant it will be to fail.

The relative strength of both these tendencies depends upon the task difficulty level preferred by the individual. When the first is stronger, intermediate level of difficulty is preferred and likelihood of success is more. Here the pride of accomplishment is high.

If the second tendency is high—that is to avoid failure—people prefer very simple tasks where the probability of failure is low or very difficult tasks where most of the individuals fail. Here, one can blame the difficulty level of the task.

2.6.1 THE RELATION BETWEEN ACHIEVEMENT MOTIVATION AND EMOTIONS

Emotions motivate human beings. Its effect on behavior is well documented. Various emotions have a very specific effect on motivation. Aroused interest regarding a particular phenomenon enhances curiosity and urge to explore. Adults as well as young children and even lower level species show interest in exploring things about some new place or new thing. The individual attends to the object of interest and interacts with the environment wholeheartedly. The achievement of required knowledge is a pleasurable activity.

Different experiences and emotions associated with it motivate the individual to get involved in some activities. Say for example, after going to America for further education a student may feel so lonely that he or she will increase emotional bonds with Indian friends studying in his or her class. In the same way, the fear of social rejection may lead to motivation for conformity, and anger may lead to increased activity.

If an individual is highly motivated but cannot perform that particular activity properly due to restrictions in the organizations, the person will be frustrated and may change his or her behavior, aspirations, and future plans.

2.6.2 THEORIES AND IMPLICATIONS

There are many theories and models of motivation. Freud (1953) gave the concept of unconscious motivation. The first type of unconscious motivation includes the urge toward life, procreation, and self-preservation. The second is the urge toward death and self-destruction. Hull (1934) gave the primary and secondary drives. Drive theories of motivation were given around the 1920s. Behavior is motivated by a desire to reduce internal tension created by biological needs. Unsatisfied biological needs "drive" the person to behave in a particular way which leads to drive reduction. If a particular behavior satisfies a drive, the same is repeated when the individual feels the same need again.

Famous drive theorists Woodworth and Hull believed that drives are triggered by an internal mechanism called as homeostasis.

Physiological drives are related to physiological balance such as temperature regulation, energy maintenance, etc. If any of these mechanisms is disturbed, the organism wants to regain the balanced state. Drive activates the need for balance. The drive is directed to regain homeostasis.

It is comfortable and pleasant to regain the balance. Around the 1940s, goal-related theories of motivation were given which put forth the idea that human beings' behavior is oriented to get reinforcement, rewards, and recognition. Famous learning theorist Tolman has proved it even in case of lower level species like rats. Expectations that a particular behavior will lead to a particular reward or goal motivates the organism's behavior.

Arousal theory is based on the concept that very high and very low arousal or environmental stimulation is unpleasant. When the stimulation is too low the individual gets bored and tries to increase arousal. When it is too high, one is motivated to reduce it. The optimum level depends upon the individual's ability to deal with the situation, and many other environmental determinants. According to Zuckerman the individuals who are sensation seekers have a need for a unique, varied, and complex stimulation from the environment. Sometimes that is risky, but they value novel experiences.

There are many physiological theories explaining motivation. One classical theory of such sort was given by Morgan in 1943 (Watson and Morgan, 1980). It gives the idea of a central motive state. It says that it is the state of nervous activities in the central nervous system that predisposes the organism to react in a certain way to a particular stimulus or group of stimuli and in a different way to other. This state can be aroused by internal stimuli as chemical or hormonal changes in the blood or external stimuli as well. Central motive state may be regulated by the forebrain, the brainstem, and the hypothalamic centers.

Among humanistic theories of motivation, Rogers and Maslow have given basic and widely accepted theories. They have emphasized cognitive and psychological components of human motivation. The perception of the world, thinking about self, beliefs about one's abilities and skills, as well as the perception regarding others becomes important. People are motivated to reach their highest personal potentials. This motivation is generated because of complex and complicated interaction of heredity and environment.

Maslow's need hierarchy and its application occupy the prime position. Hence let us discuss it in detail. There are five basic needs in Maslow's theory. These are:

1. Physiological needs
2. Safety needs
3. Love and belongingness needs
4. Esteem needs
5. Need for self-actualization

1. Physiological needs

Physiological needs such as hunger, thirst, and sleep are very dominant and motivate an individual. Unless these are satisfied, the remaining motivators cannot be of any significance. Individuals who are coming from very poor families and who do not eat properly cannot concentrate on their lessons in school or workplace. They become non-interacting and their interest level also goes down. Their cognitive and other potentials cannot be utilized in this situation.

2. **Safety needs**

   This is the need of security, protection, stability, as well as freedom from fear and anxiety. It also includes the need for structure and limits. Students who are afraid of their own parents, teachers, peers, or anyone else in school generally lag behind in studies. Others also may suffer equally if their safety needs are not satisfied. They are not comfortable.

3. **Love and belongingness needs**

   Love and sense of belongingness are essential for good mental health. This is a need to avoid loneliness and isolation. Parental acceptance and love, and sense of belongingness experienced in family as well as in peer group result in happy and healthy personality. If these needs are not satisfied, poor relations with others may lead to poor motivation, poor self-concept, and poor academic and other achievements.

4. **Esteem needs**

   This includes others' reaction to the individual and his or her opinion about himself or herself. We want favorable evaluation by others which should be based on appropriate achievements. Our sense of self-worth and that of competence depend on these two things. Parents and teachers should always remember that the reinforcement they give is essential for satisfying esteem needs of children. Hence, appropriate praise should be used while interacting with parents.

5. **Need for self-actualization**

   According to Maslow, it is the tendency to feel restless if we are not being all that we can be. We have to utilize all our potentialities to the fullest extent to feel the satisfaction of being competent and fulfilled. Many a time, it is observed that we do not think about our potentials and cannot identify our own good qualities and aptitudes. We are generally taught to evaluate ourselves only with reference to others and with reference to the tasks that we are doing. However, we must find out our potentials and develop them to get a sense of self-actualization. It is worth noting that very few people can reach this level. According to Maslow only 1 percent people can really achieve self-actualization. However, we can experience and enjoy moments of satisfaction by utilizing our own abilities for achieving something that is socially creditable.

Maslow was interested in people who use their potential to the fullest extent or who do their best they are capable of doing. It is the most important intrinsic motivation. The goal of life is growing and developing to the fullest extent. Such people are more devoted to their work. They are more self-disciplined and for them work is exciting and pleasurable. They are more interested in the welfare of others that means they are interested in not only their family members but the whole mankind. They are autonomous, independent, and true to themselves in face of rejection and unpopularity. They take their own decisions. Maslow's theory gives us a generalized understanding of human motivation. Unless and until the lower order needs are satisfied, we cannot think of fulfilling the higher order needs. The teachers must take into consideration various facts of students' lives and then try to motivate them for better achievements. Maslow's theory is applied in different ways to people coming from different socioeconomic status. Those who are coming from low socioeconomic status have to devote more time for fulfilling their basic needs, but those who are from a high socioeconomic class need not worry about fulfilling their basic needs. Their concern may start from a higher level. Those who are from the middle level may devote less time for both the ends, that is, for basic physiological needs and very high needs of self-actualization. For them, social needs become most important.

Recently, some theorists have proposed a new perspective and argued that higher needs are not fundamental. They are pursued in service of esteem needs that people seek beauty, knowledge, and self-actualization to impress others. Needs related to reproductive fitness are proposed to have the upper level. The top three needs are: the need to find a mate, need to retain the mate, and the need to successfully parent offspring. This is, however, a controversial issue.

Some other researchers also have given various theories about motivation. Bruner has given the idea of discovery learning for stimulating students' motivation. In this type of learning, an individual student behaves according to his or her own perception of the environment so that he or she sees a meaning in knowledge, skills, and attitudes as he or she himself or herself discovers all that. Weiner (1990) has given the importance of attributional style. Attribution theory depends basically on three assumptions. These are:

1. Individuals wants to know the cause of his/her own and others' important behavior.
2. These causes are not randomly assigned to behavior.
3. The causes assigned affect the subsequent behavior.

Weiner (1990) stated that there is a relationship between the type of attribution, stability of attribution, its resistance to extinction and the expectancy of future goal attainment. There are cognitive and emotional reactions to it.

If Vishal fails in maths and says, "I failed because I did not try hard." This leads to a feeling of shame and guilt. If Karan also fails and says, "I failed because I do not have enough intelligence." This leads to a feeling of low self-esteem, lack of self-worth, and hopelessness. Knowing how students explain their behavior and what is their attributional style is necessary for maintaining their motivation. Students attributing their behavior to their ability, effort, task difficulty, or luck can help teachers to improve students' self-concept by realistically examining their abilities with reference to the task and, thus, helping in motivation and achievement. Skinner (1971) believed that the proper use of reinforcement or reward can improve motivation and performance.

Bandura (1977) has given the idea that the observation of model behavior and self-knowledge are the important motivating forces. It is related to imitation. The implications of these theories are very important for teachers. The research that is done about interest, curiosity, and other related factors suggest the following things: 1. What exactly is to be accomplished should be communicated clearly to the students. 2. What are the objectives and how they are to be achieved should be explained. 3. By posing questions related to the topic, the teacher can intellectually tease students to exploring new ideas. 4. Stimulating a cognitive conflict causing some apparent confusion, and simultaneously providing cues for a solution is better for motivation. 5. Opportunity should be given to students to select the topics that they are curious about and freedom along with direction to explore for themselves. 6. Teachers and other significant adults can demonstrate the model resourceful behavior so that the students can also use similar strategies to solve their problems. 7. Participating in meaningful projects with connections to the world outside classroom motivates students. Ambiguity regarding the exact goals as well as expressing negative expectations are proved to be detrimental to motivation. Threat regarding the consequences of failure and the loss of self-concept should be avoided. If no feedback or reinforcement is given, it is difficult to maintain motivation to continue the activity. The student gets frustrated in that case. If tests are taken regarding the concepts not taught or if the lesson is too difficult students may get demotivated. It is also proved that social approval contributes to motivation. Verbal praise is useful to motivate the students in the classroom.

2.6.3 THE MEASURES OF ACHIEVEMENT MOTIVATION

Researchers have given various ways to measure achievement motivation. Three of them commonly used are:

1. **Self-report inventories**—Here the person gives responses to some questions or statements. There are limitations of such type of measurement like for creating good impression the individual may give fake responses. However, if properly constructed and adequately administered, these may give valid results. They save time and energy as group assessment is possible and are easy to score.
2. **Projective techniques**—Here ambiguous stimuli are given. The individual is asked to complete statements or write stories about pictures or some such thing where he or she is to provide some details from his or her own stock of ideas. This technique requires a lot of training.
3. **Actual behavior**—Here the evaluation of an individual's behavior is taken as a basis of measuring motivation. It is very reliable but consumes time for individual assessment.

We are capable of understanding our motivation and can try to improve the same by using positive self-talk and added efforts. We can give positive feedback to ourselves even for small achievements. We should be kind enough to forgive our mistakes and give ourselves some margin to err.

2.7 SUMMARY

Motivation plays a very vital role in deciding the behavior of all living beings. Our behavior depends on what exactly we want to achieve and how motivated we are to achieve that. Along with physiological drives, we are motivated by psychological and social aspirations. All great people struggle hard to achieve something which any ordinary person may not be able to achieve.

Theories of motivation like that of Maslow have given basic facts of motivation. The hierarchy of motivation is such that unless and until the lower level needs are satisfied, the higher order needs are of no use to activate human behavior. The applications of motivation are everywhere in human and animal lives. Its applications are equally important at home, in school, in industry, in other organizations, and even in social life.

If students are motivated to learn new things, their future will be much better than others. Motivation is so important in human life that a lack of motivation can be considered as detrimental to all aspects of life. Those who are motivated to achieve self-actualization are contributing to civilization. If we are not motivated to use our hidden talents, it will be wasted completely.

QUESTIONS

1. Define motivation. What are the types of motivation?
2. What is conducive environment for motivating the students?
3. Discuss Maslow's theory of motivation.
4. Explain the importance of the concept of self-actualization in human life.
5. Discuss the determinants of motivation.
6. What are the strategies to motivate students in classroom environment?

APPLICATION ORIENTATION

1. Collect information of two such individuals who have achieved some extraordinary credits in spite of handicapping conditions or chronic disease from newspapers or web, and compare their lives with that of others leading normal lives.
2. Identify whether the persons are intrinsically motivated or extrinsically motivated.

   a. Shobhana works very hard as she wants to go abroad for further education.
   b. Vijay works very hard to help the needy persons to make their lives better.
   c. Mother becomes happy when she can take care of her young ones.

3. Write down what would you like to achieve during:

   a. This week
   b. This month
   c. This year
   d. Next five years

SUGGESTED READINGS

Atkinson, J. W. and Feather, N. T. (eds). (1966). *A theory of achievement motivation*. New York: Wiley.

Bandura, A. (1977). *Social learning theory*. Englewood Cliffs, NJ: Prentice Hall.

Bruner, J. (1966). *Studies in cognitive growth*. New York: Wiley.

Feldman, R. S. (2011). *Understanding psychology*, 10th ed. New York, NY: McGraw Hill.

Freud, S. (1953). *An outline of psychoanalysis*. London: Hogarth Press.

Halonen, J. S. & Santrock J. W. (1999). *Psychology context and application*. New York: McGraw-Hill.

Hull, C. L. (1934). The concept of habit-family hierarchy and maze learning. *Psychological Review, 41*, 33–52, 134–152.

Maslow, A. H. (1970). *Motivation and personality*, 2nd ed. New York: Harper and Row.

Maslow, A. (1987). *Motivation and personality*. New York: Harper and Row.

Mcentarffer, R. & Weseley, A. J. (2012). *Barron's AP psychology*, 6th ed. First E book. http://www.Amezon.com/Barron'sAPPsychology-6th edition/dp/143800270X.

Murry, H. A. (1938). *Explorations in personality*. New York: Oxford University press.

Skinner, B. F. (1971). *Beyond freedom and dignity*. New York: Vintage books.

Rogers, C. (1951). *Client Centered Therapy: Its current practice, implications and theory*. London: Constable.

Watson, J. B. and Morgan, J. J. B. (1980). The original drive theory of motivation. *Bulletin of Psychonomic Society, 16*(4), 314–316.

Weiner, B. (1990). On perceiving the other as responsible. In R. Dienstbier (Ed.), *Nebraska symposium on motivation*. Perspective on motivation. Lincoln, NE: University of Nebraska Press.

3 | Creativity

After reading this chapter you will be able to:

1. Discuss the nature of creativity.
2. Explain various factors affecting creativity.
3. Know the stages of creativity.
4. Enumerate personality traits of a creative person.
5. Describe the ways of enhancing creativity.
6. Use the information for enhancing your own creativity.

3.1 INTRODUCTION

Right from the childhood Gregor Mendel was interested in cultivating different types of plants. As he grew older, in spite of different odds, he continuously did some experiments and cultivated thousands of pea plants for many years. He tried to manipulate various characteristics of plants and derived laws of inheritance. He was the one who gave the basic laws of genetics more than 150 years ago in 1860.

How could Mendel generate number of new ideas and genetic combinations? What compelled Mendel to continuously struggle hard for preparing various hybrid plants and give many beneficial products to mankind? When the environment was not conducive, what resulted in his ultimate involvement and tremendous efforts? Creativity is the most significant answer.

As we will discuss the nature and characteristics of creativity, and the personality of a creative person, you will be able to understand it better. Let us also get an insight into various strategies to enhance creativity.

Human life without creativity would be impossible even to imagine. There would have been no improvement in the life style, the daily routine, knowledge and understanding as well as the treatment for various diseases. Life would have been the same as it was billions of years ago. In a way, it can be said that the existence and welfare of mankind depends on its creativity. Whole civilization changes only on the basis of creativity. New solutions to old problems, improving the currently available products, processes, and ideas, result in the progress of mankind. Through ages and generations man is struggling hard to make human life more and more comfortable only with the help of creativity.

Creativity is the most important and highest cognitive process. The advancement of science and technology and medicine are well-known examples of creativity. We use mobile phones, televisions, DVDs, computers, laptops, and palmtops which are basically products of human creativity. Every day new models are made available, and improvement is a continuous process. The great inventions in the field of medicine like that of insulin are capable of saving billions of lives.

Creativity is something that is original and practical. That is why it is rare. It is to find out alternatives to solution to various problems, words, procedures, things, materials, energy, organizations, and so on. Creativity is creating something new totally or partially. It may take any form. It can be a poem, a painting, investigation regarding some commodity, or a new social work like coming up with an institute for AIDS patients. So, we can label many people as being creative. Some examples are Mahatma Gandhi, Mother Teresa, Homi Bhabha, Shakespeare, Leonardo da Vinci, as well as Baba Amte.

Creative problem-solving increases production, problem-solving capacity, satisfaction, and self-worth of the individual.

Creativity is the highest cognitive process.
The existence of mankind depends on its creativity.
Creativity is original and practical.

Creativity is finding alternatives to:

Words
Procedures
Things
Materials
Energy
Organizations

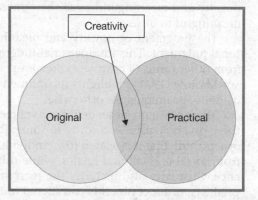

Creative problem-solving increases:
Productivity
Satisfaction
The problem-solving capacity
Self-worth

3.2 NATURE AND DEFINITIONS OF CREATIVITY

Creativity is very difficult to define. It includes work of Madam Marie Curie, Einstein, and that of Kishor Kumar and A. R. Rehman. Creativity is some creation that is original and useful in day-to-day life situations. Some definitions of creativity are given as follows.

Papila and Olds (1987) have given the definition as: "Creativity is the ability to see things in a new and unusual light, to see problems that no one else may even realize exist and then to come up with new unusual and effective solution."

Four basic criteria to be used for creativity as per Newell, Shaw, and Simon (1963) are that it:

1. Is novel and useful.
2. Is different from old accepted ideas.
3. Requires intense motivation and persistence.
4. Organizes the ambiguous and unclear situation in a coherent, clear, and new way.

Some other researchers have defined creativity in terms of a process.

A creative process is one by which something new is produced—an idea or an object including a new form or arrangement of old elements. The new creation must contribute to the solution of some problem.

Creativity is also defined as a construct similar to intelligence, but it differs from intelligence in that it is not restricted to cognitive or intellectual functioning or behavior. It is a complex and complicated interaction between motivational conditions, personality factors, environmental conditions, chance factors, and even products.

> Papilla and Olds (1987) have defined creativity as:
>
> The ability to see things in a new and unusual light, to see problems that no one else may even realize exist, and then to come up with new unusual and effective solutions.

Recently, creativity has been conceptualized in three different ways. Creativity is a novel and personally meaningful interpretation of experiences, actions, and events. However, the novelty and meaningfulness of these interpretations need not require being original or even meaningful to others.

The judgment of novelty and meaningfulness that constitutes creativity is an intrapersonal judgment. This intrapersonal judgment is what distinguishes this concept of creativity from other forms of creative expressions.

Maslow (1971) highlights its uniqueness as personal experience. He was not interested in its utility or uniqueness otherwise.

There are many other definitions of creativity. However, there is a lack of agreement among these psychologists. According to some, it is a component of cognitive behavior, while some others think that it is related to an individual's total personality. Some highlight its importance from social and cultural angles, while others insist that it is an individual's personal experience. Creativity also includes the rearrangement or reshaping of the already-existing ideas, products, or processes. It is considered in two ways: one as a product and other as a process.

Let us consider the nature and characteristics of creativity.

1. It is proved that creativity is universal. It is seen among people coming from all ages, locations, cultures, castes, creeds, and communities. Genderwise also there is no difference in creativity, which means that creativity is found equally in both men and women. This obviously means that all of us have creativity to some extent.

2. Creativity can be enhanced. Though it depends to some extent on heredity, environment also plays an important role in its expression. If the environment is conducive and training is given, creativity can be nurtured.

> Characteristics of creativity:
>
> 1. It is universal.
> 2. It can be enhanced.
> 3. It is self-expression and carries ego involvement. It is not essentially related to very high intelligence.

3. Creativity is all about producing something novel. It may not only be a totally new idea or object, but a novel combination of separate elements, principles, or a modification. For example, creating a fan which can be operated by battery and which you can carry in your pocket is creativity. Creativity is divergent thinking! It is not restricted to the rigid one-to-one thinking or the convergent-type thinking, but is open thinking—with numerous alternative solutions to one question. If the alternatives are unconventional, there is more creativity.

4. Creativity is self-expression and carries ego involvement. May it be a painting, a poem, a design of a building, or a movie, the creator's ego is involved in it. It is related to the individuality and identity of the individual.

5. Creativity is not essentially related to very high intelligence, though normal intelligence is a prerequisite for it. It means that every creative person is not gifted and that all gifted persons are not creative. Thus, the correlation of creativity and intelligence is not simple and may vary with the range of intelligence.

6. There are two basic types of creativity. One is pure creativity and the other is applied creativity. Pure creativity is basically used for self-expression and the person concerned gets a sense of satisfaction as well as a sense of achievement only because of self-expression. We can think of a painting in this case. Applied creativity, however, has a particular intention. A scientist trying to find out a specific robot that will be capable of performing brain surgery is applied creativity. There is a particular intention and an obvious application of the output of applied creativity and a group of people or the whole mankind gets its benefit.

> There are two types of creativity:
>
> 1. *Pure creativity*—one that results in self-expression, satisfaction, and sense of achievement.
> 2. *Applied creativity*—one that has a particular intention. Beneficial for a particular group of people or whole mankind.

Another classification is creativity related to everyday life and major or eminent creativity. The latter two forms of creativity rely on interpersonal and historical judgments of novelty, appropriateness, and lasting impact.

7. Measurement of creativity is very difficult. Three things are measured about responses—fluency, flexibility, and originality. Fluency is number of responses given in the available time, flexibility is various groups of ideas used for giving these responses, and originality is a new combination of known matter or entirely new suggestions.

3.3 FACTORS AFFECTING CREATIVITY

Creativity depends on natural gifts such as intelligence and ability to deal with various new ideas. Education, training, as well as opportunity for expression of creativity play an important role in actual creativity used by the individual. Proper care to create conducive environment adds into the possibility that creativity will be fostered.

Creativity = Knowledge × Imagination × Analytical thinking

In this formula the interaction of three cognitive variables is considered as essential for creativity. Here cognitive means how we acquire a process and store the information available in the environment.

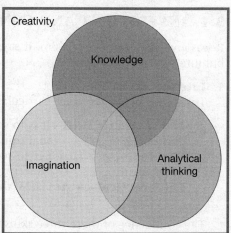

Knowledge contributes a lot in creativity. It adds into the number of alternatives available for reorganization and reconsideration. Let us take for example verbal creativity. It is obvious that an educated person will be in a better position to think about various words, their exact meaning, hidden meaning, grammatical constructions, and change in the meaning with change in the structure and similar other aspects.

Imagination is the origin of creativity. One has to think about hypothetical combinations of commodities, ideas, behavioral patterns, and so on. Playing with such imaginations is essential for creating new ideas and generating impossible solutions of various problems.

Analytical thinking is useful for assessing the utility of the ideas created and the new solutions suggested to old problems. One has to see as to what extent are the ideas generated applicable in day-to-day life situation. Intrinsic motivation is essential for any creative expression.

Another formula regarding creativity is:

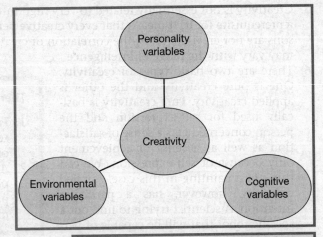

Creative problem solving increases-
Productivity
Satisfaction
Problem-solving capacity
Self-worth

Creative achievement = Cognitive variables × Environmental variables × Personality variables

This formula considers variables other than cognitive ones also.

3.4   INVESTMENT AND CONFLUENCE THEORY OF CREATIVITY

It was given by Sternberg (2006). It says that creativity requires the interaction of six distinct but interrelated resources:

1. **Intellectual skills**
   Three intellectual skills are particularly important:

   a. **The synthetic skill**—It is to see problems with new points of view and to get rid of the bounds of conventional thinking.
   b. **The analytic skill**—It is to recognize which of one's ideas are worth pursuing and which are not.
   c. **The practical–contextual skill**—It is to know how to persuade others regarding one's ideas.

The confluence of these three skills is also important. Only analytic skills lead to powerful critical thinking which cannot be creative.

Synthetic skills result in new ideas but they are not scrutinized for improvement and are made to work. Practical–contextual skills result in societal acceptance of ideas only because the ideas have been good and powerfully presented.

2. **Knowledge**
   On one hand, enough knowledge of the field is a must. On the other hand, knowledge about a field can result in a closed and entrenched perspective, resulting in a person's not moving beyond the way in which he or she has seen problems in the past. Knowledge, thus, can either help or hinder creativity.

3. **Thinking styles**
   Thinking styles are preferred ways of using one's skills. In essence, they are decisions about how to deploy the skills available to a person. With regard to thinking styles, a legislative style is particularly important for creativity, that is, a preference for thinking and a decision to think in new ways.

   This preference needs to be distinguished from the ability to think creatively.

   Someone may like to think along new lines, but not think well, or vice versa. It also helps to become a major creative thinker, if one is able to think globally as well as locally, distinguishing the forest from the trees and thereby recognizing which questions are important and which ones are not.

4. **Personality**
   Numerous research investigations have supported the importance of certain personality attributes for creative functioning. These attributes include, but are not limited to, willingness to overcome obstacles, willingness to take sensible risks, willingness to tolerate ambiguity, and self-efficacy. In particular, buying low and selling high typically means defying the crowd, so that one has to be willing to stand up to conventions if one wants to think and act in creative ways. Often creative people seek opposition; that is, they decide to think in ways that countervail how others think. Note that none of the attributes of creative thinking are fixed. One can decide to overcome obstacles, take sensible risks, and so forth.

5. **Motivation**
   Intrinsic, task-focused motivation is also essential to creativity. The research of Amabile (1983) and others has shown the importance of such motivation for creative work and has suggested that people rarely do truly creative work in an area unless they really love what they are doing and focus on the work rather than the potential rewards. Motivation is not something inherent in a person. One decides to be motivated by one thing or another. Often, people who need to work in a certain area that does not particularly interest them. They will then look for some angle on the work they need to do and what makes this work appeal to rather than bore them.

6. **Environment**
   Finally, one needs an environment that is supportive and rewarding for creative ideas. One could have all of the internal resources needed to think creatively, but without some environmental support (such as a forum for proposing those ideas), the creativity that a person has within him or her might never be displayed.

7. **Confluence**
   Concerning the confluence of these six components, creativity is hypothesized to involve more than a simple sum of a person's level on each component. First, there may be thresholds for some components (e.g., knowledge) below which creativity is not possible regardless of the levels on other components. Second, partial compensation may occur in which strength on one component (e.g., motivation) counteracts a weakness on another component (e.g., environment). Third, interactions may occur between components, such as intelligence and motivation, in which high levels on both components could multiplicatively enhance creativity.

While discussing the aspects of creativity, Guilford (1986) considered creative thinking as involving divergent thinking, which emphasizes fluency, flexibility, originality, and elaboration. Guilford, however, noted that creative thinking is not the same as divergent thinking, because creativity requires sensitivity to problems as well as abilities to redefine, which include transformations of thought, reinterpretations, and freedom from functional fixedness in driving unique solutions. In order to develop Torrance Tests of Creative Thinking (TTCT) and in its further revisions, Torrance (1974) has explained six components of creativity. He has described these aspects of creativity in terms of their mode of measurement. These aspects of creativity are:

1. **Fluency:** The number of relevant ideas, for example, shows an ability to produce a number of figural images.
2. **Flexibility:** It is an individual's ability to produce not only a large number of responses, ideas, or solutions to a problem, but also a variety of responses, ideas, or solutions to a problem.
3. **Originality:** The number of statistically infrequent ideas indicating an ability to produce uncommon or unique responses.
4. **Elaboration:** The number of added ideas and demonstrates the subject's ability to develop and elaborate on ideas.
5. **Abstractness of titles:** The degree beyond labeling and is based on the idea that creativity requires an abstraction of thought. It measures the degree to which a title moves beyond concrete labeling of the pictures drawn.
6. **Resistance to premature closure:** The degree of psychological openness based on the belief that creative behavior requires a person to consider a variety of information while processing information and to keep an "open mind."

3.5 STAGES OF CREATIVITY

The history of research on stages of creativity began with Graham Wallas (1926) who suggested that creative thinking follows four successive steps.

3.5.1 STAGE OF PREPARATION

The subject begins to gather information about the problem to be solved and attempts some solutions. This stage is characterized by a state of trial and error in learning. Therefore, the individual is advised to learn as much as possible about the problem area. In preparation, the thinker begins recalling personal experiences and investigating in all different directions to gather information about the problem to be solved. The object of defining the focus question of interest is to list all concepts associated with the focus question.

Since the goal of this procedure is to generate the largest possible list, the thinker should not worry about redundancy, relative importance, or relationships at this point.

3.5.2 STAGE OF INCUBATION

In the second stage the solution exists but is not clear. The individual must not intentionally work on the problem. Instead, it is allowed to sink into the unconscious. The individual is advised to relax and reflect on his or her focus question that might lead him or her to modify the focus question.

3.5.3 STAGE OF ILLUMINATION

In the third stage, the problem-solver suddenly experiences insight into the problem when a new solution, idea, or relationship emerges. In other words, the individual attempts to reformulate his or her ideas or to formulate new ones. The individual is more active and more conscious work is needed in this stage. Thus, he or she attempts to reformulate his or her ideas or to formulate new ones.

3.5.4 STAGE OF VERIFICATION

In the stage of verification, the thinker tests, tries, and checks the solution he has arrived at. Since this stage is the final one, the thinker may well make some modification to his or her ideas which he or she reached at in the previous stages. Thus, he or she may need to review his or her concept map as he or she gains new knowledge or new insights.

In some situations, the above stages may appear in a different order, or combined into two or three stages. They also do not occur regularly. For example, sometimes the subject's knowledge of the problem area allows him or her to pass over the first stage (preparation) and move on to the next stage (incubation) or even to the third.

The relation between intelligence and creativity is a controversial issue.

Most of the studies concerning the relation between intelligence and creativity proved that it is not very strong

Guilford (1967) suggested that a minimal level of IQ which is slightly higher than average may be necessary, but not sufficient, for creativity. It means that there are many other factors necessary for the development of creativity. Creative achievement is thought to be impossible below this level of intelligence.

One more idea is that creativity is dependent on domain-specific knowledge, which in turn depends on the amount of exposure to and expertise in a given field and deliberate practice.

Researchers have proved that intrinsic task motivation is essential for creativity. Relevant skills, relevant processes, and intrinsic work motivation play an important role in creativity. There is some overlapping area of these three and that is the area of creativity.

A lot of research has been done regarding what blocks the expression of creativity. Some factors are internal and some are external. Internal factors are a lack of motivation, lack of interest, and lack of opportunity and rigidity. External factors include socialization agents such as parents, teachers, and their practices that inhibit the expression of creativity. Specially, our Indian formal education system does not give much opportunity to solve problems creatively. There is only one correct answer to every question, not only in mathematics but also in languages used in our schools. It is observed that parents unnecessarily give readymade answers to their children. As can be easily understood, essay writing is the only possible opportunity for using creative ideas for school children. However, teachers and parents dictate even essays and compel children to memorize the same and write it accordingly. This is detrimental to the development of creativity. Hence, one should compensate for that and give some more opportunities where creative problem-solving is possible.

3.6 PERSONALITY OF A CREATIVE PERSON

A lot of research has been done regarding the personality and behavior of a creative person. Some common characteristics of a creative person are:

1. Flexibility
2. Insight
3. Tolerance of ambiguity
4. Self-evaluation
5. Risk taking
6. Originality
7. Capacity to visualize
8. Intelligence
9. Knowledge
10. Independence
11. Fluency
12. Sensitivity
13. Curiosity
14. Imagination
15. Perseverance
16. Independence
17. Enthusiasm
18. Self-sufficiency
19. Involvement in unconventional ideas
20. Strong personality

A creative person is inventive, resourceful, reflective, individualistic, self-confident, and self-directing. He or she is interested in a wide variety of subjects. Being humorous is another characteristic of a creative person.

Self-perception of creative individuals is different from that of less creative individuals. A creative individual perceives himself or herself as independent, inventive, having individuality, insight, versatile, and having determination. They also think that they are enthusiastic, industrious, having more ego strength, self-sufficient, self-directing, and strong and that they enjoy abstract thinking.

As compared to that a less creative person perceives himself or herself as more reliable, dependable, conventional, having a good character, and having concern for others. However, they think that their ego strength is poor, and that they are less self-sufficient and less self-directing. They also know that they have weak personality and are less involved in abstract thinking.

The creative students:

1. learn the strategies needed to solve problems they encounter;
2. do not keep quite when the problems become tough, they persevere;
3. are more fluent than most other students;
4. propose novel ideas that are also practical;
5. demonstrate a lot of flexibility of mind;
6. recognize the elements.

3.7   ENHANCING CREATIVITY

Thomas Edison used to say that creativity is 1 percent inspiration and 99 percent perspiration. As it is said creativity is a universal phenomenon. It is seen everywhere, irrespective of caste, creed, and community as well as age and gender. The only thing is we do not use it and its existence remains dormant for the whole of our lives.

Creativity can be enhanced only if a conducive environment is provided to an individual. That basically includes the following dimensions:

1. **Psychological safety**

   Creativity essentially needs freedom of expression. Children should feel free to say whatever they want to. If they think they are safe, their thoughts, ideas, and new solutions will not disturb their status and interpersonal relations, and they will not be criticized for suggesting something crazy, thus, will be more creative. Students should be allowed to express whatever comes to their mind regarding a given topic in front of teachers and classmates at school, and parents at home.

2. **Sense of inherent worth**

   The expression of creativity requires satisfaction with self. Individuals should be satisfied with their self-worth. If you think that you are capable of suggesting something, some solutions to the problems of parents or some problem of the whole class, you will feel comfortable while suggesting that. Self-confidence and self-worth are essential for this.

   The knowledge regarding self, acceptance of self, and opportunities to prove self help in the enhancement of self-worth.

3. **Absence of judgment and threat**

   Many parents and teachers constantly evaluate and criticize ideas of children. Sometimes it is threatening for students to solve problems in different ways. Ridiculing and making fun of new ideas are common. This should be avoided and significant adults should take things seriously at least for consideration.

4. **No need for being defensive**

   Openness of atmosphere reduces defensiveness substantially. Any person who is defensive hides his or her own feelings and real emotions. The adults should see to it that they do not make children feel awkward about their self-expression.

Many more things can be listed which mean the same, for example, there should be a possibility of thinking, feeing, and expressing innermost thoughts. There should be complete psychological freedom, security, and openness.

Educational psychology has given some suggestions for creating a conducive environment for enhancing creativity. These are given below. Significant adults should respect child's right:

What blocks creativity?

1. Internal factors:

   a. Lack of motivation
   b. Lack of interest
   c. Lack of opportunity
   d. Rigidity.

2. External factors (socialization practices of):

   a. Parents
   b. Teachers
   c. Significant adults

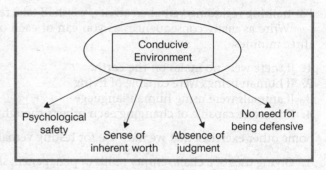

1. To initiate his or her learning efforts.
2. To reject ideas of adults.
3. To ask questions.
4. To take time to plan for imaginative activities.
5. To take part in freewheeling discussion.
6. To express his or her aesthetic interests.
7. To get encouragement for new ideas and activities.

Let us take for example one of the various methods of enhancing creativity. Let us consider two types of creativity—verbal and nonverbal. For verbal creativity, you can think of the following exercise.

3.8   VERBAL AND NONVERBAL CREATIVITY

For training regarding verbal creativity, we shall take few items useful to test creativity.

Write as many consequences as you can of each of the following imagined situations in three minutes.

1. If there were no males on the Earth.
2. If human beings were capable of flying.
3. If animals were using human language.
4. If we were capable of changing each other's thoughts.

Some other exercises that we may use for testing verbal creativity are:

1. Giving uses of a chalk, empty refills of pen, pencil, stone, and so on. Here also we start from very familiar ideas and then come up with rare ones.
2. Playing with words, like changing their order of letters and making new words. For example, "tub" can become "but," "rat" can become "tar," or "own" may become "now." One may also increase the number of letters and make it more challenging.
3. Asking a child to list words sounding alike such as cat, rat, mat, fat, and hat; just, must, and rust; or page, rage and cage.
4. Utilizing synonyms or antonyms, changing the grammatical structure of the sentence and seeing how the meaning changes. Even separating a word in two or three parts may lead to different meanings. For example, a word mango can be divided into the words man and go, where the meaning changes completely.

As far as nonverbal creativity is concerned, again we can think of many games and stimulating exercises. To give some examples, here we use the following alphabets. What you have to do is add lines and prepare pictures of various sorts and suggest meanings of the picture, thus, suggested.

Y   L   M   O

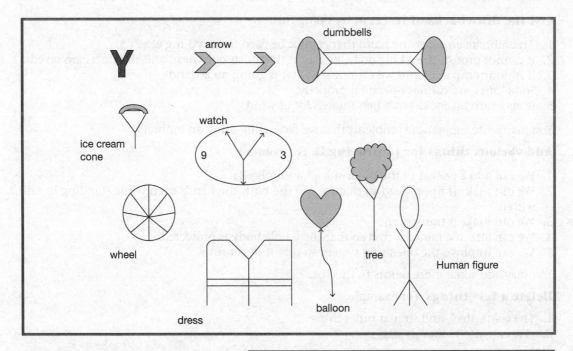

You will be able to see that you can add many sizes, shapes, and lines to already given figure. You can prepare flowers, huts, shirts, trees, arrows, and even lord Ganesh out of basic alphabet Y. You will be capable of drawing the Sun, balloon, flowers, human face, animals like cats, human figures, etc. using the other basic figures given.

There are other examples where creativity can be applied. It means that we have to train ourselves to solve practical day-to-day life problems.

Let us take one example of this type. We have to consider a commodity that we use in everyday life. Here, let us think about an umbrella—any ordinary umbrella.

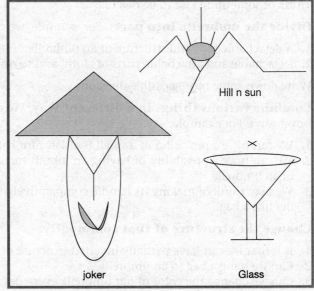

List the drawbacks of it. Let us try doing this:

1. An umbrella engages one hand that cannot be used for anything else.
2. It cannot protect the whole body, hence, at the most, only head and shoulders are saved.
3. It is nontransparent and we cannot see what is going on around.
4. Sometimes, we cannot operate it properly.
5. It may turn upside down when there is lot of wind.

You may write some more problems that we face while using an umbrella.

Add various things for improving it. For example:

1. We can add a pocket to the inner side of an umbrella.
2. We can make it fit on head so that we can use both the hands even while standing in rain with it.
3. We can make it transparent.
4. We can attach a raincoat to it so that the whole body is protected.
5. We can improve the operating system so that it never rusts.

You may add some more points to this list.

Delete a few things. For example:

1. The color, steel, and similar other things.
2. We can also reduce its size.

Think of something else to be deleted.

Divide the umbrella into parts. For example, we can think of:

1. A detachable roof and structure of an umbrella.
2. Detachable and attachable parts of cloth, and so on.

Write down some more possible divisions.

Combine various things in a different way. We can think of combining various parts in novel ways. For example:

1. We can have a provision of a small transistor for listening radio while walking.
2. We can have a possibility of having an inbuilt torch or place to hide a knife in the handle of an umbrella.
3. We may think of making its handle comparatively bigger so that we can hang it on shoulder like a bag.

Change the structure of that commodity:

1. Is it that we can have partially inverted structure of an umbrella?
2. Can we hang a bag to an umbrella?
3. Can we change the color of our umbrella every day to match our dress?
4. Can we introduce air in the cover of an umbrella to reduce its weight?

Think of some more changes in structure of an umbrella.

You must have understood that we can think about anything that we use in our day-to-day life situations, any commodity, any behavioral pattern, or any type of game and improve it to a large extent. Creativity is something that we have to use in every area of life, every now and then, and it is obvious that it helps us to improve our lives. Even a housewife is capable of using a lot of creativity for the different ways of cooking, reorganizing the kitchen, saving her time while cooking, and saving energy and resources like gas needed to cook.

A learner can also use creativity for better understanding, better remembering, and even writing at the time of examination. Educational psychologists gave this model of creativity long ago which is now being used in every sphere of life especially in industries and offices, for advancements of science and technology, and in each and every activity that involves human beings.

Creativity can be fostered by using various tricks. Some important ideas are given in this unit. Creativity can be of great value to everybody if we reconsider the issues in a different light.

3.9   SUMMARY

This chapter deals with the highest cognitive process of human beings, that is, creativity. There are different types of creativity: verbal and nonverbal, pure and applied. Creativity is something novel and useful. Originality, fluency, and flexibility are the dimensions of creativity. Creative problem-solving is always beneficial. It is worth noting that creativity in universal and can be enhanced. Psychological safety and conducive environment lead to increased creativity.

QUESTIONS

1. Define creativity and explain its types.
2. What type of personality is seen among creative individuals?
3. Describe various factors affecting creativity.
4. Discuss the stages of creativity.
5. Elaborate the ways to enhance creativity.

APPLICATION ORIENTATION

1. Find out different uses of some waste material like plastic bags and suggest how it can be used for benefit of the poor.
2. Observe various activities in the kitchen and find out creative ways to save energy and time of your mother.
3. Try to organize study materials in a new, easier way to remember. Organize competition regarding the same.

SUGGESTED READINGS

Guilford, J. P.(1967). *The structure of intellect*. New York: MacGraw-Hill.
Guilford, J. P. (1986). *Creative talents: Their nature, uses and development*. Buffalo, NY: Bearly Ltd.
Maslow, A. H. (1971). *The farther reaches human nature*. New York: Yiking Press.

Morgan, C. T., King, R. A., Weis, J. R., & Scooper, J. (1993). *Introduction to psychology*. New Delhi: Mc Graw-Hill.

Newell, A., Shaw, J. C., and Simon, H. A. (1958). Elements of a theory of human problem solving. *Psychological Review*, 23, 342–343.

Newell, A. and Simon, H. A. (1963). *Human problem solving*. Englewood Cliffs, NJ: Prentice Hall.

Papila, D. E. and Olds, S.W. (1987). *Psychology*. New York: McGraw-Hill.

Sternberg, R. J. (2006). The nature of creativity. *Creativity Research Journal*, *18*(1), 87–98.

Sternberg, R. J., & Lubart, T. I. (1999). The concept of creativity: Prospects and Paradigms. In R. J. Sternberg (ed.). *Handbook of creativity*. London: Cambridge University Press.

Torrance, E. P. (1974). *Torrance test of creative thinking*. Bensenville, US: Scholastic Testing Service Inc.

Wallas, G. (1926). *The art of thought*. New York: Harcourt Brace.

4 Values and Ethics

Objectives

After reading this present chapter, you will be able to:

1. Realize the importance of values in human life.
2. Understand nature and significance of ethics.
3. Learn about moral development.
4. Know the functions of work ethics.
5. Analyze the concept of character building.
6. Accept the idea that training can improve your work ethics.
7. Notice sexual harassment of women.
8. Improve your work ethics.

4.1 NATURE AND SIGNIFICANCE

Two sisters basically from Indian family were born and brought up in America. They were in their teens and facing intense value conflict due to differences between Indian and American cultures. Parents were very strict and totally against any premarital sexual pleasure. They wanted that their daughters should lead a life exactly according to their expectations and settle down in India after marriage. So the girls were not at all mixing with guys and were isolated and made fun of in their school. Every one used to criticize their behavior and express doubts whether they are normal or otherwise. They used to feel extremely awkward and trauma of social rejection was beyond their tolerance. One fine morning both of them killed themselves by jumping from 12th floor of their school building.

What is the basic reason behind the restrictions the parents were forcing them to follow? Why these two young ladies could not adjust with the situation? Can value system have an impact on every aspect of human life? This true story basically is about severity of value conflict. Let us discuss the importance of it in our lives.

Vinay is a third-year student of physiotherapy. He has to treat many patients every day. Once he was told to treat a patient and give a particular passive exercise to a patient ten times. Vinay gave the exercise only thrice and continued this practice every day. After seven days' treatment was over, it was seen that the patient was still suffering badly and the expected improvement was not achieved.

There are many people in the world who say something else and do something else. Few significant adults also give this message "do as I say and don't do as I do." Such people cannot gain respect by others. Ethics are regarding congruity between values and actions. There is a social role where the individual is supposed to behave in a particular way. Social acceptance also can be achieved with an ethical behavioral style. In ethical behavior, it is not just overt behavior but complete internalization of values that must be achieved.

What is good and what is bad is defined by many generations. Every society, culture, and subgroup of a community expects a particular type of decency and maturity, and a particular understanding in the members while they interact with each other. Any civilized society demands not only the postponement of instinctual satisfaction but also the radical modification of instinctual needs and sometimes its complete and permanent inhibition. Any illegal, irresponsible act done against anyone is unethical. Stealing, shoplift, vandalism, false records, breaking confidentially, ignoring safety rules, poor client service, or any other type of irresponsible behavior is unethical.

4.2 VALUES

Values are one's personal treasure. Values are the things that are important to us. They are deeply held beliefs that we usually internalize during our upbringing and develop further as we grow older. Values are learnt or chosen, are parts of our consciousness, and are specific to us. Values are open to change. One may not maintain absolutely identical values throughout one's lifetime. Values form the basis of why we do what we do. They help the individual to decide the preference, even of needs.

As is obvious, it is something that the individual values the most and strictly behaves accordingly even when his or her life is at stake. Many a time, an individual gets involved in doing something that is unpleasant only because of his or her values.

Raman is attached to his father and respects him a lot. He wants to fulfill all the dreams of his father. Unfortunately, his father met with an accident due to which he is bedridden for last six months. Raman does everything for his father: feeds him, does everything for his personal hygiene, brings medicines, and so on. There are many unpleasant things that he is doing regularly, but these are because of his values and priorities.

Life orientation is achieved with the help of values. Values and moral rules are manmade resulting from cultural evolution. They are taught to the next generation so that they lead a life substantially disciplined than lower level species.

Allport (1968) defines values as meanings perceived related to self. To value self means to prefer it, invest energy in it, and to work for it. It is related to motivation. Types of values:

1. **Theoretical**—truth, knowledge, critical thought
2. **Economic**—practical, useful payoff
3. **Aesthetic**—elegance of an act
4. **Social**—love of others, sympathetic, and unselfish attitude.

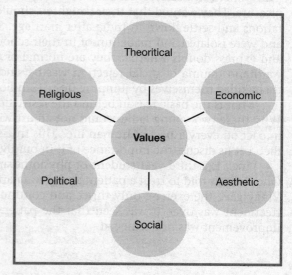

5. **Political**—power and control
6. **Religious**—contemplativeness

Values are related to human mental health. Life orientation is achieved by values. Values are the psychological center of gravity. Value plus identity is equal to character. Values can be considered as a continuum. One can place oneself somewhere on that continuum, for example:

Creativity	destructiveness
Freedom	compulsion
Strength	weakness
Cooperation	competition

Spiritual life largely depends upon family. Sometimes exactly opposite values are taught in the family such as spiritualism, work is worship, pretension of good relations, pleasure principle, creativity, duty, discipline, and self-control.

Values are seen not only in behavior across situations, but they affect every choice of the individual even as an adult. In an organizational setup also it becomes essential to understand value system of the individual to understand his or her decisions. Emotions and their expressions are related to values. Cognitive dissonance depends on the value system of the individual. Human relations are also affected by values of the individuals.

The development and clarification of values are based on various processes. They are:

1. **Thinking**—Independent analytical thinking involving critical evaluation and understanding is necessary for the development of proper values. If independent and objective thinking cannot be achieved, the person will depend on others for evaluating and deciding the priorities of his or her life. Critical thinking helps to differentiate between facts and opinions. One can find out if a particular thing can be accepted as truth based on the available proofs. If the individual is not capable of all these, then he or she will depend on what others say and how they interpret the world.
2. **Feelings**—Accepting and evaluating own feelings help the individual to understand what the ultimate satisfaction is and how to gain it. This leads to a clear understanding of what one wants to achieve in life.
3. **Communicating**—The reevaluation of values take place when one interacts with others. Carefully understanding others' messages, observing their style of communication including emotions, their expressions, nonverbal communication, and attitudes help clarifying one's values and sending clear messages about them.
4. **Choosing**—Selecting values without outside pressures is essential. Alternative courses of actions and their consequences must be considered for this.
5. **Acting**—Repeatedly behaving in a particular way and consistently accepting that action as the best make values more stable. Then, it can be generalized to other areas of life.

Everything starts from one's core values. These are the values that one consistently ranks higher than others. The identification of core values results in a definite picture of the kind of person one wants to be and the kind of life one wants to have.

Anup is born and brought up in a value-based family. Right from childhood he was following the ultimate values and was never involved in any wrong deed or dishonest behavior. He is working in a semigovernment organization since last 10 years. Now he has to shoulder the financial responsibility of the organization. He discovered that all his colleagues and superiors are paid extra money and gifts for sanctioning some tenders. If he denies that offer, they become anxious and start showing mistrust. This affects his interpersonal relations and his chances of promotion. Hence, he has also started accepting these gifts and now he is accepted as a group member.

Slow erosion of one's core values over time is called as value drift. This may result from constant pressure, unwanted experiences, and consequence-oriented behavior of the individual. A person having very intense ideas and values against corruption may slowly get involved in the same practice because of ample opportunities and pressure from superiors as well as general atmosphere in the organization.

Aasha and Sudha are third-year engineering students. They have been classmates since fifth standard. Aasha is always interested in impressing others and attracting attention of teachers of opposite gender. She wears provoking dresses which are short and fashionable. She is always excited and tells sex-related jokes to her friends. Sudha is a simple and a gentle girl. She is sincere and hardworking. She concentrates her attention on studies and related activities. She is soft-spoken and respects others and helps all her friends. Both of these young ladies have exactly opposite value systems, and hence, they cannot get along well with each other. They just cannot tolerate each other's presence.

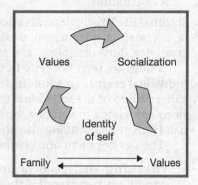

One of the major causes of conflicting interpersonal relations is the clash between the personal values of different individuals who have different abilities, aptitudes, interests, family backgrounds, religious experiences, education, role models, and media exposure.

4.2.1 Determinants of Values

The determinants of values are based on the interaction of the individual with others.

1. **Family**—Practices adopted by parents to shape the personality of the child.
2. **School**—Playing with age-mates is important.
3. **Cultural factors**—Everything passed on from generation to generation by significant adults.
4. **Personal factors**—Attributes and qualities and characteristics with reference to intraindividual interaction.

Family affects values and values affect family. So, they are influencing each other. If there is any value conflict in the family, it is necessary to resolve it by positive strategies. If some negative elements crop up, even the family may dissolve. Different families preach different values: values for work, regarding personal development, spiritual life, or pretending things only for social status. Some other values are pleasure principle, freedom of expression, spontaneity, creativity, self-discipline, self-control, power, and money. Sometimes negatively oriented values like cutthroat competition, selfishness, and inferiority are also imbibed by children in their own families. If family values are like sacrifice for each other, cooperation, sharing, affection, and similar things, children become emotionally healthy and happy. They enjoy appropriate warmth and close family relations and become confident, independent, and competent. Otherwise, they suffer emotionally, socially, and face personality problems.

All these correlates, in turn, are strongly associated to the mental health of the individual. The person may experience internal value conflict when forced to choose between two or more strongly held values. A college student who wants to buy a motorcycle for himself but knows that parents will not be able to afford it is in a fix as to how to manage. He can neither cheat them nor neglect his requirement as he has to travel a lot for going to his college. The resolution of internal value conflicts depends on the individual's willingness to rank own core values in the order of their importance to the individual. Prioritizing values helps to make decisions when life gets complex and choices become difficult.

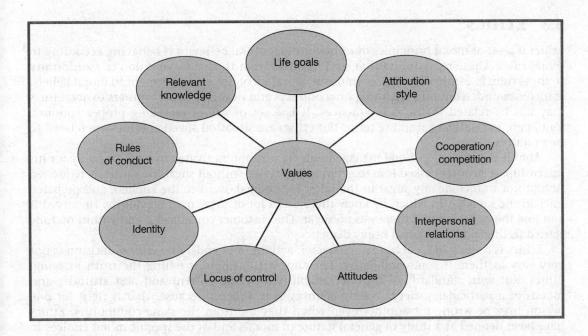

Solving the conflicts resulting from differences in various correlates of values requires effective human relation skills. Nonjudgmental attitude, accepting others as they are, and maturity to understand human nature are essential for solving such interpersonal conflicts.

Many individuals openly criticize others' behavior and character as a whole. Here, the individual wants conformation that his or her own values and character are more socially acceptable. Conformity can be healthy or defensive.

When one confronts others' lapses in character, it leads to strengthening own integrity.

They help us to prioritize needs. Values are especially useful in explaining why we do things that we don't actually like doing.

Modern Indian society is going through tremendous change regarding values. The loss of consensus and self-oriented attitudes is seen very commonly. Losing values, or not knowing which values to choose, can be devastating. In some other countries, it is seen that loss of stable values within a short duration can have horrible effects on society.

Researchers have identified 10 universal values in a cross-cultural perspective.

1. Power
2. Achievement
3. Hedonism
4. Stimulation
5. Self-direction
6. Universalism
7. Benevolence
8. Tradition
9. Conformity
10. Security

Self-direction and achievement values enhance self-development.

4.3 ETHICS

Ethics is a set of moral principles of right conduct. Moral behavior is behaving according to moral rules. These rules are positive and negative, that is, the dos and don'ts. Conformity to these rules is admired by the community. Moral ideology is commitment to moral beliefs. It includes understanding regarding how one acts and how one expects others to act. Ethics may not be related to the consequences. It is a set of values regarding proper conduct. Values are in relatively absolute terms but ethics are situation specific. Ethics are related to one's duties.

Abhijit is a student of hotel management. He was not motivated to work sincerely for his internship. A customer asked him to get pineapple juice without sugar. He earnestly requested Abhijit not to include any sugar in the juice. He nodded, went to the kitchen, and prepared juice in the same jar in which he knew there was a lot of sugar used previously. He served it and told the customer that there was no sugar. The customer consumed it and within no time started feeling giddy as he had heavy diabetics.

Ethics is a study of ideal human character, actions, and ends. Any ethical decision is not very easy as there is some ambiguity. The simplest example is telling the truth or lying. Ethics deal with standards of conduct established by the current and past attitudes and moods of a particular society. Exactly defining it is difficult because what is right for one person may be wrong for another even when they are from the same community. Ethics have been defined as a study of general nature of morals and of the specific moral choices to be made by a person. Here, choices are important because examining and becoming aware of one's own values and being responsible for the consequences of one's own actions plays a major role. The motivation to act ethically may be self-imposed, socially mandated, or spiritually inspired. One must have this understanding of right and wrong, good and bad, and virtue and vice.

Ethical behavior is making for the greatest good, for greatest number, and fulfillment in one's own life and the lives of others. Ethical qualities are love, justice, and courage. Love includes selfless behavior, cooperation, kindness, consideration, unity, and sympathy. Love implies loyalty, and loyalty in turn demands courage.

Nina and Rita are friends. They are attending a college where most of the students are coming from a particular religion. Rita is the only one who is from a different background and religion. As a consequence, she is not accepted by her classmates and even by her teachers. She is not given any opportunity and is not given any importance while making decisions in the group. She feels lonely and isolated. Nina is very kind and considerate. She understands Rita's problems and tries to help her in every sense. Sometimes she fights for her rights and rejects some opportunities only because Rita is not getting them. Nina fights for friend's rights.

Concern for others and respecting everyone's rights are part of ethical behavior. Fighting against injustice is also expected in ethical behavior.

Everyone is interested in knowing how others keep moral rules, because if someone breaks the rules, others also suffer. Hence, in every community, it is essential that the offender is punished, legally or socially. If the individual has more empathy for the person who suffers, then he or she will make special efforts for punishing the offender. The contemporary example is the ill known case of Nirbhaya who was gang-raped in Delhi in December 2013. Huge crowds showed agitation and tried to express the urge for punishing the offenders by protest.

In childhood, ethical understanding is narrow and specific. Then, gradually the child generalizes these concepts. A well-known psychologist Piaget has examined how children's concept of justice changes. To start with, it is a rigid and an inflexible notion of right and wrong. Gradually, the relative nature of ethics is understood. Sometimes, lie is also justified, is realized. In socialization, discipline plays an important role in the development of a moral code. The development of conscience is also associated with socialization. It is related to shame and guilt. Guilt is negative self-evaluation which occurs when the individual does something against conformity. Shame is an unpleasant emotional reaction to negative judgment of self resulting in self-depreciation. Shame depends on external sanctions; however, guilt depends on both internal and external sanctions.

By adolescent years, every individual should be able to learn what a group expects and then being willing to mold his or her behavior should conform to it without anybody's supervision, guidance, and threats of punishment. He or she should be able to control his or her own behavior and shoulder one's responsibility.

For making right ethical choices, one must focus on the following issues.

1. One should distinguish between the right and wrong. Objectively thinking and determining the right path is essential for restraining from choosing the wrong path. It is tempting to tell lies and bunk the classes, but it is for sure that it is going to spoil one's own grades and human relations.
2. Just because one has the power to do something does not mean it is the proper thing to do. Many children and even adolescents enjoy harassing young puppies or kittens, spoiling public property, and teasing the handicapped. They can do it but they should not as it is very unfair to behave like that.
3. Even if one has the right to do something does not mean it is right to do it. Say for example, everyone has a right to decide how to utilize one's leisure time, but if some family member is not well and needs assistance, that should be given priority.
4. Only because one wants to do something does not mean one should do it. Many adolescents want to smoke and drink just for the sake of thrill; they should always remember that it may lead to some unwanted habits and health problems.
5. Choose to do more than the law requires and less than the law allows. One should be very particular regarding one's behavior and legal limitations. Immediate gratification leads to shortcut methods to satisfaction which are against the social and legal sanctions.

Satisfaction through nonfinancial resources that make the biggest contribution to a fulfilling life should be focused on.

Progress and prosperity have almost identical meanings to many people. They equate progress with the acquisition of material things.

4.3.1 ETHICAL SENSITIVITY

What all is essentially to be understood for ethical sensitivity? The following are some important things:

1. Effectiveness of work depends on skills and experience.
2. Excellence depends upon values.
3. Skills are not enduring.
4. Skills change, values don't.
5. Orientation should be decided with the help of a pious mind.
6. The prime requirement of leadership is self-discipline.
7. The expectation that a person should be good and act good.
8. Good things do not happen easily. Efforts are essential to make them happen.

9. Simple living and high thinking should be practiced.
10. Facilitation, follow-up and motivation through support are essential.
11. One has to trust oneself.
12. Any unfair means results in injustice to someone. Hence, it should be avoided.
13. Involvement regarding work is one important issue.
14. Sincerity and enthusiasm for work give better results.
15. Avoid anger, selfishness, jealousy, and hostility.

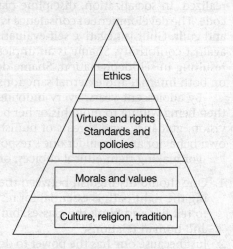

Character is defined as those attitudes and dispositions within an individual which relate to the behavior that is subject to moral evaluation by the society.

The standards of behavior approved, including honesty, integrity, and moral strength, are called the character of the individual. It is the center of human life and the quality that earns respect.

The basic ingredient of character is integrity that is exhibited when the individual achieves congruence between what he knows, what he says, and what he does. When behavior is in tune with professed standards and values and when the individual practices what he or she believes in, integrity is achieved.

4.4 MORAL DEVELOPMENT

Right from the beginning, parents and other family members teach moral values to their children. Moral development is the way the child learns to distinguish between right and wrong. It is the process by which the child develops conscience and learns to judge for oneself what is right and wrong. It requires the child to understand the situation and other people's points of view before making any kind of judgment.

This ability to make a judgment develops gradually. Parents shape the behavior of their children by punishing, rewarding, and setting an example. Punishment may be associated with withholding affection or associating fear, pain, or anxiety with bad thoughts and actions. Rewards are used to teach moral values by praise, smile, hugs, attention, and gifts given after prosocial behavior. Younger children are unable to understand the real meaning of their behavior. If one has to understand and label a child's behavior who brings his or her friend's toys, it is a must to interpret it with reference to the child's age. If the child cannot understand the meaning of stealing, his or her behavior should not be labeled as stealing. He or she is too innocent to steal.

During the elementary school years, the child begins to understand other people's points of view and the contexts in which he or she holds such views. The child, therefore, becomes gradually capable to reason out things in a better way.

According to Freud (1953), superego suppresses, neutralizes, or diverts instinctual forces which may result in violating moral rules. Superego also holds some ego ideals which the society appreciates. It represents the voice of the parents and the society at large. The basic mechanism of the development of superego is identification. The child adopts the attributes of others and tries to behave as if he or she were they. Resistance to temptation is an important prerequisite of moral development.

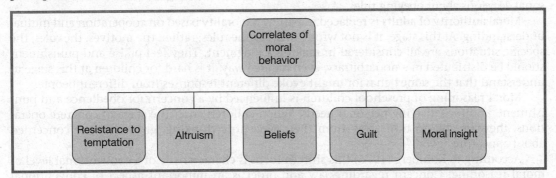

Resistance to temptation and guilt are two important issues as the individual has to control his or her own behavior with reference to various opportunities to enjoy in a socially unacceptable way. If the individual cannot control his or her thoughts and behavior, his or her moral development will be hampered.

Moral development is highly dependent on cognitive development. The ability to discriminate between right and wrong requires the cognitive structures that help the child to see the different aspects of a related issue.

There is a close relationship between moral and social development. Moral issues are essentially a part of the social ethos of a given society at a given time.

4.4.1 THEORIES OF MORAL DEVELOPMENT

Jean Piaget and Lawrence Kohlberg's theories of moral development are very well known and well accepted.

4.4.1.1 *Piaget's Ideas about Moral Development*

Piaget has given a stage theory of cognitive development. Moral development is clubbed with cognitive development. Acting morally is an intelligent adaptation to one's social environment. In Piaget's (1952) views, the child enters a new stage of moral development when he or she enters the stage of concrete operations at the age of 7 which continues till 11 years. During this stage, appropriate use of logic, more mature adult like thought process, solving problems in concrete and logical manners are achieved, but children lack hypothetical abstract thinking. He called it heteronomous morality or moral realism (heteronomous means under an outside authority). During this stage rules are regarded as unchangeable, absolute, and imposed by an external authority. Egocentrism of young children encourages them to adhere to three beliefs:

1. **Imminent justice**—Wrong doing invariably leads to punishment.
2. **Objective consequences**—Morality of an act is judged by its objective consequences, not the objective intentions of the persons.
3. **Absolutism**—Young school children believe in the absolutism of a moral perspective.

They believe that there is only one correct moral conclusion per circumstance. The stage of autonomous morality or morality of cooperation—a new stage—is achieved around the age of 10.

As children become less egocentric by the age of 9 or 10, they are also able to realize that rules are not fixed but arbitrary. They come to know that rules can change and it is possible to make personal decisions about obeying rules.

Moral authority of adults is replaced in part by a morality based on cooperation and mutual understanding. At this stage, it is not wrong to break the rules; rather, the motives, the rules, the specific situations are all considered in making a judgment. They feel praise and punishment should be distributed in a nonarbitrary, even handed way. It is hard for children at this stage to understand that the same behavior might evoke different responses from different people.

Moral reasoning of preschool children is influenced by a concern for obedience and punishment, and for satisfying personal needs. When children enter the stage of concrete operations, they are able to turn away from their egocentric thinking, growing more concerned about appearing "good."

According to Kohlberg (1976) this shift in focus is characteristic of a conventional level of moral reasoning. Concern regarding law and order is an important aspect of conventional reasoning. Rule breaking is considered to be inherently immoral because it creates chaos in a stable social system. Reasoning at this level fits what many societies consider to be acceptable moral rules.

4.4.1.2 Kohlberg's Theory of Moral Development

Lawrence Kohlberg extended the ideas of Piaget and other pioneering work by creating a comprehensive three-stage theory. Kohlberg studied moral development by posing moral dilemmas to groups of children as well as adolescents and adults. These dilemmas were in the form of stories. One of Kohlberg's best-known dilemmas involves a man named Heinz who must choose between stealing medicine and letting his wife die.

In Europe, a woman was about to die due to a particular kind of cancer. There was only one drug that the doctors said might save her. The drug was expensive, that is, $2,000 for a small dose of the drug. The sick woman's husband, Heinz, went to everyone he knew to borrow money, but he could only get about $1,000. He told the druggist that his wife was dying and asked him to sell it cheaper or let him pay later. But the druggist said, "No, I discovered the drug and I'm going to make money from it." So, Heinz got desperate and considered breaking into the man's store to steal the drug for his wife. Should Heinz steal it?

Instead of the answer, Kohlberg analyzed the reasons children gave for their answers. He identified three general levels of moral reasoning—preconventional, conventional, and postconventional—and described two stages at each level.

1. **Level 1**

   a. *Stage 1 (obedience and punishment orientation)*—Preconventional morality comprises stages one and two. The first stage is where rigid rules based on punishment and obedience are followed to avoid punishment.

   b. *Stage 2 (reward orientation)*—In the second stage, rewards are related to behavior. Rules are followed only for benefits of self and rewards.

2. **Level 2**

   a. *Stage 3*—Conventional morality is seen in stages three and four. Children follow rules just to get respect of others and get remarks such as "good boy," and "good girl."

   b. *Stage 4*—People approach moral problems as responsible members of society. Reasoning is used to decide what decision should be taken.

3. **Level 3**

   a. *Stage 5*—Postconventional morality is the characteristic of stages five and six. Here, universal moral principles of morality are taken into consideration than relatively flexible rules of a particular culture and community. Here, individuals' rights and democratically accepted laws are the basis of behavior.

   b. *Stage 6*—The individuals obey laws because they accept that laws are based on universal ethical principles. This is the stage of morality of individual principles and conscience.

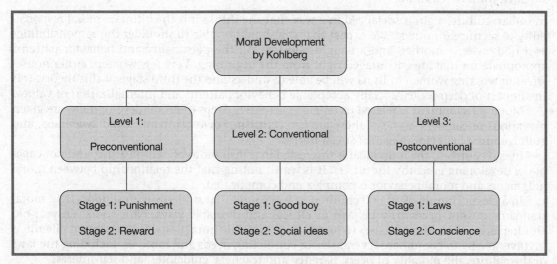

According to Kohlberg, there is a fixed sequence of stages of moral development. Until adolescence, one cannot reach the highest stage. Of course, everyone cannot reach the highest stage as it depends on intelligence and cognitive development.

Moral development of women has recently been considered by a psychologist called Gilligan. Three stages are given in this theory. There is a difference between how girls and boys develop morality. It is because the child-rearing practices and aims for these two genders are totally different. Boys perceive morality in terms of justice and fairness; on the other hand, girls perceive morality in terms of responsibility toward individuals and willingness to sacrifice themselves to help specific individuals within the context of a particular relationship. Compassion for individuals is a greater factor in moral behavior of women.

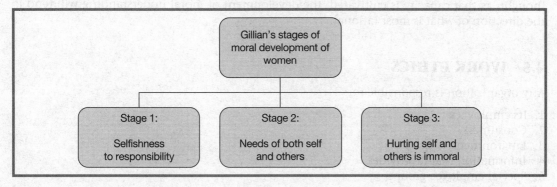

1. **Stage 1 (orientation toward individual survival)**—What is practical and best for self. Then there is a gradual transaction from selfishness to responsibility which includes what is best for others.
2. **Stage 2 (Goodness as self-sacrifice)**—The initial view is that women should sacrifice for others. Gradually, it changes to include needs of both, self and others and from goodness to truth.
3. **Stage 3 (Morality of nonviolence)**—Moral equivalence between self and others is established. Hurting anyone including self is seen as immoral. This is the most sophisticated form of reasoning.

In Indian culture, a girl is socialized in a way that she thinks it is the ultimate moral responsibility to sacrifice for others. We expect that she should be able to shoulder the responsibilities as a housewife, a mother, and a daughter-in-law. All the personality and behavior patterns appropriate for that are encouraged right from the beginning. Very few women, either housewives or working women in India will be able to understand the third stage of this theory. It is the impact of deep-rooted socially acceptable behavior patterns and internalization of values.

Moral development is related to religious activities. Steps of moral development are given by various researchers. Some of these are ego centrism, socio centrism, social awareness, and guilt feeling if behavior is against social norms.

In ego centrism, the individual is interested in selfish motives, self-pleasure, and not capable of developing empathy for others. It is worth noting that the relationship between moral judgments and moral behavior is complex and complicated.

In a classical study of 10,000 children, it was found that students who support rigid moral standards do not necessarily behave in ethical and desirable ways. Nine-to-eleven-year-old children are quick to find excuses to justify their own rule infractions. Solving moral dilemmas involves trying to coordinate several sets of conflicting needs and motives, including the laws of the culture, the morality of peers, parents' and teachers' guidelines, and self-interest.

The third and fourth graders may be able to identify the moral of a story but may not be able to apply it. Moral decision-making benefits from practice and maturity and from specific instructions on how to generalize moral principles to life.

Children also need to be motivated for some practice in making decisions based on moral reasoning. Moral development can be encouraged by using the challenge of self-examination to create opportunities to encourage a sense of dysfunction.

Kohlberg argues that with the development of processes of rational reasoning and exposure to proper education, the individual will recognize the conceptual inadequacies of the lower level of understanding and adopt a higher, more rationally defensible conceptual level. The underlying assumption is that in a creature endowed with the capacity for rational thought, as that capacity is cultivated, the development of moral understanding will tend in the direction of what is most rational.

4.5 WORK ETHICS

Any organization is responsible for:

1. Its employees
2. Consumers
3. Environment
4. Information that it provides
5. Special employee groups
6. Dependent small business

As far as environment is concerned, a chemical factory is responsible for polluted water that it is disposing in a river or toxic gases that it produces. It is unethical to neglect these issues and exploiting others.

In the same way, even personal conduct should be evaluated such as smoking in the office and using office phone for personal reasons.

Differences in ethical standards are associated with the following factors:

1. Supply of workers
2. Skill level
3. Level of productivity
4. Level of motivation
5. Attitude to leadership
6. Reaction to discipline
7. Expectations about job security
8. Attitude toward status and rank
9. Attitude toward different races and gender

4.5.1 DEVELOPING WORK ETHICS

Work ethics are enhancing positive things such as cooperation, cordial relations, and a proper way of interacting with each other. It is necessary of young adults to understand that when they start their college education, or a job, they should be aware of the fact that their behavior will be evaluated continuously by seniors and colleagues. From the first day of their job they should remember some basic things. Actually, work ethics are many. However, some most important things are given below:

1. Do not criticize your teacher, boss, or any authority person.
2. Creating and maintaining good impression in the organization may be a college or an office.
3. Maintaining good relations with your colleagues—showing extreme emotions especially negative ones creates a bad impression.
4. Do not comment on personal lives of colleagues or classmates. Many a time, we do not know the truth completely and unnecessarily get involved in such gossips which are detrimental to good interpersonal relations.
5. Do not compare self with colleagues.
6. Do not interfere with others' jobs, concentrate on your own.
7. Do not break the dress code in your college or organization.
8. Do not discuss your family matters in the office, college, or when you have to maintain formal relations.
9. Do not bring your family members to the office or college.
10. If you are doing some work, discuss it with others and authority persons, so that they can remember it when they have to evaluate you or select people for a particular activity.
11. Praise others for whatever they are doing. Appreciate their efforts.
12. Keep yourself informed.

Simrun never used to study properly. She always used to depend on her friend Rita who used to have the exam number prior to Simrun. Rita was kind hearted and used to help everyone. Even at the time of examination, Rita used to show her answer sheet to Simrun. Rita was a bright student who was motivated to study well. So, both of them used to get good grades. This behavior is unethical on part of both the students. Helping others in wrong ways should never be encouraged.

Rationalization is also commonly seen like "everyone does it," "I am not paid enough," "they do not deserve my loyalty." How to reduce unethical behavior?

Individuals should be motivated to increase loyalty by giving awards, benefits, consistent treatment, recognition for good deeds, and clearly discussing things with the subordinates and students. If you are not clear about what is ethical, ask some questions to self: Is it legal? Is it against the policies of the institutes? Could it harm someone? If anyone I knew saw me, would I feel uncomfortable?.

4.6 CHARACTER BUILDING

Spiritual and moral development essentially are related to a philosophical perspective. There are various dimensions of the philosophical perspective.

Every action of human beings, day-to-day interactions with others, goals and aspirations, and similar other things are decided by one's philosophy of life and value system. It is necessary to think about:

1. What is important in one's life? If one makes it clear, many things about one's life will be clear.
2. Which of the activities are related to goals in life and significant for the individual will be understood properly.
3. Understanding what is important leads to selecting what one wants to achieve in life.
4. What helps in achieving the goal?
5. An objective perspective regarding self, goals, and environmental issues can be obtained. Hence, what one can achieve and what one may not be able to achieve is clear.
6. Understanding regarding how to behave and interact with others is enhanced.
7. One becomes a well-behaved, good citizen who does all the duties essential for that.

When one thinks about it, one may realize that what exactly he or she wants to achieve and what should be done to achieve that is not understood properly. If one does not understand that, it is obvious that whatever he or she is doing may not be useful at all.

All philosophical thoughts are directing human life to the ultimate values and want individuals to be kind, courageous, generous, and oriented toward justice and peace. One has to decide the path that one has to follow.

Spiritual dimension is one's core commitment to one's values. It is extremely important and secret area that influences one's whole life. This is related to one's inspiration. This is the link between a man and the timeless truths of all humanities. By strengthening this bond, one feels as renewed and recommitted. It gives power and multiplies one's energy.

For generations people are involved in defining moral character and moral development. In any civilized community it becomes essential to train young ones so that they become capable of shouldering the responsibility of preserving the moral characteristics of the community. They should become good adults.

4.7 RELATIVITY

It is essential to accept that the nature of perceived goodness is relative. It is culture specific, gender specific, age specific, environment specific, and so on. Obviously, there is no prescribed way in which one should always behave. It should not be restricted to outer behavior or rules and regulations. It is customary in the Western style of discipline that adults while scolding children say, "Behave yourself." However, in Indian sense, moral development is internalization of values. It is not just behaving in a particular way but understanding and accepting that this is the most appropriate way of interacting with others. In only "behaving" there is a possibility of having different views and values and a different sort of behavior. Both doing bad deeds and hiding them are possible in that. Moral development is far more than good manners. This is ethical, value-oriented behavior which is taking place according to the internalized value system.

Even values are not fixed. They are relative. Exact definition is difficult to achieve. Ethical behavior is making for the greatest good for the greatest number and fulfillment in one's own life and in the lives of others. The most important ethical qualities are love, justice, and courage. It includes affection, just behavior, cooperation, kindness, understanding, and sympathy. Though it is difficult to experience equal affection for all human beings in the world, but treatment which causes injustice can be avoided.

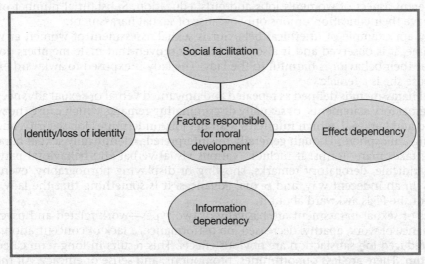

Character can be defined as that attitude and disposition within an individual which relate to the behavior that is subject to moral evaluation in his or her society. Social approach says that an individual is encouraged to behave in a particular way. Psycho-analytical approach says that all good things are a result of superego of the individual. Learning theory approach highlighted discipline and practices of upbringing in character development. According to cognitive development theory, to behave morally is to behave rationally. It is intelligent adaptation to one's social development.

Any civilized society expects not only delay of gratification or postponement of instinctual satisfaction but also radical modification of instinctual needs and sometimes their permanent inhibition. According to Freud, superego neutralizes those instinctual forces which if acted upon may violate moral rules. Superego also holds some ideas that are appreciated by society. Superego represents the voice of the parents. By identification, the individual imitates and adapts values and attributes of the parents. Conscience is formed by identification with the authority figure or aggressor. When father scolds his child, aggressive tendencies in the child arise, and since they cannot be used against father so they turn to the child who punishes himself.

Good character is associated with good values. Humility, integrity, compassion, resistance to temptation, altruism, moral insight, and belief are the most important of them. It does not mean that harsh punishment leads to better moral development. When forbidden impulses arise, aggressive tendencies of superego are evoked to keep the ideas away from conscious. In this process, guilt is also generated if control is not complete.

According to learning theory, parents shape the behavior of their children by punishing, rewarding, and setting examples, that is, by negative and positive reinforcement, and modeling.

Resistance to temptation, if absent, leads to conflicts even in adults. Intelligence and female gender are related to better resistance. Teenagers are weak in that. Low self-esteem and neuroticism lead to poor resistance. Rejecting and neglecting the child leads to criminal tendencies. Values and family both affect each other.

4.8. SEXUAL HARASSMENT

Let us take an example of unethical behavior which is subtle but very harmful to the victim.

In a country like India, sexual harassment of women is very common and taken for granted as an inherent aspect of women's jobs and girls' education. Substantial number of girls and women leave their education or jobs only because of sexual harassment.

A very apt example of unethical behavior is sexual assessment of women at workplace. Many a time, it is observed and is also scientifically proven that male members do not even accept that their behavior is harmful to the lady. The lady is exposed to awkward experiences only because she is a female.

Sexual harassment is defined as repeated and unwanted verbal or sexual advances, sexually explicit derogatory statements, or sexually discriminating remarks which cause the worker feel threatened and harassed, which interferes with her job, undermines job security, and creates a threatening atmosphere. Though generally misinterpreted, scientifically sexual harassment at workplace takes many forms: it includes various visual verbal and behavioral patterns from leering to ridicule, derogatory remarks, showing or displaying pornography, even touching own body in an indecent way, and sexual advances. It is something that the lady has never invited, but she feels awkward about it.

Effects of sexual harassment are basically of two types—work related and psychological. The avoidance of work, apathy, decreased job performance, a lack of concentration, absenteeism, and reduced job satisfaction are obvious effects. This results in long-term career damage of the victim. There are less opportunities, promotions, and sense of efficacy. All these things create an impression that women are not interested in job opportunities and lack the sincerity necessary for the same.

Psychological ill effects are detrimental to mental health. A lot of suppressed anger, guilt, shame, fear, nervousness, anxiety, tension, stress, depression, and decreased creativity are seen as long-term effects of sexual harassment. Physical health also is affected. Headaches, nausea, helplessness, sleeplessness, and effects from ulcer to cancer are reported by researchers. Retaliation is not possible due to fear of character assassination.

Respecting women working in the organization and girls studying in one's school or college is a must to avoid such malpractices. It is against the human rights of women to trouble them only because men can easily do that. Such behavior may lead to a lack of respect for the person may he be a boss, a principal, a teacher, or a student.

4.9 MANNERS AND ETIQUETTES

Shivam is a second-year student of a professional college. He is not interested in studies but wants to enjoy life. He along with his friends sits on the stairs and continuously smokes. He passes some derogatory remarks when some girls enter the building. He also comments on teachers such as Mr Fatty, Mr Oldy, and so on. He thinks that he is very popular as he is daring.

Etiquettes and manners are a code of conduct in social situations. In interpersonal relations, etiquettes are appropriate behavior or practices according to social convention. It depends on social norms, culture, and tradition as well as on the socioeconomic status. All social interactions are influenced by manners and etiquettes. In all types of occasions where formal as well as informal interactions take place, these etiquettes direct individuals. Cultural impact is most significant in deciding exact manners and etiquettes.

Manners are associated with making good impression and improving self-concept. In all social situations, manners are essential for creating good impression. Formal mannerism, showing respect and politeness are some important elements of manners. Courtesy, consideration for others, and understanding the other individual's position and status are also associated with that.

Manners and etiquettes are becoming more important in the corporate world. Especially managers, officers, and people from any high-status occupations are expected to observe them carefully. They are behavioral styles like table manners.

In organizations, during daily routine work also manners and etiquettes must be practiced to maintain a smooth working atmosphere. One example is telephone manners and etiquettes. They are:

1. One should answer the phone in three or less rings.
2. It is necessary to ask the individual whether he or she has time to talk.
3. One should answer with one's name and name of the department.4. Official calls should be made during office hours only.
4. Return calls should be done within 24 hours.
5. Personal information of coworkers should not be given on phone.
6. If the connection is lost, one should call again and should not wait for the other person to call, especially when one is the caller.
7. Thank the concerned person within 24 hours.
8. If someone else breaks these rules, one should not pay any heed to it.

4.9.1 Developing Good Manners and Etiquettes

For developing good manners and etiquettes, one should try to practice the following styles specially while interacting with others at a public place:

1. One should not communicate impulsively. One must think before communicating.
2. Speech should be clear and distinct. Stammering and stuttering along with unwanted utterances like um or unnecessary repetitive words decrease the effectiveness of communication.
3. Selection of appropriate worlds in the given situation to communicate proper emotions enhances the impressiveness of communication.
4. One should use soft and socially approved expression and avoid expressing negative words and abusive language.
5. No one should talk about physiological aspects like some exceptionality in structure or handicapping conditions, as well as no remarks should be passed about hard realities of life.
6. Using inappropriate and socially unappreciable nonverbal messages should be avoided as that creates a bad impression. Pointing to someone, staring at the person of opposite sex, and unnecessarily moving hands and legs while communicating are detrimental to good manners.
7. Respect, politeness, and appropriate nonverbal strategies for expressing the same are useful to create a good image.
8. One should avoid talking ill behind the back and gossiping.

9. One should avoid rude expressions and unprofessional words regarding any thing and anybody.
10. Culture-specific and socially accepted style of greeting others, thanking them, and expressing apology, like for example, when one is late.
11. Hygiene of self and others should be protected. While coughing and sneezing, one should cover nose and mouth properly and turn away from phone and people.
12. Showing interest in what others say and paying attention also is essential to express courtesy.
13. Interrupting others when they are talking and belittling them must be avoided.
14. Respecting self and others for being agreeable and acceptable.

Such type of manners and etiquettes are to be observed for other things such as table manners, dress fashion, and mannerisms while interacting in public, with a person of opposite gender or with elderly. Nowadays all these things are becoming so important that even formal training regarding the same is given to newly selected members of organizations.

Good manners and etiquettes create a pleasant atmosphere, and if we behave in an appropriate way, others also reciprocate similarly. However, it should be remembered that internalization of values is more important than just overt behavioral discipline.

4.10 SUMMARY

This chapter discusses in detail the nature and significance of values in human life. Different types of values and theories of moral development are discussed in detail. Ethics are about behavior as related to values. In day-to-day life how people behave and what are its consequences on others is an important issues. Ethics depend on the whole socialization of an individual, his or her integrity and values. Various cultures expect different ethics.

Sexual harassment of women at workplace is the most obvious example of unethical behavior. It is troublesome to the victim, illegal, and an irresponsible behavior. Good manners and etiquettes are essential for creating proper impression and maintaining adequate self-image in an organization. It may be a school, college, or a workplace.

QUESTIONS

1. Elaborate the nature and significance of values.
2. What are the different types of values?
3. Describe the concept of ethics. Give examples.
4. Discuss the various theories of moral development.
5. Elaborate different correlates of values.
6. Discuss the consequences of sexual harassment of women at workplace.
7. How to develop good manners and etiquettes?

APPLICATION ORIENTATION

1. After substantial introspection you should write down your core values. Which of your major decisions and behavior patterns are affected by your values?
2. Trace back the development of your values. Can you remember any ideal person that you are imitating or used to imitate when you were young?

3. Write down names of five individuals whose values and morals are so strong and positive that they are devoted to some social cause.
4. Discuss the perception of sexual harassment of your classmate from other gender. Do you find that it is different from yours?
5. Can you remember anyone whose manners and etiquettes are so bizarre that everyone criticizes the person? Discuss with your friends and get a feedback from them regarding the appropriateness of your manners and etiquettes.

SUGGESTED READINGS

Allport, G. W. (1968). *The person in psychology*. Boston, MA: Beacon press.

Berk, L. E. (2006). *Child development* (7th ed.). New Delhi: Pearson Education.

Boniwell, I. (2012). *Positive psychology in a nutshell*. New York: McGraw-Hill.

Elliot, S. N. et al. (2000). *Educational psychology: Effective teaching, effective learning*. New Delhi: McGraw-Hill.

Eysenck H. J., Arnold, W. J., & Meili, R. (1975). *Encyclopedia of psychology*. Fontana, CA: Fontana/Collins.

Freud, S. (1953). *An outline of psychoanalysis*. London: Hogarth Press.

Kolberg, L. (1976). Moral stages and moralization: The cognitive developmental approach. In T. Lickona (Ed.), *Moral development and behaviour*. New York: Holt, Rinehart and Winston.

Piaget, J. (1952). *The origins of intelligence in children*. New York: International University Press.

5 Self-management

Objectives

After reading this chapter, you will be able to:

1. Understand the significance of self-management.
2. Know various dimensions of self-management skills.
3. Define social competency behavior.
4. Think critically about value orientation.
5. Understand various life goals and the importance of selecting them.
6. Utilize the knowledge of all these things for enhancing self-management skills.

5.1 SELF-MANAGEMENT SKILLS AND SOCIAL COMPETENCY

5.1.1 NATURE AND SIGNIFICANCE

Sudeep is an irresponsible and a happy-go-lucky person. As he is appearing for 12th and CET for engineering, his parents have made a provision for various coaching classes and additional guidance for him. Sudeep, however, is not very serious about his studies and enjoys movies, and parties with his friends instead of going to coaching classes. He is also interested in challenging his friends and wants to win every bet. Once he went to the second floor of his college and only for winning a five-hundred-rupee bet, he jumped from there.

Why are adolescents doing such things that are harmful to them and detrimental to their future? Why can such a person not evaluate objectively the long-term consequences of their own behavior? Parents or teachers are not supposed to be responsible and they are not available to supervise all the activities of these adolescents and young adults. Why can one not shoulder the responsibility of his or her own self?

Overinvolvement of parents spoils the person and, thus, overdependence and laziness may result. We have to be independently self-nurturing and mature enough to manage our own self.

The best example of self-management is seen in the nature. No help is given to a butterfly when it comes out of its cocoon, otherwise it always remains weak and dies soon.

The whole science of psychology is oriented toward the all-sided development of an individual. Here one has to consider not only achievements but psychological harmony, maturity, and socially acceptable behavioral patterns. Acquiring high and appropriate life goals is essential to give proper direction to an individual's life. Importance of value system in integrating human life cannot be underestimated at any given point of time. Managing self-competency involves the overall ability to assess one's own strengths and weaknesses, and pursue well-accepted professional and personal goals, balance various areas and roles of one's life, and maintain motivation to learn new skills and appropriate behavioral changes. In self-management, one has to shoulder the responsibility of managing self and basic tasks such as education or career over time and through stressful circumstances. One who can manage self can manage all the remaining challenges in life.

As children grow older they are expected to be independent in various activities and manage on their own. In the same way, a young adult should be able to lead an individually satisfying and socially useful life .The basic assumption is that one is responsible for whatever happens to one's life. The individual should be able to lead his or her life independently and should be in a position to guide one's own activities. If one is not capable of managing self, it means that he or she is allowing others to control his or her life. Self-management skills and skills of social competency are required for achieving this goal. There are ways and means to learn self-management and social competence. It adds into our repertoire the knowledge regarding how to improve our behavior and achieve better goals.

Self-management needs methods, skills, and strategies by which the individual can effectively direct his or her activities toward appropriate goals. It includes goal setting, decision-making, focusing, planning, scheduling, self-evaluation, self-intervention, and efforts toward self-development. Self-management should be oriented toward making the individual's psychological status balanced and self-directing. The person should not require anybody else's help to lead a socially acceptable and still satisfactory life. It is worth trying for oneself and others.

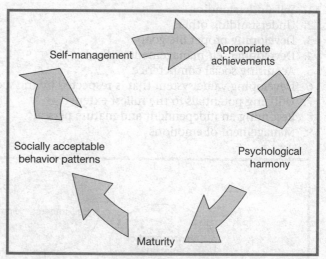

One should be able to lead a socially effective and individually satisfying life.

One should be able to shoulder the responsibility of one's life, decisions, as well as actions.

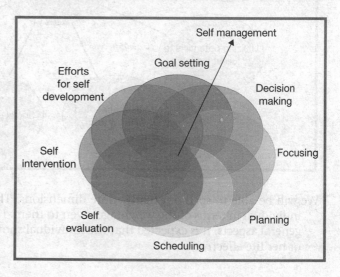

These activities are oriented toward the all-sided development of the individual. It includes emotional, social, educational, occupational, and cognitive development of the individual. It is also to be noted that motivation should be from within. A person should contribute to his or her development. No one else can change our life, only we can do that. So it is a must that the person should be able to decide as to what he or she wants to achieve.

The various aspects to self-management are:

1. Self-understanding
2. Understanding others
3. Developing proper life goals
4. Developing self-management skills
5. Acquiring social competence
6. Developing value system that is respected by the society
7. Utilizing potentials to the fullest extent
8. Becoming an independent and mature person
9. Management of emotions

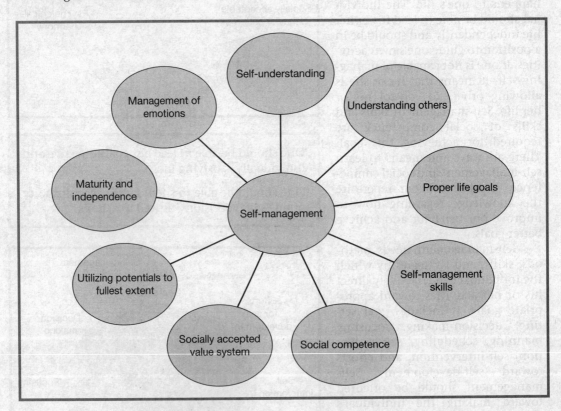

We will be able to spell out many more dimensions. These aspects will be different for each individual in terms of the weightage given to them. However, these are the most important general aspects. It is expected that the individual should be independently dealing with his or her life effectively.

5.2 SELF-MANAGEMENT

Self-management is the deliberate applications of counseling principles to oneself by oneself. It is oriented toward enabling each individual counselee to be his or her own counselor. According to traditional meaning, self- management is self-control but as per the new idea, it is self-discipline. The reasons behind it are as follows:

1. First thing is we do not want the individual to be dependent on anybody else as and when there is a confusion or a decision is to be taken. The elderly person may not be available or may leave the station or country for some work.
2. Self-confidence has to be achieved by the individual to deal with his or her life and develop ways to tackle his or her own problems. Generating opportunities for self and giving a chance to try as well as margin to err may enhance self-confidence.
3. Self-management is based on internalization of values by the individual. If there is an ornament worth ₹50,000 lying on the ground and there is no one around, then what a student will do depends on whether he or she has internalized the ultimate values like honesty. If yes, then he or she will take it and submit it to the college office or principal's office and display a notice on the board about it. However, if the person only wants to show that he or she is honest, he or she will look around carefully and then after making sure that no one is observing, will pick it up and keep it in his pocket. Here, the only concern is about being caught by others and the individual is not really honest but wants to pretend it.

Once internalization takes place, the individual himself or herself can monitor his or her feelings, behavior, and interaction with others. In that case, external control and supervision or threat are not necessary.

Once achieved, self-management skills are useful for the whole life of the individual. In long run, the individual does not need anyone to help him or her in case of important decisions.

Pranoti is studying in second year in a management college where all her classmates are from very well-to-do families. They spend a lot of money every day during lunch break and purchase luxury items such as cold drinks and pastries. Pranoti does not get that much of pocket money from her parents and, hence, cannot do all these things. She wants to be with her classmates and enjoy, hence feels unhappy. So she started asking her parents for more pocket money. Her mother told her that it was difficult due to her father's health problems and limited income of the family. Gradually, Pranoti realized that her life is different from that of her friends' and started eating her own tiffin and spending more time in the library instead of accompanying them to the canteen. She did not ask for more money and at the same time found out an alternative acceptable activity for herself. Now even if Pranoti gets some extra money, she never spends it on unnecessary things.

Let us consider the procedure of self-management. The individual is to encourage himself or herself to go step by step and try to improve his or her self-command. Following are some important steps:

1. **Identifying the target behavior**

   The first step is to identify what exactly one would like to achieve. It is the precise identification of what it is that has to be changed. It can be some behavioral pattern that the person wants to achieve or something that he or she wants to extinguish. It may be some behavior that is only weakly established and the person wants to strengthen. The person also should understand what other environmental and personal factors are responsible for that particular thing. Understanding cause–effect relations is essential before starting self-management program. Those specific behavior patterns are the target behavior that one wants to change. Contributing factors should also be controlled. All the while we are talking about the behavior pattern that the individual himself or herself wants to change, and not about something that someone else wants the individual to change. If the person is changing his or her behavior as per someone else's wish, it cannot be called as self-management, which is the ability to manage one's own behavior with the use of self-reinforcement. Self-reinforcement is much more effective than similar reinforcement given others.

2. **Acquiring baseline data**

Second step is acquiring baseline data like knowing under what conditions and how often unwanted behavior occurs or conditions and frequency when wanted behavior does not occur. Sometimes target behavior is ambiguous and vague. In this case, more details regarding the intensity and duration as well as the length and conditions accompanying that behavior are essential.

3. **Setting up a contingency management plan**

This is the plan of rewarding oneself for acting in a preferred way and punishing oneself for getting involved in an unwanted behavior. For minor achievements, we have to think of small rewards, and for a substantial achievement, a major reward is to be given. One has to break down the target behavior into small segments. This leads to a better understanding of how one has to stop acting undesirably and how he or she has to begin practicing the wanted behavior.

Yogendra has always been a lonely child who cannot make friends. He, first of all, should accept this idea that he has to change his behavior and style of interaction with others. Then Yogendra will be motivated to modify his behavior and see the effect. What type of behavior leads to friendliness and unfriendliness is to be considered in detail. As Yogendra wants to be a self-managing person he has to start changing his behavior and rewarding himself for even minor changes. The first change is that now Yogendra has started smiling at his classmates which he never used to do previously. The next step will be giving simple greeting along with smile. The third stage will be giving some complimentary comments with a

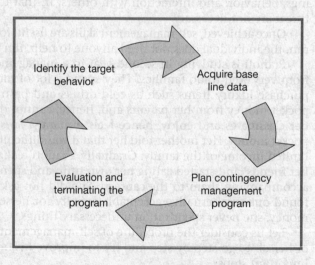

smile and a greeting. Here, we have to think of some reward that he likes. It can be anything such as buying a gift, eating something, or playing some game. Rewarding oneself with the help of self-talk, evaluating effects of behavior change, and giving feedback to oneself are also effective.

As far as diminishing undesirable behavior is concerned, punishing self if involved in that type of activities is a must for self-management. The punishment may be something like the loss of a desired leisure such as restrictions on television viewing.

4. **Ending the procedure**
   In this last stage, assessment is to be done whether the desired behavior has been achieved or undesirable behavior has been diminished. If that is achieved, the contingency management program can be terminated. Here, it is essential to decide if the premature withdrawal of contingency management is taking place. A patient who is feeling better after taking a medicine for some time feels that it is not necessary to continue medicine and stops taking it. This may result in reemergence of the same complaint again. A similar situation may result if the evaluation of the changes in behavior is not done properly.

5.3 SOCIAL COMPETENCY BEHAVIOR

As we have already discussed, the ultimate goal of self-management is to help an individual to lead an individually satisfying and socially effective life. Every society, every religion, and every educational institute wants an individual to function effectively in the society. It includes getting along well with others is valued by all social institutes—family, school, religious organizations, social organizations, and so on. Man is a social animal and our happiness largely depends on our relationships with others such as our parents and siblings, teachers, fellow beings, and other significant people in our lives. As a member of a group we must be able to understand others' emotions and accept them as worthy individuals.

Some important goals in this domain are discussed as follows:

1. **Identifying perceptions and feelings**
   While interacting with others in day-to-day situation, one does not and cannot identify perceptions and feelings of others. However, these skills are essential for developing and maintaining proper relations with others. These skills can be learned if systematic efforts are done for the same. While discussing communication, the role of various other skills such as verbal and nonverbal in interpersonal relations has been discussed. All these things are essentially to be considered here. The use of appropriate nonverbal communication strategies and verbal modes of communication help any individual to establish cordial relations and maintain them. Every individual should be given an opportunity to learn more about these things which are important in day-to-day life situation. Skills required in verbal communication include: attentive listening, use of socially acceptable apt words, avoiding hurting others' feelings, being assertive, and respecting others as worthy individuals are essential for better communication.

   Some useful strategies for understanding others are:

   a. **Restatement**—Restating ideas and experiences expressed by a speaker is another strategy worth considering. This leads to better understanding on the part of the listener.

   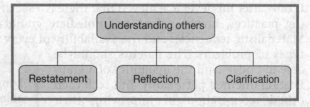

   b. **Reflection**—This is all about reflecting feelings and perceptions of the speaker. It is a must to develop this capacity to understand other person's feelings. It enhances the understanding of the listener about the perceptions of the speaker and reassessment of his or her own perceptions and feelings.

c. **Clarification**—This goes beyond restatement and reflection because it is integrating the whole process of communication and making it more meaningful. Sometimes, even the speaker fails to do this and is not aware of the meaning. It includes the clarification of concepts, events, feelings, and a relation between all these elements.

All these things are similar to the concept of emotional intelligence. It is social intelligence that involves the ability to monitor one's own and others' emotions, to discriminate among them, and to use this information to guide one's thinking and actions. Empathy and handling relationships are included in this with self-awareness, managing oneself, and motivating oneself to manage impulses.

5.4   VALUE ORIENTATION

The image that an individual holds of himself or herself as an independent individual and in relation to others is intrapersonal self. What does one think about himself or herself? What does he or she value the most? What attitude does he or she hold? And, how does he or she evaluate that limitations and assets are important things. Beliefs represent the organizational strategies of the individual through which the person puts everything that he or she knows together.

Values refer to guideline for behavior. It is centrally located in an individual's belief system about how one ought and ought not to behave and about goals which are worth attending. It constitutes desirable modes of conduct and ultimate goals to achieve. Interpersonal self is the actual relation with others. It is the complex interaction between intrapersonal self, interpersonal self, and ideal self, that is, what one wants to achieve that decides values.

Each and every religion in the world wants its members to develop tolerance for the delay of gratification. When an individual wants something he may not get it immediately. All cultures want to socialize its members to have self-discipline. Let us elaborate an example. The age of marriage in India is not the same as the age of physical maturation. Any individual matures physically during the middle of teenage, but the society and Indian culture want him or her to get sexual satisfaction only after early or mid-20s. If we consider social expectations and approval, premarital and extramarital sex are not accepted. Though it is a controversial issue, the influence of Western culture has been changing young adults' behavior which may prove to be hazardous not only psychologically and socially but also physically. The obvious example is that multiple sex partners may lead to the risk of HIV and AIDS along with many other infections and psychological and social problems. For generations, the society expects that the individual should get enough education or training regarding skills, some occupation, and should be able to shoulder the responsibilities of his or her family and children. It is only after this level is achieved that there is a social sanction for marriage. Faulty child-rearing practices, however, lead to immediate gratification-oriented personality of children. Materialistic tendencies and the availability of every pleasure during childhood lead to these types of problems. The parents should be able to understand the dynamics of a gratification-oriented personality and seek each others' cooperation in improving their child's habits and perception.

A very interesting experiment was conducted in 1972 by Walter Mischel, with pre-school children. They were given a choice of either eating a favorite food immediately or

Longitudinal research revealed that those able to resist temptation were significantly more competent as adolescents and their academic achievement was better even after 18 years. The advantages were seen 40 years later also.

waiting for 15 minutes and getting two of the same sort instead. In 2011, it was found that children better at delaying gratification carried this competence to adulthood, also showing consistent differences in certain areas of brain linked to addictive behaviors.

The capacity to sustain efforts and keep working even in the face of obstacles has recently been found to be more important than IQ in predicting academic achievement and long-term success (Duckworth et al., 2007). Finally, emotional control, or the ability to manage impulses and emotions, is another essential skill underlying personal development.

Simba is the only child in a middle-class family. He is 18 and doing his graduation. He thinks that his parents are supposed to provide everything not only for his education, but for all sorts of comforts and leisure time activities. He has been expecting that the parents should spend extra amount for various admissions, coaching classes, fun trips and parties, and even for his foreign trip. Simba is attracted toward a college mate who is a simple, sincere, and value-oriented young lady who wants to get good grades. She is not interested in anything else and is not paying any heed to Simba. He gets extremely upset and annoyed, and is ready to do anything to get her love. Sometimes he also thinks of using unfair means to get her love.

Extreme reactions to minor frustrations are seen in case of these children even in their latter life. Temper tantrums, maladjustment, and undue importance given to simple things are seen in their interactions. They become egocentric and selfish. Such individuals face problems when they become young adults as their parents cannot provide everything that they want to get at that stage of life. For example, no parent can get their child admitted to a government medical or engineering college if their son or daughter could not get a rank necessary for that.

The delay of gratification is one important strategy that is used in Indian culture. For generations, it has been customary in middle-class families to teach children to pray before they eat. Even when they are extremely hungry, and food has already been served, it is a must for them to pray, at least for two minutes, and only then are they allowed to eat. This increases the tolerance of delay between a drive and its gratification. In a way, it increases frustration tolerance. For self-management, it should always be considered as one important issue that frustration tolerance contributes a lot in psychological balance and integrity along with socially acceptable behavior.

5.5 LIFE GOALS

For the highest meaning of life, everyone must develop satisfactory life goals. It is the unifying whole which binds together all aspects of and activities of one's life in one consistent and significant whole.

It is something that a person believes is valuable and is oriented toward achieving it. Life goals are related to a set of values. The person may or may not be able to achieve these goals but tries to move toward them for the whole of his or her life. A scientist may not be able to find out effective drug to treat AIDS though still he or she may devote whole of his or her life for that. It is the center of integration of an individual's physical, intellectual, and emotional aspects.

In every sphere of life, well-being depends on our ability to choose a direction in life and to form intentions. Life goals are core goals, personal strivings, life tasks and aspirations, and specific motivational objectives which give direction to our lives.

Well-being is related to goals that are attainable, realistic, and feasible. Goals should be personally meaningful, related to intrinsic and congruent motives and needs. They should not be conflicting.

Harmony between motivation and goals leads to great satisfaction.

According to some experts, well-being is higher when people select goals that are based on identified, integrated, and intrinsic motivation. Self-concordant goals are associated with pleasure and happiness. They fulfill the innate psychological needs. In the long run, the individual puts in more efforts to achieve these goals. When these goals are achieved, well-being becomes enhanced even further.

Certain goals are more likely to contribute to the well-being than others. Erich Fromm (1994) gave two types of orientations. First is "having orientation" that is related to obtaining material pleasure, wealth, and status, and the second is "being orientation," for example, self-actualization. People with a being orientation are happier. Some other researchers also proved that focusing on extrinsic goals such as money or fame leads to inferior outcomes as compared to intrinsic aspirations as self-acceptance and affiliation. Extrinsic goals are associated with lower self-esteem, more drug use, more television watching, and more difficult and less satisfying relationships.

The congruence between the values a person holds and their goals is also important. There are 10 universal values—power, achievement, hedonism, stimulation, self-direction, universalism, benevolence, tradition, conformity, and security.

Sometimes people choose to pursue goals that are less important but urgent and attract more attention, for example, doing a job or daily chores or the fear that they may not be able to accomplish something they want to. Frequently, it has been just hard to keep going due to the lack of energy and give up before achieving a desired goal. Well-being is related to goals that are attainable, realistic, feasible, personally meaningful, intrinsic and congruent with motives and needs, and not conflicting.

Dileep is oriented toward saving the environment. He knows that he alone will not be able to change the environment but he is doing everything that one can do for avoiding pollution and becoming environment friendly. He does not use a car or a scooter as it creates pollution, does not iron his cloths as it is wastage of electricity, and saves every drop of water. So, he has to walk or use bicycle, has to wear cloths which are simple, only cotton, not ironed, and so on. Still, he continues to do all these things with great devotion as it is his life goal.

It is a challenge to select a life goal suitable to one's abilities, needs, and interests. The goal should have the promise of attainment. Human life is limited. If a person cannot decide what is important and what is not, he or she will be wasting his or her time unnecessarily. Parents, teachers, counselors, and the whole socialization process are responsible for the selection of life goals.

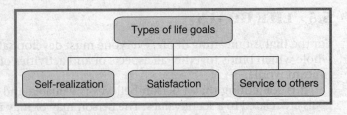

In short, the major life goals are as follows:

1. **Self-realization**—It is the discovery of the authentic self. It is freedom from external coercion such as social, cultural, political, or economic. Maturation of personality is essential here. Freedom from assumptions and preoccupations results from it. Experiencing reality of the world without any psychic restrictions can be achieved with self-realization. Individual should be able to understand the relationship between self-concept and life goals. If both of them are in congruence, the individual obtains satisfaction out of it. With self-realization the individual is capable of objectively and openly understanding the world without any filters.

2. **Service to others**—Every religion pleads the importance of service to others. Great people like Mother Teresa worked for it and devoted their lives for serving others. It is a socially respectable goal. Many individuals serve the needy and deprived as per the available time and energy. Though they cannot devote their whole life, they find some time out regularly to serve the poor or handicapped. A teacher may teach students from slum areas during evening without charging them anything for that. A housewife may read textbooks loudly for the blind or a student may share his or her books with his or her friend who cannot afford to buy them.

3. **Satisfaction**—For self-management, one has to focus on socially acceptable satisfactions. For example, an adolescent may either be satisfied by drug abuse or get satisfaction by playing cricket. If the individual is oriented toward getting satisfaction by doing socially undesirable things, he or she should try and understand the danger in that. Ideal situation will be where the individual gets satisfaction in every sphere of life—from home and family, from education, from peers, and so on. The student should discuss these things with teachers, parents, and counselors.

One more important aspect of self-management is management of emotions. Emotional intelligence is the capacity to recognize one's own and others' emotions, including self-awareness, self-motivation, being empathic, and having social skills.

All philosophical thoughts are directing human life to the ultimate values and want the individual to be kind, courageous, generous, and oriented toward justice and peace. One has to decide which path one has to follow.

There are various philosophies regarding life. Some well-known ones are listed as follows:

1. Hedonists put forth the view that one should live for today. One must try to get as much pleasure as possible. However, it is obvious that one must always respect social norms and should avoid anything that is not acceptable to society. One more point explained by him was that extreme pleasure may result in sorrow.

2. Some Greek philosophers were interested in the idea of avoiding pain. According to Epicurus one should try to gain as much pleasure as one can but try to avoid pain. Whatever one cannot achieve should be given up. No one can get everything that one wants to. Hence, one should train oneself to forget about things which are beyond one's reach and concentrate more on mental satisfaction than material or physical pleasure.

3. Aristotle put forth the idea that man should look at life as a compromise. No extreme ideas should be entertained. This will lead to a happy balanced life. With all special abilities, man should find out this balance point.

4. One more philosophy is, whatever happens, is for good. Stoics philosophy says that only God knows why things are happening in a particular manner. As we do not know the complete picture, we think otherwise. One should be able to control one's emotions.

5. One more view is that the aim of life is peace of mind. Nothing matters, after all, more than that.

6. Search of knowledge leads to all good in life. A person will be happy only when he or she is good or virtuous only by attending knowledge. Things such as courage, wisdom, and justice are important to achieve in life with the help of knowledge.

7. Christian philosophy says that God will give all happiness. Those who are good natured only will believe in God.

8. Bentham says that one should try to get and give pleasure to others. Along with one's happiness and welfare, one should think about others' happiness and welfare.

9. Indian theory of Karma assumes that whatever the person experiences depends on his or her prior deeds and their appropriateness.

It is essential to preserve and enhance balanced, healthy life. For that, many a time one has to renew four important dimensions of one's nature—physical, mental, social and emotional, and spiritual.

Spiritual dimension is one's core commitment to one's values. It is extremely important and secret area that influences one's whole life. This is related to one's inspiration and the link between man and timeless truths of all humanities. By strengthening this bond, one feels as renewed and recommitted. It gives power and multiplies one's energy.

For generations people are involved in defining moral character and moral development. In any civilized community it becomes essential to train young ones so that they become capable of shouldering the responsibility of preserving the moral characteristics of the community. They should become good adults.

Every action of human beings, day-to-day interactions with others, goals and aspirations, and similar other things are decided by one's philosophy of life and value system. Following are the necessary points that one should know:

1. What is important in one's life? If one makes this clear, many things about his or her life will be clear.
2. Which of the activities are related to the goals in life and significant for the individual?
3. Understanding what is important leads to selecting what one wants to achieve in life.
4. This helps in achieving the goal.
5. An objective perspective regarding self, goals, and environmental issues should be obtained. Hence, what one can achieve and what one may not be able to achieve become clear.
6. Understanding regarding how to behave and interact with others is enhanced.
7. One becomes a well-behaved good citizen and performs all the duties essential for remaining the same.

If we cannot understand what exactly we want and to achieve that what should be done we will be aimlessly doing something and wasting our life. If one does not understand the destination, it is obvious that one would wander. With distorted perceptions, and lack of self-management skills, one would land in trouble as he or she will be able to realize it only when it is too late.

5.6 SUMMARY

Self-management is a very significant aspect of human life. The person who develops self-management skills becomes mature enough to deal with his or her life and achieve socially effective and individually satisfying lifestyle. Values essentially are core to personality and behavior of any individual. They play a very salient role in human life. Life goals should be consistent with values. There are different types of goals. Some of them are self-oriented and some are other-oriented, some are based on extrinsic motivation and others on intrinsic motivation. Material and money orientation leads to limited satisfaction but goals like self-actualization result in far better outcomes.

If proper life goals are not developed, the individual will be misguided by temporary pleasure and immediate gratification which is detrimental to the whole life. Different philosophers have given varied philosophical views to make human life more balanced and sound.

QUESTIONS

1. What are self-management strategies?
2. Discuss the concepts and types of life goals.
3. Describe gratification orientation.
4. What are social competency skills?
5. Discuss the importance of value orientation.

APPLICATION ORIENTATION

1. Prepare a list of your needs where their gratification is delayed by your parents. What is your reaction to it? What do you think is your parents' intention?
2. Which of your activities are only individually satisfying? Which of your activities are socially acceptable? Enumerate your behavioral patterns that are both individually satisfying and socially acceptable.
3. What are your life goals? What are your aspirations? What would you like to be after 10 years?
4. If you make a mistake what is your reaction? Objectively evaluate your reaction. Do you justify and defend your error, or accept that it is your mistake? Do you feel awkward or guilty or you can forgive yourself?

SUGGESTED READINGS

Baron, R.A., Byrne, D., and Branscombe. (2008). *Social Psychology*. New Delhi: Pearson Education

Duckworth, A. L., Peterson, C., Mathews, M. D., and Kelly, D. R. (2007). Grift: perseverance and passion for long term goals. personality processes and individual differences. *Journal of Personality and Social Psychology, 92*, 1087–1101.

Eugene, M. (2000) 3rd ed. Business Psychology and Organizational Behavior. Sussex: Psychology Press Limited.

Fromm, E. (1994). *Escape from freedom*. New York: Holt Paperbacks Owl Books.

Ilona Boniwell (2012) Positive psychology in a nutshell. New York: Open University Press, McGraw-Hill.

Communicating and Thinking

2

6 Communication

Objectives

After reading this chapter you will be able to:

1. Understand the importance of communication in human life.
2. Know nature, functions, and models of communication.
3. Evaluate your own style of communication.
4. Improve your strategies of communication.
5. Describe how gender affects communication.
6. Explain the concept of communicating rationally.

6.1 INTRODUCTION

A doctor and a nurse fell in love and got married. They were blessed with a son. By the time the son was 9 years old, their hospital became one of the leading hospitals in the city. Once their son met with an accident and was unconscious. Immediately, he was brought to their hospital. Due to brain injury it was essential to operate him. The doctor was to operate him. The son was taken to the operation table. There he suddenly opened his eyes and said, "This is not my father!!"

Why did he say that?

This is a very well-known story about communication and is a demonstration as to how communication fails.

The answers to this question are generally generated by anticipating that the son's medical condition was such that he could not recognize his father, as he was wearing a mask or something like the doctor was not his biological father, and so on. However, the reason was that the doctor was not his biological father. In Indian culture, very few individuals are capable of understanding this—readily realizing this—not his father but his mother was a doctor. The gender of the doctor and of the nurse was not mentioned anywhere. However, almost all individuals are ought to assume that the doctor must be a male and obviously the nurse must be a female.

Male domination imbibed during socialization in the Indian scenario is responsible for this type of misunderstanding in communication.

Let us see how do we communicate? How the receiver interprets the message? How much accuracy can be expected? How to enhance it? What are the correlates of communication? What are the different styles of communication?

6.2 NATURE, IMPORTANCE, AND DEFINITION OF COMMUNICATION

Communication is as essential for the survival of human beings in social life as breathing is for survival in physiological sense. Survival of all living beings depends upon communication which is human connection. Even a newborn baby will not be able to survive without communication. Though not elaborate in terms of language, the baby expresses feeling of discomfort and attracts attention of its mother. The person who is pretty old and seriously ill and is going to die after sometime also heavily depends on communication every moment. Hence, communication is essential for everyone. It is a universal and a lifelong process. All living beings communicate with each other. However, human communication is much more elaborate than communication of other species. Human communication is sharing of experiences indirectly with the help of symbols. This is unique and is seen only in case of human beings, as creating and using symbols are the highest cognitive abilities available only to humans.

> Communication is a process of creating a meaning between two or more people.
>
> Communication is essential for survival in social life of human beings.

Communication is the most significant aspect of human life as each interpersonal relation develops and is maintained only on the basis of communication.

This diagram shows that in human communication, by and large, if we take an average, listening is 45 percent, speaking is 30 percent, reading is 16 percent, and writing is only 9 percent of all the communication done.

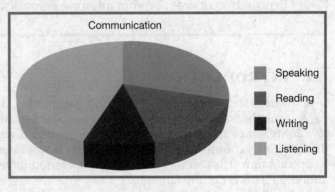

Right from the beginning, an individual's self-identity, self-concept, and self-worth depend upon communication and feedback from others. Research has proved that isolated people face many serious health problems and die prematurely.

Human beings depend upon each other for everything and human relations result in either happiness or unhappiness.

6.2.1 DEFINITIONS

There are different definitions of communication. It is broadly defined as sharing of experiences. Symbols are used in communication for representing something and creating meaning related to something that may not be present in the immediate environment. Goyer in 1970 has stated that human communication is sharing experiences indirectly and vicariously. Tubbs and Moss (1994) have expressed the idea that human communication is a process of creating a meaning between two or more people. It is a social interaction where two agents share a common set of signs and semiotic rules. These rules are syntactic, pragmatic, and semantic.

According to Drafke and Kossen (1998), communication is a two-way process resulting in the transmission of information and understanding between individuals. It is the exchange of thoughts, messages, or information by speech, signals, writing, or behavior between a sender and a receiver.

Recently, the concept of manipulative communication was given by Bryenton, which specifies that communication is intentional or unintentional ways of manipulating words and gestures to get what one wants by demeaning, discounting, attacking, or ignoring instead of respectful interaction, sarcasm, rudeness, swearing, and criticism.

There are numerous functions of communication from pleasure to treatment and in day–to-day life one has to communicate for any interaction or work.

The range of messages is from survival needs to some creative piece of research. That is why, though human beings have been communicating for generations, it is necessary to think about its improvement.

Business relations obviously depend on communication more than anything else. Appropriate on-the-job communication is essential for getting ahead in the job. In business, communication of honesty, sincerity, spontaneity, and at the same time maintaining business ethics is essential. That makes it even more challenging. Sometimes, not saying or doing any-thing communicates many things.

Nisha and Payal are colleagues who are working in the same office for last 5 years. When they cross each other they do not even look at each other. Are they communicating anything? Some of you may think that nothing is communicated. However, yes definitely something is communicated!! Either they hate each other, one of them holds the other in contempt, they believe they are superior to each other, they are arrogant or they feel something that is extremely negative. Such type of mentality is seen in various Indian organizations.

Communication is essential for expressing self in terms of emotions, ideas, and attitudes, as well as for evaluation, treatment, teaching–learning, and every human transaction. In short, communication is a science in itself. For any type of sales or services, for example, communi-cation becomes the most important skill.

There is a difference between the speed of talking and the speed with which one can make the message meaningful. Generally, the speed of speaking is 150 words per minute; however, the capacity to listen is 450 words per minute. As a consequence, one gets some extra time for making the message meaningful. Thinking of something else while listening to a lecture or during any other type of communication is a common practice. So, many a time while thinking of other things, a fake impression that the message has been understood is passed on, when in reality, it is not the case. It is scientifically proved that most of the time one neglects the nonverbal cues and gets only 25 percent of the message neglecting the rest 75 percent. For the communication to be effective, one has to concentrate on the message in every possible way and try to under-stand as much contents as possible along with the feelings and emotions expressed in that.

Hence, communication is essential for making sense of the world and sharing that with others. For appropriate communication, one must be a sensitive and accurate receptor of all channels of communication. One has to express that the message is understood. Being aware of and assessing the impact of communication on the client is also recommended. It is a skill-ful job and a scientific art.

Let us consider some important dimensions of the same.

6.3   BASIC MODELS, DETERMINANTS, AND TYPES OF COMMUNICATION

Researchers from various fields such as psychology, education, management, and similar other disciplines like sociology have been working for understanding various aspects of human communication. The basic characteristics and processes of human communication have been the focus areas of research for last more than 75 years all over the world. Considering its importance, sound theory of communication is essential as it is always useful for better application of the principles of communication.

The basic model of communication is as given below:

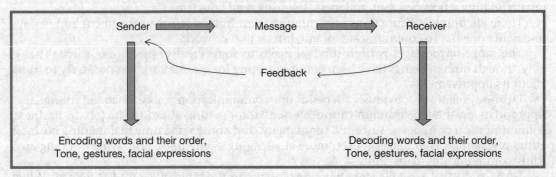

There is a sender, a receiver, and a message. Without feedback, communication cannot be complete as it is essential to ensure that the receiver has understood the message sent by the sender. The sender filters semantics, emotions, attitudes, role expectations, gender bias, and nonverbal messages. While receiving the message the receiver also filters the same. The sender selects words, their order, tone, gestures, and facial expressions which together are called encoding. The receiver has to decode all these things as per his or her interpretation. Hence, if one concentrates only on words, the possibility of misinterpretation increases which leads to miscommunication. Both the sender and the receiver share the responsibility of effective communication. That is why feedback becomes important. The speaker should not assume that everyone knows the exact meaning of the message that he or she is delivering and the listener should not assume that he or she knows exactly what the speaker wants to say.

Emotions are one of the most powerful filters. They lead to a pro or an anti point of view. The focus is not content but feelings. Attitude may facilitate or hinder interpersonal communication.

In Tubbs' communication model (1994), different roles of two individuals while communicating are taken into consideration. Both of them are sources and receivers of communication. Both are influenced by one another. In day-to-day life, communication is spontaneous and unstructured; hence, their roles also overlap. This transactional viewpoint of communication emphasizes simultaneous and mutually influential nature of communication.

In 2008, Barnlund gave the transactional model. Here, the individual is simultaneously sending and receiving messages. In some recent models, it has been proposed that how an individual communicates is a determining factor of the way how the message will be interpreted.

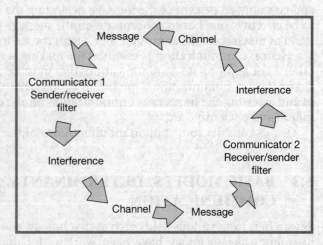

6.3.1 DETERMINANTS OF COMMUNICATION

Select one unknown college mate of your own gender. Do not discuss anything with each other. Both of you should write down only one word describing each other. Then write down the word you think the other person must have written for you. Write down the expected similarities and differences in you and your partner. Write down the similarities and differences your partner must have written.

Now keep the papers aside and discuss something with your partner for five minutes. Then discuss whatever is written on the papers and find out the discrepancy.

You will be able to see that we take things for granted and unnecessarily keep on evaluating each other.

Communication is a very complex process. Some characteristics of both the individuals play an important role in the process of communication. These are mental capacities useful for utilizing knowledge, attitudes, and emotions for communication. In a way, the input for communication is collected from all the stimuli of physical and social world, from the past and the present, that give information about it. Any communication in two individuals A and B depends upon:

1. Who A thinks he or she is?
2. Who A thinks B is?
3. Who A thinks B thinks A is?
4. Who B thinks A is?
5. Who B thinks he or she is?
6. Who B thinks A thinks B is?

If this is the situation when only two individuals are communicating, the complexity increases with number of members communicating with each other simultaneously.

The complex process of communication depends on the following things:

1. **Context**

   a. Physical—intensity and background stimuli.
   b. Social—who is talking to whom and where.
   c. Historical—past experiences of the individual in that particular circumstance or interaction with that individual.
   d. Psychological—emotional reactions of the individual, curiosity, interest, and comfort.
   e. Cultural—cultural ways of expression and cultural differences among the two persons communicating.

2. **Status/characteristics of participants**

   a. Physical traits—age, sex, and so on.
   b. Psychological attributes— values, attitudes, and so on.
   c. Personality characteristics—introvert or less interested in communication, extrovert or talkative, and others alike.
   d. Style of emotional expression—excessive emotional expressions or less overt expression of emotions.
   e. Social experience and socialization—the process of bringing up children, impact of social interaction, and childhood experiences.
   f. Knowledge and skills—regarding the subject of communication as well as about communication itself.

3. **Message**

   a. Meaning—intention of the sender to communicate a particular message.
   b. Symbols—exactness of verbal and nonverbal symbols used to express a particular idea.
   c. Encoding and decoding—difference between the ways in which a particular message is interpreted by a sender and a receiver.
   d. Organization—the organization of verbal and nonverbal indicators.

4. **Channels**

   a. Sensory—auditory, visual, tactile nature of message, or even odor or taste as stimulus to be interpreted.
   b. Noise—background noise or background disturbances.
   c. External—environmental stimuli.
   d. Internal—thoughts or feelings due to which the interpretation of message is distorted.
   e. Semantic—different meanings and ideas associated with a particular word or action.

5. **Feedback**

   a. Sense modality used for feedback—heard, seen, or understood by other means.

Any disturbance related to these leads to blockades of communication.

Role expectations are also responsible for making the message meaningful. One expects that a person will communicate the same thing as he or she is playing a particular role. Like for example, most of the employees think that the boss is going to give some negative feedback, or in a typical traditional Indian family, a daughter-in-law thinks that her mother-in-law is going to scold her. This kind of mind-set itself may color perception regarding the message.

6.3.2 Types of Communication

There are different types of communications. The basic types are impersonal and interpersonal communication. Impersonal communication is one-way communication such as giving basic information using circulars, bulletins, and e-mails. Interpersonal communication is face-to-face interaction in which the people involved talk and listen in a way that maximizes their own and others' humanness. Interpersonal communication takes time. The goal of interpersonal communication is more than just giving information. It is the most important and influential type of communication in deciding interpersonal relations and happiness of any individual. Hence, it is a fertile field of research. One more essentially important type of communication is intrapersonal communication. This is communication of any individual with self. It may be labeled as self-talk. This is related to self-understanding, self-confidence, and self-worth in general.

6.3.2.1 Other Common Types of Communication

1. Oral or spoken and written
2. Formal and informal
3. One-way communication—such as, television, radio, or newspaper—and two-way communication—like an interview
4. Upward, horizontal, and downward
5. E–communication and Indirect communication—like art work
6. Intrapersonal and interpersonal communication

Some psychologists divide communication into syntactic, pragmatic, and semantic. The data do not only include words but nonlanguage sounds and body language. From this point of view, it is impossible not to communicate.

Scheflen (1968) has outlined channels of communication as:

1. Language modalities—including linguistic such as lexical, stress, pitch, and juncture.
2. Nonlanguage modalities—nonlanguage sounds and vocal modifiers.

Under the nonlanguage modalities kinesics and postural dimensions are considered. That is, voluntary and involuntary behavior, facial expressions, tonus, and positioning. Tactile communication is also equally effective. Odorifics, proxemic and artifactual including dress, cosmetics used and decor as well communicate many things. Researchers have studied 135 gestures and expressions of body, head, and face indicating different messages. In a way it can be said that the whole body, gestures, and glance speak. Though it is somewhat ambiguous and overlapping, when verbal communication is not clear, people believe in nonverbal communication.

Mehrabian in 1968 has used electronic filter and has divided the total message quantitatively. Only 7 percent of the message is communicated verbally, 38 percent vocally, and 55 percent with the help of facial expressions and other modes of nonverbal communication.

It is because of this fact that verbal message communicates very little; if one focuses only on words, the chances of misinterpretation increase.

When there is any discord between you and your friend or you and your sister, what do you insist on? Many a time, you insist on a particular word used by the other person and keep on arguing how inappropriate it was and want to prove that he or she only wanted to abuse you. However, no word has exactly the same meaning on every occasion and with reference to every type of tone, facial expression, and context.

There are many ambiguities in any communication .The meaning which one wants to communicate is never the same that the receiver understands.

Messages are divided by two ways:

1. Intentional and unintentional
2. Verbal and nonverbal.

If both these ways are mixed, there are four types of messages:

1. Intentional verbal
2. Unintentional verbal
3. Intentional nonverbal
4. Unintentional nonverbal

These types can be explained as follows:

1. **Verbal messages**
   These constitute of one or more words spoken. Intentional verbal messages are conscious efforts to communicate with others through speech. The use of common symbols is essential for proper communication.
2. **Unintentional verbal messages**
   These are the words that the sender says without meaning to. According to principles of psychoanalysis, these are unconsciously motivated. Slip of tongue is the best example of such a communication. The person who is communicating may not be aware of what has been communicated till the time he or she gets some feedback from others.
3. **Intentional nonverbal messages**
   These are the messages that an individual wants to transmit. One may greet the other person only by waving a hand, smiling, or nodding his or her head without words.

4. **Unintentional nonverbal messages**

   These are the nonverbal messages transmitted without control. Sometimes these messages are contradictory to the intentional verbal messages and convey the real meaning of the message. A student who is afraid of presenting a paper in front of the class may say that he or she is not afraid but is unwell and shows all signs of stress and fear. Controlling unwanted nonverbal expressions is a difficult task.

Channels are related to two aspects—one is sensory like sight, hearing or touch. The other is organizational communication such as newsletter, notice board, etc. For communicating many cues multiple-channel communication is recommended.

When communicator "one" says something, communicator "two" listens. The four basic processes involved in listening are:

1. Attention
2. Hearing
3. Understanding
4. Remembering

Individual differences with reference to socialization, cultural background, and physical and psychological filters play an important role in listening. Hence, feedback is essential to check information about the accuracy of communication.

6.3.2.2   Verbal Communication

All social processes depend upon speech. Hence, it is almost the essence of our life as a social being. Communication is a social technique. Without it there will be no common meaning, and concepts, no action that provides information and instructions, no give and take of knowledge, and no social organizations. Speech communication is the basic form of adaptation to the environment. All types of communication convey both content and relationship. While words can be used to communicate almost anything, relationship is basically communicated with the paralinguistic and nonlanguage modalities. This is actually the true message or the true meaning of the verbal message.

Adequate research evidence is available to indicate the importance and functions of verbal communication.

Communication as a science is based on some basic principles like each individual is a worthy person and deserves to be respected. This respect is to be expressed with the help of verbal communication. Everybody is unique and, hence, should be valued.

In verbal communication, it is a must to remember that both the parties should be able to enjoy equal status and freedom. No verbal expression should be indicating any general evaluation of the other's behavior. No remarks should be passed to compare an individual's behavior with social mores, norms, and morals.

Verbal communication contributes significantly to maintain good human relations. For effective verbal communication one should avoid certain expressions which may lead to unpleasant consequences.

6.3.2.3   Nonverbal Communication

Even in day-to-day life situations it is accepted that actions speak louder than words. The body speaks, glance speaks, and everything regarding speed of movement as well as distance that one maintains while communicating speaks. Giving accent, complimenting, contradicting, regulating, repeating, and substituting are the basic functions of nonverbal communication. Nonverbal communication is different when one likes the individual with whom he or she is communicating, dislikes the individual, or does not know the individual at all. It is communication without words. Sometimes nonverbal vocal communication is also considered an important issue. However, nonverbal, nonvocal communication is given much more attention by researchers. If all verbal, nonverbal, and behavioral communication is taken into consideration, it is impossible not to communicate. Out of the total time for which the individual is awake, 90 percent of the time, the individual is communicating something to someone.

Apart from verbal expressions, a person's body is also a source of many additional cues of communication. Body expression and experiences such as tension, tapping, stroking, fidgeting, rocking, or constricting are important sources of information and awareness. In terms of nonverbal communication, researchers have concentrated their attention on the meaning of various acts. It is proved that a specific act has a specific meaning. The ability to interpret such acts adds to an individual's repertoire of skills. Understanding nonverbal communication of the communicator is far more useful than just listening to the words. In case of some communicators many feelings and attitudes cannot be verbalized adequately. Hence, it is essential to be watchful and alert to take a note of the nonverbal communication even if it appears to be redundant at that given point of time. It requires sensitivity, training, and skills.

Indicators of nonverbal communication

Eyes, head and face, mouth, gestures, touch, postures, distance, walking style, and status symbols play an important role in nonverbal communication. Appearance, face, gestures, gaze, spatial behavior, bodily contact, and almost everything influence communication to a substantial extent. Simple acts as scratching head, resting face on hand, crossing arms across the chest, biting fingers, and many other types of nonverbal communications are common. Facial expressions as well as eye contacts also declare many emotions. If the listener is reluctant to communicate, he or she will not look at the communicator or if at all he or she looks, it will be very brief.

Eyes are the most important means to communicate relations. Even no eye contact communicates many things. Gestures, postures, touch, as well as the distance we keep while communicating tell something about one's relation with the receiver. In short, what we can say is that **communication is the most powerful way of developing, maintaining, and expressing human relations.**

There is a controversy regarding whether the person is aware of his or her own nonverbal communication and if it is intentional or there is hardly any awareness and it is unintentional. Another important issue is whether the origin of nonverbal communication is biological or cultural. Whatever may be the case, nonverbal communication was also used by primitive man who could not use language, and it was useful for communication at that time also. As it is generally accepted that there is some ambiguity in nonverbal communication, researchers have checked for the percentage of agreement among various trained judges about it. For example, it has been reported that the percentage of agreement is very high in this case as shown in the box.

- Hand movements—69 percent
- Head nods—66 percent
- Head turned away—85 percent
- Head support—90 percent
- Low face movements—87 percent
- Smile—83 percent
- Upper face movements—80 percent
- Hand movements—80 percent
- Hand gestures—95 percent
- Body position-forward, upward or backward—100 percent
- Arm movements—96 percent.

There are some elements of social behavior useful for communication. Even appearance, gaze, spatial behavior, bodily contacts, personality, and social attitudes indicate some things. It can be seen that one can interpret nonverbal communication only after proper training. In the same way, paralanguage also helps to understand the message. Researchers like Matarazoo and others have developed a paralanguage measure. Highly reliable findings of the "duration of utterance," "duration of latency," and "percentage of interruptions" are reported even on audiotape. Audiotape and exact written transcript show a correlation as high as 0.92 in the interpretation of paralanguage. The simplest example is speech–disturbance ratio. There are many indicators of emotional disturbances, like when an individual becomes anxious, it is reflected in his or her word frequency. It is well documented that paralanguage and kinesics are related to emotional state.

Interpreting nonverbal communication accurately means understanding the world of the individual from his or her own point of view.

Researchers have proved that omissions and intruding incoherent sounds indicate some emotional disturbances. In some other research, it was found that a speaker relaxes either very little or to a great deal when he or she dislikes the person talking to him and to a moderate degree when he or she likes the person moderately. Both relation and content are expressed more clearly by nonverbal communication strategies. The more you like a person, the more time you like to spend looking into his or her eyes as you talk.

If a figure like a circle on the right hand side of the top of a triangle placed in the left corner of a parallelogram is to be drawn only on the basis of verbal instructions and without any hand movements, facial expressions, and repeated explanations, it becomes very difficult to understand how to draw it. However, if a similar figure is explained with the help of facial expressions and other nonverbal communication strategies, it becomes comparatively easy.

Ask your friends to draw this figure without showing it to them and when you describe it only with the help of words. Then see the different figures that they will draw.

Sometimes the nonlanguage channel communication is controversial to language channel communication. Like for example, a young lady may smile while telling how unhappy she is or a child may say that everything is fine when he or she is almost in tears. Nonlanguage channels and paralinguistic channels more accurately express emotions and intentions and at the same time are interpreted in a better way as compared to language channels. An adolescent may express something by action which he or she cannot express by words either because of social barriers and fear of consequences. Likewise, an adolescent may bang a door if his or her father asks him or her to spend less money for fun.

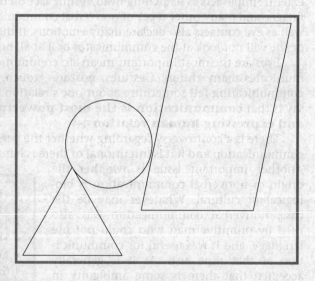

Most of the times, there is some inconsistency in verbal and nonverbal messages. That is exactly why a good communicator must be able to interpret and receive all communication modalities. Training is essential for that and techniques like tape recording of audiovisual aspects of communication may enhance the awareness of the speaker and the receiver.

A reader may identify his or her own communication style when he or she feels:

1. Angry
2. Tensed
3. Delighted
4. Upset
5. Unhappy

Tone is capable of changing the meaning of any communication. If the mother of a 10-year-old child scolds him or her for drawing on the wall and says, "Don't be crazy," there is a particular meaning to the word crazy similar to mad or immature. However, think of a young newly married couple. Think that the wife is blushing and saying to her husband, "You are crazy," the meaning of the word crazy differs here a lot. The same words uttered in different ways indicate different meanings and emotions. If one screams loudly, the message will be interpreted otherwise than if the same message is given by the same person softly.

6.4 COMMUNICATION STYLES

There are different ways in which communication styles are classified. In day-to-day life one can observe four basic styles of communication.

1. **Clear and direct communication**
   It is the most simple and appropriate style of communication. Here, the message is stated plainly and directly. It contains the statement of what has happened and what is one's emotional reaction to it. For example, the mother says to her daughter "I was disappointed when you did not complete your homework on your own."
2. **Clear and indirect**
   In this second style of communication, the message is clear, but it is not directed to the person for whom it is intended. The person will state something as a general remark—"It is unfair when someone just neglects one's responsibility."
3. **Masked and direct**
   Masked and direct communication occurs when the content of the message is unclear, but is directed to the appropriate person. For example, in case of a family, the mother will say, "Now a days, students just don't work as hard as they used to."
4. **Masked and indirect**
   Masked and indirect communication occurs when both the message and the intended recipient are unclear. In unhealthy family relationships, this type of communication tends to be very common. For example, the mother will say "Youth today are insincere."

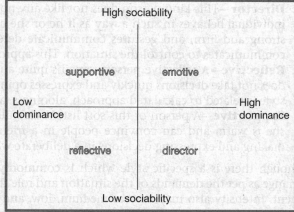

Some other researchers have considered dominance and sociability as basic dimensions in this relation. A vertical and a horizontal continuum may explain four types of communication. High sociability to low sociability and high dominance to low dominance are the two continuums.

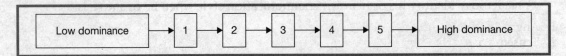

One has to determine his or her place on the dominance scale; think about others and their place on this continuum according to you. Low dominance people are characterized by a tendency to be cooperative and eager to assist others. They tend to be low in assertiveness and are more willing to be controlled by others.

High dominance people give advice freely and frequently initiate demands. They are more assertive and tend to seek control over others.

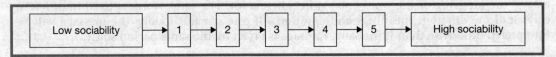

The dimensions that are considered for placement on sociability continnum include being open, friendly, talkative and quality of being easy to get to know. It can be defined as the tendency to seek and enjoy social relationships. Sociability can also be thought of as a measure of whether you tend to control or express your feelings. Those high in sociability usually express their feelings freely, whereas people low on the continuum tend to control their feelings. The person who is low in sociability is more reserved and formal in social relationships. Their behavior is indifferent. Extreme positions in both cases may lead to social problems.

Dominance is to be taken as the *x*-axis or the horizontal axis, and sociability as the *y*-axis or the vertical axis. The model is divided into quadrants, each representing one of the four communication styles: emotive, director, reflective, or supportive.

1. **Emotive**—High sociability and high dominance indicate emotive style. An emotive person talks loudly and is involved in vigorous hand movements. Such a person displays action-oriented behavior and is constantly on the go. Emotive type of communication is associated with informal style where the person starts communicating freely, immediately after formal introduction. It is easy for him or her to convince others. This style indicates that the person will put forth his or her viewpoint dramatically and forcefully.
2. **Director**—This kind person does not like any nonsense and has got serious attitude. The individual behaves in such a way as if he or she cannot have fun. His or her opinions are strong and firm, and gestures communicate determination and indifference. He or she communicates to control the situation. This approach is formal.
3. **Reflective**—A reflective person remains quite and wants to spend time alone. He or she does not take decisions quickly and expresses opinions in a formal and deliberate way. This style is related to calculated approach, aloofness, and reviewing details.
4. **Supportive**—A person of this sort listens carefully, and is cooperative and patient. He or she is warm and can convince people in a friendly manner. He or she is interested in making and expressing decisions in a deliberate way.

Though there is a specific style which is commonly used by an individual, the styles may change as per the demands of the situation and role that the person is playing in that environment. Intensity also may vary as medium, low, and high. No method is effective if there is rigidity and excessive use of a particular style. Every method has its own advantages and disadvantages. Emotive is refreshing, directors get the advantages of thoroughness and determination. Supportive people are admired for easygoing responsive style. Emotional control and industriousness are advantages that are associated with reflective style. However, there are also some disadvantages associated with every type. A person who is supportive is interested in pleasing everyone and cannot take a firm stand regarding anything. He or she is constantly in need of assurance and apologies very often. The director is very cold and uses closed words. An emotive uses emotionally loaded language and may hurt anyone. Reflective does not take any decision and does not express emotions. What is most valued is the capacity to get along well with any type of person having any style. This capacity is called as versatility. Others can freely communicate with a versatile person and he or she does special efforts for becoming acceptable to others.

Many such styles have been given by researchers. Driver, analytical, expressive, and amiable are four such basic styles. Here, assertiveness and responsiveness are the two dimensions covered. Those who are highly assertive and less responsive are called as drivers. They are aloof, cool, and highly task oriented. Such individuals control their emotions. They focus on work and accomplishments. They display awards and strive for efficiency. They are always busy in their office work.

Individuals who are low on both assertiveness and responsiveness are labeled as analytical. These individuals like structure and system. They are organized and are not comfortable when they work with others. For them, job is more important than relationships.

	Low responsiveness
ANALYTICAL	DRIVER
AMIABLE	EXPRESSIVE
	High responsiveness
Low assertiveness	High assertiveness

Expressive individuals are high on both assertiveness and responsiveness. On the one hand, they want to manage their relations and on the other, they are impulsive and emotive. They use various tricks and indirect verbal and nonverbal methods to express their emotions. Their style in general even to get work done is based on emotional exchange.

Amiable individuals are less assertive and more responsive. They are more concerned about relationship than work. They generally fulfill social needs of others. Need for affection and that of inclusion is more in case of amiable individuals. They make others comfortable. There are no barriers in their communication and they communicate more freely with others.

6.4.1 Common Types of Communication Styles

There are some common types of communication styles. Some examples are given as follows.

1. **Noncommunicative person**—This person concentrates on what he or she thinks and what he or she wants, and does not take the listener into consideration. His or her message may cause confusion but he or she is neither aware nor concerned about it. Confusion in his or her mind is related to other behavioral confusions. In case of these individuals, special efforts are necessary to understand their message.
2. **Overly logical speaker**—Some individuals have the need to be precise and accurate in what they say. This is seen in an exaggerated manner in some personality types like obsessive personality. The person wants to win and control the situation. Here, postures and movements are also extremely rigid.

3. **Under-talker**—These people believe in self-protectiveness that may arise from a sense of inadequacy or fear of making an error. Here, paralinguistic and nonlanguage cues indicate the psychological state of the individual. Sometimes indirect verbal cues such as unsolicited denial (i.e. denying something one has not been accused of) are seen.

4. **Over-talker**—This person is typically not a listener. He or she may be basically an anxious and insecure person. Some individuals whose communication pattern otherwise is not over-talking may use this style in situations of tensions where they feel threat. Typically, there is a high output of words in a fast rate of speaking, a higher than usual speech, and greater physical movement.

5. **Tangential speaker**—This type of speaker counters the other person's statement by throwing in side remarks and irrelevancies. The power- and control-oriented individuals may use it to disrupt someone else's communication by putting the other person off his or her stride and controlling the situation.

6. **Helpless speaker**—On the one hand, this person asks for help and on the other accuses that the other person is not capable or willing to fulfill his or her demands. The general feeling and expression is, "There is no one who cares for me and listens to me."

7. **Combination of patterns**—This is a person who may use different patterns at different times or even in combination. For example, a person who is overly logical may also be an over-talker.

The nonlanguage channels are by and large consistent with language patterns. An over-talker generally uses a great deal of gestures and facial expressions. The overly logical speaker may be rigid in postures and gestures. He or she uses words distinctly. The noncommunicators use hardly any nonlanguage communication.

6.5 CULTURE AND COMMUNICATION

Communication essentially depends on culture. In a country like India, there are many cultural variations. It is related to language, the socioeconomic status, geographical areas, religion, caste, creed, and community. A very common expression of affection in slum area will lead to a horrible consequence in a colony of very well-to-do educated people.

Culture also affects the directness and necessary context in communication.

6.5.1 INDIRECT- OR HIGH-CONTEXT COMMUNICATION STYLE

Context means the amount of innate and mostly unconscious understanding that a person can be expected to bring to a particular communication. In high-context collectivist and homogeneous cultures, such as Thailand, people are expected to have the understanding of how most interactions will take place, of how they and the other person will behave in a particular situation. They know and understand each other quite well, and they have indirect style of communication. They rely less on words to convey meaning and more on nonverbal communication. Manipulating the context is enough for them for communicating something. In this situation they work closely together and know what everyone else knows. Communication exchange is also useful for maintaining harmony.

6.5.2 DIRECT OR LOW-CONTEXT COMMUNICATION STYLE

Cultures like those of the United States tend to be more heterogeneous and individualist. Less can be assumed and is known about the other person. Everyone is self-oriented, self-reliant, and emotionally detached. Hence, they have to depend on verbal communication. Here, giving information is the basic purpose of communication.

6.6 EFFECTIVE COMMUNICATION

Communication is effective only when the message initiated and intended by the sender corresponds closely with the message perceived and responded to by receiver.

R/S = receiver's meaning/sender's meaning = 1

Researchers have proved that such perfect correspondence is never achieved in day–to-day life situations. On the other hand, many a time a zero mark is the output of communication. This means that there is no correspondence between the response the communicator wants to produce and the one that he or she receives.

The effectiveness of communication can also be measured in terms of possible outcomes. Five important aspects from this perspective are:

1. **Understanding**—accurate reception of the contents of the intended stimuli.
2. **Pleasure**—it depends upon feelings about those with whom communication is done.
3. **Attitude influence**—it is the process of changing and reformulating attitudes of the receiver.
4. **Improved relations**—effective communication results in improved relations between the sender and the receiver of any message.
5. **Action**—effective communication has the power to change the action of the individuals involved.

Hence, communication should be effective in every aspect—cognitive, affective, and conative.

6.7 COMMUNICATING RATIONALLY

Vinit was taken to the hospital when he met with an accident. There was a hairline fracture in his hand. As plastering was not necessary, a bandage was used to support his hand. He was treated by a young doctor who was very pleasant and soft-spoken. His communication style was very attractive and friendly. When Vinit was discharged from the hospital, he wished him luck. However, within three days again he was taken to the doctor due to extreme pain in his hand. Vinit never knew that weight lifting is strictly prohibited in fracture, and the doctor never told it to him. Vinit lifted a bucket full of water and it resulted in a major complication.

If a doctor does not tell the reality regarding health conditions of the patient but talks very nicely to the patient and his or her relatives, what will be the consequence? What will the impact of that communication be? Will it be positive or negative? Was the communication pleasant? Was it done using all important verbal and nonverbal styles useful in that situation? Was the communication of the doctor effective? Was that rational and objective? Whatever are the effectiveness indicators, the best communication is always rational. Communication is useful, mature, and worthy if and only if it is rational and gives objective information.

Though the concept of rationality originated from philosophy, many other branches of science are developing it further and applying it to their area. These branches are psychology, politics, sociology, economics, and evolutionary biology.

Many psychologists put forward the view that human beings are rational in principle, but they err in practice as there are various factors detrimental to rationality.

Rational decisions in organizations are optimal decisions. Practical rationality is a strategy for living one's best possible life, achieving one's most important goals, and one's own preferences.

Rationality is holding oneself responsible for or accountable to the bounds of logic and evidence. Obviously, its relation with factual and objective world is very strong. Think about some communication which is not based on reality, and is not objective. It will be not only a waste of time but may prove detrimental to the receiver. Sometimes, it is uncomfortable to do so, but still when we are observing rationality we try to avoid various biases. We accept the fact that emotions and intuition are more useful and much more valuable if combined with thoughtful analysis while communicating.

A 10 year-old child was brought to a well-known psychologist. The major complaint was slow learning and academic failure. After some tests and discussions, the psychologist told the parents about what type of education will be appropriate for the child and highlighted the areas in which the child will be able to work more comfortably. Instead of mentioning the label that the child was a boarderline retarded individual, he was explaining the areas where the chances of success are more. She was both understanding the feelings of parents and using scientific reality for better results of communication.

Reasoning guides us for better understanding our feelings with reference to causes, and impact on behavior. In rationality, we are interested in accepting our own limitations in thinking and encourage others to give us feedback about that, so that we can improve upon it.

Rationality is the habit of acting by reason, which means in accordance with the facts of reality. The only alternative is acting by whim. This is because an action based on a belief in a particular cause–effect relationship will not occur if that relationship is invalid. Any deviation can have long-term problems, since one's knowledge is often derived from his or her previous knowledge. To accept a false belief once can have the effect of polluting all further knowledge.

It means accepting only that which you have a reason to believe in is essential. One has to use logic to weed out any contradictions. It means when you have to accept the judgment of others, you use your own mind to determine whether you should. Is the person educated in that field? Is it a must to accept it as it is? What are the other ways or options to think about the issue?

Rationality is in your self-interest because the only way to achieve desired outcomes is to act according to reality. To understand reality, one must use reason consistently, until the mistakes are cleared away and the new knowledge reevaluated. If a person has been, even slightly, influenced by personal emotions, feelings, instincts, or culturally specific moral codes and norms, then the analysis may be termed irrational, due to the injection of subjective bias. That is why it is difficult to achieve.

6.8 SUMMARY

Man is a social animal. We do not live in isolation.

For almost all the time when we are awake, we are communicating something to someone, verbally or nonverbally. We communicate for various purposes. Our satisfaction and happiness, self-concept, and interpersonal relations, in fact, everything in social as well as personal lives depends on communication. According to various researchers, communication has to be a two-way process and the responsibility of effective communication is to be shared by both the individuals involved. Verbal and nonverbal communication along with tone are to be considered and interpreted for communicating effectively. There are different styles of communication. We should identify our own style and others' styles so that good interpersonal and intrapersonal communication can be maintained.

QUESTIONS

1. Describe the significance of communication in human life.
2. Explain how communication is a joint responsibility of the sender and the receiver.
3. Discuss various determinants of communication.
4. Describe the causes and consequences of ambiguity in verbal communication.
5. How effective is nonverbal communication? Give relevant examples from the Indian scenario.
6. Give types of communication styles. How does it affect an individual's interpersonal relations?
7. How can one enhance the effectiveness of communication? Enumerate the advantages of effective communication?

APPLICATION ORIENTATION

1. Try the following exercise repeatedly in a small group of friends. Each one should talk for five minutes regarding some social problem. Others should objectively evaluate various aspects of communication, for example, one of the observers should evaluate tone, someone should evaluate facial expressions, and so on. Give feedback to the speaker one by one. Now with these modifications, ask the individual to again talk for five minutes. Continue this till substantial change and understanding results.
2. To what extent do you think that you are aware of your own nonverbal communication especially when you are quarreling with your sibling or friend? Discuss with them regarding your nonverbal communication. Introspect regarding the exact emotions you want to communicate and the understanding of others.
3. Give some examples of interactions when communication was substantially distorted and resulted in misunderstanding. Discuss its causes with the person with whom you were interacting.

SUGGESTED READINGS

Drafke, M. W., & Kossen, S. (1998). *The human side of organization*, 7th ed. Boston, MA: Addison-Wesley.

Helgeson, V. S. (2006). *Psychology of gender*, 2nd ed. New Delhi: Pearson Education.

Tubbs, S. L. and Moss, S. (1994). *Human communication*. New York: McGraw-Hill College.

Goyer, R. S. (1970). Communication, Communicative process 20 meaning: Toward a unified Theory. *Journal of Communication, 20*(7), 4–16.

Scheflen, A. E. (1968). Human Communication: Behavioural programs and their integration in interaction. *Behavioural Science, 13,* 44–55.

Mehrabian, A. (1968). Communication without words. *Psychology Today, 2*(9), 52–55.

7 Thinking and Reasoning

Objectives

After reading this chapter you will be able to:

1. Understand the nature and types of thinking.
2. Know the importance of concepts.
3. Explain the scope of reasoning.
4. Describe theories of thinking.
5. Elaborate the nature of attributional style and its effects.
6. Realize the nature and steps of problem-solving.
7. Differentiate between different types of decisions.

7.1 INTRODUCTION

Sandeep is a 14-year-old student from a lower class family. As he is the only son, parents are concentrating their attention on his education. His two sisters help their mother to earn by preparing and selling pickles. They are school dropouts as their family cannot support their education. Sandeep, on the other hand, is free to study and go to tuition class. He, however, thinks that he is being treated in an unfair manner and is expected to get good grades. He thinks that going to school and attending class is boring and wants to stay at home like his sisters do. He thinks that he is the most unwanted child in the family.

Why is Sandeep so confused? Why does he have a distorted thinking process?

Human beings can acquire a lot of information from the environment and store huge amount of that information in long-term memory. This information is manipulated and transformed through thinking that is the manipulation of the mental representations of information in the form of word, visual image, sound, or data. Human beings can think about the present, the past, and the future. We can think about reality and fantasy. General intellectual abilities, concept formation, language as well as reasoning power and the ability to think critically are necessary for thinking. As this is a special power of human mind which is responsible for the advancement of science and technology, a lot of research has been done by psychologists for enhancing this power and using it in day-to-day life situations.

7.2 NATURE AND TYPES OF THINKING

All achievements of every individual result from his or her thought process. From a psychological perspective, thinking is characterized as a complex, analytical, synthetic activity of the brain and every mechanism which is capable of processing the information received.

It is impossible to underestimate the importance of thinking in human life. Thinking makes human life different from that of animals. One's behavior, understanding, and emotional experiences depend on thinking that is not only associated with problem-solving, but with every minor decision that one has to make. Thinking is the act or process of having ideas or thoughts including reasoning, problem-solving, decision-making, formation of mental models, and contemplation of knowledge, beliefs, and opinions. The difference in the types of thinking is relative and depends on many things as experience, diverse subjective attitudes, and objects about which thinking process is utilized.

With the help of figurative and pictorial imaginary representations, ordering according to similarity or equality and differences is done. Objects with the same qualities in terms of various senses are treated together. Those that are different are separated. The action of ordering with the help of figurative and pictorial images is called as intuitive thinking. Young children are more prone to such type of thinking.

> Thinking is defined as establishing of order in apprehended world. This ordering is related to objects and their representation, as well as to the relationship between objects and order of relationship between their representations.

Thinking is the basic cognitive skill necessary for each interaction with the environment and with oneself. So, inter- and intra-individual relations also depend on a thought process. It has been defined as the process involved in manipulating information, either collected through the senses or stored in memory from previous experience, so as to be able to respond to the immediate situation.

Anyone who suffers from problems related to thinking may suffer from thought disorder which means a pathological disorder of thought. It includes delusion, flight of ideas, loosening of association, etc. leading to schizophrenia and similar disorders.

Only being intelligent is not enough for critical thinking, one should know how to use that intelligence and know a rational view point.

The stages of thinking are:

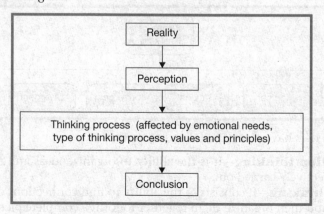

The relation between thinking and language is complex and complicated. Language is not only a means for expressing thought but a basic element of mechanism of thinking. With the help of language, abstractions are made from immediate objective impressions and behavior, which are replaced by thought, images, and schemata in combination with outer and inner language.

7.2.1 CLASSIFICATION OF THINKING

There are different ways in which thinking is classified. The most obvious distinction is autistic and rational thinking.

1. **Autistic thinking**—This thinking has no rational purpose. It is the brain's manipulation of the information available to it, from the senses or from stored material, without any particular purpose. Thinking is called autistic when ordering of experienced world takes place as per feelings and motivation. Hence, people, things, and objects coincide with the inner state. If wish fulfillment determines the result of thinking, the thought process is primary. Daydreaming is an example of autistic thinking.
2. **Magical thinking**—This is the ordering of objects, people, and their representations in a way as if they are capable of acting like human beings. This is also found in young children.
3. **Rational thinking**—It is logical, rational, and directed toward a purpose. When you are solving the clues in a crossword puzzle you are engaging in rational thinking.

   If representations, thoughts, and their relations cannot be expressed like imagery, thinking is nonintuitive. It is abstract and conceptual.
4. **Convergent thinking**—This produces responses that are based primarily on knowledge and logic. There are fixed rules and systematic strategies in convergent thinking. There is only one correct answer to any problem. The obvious example is mathematical problems.
5. **Divergent thinking**—It refers to the ability to generate many unusual responses to questions. Sometimes it is referred to as productive thinking which requires insight and creativity. According to gestalt view, a thinker must see a new way of organizing the problem, and a new way of structuring the elements of thought and perception.

   It is also called as innovative thinking which involves generating new ideas or new ways of approaching things to create possibilities and opportunities.
6. **Reproductive thinking**—This is based on memory and whatever strategies the individual has stored in his or her repertoire and application of tried and well-known paths to solution.

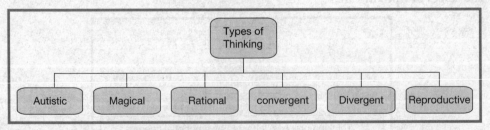

Some other researchers have given the following types.

1. **Implementation thinking**—It is the ability to organize ideas and plans in a way that they will be effectively carried out.
2. **Conceptual thinking**—It consists of the ability to find connections or patterns between abstract ideas and then organize them together to form a complete picture.

3. **Intuitive thinking**—It is the ability to take what you may sense or perceive to be true and, without knowledge or evidence, appropriately factor it into the final decision.
4. **Critical thinking**—It is the mental process of objectively analyzing a situation by gathering information from all possible sources, and then evaluating both the tangible and intangible aspects, as well as the implications of any course of action.

It is not thinking negatively with a predisposition to find fault or flaws. It is a neutral and unbiased process for evaluating claims or opinions, either someone else's or our own.

Critical thinking does not mean that people think exactly alike. People who have different values or principles can reach entirely different conclusions. Differences in perception and emotional needs prevent us from thinking the same way.

Critical thinking is essential for solving more complicated problems in day-to-day life. These problems do not have an answer key. They have uncertain boundaries, incomplete data, and sense of urgency. Critical thinking is defined as grasping the deeper meaning of problems, keeping an open mind about different approaches and perspectives, and deciding for oneself what to believe and what to do. For this one has to:

1. learn to recognize when does a problem exist;
2. define problems more precisely;
3. cope with poorly structured problems;
4. deal with problems which are not self-contained;
5. address problems with no clear-cut criteria;
6. manage risky personal issues.

Problem-solving in classroom and laboratory situations are totally different as compared to day-to-day life situations. However, thinking critically helps. Making sense out of one's own behavior, evaluating the accuracy of the claims of behavior, and making wise personal choice are essential in problem-solving.

Critical thinking hardly considers feelings or emotional thinking. Emotions give our lives meaning, pleasure, and a sense of purpose. Critical thinking cannot possibly fulfill this role. Still, important emotional decisions such as deciding about a life partner should include critical thinking.

There are different types of thinking which serve different purposes.

Following are the steps that should be followed to enhance critical thinking:

Step 1: Adopt the attitude of a critical thinker.
The first step to becoming a proficient critical thinker is developing the proper attitude. Such an attitude includes the following characteristics.

1. Open-mindedness
2. Healthy skepticism
3. Intellectual humility
4. Free thinking
5. High motivation

For being both open-minded and skeptical, one has to find out facts and information sources. It is necessary to support issues we intend to judge and examine issues from as many sides as possible, rationally and objectively looking for the good and bad points.

For finding out truth as far as possible, one should accept the errors one is making.

It is very common that there are flaws in our beliefs. We should be ready to examine new evidence and accept conclusions objectively. Many issues are beyond clearly labeling as right or wrong, but a combination of both. To think freely, keeping aside social pressures to conform is essential. This can be quite difficult but one should be able to do it till the evaluation is complete.

Finally, a critical thinker must have a natural curiosity and be highly motivated to put in the necessary work sufficient to evaluate the multiple sides of issues.

Step 2: Recognize and avoid critical thinking hindrances.
In each day of our lives we become exposed to things that hinder our ability to think clearly. They may be unintentional and natural human limitations or manipulative. We must know how to recognize and avoid it.

Basic human limitations are misconceptions due to faulty logic or perception, or psychological and sociological pitfalls. Thinking is also restricted by the language we use.

Step 3: Identify and characterize arguments.
Critical thinking needs the ability to recognize and construct a proper argument. It is associating a reason to support the conclusion.

Step 4: Evaluate information sources.
If the facts supporting an argument are erroneous, so will be the argument. A critical thinker must have a sound approach for evaluating the validity of facts. A critical thinker should find out information sources which are credible, unbiased, and accurate.

Step 5: Evaluate arguments.
It is the process to assess whether: (a) assumptions are warranted, (b) reasoning is relevant and sufficient, and (c) unreliable information has been omitted.

A warranted assumption is one that is either known to be true or reasonable to accept without requiring another argument to support it.

Reasoning. This is evaluating arguments to assess the relevance and sufficiency in support of the argument's conclusion.

Omissions. This is the final step to evaluating arguments and attempts to determine if important evidence has been omitted or suppressed either intentionally or unintentionally.

7.3   CONCEPTS

In any type of thinking we depend on concepts. Concepts are the most essential prerequisite of thinking. Concepts are categories used to group objects, events, and characteristics on the basis of common properties. This is a special ability to categorize which helps us to make sense of information in the world. Without concepts, it would have been impossible to process information effectively. Otherwise processing information about each object as a unique identity is difficult to imagine. Concepts help us to relate experiences with objects. It is only because of concepts that we can use efficient ways to apply the power of learning, memory, thinking, and problem-solving. Generalization, discrimination, and abstraction are the three stages of concept formation. Finding out essential similarities, then the finer details of the groups of objects, and ultimately the capacity to think about the object when it is not available to our senses are included in concept formation. For example, first of all the child finds out that all dogs have common characteristics such as four legs, two ears, one tail, and fur. After that he or she has to understand the difference between a dog and a cat though many characteristics are similar. The difference in their size, their exact appearance, and voice are to be taken into consideration to distinguish between the two species. Then, a stage comes when the child can understand the meaning of words such as a cat and a dog and can imagine about them. All these things are included in concept formation.

There are two basic types of concepts—concrete and abstract. Concrete concepts are: "car," "table," "chalk," "paper," "boat," and so on. Concrete terms are the terms indicating some objects that we can experience with the help of our senses. That means we can see, touch, weigh, smell, and taste these objects. On the other hand, abstract terms indicate something that we cannot inspect with our eyes and that are not available to other senses also. Simple examples of abstract terms are "freedom," "sincerity," "friendship."

Concrete terms are easy to learn as compared to abstract concepts. Their imagery arousal value is more than abstract concepts. One can easily imagine about a concrete term and associate it with other ideas.

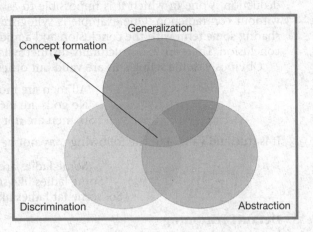

7.4 REASONING

Reasoning is a cognitive process or a mental activity directed at finding the solution of a problem and transforming information to reach conclusion. Here applying formal rules of logic or some other rational procedure is essential. Inference plays essentially important role in reasoning. It is reasoning from premises to conclusion.

There are different types of reasoning. Some important ones are stated below.

1. **Conditional reasoning**

    It is a form of logical reasoning based on conditional statements or conditional propositions like if p then q.

    P is the antecedent and q is consequent. Example, if this substance is glass, it will break if dropped from height. The conditional statement is logically equivalent to not p and not q.

    A subjunctive conditional is a conditional statement in which:

    The antecedent and consequent are both hypothetical. For example—If the Himalayas, will melt, the whole nation will drown.

2. **Counterfactual conditional reasoning**

    This is a form in which the antecedent is not only hypothetical but also false.

    If there were no oxygen on the Earth, there would have been no living beings. Counterfactual reasoning is based on the following type of statement. Counterfactual conditional is a proposition in which p is assumed to be false, and q hypothetical. This is necessarily true. For example—if 5 + 5 = 12, then man is able to fly.

3. **Inductive reasoning**

    This is the form of reasoning where we go from specific to general. The simplest example is—You need oxygen for survival. You are a human being. So, all human beings need oxygen for survival.

4. **Deductive reasoning**

This is the reasoning from general to specific. From observing many cases we can draw a conclusion about a specific case. For example—All cows have four legs. Kapila is a cow. So, Kapila has four legs.

Here, the conclusion is inferred from a set of premises that logically imply it. A validity deduction is one in which it is impossible to assert the premises and deny the conclusion without contradiction. One example is syllogism. In syllogism, there are two propositions sharing some term with the conclusion and a middle term with each other but not with the conclusion. There are 256 structurally distinct syllogisms; however, only 24 of them are valid.

Obviously, some syllogisms are valid but others may not be. For example,

All men are mortal.
No gods are mortal.
So, men are not gods.

It is true and valid. But the following may not be true.

Some ladies are fat.
Some ladies like singing.
So, some fat ladies like singing.

5. **Default reasoning**

Here, default is assumed to be true by default, but can be rejected if further premise is added. So, this is not really logical. For example—

Birds fly.
Tweety is a bird.
Therefore, tweety can fly.

However, if you add some further premise and think more carefully, it becomes defeasible. For example—Tweety is a penguin.

6. **Deontic reasoning**

The concept of deontic reasoning is related to moral value judgment and is less likely to fulfill the expectations of logic. It is reasoning about obligation and duties in relation to ethical and moral actions. "If a boy is under 16, he should never smoke." There is every possibility that in some cultures and some climatic conditions it is allowed and, hence, may not be interpreted as a taboo or prohibition.

There are many more examples of reasoning and various rules related to them. However, on the basis of the examples given earlier, you will be able to understand that reasoning is related to logical rules of thinking. When we think of there being a logical error, our thinking and the conclusions we draw may be distorted.

7.5 THEORIES AND FACTORS RELATED TO THINKING

Various theories have been given by different experts to explain the nature, mechanism, and development of thinking. Some important ones are given as follows:

1. **Behavioristic theory**

According to this theory, thinking behavior is learned or acquired. Some pioneering workers put forth the view that thinking begins as a result of some stimulus. A particular stimulus results in a particular thinking response. Hence, they wanted to explain it with the help of conditioning. Both classical and instrumental types of conditioning were included in this type of thinking process. Both types of conditioning are dependent on the principle of reinforcement. In classical conditioning, it is just a sequence of action that one has to learn and in instrumental conditioning, one has to operate on the environmental stimuli and give a particular response to get reinforcement.

2. **Motor theory of thinking**

Watson (1913) viewed thinking as subvocal speech. The process of thinking inevitably involves inner language. This was a motor theory of thought. Some work was done with deaf-mutes. It might be expected under Watson's theory that they would move their fingers more than a normal group of adults when they are thinking as they use their fingers for sign language. There was a high correlation between motor activity in the fingers and thinking of the deaf than in a hearing group of adults. Skinner (1938) later viewed thinking as private behavior as opposed to overt behavior, and believed that it was similarly subject to stimulus control and reinforcement. He attempted to show that both overt behavior and thinking were controlled by conditioning. In overt behavior, there is an interaction with someone else, while with thinking, individuals are their own listeners.

3. **Gestalt theory**

In this theory, the importance of the organization of perceptual field in the process of thinking is highlighted. According to this theory, thinking is always purposeful and goal oriented. We have to consider the whole context in which thinking takes place. One should be set for reorganizing and restructuring the perceived field for an effective solution of the problem that one wants to solve.

The gestalt principle that human beings generally try to make the environmental stimuli as meaningful as possible also plays an important role in thinking. This is the adoption of the good form or prägnanz.

As far as gestalt principles are concerned, it is easy to demonstrate the idea of prägnanz. Suppose you see a figure like this:

```
          ^   ^
        ( 0   0 )
        (   -   )
```

You may not perceive it only as some signs available on the computer but something else. It is not continuous, nor a drawing of any living being. Still you may perceive it as an owl. We generally make the stimulus as meaningful as possible.

4. **Cognitive approaches to thinking**

Researchers in the field of cognitive psychology focused on mental processes which occur during thinking. The idea of heuristic strategies was given by Miller and Milner (1960). It is based on understanding the human strategies to solve problems. The complexities of a problem might be simplified by working out a series of rules of thumb. These could then be applied one at a time. We will discuss it afterwards in this chapter.

5. **Information processing approach**

This is the most recent approach to explain thinking. In information processing approach, the way in which we process the environmental information is taken into consideration.

The depth of processing depends on the nature of the environmental stimuli and the strategies one is going to use for favorable changes in the same. The salient stages of this approach are:

a. Registering the information available in the environment.
b. Retrieval of information from memory.
c. Using the information from both these sources.

So, in a way it is about considering how we acquire, organize, store, and use the information for planning purposeful behavior. In this approach, we consider everything regarding sensation and perception, organization in memory, as well as types of memory such as sensory, short-term, and long-term, retrieval and forgetting, and all other cognitive processes essential for thinking. This is based on the experimental research done and, hence, is more acceptable.

6. **Developmental theories**

a. Piaget's theory has given an account of how thinking process develops. First is the sensory motor stage, till 2 years, where sensory and motor activities are more important as there is very little mental manipulation of objects and ideas that is possible. Object permanence and differentiation between self and others are achieved by the end of it. At the preoperational stage (2–7 years), the use of language and images helps in the thinking process. During the concrete operational stage (7–11 years), logical thinking regarding concrete terms is achieved. Here classification, conservation, and concepts of number are developed. The last stage is that of formal operation (12 years and after). The ability to think about abstract terms, test hypotheses, and solve problems which do not exist in the immediate environment are the basic achievements during this stage. This is the highest stage. Though criticized heavily, this theory is useful to get a clear idea regarding a learners' level of understanding.

b. Sullivan's basic modes theory has three stages of cognitive development according to Sullivan. They are called modes. These stages are:

   i. Prototaxic mode
   ii. Parataxic mode
   iii. Syntaxic mode

In the prototaxic mode, during infancy there is no definite structure of the thought process. Everything is vague. Only basic pleasures and apprehensions are experienced. In the parataxic mode, a child differentiates between self and the world that means the objects and the persons around him. Only concrete manipulation of things and objects is done. During the last stage that is the syntaxic stage, symbolic representations, images, logical thinking, and abstract reasoning are achieved by the individual.

c. Bruner's theory gives the stages of cognitive development as enactive, iconic, and symbolic representations. During the first stage, the child interacts with the environment only through his or her motor responses. These motor responses and movements are associated with child's representation of things. The next iconic representation stage is characterized by mental images and mental pictures. In the final stage of symbolic representation, words, symbols, and other imaginary abstract phenomena are used for thinking. They are not dependent on motor activities and sensory images.

7. **Psycho-analytical theory**

Freud has given two basic ideas that are predominant in deciding not only emotions and behavior but the whole thought process of human beings. These are the satisfaction of sex drive and the role of unconscious. According to him nine-tenth of one's psyche consists of the unconscious and the subconscious. Hence, according to Freud, wish fulfillment, dreaming, and unconscious morbid thinking is a major part of the thinking of human beings.

Where physiological needs are not fully satisfied, their memory is brought into play. This memory is associated with the kind of excitation that actual food, warmth, and contact evoke.

For example, a hungry infant hallucinates about food, but this hallucination is not in itself satisfying. Some of the energy released is devoted to actually obtaining food. This is essentially autistic thinking, driven by emotions. Freud makes a distinction between the primary and secondary thought processes. According to him, secondary thought means a rational conscious thought. Primary thought processes are unconscious. There are three separate levels of thinking:

a. **Preconscious thought**—These are thoughts and ideas which are not part and parcel of our consciousness. So no attention is devoted to them.
b. **Conscious thought**—One pays attention and engages actively in dealing with them.
c. **Unconscious thought**—These thoughts are inaccessible to our consciousness but play a significant role in determining our behavior.

The relation between thinking and reasoning with communicating is so obvious and important that it is impossible to think about communication without thinking and reasoning. It is equally true regarding interpersonal and intrapersonal communication. Understanding and responding to any type of communication totally depends on the appropriateness of the thinking process. If thinking is not systematic and objective, it will affect communication. The person will not be able to receive the real message sent by others and as a consequence his or her response will be distorted.

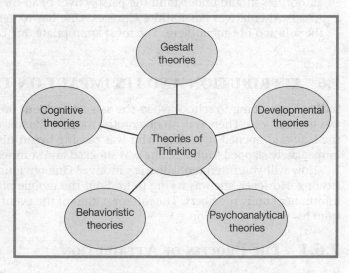

Many researchers put forth the idea that if thinking skills are improved, one may not only get various benefits regarding cognitive achievements such as good grades and success, but can also enhance social life, interpersonal relations, and emotional balance. One can turn negative tendencies like aggression in positive emotions, and even reduce temper tantrums. In a way, thinking is a tool for adapting oneself to the environment. The evolution of culture, art, and technology depends on the thought process. Education system in India is by and large information oriented and memory based. Readymade answers are given to the students and they just have to memorize them. Tendency of the students to explore and find answers on their own is not developed. That is exactly why sometimes partially educated people are very well known for their innovations and self-directed achievements. Indian education focuses on logical and critical thinking and neglects the development of innovative thinking among students. Being correct is the only emphasis. Though at least normal intelligence is necessary for higher quality thinking, it does not mean that those who are very intelligent are good thinkers.

For improving thinking skills de Bono (1985) has devised some thinking formulae. Most important of them are: (a) AGO, (b) CAF, (c) PMI, (d)OPV, (e) APC.

1. AGO stands for Aims Goals Objectives. As deliberate thinking depends on the will power, the thinker should be aware of the aims, goals, and objectives. In other words, a sense of direction is required for thinking effectively.

2. CAF means Consider All Factors. One has to carefully take a note of all factors regarding an issue to analyze it. This reduces the error of partial perception and related problems in thinking.
3. PMI is considering Plus Minus Interesting. First we have to write down all the positive aspects of a solution. Then, we have to write down all the negative aspects. Lastly, we write down the interesting ideas regarding the same. It is easy to arrive at the best suitable solution of the issue or problem.
4. OPV means Other People's Views. Considering the perspective of the significant people involved in or affected by the decision or solution helps a lot. For example, a change in the structure of an educational degree course mainly affects the students, teachers, management, and parents either directly or indirectly. So, before implementing a new policy, the authorities should understand the perspectives of all these groups.
5. APC is Alternatives Possibilities Choices. One has to generate all possible alternatives for the solution of the problem. The most appropriate one is selected.

7.6   ATTRIBUTION AND ITS IMPACT ON THINKING

Sadhana was going to school when she saw an accident on the road. A lady was injured and was unconscious. There was no one on the road. Sadhana went running and took the purse of the lady and opened it. A man who was passing by on his two-wheeler stopped to see and immediately slapped Sadhana. She was shocked and stunned.

How will you interpret Sadhana's motive? One obvious meaning is she was interested in stealing. However, she was trying to find out the mobile phone of the lady so that she could inform her family members. The interpretation of the event and behavior of the man resulted from his wrong attribution.

7.6.1   THE PROCESS OF ATTRIBUTION

It is about an individual's understanding of the reasons behind peoples' behavior and events in his or her own life. Attribution theory is concerned with how individuals interpret the cause and effect of various events and how this relates to their thinking and behavior.

The behavior of an individual is attributed to an external cause when external reasons are more plausible. If your friend comes late, you may say that it is because heavy rain and traffic jam that he or she is late. During rainy season this is the first interpretation that comes to our mind.

On the other hand, behavior will be attributed to dispositional factor when external causes are unlikely. Dispositional factors are regarding the person. You may attribute delay to the careless attitude of your friend and say that may be his or her bike is not properly maintained and, hence, must have broken down, or no petrol must be there in the tank.

Causes: (a) related to the actor, (b) related to the entity, and (c) related to the circumstances.
Any observer can use one of the three specific types of causes to explain an effect:

1. **The actor**—The individual who is demonstrating the behavior. If a mobile is not working properly, one can easily blame the user and say, for example, "Abhay must have misused it."
2. **The entity**—The target person or thing at which the behavior is directed. Another explanation is that the mobile was old and, hence, is not repairable now.
3. **The circumstances**—The setting under which the behavior occurs. It must be due to humidity in the air that the mobile is out of order.

If there is substantial agreement between the explanations given by others, it is called as consensus. Say for example, all family members think that Abhay is irresponsible and has spoiled the phone. If the actor behaves in the same or similar manner on other occasions, it is consistency. If Abhay's father generally blames everyone in the family when something gets damaged, this may be a consistent behavior. And if he always blames Abhay when something wrong happens, and attributes it to his irresponsible behavior, this tendency is called as distinctiveness.

Sometimes some evidence is available and sometimes no information is available. So the person has to infer on the basis of his or her own interpretation.

7.6.2 CORRESPONDENT INFERENCE—FROM ACTS TO DISPOSITION

A person's behavior can be used to make inferences about his or her personality and the motive behind his or her behavior. But the question is whether these two things match with the other things. This is correspondent inference. The more the behavior appears to reflect the underlying disposition, the greater the correspondence between these two factors is.

Kishor hates his brother and has got a lot of sibling rivalry. However, when some guests came to them, Kishor pretended to have respect for his brother and praised him in front of them. The guests were impressed to see that.

Social desirability modifies an individual's overt behavior. It also influences the attributions that one makes. Generally, the greater the social desirability of an action or behavior, the more difficult it will be to understand the intention fully.

7.7 PROBLEM-SOLVING

The most obvious activity related to thinking and reasoning is problem-solving. Life is full of various problems. Every now and then we are involved in solving some problems. Though it has a negative meaning, problems and problem-solving is essentially an inherent part of human life. An individual's achievements, progress, as well as daily activities depend on problem-solving. By and large, we are interested in products of problem-solving and neglect the actual process and different types of thinking and knowledge involved in that.

Problem-solving is an attempt to find an appropriate way of attending a goal when the goal is not readily available. Generally, there is a barrier to a solution. As a consequence, it is difficult to solve the problem, which means it prevents the goal from being achieved. A problem situation assumes that a situation identified as a problem. If we do not consider that as a problem, we will not try to change the situation. The goal of cognitive psychology is to increase the efficiency of problem-solving and decrease the cognitive load of the learner. It is the fastest and the best solution that one should get with minimum efforts.

Let us take an example. Children from first standard find it difficult to master the table of 9. They have to learn it by heart without understanding or making it meaningful. They are taught the rote learning method. However, if we teach them to memorize with the help of folding fingers, it is very easy. First, fold one finger, that is, 1 × 9, thus the first finger is folded and nine are remaining. That means one nines are nine. Then fold the second finger to indicate twos. Now the first finger stands apart to indicate 1 and 8 separately. So, nine twos are 18. Now, fold the third finger indicating 2 and 7, that is, 27, and so on. It becomes so easy that the cognitive load reduces and any moment the child can recollect the figure.

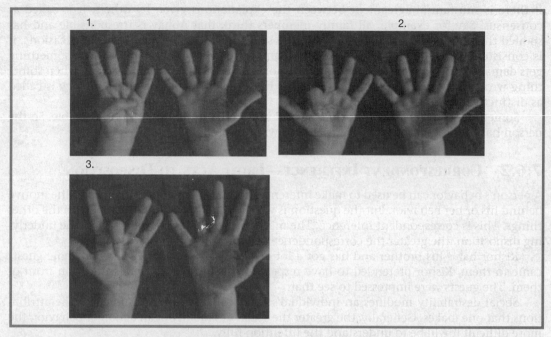

There are many other methods like that. Write 9, 8, 7, 6, 5, 4, 3, 2, 1, 0, and keep on writing 0, 1, 2, 3, 4, 5, 6, 7, 8, 9 before these digits. It will become 9, 18, 27, 36, 45, 54, 63, 72, 81, 90.

Problem-solving includes some specific given position and a wanted goal position. We have to operate on the information given and create a situation similar to goal point or wanted position. The thought process involved in a person's effort to remove obstacles in the way to achieve the goal state is called problem-solving. Such a process is involved in critical thinking for taking many important decisions of life as well as for solving simple routine problems.

Much of the advancement in science and technology takes place because of problem-solving. Hence, it is one of the most important cognitive activities of human beings.

7.7.1 NINE DOTS PROBLEM

```
*   *   *
*   *   *
*   *   *
```

In this problem, you have to join these nine dots without lifting your pencil and without rewriting on the already drawn line using only four straight lines. When there will be any change in the angle of the line we will consider it as a separate line. (For solution see the last page of this chapter.)

7.7.2 TYPES OF PROBLEMS

There are different types of problems in day-to-day life also. Human beings every now and then complain that there are many problems, but if there is no problem, they invite some. As human brain needs some stimulation, we wish to get involved in some intellectually stimulating activities. That is why we solve crosswords, anagrams, and matchstick problems or play scrabble as a pass-time activity.

Problems can be divided into various ways: simple and complex problems, well-defined and ill-defined problems, adversary and non-adversary problems, and potentially solvable and impossible to solve problems. Some common types are given as follows.

1. **Simple and complex problems**
   Simple problems have limited subproblems and they take comparatively less time to reach the goal. Complex problems have many subproblems, there are many steps and they are time-consuming.

2. **Well-defined and ill-defined problems**
   Well-defined problems have a clear, specified beginning, a clear end point, and a definite tool or technique to be used for solving the problem. A problem is well defined if there is a definable initial state and a goal state, specific definite steps, and well-accepted explicit rules regarding solving it.

   Ill-defined problem on the other hand lacks clear specification of at least one of these three. An ill-defined problem is the problem where the initial state, the goal state, and the rules are ambiguous and are not clearly defined. Writing a "good essay" is a simple example of ill-defined problems.

3. **Adversary problem**
   It involves competition of two or more persons when only one of them can win, and hence, the problem arises. Nonadversary problem does not include competition.

4. **Solvable and nonsolvable problems**
   These are also different in the sense that there are certain things that human beings will never be able to achieve like travel with a speed more than light.

5. **Problems of inducing structure**
   Problems of inducing structure require determining a relationship among several elements of the problem. In analogy, one is required to find a structure in some elements with clearly defined rules, like, "Chalk is to board as pen is to paper." There are different cognitive activities necessary for this type of problem-solving. They are attribute discovery, encoding, and comparing encoded attributes and evaluating attribute-based structure among the elements.

6. **Problems of transformation**
   Here the main task is to find out a sequence of operations to transform the initial state into the goal state. A classic example of such a problem is the matchstick problem where a particular design of sticks is given depicting say six squares and you are supposed to shift only a limited number of sticks and make say four squares out of it.

7. **Problems of arrangement**
   Problems of arrangement require the rearrangement of the elements of the problem according to a particular criterion. In some of such problems, the arrangement criterion is predefined, while in others it is to be discovered.

In a simple anagram problem, one has to reshuffle the given letters and make a meaningful word. If "utb" is given, one should prepare the word but or tub.

Like that there are different types of problems and even different combinations of the above-stated problems.

7.7.3 APPROACHES TO PROBLEM-SOLVING

1. Traditional approaches

Traditional approaches explain problem-solving in terms of principles of associative learning and conditioning. Already learned stimulus response associations are used for problem-solving. The problem reminds the individual of some known associations. Some of them are correct and others are not. If strength of wrong associations is equal or more than the correct ones, the problem becomes difficult. If strength of correct associations is more, the problem becomes easy. Due to previous experiences some associations are strengthened and others are weakened. Those that are useful for successfully solving the problem are strengthened and those associated with failure are weakened. The rearrangement and transfer of the already learned ideas are focused.

2. Common strategies

Some common strategies that people often employ in problem-solving include:

a. **Hypothesis testing**—This involves assuming a possible explanation to a problem and trying to prove or disprove the assumption.

b. **Reduction**—Problem-solving may also be done by transforming the problem into another problem for which solutions exist and this is called reduction.

c. **Root cause analysis**—This involves eliminating the cause of the problem for solving it. In day-to-day situation this is very effective.

d. **Trial and error**—This is one of the most widely used methods where one keeps on testing various possible solutions until the right one is found. It is time-consuming. It may or may not solve the problem.

e. **Gestalt approaches**—Problem-solving by insight—Significance of the structure of the problem situations and of new combinations of old ideas are highlighted by Gestalt. Rearrangement of ideas and objects helps problem-solving. Kohler (1925) had demonstrated it even for lower level species like monkeys.

This correct reorganization generally occurs as a sudden insight. After many inaccurate attempts the individual gets this solution.

3. Heuristics and algorithms

a. These are some strategies which differ with respect to time and efficiency of problem-solving. **Algorithm**—If one is trying to solve a problem to find out the square root of 476, one has to follow a sequence of steps to get the correct answer. There is no other option than to follow these steps. That is called as algorithm. An algorithm invariably leads to the solution if it is used properly. It is a procedure of steps that does guarantee a solution if one follows the steps correctly. These rules constitute an algorithm because a correct answer is guaranteed if one follows the rules.

In systematic random search we try out all possible answers using a specified system. This method is somewhat more efficient than the unsystematic random search, but it is highly time consuming when there are many alternative answers. Given a three letter anagram, this type of strategy works, but for solving a longer anagram, such as NOPAOLRHOGTY, it is extremely time consuming. It is because in an anagram problem, an algorithm would be attempting all the possible letter sequences until the correct and meaningful word is found.

There are four essential properties of an algorithm:

(i) Each step of an algorithm must be exact. An algorithm must be clear, precise, and unambiguous, so that there remains no uncertainty.

(ii) An algorithm should be stopped after the solution is achieved. If the process does not stop when executed, one will not be able to get any result from it. Therefore, an algorithm should have a specific limited number of steps.

(iii) An algorithm must be general. This means that it must solve every instance of the problem.

Although an algorithm is a guarantee to reach to the solution, the efforts in terms of cognitive processing and time essential for that is so great that human beings rarely use this strategy. It is more useful for computer applications.

b. **Heuristics**—In this method, one has to select the most relevant alternative for solving the problem. This is a kind of shortcut which saves time and cognitive efforts. However, it does not guarantee a solution. Heuristics are rules of thumb that help us simplify and solve problems. Heuristics do not guarantee a correct solution to a problem, but when they work, they permit more rapid solutions.

The simple example is solving anagrams. Here, the unsystematic random search technique is more useful. Unsystematic random search means that we try out all kinds of possible answers but make no attempt to be orderly in our search and keep no record of our previous attempts. As a consequence, we may repeat a response that has already been proved to be wrong. Even then it saves time and energy.

A heuristic device for solving the anagram problem would be to look for familiar letter combinations. Some important heuristics are discussed follows:

(i) **Working backward**—Starting from the goal state and moving backward to the initial state is called as working backward. This strategy is very useful in solving problems like a paper–pencil maze. It is very beneficial when the initial state is ambiguous and the end state is quite clear.

Working backward helps when one begins to see subgoals by starting with the final goal. Once this series of subgoals projecting backward from the goal state is understood, then working in a forward direction becomes easy. This method is less effective when the goal state is not well defined.

(ii) **Analogies**—This is based on similarity between problem-solving strategies of old and new problems. One has to use experiences of strategies used to solve past problems for solving a current problem.

(iii) **Means end analysis**—It is a strategy in which the problem-solver divides the problem into a number of subproblems, or smaller problems. Each of these subproblems is solved by detecting the difference between the original state and the goal state, and then reducing the difference between these two states. Hence, it involves a search for operations that will reduce the difference between the present state of knowledge and the goal state. Finding out a difference between the original problem state and the goal state is the first step. Which method can be used to decrease the difference between the two stages needs to be decided.

Dividing the problem in a subgoal helps is the next stage. A similar procedure is to be used for the subgoal. After successfully completing each goal, one gets closer to the ultimate goal. It is essential to constantly monitor and evaluate success regarding short-term goals and its relation to the ultimate goal.

4. **Some specific techniques of problem-solving**
The way in which a problem can be solved depends to a great extent on the nature of the problem itself. This is called the domain-specific problem-solving approach, applicable and useful for solving only a limited class of problems.

a. **Generate and test techniques**—If one has to write down 10 words beginning with the letter z and having five letters, one generally uses the generate and test technique. It consists of generating possible solutions and then evaluating them. There is every possibility that one thinks of various words which are not fulfilling the criteria say having three, four, or seven letters, then one has to discard them.

   If there are numerous possible answers and there is no specific criterion, this method is less effective. If you cannot remember your ATM number or password of some important account, you may keep on guessing and trying various options and fail to get the correct one. Gradually, it becomes impossible to remember the already-tried wrong answers. Efforts are wasted and one gets annoyed and frustrated. If the options are limited this strategy is more convenient.

b. **Planning strategy**—In this heuristic, the problem is divided into two types—simple aspect and complex aspect. First, the simple aspect of the problem is solved and then the complex aspect. It is useful if the aspects that are ignored can easily be worked into the solutions to the complicated problems. It is our regular practice to use this method while finding out the total interest of a specific amount for a particular period with a given interest rate. First one keeps aside the number of years and finds out the interest of that amount only for one year and then multiplies it with the number of years.

c. **Thinking aloud**—verbalization of information at the time the individual is attending to it—Concurrent verbalization gives valuable information regarding actual problem-solving. When subjects think aloud, they put into words various cognitive processes used for solving that problem. This gives a description of the subject's solution strategies and their sequence. This verbal description is called a protocol.

Newell (1980) recommended a series of steps in order to clarify the protocol.

1. The protocol needs to be divided into phrases, or descriptions, of single acts.
2. The construction of a problem behavior graph or description of the way in which the subject moves around in the problem space is useful.

Some other experts have given inference, classification, evaluation, actual action, and contradiction as vital parts of problem-solving.

Newell and Simon have suggested that the objective structure of a problem can be characterized as:

1. A set of states, beginning from an initial state
2. Involving many intermediate states
3. Ending with a goal state

There is a whole space of possible states and paths through this space, and only some of these will lead to the goal state. This problem space describes the abstract structure of a problem.

If problem-solving is considered as modeling, the construction of situation-specific model is highlighted. A goal must correspond to the desired state of ones knowledge about the world.

7.7.4 Steps and Styles of Problem-solving

Steps of problem-solving are serial. We should have memory aid, and experience, as well as familiarity that may increase our efficiency.

In any type of problem there are three stages for solving: preparation, production, and evaluation. Incubation also helps in creative problem-solving.

1. **Preparation**—In this stage, information is collected from the environment and understanding the actual nature of the problem is facilitated. What are the givens of any problems must be clear for deciding the nature of operations to solve that problem. It is to understand different aspects of the problem including issues, obstacles, and goals involved, and for constructing an internal representation. Background knowledge is essential for that.

   For understanding a problem, paying attention to the important information in a problem and ignoring the information that is irrelevant is a must. The next step is to find an appropriate way to represent the problem by using symbols, lists, matrices, graphs, and images. Sometimes we have to divide the problem in parts so that we can solve it easily.

2. **Production**—It includes actually producing the solution. Operating upon the given information is a function of this stage. Here, retrieving the facts from long-term memory, scanning the information from the environment, operating on the contents of short-term memory, maintaining the information of previous stages in short-term memory, and also storing information in long-term memory for future use is done.

   The next stage is finding a variety of potential solutions on the basis of one's past experiences, available resources, and thinking critically about the problem.

3. **Evaluation**—Moving closer to the goal and learning about major obstacles and costs of the selected solution, and ultimately selecting the best solution are the basic tasks of this stage. Various strategies are used for that. Then, the comparison of the solution with the representation of the problem is done. Sometimes the evaluation stage leads to the conclusion that the problem has not been solved adequately, and thus, one starts from an earlier stage, depending upon the source of the inadequacy.

   For example, after solving a product movement correlation example, we arrive at a conclusion that has the value 2.47; this has to be wrong as any correlation is within the range of −1 or +1 and cannot be more than that. If the answer is wrong, we have to go back to stage one and start solving the same problem from the beginning.

4. **Incubation**—Many researchers have proved that incubation helps in problem-solving. Incubation is actually time off or the rest period. If we cannot solve a problem, we generally take some time off and take a cup of tea. Again, we go back and start dealing with the problem and we can solve it. Some educational psychologists think that it reduces fatigue and frustration generated by failure to solve the problem. If we are frustrated we react to the frustration than to the actual problem. After rest we can have a fresh look and notice our mistake. It is also suggested that we are unconsciously working on the problem and get a solution when we are overtly not thinking about it. Incubation is proved to be especially useful for creative problem-solving.

Simple laboratory experiment can be done to see the effect of incubation on the efficiency of problem-solving. Consider two groups of individuals: let one of them work continuously for long hours and the other one rest in the middle of the task. If these two individuals have a similar level of intellectual abilities and familiarity of the task, you will be able to see the difference in their performance. Generally, rest helps in problem-solving.

Gestalt psychologists suggest that problem-solving behavior also follows the stages that are followed in creative thinking: preparation, incubation, illumination or insight, and verification.

7.7.5 Types of Problem-solving Styles

There are different styles of problem-solving. Some commonly seen are:

1. **Intuitive problem-solving**

   If somebody is solving problems only on the basis of the thought, "I take action and rely on my instincts to point me in the right direction." They rely on own experience and judgment and quickly size up a situation and take an action. It is the way experience is translated into action.

   Following are the problem-solving skills involved:

   a. Recognition—recognizing early signs of problems.
   b. Sizing up the situation quickly—getting a detailed gestalt picture.
   c. Projection—quickly seeing the likely outcome of each possible response.
   d. Action—ability to decide and act without deliberate analysis.

   There is a strong correlation between experience and intuitive decision-making. The knowledge of that particular area is essential for this.

   Risks:

   a. Speed of action maybe risky if the internal signals are distorted. Not verifying accuracy leads to solving strategies risky in other situations.
   b. Others may not support your decisions as they may perceive it distorted understanding leading to too early action.
   c. Use of past knowledge for gaining insight is a must.

   Hence, it is not the proper way to deal with problems; decisions may be inaccurate and may not be useful in new situations or complexity. Sometimes others may be involved in problem-solving.

2. **Analytical problem-solving**

   It involves thinking about the problems and alternatives for problem-solving, selecting the best for action, and analyzing the situation before action. Collecting information and organizing the situation to accurately define the problem is a must. It also involves applying tools for measurements, identifying relations and interactions, and finding out clues that help in understanding the problem as well as benefits and risks of each alternative and then selecting the best. Consistency of the thought process is important.

   Risk:

   One may unnecessarily keep on applying it to all problems where rigorous analysis is not needed.

7.7.6 Factors Affecting Problem-solving

The effectiveness of a problem-solving behavior is measured on the basis of two criteria—the time taken in solving the problem and the probability of getting the solution. An effective solution of a problem is dependent upon a number of factors.

These include:

1. **Nature of the problem**

   The magnitude of the problem, the difficulty level, and the degree of difference between the initial state of the problem and the final goal are the basic issues. As the size of a problem increase, the number of elements present in the problem space, and difficulty to reach solution as well as time for solution increases, for example, an increase in the number of letters of the anagrams enhances the difficulty level of the problem. So, if there are more steps and longer blind alleys, difficulties are magnified. These are multistep complex problems. There is a positive correlation between the number of steps and the difficulties encountered. Knowledge, experience, and aptitude help in problem-solving.

2. **Degree of difference between initial and goal stages**
   Greater the difference between the initial and the goal states, less is the likelihood of easy solution. Here, problem space is more disorganized and more steps are required to reach to the solution. For example, a larger maze. Familiarity may decrease the difficulty level.

3. **The perceiver's set**
   It is defined as a tendency to perceive and respond to a particular stimulus in a stereotypical way. When a person successively and systematically perceives and responds to the problems, in a similar way, a set develops. A set may have a facilitatory, as well as inhibitory effect on problem-solving. If a useful set is already saved in memory, the solution may become easier. But if the set and the expected ways of solving a problem are different, it may hinder problem-solving.

	Jar A	Jar B	Jar C	Exact amount we want to measure
1)	17	7	4	2

Find out a formula to solve this problem.

   Is it A – B – 2C?

	Jar A	Jar B	Jar C	Exact amount we want to measure
2)	22	9	3	7

Can you use the same formula?

	Jar A	Jar B	Jar C	Exact amount we want to measure
3)	30	19	3	5
4)	20	7	5	3
5)	28	7	5	11
6)	17	7	3	4

You have to solve the following problem by developing a formula. Suppose there are three jars A, B, and C. Their capacity is given along with the exact amount of water in cc that we want to measure.

Have you used the same formula for all the problems? If yes, again look at the last problem. Can you find some other way?

Yes, there is another way to solve this problem and it is the shortest way possible. You can use only jars B and C and get 4 cc of water.

This is called as Luchin's water jar problem. This is the demonstration of a set and how it affects effective problem-solving. In this case, the individual in affected by a self-induced set which is adversely influencing problem-solving. Functional fixedness also is similar to what we have just discussed.

However, the effect of a set can be minimized by increasing the time interval between practice and problem-solving, by clear instructions regarding neglecting previously learned rules, and by introducing some exceptions in practice.

4. **Functional fixedness**

It is the inability to solve a problem because it is viewed only in terms of usual functions. If the problem is usual, it is solved easily. If it involves something new, it becomes tricky. A negative set is induced by the way we classify objects on the basis of their use in our daily life. Functional fixedness refers to the tendency to perceive the objects with their customary and stereotypical use.

5. **Hints**

Even when hints are given they may or may not be effective. First of all the relation between solution and hint may not be clear to the problem solver. Sometimes hints may decrease inappropriate attempts to solve the problem, but it may not happen. If hints are given before problem-solving starts, they are more effective. If the problem requires the production of familiar ideas, which is reproductive thinking, it is easy. In that also if the words of high frequency are to be recalled, it takes less time and is very easy to solve that problem. If there are more cues leading to the solution, it becomes clear to us and the problem-solving capacity is enhanced.

7.7.7 LIMITATIONS OF HUMAN INFORMATION PROCESSING

There are many limitations regarding human problem-solving. If there is no paper and pencil we cannot even solve simple problems like 249 × 289. The basic limitation of human information processing is that we have to hold the necessary information in our short-term memory and operate upon it. Short-term memory is available only for few seconds. It is difficult to complete the operations within that period. Holding the information in short-term memory and at the same time retrieving back the relevant information from long-term memory and combining these two for further operations is necessary. Our attention also is limited and selective. Hence, everything cannot be attended to. Out of huge amount of information available in the environment to our senses, we can attend to very limited information. The information that is attended to is immediately lost if it is not rehearsed and intentionally remembered with specific processing and motivation. One more thing is that our processing capacity is limited. Like a computer, we cannot solve complex and complicated problems in less time. We have to solve the problems step by step and sequentially. Neither can we skip a step nor can we easily reverse the processing.

There are many other factors that are directly related to problem-solving along with other cognitive tasks. They are two types of factors—one individual related and others are problem related. In the first type, exact knowledge, age, education, familiarity to the type of problem, practice, etc. are included. In the second type, we consider if the problem is rare or common, new or old, sudden or slow, having specific important intention or pass-time activity, and similar other things. A very useful method of problem-solving is given by Bransford and Stein (1984) which is called as the IDEAL method. In this method:

I	stands for identification of the problem.
D	stands for defining and presenting the problem.
E	stands for exploring possible strategies.
A	stands for acting on the strategies.
L	stands for looking back and evaluating the effect of our activities.

A comprehensive model regarding problem-solving was given by Robertson in 2001. According to this model, problem-solving depends on external and internal factors. External factors that play an important role in problem-solving are details of the problem itself, its context, social setting, and the whole culture. Personality and motivation are the prominent internal factors that interact with cognitive factors. A cognitive system includes a perceptual system and some variable factors such as long-term memory, knowledge base, chunk size, and methods. It also includes comparatively less variable factors such as processing speed, learning rate, and forgetting. Biophysical system means that sympathetic and parasympathetic systems interact with cognitive system in problem-solving.

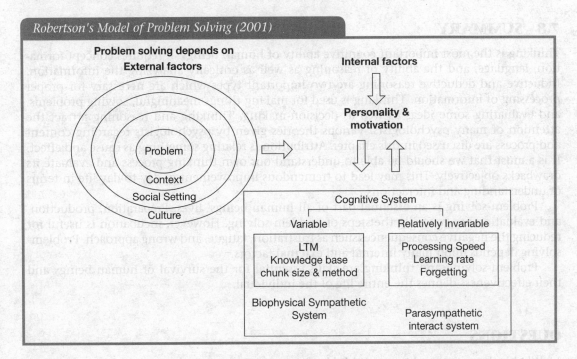

7.7.8 CREATIVITY AND PROBLEM-SOLVING

As there is a separate chapter on creativity, let us not discuss the basic things again. Creativity plays an important role in problem-solving by insight, and insight plays an important role in creativity.

It requires three separate problem-solving skills:

1. Selective encoding
2. Selective combination
3. Selective comparison

These are discussed in detail as follows:

1. **Selective encoding**—While solving a new problem, we are often confused due to large amounts of useless information. As an insight arises, we determine which information is relevant for further consideration.

If one is involved in irrelevant information, it will take a toll of time and efforts along with the risk of making a wrong and less effective decision.

2. **Selective combination**—Many a time, one has all details and pieces of information regarding the solution, but we do not know how to put them together. An insight arises when one finds out a novel way of combining the elements of the solution. An innovative way leads to more creative problem-solving.

3. **Selective comparison**—When we solve a problem, we often use a model solution that we have stored in our repertoire of past memories. Insight occurs when we discover that a more novel comparison leads to unforeseen consequences.

7.8 SUMMARY

Thinking is the most important cognitive ability of human beings. It requires concept formation, language, and the ability of reasoning as well as critically analyzing the information. Inductive and deductive reasoning are two important types which are necessary for proper processing of information. Thinking is used for making things meaningful, solving problems, and evaluating some ideas as well as decision-making. Thinking and reasoning attract the attention of many psychologists. Various theories given by psychologists regarding content and process are discussed in this chapter. Attribution is relating something as cause and effect. It is a must that we should be able to understand our own thinking process and evaluate its drawbacks objectively. This may lead to tremendous improvement in day-to-day life in terms of understanding and interactions.

Problem-solving is an essential part of all human beings' lives. Preparation, production, and evaluation are generally the steps of problem-solving. However, incubation is useful for reducing the negative consequences such as frustration, fatigue, and wrong approach. Problem-solving depends upon many internal and external factors.

Problem-solving and thinking are skills essential for the survival of human beings and their effectiveness defines the entire life of the individual.

QUESTIONS

1. What is the nature and types of thinking?
2. What is reasoning? What are its types?
3. Discuss the important theories of thinking and its importance in human life.
4. Which cognitive skills are necessary for thinking?
5. What are the limitations of human information processing?
6. Explain the various stages of problem-solving.
7. What are the factors affecting problem-solving?
8. What are algorithms and heuristics? Give one example each.
9. Explain the stages of decision-making.

APPLICATION ORIENTATION

1. Enumerate errors that we make with reference to reasoning. Take one example and analyze your wrong decision.
2. Discuss with friends your style of thinking. Can you accept that objectively? What improvements are necessary in it?
3. If you have to make a decision regarding purchasing a two-wheeler, which steps would you follow? What information will you collect and analyze?
4. Give five examples when you use heuristics and when you use algorithms.

SUGGESTED READINGS

Bransford, J. D. and Stein, B. S. (1984). *The IDEAL problem solver: A guide for improving thinking, learning, and creativity.* New York: W. H. Freeman and company.

Feldman, R. S. (2008). *Essentials of understanding psychology.* New Delhi: McGraw-Hill.

Galotti, K. M. (2008). *Cognitive psychology in and out of the laboratory.* Canada: Nelson Education.

Hunt, R. R., & Ellis, H. C. (2006). *Fundamentals of cognitive psychology.* New Delhi: McGraw-Hill.

Kohler, W. (1925). The mentality of apes. New York: Harcourt, Brace.

Miller, G. A. and Milner, A. F. C. (1960). Review of plans and structure of behaviour. *Canadian Journal of Psychology, 14*(4), 281–282.

Newell, A. (1980). Reasoning, problem solving and decision processes: The problem space as a fundamental category. In R. Nickerson (Ed.), *Attention and performance* (viii, pp. 693–718). Hills Dale, NJ: Erlbaum.

Reed, S. K. (2010). *Cognition: Theories and applications.* London: Cengage.

Skinner, B. F. (1938). *Behavior of organisms: An experimental analysis.* New York: Appleton-Century.

Solso, R. L. (2006). *Cognitive psychology.* New Delhi: Pearson Education.

Sternberg, R. J. (2009). *Applied cognitive psychology: Perceiving, learning, and remembering.* London: Cengage.

Watson, J. B. (1913). Psychology as the behaviorist views it. *Psychological Review, 20*, 158–177.

8 | Proactive Thinking

Objectives

After reading this chapter you will be able to:

1. Understand your mistakes while being reactive.
2. Learn the concept of proactive thinking.
3. See the advantages of proactive thinking.
4. Try to enhance proactive thinking and behavior.
5. Learn more about other effective thinking patterns.
6. Think about goal orientation.
7. Know the importance of putting first things first.
8. Think win/win where both the parties win.
9. Realize the necessity to understand others.

8.1 NATURE OF PROACTIVE THINKING

Shiv was going to his college and was getting late. He was driving his motorbike at full speed. All of a sudden, another person on a motorbike came from the other side and they met with a minor accident. The fellow started abusing Shiv and was very aggressive. Shiv also started using slang language and blaming the other person. They got involved in a serious dispute. Shiv could not go to his college for the whole day as he had to stay in the police station.

Who has decided what Shiv has done for the whole day? Why is it that Shiv had permitted someone else to decide his mood? Why did Shiv become more aggressive?

If someone abuses you what do you do? Can you control your reaction?

As we interact with the environment, most of us get involved in competing with others. We do not think about who the other person is, what is his status, should we interact with him as if we were on par with him, and so on. Hence, our mental status, mental setup, and mood depend on what the other person says and how he or she behaves.

We are completely surrendering ourselves to the environmental stimuli and especially to anyone who may interact with us even when the person is completely unknown. This means that someone else is going to decide what type of activities we are going to do, what we are going to experience, and whether we are going to utilize our time properly or will waste it.

Reactivity is crisis-based thinking. It is coming up with a solution after the problem emerges. It is something like firefighting. A person with such thinking is driven away by the environmental forces. They are more prone to stress. There is no initiative that is taken by a reactive person. Proactive thinking and proactive behavior mean anticipatory, self-initiated behavior. Such thinking is change oriented and leads to acting in advance of some expected future situations. It is controlling things and making something happen. Generally, people react to environmental stimulation and try to adjust with them. They wait till something happens. A proactive individual is oriented toward initiating change. Such individuals do not need any order or instructions while working in an organization. They can guess the changes and change their behavior.

The concept is borrowed basically from classical ideas of psychology where it indicates something like conditions prior to learning. Concepts such as proactive and retroactive interference are commonly used in psychology.

A proactive person shoulders the responsibility of his thinking, and behavior, and is ready to face the consequences. A reactive individual on the other hand tries to look for the causes in the environment.

Proactive thinking is related to the awareness of the available choices for responding to a given situation and is based on the understanding that we are responsible for our actions and lives. Behavior is a function of decisions and not conditions.

Five ways to be proactive:

1. **Predict**—Developing foresight and learning to anticipate problems are essentially the first stages of being proactive. One has to imagine future outcomes. Simultaneously, one has to be logical and creative. One should be logical for predicting environmental changes and creative for imagining options available for reacting.
2. **Prevent**—One should not be powerless. It is necessary to control and change the environment. It is a must to have the courage to face or confront the changes and bear them head on.
3. **Plan**—It is necessary to plan for long-term consequences of the ever-changing interactions of the person with environment. One has to bring future in planning the present. Students should also plan their future in terms of what they want to be, say after five years.
4. **Participate**—Being active is always beneficial than observing passively. Taking initiative to exert one's power enhances proactive behavior.
5. **Perform**—Timely effective action and being responsible for one's own decisions leads to better performance. It is thoughtful action which helps than impulsive reaction.

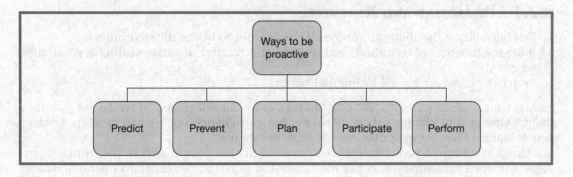

8.2 BEING PROACTIVE

An individual's mental status, thoughts, and feelings are not equal to him or her as a whole. If one uses a social mirror as the only mirror for understanding self, it will be a distorted image that he or she will receive. Remarks of others reflect their personality problems and their weaknesses.

There are three things that are responsible for the behavior of human beings. These are:

1. **Genetics**—as one cannot change the genetic aspects, one has to accept them as they are.
2. **Psychic**—psychological status and interactions comprise of a psychic dimension. It decides human behavior.
3. **Environmental**—conducive or unpleasant environment decides an individual's behavior.

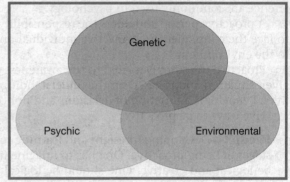

Most of the human behavior is S-R or stimulus–response type of behavior. However, there is an individual between the stimulus and the response. It is useful to explain different responses of different individuals to the same stimulus. There is a freedom to choose that makes a difference. Self-awareness, imagination, conscious understanding, and independence taken together are useful to choose among many possible responses. Proactivity is accepting the responsibility of one's own actions and life. One's behavior is a function of one's decisions and not of conditions. Values are more important than feelings. One has to take initiatives and responsibility to make things happen. Responsibility is the ability to choose a response and it leads to the tendency to not to blame the circumstances and conditions for one's behavior. One's behavior is one's conscious choice based on values than product of feelings and conditions. If one's life is a function of feelings and conditions, he or she has chosen to empower those things to control oneself. This is being reactive. If the environment is good, they feel good. Proactive people carry their environment with them. They are value driven and, hence, produce good work in spite of poor environmental support.

8.2.1 PROACTIVE AND REACTIVE

1. Responsibility is the ability to choose a response, not to blame the environment.
2. If life is a function of conditions and feelings, it is reactive. If social weather is good, they feel good.
3. Proactive people are guided by internal values.

As Mahatma Gandhi has said, "No one can take away our self respect, if we do not give it to them." One cannot change others' behavior, but can change one's reaction to it. Reactive people blame others for their own misery, proactive do not.

Sheela is a married young lady who is pursuing her last year in architecture. Since morning she is upset and annoyed as her mother-in-law is giving her constant instructions and passing derogatory remarks regarding every small thing done in the kitchen. That is a regular problem and is irritating for Sheela. She discussed this with her husband again and again but all is in vain. Sheela gets disturbed in the morning and, hence, can neither peacefully concentrate on her classes nor study properly. She failed in two subjects and blames her mother-in-law for that.

It is not someone else's behavior but one's reaction to it that is more harmful. Sheela should take the remarks as a casual activity and try to forget them after that work is over. Overemphasizing them creates a problem.

Reactive people feel good when others treat them well. Hence, the social weather decides their behavior. If it is not good, they become defensive. It is the behavior of others that decides their behavior. So, others' weakness becomes their controlling factor. On the other hand, proactive people are guided by their internalized values. They are also influenced by the environment, but their response depends on their values.

No one can insult the individual without his or her consent.

Reactive people explain their misery in the name of circumstances and someone else's behavior. However, whatever one faces today is a result of one's decision that was taken yesterday. Others' should not be able to decide an individual's mood and behavior. It is not the impact of experiences but one's reaction to these experiences that hurts the individual. Actually, no one can hurt an individual's basic identity and basic character. With the help of intrinsic power, everyone can find out proper alternatives for a given situation.

Some people wait and think that someone will do something for them. However, if one's own initiative and resourcefulness are used, problems can be solved in a better way. With the help of brain storming, one can find out what exactly is he or she experiencing, what is the stimulus associated with that, what will happen in future, what response should be given, etc. These points should be discussed and better understanding can be achieved. This aids in problem-solving.

The difference between reactive and proactive languages is significant.

Reactive Language	Proactive Language
1. There is nothing I can do	1. Let us find alternatives
2. I am what I am	2. I will try to behave in a different way
3. I become mad because of them	3. I can control my emotions
4. I would not allow that to happen	4. I shall do effective presentation
5. I have to do it	5. I will choose appropriate response
6. I cannot	6. I choose
7. I must	7. I prefer
8. If only	8. I will

The real meaning of "I have to do it" is "I prefer doing it." Reactive language is self-fulfilling prophecy. Reactive people blame others, environment, stars, or something like that. Their emotions depend on the environment and they are not the master of their emotions.

All of us are concerned about many things in the environment. We are worried about our future, our family members, pets, relatives, community, city, nation, and sometimes the whole mankind. Hence, our circle of concern can be huge. However, we do not put in our efforts to change everything about which we are concerned. Like for example, we do not take an initiative to save the environment, for global peace, and so on. On the other hand, we struggle hard to help our family members and friends, and keep our premises clean.

The activities of reactive and proactive people in this regard are not the same. There is substantial difference between the relationship of proactive and reactive people's circle of concern and circle of influence.

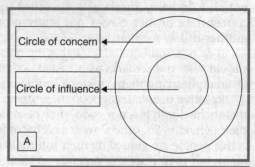

The larger circle in the figure is the circle of concern. Here, the individual is concerned about issues such as national income, pollution, and so on. The individual is concerned about these issues but cannot change the scenario. The small circle is that of the circle of influence. Here, the individual devotes time and energy to change the situation.

For proactive people positive energy enlarges the circle of influence and it becomes larger. There is a substantial overlap between the two circles (as seen in Figure B). It obviously means that proactive individuals will try to change many things about which they are concerned. They will help the poor or change their lifestyle to save energy.

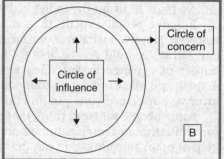

However, for reactive people, negative energy reduces the circle of influence (as shown in Figure C). Hence, the circle of influence becomes smaller and the circle of concern remains larger. In this case, for example, reactive people will not do anything even for their family members or friends. They will use their time, efforts, and money for very limited reasons.

If influence is more than concern, it may lead to a selfish lifestyle (as shown in the figure). It means that the person is focused on the circle of concern and is not ready to think about other issues though he or she can. A top businessman refusing donation for a cancer hospital is a typical example of this sort. This is a reactive style. Proactive people have a circle of concern as big as that of influence. They use influence effectively. One should always try to expand the circle of influence.

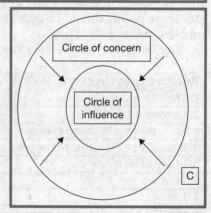

8.3 OTHER EFFECTIVE THOUGHT PATTERNS

Those who want to be successful in their lives should develop some habits which are essentially important to guide their ideas, attitudes, and behavior.

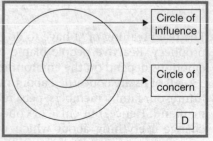

Covey in his very well-known book *The Seven Habits of Highly Effective People* has discussed habits of effective people in detail (1997). Here, habit is considered to be an intersection of knowledge, skills, and desire. Knowledge is a theoretical paradigm which contents the knowledge of what to do and why. Skill is knowing of how to do it. Desire is the motivation—the want to do a particular thing. By working on knowledge, skills, and desire, one can improve and reach to new levels of personal and interpersonal effectiveness. Effective habits are internalized principles and patterns of behavior. Happiness can be defined as the fruit of desire and the ability to sacrifice what one wants now for what one wants eventually.

The last idea is exactly like the delay of gratification. The postponement of satisfaction is essential and expected by any culture and society. Every culture and religion expects that the members should be able to master these skills of self-discipline and should be able to wait for satisfaction till the society permits the same. The simplest example is the duration between some need or drive and its fulfillment. As is stated elsewhere , the society expects that growing individuals should postpone marriage till they become responsible to shoulder responsibilities of a family. If such type of self-discipline is not developed, the individual will be gratification oriented and behave against social expectations, and ultimately, this will result in various problems not only in his or her life but in the lives of family members and even in the society. Gratification orientation leads to the desire to get every satisfaction immediately. This leads to poor personality organization and affects the behavior, motivation, and all social interactions.

If one considers a continuum of maturity, there are three aspects to it. One is dependence, second is independence, and third is interdependence. To start with, all humans are dependent on others even for the smallest needs in childhood. Here, someone else takes care and if not then that person is to be blamed. Then, as the individual grows older, he or she becomes more and more independent—physically, mentally, emotionally, and financially. Here, the individual can choose, can work for himself, and be responsible for his or her actions. The individual becomes self-reliant. As maturity of the individual increases, the awareness that human life is interdependent also increases. Interdependence is the stage where the individual understands that in human life cooperation is important. If joint efforts and joint use of talents is done, output is far better than an individual's independent output. These people combine their efforts with the efforts of others to achieve their greatest success.

Dependent people need someone to help them. Their self-worth and feeling of security depend on others' opinion regarding them. Those who are independent do not depend upon others—their reactions, their liking, or the way in which they treat these individuals. Independent individuals do not understand the importance of interdependence and, as a consequence, cannot become good leaders, or effective members of a team. Interdependence is essential not only for marriage and family life but for organizational success also.

Interdependence is a far more mature and a more advanced concept. It is the realization that combined efforts are better than an individual's efforts. In personal life, one has to depend on others for the give and take of love and affection, emotional support, and friendship. Only those who are independent can opt for interdependence; however, those who are dependent cannot opt for it as they do not have any contribution of their own to combine with others.

For private victory, the following things are necessary:

1. Being proactive
2. Beginning with the end in mind
3. Putting first thing first

After this, an individual can achieve independence.

Then comes public victory. For this, the essential things are:

1. Thinking win-win
2. Seeking first to understand, then to be understood
3. Synergizing
4. Sharpen the saw

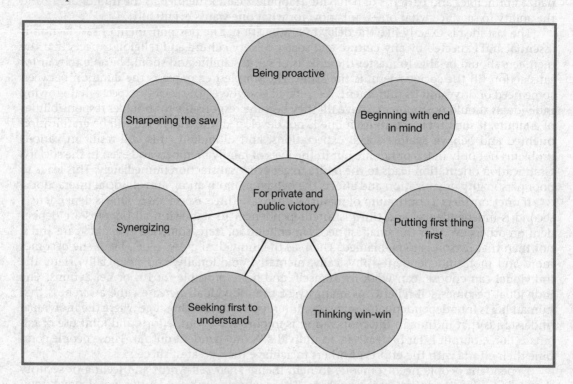

8.4 BEGIN WITH THE END IN MIND

To begin with end in mind means that one must start putting in efforts with a clear understanding of what exactly one wants to achieve. Every step should be in a right direction. A clear understanding of where one is also is essential to decide the exact plan of action. Otherwise, devoting time and energy along with efforts is of no use. Many well-educated people reach a destination that they never wanted to reach and that was not so important for them. One has to make sure what he or she wants to achieve—money, fame, promotion, authority, and so on. Otherwise what matters most is neglected. One may work very hard but all the efforts may be ineffective. For self-awareness, proactivity, and personal leadership, two things assist mankind. These are imagination and conscience. With the help of imagination one can visualize the uncreated world of potentials. Through conscience one gets the knowledge of universal laws and principles.

As is discussed at length in Chapter 1, the whole science of psychology depends on the principle of individual differences. As there are individual differences in all characteristics such as abilities, aptitudes, interest, personality characteristics, socialization, motivation, and so on, success should not be measured using the same criteria. Each individual is a unique combination of different qualities; his or her success also may be in different fields. Like for example, many scientists were underachievers in or dropouts from schools. Their potentialities in a particular area were recognized only after many years. If one can understand one's potentialities and drawbacks, one will be able to accept oneself. This accepting of oneself is the first step to utilizing one's potentialities to the fullest extent and trying to improve shortcomings.

It is only after self-understanding and self-acceptance that one will be able to decide his or her definition of success. It may be totally different from not only others' definition but one's own definition prior to self-understanding. The appropriate definition of success is a must so that the individual directs all his or her efforts to achieve it.

Dinesh is the youngest and the only son of a principal, born after three daughters. His father always wanted Dinesh to be an engineer and right from high school he was admitted to technical subjects. Even at the age of 14, he used to dislike his practicals and used to get upset by the forceful attitude of instructors over there. Dinesh loved to draw, play table tennis, and was involved in poetry. He himself used to write poems and get awards for the same. Dinesh was admitted to a science college by his father and he lost interest in studies. He wasted his time and did not study properly during 12th standard. As a consequence, he could get only passing grades. His father tried his level best but Dinesh could not get admission in any one of the engineering colleges. Ultimately, he was admitted to a diploma course. He was feeling nervous and depressed. He actually never wanted to do engineering and wanted to pursue literature studies and wanted to have a bright career in table tennis.

Since then, for the last 25 years he is working in an unwanted field and wants to compensate for it by alcohol abuse and is very aggressive and unpleasant.

Like one plans and prepares a blueprint before the actual construction of a building is done, every successful person plans what exactly he or she wants to achieve in life and then starts attempting it. If one starts working on things without planning properly, it will be difficult for him or her to get satisfactory results. If self-awareness and optimum planning is not accomplished, one empowers others to influence one's future. It is only reactive to live a life as per the environmental demands and others' convenience. It may not be what one wants to achieve. It is someone else's agenda. One should not live with the scripts written by others. Here again, imagination and creativity work very well. If a person is concentrating on short-term goals, he or she will never be in a position to achieve long-term goals.

Actually, what matters most gets buried under layers of immediate concerns, pressing problems, and outward reactive behavior. The examination of deepest values becomes essential in such cases. If one's activities are not in congruence with deepest values, it obviously means that one has not planned one's life from proactive perspective. Instead of memory one should think about plans based on imagination.

When Sarita completed her MBA, her parents were eager to take a decision about her marriage. She wanted to have a bright career in corporate and utilize her cognitive abilities and skills to fulfill her dreams. However, as per her parents' wish she had to marry a person who was settled in Japan. Afterwards, when she went to Japan, she discovered that it is a must for her to learn Japanese language even for day-to-day activities and could not get a job as her residence was in a rural area. Sarita was reluctant to accept her status as a housewife. She was nowhere.

One has to plan on the basis of one's potentials and should become the first creator of his or her lifelong achievements. Decisions are to be taken on the basis of deep values. One has to act with integrity. One does not have to react to emotions and circumstances. One has to be proactive and value driven.

To achieve this, one has to start working at the very center of the circle of influence. One's vision, values, and understanding play an important role here. What is the center of the circle of influence should be understood with reference to talents and areas of contribution. Then focused efforts to achieve greatest results are needed.

Whatever is the center of one's life, it becomes a source of one's security, guidance, wisdom, and power. Security is identity, sense of worth, self-esteem, emotional anchorage, and basic personal strength. Guidance is a source of direction in life. Wisdom is one's perspective on life, sense of balance, and relation between various principles. It is the gestalt view or all-sided understanding. Power is the capacity to act, the strength to achieve something. It is the vital energy to make choices and overcome deeply embodied inefficient habits and to cultivate better habits. This decision about the center is of utmost importance as the center selected should be able to provide high degree of security, guidance, wisdom, and power which empower proactivity and give congruency and harmony to every part of life. Some people are oriented toward money, pleasure, self, family, religion, or something like that. However, some of the individuals are oriented toward more than one thing. Once the emission of life is decided, exact roles and appropriate involvement in these roles are to be determined. The relation of these roles to various goals should also be clear.

8.5 PUT FIRST THINGS FIRST

Independent will make effective self-management possible. It is the ability to make decisions and choices and act accordingly. Integrity, value one places on oneself, reflects in the ability to make and keep commitments to self. This honor with the self is essential for proactive growth. One has to learn this self-discipline which should be from within. It should be a function of one's independent will. Here putting first things first is effective. This habit is related to life and time management. Time management has been the area of concern for many years. To start with, people were interested in recognition and inclusion of demands placed on the individual within the same time frame. Second, the idea to deal with a given time was scheduling time with the help of calendars and appointment books. Third type of idea related to it is regarding clarifying values and comparing the relative worth of activities based on their relationship to the values. It is highlighting the importance of planning short-, intermediate-, and long-term goals and maintaining harmony of these goals with values.

It is well accepted today that efficient planning and control over time are counterproductive. Efficiency focus creates expectations that clash with opportunities to develop rich relationships, to meet human needs, and to enjoy spontaneous movements in daily life. Too strict scheduling may restrict other opportunities.

Basically, the issue in time management is not only to manage the time but to manage oneself. It is necessary to enhance relationship and accomplish results simultaneously.

Human beings spend time in four ways. Considering two dimensions of activities that occupy time—namely important and urgent—one may divide activities into four types. These are:

1. **Activities that are important and urgent**—this includes pressing problems, crises, and deadline-driven projects.
2. **Activities that are important but not urgent**—it includes prevention, utilization of potentials, relationship building, recognizing new opportunities, planning, and recreation.

3. **Activities that are not important but urgent**—interruptions, calls, mails, popular activities, some meetings, etc.
4. **Activities that are neither important nor urgent**—time wasters, some pleasant activities, calls, and mails.

Four types of activities

S.No.	Important	Urgent
1.	Yes	Yes
2.	Yes	No
3.	No	Yes
4.	No	No

Urgent matters are usually visible. They may be easy to do but insist on action. They may be pleasant and fun to do but unimportant.

Important-matter activities are those that contribute to one's mission, values, and high-priority goals. Generally, urgent matters get attention as they are time bound. However, the matters that are not urgent but are important are generally neglected or postponed. Many people's time and energy is consumed only by urgent things. This aspect becomes bigger and bigger as the individual gets involved in it.

Prachi is a married lady having a kid of two years. Her mother-in-law is also staying with her and is suffering from old-age problems. Prachi's husband works in a company, but his earnings are not sufficient as they live in Delhi. Prachi is motivated to work and is doing a correspondence course, which increases the possibility that she will get a good job. Every day she decides to study but then is supposed to take care of her house, look after the baby, and serve the old lady. After doing all these things she is so tired that she has no energy left and also does not get time to study. At the time of examination, she feels that she is not ready for them.

As the individual is diverted to urgent matters, the matters that are related to long-run goals do not get any time. These are the activities that are most significant for an individual's future and for the use of potentials. They require more initiative and more proactivity.

Generally, the first type of activities take a lot of time; the remaining time is devoted to the forth type of activities. The result is obvious that very little time is devoted to the second and third types of activities.

Some other people spend a lot of their time in third type of activities thinking that they are doing the first type of activity. They keep on attending the urgent things assuming that these things are important. However, in reality, the urgency is based on someone else's expectations and priorities.

The consequences of attending to various types of activities are also different. Type one activities result in stress, burnout, crisis management, and putting out fires. Those who are involved in third type of activities face problems such as feeling victimized, broken relationships, visualizing plans and goals as worthless. There is focus on short-term goals and they are involved in crisis management. Those who focus their attention on the third and fourth types of activities, generally, lead an irresponsible life. They depend on others for basics, and are fired from jobs.

Effective people stay away from the third and fourth types of activities, as these activities may be urgent but are not important. They are always more involved in activities of second type that are not urgent but are important. Hence, they do not get involved much in first type of activities that are urgent but not important.

It is obvious that effective personal management is related to important matters. It results in balance, discipline, control, proper vision and perspective, and a few crises. This deals with things such as long-term planning, preparation for the same, preventive maintenance, as well as concentrating on things that are important forever.

Effective people are not problem minded, they are opportunity minded. They keep the activities which are urgent and not important at a low level, and devote time for capacity building and self-actualization. This increases their effectiveness. For achieving this goal, an individual has to cut down other activities which are less important. One should have the courage to say no to other activities that may act as a hindrance and lead to waste of time and energy. One should be assertive and able to say no without any unpleasant feeling.

One always says no to something, either to urgent or important things. One has to take a decision regarding how important are his or her long-term goals and what exactly he or she wants to achieve in life. Otherwise, one will not be able to achieve the best and neglect his or her unique contribution. For this, prioritizing is essential.

The way one spends one's time basically depends on the way in which he or she perceives his or her time and priorities. For being effective, one has to invest more and more time in important matters and manage the remaining things accordingly.

A temporary sense of achievement can be achieved by doing some urgent important, urgent unimportant things, or things that are neither urgent nor important. However, they are neither associated to one's priority nor to one's values and ultimate goals, or the purpose of life. This is related to the sense of control and enhances the sense of self-esteem.

If there is no planning done to manage one's roles in a balanced way, it is detrimental to the effective use of time. If the day is overscheduled, it results in frustration and the wish to escape. The individual may be more interested in nonsignificant and nonurgent matters. It strains human relations.

For staying in second type of activities, that is, important activities, one has to think about six important criteria. These are:

1. **Coherence**—There is harmony, integrity, and unity in vision and mission, goals and roles, priorities and plans, and desires and disciplines.
2. **Balance**—There should be a balance between different roles and priorities. One has to keep in mind the importance of health, family, professional, and personal development.
3. **Quadrant 2 focus**—It is necessary to think about prevention than prioritizing crisis. One should not prioritize what is there on the schedule but schedule the priorities.
4. **The people dimension**—The effectiveness of dealing with people is also one important aspect. Many a time schedules are not as important as people are. So, one has to reschedule everything for people.
5. **Flexibility**—The planning one does should be flexible. It should change according to one's needs, style, and environmental demands.
6. **Portability**—The planner should be portable and one should be able to go to various places so that data are available as and when needed.

There are four activities for concentrating on self-management and concentrating on quadrant 2.

1. **Identifying roles**—Identifying one's key roles such as parent, officer, life partner, etc.
2. **Selecting goals**—Selecting two or three important accomplishments that one wants to achieve in every significant role in the next seven days. These short-term goals will be tied to long-term goals.

3. **Scheduling**—Thinking about the next week and scheduling time to achieve these short-term goals is the next stage. One has to translate each goal into a specific day of the week. If there are some other activities already on the schedule, evaluate their relation with your long-term goals and reschedule the whole thing, if necessary. Then it becomes essential to think about the actual action plan. Some time should be available to handle unexpected events and to give more time to some relations or to enjoy life spontaneously.

4. **Daily adapting**—Daily planning becomes a matter of daily adapting. It becomes essential to prioritizing activities and responding to unexpected events, changes in relationships, and events.

    Every morning, one has to review the schedule to find out a proper arrangement for value-based decisions and unexpected events. Though activities cannot be divided as important and not important, there should be a balance in activities and important activities should get enough time and energy.

    It is obvious that scheduling activities without even knowing their relation with values and personal mission is not effective. There is every possibility that one may be doing activities that one need not do at all and unnecessarily giving them priority.

5. **Living it**—Self-awareness and conscience can provide a high degree of security, guidance, and wisdom to empower one to use independent will and maintain integrity of being truly important.

    One's frustration is a function of one's expectations. It is the reflection of social mirror rather than own values and priorities.

    People are more important than schedules. So, one should be flexible. One should consider his or her needs effectively and then may change the schedule accordingly.

6. **Delegation**—Increasing p and pc: Delegating to other people is one way of being effective. Many people refuse to delegate to others because they feel that it takes too much of time and efforts and they could do the job better themselves. However, effectively delegating to others is the most powerful high-leverage activity. Transferring responsibility to other skilled and trained people enables one to devote one's time and energy to other higher order activities. Delegation means development of the individual as well as the organization. It is related to public victory and is included in habit four, that is, think win win . Delegating is the best policy to be interdependent. Effective delegating results in huge amount of output as compared to input.

Swapnil is now 18 years old. However, his father never allows him to touch the bike or car. His father never allowed Swapnil's sister Varsha who is 22 years old to learn driving. Their mother is out of question as she knows that she does not have enough confidence. As a consequence, every time whenever the family members go out, Swapnil's father has to drive. Whenever, he is out of station, all the family members are deprived of using their car. Once when the father was out of station, Swapnil's grandfather became seriously ill and no alternative arrangement of a vehicle was possible. The whole family suffered. The lack of trust regarding others' capabilities is detrimental to delegating.

There are two types of delegations. First is gofer delegation and the other is stewardship delegation. Gofer delegation means a delegation where one is told all what he or she has to or must do and the way in which it is to be done. Here, the person who is delegating is interested in close supervision, is focused on the methods, and is responsible for the results. However, the basic question is, Is it possible to supervise or manage many people regarding every move they make? The other type of delegating is far more mature and effective as it appreciates self-awareness, imagination, and conscience and free will of others.

Stewardship delegation, is focused on results than methods. It gives people a choice of methods and make them more responsible for the results. It takes more time in the beginning. However, this is the time best invested. It leads to the best results. It involves mutual understanding and commitment about expectations in five areas.

1. **Guidelines**—It is necessary to identify the parameters within which the individual has to function. These should be as few as possible. Otherwise, the initiative is killed and people are sent back to the gofer type. The failure paths of the jobs and blind alleys should be discussed with the individual. In this way, the individual knows what is not to be done and no one has to guide them on what to do. . It is always better if the individual learns on his or her own. Asking the individual to shoulder the responsibility helps, as he or she has to function within the guidelines given.

2. **Resources**—Identifying human, financial, technical, and organizational resources to be used for accomplishing goals is the next stage.

3. **Accountability**—Communicating standards of performance that will be used for evaluation and time for evaluation is helpful for neat planning.

4. **Consequences**—Specifying consequences of the evaluation of performance is further helpful. Awards and rewards as well as new opportunities associated with the present performance should be made clear. This is beneficial to maintain motivation.

Trust is the highest form of human motivation. It brings out the very best in people. It takes time and patience. It assumes that if people are trained and given opportunities to develop, they rise to the level of trust.

If stewardship delegation is done appropriately much more work can be accomplished in much less time. It is beneficial to both the parties. The focus here is on effectiveness with people and not of efficiency with things. In the long run, it saves time. In such cases, the individual becomes his or her own boss and is committed to the desired goal. He or she is eager to use all his or her potentials and creativity for the job to be done. With more mature people, one can expect fulfillment of more challenging results, with fewer guidelines, less frequent accountability, and less measurable but more discernable criteria.

This leads to both personal and organizational growth.

8.6 THINK WIN/WIN

A commendable style of interaction in Japan starts from childhood. If there is a competition, Japanese children greet each other and say, "Let us win." There are many social workers who work for others and want them to get the facilities and opportunities.

When we interact with others, we think about the consequences of the interaction. Many a time, people are interested in their own benefit and do not think about the other person, party, or organization. They want the benefits and awards, and want the other person to lose the competition. There are some others who want that everyone should get the benefit and the awards and rewards.

There are six paradigms of human interaction. These are discussed in the following sections.

8.6.1 WIN/WIN

This type of interaction seeks mutual benefit in all sorts of interaction. Here, the solutions are mutually satisfying and mutually beneficial. Both the parties feel good about the solution and feel committed to the action plan. Win/win is based on the perception of life as cooperative not competitive. It assumes that there is plenty for everybody. Hence, one person's success is not achieved at the cost of other's failure. Here, the basic idea is that if neither of the solutions proposed by both the parties is satisfactory, they should generate a third, more efficient, and more beneficial way of solving the problem. There are five dimensions of win/win: self-awareness, imagination, conscience, and independent will. It involves mutual learning, mutual influence, and mutual benefit. Five interdependent dimensions of life are covered in win/win. These are character, relationship, agreements, system, and processes.

Three character traits are essential for win/win. These are integrity, maturity, and abundance mentality. It is difficult to think about win/win without integrity. The value system results in the quality of commitment. If value system is poor, commitment also is poor. Without trust, win/win becomes a meaningless technique.

Maturity is a balance between courage and consideration. On the one hand, there is courage necessary for the expression of personal feelings and convictions, and on the other the other hand, consideration for others' feelings and conviction should be dealt with. If the issue is important for both the parties, it is essential to balance both. To achieve win/win, one should have both courage and consideration.

Actually, courage and consideration are the two dimensions which decide whether the situation will result in win/win, lose/win, lose/lose, or win/lose. If the status of both consideration and courage is high, it results in a win/win situation. If both courage and consideration is low, it results in lose/lose. If of consideration is high and courage is low, it leads to lose/win. And, when that of courage is high and consideration is low, it will result in win/lose.

Courage high consideration high	Win/win
Courage low and consideration low	Lose/lose
Courage high and consideration low	Win/loss
Courage low and consideration high	Lose/win

8.6.1.1   Abundance Mentality

Some people have scarcity mentality. They think that there are only limited things available in life. If one gets a bigger share, the other will get less. Hence, they are not ready to share success, power, and recognition with anybody. They cannot be genuinely happy when others succeed. They interpret that someone's success is their failure. They are always comparing and competing. They prefer people who are weaker and do not challenge them.

On the other hand, those who have inner sense of personal worth and security, they have abundance mentality. They think that there is enough for everybody. Hence, they are ready to share success, prestige, and power. They are more open and creative. They appreciate uniqueness, inner direction, and proactivity of others. This is public victory which gives beneficial results for everyone. Here, making things happen together, communicating with each other, and working together result in such things which are better than what each one can accomplish by working independently.

Trust is essential for maintaining appropriate relations. Without trust, only compromise is possible. There is no credibility, mutual learning, communication, and expression of creativity without trust. In win/win agreement, five elements are made very explicit.

1. **Desired results**—Identification of what is to be done and when it should be done.
2. **Guidelines**—Specification of parameters within which results are to be accomplished.

3. **Resources**—Identification of human, financial, and personal or organizational resources available.
4. **Accountability**—Setting up standards of performance and time of evaluation.
5. **Consequences**—Specifying good and bad consequences as a result of evaluation.

8.6.2 WIN/LOSE

It is an authoritarian style. The individual is interested in winning at the cost of others. Such individuals are prone to use position, power, credentials, possessions, or personality to get their way. Some child-rearing practices are associated with this mentality. If parental love is conditional, the indirect message given to the child is that he or she is not intrinsically valuable or lovable. Value lies outside them. It is the comparison with someone else or some expectations. Such practices of parents are affecting highly vulnerable and dependent children and they are molded to a win/lose mentality.

Peer influence also is associated with win/lose mentality as peer acceptance and conformity to their expectations and norms lead to a sense of competition. Even in academic evaluation, individuals are not graded on the basis of comparison between their potentials and achievements but only on the basis of comparison with others. There are no intrinsic values. Everything is extrinsically defined. So, it is based on competition not cooperation.

However, in real life it is not always competition. Like for example, in marriage, if both the partners are not winning, both of them are losing. Same is true for organizations. If there is no cooperation, the organization will deteriorate. The win/lose mentality is detrimental to cooperation.

8.6.3 LOSE/WIN

It is worse than win/lose because it has no standards, no demands, no expectations, and no vision. An individual with such mentality wants to please others. He or she is oriented toward popularity and acceptance. These individuals are influenced by the ego strength of others. They have no courage to express their own feelings and thoughts. They give up easily. The win/lose type of people like lose/win people as they can easily exploit them. Those having lose/win mentality suffer from suppressed emotions and psychosomatic illnesses along with a lot of resentment, disillusionment, and disappointment. This leads to a lot of negative feelings and disproportionate anger to minor provocations and cynicism. All these things negatively affect their self-esteem and relations with others.

8.6.4 LOSE/LOSE

Rushin was extremely hostile about his classmate Sudhir. He wanted to teach a lesson to him. Sudhir always gets good grades and can maintain good impression in college. Rushin prepared a cheat sheet for the final examination and kept it under the table of Sudhir's examination seat. As was expected, Sudhir was caught by the supervisor and he could not write the paper. Afterwards, the teacher could easily understand that it was Rushin's handwriting and, thus, he was also debarred from the examination.

When both the parties are stubborn, ego invested, and determined, the result is a lose/lose situation. For example, only because the individual wants to teach a lesson to the other, he or she does not mind even if it results in his or her own loss. Such individuals are focused on their enemy and are so obsessed by his or her behavior that they become blind to everything except their desire for that person to lose. They are highly dependent people without their own direction.

8.6.5 Win

These type of people do not want others to lose. That is irrelevant for them. When there is no competition, this is the most common approach. These individuals just secure their own end and leave others to secure theirs.

Which option is the best depends on many things. When a relationship is important and an issue is not really important, lose/win is the preferred strategy.

When the efforts and time necessary to win are more than its worth, one may prefer lose/win. If achieving a particular goal is against one's value system, one may prefer lose/win.

In business, one has to think about long-term win and surrender short-term wins. Like for example, for achieving long-term trust of a customer, a shopkeeper may reduce the price of a commodity. In case of win/lose, it affects the attitude of the other person toward the individual, which might affect the effectiveness of the organization.

8.6.6 Win/Win or No Deal

No deal basically means that if there is no solution that leads to win/win, it is beneficial to agree than to disagree agreeably. That is no deal. If values and goals of the two parties are exactly opposite of each other, it is better not to get involved in any deal. It is better not to push each other. It gives a lot of emotional freedom. Just to maintain a relationship people keep on doing compromises one after the other. This creates problems for the individual and for business.

8.7 SEEK FIRST TO UNDERSTAND THAN TO BE UNDERSTOOD

In an organizational setup, medical practice, or even at home, it is necessary to take time to understand and diagnose before doing anything else. It is essential for effective interpersonal communication. If there is no understanding, there is no open and free expression. The person may not feel safe enough to open up. Trust requires a particular style of communication. Unless the speaker is influenced by the uniqueness of the individual, the individual will not be influenced by his or her advice. Empathic listening is the best way to build trust.

Generally, people are interested in being understood first. They do not listen with the intent to understand. They listen to reply.

They are either speaking or preparing to speak. They are filtering everything through their own paradigms and projecting their own ideas while interpreting others' communications.

They are either interested in proving their point or disapproving others' point. This practice is detrimental to interpersonal relations.

8.8 SUMMARY

This chapter presents a clear picture of how we generally interact with the environment and how we should do it ideally. Mostly, we are reactive, and so our psychological status depends on someone else. We should be able to decide our own agenda and mood. No one else should be allowed to interfere with it. Being proactive is essential for that.

Proactive thinking is controlling and managing one's own mental state, shouldering the responsibility of own actions, and maintaining one's mood irrespective of environmental stimuli.

Other effective thought and behavior processes as given by Covey are also equally important. Differentiating between urgent and important, thinking about success for everyone, trying to understand others, and then explaining our views are some ideas. If we practice these things in day-to-day life situations, we will be able to plan our activities in a better way. We will be goal directed. We will be able to save our time and communicate properly.

All these thinking and behavior patterns are most effective in human life.

QUESTIONS

1. Explain the nature of proactive thinking.
2. What are the other effective thought patterns?
3. Describe what is meant by beginning with the end in mind. Give an example.
4. What are advantages of putting first things first?
5. Explain thinking win/win and win/lose.

APPLICATION ORIENTATION

1. Analyze one's own behavior and write down three incidents when you have acted reactively and the cost was very high.
2. What is your general tendency regarding giving preference to work? Is it important or urgent that you do as your priority?
3. Which is your general style of interacting with others? Is it win/win, win/lose, or lose/win?
4. What are you concerned about? Describe in detail how would you deal with these things.
5. Do you think that you plan all your important activities and know exactly what you want to achieve after completing that activity. Give three of your short-term and two long-term goals.

SUGGESTED READING

Covey, S. R. (1997). *The seven habits of highly effective people*. London: FranklinCovey and Pocket Books.

Positive Thinking

After reading this chapter you will be able to:

1. Realize the importance of positive thinking in human life.
2. Understand how to change negative thoughts.
3. Know step-by-step enhancement of positive thinking.
4. Find out the relation between stress reduction and positive thinking.
5. Apply the knowledge for self-improvement.

9.1 NATURE AND SIGNIFICANCE OF POSITIVE THINKING

A child of 10 years lost his arm in a railway accident. After extreme struggle for years he became an international volleyball player. When asked about his amazing achievements he said, "As I have only one hand I don't have to decide which hand is to be used. This saves my time and energy."

There are many such things which are really worth considering. Edison was 67 years old when his laboratory was completely destroyed due to fire. He exclaimed, "That is good ... all mistakes have disappeared ... let me start a new." Within three weeks he invented the phonograph. Actually, Edison's 10,000 experiments were sheer waste. Those who think positively never give up.

Positive thinking is the faith that positive attitudes towards life result in positive output. As exercise is to physical health, positive thinking is to mental health. It is proved that those who think positively get their goal soon as compared to those who do not. Those who think negatively act slowly with doubts about the possibility of getting success. Positive thinking is a part of personality characteristics and general expectations depend on that. Positive thinking is associated with the feeling of subjective well-being.

Almost all human beings aspire for something in life. They work hard for that achievement: it may be only earning bread and butter or some dignified goal such as highly intellectual activities like doing some important research. Every day as one works for routine jobs and day-to-day activities, he or she may not get time to think about one's personal happiness and satisfaction. No mental energy is available to give a positive feedback to one self, feel completely relaxed, and generate positive attitude towards life and self. One is completely engrossed in solving the difficulties of daily demands and keeps on working hard without any consideration of self and personal well-being. Actually, in any stage of life one should start rethinking about how to feel good and understand self-worth. One should start satisfying the urge to utilize potentialities to the fullest extent. Say for example, if one likes singing one should start getting training in singing at any stage of life, even at the age of 50. One should appreciate one's achievements, accept that one is struggling hard for years and give due positive reinforcement to self. For that, one has to see the starting point, in the sense all the odds and difficulties one has encountered and where one has reached and how much efforts one had to put in for that. One has to remember that life is just a journey and that there is no particular destination where one has to reach. It obviously means that life is the "present." There are certain things that one cannot change in life and one has to accept them as they are. For example, one cannot correct the mistakes that one has done in the past, and one cannot change one's past experiences. Thinking and rethinking about all these things is not going to help the individual but may unnecessarily waste his or her psychological energy. Thinking about what positive things may happen in one's life is essential for positive thinking.

All great people have worked and achieved their goals against many odds. Mahatma Gandhi, Abraham Lincoln, Madam Marie Curie, and many great people have worked against environmental hurdles. They never complained about the limitations and problems. Their positive thinking gave them a lot of strength and motivation.

Those who think positively are positive even when they are under stress. They recover soon in case of disease and surgery. Even after some serious disease like breast cancer women who think positively recover soon and start their routine early. This effect is mediated through coping mechanisms. Whether the coping style will be problem focused or emotion focused depends upon personality. Problem-focused coping is associated with the idea that something can be done about the problem. If the person thinks that nothing can be done about the problem he or she will become helpless. An optimistic person thinks positively and when there is any ambiguity he or she expects a good outcome. The person thinks about the bright side of the environment and expects that something good is going to happen in one's life.

Active coping strategies may lead to attempts to acquire social support. Not doing anything to improve the conditions and blaming oneself are associated with the lack of positive thinking. Accepting truth as it is and as far as possible trying to do a better job are signs of positive thinking. Not accepting facts and avoiding ways to adjust

> Positive thinking is a part of personality characteristics and general expectations depend on that. It is associated with the feeling of subjective well-being.

with the environment are related to negative thinking. Those who are not positive thinkers depend on God for everything. This overdependence leads to inactivity, anxiety, hostility, and arising of the negative side of self and the world. It leads to the lack of satisfaction—in the family and on job—conflicts, and somatic complaints. Depressive attribution style is also a result of negative thinking.

9.2 WINING NEGATIVE THINKING

The reader may stop for a while and imagine that he or she has a limited life due to some terminal disease, say for six months, and wants to do many things during that span. The reader may prepare a list of such activities and then he or she will be able to notice that these are the activities that he or she has been wishing to do for many years and just neglected them. The basic questions that one should ask are: Why to wait for such a situation? Why not fulfill one's wishes and be happy in a normal environment?

Negative thinking concentrates on the limitations of self. Thinking that one is less than others leads to anger, frustration, envy, internalized anger, and similar other emotions. These emotions lead to the overutilization of neurohormones of brain such as serotonin and nonepinephrine. It leads to depression, mental and physical, which increases the possibility of ulcers, spastic colon, and other problems.

Negative self-talk actually emerges from an individual's own misperceptions, lack of information, and distorted ideas. They overpower logical thinking and reasoning. Some common forms of negative and irrational self-talk include:

1. **Filtering**—An individual magnifies the negative aspects of a situation and filters out all positive ones. After getting appreciation for a completed job if one is thinking only about a small error that one has committed, the individual just forgets about the compliments received, the hard work, and the accomplishments.
2. **Personalizing**—If something bad happens, the individual starts blaming self. Like if a party is canceled, he or she may think that it is because no one enjoys his or her company.
3. **Catastrophizing**—It is anticipating the worst. If the individual has to travel by air, he or she will start thinking about the various disasters like air crash.
4. **Polarizing**—It is interpreting things either good or bad, like if one has not achieved total success, it is failure. In this type of interpretation, there is no possibility of in-between interpretations.

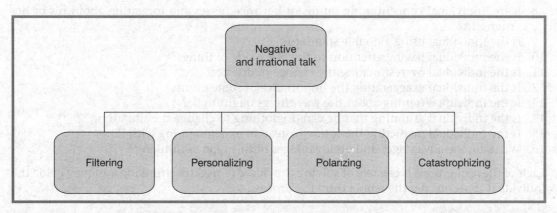

For positive thinking one must challenge irrational thinking with rational positive thoughts. If one does this then gradually self-talk may become realistic and self-affirming. One has to stop thinking and evaluate whether thoughts are positive and negative. If they are negative, reinforcing positive rational thoughts becomes a must. A simple rule to enhance positive thinking is that one should not say anything to self that he or she would not say to others. Some examples of common negative self-talk and positive conversion of the same are given as follows:

Negative Self-talk	Positive Conversion
I have never done it before.	It is an opportunity to learn something new.
It is too complicated.	Let me tackle it from a different angle.
I don't have the resources.	Necessity is the mother of invention.
I don't have enough time.	Let me evaluate and rethink about priorities.
It is not going to work.	I can try to make it work.
It is too radical a change.	Let us take a change as a challenge.
No one communicates with me.	Let me see if I can communicate with them.

Gradually one may change from concentrating on limitations to optimistic views and motivation.

For winning negative thinking, one should love people and use things, not love things and use people. A worthwhile self-concept and a positive competent self-image are the requirements for success and happiness in life.

9.2.1   CHALLENGES TO NEGATIVE THINKING

One may ask various questions to oneself and introspect to find out the objective answer to them. It may help overcoming negative thinking.

1. Is the person confusing a thought with a fact?
2. Is the individual jumping to a conclusion?
3. Is the individual assuming his or her view towards things is the only one possible way of looking at them?
4. What is the effect of thinking the way the individual does?
5. Is the individual asking questions which have no answers?
6. What thinking errors is he or she is making?
7. Is the individual concerning himself or herself as a total person on the basis of a single event?
8. Is the individual concentrating on his or her weaknesses and forgetting about his or her strengths?
9. Is the individual using a double standard?
10. Is the individual paying attention to the black side of things?
11. Is the individual overestimating the chance of disaster?
12. Is the individual exaggerating the importance of some events?
13. Is the individual fretting about the way things ought to be?
14. Is the individual assuming that he can do nothing to change the situation?
15. Is the individual predicting the future instead of experimenting with it?
16. What are the advantages and disadvantages of this type of thinking?

Each of these questions is capable of solving the riddle of negative thinking and may guide the individual to reconsider the whole thinking process.

9.3   CORRELATES OF POSITIVE THINKING

Many aspects of personality and general attitude are correlated to positive thinking and exactly opposite are the correlates of negative thinking.

Correlates of Positive Thinking	Correlates of Negative Thinking
High self-esteem	Low self-esteem
Acceptance of others as they are Optimism	Being critical of others Pessimism
Assertiveness in interpersonal relations	Passive in interpersonal relations
Acceptance of environment	Blaming the environment
Rear anger	Frequent anger
Positive planning	Always lacking time
No demand for help but accepts if given	No acceptance of help by others

Correlates of Positive Thinking	Correlates of Negative Thinking
Hopes that everything will continue properly	Expects perfection
No unnecessary guilt-unloading on others and no expectation of guilt by others	Guilt unloading on others
	Excess guilt feelings
Persuades others	Manipulates others
Feels responsible for one's actions	Depends on God for everything
Reasonable rules of conduct	Strict rules of conduct
Reasonable character	Devoid of character
Control of impulses	Vulnerable to drug abuse, alcohol addiction, excess bonds to religion or work, involvement in crime

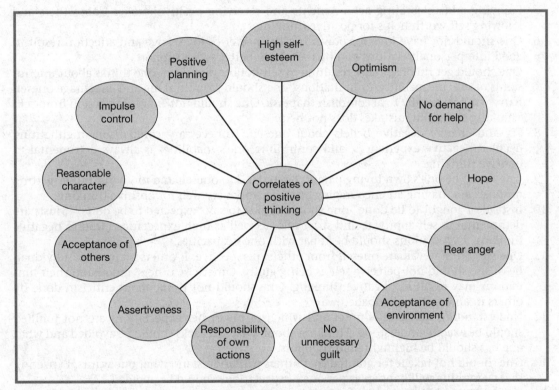

Positive thoughts can be generated and enhanced with some simple skills. One has to say a self-prayer everyday like the one given by a psychologist.

I love myself. I believe in myself. I am a unique person created by nature. I balance my emotional states. I do things which are important for me. I love to work. I keep my mind steady and fit. I love my life. I do not worry. I do not get involved in sad of anxiety provoking thoughts. I only think about happiness in life. I enjoy being myself.

I concentrate my attention on things that I can change than those that I cannot. I keep my mind so busy in positive thoughts that there is no space for negative thoughts.

I am a special person. I like myself. Every day I am improving in every way. I will be able to understand more about my potentialities..................."

The joy I get everyday enhances liking regarding life.

9.4 STEPS TO POSITIVE THINKING

1. Accept oneself as one is with all good and negative qualities, potentials and limitations, physical characteristics, appearance and habits, etc.
2. One cannot change others, but can change one's reaction about one's behavior. Thinking that others are responsible for one's negative thinking may result in more helplessness, anger, and dependence on others for mental health.
3. Awareness, courage, decision, and behavior should be the sequence of acting. The objective evaluation of the circumstances and appropriate decision regarding behavior are essential to enhance positive thinking.
4. One has to keep self-image high and should not blame oneself for temporary failures and setbacks. Underestimating self without giving optimum opportunity to develop may lead to negative thinking.
5. Enjoying and celebrating achievements and receiving positive strokes from others and knowing self-worth helps for positive thinking.
6. One should not have love for power but the power of love. Love and affection result in good interpersonal relations and this results in better social support.
7. One should get rid of self-talk resulting in self-doubt. Whenever one thinks about inferior status of self, incapability, or limitations, one should stop thinking and encourage oneself to try wholeheartedly to accomplish that task. One should not expect perfection from self. Thinking about old mistakes does not help.
8. Try and change negative beliefs about oneself. Unnecessary comparison, highlighting detailed negative experiences, and confirming one's inabilities is always detrimental to positive thinking.
9. One has to be one's own loving parent. Being kind to oneself and forgiving and forgetting mistakes and having an encouraging attitude work very well for positive thinking.
10. Instead of "ought to be done" one should decide to say "expected to be done." Musts are detrimental to self-approval, and strict rules as well as high expectations lead to negative thinking. Expectations should be at par with one's capacities.
11. One should not evaluate oneself from others' perspective. If others blame the individual, he or she should not perceive self as being guilty. Otherwise others' mood and their limitations may result in negative thinking. One should not think about criticism done by others in an emotionally loaded way.
12. Understanding why one is upset and which of his or her expectations are not fulfilled should be exactly understood. Thinking about what one lacks should be avoided and what one has should be highlighted in thoughts.
13. One should not take it for granted that others will understand what one wants. Expecting that everything will happen as per one's expectations should be avoided.
14. Everyone should have a meaningful leisure time activity.
15. Improving interpersonal relations leads to getting support and positive energy.
16. Planning exactly what one wants to do is essential. If one fails, he or she should say that he had planned to fail.
17. Only the individual himself or herself is responsible for what he or she thinks and which emotional experiences he or she gets. The individual himself or herself can change his or her thoughts.
18. Supporting others when they face problems helps the individual to be more positive about one's capacities and self-worth.

19. There is no satisfaction and happiness outside; it has to be found within oneself. A person will always be happy in spite of many environmental odds, and someone else will be unhappy even though he or she has everything in life.
20. Every day should be spent in happiness not in worries and blaming self or others. One has to find time to relax, and enjoy simple experiences in daily life.
21. One should always remember that one who does not trust self is one's own enemy who fights with self for the whole life. So, for positive thinking, trust oneself.
22. Spending enough money and time on needs of self, self-grooming, helps in maintaining a positive image and positive thinking.
23. One should accept one's mistakes than denying them. If one pretends and wants to hide mistakes, he or she wastes a lot of energy in doing that which leads to negative consequences.
24. There is no shortcut to success. One's achieving something by unfair means may lead to negative thinking and low self-esteem. A self-made person always is more confident and has a positive image of self.
25. If one is happy he or she will perceive that the whole world is happy. Hence, see the brighter side of life. One has to think of what is available and can be improved.

9.5 USE THE POWER OF POSITIVE THOUGHTS

1. Behavior and performance depend on what one communicates to oneself.
2. People feel and think low not because of the negative environment, but because they are in adverse environment because they think and feel so.
3. Positive results can be achieved only when one refrains from negative thoughts.
4. Whatever one wants to control or resist with negative responses gets stronger as one gives one's thoughts to it.
5. All that one finds disagreeable in others is a lesson for the individual himself or herself.
6. Positive thinking does not mean complacence.
7. Negative thinking has a basic thinking style that one can prosper only at the cost of others and not with them.
8. One feels threatened with every change.
9. One does not want to take responsibility of one's wrong deeds.
10. By talking negatively or proving others wrong gives a feeling that the speaker is better than others.
11. People are more likely to listen when the speaker criticizes others.
12. An individual may talk negatively about self only in the hope that others will praise him or her.
13. There is some hidden positive thing in every negative event.
14. One should not blame or judge others.
15. One should not pay any heed to subjective criticism.
16. One should not talk to oneself in a disparaging manner.
17. One has to shoulder the responsibility of whatever one goes through life.
18. One should concentrate on what others have done for him or her and not on what they have not.
19. One should not behave just to teach a lesson to others.
20. One should have a positive gesture.
21. Displaying positive thoughts everywhere, in an organization or at home, helps a lot.

Some questions to challenge negative thinking and enhance positive thoughts are:

1. What thinking errors am I making? Am I making an error like all or none? Nothing is completely right or wrong and black or white. People are not good or bad. They are a combination of the two. For example:

    Thought—I did my job very poorly.

    Possible answer—I did not do my job as good as I wanted to. However, it was not very poor. Nothing can be done perfectly. There is always some scope for improvement in everything.

2. What is the evidence? Is there any confusion of a thought with a fact? Only because one believes something is true, does not necessarily mean that it is. Is the fact accepted to be true by others? Are there any conclusive pieces of evidence available to prove that it is the truth? What are the possible contradictory pieces of evidence? On the basis of this, it is easier to conclude about whether it would stand up or will be dismissed. For example:

    Thought—When I met my colleague today he did not smile at me. I must have done something to offend him…. What is that?

    Possible answer—It is true that he did not smile at me, but I have no reason to believe that he is offended with me. It probably has nothing to do with me, maybe he was thinking of something else.

3. What are the possible alternatives? Am I assuming that my view is the only possible explanation of things? How would I have explained this situation before getting disturbed? How would somebody else explain this situation? How would the same person explain it if it would have happened in case of someone else? For example:

    Thought—This is a terrible mistake. I don't have the capacity to learn this activity properly.

    Possible answer—If I would have been healthy, or I had enough time, it was not a difficult job. Many others also fail to do the same task. It is not a serious issue. I will be able to correct it.

4. Am I jumping to a conclusion? This is the result of basing thoughts on poor and inadequate evidence. Many a time, one thinks that others are thinking critically about him or her. However, as one does not know the real thoughts, it should not be the conclusion. It may be right or may not be. One should stick to what one knows for sure. For example:

    Thought—My friend did not eat the sandwich that I prepared for him. He must have disliked the sandwich and thought that I cannot prepare even a sandwich.

    Possible answer—The factual information that I have is that my friend did not eat the sandwich. I do not know what he thinks. May be that he was not hungry. I will have to discuss with him.

5. What is the effect of thinking the way I do? What exactly do I want to achieve? Happiness? Joy? Satisfaction? Most of life? Is it that the way I think helps me to achieve these goals? Or are these standing in the way of my goals? For example:

    Thought—I had many opportunities…. However, I did not utilize them…. I have wasted my life…now I will never be able to do these things.

Possible answer—Repenting about past can make me only unhappy and depressed. The more important thing is what am I going to do with my future?

6. Am I asking questions which have no answer? Questions like how can I undo my past? Why am I of this particular gender? Why am I not born in a very rich family? Such types of questions are definitely leading to unpleasant thinking. It is a must to convert them into some answerable questions or better to forget about them. For example:

Thought—When will I be well settled?

Possible answer—There is no fixed answer to this question. Going over and over again makes me upset. Instead, I should try to work hard to achieve what I want.

7. Am I using the ultimate words in my speech and thinking? Words such as never, always, everybody, and nobody are indicating extreme viewpoints. Things are sometimes, some-where true about somebody.

Thought—Nobody is interested in my welfare. Things are always unfortunate for me.

Possible answer—That is exaggeration of facts. Somebody sometimes is not interested in my welfare or somethings are sometimes not according to my expectations are the facts.

8. Am I concerning myself as a total person on the basis of a single event? Only because one cannot accomplish something he or she is not a completely useless person. Blanket terms used to describe oneself indicate negative attitude toward self.

Thought—I scolded my roommates unnecessarily. I am a terrible person and an unpleasant roommate.

Possible answer—In the given situation with a given type of health problem and given type of pressure of work, I became irritable. It does not mean that I am always an unpleasant person or a horrible roommate. I cannot take a guarantee that I will always be capable of understanding others.

9. Am I concentrating on my weaknesses and forgetting about my strengths? Many a time, we forget about occasions when we have successfully achieved the expected goals and high-lighted when we fail. So, even if one has the capacity to deal with the difficulties encountered, one will be hopeless. For example answer:

Thought—I can't stand being jobless. I have lost my job, now there is no hope.

Possible answer—I was jobless before one year also. I did many things that I enjoyed during that period. I will try and find out a new job for myself which may be better than the previous one.

10. Am I using double standard? Am I evaluating my own performance more strictly and expecting too much from myself? Can I accept comparatively less output from others? Am I evaluating myself more critically than others? How do I react to those who are in similar situations? For example:

Thought—I am not normal. I am too upset by things and events.

Possible answer—If someone else in a similar situation gets upset, I am sympathetic to him or her. But I am not capable of showing the same sympathy to myself and give support to myself. As I help others to get a solution, I will have to help myself.

11. Am I paying attention only to the black side of things? We may think of some things that were not done properly but forget about things that went on smoothly. For example:

    Thought—That was a really terrible day.

    Possible answer—It is accepted that I had some disagreement with my father, but otherwise everything went on smoothly. Actually, I enjoyed the movie and party of my friend's birthday.

12. Am I overestimating the chances of disaster? Expectations that disaster will follow the mistake are greater in case of a pessimistic person. What is the possibility that it will happen is to be evaluated. For example:

    Thought—I could not study properly. Now I am going to fail.

    Possible answer—When was the last time that I failed? Can I study properly for every examination? I hope I will be able to pass but may get slightly less marks than usual.

13. Am I exaggerating the importance of events? What am I going to remember about its significance after one month, one year, or ten years? Nothing. If it is so, why should I give excess importance to that event? For example:

    Thought—I made a fool of myself. I will not be able to face these people again.

    Possible answer—No one or very few people must have noticed what has happened. Actually, it is not worth remembering, so even if they have noticed, they will also forget. I will probably laugh at it in the future.

14. Instead of accepting things as they are, am I fretting about the way things ought to be? Thinking again and again that world is unjust and life is difficult. For example:

    Thought—The world is cruel. Things should be different.

    Possible answer—Things are as they are. Thinking that they should be different is equal to denying the reality. Instead I must try to change it as far as I can by doing something for those who are suffering.

15. Am I assuming I can do nothing to change my situation? Pessimism is always underlying depression. Here, the person gives up before trying. For example:

    Thought—I don't think I will be able to do it.

    Possible answer—If I tell that to myself before trying, I shall never try. Let me try it in a different way. May be in the past some of my efforts were futile. But now, I will have to try again.

16. Am I predicting the future instead of experimenting with it? If I have failed in the past I don't think that I will be able to change my style in future. For example:

    Thought—I know this is not going to happen.

    Possible answer—It is the fact that it has never happened before, but it does not mean that it will not happen now. It is okay that I have never done it before, but if I want I will be able to do it.

17. What are the advantages and disadvantages of thinking this way? Are the advantages less than the disadvantages? What keeps these types of thoughts going? Can I avoid disadvantages and get only the advantages? For example:

Thought—I must be able to create a good impression during this presentation.

Advantages—I will make extra efforts to impress people. If they like my presentation I will feel marvelous.

Disadvantages—If someone does not like my presentation, I will feel terrible. Then I will think that I am not a worthy person.

Possible answer—Telling myself that I must do it creates a pressure on my mind. As a consequence, being relaxed becomes difficult. I will not be able to enjoy myself in that situation. It is illogical to think that everyone will appreciate me all the time. It is good if they do, but if they don't it is not the end of the world.

9.6   STRESS REDUCTION AND POSITIVE THINKING

Positive thinking is associated with reduction of stress. It helps in the management of negative emotions. It improves one's health—both physical and psychological. Overcoming negative self-talk by recognizing it becomes essential for that. One has to replace negative thoughts by positive thoughts. If one thinks that life is only a struggle, he or she is very unfortunate, there is always some unfair competition, then all these things are proven true in case of that person. It is something like saying television is hazardous. Actually, it is hazardous when one watches it excessively and when one watches programs detrimental to mental health. In a way, it is up to the person deciding whether he or she wants to use it this way or that way. Likewise, it is the interpretation of the environment that decides the orientation of personal thoughts. One may take it as a threat or a challenge.

9.7   EFFECTS OF POSITIVE THINKING

1. Decreased negative stress
2. Greater resistance to common infections
3. Improvement in general health
4. Reduced risk of coronary artery disease
5. Easier breathing, even in case of some lung disease as emphysema
6. Improved coping ability for women with high-risk pregnancies
7. Better coping skills during hardships

In general, harmful effects of negative stress are reduced substantially by positive thinking.

Researchers have proved that optimistic or pessimistic tendencies and personality decides how well and how long one lives. It is reported that positive thinking leads to a sense of well-being.

Many individuals seriously try to forget about negative things in life but again and again the same thought comes to their mind. It is difficult to get rid of negative thoughts. For example, if a student is insulted by his or her teacher, he or she will get upset by the same memories, the details of the events, words used by the teacher, reactions of other students, and so on. He or she will not be able to concentrate on his or her work or even on human relations. Some strategies to overcome negative thoughts are suggested by psychologists. They are:

1. A simple way to get out of this vicious circle is to write down whatever comes to one's mind or talk loudly to oneself, then reducing the pitch of voice. One has to describe all negative

feelings to oneself at least 4–5 times. Then, the next step is to recollect the mental state one was enjoying when one was happy and enthusiastic. The details of self-talk at that time also can be recollected or reconstructed. Again increasing the volume of speech and talking about positive things and aspirations helps. If one can recollect visuals, it can lead one to a better and positive mental state.

2. Instead of fighting with negative thoughts, one should start doing positive things. In the same way, instead of blaming others, it is essential to introspect and find out what one has done and what should be improved? Understanding one's limitations or limitations of one's environment helps to accept the reality and it becomes easier to overcome them. Whatever is unfair in someone's behavior actually is a lesson for the perceiver. Everyone has to see if his or her own behavior is similar to that. Finding out one's own errors and relating them to the actual outcome also helps.

3. One more frequently seen tendency is to compare oneself with someone else. As every human being is entirely different as far as mental and psychological abilities, aptitudes, and other things like family background, socialization, and value system are concerned, he or she is not comparable to others. Any comparison may lead to dissatisfaction and hostility. Hence, it leads to negative feelings. This is also related to a wrong notion that one can prosper only at the cost of others and not with them. However, that is not a case, for example, in Japanese culture, people believe in helping each other to develop and in winning with each other. Like Japan, we can also think of the let us win attitude. In any case, one need not unnecessarily waste one's psychological energy in any unwanted comparisons. As a consequence of such hostility, one starts experiencing insecurity and wants to achieve success by using any unfair means.

4. There are various ways to achieve success. It is not necessary to get involved in some unfair game to get ahead. If someone else fails, it is not equal to one's success. Subconsciously one is aware of the fact that it is not possible to succeed every time. Hence, one wants that others also should not succeed. Then, one wants to trouble them. Once it is proved that others are not able, one thinks that he or she has proved that he or she is. However, others do not think so.

5. Many a time, change is threatening. It results in change in work, responsibilities, routine, and similar other things. This is actually a negative style of thinking as one is not ready to take new challenges and learn new things. Change is a rule of life and one should accept it with open attitude.

6. If something goes wrong, it is customary to blame others for that. That is interpreted as success. Obviously, that is not taken as success but hesitation to accept one's limitations and trying to improve. Criticizing others is very easy and is a popular type of communication which leads to cheap popularity. For positive thinking, one should stop thinking and talking ill of others and of oneself. It is a must to avoid evaluating and criticizing others. One has to accept them as they are. Everyone wants to achieve something and tries to do it the way he or she thinks is the best for him or her. So, it is better to avoid evaluation. Behavior depends on the individual's understanding and maturity. Everyone's understanding and maturity levels are different. Hence, it is the best policy to avoid evaluation.

7. Once a person is involved in negative thoughts, there is no possibility that he or she will be able to generate positive ones. One has to find out hidden positive things even when outwardly things are negative. Someone may learn how to deal with unexpected stressors only because of a traumatic situation, which ultimately may generate a lot of self-confidence, how to do things in a perfect way because of a very strict father, how to build a new house as the old one is destroyed by flood, and so on. One also learns what should not be done in a difficult situation and if others are not behaving properly; one may introspect to find out if he or she is also making the same errors.

8. One should not think about subjective remarks or subjective criticism. Even when it is done by self, subjective criticism is of no use to improve one's performance. On the contrary, objective evaluation and criticism are to be taken into consideration for self-improvement. So, one should not think about a remark like "you are incapable" but rethink about a remark like "you should improve your writing skills."

9. One should not use disparaging language while talking to oneself. Many a time, one overevaluates the importance of what others say. Everyone is unique and has different potentials and limitations. Once these limitations and good qualities are accepted by the individual himself or herself, he or she should not depend on proving oneself or getting others' approval. Whatever people say, the facts about self remain the same. Nature's unique creation does not depend on anyone's words.

10. One should accept the responsibility of one's experiences. A person is himself or herself responsible for his or her own experiences and he or she should accept it. If one thinks he or she is not capable of doing his or her duties properly, others contribute to the actual actions related to it. Every individual plays a particular role. Hence, the first step to get out of negative thoughts is to improve self-concept.

11. Concentrating one's attention on what others have done for oneself is far better than thinking about what they have not. It is always a comparative statement when one says "no one is concerned about me," which actually indicates that otherwise people are doing much more. One has to appreciate that, and as a consequence, it may increase.

12. As there are many things that one cannot understand about others, instead of teaching a lesson to others, one should start interacting positively with others, and this may lead to reciprocal positive feelings.

The most important thing is that whole biochemistry of an individual changes because of positive thinking. Every cell becomes healthier and the benefit of that becomes obvious.

If one walks smartly, one feels smart; if one walks like a sick person, one feels sick. One may imitate successful people, should walk like them, talk like them, and try and think the way they do. This is the easiest way to be a positive thinker.

9.8 BOARD DEPICTING POSITIVE THINKING IN AN ORGANIZATION

In many organizations, people feel pessimistic and they do not think that anything good is going to happen there. They are not motivated to try something new and never expect better achievement. Some examples of such thoughts in an organizational situation are given as follows.

1. Terminating a new idea by saying that it is not practical. Without actual experimenting with an idea, no one can find out its real value in day-to-day life. Modifying the concept, strategy, or interpretation also becomes difficult without actual trial.

> I am enjoying life due to inherited and acquired abilties, aptitudes, and skills. Work in the present organization makes my life meaningful as I get an opportunity to utilizes all of them through it. I am motivated to do my job properly and sincerely because it enhances my self-worth and contributes to welfare of others.

2. Not trying any new idea thinking that it will be of no use. These are concluding remarks before conducting an experiment. If a player thinks this way before hitting a ball with a bat, he or she will not be able to win.

3. Thinking that there are so many questions so it is better to give up. If there are many questions, one should try to solve at least some of them. Thinking that no one will be able to solve all of them leads to a pessimistic attitude.
4. Thinking that it is difficult to deal with a particular type of activity. That is exactly why it should be attempted. If not, then there will be no improvement and no change in any given situation.
5. Being reluctant to accept new things because one has never tried it before. That is exactly why one should try it, otherwise the whole world will change, but people having this attitude will never change.
6. Mentioning that there is a lack of facilities. Facilities are made by people and are not responsible for their fate. One can do whatever is the best possible in the given environment. One should exploit the available facilities and try to change the environment.
7. Lack of proper cooperation by colleagues is mentioned as one of the most important factors detrimental to motivation and positive thinking. One should concentrate on whatever cooperation one gets and not on what he or she does not. If one talks about the available cooperation, it will increase. One must think about change in behavior and interaction which may enhance cooperation.
8. In an organization, people say that superiors cannot understand many things and hence there is no point in hoping for any change. However, everyone can use positive attitude while interacting with one's juniors and see its effects on routine jobs.
9. Generally, people blame juniors and say that their work is not satisfactory. They are reluctant to work. If this is what one thinks, it is essential to analyze one's own behavior. Double standards and neglecting others' potentials and aspirations should be avoided. The leader should work with subordinates and use their talents appropriately. He or she should give them the credit of their work and due recognition to their good qualities.

One should be optimistic about the work that one has to do on the given day. This leads to more creative problem-solving. In any institute, positive thoughts should be displayed on walls, in lifts, and staircases.

To sum up, it can be said that positive thinking can change an individual's psychological health as well as whole future. It may be in one's family, school or college, or organization where one works that the individual gets the benefits of positive thinking.

9.9 SUMMARY

Positive thinking is the faith that positive attitudes toward life result in a positive output. Positive thinking is the magic which has unique benefits in day-to-day life or even when we face some problems. It is the expectation that something good is going to happen if we keep on trying. It helps mental health. Many great people had to fight against the odds in their lives. One can prevent negative thinking and enhance positive thinking. Causes and consequences of negative thinking should be studied. Many positive attitudes, hope, optimism, and acceptance of self and environmental conditions are the obvious outcomes of positive thinking.

QUESTIONS

1. Describe the nature of positive thinking and its advantages.
2. How should one overcome negative thinking?
3. Discuss the various correlates of positive thinking.
4. What are the strategies to enhance positive thinking?
5. How is positive thinking associated with stress reduction?

APPLICATION ORIENTATION

1. Prepare a list of things that you worry a lot about. Write down the benefit out of them. Find out the root cause and actions necessary to change the situations positively.
2. Do you think repeatedly about your old mistakes, which are those? If you want to avoid it use the thought-stopping technique. Whenever the disturbing thought comes to your mind say "stop," and stop thinking about it. Give some reward to oneself for not thinking about it for a particular time. Gradually, increase the time. Keep a record of the same.
3. Select someone you often criticize for his or her inappropriate interaction style and behavior. When you tell him or her about it, does that change his or her behavior? What is the impact of such thinking on your mood? Analyze and record it repeatedly.

SUGGESTED READINGS

Halonen, J. S., & Santrock, J. W. *Psychology context and application.* New York: McGraw-Hill.
Mcentarffer, R., & Weseley, A. J. (2012). *Barron's AP psychology*, 5th ed. First E book. http://www.amazon.com/AP-Psychology-Barrons-Ap-ebook/dp/B00IGAAAGA (accessed on December 17, 2012).
Peale N. V. (2006). *Power of positive thinking.* The Quality Book Club. E book. www.amazon.com//positivethinking-Reverend—Norman-Vincent/dp/8087888235 (accessed on December 17, 2015).
Quillam, S. (2008). *Positive thinking.* New Delhi: DK Publishers.

10 | Assertiveness

Objectives

After reading this chapter, you will be able to:

1. Know the nature and importance of assertiveness.
2. Understand various types of assertiveness.
3. Learn about various skills in assertiveness.
4. Relate different strategies to assertiveness.
5. Associate personality characteristics with assertiveness.
6. Try to be more assertive in day-to-day life situations.

10.1 INTRODUCTION

Sonal was a 22-year-old girl from a rural area. Her parents were interested in finding a suitable life partner for her. A proposal was worth finalizing according to her parents, but Sonal was reluctant to even think about it. In front of all the elderly male members from her joint family who were strict authoritarian, she was asked if she was ready to accept the marriage proposal. Sonal was boiling with anger and was pretty upset. She was trying to control her emotions. Looking down avoiding eye contacts and fumbling with her fingers she murmured, "Uhm...no...not actually...in fact...I don't want to...marry him." All the family members were very happy and they were convinced that she was reluctant to accept it as she was blushing.... They ultimately decided to go ahead.

When Sonal was not interested in marrying that person why could she not tell that to her parents more clearly? Why did the parents misinterpret her message? What will be its consequence? What should be done in such a situation? Assertiveness is the only answer where the person can at least try to alter the environment. It reduces social anxiety, passivity, and hostility.

In a typical Indian scenario, this is the most common type of interaction among parents and young ladies. Why is a young girl like Sonal not capable of communicating

> Assertive behavior emerges as one aspect of emotional freedom that concerns standing up for one's own rights.
>
> It is confidently expressing oneself so that others do not take things for granted.
>
> It is preventing the injustice invited by one's own behavioral style.

her real feelings about the most important decision in her life to her parents? The only answer is that she lacks assertiveness. Hence, she cannot find a way to express her feelings and opinions without hurting others. As a consequence, she is inviting injustice leading to long-term devastating effects.

Human happiness and progress depend on effective human relations. Interpersonal relations are a major source of self-worth and satisfaction in life. It is necessary to maintain good human relations with people to get the most from life. Effective relations, in turn, depend on an appropriate expression of feelings and emotions without arousing any negative feelings in the mind of the opposite party. All these things are achieved by practicing assertiveness. Assertive behavior emerges as one aspect of emotional freedom that concerns standing up for one's own rights. For that, one must know one's own rights, do some essential things to protect them, and strive for emotional freedom. This is a way of maintaining and improving the quality of personal life, as well as personal fulfillment. It is confidently expressing oneself so that others do not take things for granted. Assertiveness is a direct, honest, and appropriate expression of one's feeling, opinions, and beliefs (Jakubowski-Spector, 1973).

10.2   TYPES OF BEHAVIOR

There are three types in which human behavior can be classified. It is actually a continuum from aggressiveness to submissiveness and passive behavior. Assertiveness is the golden mean. Albert and Emmons, in 2008, first put forth the view that response styles can be of three types—aggressiveness, assertiveness, and nonassertiveness or submissiveness. Some other researchers have given one more type called passive aggression.

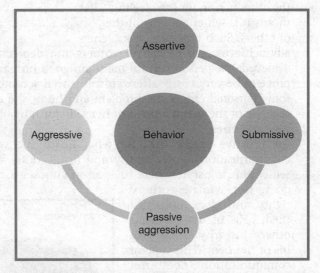

1. **Aggressiveness**

   An aggressive person tries to get what he or she wants in any way. Here, the person exploits others for self-enhancement. Aggressiveness results in insulting and hurting others and humiliating, disregarding, belittling, or overpowering them. It gives rise to

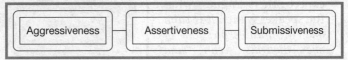

threat, fight, and manipulation. An aggressive person does not respect others' rights and does not have interest and concern for others. He or she is rude, obnoxious, loud, boisterous, domineering, and expressing superiority. The message is, "I am okay, you are not."

It means, "I am superior and right, you are inferior and wrong." There are more "you" statements to accuse others. These individuals decide for others. Others may feel hurt, humiliated, angry, worthless, embarrassed, and abused. This results in a lack of close relationship and the person gets alienated from others. Aggressiveness is expressed basically with the help of nonverbal communication along with verbal expression. The basic purpose of aggressiveness is to dominate and win at any cost where one can force the other person to lose. An aggressive person openly blames others for any problem. He or she stands very close to the other person and starts shouting. His or her voice is shrill, demanding, authoritative, and abusive. Eyes are staring, narrowed, and expressing hatred. Body posture is upright, tense, and stiff, and gestures indicate superiority. Fists are clenched, pounding, finger pointing, and many more abrupt gestures are seen. He or she never cares for what the other person must be feeling. That means it is self-enhancing at the cost of others. Such type of person gener-

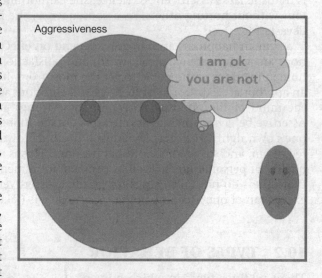

ally achieves goal by hurting others and depreciates others. Though immediate goal is achieved, the person cannot maintain good human relationship with others and this may prove to be very costly afterwards. It is well accepted that the person who is aggressive has some personal emotional problem and he or she does not shoulder the responsibility for that. He or she maintains his or her self-worth by blaming others for his or her problems.

2. **Assertivenes**

An assertive person asks for what he or she wants directly and openly. His or her communication is confidently and firmly done without any anxiety. Assertiveness is a self-enhancing style where the person chooses for himself or herself. An assertive person does not violate others' rights and does not hurt them. He or she respects others' integrity along with his or her own. This type of communication does not expect others to guess what the speaker wants. *It is calm and dignified expression of one's thoughts, feelings and emotions.* It is the most effective way of interacting with others and comfortably

maintaining good human relations. It reduces the need for approval by others. This increases the chances that the individual may get what he or she wants. It is related to enhancing self-respect and self-esteem whatever may be the end product.

The message is, "I am okay, and you are okay," where others feel respected and valued. It means, "You and I may have our differences, but we are equally entitled to express ourselves

to one another." The possibility increases that this person will be able to achieve his or her goals without any damage to interpersonal relations. He or she uses I statements, objective words, direct statements, and honest expression of feelings. Voice declares conversational tone which is firm, relaxed, and warm. He or she can maintain appropriate eye contact, and open and attentive gestures. Body expressions and movements are relaxed and straight.

The assertive formula is 'I feel _____ (a certain way) when you _____ (do a certain thing or behave in a certain way) because I want or need or feel _____ (a certain expectation from/about this act/behavior)'

3. **Nonassertiveness or submissiveness**

A nonassertive person keeps on hoping that others will be able to correctly guess his or her feelings and emotions. This type of person never tells freely what he or she wants and never explains what his or her real feelings are. They do not want to upset anyone and so do not get what they want. They are afraid of dislike and rejection. They want to avoid confrontation. There is no guaranty that nonassertiveness may result in the outcome that is expected. Losing other people's approval is usually a major issue for those who are nonassertive. However, nonassertion does not guarantee approval. Actually, the end product of nonassertive behavior is that the person becomes angry about others' behavior. *It involves violating one's own rights by failing to honestly express them and gives others a chance and opportunity to violate one's rights.* The message is, "I am weak and inferior, and you are strong, superior, and powerful."

This type of communication is actually done in such a way that it is apologetic which can be disregarded by others. In nonassertive style of interacting, the person is involved in self-denial and acts in an inhibited way. He or she thinks that his or her expectations and needs are not important and others' needs and desires are more important. He or she thinks that he or she does not deserve any special concerns. He or she depends

upon his or her fate. That means he or she depends on others for his or her achievements, is completely passive and accepts life as it is, and allows others to tell him or her with what is to be done. His or her plans are changed or influenced by others. He or she gives up when he or she suspects that conflict is going to occur. His or her style of communication is expressing apology, hedging, rambling, disconnected and indirect. He or she thinks that he or she cannot change any important thing in his or her life, is anxious and hurt and allows others to choose. However, one must at least try to put forth his or her point of view clearly so that the possibility that the other person will consider it increases. If a person is nonassertive, he or she may blame himself or herself afterward for not fulfilling his or her own expectations.

The body language in state of nonassertiveness is totally different than that of assertiveness. A nonassertive person is not interested in eye contact; his or her eyes are averted, downcast, teary, or pleading; posture is stooped; and shows distracting movements such as moving to and fro, expressing awkwardness, nervous coughing, and avoiding talking about the main issue. Excessive head nodding is also seen. Weak, hesitant, low, soft, and wavering voice expressing apology for simple things is an indicator of nonassertiveness.

4. **Passive aggressiveness**

This type of behavior involves expressing one's needs and feelings in an unclear and confusing manner. The purpose is to express oneself without having to state one's feelings openly. The hidden purpose is to get what one wants. The message is, "Actually you are not okay, but I will let you think that I think you are." This person manipulates to get what he or she wants. He or she wants to show how he or she feels by pouting, playing the martyr, pretending to withdraw, procrastinating, making empty promises, and playing helpless. Others feel confused, frustrated, distrust, and taken advantage of. This person appears to be independent and in control of the situation. He or she may achieve the desired goal, but passive aggression gives rise to the feeling of low self-esteem. Verbal language is like sarcasm, teasing, ridiculing, and false praise. Hence, the voice is sarcastic, sometimes crying, whining, monotonous, and judgmental. He or she may show impatient gestures and a disapproving style of nonverbal communication.

10.3 NATURE OF ASSERTIVENESS

Assertiveness is being firm and expressing one's views and emotions without hurting anyone. Nature has created all human beings as equal. Those who do not believe in this, have wrong assumptions while interacting with others. Colman's (2008) *Dictionary of Psychology* defines assertiveness as "an expression of one's needs, wishes and feelings frankly, honestly and directly, in a way that causes others to take them into account."

There are various definitions of assertiveness. These definitions are progressively becoming more focused and are making the nature of assertiveness more and more clear.

Some important definitions of assertiveness are given as follows.

1. Assertiveness is all a socially acceptable expression of rights and feelings (Wolpe & Lazarus, 1966).
2. Assertiveness is the ability for self-expression (Liberman, 1972).
3. Assertiveness is the habit of emotional freedom (Lazarus, 1971).
4. It is the behavior that enables a person to act in his or her own best interest, stand up for himself or herself without undue anxiety, express his or her rights without destroying the rights of others (Alberti & Emmons, 1974).
5. Lazarus in 1973 proposed the idea that assertiveness is divided in four specific responses:

   a. The ability to say no
   b. The ability to ask for favors or make requests
   c. The ability to express positive and negative feelings
   d. The ability to initiate, continue and terminate general conversation

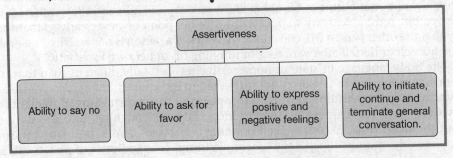

6. It has been highlighted that assertiveness involves:

   a. The ability to express positive feelings
   b. The ability to express negative feelings
   c. Self-denial

There are many aspects of assertiveness that are obviously noticed while social interaction. It shows two things essentially:

1. Respect for self
2. Respect for others

So, on the one hand, it is expressing one's needs and defending one's rights, and on the other, it is respecting the other person's needs and rights.

    Lazarus (1973) defined assertiveness as "expressing personal rights and feelings." It is protecting one's rights without violating others'. It means expressing personal likes and interests spontaneously, talking about self without becoming self-conscious, accepting compliments comfortably, and disagreeing with someone openly. One has to accomplish this without insulting, threatening, or belittling the other person. It does not involve punishment, rejection, or negative evaluation of others. Assertiveness is the application of sound knowledge of human rights in interpersonal relations. Individual's rights are as follows:

> **Stand up for one's rights**
>
> - Deny requests
> - Refuse insulting treatment
> - Express opinions freely
> - Complain about something

1. To ask for whatever one needs—Of course the other person has a right to deny that.
2. To maintain one's opinions and values and express them appropriately.
3. To change one's opinions.
4. To take decisions and experience its consequences.
5. To deny anything.
6. To become successful.
7. To say that one does not know.
8. To say yes or no to anyone's any request without feeling guilty.
9. To relate to others without depending on them for approval.
10. To learn to be assertive.

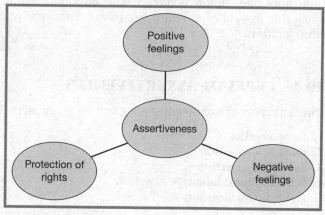

Every individual has to stand up for his or her rights. With assertiveness, one can achieve the following things.

1. One can express:

   a. Positive feelings such as,

   (i) Appreciation—within a given socially acceptable framework, one should be able to express appreciation
  (ii) Praise
 (iii) Receiving praise
 (iv) Requesting
  (v) Initiating
 (vi) Accepting criticism that is factual—this requires objectively evaluating self-behavior, styles of expression, and positive and negative characteristics. Only then can one accept factual criticism about self. Excessive ego involvement and defensive behavior are detrimental to accepting factual criticism
 (vii) Criticizing others objectively
(viii) Communicating positively.

   b. Negative feelings such as,

   (i) Annoyance
  (ii) Feeling of being hurt

2. Stand up for one's rights:

   a. Denying request
   b. Refusing insulting treatment
   c. Expressing one's opinion
   d. Complaining about something.

It is worth noting that assertiveness is learned behavior. Hence, one can improve assertiveness with practice and appropriate training. In response to a particular interpersonal interaction, how one should behave is the important thing. Different sorts of assertiveness is applicable in case of different situations. That is why different types of assertiveness need consideration.

10.4 TYPES OF ASSERTIVENESS

Different types of assertiveness are given by researchers. These are:

1. Basic assertion
2. Empathic assertion
3. Escalating assertion
4. Self-assertion/I language assertion
5. Confrontive assertion

a. **Basic assertion**

This is the simple expression of standing up for one's own rights, opinions, feelings, and beliefs. This may not consist of social skills like empathy. The simplest examples of such expressions are: "I want to study now" or "I feel like resting for a while." One should not take it for granted that everyone can easily achieve this. Let us take for example that a typical Indian housewife who is continuously devoted to the needs of her family members will not be able to say that she wants some rest when there are many things to be done such as cooking, washing, and cleaning. Though she is not well or extremely tired, she will start doing all these things.

b. Empathic assertion

These assertive people are sensitive to others and communicate that they have understood the emotions of others. After taking into consideration others' feelings they express their ideas assertively. A friend says, "I know that you are not free for the whole day but I want you to visit my place just for ten minutes." The expression of understanding the other person's problems and requirements make the speaker's communication more acceptable. As is indicated from the title itself, empathy is a must for this type of assertiveness. Hence, this requires maturity and understanding.

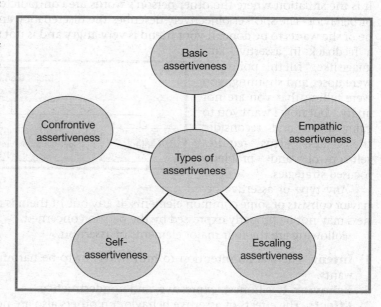

c. Escaling assertion

This is minimal assertive response that can help achieve the speaker's goal with minimum efforts. The possibility of negative consequences is comparatively less. If the goal is not achieved this way, then the speaker may become more and more assertive. For example, a teacher may tell the students, "If you fail to submit your assignment by tomorrow, I will have to increase the work." This may lead to better results and goal may be achieved. Most of the students will submit their assignments within the given time.

d. Self-assertion or I language assertion:

While expressing difficult negative emotions this type of assertion helps a lot. Instead of saying that "you have hurt me" the person says "I was hurt when you said that." This type is also useful to understand if their feelings are resulting from some violation or they are imposing their own values and interpretations on others. Let us imagine that an employee is generally supposed to work harder as compared to other colleagues and at present he or she is responsible for four projects at a time. In a meeting, while the boss is explaining all these things, the employee feels very angry and wants to scream loudly and blame the boss. However, that will lead to more problems of interpersonal relations and the employee may be punished by his or her boss. Instead of that he or she should express his or her problem with the help of I statements. In this situation, the employee can ask for advice without insulting the boss and further complications. He or she says, "I get confused when I am expected to work on four projects simultaneously. Sir, kindly tell me which of them is the most urgent, and to be completed as priority." In this case, without getting annoyed the boss may rethink about the work, may tell his or her priority, and may redistribute the work or give some more time.

e. **Confrontive assertiveness**

It is the situation where the other person's words are contradictory to his or her own actions or behavior. The speaker objectively describes the discrepancy and then assertively tells what he or she wants to be done. If your friend is very angry and is not accepting that, you may give a feedback in assertive language like, "Till this point you were upset and shouting, you were telling that you are not angry…but now I want you to calm down and reconsider the issues." This requires self-control and problem-focused strategies.

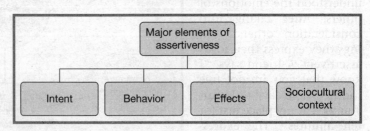

Any type of assertive behavior consists of some common elements. If any one of them is not up to the mark, assertiveness may not be properly expressed by the person concerned.

Following are the four major elements of assertion.

1. **Intent.** There is no intention to hurt others or to be harmful by stating own needs and wants.
2. **Behavior.** It is honest, expressive, and nondestructive.
3. **Effects.** The effects of assertive behavior on others also are not harmful.
4. **Sociocultural context.** The behavior that is assertive in one sociocultural context may not be assertive in some other.

Some other researchers have given four types of assertive expressions. These are:

1. Supporting and caring which are warm and nurturing appreciation.
2. Directing and guiding which include firm authoritarian style.
3. Analytic assertiveness which is thoughtful and alert.
4. Expressive assertiveness which is used to express emotions.

Some researchers have recently given nine broad areas of assertive behavior. These are:

1. Assertive talk
2. Spontaneous expression of feelings
3. Greeting others
4. Disagreement
5. Asking why
6. Talking about oneself
7. Rewarding others for compliments
8. Refusing to justify opinions
9. Direct eye contact

It is worth noting that researchers have concluded that nonverbal messages are found to be more effective by observers. Verbal assertive behavior can become nonassertive or aggressive depending on nonverbal behavior that accompanies it. For example, the duration of looking at a person, loudness, and effect of speech change the message to a large extent. The importance of facial expression, timing, fluency, and content cannot be underestimated. Making requests for behavior change and initiating interactions are the most favorable social evaluations and are rated as being highest on assertiveness. Expressing unpopular opinions is generally rated as highest on assertiveness. The relationship between any two individuals and their roles in a given situation may help or hinder the assertiveness expression. In a close relationship, people may become more expressive and willing to share their actual emotions. If there is no fear of upsetting the relationship people may criticize each other more openly. Chan in 1993 proposed three dimensions of assertiveness—expressing, confronting, and demanding—which are related to beliefs and rights differently.

It is important to consider the cultural norms of the community as culture and socialization play an important role in assertiveness. For example, in Indian community girls and women are encouraged to be nonassertive, dependent, and passive as well as submissive. Male members on the contrary are encouraged to be aggressive, competitive, objective, confident, and analytic minded. A lot of research has been done regarding gender differences in assertiveness all over the world and it has been found that male members are more assertive than females. In most of the cultures, men are socialized to dominate, exploit, and demand various rights. Girls and women, however, are socialized to think that there are no needs of their own. As a consequence, they develop no identity of their own out of marriage relationship and this condition remains the same for the whole of their lives. Hence, it is necessary to train girls to be assertive right from childhood. It is also proved scientifically that women are more assertive about expressing positive things such as praise, appreciation, affection, and concern. Men are lagging behind in this type of assertiveness.

10.5 ASSUMPTIONS AND RIGHTS IN INTERPERSONAL COMMUNICATION

There are many assumptions that exist without verification in our mind when we interact with others and interfere with assertiveness. If one considers one's legitimate rights, he or she is exactly opposite of these assumptions. Some important assumptions and corresponding legitimate rights are listed as follows:

1. **Assumption**—It is selfish to put your needs before others'.
   Right—You have the right to put yourself first sometimes.
2. **Assumption**—It is shameful to make mistakes.
   Right—You have the right to make mistakes.
3. **Assumption**—You should always try to be logical and consistent.
   Right—You have the right to change your mind and decide about different courses of action.
4. **Assumption**—It is not polite to question others regarding their actions, as they have appropriate reasons for their actions.
   Right—You have the right to protest against unfair treatment and criticism.
5. **Assumption**—You should never interrupt others by asking questions as it declares your stupidity.
   Right—You have the right to interrupt and ask for clarification.
6. **Assumption**—People are not interested in hearing that you feel bad. So, do not tell it to others.
   Right—You have the right to feel and express pain.
7. **Assumption**—When someone gives you an advice, you should take it seriously.
   Right—You have the right to ignore others' advice.

8. **Assumption**—You should be sensitive to the needs and wishes of others even when they are unable to tell you what they want.
   Right—You have the right not to anticipate the needs and wishes of others.
9. **Assumption**—You must answer if someone asks you a question.
   Right—You have the right to choose not to respond.
10. **Assumption**—When someone is in trouble, you must help him or her.
    Right—You have the right not to shoulder the responsibility of others' problems.
11. **Assumption**—You should always try to accommodate others.
    Right—You have the right to say no.
12. **Assumption**—If you want to be alone, people will think that you do not like their company.
    Right—Even when others prefer your company, you have the right to stay alone.

In short, one has the right to ask for what one needs. Of course, the other person has the right to deny that. One has the right to maintain one's opinions and values and express them appropriately. One can also change one's opinion, make decisions, and experience the consequences. Denying anything if one wants to and saying that one does not know are also one's rights. One has the right to do that without feeling guilty. We can relate to others without depending on them for approval. We have a right to be successful.

10.6   SKILLS IN ASSERTIVENESS

Thoughts, beliefs, and attitudes toward self are responsible for nonassertive behavior. First of all self-talk of the individual should be changed. Trying new solutions to old problems is also essential for assertiveness.

Along with verbal skill it is essential to have appropriate nonverbal skills to express assertiveness. If one wants to express assertiveness no ambiguity should be shown in nonverbal communication. Biting nails, hair appropriation, avoiding eye contact, and being reluctant to talk are the signs of unassertive behavior. Hence, all these things are to be avoided. There should be correspondence between verbal and nonverbal messages. If it is not maintained and they are controversial, people believe in nonverbal message.

10.6.1   Verbal Component of Assertive Behavior

1. **Clearly and firmly saying no or taking a stand.**

   a. *Position*—A statement which may be indicating acceptance or rejection in response to one's stand or any request by someone.
   b. *Reason*—Justification of one's position, request, or feeling.
   c. *Understanding*—A statement recognizing others' view point.

2. **Asking favors or asserting rights.**

   a. *Problem*—This is the statement of the position that needs to be changed.
   b. *Request*—Asking for something that may change the situation and solve the problem.
   c. *Clarification*—A statement designed to elicit additional, specific information concerning the problem.
   d. *Listening*—Good listening is the most basic skill for assertiveness. Effective listening gives confidence and helps maintaining human relations.

3. **Expressing feelings.**

a. *Personal expression*—A statement for communication of one's emotions and feelings such as affection, concern, etc.
b. *Content*—The content of verbal message for expressing assertiveness has to be culturally appropriate.

10.6.2 NONVERBAL COMPONENTS OF ASSERTIVENESS

Assertiveness involves the following:

a. **Eye contact.** Firm eye contact is essential for assertiveness.
b. **Body posture.** Upright posture as well as relaxed standing style declares assertiveness.
c. **Gestures.** Natural, spontaneous, and relaxed hand and arm gestures declare warmth, openness, and emphasis with which the assertive message is given.

 The unassertive style may include evasive eye contact, body gestures such as hand wring, hunching shoulders, covering mouth with hands, any other nervous gestures that may distract the listener. Anything that shows excessive anger such as finger pointing or shouting is also detrimental to assertiveness. It may express aggressive tendencies.
d. **Facial expressions and tone of voice.** Facial expression indicating sincerity, maturity, integrity, and urge for equal status helps in the expression of assertiveness. Tone should be gentle but firm. Screaming loudly and talking too softly are indicators of a lack of assertiveness. Screaming clearly shows aggressiveness and talking too softly declares lack of confidence and submissiveness.
e. **Fluency.** For being assertive, fluency is a must. Without fluency the message looks like submissive murmur. Hesitation and pauses declare that the person is not assertive enough
f. **Timing.** Unnecessary interruption of the other person's message or long silence is detrimental to assertiveness. Hence, these things should be avoided.

Assertiveness is avoided by many people as they are afraid of the loss of social approval, ridicule, and of displeasing others by selfish behavior. Their concern for others is more as compared to concern for self.

10.7 STRATEGIES TO BECOME ASSERTIVE

There are various steps for becoming more assertive. The first is to identify the problem situations. These are the situations where one can easily identify that his or her behavior was not assertive enough to maintain his or her self-worth. Events, people, and issues regarding which one wants to be more assertive give a clear idea that how frequently one needs to improve his or her behavior. Then one should describe the exact problem in interaction. After that one has to write a script to change. There are six things to be done, they are known as LADDER.

L	look at your needs, wants, and rights.
A	arrange time and place to discuss the situation.
D	define the problem specifically.
D	describe your feelings by using I messages.
E	express your request firmly and simply.
R	reinforce the possibility of what you want.

For becoming assertive:

1. **Mange your extreme emotions**—Emotional maturity is essential for practicing assertiveness. There is no exaggerated expression of emotions in assertiveness. One must have a balanced style of emotional expression. Understanding others' emotions and controlling own emotions are the basic skills required for emotional maturity. There is no becoming mad with anger or anguish, crying or shouting loudly with negative emotions, and insulting someone with utter dissatisfaction. Even when expectations are not fulfilled, it should be communicated with balanced style.

2. **Observe one's own expressions**—One has to stand straight, maintain eye contact—should not look elsewhere or toward floor—hold head and neck in normal position and avoid drooping shoulders and head position, and make no unnecessary hand movements. One should not communicate as whisper but should be loud enough so that the other person can get appropriate auditory stimulation and the message is heard properly.

3. **Avoid expressions detrimental to assertiveness**—Any gesture which creates impression of ambiguity, awkwardness, or physically and psychologically hurting others should be avoided carefully.

4. **Not be ashamed of what one wants to say**—Once the speaker decides to talk about a particular issue, he or she should not be reconsidering its importance. Even if the problem is very simple or the other person may be very busy or even when it is personal problem, the speaker should state it clearly and neatly.

5. **Should speak firmly and confidently**—The speaker should not suggest what he or she wants to communicate but should say it straightforwardly. He or she must know what exactly he or she wants to communicate and what he or she wants the other person to understand. He or she must select words and nonverbal communications accordingly.

6. **Should shoulder the responsibility of what one says**—The speaker should not try to save himself or herself and dodge the responsibility of what he or she wants to communicate. It should be an honest expression of what one wants to say and one must be prepared for the consequences.

7. **Should not use the words "anyway" or "anyway you like"**—One should not use such words especially when choice is given or asked for one's preference. If the other person gives a choice, the speaker should be able to decide for himself or herself and tell that clearly. The speaker should not take it for granted that the other person will be able to understand the speaker's emotions and preferences without clear communication.

   Unassertive style of expression leads to a condition where the speaker is taken for granted by the other party. This is a typical style of communication of average Indian ladies.

   In a typical middle-class family, this is a common type of interaction among middle-aged couples. The husband wants to plan a holiday outing for four days and asks his wife regarding her preference. "Where should we go? To Kashmir or to Kanyakumari?" As the wife is never encouraged to express her views openly from childhood, she says, "Actually.........anywhere...you like."

   As soon as the husband leaves for booking tickets for Kashmir, immediately she starts cursing him that he is always interested in going to the same place and she is fed up of it. As choice was given, she should have told that she prefers Kanyakumari.

8. **Should not allow or ask the other person to take decisions on one's behalf**—If the decision is not made by the speaker, it is obvious that the other person will have to take the decision on behalf of the speaker. This may lead to some sort of inconvenience of the speaker or compulsion to behave as per someone else's ideas.

9. **Should express his or her preference in a gentle way**—This should be done by using word as "this is better according to me" so that the other person is able to consider that option also. Once the speaker expresses his or her ideas, the possibility that the other person will rethink about his or her decision increases. However, if it is not expressed at all, one cannot blame the other person for taking a decision without considering the speaker's preferences.

The consequences of shyness are difficulties in:

1. Meeting new people, making friends, and getting psychological support out of these relations.
2. Overcoming negative feelings as depression and loneliness.
3. Expressing feelings, values, and attitudes.
4. Creating appropriate impression as shyness is interpreted as being weak, unfriendly, and tense.
5. Thinking clearly and communicating that to others.
6. Overcoming an over preoccupation with one's personal feelings and thoughts.

10.7.1 STRATEGIES TO ENHANCE ASSERTIVENESS

The techniques of enhancing assertiveness are also discussed by psychologists. Some important techniques are discussed as follows:

1. **Rehearsal of assertive behavior**
   The speaker should practice an assertive way of verbal and nonverbal expressions. For such practice judging one's words, tone, speed of talking, facial expressions, and bodily gestures should be monitored minutely and objectively. This can be demonstrated, for example, while dealing with a salesman. If one smiles while saying that he or she is not interested in buying a product, the salesman will continue convincing him or her. If one expresses assertively, with appropriate facial expressions and tone, it becomes effective.
2. **The speaker should continue to assert repeatedly**
   Though the other person argues in different styles, the speaker should not change his or her position and constantly express his or her opinion assertively. Whatever may be the argument of the opposite party, it becomes essential to repeatedly assert one's position.
3. **Accepting criticism comfortably**
   The speaker should not become upset or anxious while receiving criticism. He or she should control his or her emotions and without being defensive should accept that it may be at least partially true. The speaker should be able to express that he or she will consider that and think about the future decisions. If one becomes defensive, all the mental energy will be wasted in denial and there will be no possibility of improvement. In addition, one may lose emotional control if one becomes upset.
4. **Asking for feedback**
   A person who wants to enhance assertiveness, wants to know about his or her own communication, and its effectiveness. Critical evaluation by significant people is essential for increasing assertiveness. One must select the positive and constructive suggestions. One has to use negative criticism in a constructive way.
5. **Negative assertion**
   Clearly accepting one's limitations without expressing apology should be learned. When one is more open about one's drawbacks, others may change their perspective and the speaker also may get some help for managing negative emotions such as anger and irritation.

The steps necessary for becoming assertive are listed as follows. They are:

1. **Learning by imitation or modeling.** One may imitate the behavioral style of a person who is assertive and for that observe his or her behavior. Modeling is a technique of behavior therapy in which the client learns appropriate patterns of behavior by imitating another person demonstrating the target behavior either as live or on video. This is very useful in assertiveness training.
2. **Practicing assertive behavior** in different situations in day-to-day life is essential than just knowing the theory behind it. In daily life situations, one should try and practice it as a new behavioral style. Others may not take it seriously, in initial stages, as it is a changed pattern of the individual's behavior. However, practicing makes the individual more comfortable and others also gradually take it as an essentially significant change.
3. **Rewarding or reinforcing** self for assertive behavior enhances assertiveness.
4. **Feedback from others,** their changed behavior, and the reduction of negative emotions increase the possibility of assertive behavior.

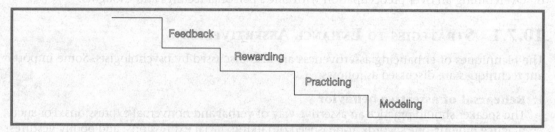

Hence, for becoming assertive, one has to learn to deny and encourage oneself to develop a belief system to protect one's rights. Specially, when one expects that the other person is going to make some important decision where the speaker is involved, all relevant communication skills should be used. One must allow oneself to make some mistakes and have the courage to shoulder the responsibility of what one says. Before the actual interaction, one must get sufficient details of the issues to be discussed, guess what the other party is going to suggest and be prepared for an answer. Asking plain open-ended questions helps to get more information from the other communicator. Being confident and assured about one's capacity to be assertive are the essential things in practicing assertiveness. Look, feel, act, and behave like an assertive person.

Researchers have suggested an action plan for overcoming negative tendencies and becoming more assertive. For that one has to:

1. Set the exact goals.
2. Relax physically.
3. Think positively about one's own abilities to interact with people.
4. Appear warm and friendly.
5. Initiate anonymous conversation with strangers.
6. Dress and groom for assertiveness and self-confidence, and model confident people.
7. Rehearse difficult interpersonal situations with techniques like role play.

10.7.2 ASSERTIVENESS IN DAILY LIFE

There are people who want to force you to accept their suggestions or make fun of you or exploit you for their benefit. It is necessary to know how to deal with them. The various strategies that one should use are:

1. **Broken record**—Over and over again one should say to a salesman, for example, "No no, still I am not interested…. I am not going to purchase your commodities."
2. **Content to process shift**—One can shift the focus of conversation from a particular subject to the analysis of interaction. For example, "You appear to be annoyed."
3. **Defusing**—One has to terminate further discussion because the other person is angry. "You are angry, let us discuss it after you calm down."
4. **Assertive delay**—One can delay the conversation till one gets further information. One can say, "I don't want to talk to you at this time."
5. **Assertive agreement**—Acknowledge the criticism that you agree with. You need not give explanation if you do not want to. You can say, "Yes you are right, I am half an hour late."
6. **Clouding**—If someone is putting you down as a person, agree in part and ignore the rest. This is agreeing without promising to change.
7. **Assertive inquiry**—Openly asking about the problem like, "What is bothering you about my speech?"
8. **Laughing it off**—If the other person is cracking a joke about your behavior then laugh—let the humor take over.
9. **Accusing gambit**—If the other person accuses you, start talking about his or her faults or simply disagree.
10. **The beat up**—If someone blames you directly, use assertive irony and say, "Thank you" without getting upset and then broken record or diffusing can be practiced.
11. **Delaying gambit**—If the other person says "let us discuss it afterwards," ask the exact time when to discuss it.
12. **Why gambit**—If someone is asking "why have you done that?" then use content to process shift. Say, "Why is it not important, the issue is I don't want to do it."
13. **Self-pity gambit**—If the other person starts weeping and wants that you should feel guilty, then say, "Yes, I know that it is painful to you but I wanted to clear it."
14. **Quibbling**—If the other person is interested in debating and saying that what you say is not legitimate, use content to process shift.
15. **Threats**—If someone threatens you to use assertive inquiry, like "what of my request bothers you?" then content to process shift may be used.

Self-talk is one of the most important considerations in assertiveness. If any new task is taken as a challenge it results in positive emotions. If there are negative self-thoughts, self-talk, and self-doubt, the person would try to avoid the task. One has to be focused and relaxed simultaneously. Managing one's stress and anxiety while communicating is essential and one has to find out ways which are effective for oneself. Self-talk leading to self-affirmation should be used constantly to increase self-worth. Thinking about others' emotions and their benefit and loss is not going to help the individual who wants to be assertive. People may or may not like his or her behavior but he or she has to be firm.

Specific exercises like role play are very effective to increases assertiveness. One can practice assertiveness in a small group of participants where everyone helps each other to practice change in behavior that is difficult otherwise. The participants play different roles and spontaneously interact with each other which help to understand the reactions of others and their view points.

As far as emotional aspects and thinking process are concerned, some principles are suggested by researchers. These are:

1. One cannot change others' behavior, but one can change the reaction to it. For example, one cannot change a colleague's habit to ask very personal questions, but one can say that he or she is not interested in discussing the matter.

2. People are not mind readers. If one does not ask for what one wants, others will not be able to know. For example, greater freedom to take decisions in office work.
3. Habit cannot justify any action. Only because the boss always takes an action, it does not mean that no one else can take it.
4. No one can make others happy. Others have the responsibility of their own actions and feelings.
5. In any relationship, there is a possibility of some disapproval. It is necessary to accept that.
6. One should not be victimized.
7. Worrying about something is not going to change it.
8. One has to adopt an attitude that is useful for doing the best one can. If someone does not like it, it is his or her problem.
9. One has to be aware of the consequences of assertiveness.

Some specialists in the area of assertiveness training follow the techniques suggested by behavior modification or behavior therapy. The aims are to extinguish unassertive behavior and patterns of responses and develop and reinforce assertive behavioral patterns. Teaching new communication skills that involve persuasion and confrontation becomes necessary. Many a time, correcting nonverbal communication also becomes a must. Assertiveness cannot be expressed only with appropriate verbal communication as inappropriate nonverbal message cuts down its meaningfulness. If one wants to give negative feedback to one's assistant without making eye contact with a voice that is almost inaudible, the message will be interpreted only as unassertive message.

Special training of assertiveness can be given with tape-recorded conversation with whom the speaker wants to improve assertiveness. The speaker is to analyze his or her own responses and modify them accordingly. Participation in exercises with others having confrontation also helps the speaker to enhance assertiveness. Techniques such as video shooting the actual performance and critically evaluating the same by a small group of individuals coming from different background and different age groups may serve the purpose of giving feedback to the fullest extent. The importance of behavioral rehearsal cannot be underestimated at any point of time.

10.8   CHARACTERISTICS OF AN ASSERTIVE PERSON

An assertive person is capable of balancing his or her life and adjusting in a better way with the help of his or her style of interaction. An assertive person:

1. Is more expressive/extravert.
2. Is able to make choices for himself or herself.
3. Feels good about himself or herself.
4. Feels that there are more chances that he or she will achieve his or her goals, which means he or she is optimistic.
5. Is open and free.
6. Maintains high self–esteem.
7. Is comfortable while accepting self-limitations.
8. Does not need constant social approval.
9. Trusts that things can be changed.
10. Is ready to try new things and make errors.
11. Respects oneself and others.

12. Is confident.
13. Is ready to accept that all problems cannot be solved as per his or her ideas.
14. Is ready for compromise.
15. Is eager to try to change his or her behavioral style.
16. Shoulders responsibility of his or her own actions and communication.

It is essential to understand the application of assertiveness in real life. The story of a young lady should be reconsidered. Sonal should express herself in a better way to increase the chances that her family understands her point of view and gives her a better opportunity to live her life in her own way. She must try to convince her father. Then, she should understand what exactly she wants to communicate and should be ready to shoulder its responsibility. She should be prepared to look relaxed and manage her voice quality. She should establish a direct eye contact, stand upright, and start talking regarding good things about her father.

> Daddy, I am thankful to God that he gave me this opportunity to be your daughter. You and mom both have done so much for me and whatever I can achieve today is only because of you. Today also whatever decision you are taking is only for my welfare. However, I want to go for further education and hence will not be able to marry someone from a rural area.

It is worth noting that Sonal has started her communication by some positive words and in a mature style she discussed her own views. She neither blamed her father nor belittled the young man. The differences of opinion were expressed appropriately.

10.9 SUMMARY

Many a time, we cannot express our point of view, perceptions, and feelings properly. If we are submissive, we invite trouble; when we are aggressive, we face problems regarding interpersonal relations. Assertiveness is the most appropriate way of interacting with others as we are not hurting others nor doing injustice to self. We do not blame others but express our feelings and thoughts clearly. We should rethink about the misconception and consider our rights while interacting with others. This enhances the possibility of getting justice without spoiling interpersonal relations.

QUESTIONS

1. Explain the nature and advantages of assertiveness.
2. Describe different types of human behavior and compare them with reference to maintaining good interpersonal relations.
3. Describe different types of assertiveness.
4. Discuss your rights in interpersonal communication.
5. Which skills are necessary for assertiveness? Discuss nonverbal communication of an assertive person in detail.
6. Which strategies should be used to enhance assertiveness?
7. What are the characteristics of an assertive person?
8. Explain the nature and advantages of assertiveness.
9. Describe the different types of human behavior and compare them with reference to maintaining good interpersonal relations.
10. Describe different types of assertiveness.

11. Discuss your rights in interpersonal communication.
12. Which skills are necessary for assertiveness? Discuss in detail nonverbal communication of an assertive person.
13. Which strategies should be used to enhance assertiveness?
14. What are the characteristics of an assertive person?

APPLICATION ORIENTATION

1. When during last month did you experience that people are taking undue advantage of your gentleness?
2. In front of whom do you think you feel angry and upset but cannot express your real feelings?
3. Introspect objectively and write down how frequently do you experience aggressive tendencies.
4. What are the effects of your aggressive and submissive tendencies?
5. Practice assertiveness while interacting with your friends and analyze the difference between their behaviors.
6. Take a careful note of your own nonverbal communication and nonverbal communication of someone who is always aggressive.

SUGGESTED READINGS

A & C Black. (2009). *Assert yourself: How to find your voice and make your mark*. London: Author.
Alberti, R. E. and Emmons, M. L. (2008). *Your perfect right: Assertiveness and equality in your life and relationships* (9th ed.). Atascadero, CA: Impact Publishers.
Bishop, S. (2010). *Develop your assertiveness*. New Delhi: Kogan Page.
Colman, A. M. (2008). *Dictionary of Psychology* (3rd ed.). New York: Oxford University Press.
Jakubowski-Spector, P. (1973). Facilitating the growth of women though assertiveness training. *The Counselling Psychology* (4), 75–87.
Lazarus, A. A. (1973). On assertive behaviour: A brief note. *Behaviour Therapy, 4*(5), 697–699.
Wolpe, J. and Lazarus, A. A. (1966). *Behavior therapy techniques: A guide to treatment of neurosis*. Oxford, NY: Pergamon Press.

11

Fallacies, Misconceptions, and Paradoxes

Objectives

After reading this chapter you will be able to:

1. Understand the various distortions in thinking.
2. Know the impact of prejudices on human thinking.
3. Learn about stereotypical thinking.
4. Analyze attribution errors.
5. Describe person perception and its correlates.
6. Understand communication bias.
7. Explain the nature of paradoxes and identify them.

11.1 INTRODUCTION

Rajendra used to stay away from the foreign students studying in his college. He always perceived them as different from Indian students. He assumed that their life style is totally lavish as they have ample of money to spend and they do not need anyone's help. Once, Sara, a young foreigner from his class, was weeping in the recess. He was surprised and tried to find out the reason. He discovered that the reason of her crying was that she could not get good grades. She came to India only because the government of her country had given her some scholarship, but she had to earn some more money for supporting her expenses. She was putting in a lot of effort as she had to cook, earn, and learn. As she wanted to save money, she used to walk many kilometers every day. She had completed her education in her mother tongue hence English medium was difficult for her. Recently, she was was diagnosed with tumor of pituitary gland. Rajendra was moved and decided to help her in every possible way.

Why did Rajendra have a distorted image of foreigners? What were his misunderstandings? What were the consequences? When could he get rid of the negative image of foreign students? Why did he decide to help Sara wholeheartedly?

We cannot perceive the world as it is. We select some information which may be insufficient and false, and on the basis of that we decide our views, opinions, and behavior. Let us discuss some common fallacies and misconceptions in thinking, and interpersonal relations affecting our social interactions.

11.2 DISTORTIONS IN THINKING AND REASONING

It is necessary that we are aware of the errors in thinking. There are many such errors in thinking. Actually, it is a science in itself. Hence, the scope of this section is very vast. However, some important distortions are discussed further.

1. **Confirmation bias and selective thinking**
   An individual tends to look for something that confirms his or her beliefs and ignores what contradict them. If one wants to prove that a particular teacher is very strict, one will be interested in every piece of evidence proving it. However, at the same time will not pay any heed to kind deeds of the same teacher. One should obtain and evaluate all the information.

2. **Partialism**
   It is assuming that the available information is equal to the ultimate truth and analyzing things on the basis of that. Many a time, what one knows and acquires through senses is only the partial truth. If we look at a notebook, it may have a beautiful picture of flowers, but if someone is looking at it from the other side of the cover page, it may not have the same. It may have the name of the company or some other advertisement. Only because we can see the flowers, we take it for granted that the other person also sees the same. If he or she says it is not, we generally argue that we can see it and there is no option than to accept it as truth. If we turn over, we will be able to see the other side and realize that what the other person said was also true. While solving day-to-day life problems, it is difficult to turn over. This leads to distorted thinking and inference.

   Anand and Suresh are good friends. They wanted the join the same college but there was a dispute regarding which college should they join? Both of them were trying to convince the other regarding different colleges as the best. Anand was interested in academic excellence and Suresh wanted more comfort and convenience. Their discord resulted in breaking their friendship. We keep on perceiving the world from our own perspective and are not ready to accept that whatever we have understood is only the partial truth.

   This error occurs when the thinker observes the problem through one perspective only. That is, the thinker examines only one or two factors of the problem and arrives at a premature solution.

3. **Adversary thinking**
   There are many alternate solutions and perspectives to every issue. However, generally what we do is considered only "either this or that" type of ideas. Right–wrong or yes–no are only primitive things. In real life, most of the time it is a combination of both or some third solution has to be found out. Adversary thinking takes place when the individual is involved in "You are wrong. So, I should be right" type of reasoning. People involved in it keep on proving that the other person is wrong. Politicians are interested in this type of thinking and they take undue advantage of it.

4. **Halo effects—Assuming consistency within a person**
   In most of the educational institutes bright students who generally get good grades are selected for cocurricular activities and to participate in various events in social gatherings. The selection method assumes that if the performance of a student in one area is excellent, he or she must be capable of also doing other activities properly.

   Halo effect is the phenomenon in which the initial familiarity that a person has positive traits is used to infer other uniformly positive characteristics. The person who is kind is expected to be honest. The converse is also true; the observation of a single negative trait can be used to infer the existence of uniformly negative traits. Here, the person who is harsh is expected to be insincere.

5. **The person—positivity bias**

   It is a tendency to perceive others as having good qualities or looking for the good in others. This bias applies to a wide range of situations and is to rate others in a predominantly positive way. A very popular singer, or an actor is perceived as being very kind and generous. Other public figures also are usually evaluated positively. People have a tendency to view others positively. This effect is not seen so vividly in group evaluations.

6. **Assumed similarity bias**

   When Kausal went to Japan, he was introduced to Kundon. Both of them were basically from Gujarat and their mother tongue was Gujarati. Kausal was very happy and had affinity for Kundon. He discussed many personal things with Kundon and assumed that he is a trustworthy person. Afterward, he discovered that all his details were misused and were publicly made fun of by Kundon.

   People not only rate others in a generally positive way but they tend to assume that others are similar to them. This predisposition is known as the assumed similarity bias. It is particularly pronounced when obvious features such as sex and race are similar, but can even occur when there are overt differences. This may lead to a wrong perception if they are dissimilar. Sometimes, the assumed similarity may also result in an accurate perception if the categorization leads to a better understanding.

7. **Initial judgment**

   Judi is a very decent person who came to Delhi for college education. She wanted a room and was hunting for the same in colonies close to her college. As these colonies belong to people from a specific community, she is not being accepted by them even as a tenant. Ultimately, she had to stay at a faraway place. At the same time, Roma stays at a faraway place only because her parents want her to stay with a family from her own community.

   In India, the intercommunity faith is remarkably low as there are many prejudices in people against each other's castes, creed, community, and religion. Here, the thinker becomes very subjective. Instead of considering the issue or problem objectively, the thinker approaches it with prejudice or bias.

8. **Arrogance and conceit**

   In this type of error very limited options are considered and the individual thinks that he or she has selected the best one. This error is labeled as the "village venus" effect to indicate the idea that villagers may think that the most beautiful girl in the world is the one in their village. This blocks creativity.

9. **Misinterpreting the cause**

   Inferences are important aspects of critical thinking. Many a time, we are confused and trapped in the pitfalls of thinking. We sometimes explain behavior only with reference to a cause. Actually, there are many reasons behind any decision or behavior. We may take coincidence as an explanation or ignore evidence that is against our belief system. Say for example, considering a dress that one wears at the time of examination as a lucky one. It is nothing but coincidence that last time pairing of that dress and good performance occurred. Actually, writing the examination paper is not related to a particular dress but to the efforts we have taken to study that subject. This is a most common fallacy in thinking.

10. **Using label as an explanation**

    Substituting labels or names for explanation of behavior is another problem. Like if someone cannot get sound sleep at night, it is called as insomnia. While explaining it the person may say that sleeplessness is due to insomnia. It is obvious that this is just using the name as if it were the cause of that disease.

11. **Misinterpreting the correlate as cause**

    Many researchers actually study correlations but interpret it as causation. Correlation means two variables are changing with each other. If one increases the other also increases and if one decreases the other also decreases. The cause behind these changes in both the variables may be the same or different. For example, there is a positive correlation between aggression and television viewing. It means that more is the television viewing greater is aggression in an individual's behavior. The researcher may interpret it as heavy television viewing is responsible for aggression. However, some emotional problem of the student may be responsible for both. This is a common error in research where the researcher is involved emotionally and wants to prove that what he or she thinks is true.

12. **Timescale error**

    Pooja is a happy-go-lucky type of a girl. Only because her friends opted for Hindi as a special subject for graduation in Arts, she also opted for the same. She also wanted to avoid extra efforts like practicals for psychology or geography. She completed her graduation but now is not getting a job.

    In timescale, partialism in thinking is seen in which the thinker perceives the problem from a limited time frame. It can be linked to shortsightedness.

13. **False memories and confabulation**

    Fantasies and projecting ideas replace some memories and fill in the gaps of memories. While interpreting data, the limitations of memory should be considered. For example, eyewitness memory. A huge amount of research is done on eyewitness memory. It is proved that a substantial number of criminals are identified wrongly as being the criminal and, hence, unnecessarily punished. Eyewitness memory depends on many factors which are related to the individual and which are not. Age, education, sensitivity, familiarity, actual violence in the crime, time gap after the incidence, and the way in which a recall interview is taken are some important factors that influence the accuracy of recall.

14. **Ignorance**

    A lack of appropriate knowledge leads to false conclusions, like a magic show is based on some tricks that we do not understand and think that it is true.

15. **Perceptual limitations**

    It can be explained by the example that we on seeing stars think that they are also as close to the Earth as the moon is. We must verify our impressions.

16. **Accepting testimonial evidence**

    Exaggerated, imaginative, and inaccurate testimonies are accepted without verification. People's accounts of extrasensory perceptions, for example, should not be accepted as factual.

17. **Fallacies due to language**

    a. *Ambiguity*—One has to avoid making a judgment based on ambiguous statements leading to many meanings.

    b. *Accepting assuring expressions*—It is something like "as every student knows." If such an expression can impress the individual, he or she will accept the statement without further analysis.

    c. *Double speak euphemism*—Accepting misleading statements used for hiding unpleasant events or ideas.

    d. *Getting impressed by jargons*—These may be used by someone just to impress others. We should be able to see the facts as they are.

e. *Being under the impact of emotional words*—This may distort the message and distract our attention to emotions.

f. *False implications*—Overtly logical statements suggesting something false should be rejected.

g. *Use of confusing nontechnical language*—This leads to some distorted meaning.

h. *Hedging language*—Giving an idea and then ambiguously rejecting it leads to cognitive confusion. For example, if a student is accused of stealing someone's mobile phone, then he or she outrightly rejects it, and then says that he or she just wanted to see that.

i. *Judgmental words*—Stating opinions as facts also is a common error. If one thinks that AIDS spreads due to hand shake, he or she will mention it as if it were a fact.

j. *Meaningless comparison*—We may be attracted to a board that reads, "Pay up to 50 percent less and buy anything." The questions to follow should be: 50 percent less than what? Is the original cost justifiable? What about the quality?

k. *Bilingualism and its effects on thinking*—These are important fields where researchers have been involved in detail to know their effects. There are two types of cognitive effects of bilingualism. One is additive and the other is subtractive. If the first language is well developed and then the individual learns the second, it is additive bilingualism; whereas, in subtractive bilingualism, some elements of a second language replace those of the first. It appears that the additive form results in increased thinking ability. In contrast, the subtractive form results in decreased thinking ability. It is necessary to have a high level of competence in both languages for a positive effect of bilingualism to be found.

18. **Fallacies based on faulty logic**

a. *Ad-hoc hypothesis*—It is something that cannot be tested independently and proved scientifically.

b. *Begging the question*—It is assuming something that we are trying to prove to be true.

c. *Superstition.* Unrelated events and coincidences are perceived as cause and effect. If an individual observes fast on a particular day and also gets a lot of money on the same day, then he or she may interpret that these two things are related.

d. *Gambler's fallacy*—If the gambler is losing many stakes, he or she will think that next time he or she will win or that picking lottery numbers not yet tried will increase the chances of winning.

e. *Forer effect*—The tendency to accept vague personality descriptions that can be applicable to most people as uniquely applicable to oneself.

f. *Post hoc fallacy*—It is the mistaken notion that because one thing happened after another, the first event caused the second. Immediately after a thunder if earthquake is experienced, it is interpreted that the earthquake resulted due to the thunder.

g. *Regressive fallacy*—It is failing to take into account the natural and inevitable fluctuations of things when assessing cause and effect. If a researcher says that conducive environment leads to the development of height and weight of children by a given amount every year, this is not true. Obviously, there are variations in exact gain in height and weight according to the stage of development, like in adolescence more gain is expected.

h. *Pragmatic fallacy*—It is arguing that something is true only because it works based on personal experience, even though the causality between it and some outcome cannot be demonstrated.

i. *Wishful thinking*—Only because we want something to happen, we keep on misinterpreting the facts. Abhimanyu's father was getting late on his birthday. So, Abhimanyu thought that his father must have gone to purchase a gift for him.

11.3 PREJUDICES

Prejudice is a preconceived irrational judgment and an expression of dislike against the members of some specific caste, creed, community, religion, race, or nation. It can be positive or negative. The most accepted definition has been given by Secord and Backman (1964) which says, "Prejudice is an attitude that predisposes a person to think, perceive, feel and act in favorable and unfavorable ways towards a group or its individual members." Prejudice is an attitude and has components that are affective, cognitive, and behavioral.

11.3.1 CHARACTERISTICS OF PREJUDICE

1. **Learned or acquired**
   It is acquired through the process of learning and socialization. During childhood we observe and imbibe views of parents and significant adults. After that we imitate parents and learn their likes and dislikes, norms, values, customs, behavior, and traditions of society. All these things result in prejudices. Directly or indirectly, children get some reinforcement for that and feel secure that they follow their parents. In a way, without experiencing anything we get readymade impressions of most of the people.

2. **Irrational**
   On one hand, rational thinking or reasoning is not at all associated with prejudices, and on the other no amount of contradictory evidence is capable of decreasing it.

3. **Functional**
   Prejudice helps the individual justify his or her hostilities, repressed desires, and strengthen feelings of self-esteem and prestige. It helps an individual justify his exploitation, and discrimination of the members of other group.

4. **Emotional overtones**
   Prejudice is accompanied by emotions. The person expresses concern, affection, care, and sympathy for members of another group. But if unfavorable, the person would show hatred and hostility. He or she will never like the person from that group.

11.3.2 TYPES OF PREJUDICE

There are different types of prejudices. Some important and common prejudices are:

1. **Racial prejudice**—Human history gives a detailed account of various examples of racial prejudices. Due to these prejudices Negros and Jews suffered a lot.
2. **Religion**—Many countries are against each other only because of differences in their religious identity.
3. **Caste prejudice**—In India, most people have a strong caste prejudice. They hate people coming from a different caste and are extremely hostile against each other. This is seen especially regarding marriage.
4. **Gender prejudice**—A very strong negative prejudice against women prevails in almost all societies around the globe. For generations, women have been thought be weak,

subjugated, dependent, and less capable in every sense. In India, it is very well documented and hinders women's self-concept and development.

5. **Language prejudice**—There are many languages in India and people have lots of unfair ideas about those who speak a different language. People are divided on the basis of language and even the states are made according to the same. People from Maharashtra and Karnataka have prejudices against each other.

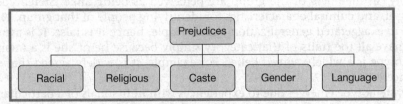

There are many other prejudices such as those regarding age, education, occupations, political parties, etc.

Discrimination is giving different treatment to individuals belonging to different social groups, communities, or religions. In case of negative prejudices, unfair treatment is given, and in case of positive prejudices, undue facilities and privileges are given to them. It is a behavioral expression of prejudice. The exploitation of weaker by more powerful is the simplest example.

11.3.3 CAUSES OF PREJUDICE

1. **Social learning**—As prejudices are learned, the environment that teaches prejudices decides the type, intensity, and nature of prejudices that one learns.
2. **Status and power structures**—Discrepancy between two groups regarding status and power results in prejudices. A group having low status is accused of low ability and motivation.
3. **Situational factors**—The situational factors in the immediate environment of the individual also lead to the development of prejudice. If an individual experiences the extreme tension due to communal riots, he or she may develop new prejudices.
4. **Psychodynamic factors**—Researches reveal that a number of psychological factors cause prejudices. People with authoritarian personality exhibit rigid thinking and punitive tendencies. They exploit others and underevaluate the juniors and submissive individuals.
5. **Historical facts**—The history of conflict between two groups results in negative prejudices. Frustration also gives rise to prejudice.

11.3.4 EFFECTS OF PREJUDICES

Avoiding the individual or group or withdrawal from the situation causing physical hurt or injury to the person or group or even killing individuals, are the consequences depending upon the intensity and environmental stimuli.

For reducing prejudices, the aspects essential are: intergroup interaction, opportunities to understand each other, working together for same goals, education explaining details and reasons of the other group's traditions, antiprejudice information, playing each other's roles, legal procedure to ban, and a personality change technique.

11.4 STEREOTYPES

One more very common phenomenon which is detrimental to appropriate thinking is stereotypes that are a cluster of beliefs regarding the members of a group generally lacking a rational basis. The concept of stereotype was introduced around 1920.

It is a belief about a particular trait being prevalent among all members of a social group.

Invariably, all members of the group are perceived as being alike. Stereotypes focus on physical, social, and cultural characteristics for identifying people of that group. This categorization leads to exaggerated generalization about people, hence it is false. It is assumed that a person will have all the traits of that category simply because he or she is a member of that group. Stereotype is a widely agreed belief. For example, it is widely agreed that science students are sincere.

Actually, stereotype emerges due to experiences with individuals of a particular group that are generalized as if they apply equally to all members of that group. Some people from every community are like that.

According to the principles of psychology, all the traits are normally distributed in every community. It means that approximately 2/3 individuals are in the normal range, 1/2 of the remaining are above average, and the remaining are below average of that trait. The normal probability curve shows it clearly.

For correcting a stereotype, even if some information and contrary proof is made available to the individual, the stereotype remains as it is. In addition, such evidence is interpreted as an exceptional case and is totally neglected.

A stereotype can have either direction, that is, it can be positive or negative.

11.4.1 DEVELOPMENT OF STEREOTYPES

As we have discussed in case of prejudices, stereotypes are also learned by socialization and imbibing views of significant others and by imitating their behavior. They are produced and also provide justification of behavior without evaluation. The same vicious circle of limited experience, knowledge, and generalization is active here. Further social interaction is affected by it. Conformity and traditional life style increases the intensity of stereotypes. It enhances a sense of belongingness and social prestige as the individual perceives the world with others in his or her group. No opportunities of getting correct information about the concerned group and a lack of interest in it lead to persistence and development of stereotypes. It directly affects all interactions.

There are various functions of stereotypes. It is a shortcut method of understanding the social behavior of others. One's expectations` and style of behavior and communication also are affected due to it, as we adjust all these things in anticipation of a particular trait. May be due to that, the interaction takes place in an expected way. Stereotypes are comparatively more stable than prejudices.

11.5 CONFORMITY AND OBEDIENCE

11.5.1 CONFORMITY

Among the various factors affecting thinking process negatively, conformity is a very commonly experienced factor.

It can change an individual's life to such an extent that the major decisions of the individual's life may be totally dependent on social expectations. The obvious example is the decision of marriage in Indian society which by and large depends on conformity and social expectations.

Nonconformity regarding such decisions leads to the possibility of social rejection and criticism by not only the society but the family also.

In 1951, Asch experimentally proved how conformity affects the thought process and decisions. In such an experiment, the task is to compare the length of lines and make a decision regarding these having equal lengths. All the others except the one under study are confederates who help the experimenter. They give wrong answers deliberately according to instructions and agree with each other. It is seen that for majority of trials the individual gives a conformity-oriented answer even when it is obviously wrong. In an original experiment, this phenomenon was observed in 75% of the trials. Approximately 25 % individuals were showing effects of conformity.

Many factors enhance conformity. The most influential factors are status, credibility, and attractiveness of other members in the group; the complexity of the task and difficulty of decision; group cohesiveness; and the fear of looking foolish. An individual's suggestibility and vulnerability to submit to the pressure of the group are also important issues.

Informational social influence occurs when one turns to the members of one's group to obtain accurate information. If the environmental stimuli are ambiguous or indicating crisis, conformity is more. When the group is large and closely interacting, its influence increases.

Research has proved that females are socialized in such a way that they are more suggestible and more likely to conform than males.

11.5.2 OBEDIENCE

This may also lead to distorted thinking, attitudes, and behaviors. When an individual has to behave exactly according someone else's orders, he or she may not feel responsible for the consequences. In Indian culture, obedience is the keyword in socialization. Offspring is supposed to obey irrespective of their age, education, and marital status. This is detrimental to an independent thinking process. The individuals are neither encouraged to understand the various aspects of the problem nor try some new idea. People do not want to be rude with the authority. Children obey simple commands first and then as they grow older, they feel compulsion to obey complex orders. This process is called entrapment.

Parents in some Indian communities behave as if they are the owners of their children. Parents decide everything, small or significant in the life of their offspring and abuse or even threaten to kill them only for conformity. There are examples of parents literally assassinating their offspring due to making their own decisions regarding marriage.

11.6 ATTRIBUTION AND ERRORS IN ATTRIBUTION

In social cognition, attribution plays an important role. It explains how people determine the cause of what they observe. Errors in attribution lead to wrong interpretation of cause and effect.

Mohan stood first in his college in the final examination of engineering. His mother was really proud of him and said that he is intelligent and his engineering aptitude is very high. This is personal attribution or dispositional attribution. His father, however, said that due to easy practical examination that he could get that rank. It is situational attribution. If his friends think that it is Mohan's regular rank and he always stands first because of his abilities, it is a person-stable attribution. If some friends think that he studied a lot for the last examinations, it is a person-unstable attribution. Similarly, if his father thinks that his teachers are pretty lenient, it is situational-stable attribution. If he thinks that a tough teacher has given an easy practical assignment, it is situational-unstable attribution.

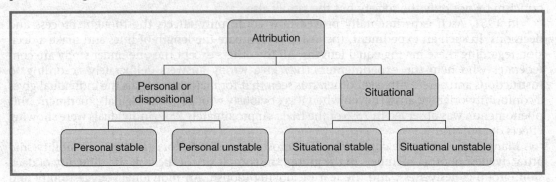

Kelley put forth a theory that explains the kind of attributions people make based on three kinds of information:

1. **Consistency**—This refers to whether the individual acts in the same way in same type of situation or otherwise. It is extremely useful when determining whether to make a stable or unstable attribution.
2. **Distinctiveness**—How do others act in such a situation is also an important issue.
3. **Consensus**—This is a particularly important piece of information to use when determining whether to make a person or situation attribution.

11.6.1 Self-fulfilling Prophecy

If without meeting an individual you have developed an idea regarding him or her only on the basis of someone else's repeated narrations, this may impact the whole interaction. You may behave in a particular way as you expect that person to interact in a specific way. If you are told that he or she is polite, you may also initiate interaction in a polite way. Now your gesture may result in his or her polite behavior.

A very well-known classic study of self-fulfilling prophecy was given by Rosenthal and Jacobson (1967) approximately 50 years ago. Some children were randomly selected for an intelligence test. The teachers were given false information regarding some of them as they were late bloomers and during that year there will be substantial cognitive gain. By the end of that year, IQ scores of these children increased more than others. This was due to teachers' expectations effect which enhanced the positive interaction and resulted in that gain.

11.6.2 Attribution Bias

A large amount of research has been done and is being done on attribution and errors of attribution. Many a time, it negatively affects interpersonal relations.

The attribution errors are distorted ways in which perceiving actions of others and the things that happen to us appears easy to interpret. Though easy, it leads to incorrect conclusions and misunderstanding regarding reality.

Attribution errors are very common. People tend to make the same kinds of errors. A few typical biases are:

1. **Fundamental attribution error**
   People tend to overestimate the importance of dispositional factors and underestimate the role of situational factors.

   Fundamental attribution error stems from people's desire to interact effectively with others. According to this view, observers increase their understanding and ability to make predictions about the world by differentially attending to the situation or person, depending on whether they are rating another person or themselves.

   The fundamental attribution error is more common in individualistic cultures like that of America than collectivistic culture like that of Japan. Importance and uniqueness of the individual is stressed in individualistic cultures and individual's link to various groups such as family or company is stressed in collectivistic cultures. In collectivistic culture, an individual's behavior is more dependent on different situations and, hence, fundamental error is less.

   When there is no substantial change in the environment, we focus on the information from the individual. If there is any change in the environment, environmental and situational explanations are accepted.

   Ross (1977) mentioned that fundamental attribution error is the tendency to overestimate the impact of dispositional causes and underestimate the impact of situational causes on other person's behavior.

2. **Self-serving bias**
   There is a general tendency that we tend to take credit for our successes but deny blame for our failures. It is taking more credit than is due for desirable outcomes, and unrealistic but useful optimism about our life prospects.

   Floyd (2009) described is the self-serving bias. It is a tendency to attribute our success to stable internal causes and our failure to unstable external causes. As we want to perceive ourselves positively, we get involved in this type of thinking. Some other experts have given this the title "the actor-observer bias."

   People tend to attribute their own behavior to external causes but that of others to internal causes. A student will think that he or she failed because the paper was difficult, and his or her friend failed due to limitations regarding his or her own abilities. Overestimating the importance of situation in explaining their own behaviors is seen in case of an actor. However, observers overestimate the importance of an actor's dispositions for causing the actor's behavior. Actually, they have access to different information. Actors have much background information about themselves. They overestimate the importance of the situation in explaining their own behaviors. Actors look at the situation, while observers look at the actors.

   We perceive our own behavior as normal and good. We generally have our friends who are having a similar background, education, age, and interests. It is a biased sample of similar others among our friends. Our own opinions are more salient in that given context. We fail to realize that our choices reflect our construal and that others have different perceptions. We are motivated to see ourselves as adequate. Still it is a misconception in judgment. If we base our future judgments on these misconceptions, it will result in inaccurate conclusions. It is always better to maintain objective evaluation and accepting oneself as one is.

   We are motivated to protect our self-esteem, so we are internally attributing success and externally attributing failure. We expect to do well in most things, which makes it logical to attribute failure to external sources.

   Floyd goes on to describe the fundamental attribution error, which is our tendency to blame other's behavior for the internal causes rather than external ones.

3. **Overattribution**

In overattribution, we select one characteristic about an individual and attribute all of his or her actions to that trait. We do not pay any heed to the real reasons for the individual's actions. Our misconceptions can cause problems in our communications and overall relationships with these individuals.

11.6.3 IMPLICATIONS

Some of our judgments are accurate and some are inaccurate. It is reported by researchers that external and visible attributes are more accurate, but inferred internal states, traits, or feelings are less accurate.

Attributional biases is associated with one's perception of the cause of our own and others' success and failure, which in turn decides the way in which we attribute responsibility or blame. Attributing own success to internal causes and failure to external causes is related to maintaining high self-esteem than the inverse style of attribution. People who attribute their own success to stable causes and their own failure to unstable causes have more optimistic expectations for the future than others. Individuals who attribute others' suffering to uncontrollable causes have more pity, less anger, and less urge to help than people who attribute another person's suffering to controllable causes.

The attributions of responsibility decide one's reaction to personal and social problems.

Dispositional attributions often elicit more punitive reactions than situational attributions for others' suffering due to health problems, fights, accidents, and disasters. Even in legal procedures, attributions play an important role in deciding the exact punishment for rape depending on the characteristics of the victim. Culture and characteristics of the victim that the killer did not know are the important issues in attributions for murder. People from collectivist cultures are less biased toward dispositional attributions for murder than people from individualist cultures.

11.6.4 GENDER DIFFERENCES IN ATTRIBUTION

Dilip stood first in 12th commerce examination and was being interviewed by local media representatives. He told them that he used to study for 12 hours a day and explained the tricks that he used for studying. He also mentioned how he maintained good physical and mental health.

Strushti stood first in 12th science examination and she stated that all the credit of her success goes to her parents and teachers. They have given her proper guidance and opportunity to concentrate on studies. She also mentioned that she is very lucky and, hence, she could achieve this success.

Subhash failed and on being asked by the teacher for the reason behind it he said that the question papers were very difficult and assessment was strict.

Manisha also was asked about her poor performance to which she accepted immediately that she could not study properly due to her mother's health problems.

Since more than 50 years, research has demonstrated that male members attribute success to their own efforts or internal attribution and girls and women attribute it to others, this is external attribution.

As far as failure is concerned, male members do not accept their responsibility and hold someone else or the environment responsible for it. Women and girls not only accept it but generalize it. It is stable internal attribution. They think that if they fail once, they will fail again. Men and boys do not generalize their failure.

It is also seen that girls and women concentrate more on their limitations than good qualities. They experience and remember more failures. They have external locus of control and low self-concept. Men on the other hand overestimate their abilities. There is a substantial difference between their actual performance and their goals. Their goals are much higher than their achievements. Ladies generally mention their goals equivalent to their achievements or just slightly above them. All these issues are related to gender differences in attribution style.

Some recent studies show slightly different results about attribution but then it depends on the culture and whole socialization of the individual. In India, socialization still teaches a woman that she is not to achieve whatever she can on the basis of her potentials.

11.7 PERSON PERCEPTION, IMPRESSION FORMATION, AND PROTOTYPE

Person perception is the study of how people perceive each other. Many factors such as impression formation, perception and related issues are included in that. The effect of information given prior to meeting an individual is also well documented. If the given information is positive, the person is positively perceived. In a classical study on person perception it was demonstrated that some information prior to meeting the individual leads to errors in perception and thinking. Kelly and Shapiro (1954) have proved that.

In one condition students were told that the new lecturer with whom they had no interaction before was a rather warm person, industrious, critical, practical, and determined. In a second condition, a group of students was told that the same lecturer was a cold person, industrious, critical, practical, and determined. After this information was given, interaction with the lecturer was introduced. There was a substantial difference between the perceptions of the students from these two conditions. Students who were told that the lecturer was cold rated him far less positively after the interaction than those who were told that he was warm, although the behavior of the lecturer was the same across the two conditions.

As far as person perception is concerned, the concept of central traits becomes a focus point. We focus on particular traits when forming overall impressions of others. They are called as central traits. These central traits are more important in deciding general the impression about anyone. They are the central points where other information about the individual is organized. The interpretation of other descriptive traits is dependent on the presence of a central trait. This is a clear distortion of information due to concentrating on a few things.

Anderson (1985) has given two models for this phenomenon: the averaging model and the additive model. The averaging model says that we find out the average of the traits as perceived in an individual. However, the additive model suggests that we simply add together the bits of information we get about a person to form a judgment.

11.7.1 IMPRESSION FORMATION

Impression formation is the rapid creation of unified perception of the personality of the other individual on the basis of a large number of characteristics.

In impression formation, primacy effect is seen and in the field of learning, primacy effect is very well documented. Say for example, you play a game where there are six or seven friends and each one has to tell a name of a film star. The first one tells a name, the second person has to repeat the name taken by the first person and then tell his or her own. The third one has to repeat the two names already spoken and then tell one more. In such a game we never forget the first one. The information which is presented first gets more importance and is remembered better. It has a stronger impact than the later information. This may lead to unequal importance that is given to the information only because of its sequence. In a research it was found that if an individual had read the information regarding an extrovert, he or she would find him or her considerably more extraverted than if he or she had read the information regarding the introvert, and vice versa. More recent work confirms that, indeed, early information is weighted more heavily than later information.

11.7.2 PROTOTYPE

Prototype is a shortcut to remember things by categorizing social information, that is, information regarding others. From this perspective, it saves the information processing capacity. Prototypes are classifying people in different categories with reference to types and intensities of the expression of traits. It helps to predict things in social life. Our expectations about others and their behavior are based on prototypes. We can plan our behavior on the basis of prototypes. It organizes the social world.

Prototype means the organization of personality types derived from person perception. This organization is resulting into schemas called as prototypes. This is an organization which leads to a classification of different traits into personality types. If commitment is the trait that we want to focus on, there are three levels. First is the superordinate level which includes prototype as a whole. Next comes the middle level which includes religious devotees and social activists, and the most specific level is regarding a particular type of people like activists in a particular area.

11.8 COMMUNICATION BIAS

In the chapter regarding communication, we have discussed various communication styles. Communication styles may generate some bias. It is a very commonly seen bias. When an individual meets someone whose style is entirely different from the individual's own communication style, this type of bias is experienced. If the styles of both the individuals are similar, this bias reduces.

For example, a quiet, reflective person may feel uncomfortable in the presence of someone who displays a dynamic, outgoing style. However, in day-to-day interaction, one has to communicate with many people having different styles and many a time there is no choice.

How can you learn to cope with communication style bias? First, you must develop awareness of your own unique style. Accurate self-knowledge is essential for developing good interpersonal relationships. The knowledge of your communication style is essential for understanding the perspective of self and others.

Then one has to assess communication style of others. The ability to identify another person's communication style, and to know how and when to adapt one's style to it, helps to maintain good interpersonal relations. Here, one can reciprocate others feelings and expressions as well.

11.9 PARADOXES IN EVERYDAY LIFE

Anuj wanted to forget about all his worries regarding studies and by and large was very upset about many things. His friends convinced him and he started smoking weed. He is regularly doing so for the last two years. He now feels very happy and describes it as "being high." Anuj feels that he has found the solution to all his problems and thinks that now he is more creative and euphoric. That means now he is very happy. However, this happiness is temporary and the side effects of weed are detrimental to health. Impaired memory and other cognitive functions, distorted judgment, and in long run other problems like infertility are reported by researchers. If a person wants to terminate consuming weed, withdrawal symptoms are beyond tolerance. As such abuse results in extreme dependence and anxiety, in this case the student who wants to be happy actually is inviting trouble. Isn't it paradoxical or controversial?

11.9.1 NATURE OF PARADOX

The Oxford Dictionary (2006) defines paradox as "a seemingly absurd or contradictory statement even if actually well founded." In 2005, it was stated that paradox is a person, thing or situation that has two opposite features and, therefore, seems strange. Say for example, it is a statement having two opposite ideas due to which it seems impossible although it is probably true. "More haste less speed" is a well-known paradox. Or "some of the poorest people live in the richest area of the country." *Oxford Dictionary of Psychology* (Coleman, 2006) defines it as "an apparently sound argument yielding either a contradiction or a prima facie absurdity." The term is also used to describe any argument that yields a surprising conclusion, or even a fact or phenomenon that seems surprising. For example, children from very rich families have more health problems. There are many types of paradoxes and huge amount of research has been done about it.

So paradox is a statement that leads to contradiction. It can be true and false at the same time or paradox is seemingly contradictory that may nonetheless be true. It may be an assertion that is essentially self-contradictory though based on valid deduction from acceptable premises. It may be statement contrary to received opinion or a common belief.

11.9.2 EXAMPLES OF PARADOXES

Prisoner's dilemma game, Skagg's Robinson paradox, paradoxical intention, paradoxical therapy, meta language, barber's paradox, duration estimation paradox, mirror reversal problem are some well-known examples of paradox in the field of psychology.

1. **Prisoner's dilemma** is a game to be played by two individuals where both the individuals get extra benefit if they use cooperative strategy than defecting strategy. If the person is considered individually he will get a higher payoff from a defecting strategy. This leads to a paradox.
2. **Skagg's Robinson hypothesis** is regarding relation between ease of learning and similarity between two tasks. When the two tasks are totally different, learning is easy. In the phase where the similarity between the original task and new task increases, learning of the second task becomes difficult. Though this idea is paradoxical, it is true and can be easily

proved by simple experiments in the laboratory situation. After that is a condition where the similarity between the tasks reaches such a point that they become identical, learning becomes very easy. So the shape of the curve is like U.

3. **Duration estimation paradox**—There is a general tendency that we accurately estimate prospective time as compared to retrospective time estimates. Prospective is signaling when we think that a specific time is elapsed. Retrospective is estimating at the end of the period how long the activity or stimulus has lasted.

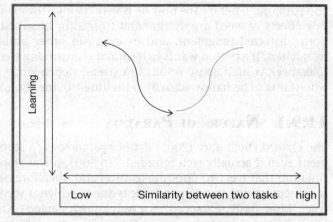

4. **Paradoxical cold and heat**—In objective or physiological sense also there are paradoxes like paradoxical cold. In that a sensation of coldness is experienced when a warm stimulus touches a cold spot on the skin. We have examples of paradoxical heat also. It is the sensation of intense heat that is experienced in the absence of a hot stimulus if the area of skin containing both cold and warm spots is stimulated with a heat grill of closely packed alternating warm and cold bars.

5. **Paradoxical sleep**—Another example is that of paradoxical sleep or rapid eye movement sleep (REM) sleep. In that case the EEG or electroencephalograph is similar to that of the waking state but the sleeper is difficult to awaken.

6. **Paradoxical theories and therapies**—There are many ideas which are used in theories and therapies. In paradoxical therapy, technics that appear on the surface to contradict the goals of treatment are used.

    In Guthrie's theory (1935), it is suggested that if a bad habit is to be corrected, ask the child to do the same thing again and again, like for example, a child has a bad habit of firing matchsticks which is risky, ask him to fire complete match boxes one after the other till he is tired and fed up of the activity.

7. **Paradoxical intention or negative practice**—It is also used to treat the patients of obsessive compulsive reaction. Here, the patient is suffering from repeated unwanted thoughts or involved in repeated unwanted actions. The patient is told to deliberately and repeatedly rehearse the unwanted pattern of thought and behavior with the aim of developing a less fearful attitude toward it and gaining control over it.

    Sometimes such instructions are given to an individual that are rendered impossible by the instructions himself or herself.

    Different types of paradoxes are given by philosophers. For example,

1. Veridical paradoxes—Here the conclusions are true.
2. Falsidical paradoxes—Conclusions are false.
3. Antinomies paradoxes—Whose conclusions are mutually contradictory.

Some well-known paradoxes in psychology are:

1. **Region beta paradox**—People can sometimes recover more quickly from more intense emotions or pain than from less distressing experience.

2. **Self-absorption paradox**—Contradictory association whereby higher levels of self-awareness is simultaneously associated with the higher level of psychological distress and with psychological wellbeing.

3. **Grandfather paradox**—You travel back in time and kill your grandfather before your grandmother conceives one of your parents. It is impossible to do it as your birth would have been impossible.

Some psychological paradoxes in everyday life can be seen very often.

1. If you love someone with great intensity, you hate him or her too with the same intensity. Say for example, you love your best friend but if he or she behaves in an unexpected way, it hurts you more than anyone else behaving in that manner.

2. If you want your children to be very unhappy, you give them everything that they demand. You may think that providing everything will make the children more happy. However, this habit leads to intense dissatisfaction as children grow up and demand something that is impossible for the parents to provide. For example, if someone wants admission in government medical college, no money can buy it but the student has to get good grades and a particular rank order. Or if one wants to marry a famous film actor or actress, parents will not be able to help it.

3. Devote lot of time in the studies of your child so that he or she loses interest in it. Many well-educated women stay back at home just to support their children in studies. They put in lot of efforts for teaching the young ones. According to the principles of cognitive psychology, the individual needs to deal with his or her intellectual stimulation independently to enjoy it. If someone interferes and gives directions for every small problem, the student will not be able to solve these problems independently. Hence, the student is fed up if everything is to be dealt with according to someone else's directions.

4. Earn huge amount of money and your happiness decreases. Those who are very rich have to take care of many things, are worried about maintaining that level of income, and feel insecure due to the possibility of robbery. Many of them have to hide their actual income as they do not want to pay huge amount of tax.

5. Fulfill every wish of your child immediately so that he or she becomes aggressive or even a criminal. Immediately gratifying every need leads to immediate gratification orientation of personality. As is covered somewhere else, this type of personality leads to impulsive behavior and undue expectations from others. Those who want everything immediately hurt others and neglect their human rights even as adults.

6. Good judgments come from experience and experience comes from bad judgment. Experience makes man perfect. It includes right and wrong decisions. Solving various problems with trials and errors also leads a sort of understanding various aspects of problem-solving. So the point that both depend on each other is true.

7. Nowadays unnecessary things are becoming necessities. All of us are consuming and using things which are actually not only unnecessary but harmful also. To take some examples, different cold drinks and ready-to-eat food lead to ill health because of use of a lot of preservatives. Some adults and young adults are abusing alcohol and drugs are obviously not necessary for healthy life.

Some other statements are:

1. If you try to fail, and succeed, which have you done?
2. Fighting for peace.
3. Don't go near the water unless you learn swimming.
4. If a person says he or she always lies, is it a truth or a lie?

One should be alert to differentiate between what such statements suggest and what those appear to suggest. Otherwise, a lot of distorted perception may lead to various problems in thinking and reasoning. It will be detrimental to human relations and any type of communication. If we cannot interpret the exact meaning of the message sent, obviously it may result in chaos. Hence, these paradoxes are to be interpreted properly.

11.10 SUMMARY

This chapter discusses various distortions and mistakes in a thinking process. Prejudices and stereotypes regarding a group of people influence our perspective about them. We process the information inaccurately and the consequences are detrimental to interpersonal relationships. Socially acceptable behavior such as conformity and obedience are exaggerations of accepting others' perspective. This also results in a lack of actively analyzing information and objectively evaluating it.

In the case of cause–effect relations also there are errors of attribution. Wrong attribution of cause and effect may mislead the individual and his or her behavior. Person perception, impression formation, and prototypes affect judgment about an individual. The communication style of the person may result in presumptions regarding the individual's nature. That affects interpersonal relations and understanding of the individual. Paradoxes deceive us regarding the meaning of the message.

QUESTIONS

1. Discuss the various distortions in thinking.
2. Explain the nature and impact of prejudices on human thinking.
3. What is stereotypical thinking?
4. Describe attribution errors. What are the gender differences in attribution style?
5. Describe person perception and its correlates.
6. What is communication bias? How to reduce it?
7. Explain the nature of paradoxes and identify them.

APPLICATION ORIENTATION

1. Observe the interaction between peers coming from different communities. Analyze what types of prejudices are prevalent in their interaction.
2. Objectively evaluate your own attribution style with reference to academic success, and failure. Discuss with friends and try to understand the similarities and differences in attribution between two genders.
3. Have you ever noticed any correlates of person perception? How does it affect interaction with the person concerned?
4. Write down 10 ideas from your thinking which are affected by different distortions and paradoxes. What may be the effect of that on understanding the issues related to it?

SUGGESTED READINGS

Allport, G. (1979). *The nature of prejudices*. New York: Perseus Books.

Anderson, J. (1985). *Cognitive psychology and its implications*. San Francisco, CA: W.H. Freeman.

Asch, S. E. (1951). Effects of group pressure on the modification and distortion of judgements. In H. Guetzkow (Ed.), *Groups, leadership and men* (pp 177–190). Pittsburgh,PA: Carnegie Press.

Dovidio, J. F., and Gaertner, S. L. (2010). Intergroup bias. In S. T. Gilbert & G. Lindzey (eds.), *The handbook of social psychology* (5th ed., vol. 2). New York: John Wiley & Sons.

Floyd, K. (2009). *Interpersonal communication the whole story*. Boston, MA: McGraw-Hill.

Franzoi, S. (2003). *Social psychology*, chapter 4. Boston: McGraw-Hill

Guthrie, E. R. (1935). *The psychology of learning*. New York: Harper.

Kelley, H. H. and Shapiro, M. M. (1954). An experiment on conformity to group norms where conformity is detrimental to group achievement. *American Sociological Review, 19*, 667–677.

Rosenthal, R. and Jacobson, L. (1968). *Pygmalion in the classroom*. New York: Holt, Rinehart and Winston.

Ross, L. (1977). The false consensus effect: An egocentric bias in social perception and attribution processes. *Journal of Experimental Social Psychology, 13*(3), 279–301.

Secord, P. F. and Backman, C.W. (1964). *Social psychology*. New York: McGraw-Hill.

Taifel, H. (1982). *Social identity and intergroup relations*. Cambridge: Cambridge University Press.

Emotions

3

12 Emotions

Objectives

After reading this chapter, you will be able to:

1. Understand the nature of emotions.
2. Know the relation between physiological factors and emotions.
3. Learn different theories of emotions.
4. Find out various correlates of emotions.
5. Understand types of attachments, love, and happiness.
6. Know the nature of fear, anger, and joy.
7. Relate gender and culture with emotions.

Sonu is a 15-year-old submissive, sincere, and introvert person coming from a high-class family. He lost his mother when he was hardly 10 years old. He stays in a joint family and his needs are taken care of by his grandmother and aunty. Both of them are very busy in household jobs and looking after other children in the family. Sonu's father generally returns after Sonu goes to bed. He feels very lonely and has no company to share his feelings and emotional experiences. He sits alone for hours and feels upset as he remembers his mother in deep grief. His younger brother Monu, who was just 7 years old when they lost their mother, however, has many friends and is always enjoying life. He generally goes to his friend's house whenever there is free time. He is an extravert and is interested in social interactions. He is satisfied and happy about his achievements and is better accepted in the family.

Why was Sonu so much disturbed for years? How in the same situation Monu could adjust better? What is the role of emotions in their exactly opposite behavior?

Emotions occupy a very significant role in human life. It is difficult to imagine how meaningless and boring human life would have been without emotions. It is related to the mental health of the individual along with satisfaction, intra- and interpersonal relations, motivation, and even cognitive processes such as learning and remembering.

12.1 NATURE OF EMOTIONS

Recently, emotion was defined as feeling, or affect, that occurs when a person is engaged in an interaction that is important to him or her, especially to his or her well-being.

Oxford Dictionary of Psychology (2008) defines emotion as any short-term evaluative, effective, intentional, and psychological state including happiness, sadness, disgust, and other inner feelings. Emotion is characterized by a behavior that expresses the pleasantness or unpleasantness of the states in which individuals are, or the interactions they are experiencing.

It is well accepted that emotions are elicited in particular environmental and interpersonal contexts.

Basic emotions are emotions that are universal and fundamentally distinguishable from one another. Human beings are born with the tendency to feel happiness, anger, and some fears. Basic emotions are happiness, sadness, fear, anger, disgust, and surprise, love, embarrassment, guilt, contempt, and jealousy.

The two basic types of emotions are positive and negative. Positive emotions include enthusiasm, joy, and love. Sometimes it is a mixture of positive and negative emotions that we experience.

Positive emotions	Negative emotions
Love	Fear and anger
Attachment	Disgust
Happiness	Jealousy
Joy	Sadness
Satisfaction	Envy
Hope	Shame
Interest	Guilt
Excitement	Contempt
Contentment	Anxiety
Pride	Hate, hopelessness, depression

Positive emotions lead to better mental and physical health, better interpersonal and intrapersonal relations, and enhanced ability to cope with stress.

Very common positive emotions are love and attachment, happiness, joy, satisfaction, hope, interest, excitement, contentment, pride, and so on. These emotions also lead to the development of physical or intellectual skills or social bonds.

Positive emotions are associated with more acceptance of others, more openness, and flexibility. They decrease the effects of negative emotions and enhance resilience. Wholehearted and spontaneous laugh helps to maintain good mental health. In childhood, some emotions are related to self-awareness and some others also require awareness regarding others. Differences of emotional expressions are also found between girls and boys. Girls often dissolve into tears or temper outbursts. Boys express their annoyance and anxiety by being sullen and moody.

For maintaining good mental health, and for every negative emotion experienced, at least three positive ones are essential. However, experiencing only positive emotions or too much of the best things can be simply detrimental.

Joy is just 10 years old, but he can manipulate everything in his family. His parents pamper him and make sure that there is no negative feeling that he ever has to face. He gets everything without asking. Many new dresses, pairs of shoes, and toys are lying in the cupboard as he did not like them. No one scolds him and in every small thing his preference is asked. Now he has started hitting his elder sister and even mother for not satisfying his expectations. School teachers have many complaints about his behavior as he is not disciplined. He takes his classmates for granted and tries to dominate them. When Joy failed in his examination and was very unhappy, nobody could help him to tolerate that frustration.

If the individual's life is emotionally satisfactory he or she will be happy, able to maintain good interpersonal relations, will take decisions wisely, and adapt to the environment comfortably.

Negative emotions and experiences play an important role in human life for general maturity and understanding. Negative emotions are unpleasant and, hence, unwanted. Negative emotions and affective states are many and diverse. They include: fear, anger, disgust, sadness, jealousy, envy, shame, guilt, contempt, anxiety, hate, depression, hopelessness, and similar other emotions.

Everyone wants to get rid of negative emotions as soon as possible. However, many a time, the immediate negative reactions of negative emotions may save us. The fear of a snake results in running away. Negative emotions may result in psychological diseases such as depression, anxiety, and phobia.

Most negative emotions are associated with a particular action; hence, only that stimulus becomes more important for the individual. This narrows the focus of attention. Positive emotions result in expanding attention.

Dr Rohit is doing his postgraduation in medicine. He is a happy-go-lucky person and belongs to a very well-to-do family. Rohit always used to underestimate pain and suffering of his patients and used to hold them responsible for their problems. Once he blamed an amputee patient that when he had met with the accident and was lying on the road, he should have told the people to take him to a super-specialty hospital.

Once while Dr Rohit was driving a two-wheeler he met with an accident and his finger was totally detached from his hand. He was experiencing extreme pain and there was no one around to help. As he was a doctor he could easily understand that immediate medical assistance was necessary, but as it was Sunday, no doctor was available around. He had to accept the idea that now that finger will not be attached to his hand again.

From then Dr Rohit has a better understanding of human suffering and has more empathy for his patients. Negative emotions and experiences are part and parcel of human life. No individual can have a completely hassle-free life without a single negative emotional experience.

Researchers have agreed upon the idea that negative emotions are beneficial and help an individual to lead a better life. The basic positive changes in human life associated with negative emotions are listed as follows:

1. Negative emotions lead to basic changes in personality of an individual. They give stability to the personality.
2. Negative emotions enhance self-understanding and improve our intrapersonal communication.
3. Learning, knowledge, and wisdom are gained from experiencing suffering and loss.
4. Positive social consequences, such as empathy, modesty, moral considerations, and care result from negative experiences and emotions.

12.2 BIOLOGY AND EMOTIONS

As it will be discussed somewhere else, there are different changes that take place during excitement and after that phase is over. First, the body accumulates its power and becomes ready for unexpected excitement or danger, and then it returns to its original calm and relaxed position.

The hypothalamus, limbic system, and ascending reticular activity system contribute substantially to physiological changes in emotions. Bodily changes associated with emotions are controlled by the autonomic nervous system and linked with the central nervous system. The autonomic nervous system consists of nerves leading from the brain and spinal cord to the muscles of various organs—heart, different glands, and blood vessels. The sympathetic nervous system which is a part of the autonomic nervous system acts during an arousal state and prepares the body by increasing heart rate, by raising blood pressure and blood sugar, and by raising the levels of certain hormones such as epinephrine and nonepinephrine. Epinephrine helps liver to mobilize glucose which leads to an increased activity of heart, brain, and muscles. This is the flight or fight reaction.

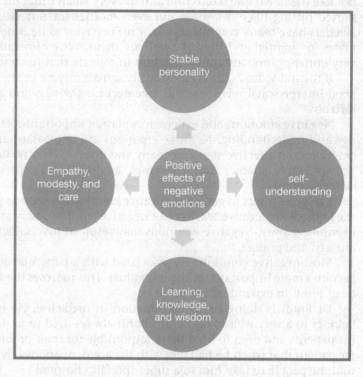

The other part of the autonomic nervous system which is called as the parasympathetic nervous system becomes active when the individual is calm and relaxed. It reduces the heart rate, blood pressure, and blood sugar, and diverts blood to the digestive tract. Though their functions are exactly opposite, both these systems are active simultaneously in case of some emotions.

Positive and negative emotional experiences depend on hemispheric dominance. The right hemisphere is linked with negative affect and the left hemisphere with positive affects.

Dominance of the left frontal lobe is proved to be related to more subjective wellbeing.

There are different types of memories and a lot of research has been done about the relation of these memories to different physiological aspects. Conscious recollections of experiences are known as declarative or explicit memories. Explicit memories can be recalled and described verbally. Implicit memories are created subconsciously like a response to dangerous or threatening situations. Emotional memories, that is, implicit memories, that evoke emotional feelings and the memories of emotional experiences, which are explicit memories, sometimes occur together, but they activate different systems in the brain. Explicit memory formation involves the hippocampus and the temporal lobe of the brain, while implicit memories involve the amygdala.

Emotional fluctuations in early adolescence are related to the variability of hormones during this period. Adaptation to hormones in adulthood leads to stability of moods. As the baby grows older, more sophisticated emotions are experienced due to the developing neuro-biological system. These are associated with the development of the nervous system. Emotions are linked with early developing regions of the nervous system, including structures of the limbic system and the brain stem.

Gradually, the maturation of the cerebral cortex results in decrease in unpredictable mood swings. And gradually the child can achieve better self-regulation. For such changes, socialization also helps a lot. For example, mother tries to generate a sense of security and stability.

Shobha was standing in the garden of her friend's house and since it was her first visit she was engrossed in watching various flowers and plants. Suddenly, a huge dog, a great den, came and stood next to her. Shobha screamed loudly, her heart was pounding, and mouth was dry. She wanted to run away but her legs were tumbling. Next time when Shobha went to the same place, the same dog came and stood next to her, but Shobha was calm and did not experience any emotional upset as she knew that it was friendly and harmless.

Physiological changes in emotions depend on the evaluation of the situation. For example, if a particular situation is judged to be very dangerous, the individual will experience sudden changes in many bodily functions. However, if the situation is not evaluated as risky, changes will not take place. Cognitive processes control this evaluation through the brain.

12.3 FUNCTIONS OF EMOTIONAL EXPRESSION

Emotions are an individual's own phenomenological experiences. It has also been discussed elsewhere in the book that no one else can really understand the exact emotional experiences of an individual. Parents many a time think that they can understand everything that goes in the mind of their offspring, but that leads to distorted images and disturbances in interpersonal relations.

It is only on the basis of external expression that any other person can guess the emotions that the person must be experiencing. That approximate understanding, however, plays a major role in the changing behavior of others also.

If you find that a friend is very upset as he or she has lost his or her grandmother, you will cancel the plan to go to a movie and spend some time with your friend and try to console him or her.

Various salient functions of expressing emotions are well known.

1. Effective communication—No communication will be effective if there are no appropriate emotional expressions. If with an emotionless face you express your gratitude toward your teacher, it will be interpreted as a formality.
2. Maintaining socially appropriate behavior and facilitating social interactions—While interacting with others, appropriate reciprocal emotional expressions enhance the feeling of being close to each other. After you get the news that your friend has got a rank in the UPSC examination, if you congratulate him or her in a flat voice, it may indicate that you are not actually happy for him or her.
3. Keeping others informed about one's own psychological experiences—It becomes necessary for one's well-being that others should be acquainted with an individual's feelings and emotions. It becomes easy for others to take care of the individual. If you are upset, your mother will try to cheer you up.

4. Stimulate others for fulfilling one's needs—It is related to the previous function. Even a young baby expresses emotions for communication of needs, comfort and discomfort, and give and take of pleasure. It may not be verbal but it serves the purpose.
5. Getting others' support and advice by declaring the intensity of emotions—It becomes essential to get support not only in childhood but throughout one's whole life. If one does not express emotions, others will not be able to help and give guidance.
6. Enjoy others' company and reciprocate their feelings and emotions—Any good interpersonal relation depends on understanding each other and give and take of emotions.
7. Emotional catharsis and improving mental health—Emotional expression helps an individual to express his or her psychological status and once he or she is free to share his or her feelings he or she feels relieved.
8. Regulating one's own behavior, understanding, and controlling one's real intentions—The objective evaluation of one's own behavior leads to monitoring one's intentions and controlling unwanted intentions.
9. Show empathy—It is only because of overt expression of emotions that one can show empathy and be close to others psychologically.
10. Molding social interactions in a particular way—This is the way in which parents and teachers discipline the children and students, and doctors give support to their patients. The whole socialization depends on this function.

12.4   EXPRESSION OF EMOTIONS

It is widely accepted that facial expressions of emotions have a strong biological foundation. Children who are blind from birth and have never observed someone's smile or frown are capable of expressing the same emotions like normal children.

Facial expression, posture, large body movements, and other gestures are associated with emotions. A lot of research has been, and is being, done on facial expressions, their relation with emotions, and understanding of the same by others. Large body movements tend to convey general emotion information. The identification of happiness, sadness, anger, and pride can be easily done only on the basis of gait.

The expression of emotions affects interpersonal relations of all sorts, for example, parent–child relationships. There is a huge amount of give and take of emotions in this relation. It demands a lot of love, affection, and emotional support to be expressed by parents. The type of parental facial expression affects the baby's emotional state and behavior such as pleasant, smiling, scary, or angry. **When a baby is exposed to quarrels of significant adults, it shows distress, gives a startled reaction, and starts crying.**

Emotions are related to behavior. When children are happy, they accept parents' suggestions and show more obedience. The role of secure attachment and related concepts, such as connectedness to parents, during childhood and adolescence, cannot be underestimated.

12.4.1   EMOTIONAL EXPRESSION AND SOCIAL RELATIONSHIP

Emotional expressions essentially play a significant role in any type of interpersonal relations. Every individual expresses emotions that are useful for the development and maintenance of relations. These emotions are dependent on the other person's response and emotional expressions. It may be any relation for that matter, starting from relations between parent and child, between siblings, with other significant adults, such as friends and teachers, and so on.

Strong emotions have the potential to cause aggressive, manipulative, impulsive, controlling, or other destructive behaviors.

Success leads to happiness and failure leads to sadness. If an individual thinks that others have intentionally blocked his or her success, he or she feels frustrated.

12.4.2 Culture

There are cultural differences in emotional expressions. However, facial expressions of basic emotions such as happiness, surprise, anger, and fear are the same across cultures. There are substantial differences in various cultures regarding when, where, and how emotions should be expressed. For example, in cultures that are characterized by individuality, such as in Australia, North America, and Western Europe, intense emotions are expressed for longer duration. In cultures such as Indian and other Asian cultures all personal emotional experiences are not openly expressed in front of others. We Indians, however, express more emotions such as sympathy, respect, and shame toward others, as we have to maintain good social relations. In various communities, in India also, there are different ways in which people express their joy and grief. Say for example, in a village, or in a particular community, ladies may cry loudly when mourning, while in others they may not. Child birth and marriage are also celebrated in a different way in almost all communities in India where a range of emotional expression is also very wide.

12.5 THEORIES OF EMOTION

There are many theories of emotions. Few important theories are given as follows:

1. **James-Lange theory** (1922, cited in Lange and James, 1962) is based on the idea that emotion is a result of physical reactions to a stimulus; the body's reaction to a stimulus precedes aspect of feeling of the emotion. The perception of a stimulus produces a specific body reaction which in turn, produces the emotional feeling. According to this theory, "we feel sorry because we cry, angry because we strike, and afraid because we tremble."

   James said that when you see a bear, you first run away then feel fear, rather than feeling fear then running away. We would not run away from a bear that is in the cage. Some interpretation and evaluation of the situation is necessary.

   In this theory, there is no mention of any intervening cognition or understanding of emotion that comes before or after the physiological arousal. The arousal itself is considered the emotional experience. The way in which one should differentiate between various emotions on the basis of physiological changes is not explained in this theory. As we know, there are overlapping physiological effects of different emotional experiences. The emotion-provoking stimulus is not considered as strong enough to produce emotional experience.

   One more point is that many of the necessary physiological responses, in particular, the hormonal action of the autonomic nervous system, are too slow to cause the emotional feeling.

2. **Cannon and Bard** gave their theory approximately hundred years ago. Cannon argued that many different emotions including happiness, sadness, and anger all seem to be accompanied by similar arousal of the autonomic nervous system that controls involuntary activity such as heart rate and hormone release. As an example, people's heart rates generally increase regardless of which emotion they are experiencing.

Cannon further suggested that physiological arousal alone cannot produce emotional reactions. For example, exercises can also increase heart rate, but may not be related to any emotions.

3. **Schacter–Singer theory** was given in 1962 and it proposed that the bodily state of emotional arousal is same for most of the emotions. Even if there are physiological differences in body's response, people cannot perceive them. Since the bodily changes are ambiguous, any number of emotions can be felt from stirred-up bodily conditions. According to this theory, producing emotional feelings results from a sequence of events. These are:

   1. The perception of a potential emotion producing environmental stimuli
   2. An ambiguously aroused bodily state resulting from the stimuli
   3. Interpretation and labeling of the bodily state

   This theory says that emotional experiences are a joint function of physiological arousal and its labeling. In case the source of arousal is ambiguous, we generally look around to find out what we are experiencing.

4. Lazarus gave the cognitive appraisal theory in 1984. This theory is based on the idea of appraisal of information from various sources like from the environment, the body, and memory. Emotions that we feel depend upon this evaluation. Thoughts about what might result from an emotional state, natural temperament or nature, and attitude are also evaluated.

   Sometimes reappraisal of the situation may completely change the emotion. For example, if your father calls you and orders you to immediately reach home, you may think that he is going to scold you. However, after you reach home you discover that your sister's marriage has been finalized and he needs your help for the party to be organized.

5. Plutchik in 1980 gave a theory of relationship among emotions. It is about basic emotions and the way they can be mixed together. According to this theory, emotions differ in intensity, similarity to one another, and polarity or oppositeness. A model is given which includes eight segments to represent primary emotions. These primary emotions which are derived from the evolutionary process have an adaptive value.

6. Leeper gave a theory in 1948. He says that all our sustained and goal-directed behaviors are emotionally toned and motivate us for long sequence behavior. In our college, we are motivated to master new things, to do good job, and get appreciation by classmates and teachers which leads to emotional fulfillment.

7. Tomkins (1962) has forwarded a theory saying that emotions provide energy for motives that give some information about needs. Emotions accompany these drives as excitement, joy, and distress which provide the energy for drives. They give power to the motives. Last two theories are about motivation and emotions.

12.6 EMOTIONAL DEVELOPMENT

The patterns of emotional development vary for children and are affected by various factors. Health, intellectual level, environment, and social reactions have been shown to affect emotional development. Child-rearing practices play a major role in children's emotional development. For example, authoritarian child-rearing encourages the development of anxiety and fear while permissive and democratic training encourages the development of curiosity and affection. Children of low socioeconomic status tend to have more fears and anxiety than those of higher socioeconomic status.

Temper tantrums are examples where the parents cannot manage to handle emotional outbursts of children. In Indian culture, a male child gets much more importance than a female child. Especially in families where gender discrimination is obvious, a young male is generally overpampered.

Harsh is the only male child and is the apple of eyes of the whole family. He is just two and a half. Whatever he wants, he wants it immediately. Otherwise he starts banging his head against the wall or floor. His mother becomes helpless and somehow manages to provide whatever he wants. This extreme emotional outburst also depends on interaction between parents and children. When parents reinforce the wrong demands of children, they are responsible for encouraging wrong emotional expressions. This is also simple classical conditioning. Here, mother's fear that Harsh will hurt himself is the decisive factor.

In adolescence, confusion regarding the normalcy of physical growth and the inability to control sexual impulses are two important problems.

Adolescents face problems such as depression, moodiness, and sadness which directly affect interpersonal relations. Ambiguous social role and vague expectations characterize their lives.

Devshish is just 16, but comparatively looks more mature and adult like. He can drive all sorts of two-wheelers and their family car. However, his mother treats him like a kid intermittently. She gets chocolates and ice creams for him and also takes all minor decisions for him. His father also, mostly, treats him like a young boy but sometimes expects very mature behavior. Devshish gets confused.

Adolescence is characterized by emotional instability and disturbed relations with parents and other family members. On one hand the impact of peers, and on the other, physiological and biochemical changes are responsible for that.

Parents play an important role in adolescents' social interactions, emotional and social adjustment, and mental and physical health.

During adolescence and young adulthood, controlling emotions and their expression is not achieved properly. During adulthood, it is better and again during old age the person becomes oriented toward more negative emotions.

As we have discussed emotions are very well communicated with the help of eye contact, facial expression, and bodily gestures. Tears in eyes, face turned downward, and walking very slowly are some examples of emotional indicators. Voice declares the emotional state of the individual such as soft or harsh voice, laughing or crying loudly, etc. As expressing emotions depends on the cultural expectations and socialization, the meaning of the same should be interpreted with caution. It is worth noting that if verbal and nonverbal messages are contradictory, one depends on nonverbal cues. Context is equally contributing to the meaning. People from diverse cultures can easily identify emotions on the basis of posed emotions though the person who poses is not from their own culture.

12.7 GENDER AND EMOTIONS

Gender is not only related to sex but to the social and psychological effects of being a male or female. It is a social and cultural construct that may dictate appropriate and ideal roles for men and women, and concepts of masculinity and femininity within a particular society. Gender roles are related to the division of labor and the division of authority, the style of emotional expression, parenting, the expectations regarding appearance, independence, intimacy, control, behavior, and many other areas.

In a male-dominated society like Indian, males are socialized to suppress most of the emotions, especially those that are labeled as feminine, and to express masculine emotions such as anger.

Statym and Sunita are twins and are 10 years old. They met with a minor accident while crossing a road. Both of them were slightly injured, however, were shocked. They started crying loudly. Their father came running. Immediately, he stared scolding Statym, "Are you a girl? Why are you crying?" He immediately went to Sunita and started consoling her and picked her up and said, "Don't worry, I will apply some medicine."

Male members are discouraged to express their weakness, pain, and encouraged to show that they are strong, and that they can manage everything. Even as adults they are expected to shoulder the responsibilities of the whole family and be the head of the family. Hence, they should make every decision objectively and systematically without considering the emotional impact of any change in life. As a consequence, even adult male members are deprived of emotional catharsis which is a must for good mental health. They are expected to maintain a mask of being capable of handling all sorts of problems and situations. Blocked emotions are troublesome to the individual. Emotional catharsis is essential for maintaining good mental health. There should be some emotional outlet for everyone. In the sense, everyone should discuss real emotional problems with someone without any loss of status. Otherwise, alcohol abuse and substance or drug abuse are commonly seen among males.

Heena's father lost his mother with whom he was very much attached. The whole family was in deep grief and Heena and her mother were continuously weeping for hours. Her father, however, was looking sad but did not weep or cry for a moment.

In Indian society, the impact of socialization is so strong that male members cannot express their emotions even after the death of their mother.

Women on the other hand are expected to develop emotions such as empathy, sympathy, kindness, helping nature, understanding, and gentleness. They are supposed to express various emotions appropriately in every social situation also. In most of the communities in India if a woman does not weep when her mother-in-law expires, people start criticizing her and generate doubts about her intentions.

Gender differences in emotional expression have been observed as early as preschool age.

Girls convey submissive emotions like sadness or anxiety and boys express disharmonious feelings such as anger and pride. Not only in Western culture like in the United States but also in Eastern culture like in India, women are expected to be more relationship oriented than men. They are expected to shoulder the responsibility of maintaining good interpersonal relations, and caring for the young ones and old as well as ill individuals. They are socialized in such a way that they should develop traits such as sympathy and empathy as well as kindness and consideration. On the other hand, men are expected to be more aggressive, self-oriented, confident, and emotionally aloof. This social sanction makes male members substantially different from females from the same community and even from the same family.

Though there are individual differences, the general impact of socialization is substantial to orient the person toward typical emotional experiences and expressions.

Women are perceived to be more emotional while men are thought to be more logical. Women experience a broad range of positive and negative emotions, more than men. They are seen as more skilled at sending and receiving nonverbal cues, smiling, laughing, and gazing.

All stereotypes about gender and emotion are not proved to be true everywhere in the world. Women are more expressive in terms of facial expressions and gestures than men. Cross-cultural studies have found that men report experiencing more emotions that are powerful like anger, while women report experiencing more powerless emotions like fear.

12.8 EMOTIONAL ABUSE

Chandu is studying in second standard. Once, when he was ready to go to school and was waiting for the school bus with his mother, he started complaining about severe stomach pain. As soon as he told his mother about it she started scolding him loudly on the road. She said that as he wants to avoid going to school, he is pretending to be ill. Chandu was shocked when she also gave him a tight slap and ordered that he has to go to school whatever may be the case.

In a country like India, emotional abuse is so common that it is generally neglected as well as taken for granted. It is considered to be the duty of parents to scold their children and give physical punishment to discipline them. It is worth noting that even when there is serio⁻ child abuse in terms of sexual abuse and the child is trying to tell that, parents general₁ neglect that message.

There are various questions that can be asked about this interaction. How is it that the mother could get clear information that there was no pain? Is she a specialist doctor? How can anyone guess so accurately the inner experiences of anybody else? What conclusions should Chandu arrive at? What are the long-term effects of such treatment given to children?

If parents do not respect children and challenge their experiences, children cannot develop trust and a sense of security. On top of it, they will not share their experiences with their parents in future and can also lie if they want to dodge any work. Chandu was emotionally hurt and the effects cannot be underestimated.

In 1976, Kempe and Kempe attracted attention to the emotional abuse of children. The central characteristic of emotional abuse of a child is that the child's emotions and emotional expressions are met with inappropriate emotional responses by the parents and other significant adults. Inappropriate generally means the expression of negative emotions such as annoyance, anger, violence or indifference. If the child is afraid of something, he or she should not be ridiculed. If a child expresses pride, excitement, or happiness after winning a singing competition and his or her father throws the certificate scolding the child that he or she should better concentrate on studies, then this will have devastating effects on the child's psychological health. Here, encouragement would have been appropriate response, but not indifference or resentment.

Emotional abuse is occurring if the inappropriateness is repetitive and occurs over a long period of time.

Emotional abuse of a child affects the child's emotional development. Healthy development involves experiencing and expressing a wide variety of emotions, both positive and negative. With emotional abuse, experiencing and expressing positive emotions becomes restricted. Additionally, negative emotions are experienced more prevalently. The inadequate development of emotional experience and expression that occurs with emotional abuse interferes with the child's ability to have healthy social relationships.

Emotional abuse results in a limited ability to understand the appropriateness of specific emotions and regulate one's emotions, alongwith expression and understanding of emotions, including empathy.

Emotional abuse is more probable if parents had experienced it when they were children, and if there is a lot of family violence and it is observed by children.

It is also seen when parents are mentally ill or are poor, isolated, unsupported, and single. Enhancing parental awareness and educating parents about the nature of emotional abuse is essential.

The abuse of women is deep rooted in Indian culture for generations. This emotional abuse occurs in intimate relationships. There are five facts reported by researchers.

1. **Degradation and humiliation**—This may be seen in husband–wife relations also and includes emotional as well as physical humiliation.
2. **Attempts to control physically and/or emotionally, or through threats**—Wives are not allowed to make any decision on their own.
3. **Rejection and/or neglect**—Violence against women includes outright rejection of the lady and neglecting her welfare.
4. **Social isolation**—Even today, a typical housewife is supposed to work inside the family in complete social isolation. Many daughter-in-laws are not given any permission even to see their own parents, to work, and to go anywhere without permission.
5. **Exploitation**—Economic exploitation, emotional blackmail, and sexual harassment are very commonly seen in Indian families.

As there are no exact legal procedures and social sanction is taken for granted, women are being abused by male members in the family. For example, in India there is no legal provision to arrest marital rape. Emotional abuse of women results in poor self-esteem, problems in other relationships, decreased efficiency and work performance, substance abuse, anxiety, depression, and increased risk for posttraumatic stress disorder. Such women are treated for these other problems as they are obviously seen. Treatments may include cognitive behavioral therapy.

12.9 REGULATION OF EMOTIONS AND EMOTIONAL COMPETENCE

All children should learn emotional tolerance as control over the environment becomes increasingly difficult. Emotional tolerance, the ability to accept and adjust to unpleasant emotional experiences, is an essential condition for emotional maturity.

Emotional regulation consists of effectively managing arousal to adapt and reach a goal.

Arousal involves a state of alertness and stimulation. Sometimes arousal is so intense that it affects proper functioning. Failure to regulate emotions results in psychological disorders. Any extreme and prolonged emotional reaction expressed in a socially inappropriate way is labeled as psychological abnormality.

Rutuja was feeling extremely happy as she could get distinction in her final year of dentistry. Just half an hour ago she got her results from the university's website. Since then she was literally screaming with excitement. Her friends also got good grades and were pleased to see that. It was a great accomplishment and lifelong satisfaction. All of them dispersed and still Rutuja was pretty excited and started dancing on the road itself. People around were surprised to see that and started criticizing her. She was not aware of that.

Intensity and duration of the emotional experience or the vividness of the expression of emotions such as facial expression and gestures should be regulated. Emotional regulation may involve increasing or decreasing either positive or negative emotions and restricting the range of emotional experiences.

Emotional regulation depends on age. The impact of extrinsic regulation is more among children and that of intrinsic is more among adults. Socialization, family environment, and parental behavior influence emotional regulation.

Harsha had a younger brother who was doing his 12th. He always used to exploit her and manipulate things. Once when she had to go for her examination, he took her two-wheeler's key and was about to leave without informing her. She saw him from the balcony and was so upset that she started screaming loudly. Even then he paid no heed to her. She could not control her anger and threw her mobile phone from the second floor.

12.9.1 Strategies to Control Emotions

In early childhood, the baby is helped to regulate emotions by parents who try to neutralize the effects of emotional outbursts with the help of facial expressions, appropriate words, and other stimuli to make the baby more comfortable.

There are two ways to help children:

1. Helping children or coaching them regarding emotions.
2. Dismissing emotions.

In the first type, monitoring children's emotions, observing their negative emotions, and using that knowledge for helping them in labeling emotions and helping them understand how to deal effectively with emotions are included. For example, when Prachi was not selected for participating in the social gathering of her high school, her mother discussed with her at length about her feelings, alternatives, and options to contribute something in social gathering and similar other activities, and in interpreting teacher's behavior in a different perspective. This discussion helped Prachi to understand strategies for handling such a situation in future. Here, parents use emotional support, praise, and are more nurturing. If parents use this strategy, children are in a better position to control and regulate their emotions and have less behavior problems.

In the second type, parents actually are unable to deal effectively with children's emotions. They lack enough understanding and skills. They either dismiss their children's emotions or reject or ignore them. If Prachi's mother were of this sort, she would have told Prachi that social gathering is not such an important event and she need not to worry about being rejected, or that being ignored did not matter much. This type of dismissing attitude of the parents forces the children to suppress their emotions.

A more advanced stage is the cognitive control which is self-initiated and depends on internal resources. Children are better equipped with it as they grow older. Changing one's perspective, associating positive things with a particular negative event, neglecting, and shifting focus of attention are the various strategies used. As children become aware of the fact that emotional outbursts are not socially acceptable and parents also do not like it, they learn how to control emotions and minimize unpleasant and negative emotions.

This leads to better coping with any emotionally arousing situation and to reduce stress for enhancing better adjustment.

12.9.2 Emotional Competence

Chapter 13 discusses emotional intelligence, and hence, we will not discuss emotional competence at length.

Emotional competence focuses on the adaptive nature of emotional experience. It requires a number of skills in social contexts. These are:

1. **Developing awareness of one's emotional state**—The individual should be able to understand, evaluate, and analyze his or her emotional experiences. It is necessary to differentiate between various emotional experiences. Even otherwise, the individual can interpret the cause–effect relation between various emotional experiences and environmental stimuli himself or herself only.
2. **Having empathy and sympathy**—Without empathy one cannot adjust one's perception according to others and be the other individual at least psychologically. If we cannot

really understand the real meaning behind one's emotional expressions and behavior, we cannot establish good interpersonal relations.

Sympathy encourages the altruistic tendencies or helping behavior. Here also, though from distance one has to imagine the other person's life, problems, and emotions, being sensitive to other's emotional experience leads to better interpersonal relations.

Detecting others' emotions includes understanding and differentiating between various emotional expressions of others. We have to understand even the mood of our parents because we should find out a proper time to ask for some favor to them.

3. **Developing appropriate vocabulary to describe various emotions**—Appropriately describing an emotion in the framework of social and cultural norms becomes essential. Many a time, young children can neither differentiate nor describe emotions—their own and others.

4. **Accepting the discrepancy between real emotions and outer expression of emotions**—Many a time, due to social pressure or social conformity the individual has to express something else than what he or she is actually experiencing. One has to recognize that inner emotional states do not have to correspond to outer expressions. It is a must to understand that even when the person is looking pleased, he or she may be very sad from within or vice a versa.

   As Prakash was selected for the republic day NCC parade which is held in Delhi, all his classmates and other friends were congratulating him. There were some classmates who were actually aspiring for the same and were feeling jealous and disappointed as they could not get the chance. However, outwardly they were showing that they were very happy and proud of Prakash.

5. **Adaptively coping with negative emotions**—Reducing unpleasant emotions by doing some other activity. When we are frustrated due to not being capable of solving a difficult mathematical problem, we keep it aside and go for a cup of tea. In case of real-life problems, some individuals get so much disturbed that they start abusing alcohol or taking drugs. This is an extreme reaction which generates new problems.

12.10   OTHER CORRELATES OF EMOTIONS

1. **Accomplishment of goals or success**

   Emotions are linked with an individual's goals in a variety of ways. Attainment of a goal leads to happiness, and if not attained, it leads to unhappiness, frustration, and anger. Success is related to self-esteem, self-confidence, motivation, and even intrapersonal and interpersonal relations.

2. **Memory**

   A very well-known experiment was given by Zeigarnik and is known as the Zeigarnik effect. In this experiment, 18–20 tasks are given to the individual who requires approximately 3 minutes for completing each task. Randomly, some of them are interrupted and for other tasks enough time is given to complete the tasks. Afterward, a recall of all the tasks is taken. Generally, it is seen that the tasks that are interrupted are recalled better. If we leave any task incomplete, there is a psychic tension that is generated. It is due to this tension that memory is affected.

Some other researchers have proved that the experience of success or failure also affects memory. Stress and severe trauma may have an impact on implicit memory systems.

Posttraumatic stress disorder is associated with the triggering of emotions by situations that are perceived as associated with a previous traumatic event. The explicit details of a traumatic event are more accurate, but implicit memory for the associated emotions and context is less accurate. Some research shows that intense, negative implicit memories such as fear and horror comparatively are accurate and stable over time, while implicit memories of other emotions are less accurate.

Emotion-arousing events are often remembered more vividly than common events. It is easier to remember what someone said in a situation than to remember the context of the situation. Emotionally charged words and sentences are better remembered than neutral ones.

Some words are more emotionally loaded than others. For example, a word like headmaster or mother-in-law has a very specific emotional background than the words chalk or brown. Here, we can understand that emotional loading has many associations and is remembered better.

As we have seen in Chapter 6, tone carries a lot of emotions. The emotional tone of voice also improves context memory. It is more effective than the content of the message.

It was found that children remembered negative emotions more easily than positive ones. That is why it is essential to be very careful while interacting with children. Girls were more likely to remember all the emotions than boys.

A lot of research has been done regarding eyewitness memory and how it is affected by emotional arousal. If there is intense emotional arousal, memory is reported to be more distorted. If the individual is more disturbed, the accuracy of memory decreases.

Learning plays an important role in emotional expression, especially of subtle emotions as jealousy. Unless we know the background of the person, it becomes difficult to identify the experience of emotions on the basis of facial expressions.

If a person is experiencing and expressing more than one emotions simultaneously, it becomes difficult to identify.

12.11 SUMMARY

This chapter focuses on human emotions and dealing with them. Emotions play a very significant role in human life. The nature of emotions is such that there are both psychological and physiological aspects of emotions. The indicators of emotions depend on the socialization of the individual which in turn depends upon culture, child-rearing practices, and experiences of the individual. Emotional expressions fulfill many goals such as enhancing effective inter- and intrapersonal relations. Emotional catharsis is a must for good mental health but male members are taught to hide and suppress them.

For emotional regulation, one should have a balanced and objective evaluation of one's own experiences of emotions. Malpractices like emotional abuse result in long-term ill effects.

QUESTIONS

1. Describe the nature of emotions.
2. Describe the effects of positive and negative emotions.
3. What are the biological correlates of emotions?
4. What are the functions of emotions?
5. How and why should one achieve the regulation of emotions?

6. Discuss and evaluate the various theories of emotions.
7. Explain salient developmental changes in emotional experiences.
8. What are the gender differences in emotions?
9. What is emotional abuse? Describe its effects.
10. How does emotional competence help us in day-to-day practices?

APPLICATION ORIENTATION

Write down the most frequently experienced positive and negative emotions. What physiological changes do you experience after that?

Discuss with your friends what will happen if you do not express your emotions at all.

Select any two individuals having exaggerated expression style and write down the indicators and effects of that style.

Find out the incidences during last week when you think your regulation of emotional expression was not up to the mark and find out what changes should be made to that.

Take interviews of five girls and five guys regarding some hypothetical life events and ask them how they will express their emotion. Find out if there are differences within the groups and differences between the two genders.

SUGGESTED READINGS

Beverly, E. (2006). *Healing your emotional self*. Hoboken, NJ: John Wiley & Sons.

Colemen, A. M. (2008). *Dictionary of Psychology* (3rd ed.). New York: Oxford University.

James ,W. (1890). *Psychology: Brief Course*. Condon: Collier Macmillan Ltd.

Kempe, R. and Kempe, C. (1976). Assessing family pathology. In R. E. Helfer and C. H. Kempe (eds), Child abuse and neglect: The family and community (pp. 116–118). Cambridge, MA: Ballinger.

Lange, C. G. and James, W. (1962). *The emotions*. New York: Hafner.

Leeper, R. W. (1948). A motivational theory of emotions to replace "emotions as disorganized response". *Psychological Review, 55*, 5–21.

McEntarffer, R., & Weseley, A. (2012). *Barren's AP psychology*. Barron first e book. http//www.amazon.in/AP-Psychology-Barrons-Ap/dp/143800270x (accessed on December 12, 2015)

Plutchik, R. (1980). *Emotion: Theory, research, and experience: vol1 Theories of Emotion* (vol. 1). New York: Academic Press.

Reevy, G. M. (2011). *Encyclopedia of emotions*. Santa Barbara, CA: Greenwood.

Strongman, K. T. (2006). *Applying psychology to everyday life: A beginner's guide*. Christchurch, NZ: John Wiley & Sons

Tomkins, S. S. (1962). Affect, imagery consciousness: *The Positive Affects* (vol. 1 ch 9) New York: Springer.

13 Emotional Intelligence

13.1 NATURE AND SIGNIFICANCE OF EMOTIONAL INTELLIGENCE

Swapnil and Dinesh both are equally qualified and they joined a multinational company in the same month. Swapnil got first class and Dinesh got second class. Both of them were facing new work demands, new responsibilities, and challenges.

Swapnil gets anxious and wants to complete his work in great hurry. He gets annoyed easily if some extra work is given to him. He cannot get along well with his coworkers and subordinates. He gets irritated and angry if others are not doing their duties on time and expresses these negative feelings with strong nonverbal communication. Dinesh on the other hand is a pleasant person. He expresses his opinions firmly but without hurting others, he never interferes in or comments on others' work. Even though he is not satisfied about a particular thing, he tries to adjust with the situation. Overall, he can get along well with others.

After one year Dinesh was selected for further promotion.

What is the problem with Swapnil? Actually, he is a bright student and has the ability to satisfactorily deal with the cognitive side of work. Why is it that he could not get promotion?

Each and every person has to work and complete the task, but no one works in isolation. One has to work with colleagues which one cannot choose. Using special skills to manage one's own and others' emotions is essential.

Out of many teachers you like a particular teacher the most. Why do you think you like that teacher? There is every possibility that some other teachers have equal or even more expertise in the subject. Then, what is the reason? Maybe one teaches well and the other does not and you like the teaching style of a particular teacher. What does it mean? While interacting with the students one respects them and the other insults them harshly. You like the teacher who knows the subject well; who is just, kind, and considerate; who respects the students; and who is not a very strict disciplinarian.

The basic difference between the two types of teachers and two employees in these examples is their emotional intelligence.

Human intelligence includes a wide range of abilities. One of the most important abilities is emotional intelligence. It is well accepted today all over the world that for being successful in life, one needs not only intelligence but emotional intelligence also. In fact, the role played by emotional intelligence is more than general intelligence. People who are talented but do not have enough emotional intelligence generally cannot adjust with their family members and colleagues, and are generally maladjusted. They do not get success which is expected on the basis of their intellectual level. Experts say that 80 percent of success is determined by emotional intelligence. One more thing which needs consideration is that intelligence without character may result in dangerous things in human life.

Emotional intelligence is recognizing, understanding, and choosing how we think, feel, and act. It includes how and what we learn, set priorities, and determine daily actions. A very well-known psychologist Goleman (1995) views emotional intelligence as very important because it allows us to exercise some self-control. Here, the idea is not to repress feelings but become aware of them so that we can cope with them more effectively.

Goleman revealed a research done at 120 companies, in which the employers were asked to describe the abilities that made for excellence in their employees. It was seen that 67 percent of these were emotional competencies and generic behavioral skills beyond IQ or expertise requirements.

Specifically, listening and communication skills, the adaptability to change, the ability to get over setbacks, confidence, motivation, wish to develop one's career, the ability to work with others and handle disagreements, and the willingness to make a contribution or be a leader were the most important ones.

According to *Oxford Dictionary of Psychology*, emotional intelligence is the ability to monitor one's own and other people's emotions, to discriminate between different emotions and label them appropriately and to use emotional information to guide thinking and behavior. Emotional intelligence is the ability underlying emotional sensitivity, awareness, and management skills which help us to maximize our health, happiness, and survival. It is simply the way of knowing how to separate healthy feelings from unhealthy ones and how to turn negative feelings into positive ones. A person with high emotional intelligence is socially poised, outgoing, and cheerful. They are not fearful or worried. They are committed to people and causes. They shoulder their responsibility and have an ethical outlook. They are sympathetic and caring in their relationship with others and have a rich and proper emotional life. They are comfortable with self and others as well as in social universe in which they live. Emotional intelligence is the ability to take the responsibility for one's own emotions and happiness. It also includes the ability to help others, identify their emotions, and benefit from their emotions.

If we compare such people with those having high intelligence, the difference will be quite clear. High intelligence quotient means wide range of intellectual interest and abilities. Such a person may be ambitious and productive but tends to be uneasy, inhibited, critical, condescending, unexpressive, and detached, as well as emotionally cold.

The concept was first formally defined by Salovery and Mayer (1990). There are four groups of competencies included in it. These are:

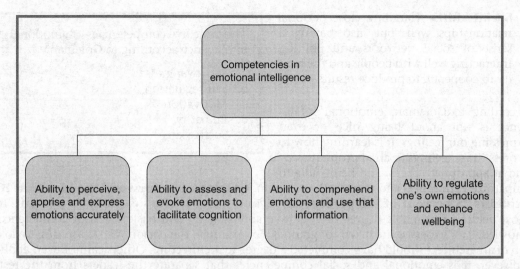

1. The ability to perceive, apprise, and express emotions accurately—Awareness regarding one's emotions, identifying one's emotions, understanding as they change, and discriminating between various physiological changes resulting from various emotions are the essential things for emotional intelligence.
2. Ability to assess and evoke emotions to facilitate cognition—This ability to facilitate cognitive assessment of emotions and take help of emotions to understand various interactions with others works well. Emotional analysis helps in learning more about the environment and others' intentions and behavior.
3. The ability to comprehend emotional messages and make use of emotional information—Recognizing others' emotions and developing empathy help in getting social signals. This ability helps in guessing and predicting others' behavior more accurately.
4. The ability to regulate one's own emotions to promote growth and well-being—Regulating one's own emotions leads to maturity in interaction and improvement in expression of emotions. This includes avoiding extreme and unpleasant ways of emotional interaction. This in turn, enhances mental health and well-being.

In 1973, Goleman's mentor David McLelland (1973) argued that traditional academic and intelligence testing was not a good predictor of how well a person would actually do in a job. Instead, people should be tested for competencies that are important to the job. Goleman gave 25 emotional competencies based on the following:

1. **Self-awareness**—Awareness of our own feelings and the ability to use them as a guide to better decision-making. The knowledge of our own abilities and shortcomings. The sense that we can tackle most things.
2. **Self-regulation**—Being conscientious and delaying gratification in order to achieve our goals. The ability to recover from emotional distress and manage our emotions.
3. **Motivation**—Developing an achievement or goal orientation, so that frustrations and setbacks are put into perspective and qualities such that initiative and perseverance are refined.
4. **Empathy**—The awareness of what others are feeling and thinking, and in turn the ability to influence a wide range of people.

5. **Social skills**—Handling close personal relationships well, but also having a sense of social networks and politics. Interacting well with people and the ability to cooperate to produce results.

> The basic five competencies of emotional intelligence according to Goleman:
>
> a. Self-awareness
> b. Self-regulation
> c. Motivation
> d. Empathy
> e. Social skills

According to Goleman, emotional intelligence is not about being nice or even expressing our feelings, it is learning how to express those feelings in an appropriate way and at appropriate times, and being able to empathize with others and work well with them. **Goleman put forward the idea that IQ explains 25 percent of job performance, and other factors explain 75 percent**. In most fields, a reasonable degree of cognitive ability or IQ and basic levels of competence, knowledge, or expertise are taken for granted. For example, the person who is aspiring to do a job of an architect should have completed a degree in architecture. Others cannot even apply. However, it is emotional and social competencies that separate the leaders from the rest. Goleman has developed various measures of emotional intelligence.

Approximately 100 years ago, a concept similar to emotional intelligence was given by a well-known psychologist Thorndike (1905). His concept is known as social intelligence which means to act wisely in human relations, and the ability to understand and manage others. Researchers have proved that emotional intelligence is positively related to an individual's performance, along with many social skills such as leadership, maintaining good human relations, conflict management, management of change, contribution to group performance and social analysis, etc., at home front and the job. Emotional intelligence results in better self-esteem, better decision–making, and wise behavioral patterns. In general, individual's behavior becomes socially more acceptable on the one hand and individually more growth oriented on the other.

Emotional intelligence was proposed as a set of interrelated abilities by Mayer and Salovey (1995). Emotionally intelligent people were thought to have the ability to reason about and use emotions to enhance thoughts more effectively than people with less emotional intelligence. Emotional intelligence involves sophisticated information processing about one's own and others' emotions and the ability to use that information to guide thinking and behavior. Individuals high in emotional intelligence are able to use their skills to pay attention to, use, and manage emotions in ways that can benefit themselves and others. This concept is based on four hierarchical branches or sets of skills: (a) managing emotions to achieve specific goals; (b) understanding emotions, emotional language, and signals conveyed by emotions; (c) using emotions to facilitate thinking; and (d) perceiving emotions accurately in oneself and others (Mayer and Salovey, 1997).

There are three models of emotional intelligence:

1. Ability model
2. Trait model
3. Mixed model

1. The ability model defines emotional intelligence as the ability to perceive and integrate emotions to facilitate thought, understand emotions, and regulate emotions to promote personal growth.

According to this model, emotional intelligence includes:

a. Perceiving emotions
b. Using emotions
c. Understanding emotions
d. Managing emotions

2. Trait model is related to the personality. According to it, emotional intelligence is the behavior disposition of self-perceived ability.
3. Mixed model of emotional intelligence was given by Goleman (1995). Here emotional intelligence is self-awareness, self-regulation, social skills, empathy, and motivation.

In 1935, Doll gave a measure of social maturity called as Vineland Social Maturity scale. This was essentially considered as a measure of a type of intelligence. Then came the concept of alexithymia which is an inability to recognize, understand, and describe emotions. Alexithymia is an indication of abnormality and is associated with schizophrenia, brain injury, Parkinson's disease, posttraumatic stress disorder, depression, and substance abuse. This is a lack of appropriate social and emotional intelligence. Many other psychologists have considered it as part and parcel of intelligence.

Goleman claimed that emotional intelligence could be more powerful than general intelligence quotient, as it accounts for over 85–90 percent of outstanding performance in top leaders and star performers. Emotional intelligence is considered as a combination of traits including happiness, self-esteem, self-management, and optimism.

The Mayer–Salovey–Caruso model proposes that there are four major branches or facets to the emotional intelligence concept (Mayer et al., 2004).

1. **Perceiving emotions**
   This is an ability to identify emotional messages in facial expressions, tone of voice, and even works of art. People who are skilled at perceiving emotions in themselves and others who have an advantage in social situations are more likely to understand things from another person's perspective and are more empathic.
2. **Using emotions to facilitate thinking**
   Emotions have the power to change the way we think. When we are happy we may think that everything is possible, whereas when we are sad, we tend to have more negative thoughts. This branch is about how emotions affect our thinking and how we can utilize our emotions for more effective problem-solving, reasoning, decision-making, and creative endeavors.
3. **Understanding emotions**
   It's not enough to notice emotions. We need to figure out the message they are carrying. Why do we have certain emotions? Where are they coming from? What are they likely to lead us to? It is important to understand, for example, that irritation may lead to anger, feeling insecure, or to unpredictable outbursts. Emotionally intelligent individuals are capable of labelling emotions with words appropriately, and also of understanding complex feelings and even contradictory emotional states.
4. **Managing emotions**
   Emotional management or regulation is not about eliminating troubling emotions, but about learning how to gain control over them. Some of us, when upset, think there is nothing that we can do about it; others believe that they can do something to make themselves feel better. Successful emotion-managers are often capable of helping others to deal with their emotions too.

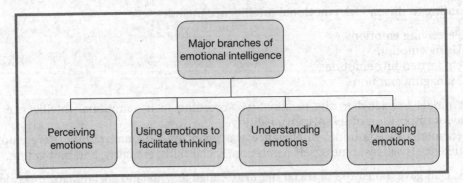

All these aspects are equally important for emotional intelligence. They are interdependent. Self-regulation essentially depends on self-awareness. Empathy and other social skills are inter-linked. As is obvious, without motivation, no one will be involved in the exercise of enhancing emotional maturity.

13.2 SCOPE AND TYPES OF EMOTIONAL INTELLIGENCE

According to Gardner (1983), there are two types of emotional intelligence.

1. Interpersonal
2. Intrapersonal

That means the first is related to interacting with others and the second is about interacting with self. For interpersonal emotional intelligence, it is necessary to understand others, their emotional experiences, general background, their motivation, style of working, and many more things. For intrapersonal emotional intelligence, communication with self becomes important. It is the capacity to prepare one's own veridical model and operate with its help. It is obviously related to insight about self. Interaction between these two forms is the base for emotional intelligence. It is worth noting that interpersonal interaction depends on intraper-sonal emotional intelligence. There is substantial overlap between intrapersonal and interper-sonal emotional intelligence. If a person cannot understand properly and objectively his or her own emotions and style of expression, he or she will not be able to understand how his or her communication affects others in terms of their emotional reactions and expressions. If one is not capable of understanding why and how others' emotions are responsible for their behav-ior, and how their behavior is responsible for others' emotions, one will not be able to main-tain good interpersonal relations.

Roma is a happy-go-lucky girl of 17 years. She takes many things casually and her mother is constantly worried about her well-being. Roma wanted to go for an overnight trip with her friends and she was not ready to compromise regarding it. Her mother also was firm and never wanted to allow her to go for that trip, especially when nobody's parents or teachers are accom-panying the youngsters. Mother was taking a very strict stand though otherwise she is friendly with Roma. In this case, if Roma is not capable of understanding her mother's concern, she will not understand whatever her mother is suggesting. Likely, she will become very aggressive and in a way insult her mother. This is not going to solve the problem.

Emotionally intelligent mother will find some solution in terms of finding out more about the atmosphere where these girls are going to stay, discussing with other parents, trying to convince Roma to change the destination to make it more safe, and floating the idea that mothers of all these girls can also go for this trip. She will ask Roma why is she so angry when she discussed some practical problems and ask her to think of being at her place and then decide what can be done in such a situation.

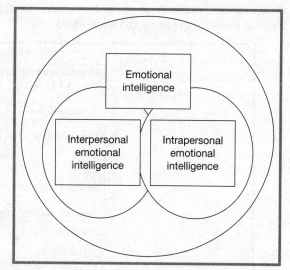

Emotional intelligence includes:

1. **Self-awareness**—Objectively observing oneself and recognizing feelings and emotions. Every moment changing emotional states are understood only by the individual. He or she is aware of the physiological impact of emotions. The person who has achieved self-awareness also remembers what types of emotions were experienced and when did they arouse. This is included in intrapersonal intelligence.

2. **Self-regulation**—Managing one's own feelings so that they are expressed in an appropriate way. One has to trace back and find out the cause of a particular pleasant or unpleasant feeling. One has to be one's own guide. One has to find out various alternative of finding out the consequences of one's behavior and resourceful behavior. Then, one has to select the best one and observe the consequences. Appropriate self-talk leads to emotional efficacy and self-confidence.

3. **Motivation**—Expressing emotions in such a way that the expression will be useful for achieving a social goal. Emotional self-control, controlling impulses, and immediate gratification orientation are the most important things in this. Immediate gratification orientation is detrimental to emotional maturity. If the person thinks about satisfying all his or her needs and desires immediately, he or she may not be able to think about others' needs and their problems.

4. **Empathy**—It is very useful to maintain interpersonal relations. Hence, is called the basic requirement for interpersonal intelligence. It includes sensitivity to others' feelings and understanding their perspective and interpretation of things and events. This gives a clear understanding of social signals.

5. **Social skills**—It includes handling interpersonal relations and recognizing others' emotions and managing emotions in others. All sorts of communication skills, and proper expression as well as negotiation skills are essential for developing social skills.

A researcher called Piaget (1968) has said that listening skills are the highest form of intelligence. Effective listening requires complete freedom from prejudices and from any filter while making communication meaningful. This leads to rapport establishment.

In effective listening, the person can interpret the verbal and nonverbal communication of the speaker properly as he or she focuses on them. This leads to a better understanding of the real message given by the individual.

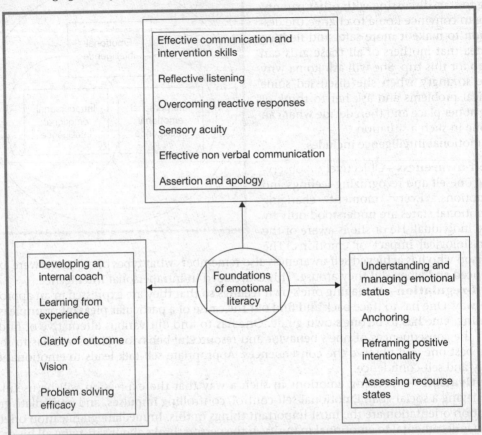

As is seen in this illustration, foundations of emotional literacy can be divided in three dimensions. First is related to effective communication skills. Sensory acuity is essential for effective communication. Verbal and nonverbal communication skills including effective listening and assertiveness are required for enhancing emotional literacy. Accepting one's mistake and extending the apology for the same also helps emotional literacy.

Being critical about one's communication and behavior, learning from experience and problem-solving capacities, and having a clear vision about future are included in the second dimension.

Third dimension is regarding anchoring, a developing clear understanding, managing emotional states, assessment of resources, and maintaining positive intentionality.

13.3 CORRELATES OF EMOTIONAL INTELLIGENCE

Emotional intelligence and maturity result in integrity, patience, and well-balanced personality. It leads to better coping strategies in any situation.

a. **Age**—Emotional intelligence and emotional maturity do not increase with age. There are many old individuals who have poor emotional maturity.

b. **Impulsive behavior**—Those who are emotionally intelligence do not show impulsive behavior. They feel certain things but do not act immediately and immaturely.

c. **Blaming others**—Emotionally mature individuals do not blame others for their own actions and emotional problems. Something like "he spoiled my mood" or "you made me angry" is not their justification of their own actions or emotional expression. They do not blame people, places, events or God and fate for their actions.

   Instead, they say that "I feel angry when you came late." Hence, there is no excuse for own behavior. This is considered as the first step to emotional maturity.

d. **Emotional honesty**—This is essentially accepting own emotions as they are experienced. Most of the emotions, especially the socially unacceptable, are not accepted by the individual. There is an inner critical evaluation that restricts such acceptance. However, unless the person understands and accepts own feelings, he or she will not be able to manage them properly. This is considered as the second stage to emotional maturity.

e. **Having the feeling of being victimized**—People who are emotionally mature shoulder the responsibility of their own actions and feelings; they do not feel that they are victimized by others.

f. **Accepting one's mistake**—Those individuals who are emotionally intelligent admit that they are wrong when they commit an error.

g. **Emotional openness**—Sharing emotions with others at appropriate time is also one important step to emotional maturity. It leads to emotional catharsis which in turn leads to better mental health. No suppression of emotions is expected.

h. **Emotional assertiveness**—Positive self-expression and expressing emotions assertively are correlated to emotional maturity.

i. **Accepting reality**—Contact with reality is related to emotional maturity which is also one of the most important correlates of emotional maturity. Relating well with others and being just to self is achieved by it.

As we have seen in the first example, the personal cost of deficits in emotional intelligence is serious and cannot be underestimated. Even if the person is intelligent and sincere, he or she may not be able to achieve what he or she is otherwise capable of achieving. It ruins careers. Hence, he or she is always an underachiever for the whole of his or her life. Not only that, such a person may face problems regarding marriage, parenting, or even poor health.

   The best thing is that emotional intelligence is not an innate ability, but can be nurtured and strengthened. Good social and emotional skills must be mastered. For any individual, the expected outcomes of emotional intelligence are:

1. **Personal effectiveness**—Where ever he or she goes, the person having emotional intelligence is always well accepted by others and can win the situation.

2. **Better performance**—In jobs and in practical academic sphere, the performance of such an individual is always better as he or she is more comfortable everywhere.

3. **Effective interpersonal relations**—An emotionally intelligent individual is always better adjusted, accepts others as they are and, hence, is better accepted by others.

4. **Better coping skills**—When the individual faces any stress, emotional intelligence results in better coping strategies and skills.

5. **Health and happiness**—Health and happiness both depend on emotional balance of the individual. If a person can understand and find out the cause of his or her emotional upsets, he or she will be in a better position to avoid such things, or can monitor and regulate his or her emotions.

6. **Improving the quality of life**—All the advantages of emotional intelligence keep an individual steady and constantly within the range of the variation of moods. This results in a comfortable and confident life. Obviously, more peace of mind is achieved and the quality of life improves.

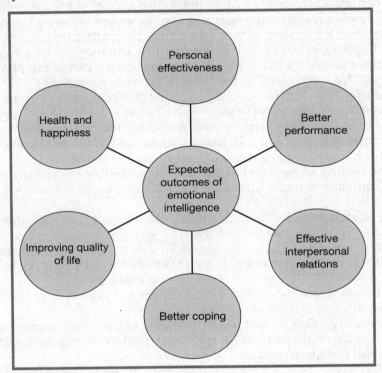

13.4 STRATEGIES TO ENHANCE EMOTIONAL INTELLIGENCE

Emotional intelligence is a personality dynamic, characteristic or potential that can be nurtured and developed. Hence, emotional intelligence of any individual can be enhanced if enough motivation and training is available. The whole process of socialization can be utilized for the development of emotional intelligence.

13.4.1 SELF AWARENESS AND ANCHORING

Anchoring is the wise use of conditioned response. One can train oneself to give a particular emotional response after one gets a particular cue. Many great people maintain their self-image and public image using this strategy. Emotional resource state or emotional state is the response given to a particular stimulus. A particular emotional state having a particular emotional, intellectual, and physical component is called as mood. Stress is the lowest type of response which basically has two options—flight or fight. Those who are emotionally literate know the benefits of anchoring. For example, a person who is participating in a running competition will think and have the image that he or she is like a leopard and can run fast. Even in stress management, what type of emotional state will be appropriate in that situation, and how can that be achieved, are important issues.

Anchoring can be learned by observing and recording our own emotional experiences. It takes time and sensitivity. The methods used for that are:

a. **Traditional diary method**—Write, in detail, all important emotional experiences regarding various daily activities like reading new books.

b. **Change in perspective**—Second type is writing about the same thing from a different perspective. If you try and interpret the same activity as a member of teaching community or as a student, you will be able to understand the other side of truth and others' perception. One has to identify changes in physiological reactions while changing the perspective.

c. **Split entry journal**—Divide a page into two parts, on one hand we have to write actually what has happened, the actual interactions, etc., and on the other hand one has to write emotional responses, physiological changes, and anchoring.

d. **Directed associative journal**—One has to write the how and why of emotional experiences. We have to underline the important words. This is useful for enhancing self-understanding.

e. **Charting the day**—Here, we should prepare a graph of emotions throughout the day. This gives a clear understanding regarding one's emotional life. It indicates patterns of responses and triggers in one's emotional expressions. The mildest and strongest feelings are seen obviously on the basis of the job. If the strongest emotions are negative, then we must try to manage it. If emotional ups and downs depend on time, then activities done at that time should be considered. Even if you take a canvas and colors to indicate your emotional experiences of the day, that gives a feedback.

f. **Speak and feel exchange**—Discuss what you feel and what are the physiological changes associated with them with someone. This skill is essential even for conflict management. The reconfirmation of these should be done by the other person as a feedback. This activity increases awareness about the relationship between mind and body. There should be no evaluation of emotional expressions of others.

g. **Reframing**—It is the ability to manage the interpretation we make regarding events of our lives. This creates emotionally useful stories as or while the incidents in our lives unfold. If someone says to a lady, "This dress suits you," her reaction depends on who said that, in which way, with reference to what, where, and other things regarding context. Ambiguity in any communication leads to negative emotions.

An emotionally literate person accepts the responsibility of his or her own experiences. Emotions are kept aside. They know they can control only themselves. If they do not, they will be facing either positive or negative overwhelming emotions. They think in terms of appropriateness of their frame of reference while interacting with others. Reframing is in a way like rationalization, not for justifying the wrong approach, but for developing healthy intentionality. Sometimes even when the individual's intentions are positive, he or she may not have any positive approach in his or her repertoire. One has to understand the interests of both parties and then try to solve the problem.

If two brothers need the same two-wheeler to go out and there is a conflict regarding it, what can be done is first find out the nature of work. If one of them is going for official work and the other is to go to a friend's house, they can solve the problem by:

a. Inviting the friend to one's house
b. Taking a hired vehicle

c. Dropping the person and bringing him back
d. Changing the timing of informal work.

This flexibility, creativity, and controlling negative emotions are products of emotional intelligence. Empathy and understanding other's emotions and perspective help are also its types.

According to Gardner there are different types of abilities to express ourselves. They are: language, movement, visual images, music, and similar other things. To express our emotional reactions, we can write, draw pictures, dance, make different nonvocal expressions such as screaming, and use combinations of various acts.

Our emotions depend on what we think and how we interpret the events. Hence, one should be capable of controlling emotions. If one interprets the world from others' perspective, then control becomes difficult. Understanding one's emotions and accepting them like, "I was feeling happy, jealous, or irritated" and also understanding its intensity becomes essential. There are people who think that there are certain things that they do not want to do but they do without their wish. That means they give up and let things happen anyway. Actually, the ideal situation is when the individual is capable of managing his or her moods; irradiating negative thoughts, fears, tensions, doubts, and unwanted ideas; learning how to maintain mental health; keeping optimistic attitude; and concentrating on the task at hand.

13.4.2 SENSORY ACUITY AND ANCHORING

If one wants to increase sensory acuity and consciousness about self, one must find out the stimuli playing the role of anchors for arousing different responses. Like a particular type of smell, a particular song, a specific photograph, or some environmental stimulus like rain or wind may be the cause of reoccurrence of a memory, images, emotions, or physical reaction. One may write down all these things in detail like increase in heart rate, tension in neck muscles, etc. After that one has to decide which type of state would be appropriate for such a situation. The basic difference between a naïve individual and an expert is related to this.

Learning to anchor and trigger emotional resource states is, thus, an important skill. First one has to recognize the relationship between emotional ups and downs with changes in voice, breathing rate, speed of talking, and vibration in voice. Then, recognize what changes take place in all these when one becomes angry, bored, irritated, depressed, happy or unhappy, and afraid of something, and what indicators of muscular stress are experienced.

For developing emotional intelligence the following skills are essential:

a. Become emotionally literate. Label your feelings than labeling people or situations.
b. Distinguish between thoughts and feelings.
c. Shoulder the responsibility of your feelings.
d. Show respect for others' feelings.
e. Use your feelings to make decisions.
f. Validate others' emotions.
g. Do not advice, command, control, criticize, and judge others.
h. Practice getting a positive value from emotions.

Learning and enhancing emotional intelligence

a. **Learn to quickly reduce stress**—Like for example, if things are not going on according to your expectations, what do you do? Say if the meeting is delayed and you are wasting your time, do you start blaming others and getting frustrated or become angry? That is not going to help. You should develop an ability to stay calm and control your upsetting tendencies in different situations.

b. **Recognize and manage your emotions**—Identifying and managing various emotions in any unwanted situation helps a lot.

c. **Connect with people with the help of nonverbal communication**—Wise use of nonverbal communication really works very well for staying connected to people. It is a must to recognize which type of nonverbal communication is specifically useful for that and intentionally suing it again and again so that one develops such habit to create a pleasing atmosphere for self and others. For example, your smiling face may reduce a lot of tension between you and your classmates who may not be very friendly with you.

d. **Use of humor and play to deal with challenges in life**—Humor can be used for positive outcomes if it is used in a healthy way. We should not make fun of others and their limitations; however, humor regarding self and our own limitations works better.

e. **Resolve conflict positively with confidence**—Every conflict can be managed positively if we wish to. Everyone has some problems and own perspectives which we may not understand easily; hence, with more efforts we have to accomplish that.

f. **Take responsibility of your own action**—Many a time, we blame someone else for our wrong decisions and problems that we face due to it. We have to shoulder the responsibility of our own deeds and decisions.

g. **Understand how your actions affect others**—When we interact with others we do not think about its effect on others. However, it is essential to understand why people behave in a particular way as they do. It gives a direction to our reactions also.

Socialization process that is conducive to enhance emotional intelligence:

a. Secure environment should be provided to children at home and students in schools and colleges. A lot of threatening and punishment, excessive harsh treatment given to children leads to emotional problems. Freedom to understand and express emotions is hampered. The individual should feel free to analyze and evaluate various experiences and to try to achieve stable self-concept.

b. Care for children is important. If parents and significant adults care for children and adolescents, they also develop a caring attitude. This leads to the enhancement of empathy and general understanding about others' emotions. It also leads to self-respect among them.

c. Adults should manage their anxiety. Many a time, overexpression of anxiety by adults leads to the introduction of similar negative feelings in mind of their offspring. Hence, open expression of such negative feelings should be avoided.

d. Feelings of children should be accepted and acknowledged. Many a time, parents and teachers do not have enough empathy to adjust their emotional state with that of children. They heavily criticize the young ones and ban their every natural feeling. In such a situation, interpersonal relations and faith disappears. Accepting and acknowledging emotions of children results in a feeling of emotional security.

e. Children should be encouraged to accept and express their feelings. Say for example, when a child is feeling upset, frustrated, or overwhelmed, it is essential to encourage the child to express and accept their feelings. At least after a particular behavior is shown, they should be asked regarding the details of emotional experiences.

f. Adults should show empathy while interacting with children. A lack of empathy on the part of significant adults may lead to serious emotional problems in children. If the experiences of a child are not understood, parents may take things for granted and project their own intentions on offspring.

g. Children should not be trained to repress their emotions. If the psychological distance between parents and their children is too much, children will not share their emotions with parents but try to repress them. As a consequence, emotional catharsis becomes difficult and mental health gets affected.

Researchers have suggested the following activities that are capable of managing emotional upsets in a better way:

a. Music and relaxation
b. Dance or outdoor play
c. Meeting friends
d. Shopping or hobbies like reading
e. Intrapersonal communication where one motivates oneself

There are some other activities which are less effective though they are considered as direct stress reduction and tension reduction activities:

a. Drug and alcohol consumption
b. Avoiding the situation or the person that causes a bad mood
c. Passive mood management as watching television or movie, eating favorite food, or sleeping

In real life, it is complex and complicated interaction of various skills that decide whether the individual will be emotionally intelligent or not. A person may fail to make good contact with others simply because he or she cannot understand nonverbal cues.

Though criticized by some psychologist due to alternative approaches, emotional intelligence seems to offer useful insights regarding complex emotions of human beings.

13.5 SUMMARY

Success in life requires emotional intelligence along with other cognitive abilities to perform the task. Understanding one's own and others' emotions is essential for properly interacting with others. There are different subskills that are associated with emotional intelligence such as empathy, communication skills, emotional sensitivity, awareness, and management of emotions. Self-awareness, emotional regulation, and motivation are also linked with it. It reduces impulsive behavior and blaming others, and enhances emotional openness. Emotional intelligence helps to maintain mental health. There are ways and means to increase one's emotional intelligence and every one should try these strategies.

QUESTIONS

1. Discuss the significance of emotional intelligence in human life. Describe the advantages of being emotionally intelligent.
2. Explain the types of emotional intelligence.
3. What are the correlates of emotional intelligence?
4. How can one enhance one's emotional intelligence?

APPLICATION ORIENTATION

1. We can maintain a written record of our own emotional experiences, especially when there is a substantial change in mood we should jot down the exact experience and the cause behind it as per our understanding. Write down the actual event and your interpretation with beliefs and intensity of change in mood.

   It is useful to understand and control emotions.

2. Challenge the beliefs that brought your mood down and think about an alternative belief. Imagine the impact of it on our emotions and its intensity.

3. What do you do when you are emotionally upset? Write down these activities and evaluate if there is any substantial positive change in your mood?

4. If you cannot get along well with someone, write down a conversation thinking that you were the other person and the other person were you. What difference does it make in your perception?

SUGGESTED READINGS

Bowden T. B. (2007). *50 psychology classics*. London: Nicholas-Brealey Publishing.

Caruso D. R., & Salovey, P. (2004). *The emotionally intelligent manager: How to develop and use the four key emotional skills of leadership*. San Francisco, CA: Jossey-Bass.

Doll, E. A. (1935). A genetic scale of social maturity. *American Journal of Orthopsychiatry, 5,* 180–188.

Gradner, H. (1983). *Frames of mind. The theory of multiple intelligence*. New York: Basic Books.

Goleman, D. (1995). *Emotional intelligence: Why it can matter more than IQ?* New York: Bantam Books.

Mangal, S. K. (2002). *Advanced educational psychology*. New Delhi: Prentice Hall.

Mayer, J. D. and Salovey, P. (1995). Emotional intelligence and the construction and regulation of feelings. *Applied and Prevention Psychology, 4*(3), 197–208.

Mayer, J. A., Salovey, P., and Cruso, D. R. (2004). Emotional intelligence: Theory, findings and implications. *Psychological Inquiry, 60,* 197–215.

McLelland, D. C. (1973). Testing for competence rather than for intelligence. *American Psychologist, 28*(1), 1–14.

Piaget, J. (1968). *Psychology of intelligence*. Totawa, NJ: Little-field Adams.

Reevy, G. M. (2010). *Encyclopedia of emotions*. Westport, CT: Greenwood.

Salovey, P. and Mayer, J. D. (1990). Emotional intelligence. *Imagination, Cognition, and Personality. 9,* 185–211.

Thorndike, E. L. (1905). *The elements of psychology*. New York: Seiler.

14 Love and Happiness

Objectives

After reading this chapter, you will be able to:

1. Learn the importance of attachment in human life.
2. Understand the nature of love and types of love.
3. Identify physiological aspects related to love.
4. Know theories of love.
5. Learn nature of happiness and its correlates.

14.1 ATTACHMENT

Sabina is a bright student. She continued her education even after marriage and managed to get distinction for postgraduation. She was eager to join a multinational company though she delivered a baby. She was trying hard and one fine morning got the opportunity, but it was in Delhi which is a faraway place from her home town. Her baby was just six months old when she left him with her in laws and joined the new job. Within just 2–3 months, her baby who was previously nice, healthy, and easy to deal with became cranky, ill, and difficult to handle. The baby was craving for his mother as was comfortably attached to her previously. His weight decreased and immunity went down.

Though the grandmother was taking care of the baby, why was he not happy? Why a stable figure of attachment becomes so important in human life?

It is reported by researchers that a substantial number of children from orphanage die within first two years not due to neglect or unavailability of food, shelter or medicine, but due to lack of one substitute mother and stable attachment.

Research regarding monkeys has proved that monkeys reared in social isolation could not show normal interaction with others. Some of them died, while others were always frightened and behaved in an abnormal manner. Even as adults they could not interact properly with other monkeys.

14.1.2 NATURE OF ATTACHMENT

Attachment has been defined by Bowlby (1969) as a deep and enduring emotional bond that connects one person to another across time and space. It may or may not be reciprocal. It is a bond of affection and loyalty. Adult–child attachment is based on the adult's responding selectively and appropriately to the child's needs. Early infant separation from mother and later maladjustment are correlated. There is separation anxiety in the young ones. In attachment, the expectation is that there should regular contact and interaction with the person concerned.

It is worth noting that attachment is seen in all living beings including human beings. You will be able to see that your pet cat takes care of her young ones and when she is away the kittens are restless.

Emotional security and psychological comfort result from stable attachment in childhood as well as in adulthood. Individuals who are securely attached to their parents in childhood are reported to have stable and satisfactory attachment with their partner in adulthood. From this point of view a strong value system supporting a stable family is essentially important not only for children but also for adults. The Indian family system has been supporting individuals from every perspective and any encroachment on the family values will be detrimental to the mental health of the whole society. In contemporary society, the impact of the Western value system is increasing and premarital as well as extramarital sexual satisfaction is resulting in deterioration of the family system.

14.1.3   TYPES OF ATTACHMENT AND THEIR IMPACT

There is a substantial relationship between the attachment in childhood and the individual's personality in adulthood. The attachment theory says that attachment increases the survival of the babies. Even a normal one-year-old child plays comfortably when its mother is around, but if she goes away, it will get upset and start crying and try to find its mother. Research has shown that securely attached children are upset when their mother leaves, but are easily soothed by her upon her return. Children who are anxious and unusually clingy are very much distressed by the separation. The basic difference is that these babies resist the mother's attempts to provide comfort when she returns and continue crying for a prolonged period of time. This pattern is called ambivalent attachment. The avoidant-type babies are little affected by the absence of the mother at least outwardly, although all physiological indicators show distress, and they actively avoid contact on her return. They ignore her presence and even looking at her as well as ignoring her invitations to interact.

Secure children grow into autonomous adults, ambivalent children into preoccupied ones, and avoidant children into dismissive ones.

Infants' attachment style depends on their parents' style of expression. If the parents are autonomous their children show secure attachment.

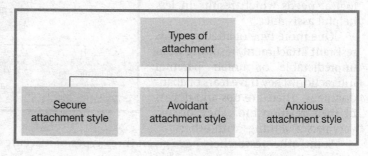

14.1.3.1   *Effects of Secure Attachment*

If we consider an adult who had secure attachment as a child, it is reported that self-acceptance, self-esteem, and self-efficacy are enhanced. Optimism, resilience, and control over emotions result from this style of attachment. Better coping with stress is also related to this style. They describe their love relationships as trusting and happy, and the partner considered a friend. The care that adults give to their romantic partner when the partners need assistance is also related to the secure attachment style. Secure adults tend to provide more sensitive and supportive care while responding to their partner's psychological needs. They are willing to turn to the partner for comfort, and they have satisfying sexual behavior.

Securely attached adults perceive relationships positively, can develop close relations with others, and have trust regarding their romantic relationships. These adults tend to have committed relationships and are less likely to get involved in temporary sexual relations.

Securely attached adults are more satisfied with their close relationships, which results in commitment and longevity. They can get and give support in distress. Autonomous adults are trusting and trustworthy, and are comfortable with mutual codependence. They can solve conflicts conductively. There is less possibility of divorce.

14.1.3.2 Effects of Avoidant Attachment

The avoidant attachment style leads to feeling uncomfortable while getting close to the partners and lack of trust. Such adults like to be independent, keep emotional distance, and withdraw easily. Individuals with an avoidant attachment history in childhood like having demanding, disrespectful, critical parents are anxious about people getting too close. They believe others dislike them and that true love does not exist. Their interactions are full of jealousy, emotional distance, and little enjoyment of physical contact. They may become workaholics or engage in affairs. They experience more depression.

14.1.3.2 Effects of Anxious Attachment

Anxious or preoccupied adults are worried about not getting enough love from their partners. They want to get very close to another person in a romantic relationship. Every moment they want to be with the partner and want his or her full attention. They are more emotional, jealous, and possessive. This leads to irritation for the partner and interpersonal relations are spoiled. Anxious adults are more likely to give compulsive and intrusive care to their partner's psychological needs which results in less helpful assistance.

One more type of attachment is resistant attachment, resulting from unpredictable or unfair parental interaction. They have fears of abandonment. There are ups and downs in their relationship. They discuss very personal things with others.

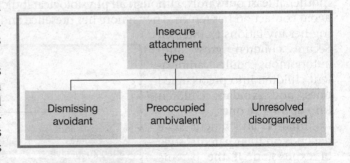

Some other researchers have given three types of insecure attachment:

1. **Dismissing-avoidant attachment**—This is a typical male adolescent attachment style. Here, the individual denies or underevaluates the importance or attachment and rejects attachment needs. The parents and offspring keep a distance from each other which lessens parents' influence. This is associated with violent and aggressive behavior in some adolescents.
2. **Preoccupied-ambivalent attachment**—Here, there is inconsistent attachment experience as the parents are inconsistently available to the adolescent. This results in an attachment-seeking behavior. Conflict with parents and anger is very common in this type.

3. **Unresolved-disorganized attachment**—Deprivation due to the death of a parent or abuse and malpractices by parents results in fear and disorientation in the child's mind. In lower socioeconomic strata where parents are not educated, abusive language and physical punishment are commonly seen.

Psychologists have given two main types of theories of attachment. They are based on what is the most important thing in forming attachment.

Learning or behavioristic theory of attachment given by Dollard and Miller in 1950 puts forth the view that attachment is basically leaned. It is the provision of food due to which the infant gets attached to someone who feeds it. It is simple conditioning through which the comfort of being fed is associated with the person, generally mother. Even otherwise, the caregiver is associated with making the baby comfortable by giving a desirable response when the baby shows signs of feeling uncomfortable like crying. Then, the baby learns to give appropriate responses like smiling and instrumental conditioning takes place that means the baby can change the behavior of the mother.

The other idea in theory of attachment is given by Bowlby (1969). The ability to form attachment is inherent and available since birth and is biologically programmed. It is necessary for survival. Crying and smiling are innate social releaser behaviors which stimulate innate caregiving response of adults. A child initially forms only one primary attachment. This forms a secure base to explore the world. Hence, it affects all future relations. If proper attachment is not formed in early years, it leads to irreversible harmful consequences. This theory is supported by experimental research.

As attachment is related to the potential capacity to love, it is the basic requirement in the emotional life of an individual.

14.2   LOVE

Shailesh was seriously ill due to kidney problem. At the age of 20, he was advised kidney transplant. Everyone at home was shocked. Doctors were hunting for a donor. His sister, Suman, however, was very eager to get the tests done to see if her kidney could be utilized. Fortunately, the doctors declared that it is okay and at the age of 22 Suman donated her kidney to him. In spite of her own operation, she also looked after him and now he is improving. Shailesh is very fortunate that his sister loves him so much.

What motivated Suman to donate her kidney to her brother? Are such bonds always so strong? If not, why?

14.2.1   NATURE OF LOVE

Love is a multidimensional emotion that is essential for human survival and happiness. It is a generalized term to indicate liking and is used to describe various types of love.

Oxford Dictionary of Psychology (2006) defines love as: "An intense feeling of fondness and attraction, deeper and stronger than liking especially when associated with romantic or sexual attachment to someone."

Though generally taken to mean as associated with sexual involvement, love is not necessarily only related to sex. The concept of love includes different shades of emotions. Love is defined as a desire to establish, maintain, or enhance a close relationship with another person or other entity like a pet, a discipline, or a philosophy.

We generally express our love for our mother, our family, our nation, our hobbies, and our most favorite subjects, for example, psychology. It is a wide range of feelings.

Though love generates positive feelings, enhances self-worth, and gives emotional support, various problems in love and love relationships are a significant source of suicides, homicides, and emotional disorders, such as anxiety and depression. Love is important not only because it can make our lives better, but also because it may become a major source of misery and pain that may result in lot of unpleasant feelings.

14.2.2 Types of Love and Their Dimensions

The basic types of love are passionate love and compassionate love.

In late 1970s, the distinction between passionate and compassionate love was proved by researchers. A very well-known psychologist Hatfield and Rapson (1994) put forth the idea that there are two basic types of love: compassionate love and passionate love. Compassionate love is characterized by mutual respect, attachment, affection, and trust. Compassionate love develops out of feelings of mutual understanding and shared respect for one another.

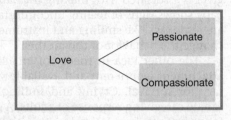

Passionate love is characterized by intense emotions, sexual attraction, anxiety, and affection. When these intense emotions are reciprocated, people feel elated and fulfilled. If it is not reciprocated, love leads to feelings of despondence and despair. Hatfield suggests that passionate love is transitory, usually lasting between 6 and 30 months.

Hatfield also suggests that passionate love arises when cultural expectations encourage falling in love, when the person meets his or her preconceived ideas of an ideal love, and when he or she experiences heightened physiological arousal in the presence of the other person.

Passionate love is equivalent to a state of infatuation. It is often characterized by excitement, moments of exultation, feeling accepted, safe, a sense of union and transcendence, and also by mood swings, anxiety, despair and jealousy. It is commonly believed that falling in love cannot be helped. Passionate love is temporary; the differences between the idealized and the actual become so prominent that they can no longer be ignored.

Compassionate love may be less intense but is lasting. It can be seen to have four elements: being, doing, staying, and growing with the other person. Being with the other refers to acceptance, care, respect, and equality. Doing with the other means having shared goals, activities, and mutual interests as well as doing sometimes involves helping, comforting, and protecting. Staying with the other is based on commitment, intimacy, and closeness. Growing with the other involves transcending one's own interests and a willingness to change. Passionate and compassionate love can coexist.

Ideally, passionate love then leads to compassionate love, which is far more enduring. Whereas most people desire relationships that combine the security and stability of compassionate with the intensity of passionate love, which is very rare.

An evolutionary approach accepts that both passionate and companionate love are helpful for the survival of the species. Passionate love leads to attraction, which can be associated with individuals entering into mating relationships that are relatively long term and lead to successful reproduction. Passionate love helps to develop potentially long-term mating relationships which include selecting the proper person, attracting partners' interests, and relationship-building behavior. It requires many changes in cognition, emotion, and behavior altering the existing activities, routines, and social interactions. It includes sexual desire, joy, jealousy, fear, anger, and anguish.

Affectionate love or companionate love is the type of love where the person wants to be with the partner and have a deep, caring affection for the person. Companionate love, which includes love between parents and the love of parents for their children, increases the probability of survival of the child.

As love matures, passion tends to give way to affection. **Intimacy and commitment are the two important aspects having significant relations with love**. Intimacy is considered as basic and commitment as secondary. Love in long-term relationships is associated with intimacy, trust, caring, and attachment and all these things are necessary for sustaining the relationship. Companionate love is a relationship built on a mutual expectation that an individual and his or her partner will be responsive to each other's needs. Stable marriage is linked to health benefits and a sense of well-being.

You will be able to realize that there are many concepts and theories related to love and it is a fertile field of research. One more interesting model is explained as follows.

14.2.3 THE COLOR WHEEL MODEL OF LOVE

In 1973, Lee compared styles of love to the color wheel. Like three primary colors, there are three styles of love: (a) Eros, (b) Ludos, and (c) Storge. Like colors, emotions can be combined to create different secondary love styles. For example, a combination of Eros and Ludos results in Mania, or obsessive love. Following are Lee's six styles of loving:

1. **Three primary styles:**

   a. Eros—Loving an ideal person
   b. Ludos—Treating love as a game
   c. Storge—Treating love as friendship

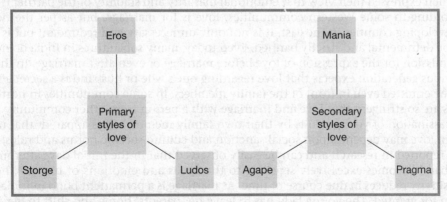

2. **Three secondary styles:**

   a. Mania (Eros + Ludos)—Obsessive love
   b. Pragma (Ludos + Storge)—Realistic and practical love
   c. Agape (Eros + Storge)—Selfless love

In all there are six different styles of love. These are:

1. Manic love is slightly abnormal having love and hate together or fear of getting close to the loved one. It is a combination of anger, jealousy, intense arguments, leaving each other, and intense reunion with passionate sexual exchanges.
2. Ludos is a game of love. It is pleasant and shallow mutual enjoyment. The partners do not need to be, unique.
3. Pragma is love based on pragmatism. Here, love depends on the fulfillment of conditions such as good looks, money, and reputed family. A typical example is arranged marriages in Indian society.
4. Eros is intense, passionate love. Eros is a desire to have, to possess, and to retain. Lack of trust leads to unhappiness and suffering.
5. Storge is the love related to friendship. It is an unconditional love resulting in happiness. Sexuality is not so important in this.
6. Agape is based on sacrifice and selflessness and is concerned with the partner's wellbeing. It accepts, protects, and expects nothing in return.

Romantic love is passionate love, or Eros, which is strongly related to sexuality and infatuation. It is very strong in the early part of a love relationship.

Sexual desire is accepted as the most important ingredient of romantic love. The scientific evidence, however, suggests that they are empirically and functionally distinguishable. For example, recent MRI or magnetic resonance imaging studies prove that romantic attraction and sexuality involve different brain systems.

14.2.4 RELATION BETWEEN MARRIAGE AND LOVE

Is love necessary for marriage? Most college students in the US, Japan, and Brazil think that love is essential for marriage. However, students from Pakistan and India think that it is acceptable to marry without love. Males from China think that good health of the partner is essential and women expressed their view that emotional maturity and stability of the partner is a must.

According to some Western communities, love is for marriage, but as per the norms of some developing counties in the east, it is not only unnecessary and redundant but is considered to be detrimental and strictly banned. Even today, many subcultures in India do not sanction permission for the expression of love before marriage or even after marriage. In the sense, the previous generation expects that love regarding one's wife or husband is a secret affair and not to be permitted even in front of the family members. In some communities in north India, the rules are so stringent that love and marriage with a person from other community leads to even assassination of young adults by their own family members. It is apparent that manifestations of love may depend upon social sanction and culture-specific norms and rules.

It is reported in research and can be easily observed that in the initial days after marriage, the husband becomes excessively sensitive to the needs and emotions of his wife; however, this sensitivity reduces in due course of time. As marriage is a permanent bond in India, things are taken for granted. The young lady has to leave her parents' home and shift to her in laws/husband's house; she is supposed to mold herself according to their expectations.

14.2.5 PHYSIOLOGY AND BIOCHEMISTRY OF LOVE

Research in the field of neurochemistry link between neurohormones and experience of love. For adequate sexual behavior, the normal level of testosterone is essential in both males and females. Dopamine, norepinephrine, and serotonin are more commonly found during the attraction phase of a relationship. Oxytocin and vasopressin are associated with long-term relationships characterized by strong attachments. Serotonin results in infatuation on one hand and produces recurring thoughts on the other. That is why people experiencing infatuation cannot think of anyone else. It is also proved that antidepressants decrease one's ability to fall in love as they suppress serotonin. The long-term attachment after the initial passionate phase of the relationship ends is related to oxytocin. A protein molecule of the nerve growth factor is high when one falls in love for the first time, but these returns to previous levels after one year. Two areas associated with love are foci in the media insula which is responsible for instincts and the anterior cingulate cortex associated with euphoria.

14.2.6 THEORIES OF LOVE

There are many theories of love. Some important ones are:

1. Psychologist Zick Rubin (1973) gave the idea that romantic love is made up of three elements:

    a. Attachment or the need to receive care, approval, and physical contact with the other person.
    b. Caring which involves valuing the other person's needs and happiness as much as one's own.

2. Intimacy or the sharing of thoughts, desires, and feelings with the other person.

14.2.6.1 Triangular Theory of Love

According to Sternberg's Triangular Theory (2004), there are three components of love: intimacy, passion and commitment. Different combinations of these three components result in different types of love. For example, a combination of intimacy and commitment results in compassionate love, while a combination of passion and intimacy leads to passionate love.

According to Sternberg, relationships built on two or more elements are more enduring than those based upon a single component. Sternberg uses the term "consummate love" to describe a combination of intimacy, passion, and commitment. While this type of love is the strongest and most enduring, Sternberg suggests that this is rare. Intimacy has to do with emotions of the sexual component, as well as romance, which is the physical arousal component.

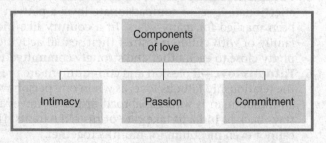

Intimacy is related to tenderness, warmth, concern for others, and the desire for the partner to reciprocate. This level of attraction is never seen in the long run. Passionate love is seen in the beginning of a relationship. It is the courtship period when sexual attraction is the focus point. Sexual attraction gradually decreases afterwards.

Companionate love is formed with intimacy and commitment. Affection, care, and warmth play an important role here. Commitment leads to the survival of the relationship. The expression of wholehearted acceptance of the partner, respecting the partner, and being sensitive to his or her needs enhance it. Different degrees of these three dimensions result in different types of love.

Type of love	Intimacy	Passion	Commitment	Example
1. Nonlove	No	Absent	Absent	Casual interaction
2. Liking	Yes	Absent	Absent	Good friend
3. Infatuated love	No	Present	Absent	Temporary sexual relations
4. Empty love	No	Absent	Present	Arranged marriage staying together for children's sake
5. Romantic love	Yes	Present	Absent	Happy dating but no plans for marriage
6. Companionate love	Yes	Absent	Present	Enjoyable relations even without sex
7. Fatuous love	No	Present	Present	Deciding about long term relations after short term interaction
8. Consummate love	Yes	Present	present	Loving, sexually satisfying long term relations.

In any relationship, each of these dimensions are developed in differing degrees, giving rise to eight types of love:

1. **Nonlove relationship**—If all three components are absent.
2. **Friendship**—A relationship based on intimacy only is a friendship. Here, irrespective of gender, the partners are not involved in any sexual interest.
3. **Infatuation**—According to Sternberg, if passion is the only ingredient, it is merely infatuation. This might happen in an affair or a very temporary sexual relation. Infatuation is often felt as love at first sight.

   Passionate love is often shortlived; it is no wonder that intimate relationships frequently suffer from a lack of longevity.
4. **Empty love**—Based on commitment, empty love is all that is frequently left after the passion has gone.
5. **Compassionate love**—A mix of intimacy and commitment but low in passion is called affectionate love, or compassionate love; a pattern often found among couples who have been married for many years. In a country like India, married couples staying in a joint family or with children restrict their sexual activities to a large extent. However, they feel pretty close to each other and strongly committed to each other.
6. **Fatuous love**—If passion and commitment are present but intimacy is not, Sternberg calls the relationship fatuous love, as when one person worships another from a distance. When an Indian man is working abroad or has to travel all over the world for his duty, his wife stays back in India to take care of his old parents. Here, she loves him wholeheartedly but cannot even meet him for months together.
7. **Romantic love**—Here, both intimacy and passion work together.
8. **Consummate love**—The presence of all three indicates consummate love. Sternberg believes that if a relationship is based on a single element, it is less likely to survive. Consummate love is the relationship best or ideal relationship that is difficult to achieve and to maintain.

Any of the three love features can be associated with either type of love. For example, an individual can feel a sort of passion for a platonic friend—the passion is nonsexual. Researchers have been working to find out the factors responsible for liking each other. We like others who are similar to us, with whom we come into frequent contact, and who reciprocate positive feelings.

14.2.7 CORRELATES OF ATTRACTION

Similarity, proximity, and reciprocal liking are responsible for attraction. Research indicates that attraction is developed regarding those who share our attitudes, backgrounds, and interests. If we are going to the same college or the same coaching class, and have the same subject as specialization, there is every chance that we will be attracted to each other's company.

Proximity means nearness. The greater the exposure one has to another person, the more are the chances to like that person. Those classmates who are staying close by generally accompany each other and interact constantly. This leads to attachment as they know each other very well. Thus, the more someone likes you, the more you will like that person.

Physical attractiveness leads to liking. There are many benefits of being nice—looking in social life, and in interpersonal and intrapersonal relations. Research has demonstrated that good-looking people are perceived as having all sorts of positive attributes including better understanding, better intelligence, good personality, and more competencies. Close relationships are often built through a process of psychological self-disclosure.

14.2.8 GENDER DIFFERENCES

Women believe that emotional security is more important in love than men do.

In traditional Indian culture, there was hardly any importance given to the expression of love in married life. Even without any formal meeting, the groom and bride were supposed to marry according to the decision made by their families. Even after that there was no social sanction for the expression of love and affection. Family bonds were very strong and social pressure used to make marriage a permanent commitment.

It is essential to reciprocate the feelings of one's partner, otherwise the relationship does not sustain. If one partner betrays other's trust, or exploits emotionally or financially, it results in depression, obsessive thoughts, sexual dysfunction, and self-condemnation. If one partner is dominant and forces the other to be submissive, it makes the relation unpleasant. Hence, if one wants to maintain a particular relation, it is necessary to be consistent, honest, caring, and being trustworthy while interacting with the partner.

14.3 HAPPINESS

Yogesh is a juvenile diabetic patient. He is suffering from it since he was two years old. Now he has to take insulin thrice a day. He has learned how to inject it when he was hardly eight years. He is doing his MBA for which he has to stay in the hostel and manages everything on his own. Yogesh is never sad and unpleasant. He is very social and loves all his friends. He enjoys the company of his classmates and hostel mates. Unless he himself tells that to anyone no one can guess that he has some chronic problem and is suffering so badly. Yogesh is happy in his life.

What makes Yogesh so strong to be happy in spite of various health problems? Why some individuals are not happy though they have no substantial problem? What are the factors responsible for happiness and unhappiness?

14.3.1 NATURE OF HAPPINESS

The ultimate goal of human life is achieving happiness. Whatever are the ways to achieve it, everyone wants happiness. Considering this fact, many psychologists are involved in finding out more about it. Happiness means subjective wellbeing. Some students may be very happy to get an opportunity to get training in NCC, but others may feel that it is taxing and boring. It means that the same condition results in happiness for one person but leads to unhappiness in case of another. As a consequence, perception and exact meaning of happiness can be different for everyone. It can be some temporary or short-term achievement such as getting good grades in term-end examinations, meeting a friend after two years, or some long-term positive feelings as getting a good life partner or building a huge house. According to some experts, joy is an immediate positive reaction to a particular event, whereas happiness is the state of positive feeling that is long-lasting. Maximum and intense positive affect and rare negative affect are expected for feeling happy.

There are some behavior indicators of happiness. People often state that they aspire to be happy, and people wish happiness for their loved ones.

Happy people tend to act differently than unhappy ones. Happy people are more sociable and generally behave in a more optimistic way, take more risks, and be more assertive. When an individual is happy, he or she tends to become more outgoing and proactive.

The expression most associated with happiness is smiling. Duchene smiles are true indicators of happiness which involve a smiling mouth, raised cheeks, and smiling eyes. Of course, it is not always true that a person who is happy will smile.

14.3.2 Physiological Changes Related to Happiness

Physiological changes are overlapping with some other emotions and, hence, give an ambiguous picture. Joy leads to slightly increased heart rate; such increase also occurs with fear or anger though with more intensity. When people are either happy or angry, the frontal cortex of the left hemisphere of the brain is more active, Dopamine, a neurotransmitter, may be higher in happy people. Also, endorphins, neurotransmitters which inhibit pain, may be present more in happy people.

Happiness is partially determined by genetic factors. It has been proved in studies of identical twins where the genetic similarity is maximum. Specifically, identical twins reared in different circumstances have very similar levels of happiness.

In 2002, Seligman gave a formula of happiness. It is:

$$H = S + C + V$$

where H stands for happiness, S for a set range. S is a genetically determined level of happiness, which remains relatively stable throughout the lifespan and returns to its original level soon after significant life events. Its contribution in happiness is up to about 50 percent. C is the circumstances which account for about 10 percent. We may or may not be able to change the environment. V is factors under voluntary control. They are intentional efforts of the person which accounts for approximately 40 percent.

Some other researchers were eager to know the components of happiness. They have recently put forth the view that happiness is a product of not material objects, but the feeling of independence, competence, and relating well to others. Young adults mention the fulfillment of their psychological needs as the cause of happiness such as getting a scholarship, a job, or purchasing a house. When their psychological needs are not satisfied, they become most unhappy. Of course, which psychological needs will be prominent in deciding it basically depends on socialization and culture. In self-oriented cultures, it is regarding self and in others, it is a group activity and achievement.

14.3.3 Correlates of Happiness

The personality of some individuals is oriented toward happiness. As we generally experience that some people are always happy. They never have any complaints about the environment.

They interact with others in a pleasant way and are altruistic. Some others are always unpleasant and never satisfied. Some important findings are listed as follows:

1. **Self-esteem**—Happy people have appropriate self-esteem. Particularly in Western cultures, it has been proved. They see themselves as more intelligent and better able to get along with others than the average person. In fact, they often hold positive illusions or moderately inflated views of themselves as good, competent, and desirable. It may or may not be true of other cultures.
2. **Internal locus of control**—Happy people have a firm sense of control. They feel more control of events in their lives. They experience less learned helplessness.
3. **Optimism**—Happy individuals are optimistic. Their optimism permits them to persevere at tasks and ultimately achieve more. In addition, their health is better.
4. **Trust**—Happy people trust others and are perceived as being trustworthy by others. This contributes to a better image in the society and improved interpersonal relations.
5. **Absence of tension and undue anxiety**—Happy people are more relaxed and less tensed. They do not suffer from exaggerated anxiety. This results in better mental health.
6. **Extraversion**—Happy people are found to be more extravert. Hence, they enjoy more social interaction. They are more popular and less lonely.
7. **Hardiness**—Happiness is positively related to hardiness or the capacity to deal with stress and negative experiences. It is the capacity to deal with unpleasant situations in a positive way. It results in better health.
8. **Easy to get along with**—Happy people have welcoming gestures and they get introduced to people very easily. They interact with others in a pleasant way.
9. **Maintaining good interpersonal relationships**—Happy people can easily maintain good interpersonal relations and enjoy good interaction. Their social adjustment is appropriate.
10. **Emotional stability**—Happy individuals enjoy emotional stability as their negative experiences are neutralized to some extent due to their happiness.
11. **Commitment**—It is seen in research that happy people are more committed to a task or a relationship.
12. **Accepting challenge**—Happiness leads to readiness to accept more challenges and deal with them in a better way.
13. **Rich social life**—To be happy we need to spend six to seven hours a day in social settings irrespective of whether the individual is an extravert or an introvert. The most obvious difference between the happiest individuals and others is that happy people have a rich and satisfactory social life. Otherwise, there is hardly any difference in their daily activities.
14. **Relationship with family and friends**—Relationships with family and friends are related to life satisfaction and happiness. Happy people like to be around other people. They tend to have a supportive network of close relationships.
15. **Physical health**—Physical health contributes to happiness as the individual is free to enjoy various activities.

Other correlates are financial security, self-development, getting a good job, faith, and enjoyment of daily activities. Losing a spouse because of either death or divorce and losing a loved job can both lead to long-term decreases in overall happiness.

Rosy has been a very pleasant person right from her childhood. She is motivated and sincere. She always wanted to be economically independent and do a job after she completed her degree in mathematics. She was very happy to get it in a reputed company. Immediately after few months she got married. Due to various responsibilities at home and health problems of her mother-in-law, she had to leave her job without her wish. Rosy became very unhappy and was getting bored at home. There was nothing new, nothing intellectually stimulating in her life. Her sense of happiness decreased to such an extent that now she feels that she is wasting her life and her talents, and that she cannot enjoy anything. Now she very rarely feels satisfied and happy.

14.3.4 MATERIAL PLEASURE

Economic stability is the primary thing essential for happiness. However, that is not all. Money cannot buy happiness in life. You must have seen people who are very rich but not necessarily happy. Money can buy comfort and commodities but not psychological peace and happiness. A student who is very wealthy may not be happy as he or she may not get love and affection of his or her parents or cannot fulfill his or her dream of getting admission to IIT. Happiness is related to the quality of life with reference to an individual's expectations and aspirations and actual achievements.

There is a weak relationship between happiness and many life circumstances that we consider important such as gold, silver, diamonds, cars bikes, huge houses, and children of a preferred gender.

Although some correlates are often considered to be the causes of happiness, they may as well be its consequences. For example, it may be that having good life partners leads to happiness or that those who are happy attract a good life partner. These are interdependent.

14.3.4 DIFFERENCE BETWEEN ACTUAL AND EXPECTED LIFE

Satisfaction depends on the desired state in all spheres of life. The idea of the desired state depends on what the individual expects, what are his or her values and general philosophy of life, and comparison of oneself with others. Culture and general life style of the community also play an important role. Hence, a person who is coming from a low socioeconomic status and who is not very well educated also may be very happy. It depends on general understanding, religious and spiritual standing, and the degree of materialistic tendencies of the individual. There are examples of saints who were very poor but still used to give away everything they own to more needy people.

Payal is a good-looking physiotherapist. She is a motivated person and wants to win every race. She tries to get first rank by hook or crook in every examination or race. Immediately after her graduation, she was appointed in a superspecialty hospital. However, she has never been happy as she knows that two of her classmates are going abroad for further education.

There are different dimensions and different developmental tasks of a male's and a female's life; their happiness may be defined differently. Especially in Indian culture, division of labor is so stringent that they are supposed to achieve totally opposite things in life. In the West, however, men and women generally are made happy by same sorts of activities—but not always. Most of the time, adult men and women achieve the same level of happiness from the same things, such as meeting old friends. But there are some differences. For example, women get less pleasure from being with their parents than men as women generally help their parents and men enjoy a lunch or dinner.

Most people are at least moderately happy most of the time. In both national and international surveys, people living in a wide variety of circumstances report being happy.

14.3.5 CONSEQUENCE OF HAPPINESS

Since centuries, philosophers and theologians are trying to understand the exact nature of happiness. Now health psychologists are focusing on the question by investigating subjective wellbeing, people's evaluations of their lives in terms of both their thoughts and their emotions. In any of the ways, subjective wellbeing is the measure of how happy people are.

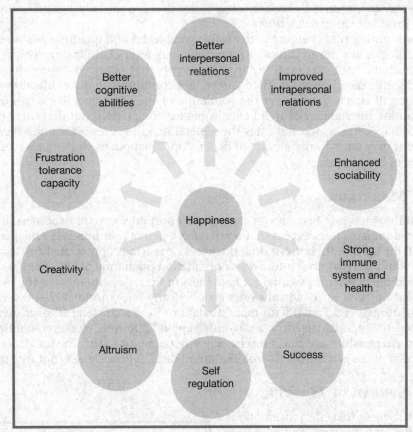

Life satisfaction is one's assessment of one's own life. If the difference between real and deserved situations is more, it is dissatisfaction. If it is negligible, it is a state of satisfaction. Happiness leads to feeling good. Positive emotions and a sense of wellbeing result in:

1. Better interpersonal communication
2. Improved intrapersonal communication
3. Enhanced sociability
4. Health and strong immune system
5. Success
6. Self-regulation
7. Altruism
8. Creativity
9. Frustration tolerance capacity
10. Better cognitive capacities like more focused attention on the task.

As a result of all of these, the individual enjoys longevity. Happiness is comparatively a stable characteristic. It varies due to some major life events, experiences, and changes.

Research has proved that there are no substantial gender differences, race differences, or even economic status differences in happiness. The adaptation theory says that although happiness reacts to negative and positive life events, it returns to the original status shortly afterward.

Like for example, though after winning a lottery the individual's level of happiness increases for a year, it returns back to the original level after that. It is also reported by researchers that after serious injuries in accidents happiness declines initially, but generally it returns back to the prior level after some time.

It is worth noting that even the patients like paraplegics and quadriplegics seem to adjust to their conditions and revert almost to their previous level of wellbeing. This is called the "hedonic treadmill." Some experts say that life events that occurred during the last two or three months influence wellbeing. There are certain conditions that are difficult to deal with and have their ill effects throughout the whole life of the individual like death of a parent. While explaining the stability of well-being, some experts pointed out that there is a general set point for happiness which indicates the general happiness level for one's life. Although specific events may temporarily elevate or depress one's happiness individuals return to their general level of happiness.

14.3.6 MARRIAGE

In Indian culture, marriage becomes an extremely important source of happiness. It is because the traditional Indian values expect that marriage is a permanent bond and the person has to cherish it till the last breath. It means that divorce is not socially appreciated and leads to social stigma. In addition to that, the culture does not sanction premarital or extramarital sex. Hence, getting a good life partner is essential for happiness in life. Specially most of the Indian ladies are dependent on their husbands not only economically but emotionally and socially; their happiness is strongly associated with marital relations. Research done all over the world has shown that marriage usually leads to a rapid increase in happiness. However, unfortunately, it comes down after a while and never reaches the original point again. The incidence of suicide among married males is less than that of unmarried ones but the same is not true for women.

14.3.7 SPREAD OF HAPPINESS

New research suggests that effects of emotions influences the environment and also can spread beyond our immediate social circles to people who are not known to the individual. Researchers have recently studied emotions in a very large group of interrelated people. They found that friends of happy people were 15 percent more likely to be happy themselves, and that the friends of friends of happy people were 10 percent more likely to be happy—even if they did not know the happy person directly. The influence of a happy person could even be found in unknown people who were three degrees of separation away—their friend's friend's friend. They even have proved that people who are smiling in their Facebook photographs tend to have friends who do the same. The social contagiousness seems to be stronger in mutual friendships (Christakis & Fowler, 2008).

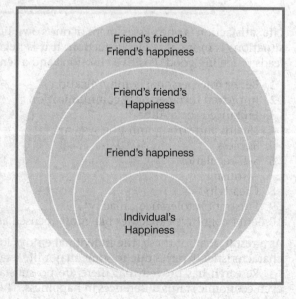

14.4 SUMMARY

This chapter explains the nature and types of attachment, love, and happiness. All these three things are essential for normal and healthy human life. As there is a clear link between love and attachment, childhood experiences contribute a lot to it—directly or indirectly. Love and its quality as well as durability depend on a combination of its various components. It can either increase or decrease an individual's happiness. Physiological changes linked with love are useful for creating a positive psychological output.

Happiness does not depend only on material pleasure or any specific thing. It is a subjective feeling that has to be associated with different things and achievements. There are many benefits of feeling happy which are seen in day-to-day life. If one if happy, one can make others' happy.

QUESTIONS

1. Describe the significance of attachment in human life. What are the types of attachment? Explain the concept of healthy attachment.
2. What are the effects of secure, anxious, and avoidant attachment on the individual concerned?
3. Describe the types of insecure attachment. What are their consequences?
4. Compare and contrast passionate and compassionate love.
5. Describe Lee's six styles of loving.
6. Discuss the physiological correlates of love.
7. What s the role of intimacy, passion and commitment n relationship?

ACTION ORIENTATION

1. Objectively analyze and identify your own attachment style with your parents. Enumerate the consequences according to you.
2. What are the correlates of different expectations about life partner in our culture?
3. Interview five persons each of both the genders coming from different age groups and elaborate the relationship between their happiness and material pleasure.
4. Discuss in detail your experiences regarding consequences of happiness and unhappiness.

SUGGESTED READINGS

Boniwell, I. (2012). *Positive psychology in a nutshell* (3rd ed.). Milton Keynes, UK: Open University Press.

Bowlby, J. (1969). *Attachment and loss* (vol.1). New York: Basic Books.

Christakis, N. A. and Flower, J. H. (2008). Dynamic spread of happiness in large social network: Longitudinal analysis over 20 years in the Framingham heart study. *British Medical Journal, 337*(337), 23–38.

Dollard, J. and Miller, N. E. (1950). *Personality and psychotherapy*. New York: McGraw-Hill.

Colman, A. M. (2007). *Dictionary of Psychology*. New York: Oxford University Press.

Hammer, W. D. (2015). Psychology applied to modern life: Adjustment in 21st century (10th ed.), Las Vegas; Wayne Weiten University of Nevada Las Vegas.

Hatfield, E. and Rapson, R. L. (1994) Love and intimacy. *Encyclopedia of Mental Health* (vol. 2). New York: Academic Press.

Lee, J. A. (1973). *Colors of Love: An exploration of the ways of loving.* Toronto: New Press.

Prior, V., & Glaser, D. (2006). Understanding attachment and attachment disorders: Theory, evidence and practice. Child and Adolescent Mental Health. London: RCPRTU.

Rubin, Z. (1973). *Liking and Loving: An invitation to social psychology.* New York: Holt Rinehart and Winston.

Seligman, M. E. P. (2002). *Authentic happiness: Using the new positive psychology to realize your potential for lasting fulfillment.* New York: Free Press.

Sternberg, R. J. (2004). A triangular theory of love. In H. T. Reis and R. E. Rusbult. *Close relationships.* New York: Psychology Press.

15 | Anger and Fear

Objectives

After reading this chapter, you will be able to:

1. Understand the nature and causes of anger.
2. Know the functions and expressions of anger.
3. Learn the ways to manage anger.
4. Analyze your own anger and causes related to that.
5. Remember the disadvantages of extreme expression of anger.
6. Acquire information regarding the nature of fear.
7. Relate various causes and consequences to fear.
8. Apply the various strategies to overcome fear for daily life.
9. Know the nature of anxiety.

15.1   INTRODUCTION TO ANGER

A man was extremely angry and was throwing things around. He was kicking the door and banging plates and mugs. Simultaneously, he was shouting loudly and finally he broke the window glass with his fist. His hand started bleeding badly and he was taken to the hospital immediately. Aman was blind with anger.

Aman is the only offspring of a very well-to-do family and is overpampered by his parents. Today he wanted a new android mobile phone but could not get the money essential for that. His father was out of station and mother was unable to give him thousands of rupees immediately.

Was his anger justified? What are the consequences of his anger? Was it detrimental to his mental as well as physical health? What are the ways to cope with such a situation?

15.2   NATURE OF ANGER

Anger is an emotion characterized by antagonism toward someone or something which has done something wrong to the individual deliberately.

Anger is a natural, adaptive response to a situation where the individual perceives some threat. Certain amount of anger is essential for the survival of all living beings. Anger essentially helps us to fight back and to defend ourselves when we are attacked.

While understanding the nature of anger, it is essential to understand that various definitions of anger depend on different perspectives of perceiving anger. The most significant ideas that are associated with anger are:

1. Anger is the emotional state associated with a wish to hurt someone (Kalat & Shiota, 2007).
2. As per the functional view, anger is related to self-defense or to the overcoming of obstacles that stand in the way of reaching a goal (Saarni et al., 2006).
3. Anger is experienced when the individual feels he or she can still influence the situation or cope with it.
4. Stimulus response viewpoint specifies that it is typically a response to an unpleasant real or imagined stimulus like threat.

Anger is a drive; it is associated with a compulsion to respond to whatever caused it. It is related to one's psychological interpretation of having been offended, wronged, or denied and is a tendency to react through retaliation. It is a strong emotional response to a perceived provocation. It is an emotion characterized by antagonism toward someone or something which has done something wrong to the individual deliberately.

There are different ways in which anger is classified. It depends upon the intensity, causes, style of expression, and individual's personality related to anger.

Three types of anger are recognized by psychologists. First two types are episodic. These are:

1. **Hasty and sudden anger**—It is connected to the impulse for self-preservation. Humans and animals show it when trapped.
2. **Settled and deliberate anger**—It is a reaction to perceived intentional harm or unfair treatment by others.
3. **Dispositional**—It is related more to character traits like irritability, sullenness, and churlishness.

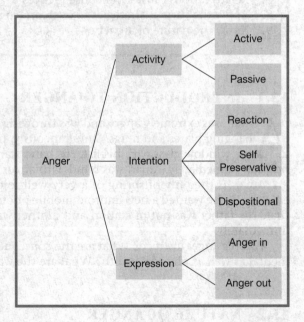

Some other experts have given passive and aggressive anger. In passive anger, the person is aloof, blames oneself, and expects failure. Aggressive anger leads to forceful fast action to harm others. These individuals blame others and neglect others' rights. With reference to intention there are three types of anger. First is when anger is a reaction, second is when anger is utilized for self-preservation, and third is when the intention is dispositional. As far as expressions are concerned, anger in and anger out are distinguished by researchers. In anger out, the expressed anger is oriented toward others and in anger in it is turned inside the individual.

15.3   CAUSES OF ANGER

Why is it that some people become angrier more easily and more frequently?

There are individual differences regarding the causes of anger. It is proved in scientific research that there are individual differences even among young children regarding anger. Some are more irritable and get angry very easily while in the same or similar situation others may not. It is concluded that there are some genetic and physiological causes for anger.

Causes of anger can be divided as internal and external causes:

1. **Internal events**
   It involves thinking and worrying about personal setbacks or rethinking about injustice done by others. Even memories of events when one was angry result in anger. Anger and blame generally accompany each other. However, blaming an individual is not necessary for anger. We may blame the environment as well.
2. **External events**
   For example, a bus conductor who refused to return your change even when it is available, delayed metro train, or blocked roads due to heavy rain.
3. **Gender**
   In Indian culture, male members are expected and accepted to be very prone to anger. It is a socially approved behavior pattern of males. According to them, it is the best way to control family members and subordinate staff. The expression of anger can be used as a manipulation strategy for social influence.

15.4   TYPES OF ANGER EXPRESSION

According to Deffenbacher and Mckay (2000), some people really are more prone to anger than others. They get angry more easily and more intensely. Some others do not show their anger outwardly but are chronically irritable and angry from within. They are grumpy. They do not shout and throw things, curse others, but they may withdraw socially, sulk, or get physically ill more often.

1. **Low frustration tolerance**—Low frustration tolerance or low inconvenience tolerance, or annoyance tolerance are the basic reasons for anger. If the situation is somewhat unjust, individuals get furious.
2. **Remote events**—Anger can be of multicausal origin, some of which may be due to remote events; we generally find only one cause for our anger. Anger experiences are interrelated to environmental stimuli and temporal context. Sometimes some environmental stimulus may not lead to anger immediately after encounter, but may be interpreted in a different way afterward and result in anger.
3. **Perceived intentions of others**—Angry persons usually find the cause of their anger in an intentional, personal, and controllable aspect of another person's behavior. This explanation, however, is based on the intuitions. These intuitions and interpretation of cause–effect relations of the angry person may not be accurate as he or she cannot objectively analyze and evaluate these things. In a way, the angry individual also loses the self-monitoring capacity.

   In older children also thwarting of desires, interruption of activities in progress, constant fault finding, teasing, and unfair comparisons with others are some of the factors resulting in anger.

One leading theory regarding the causes of anger is Berkowitz's (1969) cognitive neoassociationistic model of anger generation. It states that either pain/discomfort or believing that someone has hostile intent toward the individual causes anger. However, generally situations that are unpleasant, unfair, and intentionally caused by someone else lead to anger.

According to the appraisal theory of aggression, the appraisal of hostile intent is necessary for anger, and adding pain or discomfort will increase the anger.

Sara was upset from the morning. She was very angry because of mother's behavior. Her mother had brought a sweater for her which was slightly short. Sara never wanted a short sweater. She started blaming her mother and accusing that she has intentionally brought such a sweater for her. Sara said that she cannot understand today's fashion and is not bothered about her. Mother also got angry and blamed Sara as she is not sharing any responsibility of household chores. Both of them started quarrelling.

Children, especially infants, become frustrated and then angry, then perhaps aggressive, without any appraisal of hostile intent. Most researchers believe that very young children are not attributing blame. However, adults are more likely to add a cognitive component to their experience of anger and more often attribute blame.

4. **Anger expressed by others**—As is commonly observed in day-to-day life anger precipitates anger; it spreads like action and reaction. For example, road rage or quarrels when one is standing in a queue and an individual tries to go ahead, etc.

5. **Biological mechanisms**—Some biological mechanisms are responsible for excessing anger and aggression. Damage to the prefrontal cortex of the brain is linked with increased aggression. It is also reported that imbalance of the hormone testosterone and the neurotransmitter serotonin also cause excessive anger. The part of brain that is activated due to anger is the lateral orbitofrontal cortex.

According to Encyclopedia Britannica, an infection may lead to pain as well as anger. It is also accepted that chronic diseases may lead to decreased frustration tolerance and increased anger with irritability.

15.5 FUNCTIONS OF ANGER

Anger can be a good thing if it is within limits. It gives the opportunity to fulfill the requirements of emotional catharsis. It can give the individual a way to express negative feelings, for example, or motivate one to find solutions to problems.

Anger can be useful even for mobilizing psychological resources and for boost determination toward the correction of wrong behaviors and the promotion of social justice. There are occasions when even unknown people come together and show their anger collectively. In case of a cool-headed crime or the exploitation of environment, activists along with common men express their agitation and grievances. Anger can be destructive when it does not find its appropriate outlet in expression. It can result in destructive display of verbal aggression, possibly permanently harming relationships, or of physical aggression, potentially leading to a serious injury that ruins the lives of both the individuals involved.

15.6 CONSEQUENCES OF ANGER

According to Spielberger (1999), anger is "an emotional state that varies in intensity from mild irritation to intense fury and rage." Anger is a completely normal, usually healthy, human emotion. But when it gets out of control and turns destructive, it can lead to problems—problems at work, in personal relationships, and in the overall quality of life. It results in the feeling that one is at the mercy of an unpredictable and powerful emotion.

1. **Physiological changes**

   Like other emotions, anger is also accompanied by physiological and biological changes. Physiological responses to anger include an increase in the heart rate, preparing the person to move, and increase of blood flow to the hands, preparing them to strike. Perspiration increases when anger is intense. The release of glucose stored in the liver and muscles as glycogen results due to anger. In anger, the pituitary gland also influences testosterone levels, which in turn affect anger again.

   Hormonal problems also result in anger and aggression. Excess testosterone among male members leads to anger and aggression. Premenstrual hormonal disturbances in females also lead to irritation, anger, aggression and anxiety as well as mood swings. Imbalance of the neurotransmitter serotonin is also reported to be associated to anger and aggression. As far as physiological correlates of aggression are concerned, it is reported that consumption of alcohol, amphetamine, and cocaine leads to aggression.

2. **Cognitive effects**

   We generally describe a person who is very angry as being "blind with anger" which obviously means that his or her perceptions are distorted and he or she cannot process the information properly. Anger makes it difficult to think appropriately and is detrimental to one's physical and mental health.

   There are harmful effects of suppressing anger. An angry person can very well be mistaken because anger causes a loss in the self-monitoring capacity and the capacity to observe objectively.

   Anger, in its strong form, impairs one's ability to process information and to exert cognitive control over one's behavior. An angry person may lose his or her objectivity, empathy, prudence, or thoughtfulness and may cause harm to others or self.

   Sunit has lost his money that was given to him for the payment of fees. When his father was told about it, he was furious. He claimed that Sunit must have spent the money for fun. He was not listening to what Sunit was trying to tell and how and where the money was kept. He was just screaming and slapped Sunit. Sunit was extremely hurt and was feeling helpless.

   An angry person focuses attention only on anger-causing events. Anger leads to the anticipation of more things which lead to anger. For example, even if your friend always helps, if he or she fails to do so recently, you may forget about what he or she had been doing but just concentrate on what he or she has done just now. Anger also affects trust negatively, and less positive qualities are seen in the person who is blamed for anger. Correspondence bias or the tendency to blame a person's behavior more on his or her nature than on his or her circumstances results from anger. You may blame your brother for coming late and think that he is irresponsible, when actually it is due to a punctured tyre of his two-wheeler that he is late. Anger generates more negative opinions and prejudices about others.

   Angry individuals process information in such a way that stereotypes become prominent. In anger, superficial impression is focused on and analysis of details is not done. An angry person tends to place more blame on another person for his or her own misery. Once he or she accepts that idea, it again generates more blame on that person. This goes on and on.

   When Anjali wanted to decide about her one-day trip, Leena suggested that she should go to see a nearby museum. When Anjali went there she found that there was no convenient bus or train to go there and things displayed were so old that Anjali was bored. She started blaming Leena for spoiling her day. However, it was her responsibility to ask more about the place before going there.

Anger makes people think excessively optimistically. Even when one hits a door, the possibility that he or she will be injured is completely neglected. Dangers and risks are underestimated, and unfortunate events seem less likely. For example, an angry young man driving with tremendous speed to overtake someone who has insulted him never thinks of the possibility of an accident.

3. **Behavioral changes**

The expression of anger is powerful, including aggressive feelings and behavior. The external expression of anger can be found in body language, facial expressions, physiological responses, and at times as aggression and violence. Humans and animals, for example, make loud sounds, attempt to look physically larger, bare their teeth, and stare.

Anger is not equal to aggression. There is a sharp distinction between anger and aggression. However, excessive anger directly leads to aggressive behavior.

The pain or discomfort resulting from a specific event or evaluation of someone's behavior as hostile may lead to aggressive behavior. There are various levels indicating the intensity of anger leading to aggression. We may think of a verbal aggression between sister and brother, or extreme aggression between two criminals trying to kill each other.

Aggression may be a form of expression of anger but it may or may not be always seen. It depends on the individual's nature, style of anger expression, socialization, and culture. Aggression can be verbal or physical, direct or indirect. It is proved that anger and aggression mutually influence each other. While anger can activate aggression or increase its probability or intensity, it is neither a necessary nor a sufficient condition for aggression.

15.7 EXPRESSION OF ANGER

Socialization process as a whole gives orientation regarding the appropriateness of anger and anger expression. Some cultures discourage it but others do not. If constructively managing anger is taught and practiced by the parents, it enhances the possibility that children will learn the same. If the families have a history of violence and aggression, and do not have conducive emotional communication, anger prevails in children.

Irrespective of cultural differences, facial expressions of anger are universally understood. Researchers involved in cross-cultural research on emotional expression found that people around the world recognize an angry facial expression without fail.

The face becomes flushed and eyebrow muscles move inward and downward. Angry persons fix a hard stare on the opponent. Nostrils flare and jaw shows clenching gestures. These facial expressions are seen even in children. Tension in the skeletal muscles including raising arms and other actions are useful for getting ready for a fight or flight. It generates the feeling of strength and self-assurance.

Hurlock (1980) while considering anger among children, divided responses to anger into two categories. They are:

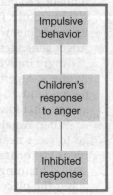

1. **Impulsive behavior.** Impulsive responses include aggressive behavior. You must have seen children hitting others or throwing things when they are angry. Temper tantrums are typical examples of children's expression of anger.

2. **Inhibited response.** These responses are kept under control. Children may withdraw into themselves. They express their anger by acting hurt or being sullen. They show that they are feeling sorry for themselves, or sometimes they express it by threatening to run away.

We cannot express our anger as and when we want to. There are social pressures and limits of socially acceptable behavior, values taught during socialization, and legal restrictions on it. Even if we are very angry, we do not even think of being aggressive while interacting with our grandmother. We either express or suppress our anger. Sometimes one can calm down.

If one can express anger in an assertive way, then that is the best expression as there is no aggression and no harm to others. It is the healthiest way as you respect yourself and respect others.

There are two types of anger expression—anger out and anger in. Anger out is anger expressed against someone, and anger in is anger turned inward that is against oneself. Actually, one should be able to suppress anger and convert it in a constructive manner. If unexpressed anger is turned inward, it may cause different health problems such as hypertension, high blood pressure, or depression. These problems, in turn, result in other problems also such as disturbed interpersonal relations, pathological expressions of anger—such as passive-aggressive behavior and cynical and hostile ways of behavior. Clear indications of such psychological state are putting others down, unnecessarily criticizing everything, and making sarcastic comments.

A true story of a government officer may be useful to understand the consequences of too much anger. He was a very sincere and a strict officer who wanted everyone in the office to work exactly according to the rules and wanted everything to be done perfectly. He used to be very angry in the office and screamed for scolding his subordinates. Once when he was extremely angry and started screaming very loudly, he fell unconscious in the office.

When we do not control our emotions, such thing can happen to us also. When you become angry, one person definitely suffers and that is you. One must find out better ways to deal with anger.

15.7.1 PASSIVE ANGER

Passive anger can be expressed in the following ways:

a. **Dispassion**—There are different indicators of dispassion such as not responding to another's anger; a fake smile; looking unconcerned about important decisions or taking ambiguous stand; getting involved more in machines, objects, or intellectual pursuits; and talking of frustrations but showing no feeling. Evasiveness, paying no heed to others when they are in crisis and need help, avoiding conflict, and not arguing back are clear examples of such anger.

   Rahi and Eshita are roommates in the college hostel. Rahi was very angry yesterday as Eshita went to her relatives without informing her. Today when Eshita was feeling unwell due to stomach pain Rahi did not pay any heed to her. Eshita wanted a tablet but Rahi did not even get that for her. She was comfortably enjoying her music and went for her classes as usual. Actually, she knew that Eshita needs some help when she is not well.

b. **Defeatism**—It is the tendency to give up. Expecting failure for oneself and others, depending on unreliable people, and underachieving, are the examples of such behavior. Underachievement essentially means that a student does not achieve according to his or her abilities and potentials. Those who drive recklessly and are accident prone are in a way practicing defeatism. Such people get irritated and express frustration at insignificant things but ignore serious things.

c. **Obsessive compulsive behavior**—This involves expecting everything as being perfect, extremely clean, and tidy. Some people keep on making sure that things are done properly such as a door is locked, hands are cleaned, and so on.

d. **Psychological manipulation**—This is misusing psychological factors for creating false impressions. Some examples are emotional blackmail. False tears, provoking others to aggression without getting involved in it, intentionally spoiling relations with someone for some advantage like political advantage, and intentionally withholding resources are some examples of the same.

e. **Secretive behavior**—Back biting, gossiping, putting people down, and stealing are a few examples of secretive behavior.

Sudeep was very upset and angry as instead of him Immanuel was selected in the college cricket team. He did not utter a single word in front of the selection committee but started spreading fake information about how Immanuel impressed the committee and used unfair means. He was trying to create an impression that it was injustice to him.

f. **Self-blame**—Always thinking that one's performance and behavior are not up to the mark and devaluating one's worth are related to self-blame. The behavioral patterns seen in self-blame are apologizing too often even without any substantial reason, being overly critical about every minor thing, and asking others to critically evaluate one's behavior.

15.7.2 AGGRESSIVE ANGER

Expressions of aggressive anger are destructive, harmful, reckless, and abusive. Aggressive anger leads to destroying things, as well as human relations. It includes mistrust, showing off, not listening to others, and not considering others' emotions. It is characterized by threatening others, physically hurting people, and exploiting others. Hurtfulness includes physical violence, verbal and physical abuse, sexual abuse, and even rape or murder. Road rage is also one example of aggressive anger.

As is indicated elsewhere, a bright young nurse called Aruna Shanbag from K.E.M. Hospital Mumbai scolded a ward boy for his misappropriation of money. He was very angry and wanted to take revenge. He planned accordingly and attacked Aruna in the changing room when she was completely unaware. His anger took a terrible turn and he raped her and injured her with a dog chain around her neck. She was in coma for more than 42 years.

Blaming others without a substantial reason and getting involved in drug abuse are also considered as expressions of anger. There are some other expressions such as manic and fast speaking and walking or driving too fast, and working too much and expecting that others will also do the same. There are anger expressions which are related to selfishness and not paying any heed to others' needs.

15.8 ANGER MANAGEMENT

There are various ways to manage anger in a conducive way. Following are the common strategies suggested by psychologists:

1. **Acceptance of reality**
   There are many things that cannot be changed in human life. We cannot change our biological parents, complete appearance, blood group, childhood experiences, genetic problems, and past experiences. Say, for example, if a student who is suffering from diabetes starts blaming the parents as being responsible for it, it is not going to change his or her status as being diabetic. May be that the parent were completely unaware of this possibility when the child was born. Sometimes, our anger and frustration are caused by very real and inescapable problems in our lives. There are many problems which cannot be solved at all. One has to accept the reality and find out ways to handle the problems and face the situation properly.

   Hence, it is a must to deeply analyze the causes and consequences of anger and decrease its occurrence.

2. **Mature communication style**

   Angry people tend to jump to a conclusion. In a great hurry and under the impact of anger they act on these conclusions, which may be inaccurate. When we are angry we should not immediately say and do whatever comes to our mind. Thinking coolly, changing perspective while thinking, listening carefully to what the other person is saying, and taking enough time before giving any response are essential for minimizing the ill effects of anger on interpersonal relations.

   Even if someone is being criticized he or she should not feel defensive. Fighting with the individual who is criticizing should be avoided. Trying to understand the real message, with interpretation of verbal, nonverbal, and hidden messages, helps. Objectively analyzing the situation helps to reduce anger, but it requires empathy.

3. **Cognitive restructuring**

   Anger is associated with extreme verbal expression which is unpleasant for others. Such type of communication hurts others, such as abusing and cursing. It is essential to replace these thoughts with more rational ones. Instead of saying, "something is awful, it's terrible, everything's ruined," one has to convince himself or herself that "it's frustrating, and it's understandable that one is upset about it, but it's not the end of the world and getting angry is not going to solve any problem." As far as verbal expression of anger is concerned, one should avoid terms like "always, never" and such other strong expressions. The basic problem is one thinks that his or her anger is justified and that there's no way to solve the problem. This only leads to alienating and humiliating others. A logical and more balanced perspective is essential for defeating anger.

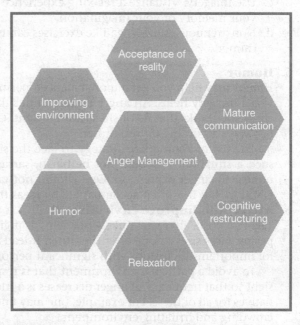

   Generally, disappointment regarding not getting the expected just and fair treatment from others results in anger. One should convince oneself that things always do not happen according to one's wish. So one should say, "I would like something to happen in this way" than "I must get it." Some frustration, disappointment, and hurt are part and parcel of life but getting angry is not the solution. If one is in a situation where others are hostile and competitive, it is difficult to expect fair and just treatment in the group. Some angry people use this anger as a way to avoid feeling hurt, but that does not mean the hurt goes away.

   It is essential to not only control anger out or anger in but constructively manage it. Anger management is very useful to maintain good mental health. The goal of anger management is to reduce both unpleasant emotional feelings and the physiological arousal that anger causes. One cannot get rid of, or avoid, the things or the people that enrage the individual, nor can one change them; however, one has to learn to control one's own reactions. We cannot select our classmates, our teachers, our colleagues, and neighbors. However we have to interact with them irrespective of whether we like them or they behave in a way that irritates us. Actually, one does not have any choice even regarding parents and siblings. You cannot change them but can change your reaction to their behavior and manage your negative reactions. Being too angry leads to out of control behavior, which is frightening also.

4. **Relaxation**

Simple relaxation techniques, such as deep breathing and relaxing imagery, can help to calm down angry feelings.

Some simple steps that you can try are:

a. Breathe deeply, from your diaphragm.
b. Slowly repeat a calm word while deep breathing. It may be something related to a religious idea like "Om" or something relaxing.
c. Use imagery. Visualize a relaxing experience or place where you have been from either your memory or your imagination.
d. Nonstrenuous, slow, yoga-like exercises can relax your muscles and make you feel much calmer.

5. **Humor**

Humor may help you get a more balanced perspective and release the tension. Even funny visual imagery helps. An angry person thinks that things ought to go his or her own way. He or she thinks that he or she is always right. Others are indecent and behave in undignified ways according to him or her.

The use of appropriate strategy to face the situation more constructively is essential in such a situation. It should not be harsh, sarcastic humor, as that's just another form of unhealthy anger expression. One should not take things too seriously. Anger is a serious emotion, but it is often accompanied by ideas that, if examined, may lead to laughter.

6. **Attempt to improve environment**

Taking a break after stressful events helps as it gives breathing time to the individual. If the person faces stresses one after the other, it leads to more anger. Selecting appropriate time for important discussions with significant persons helps to reduce anger.

To avoid a particular environment that is responsible for anger or a particular person or sight so that frequency of anger decreases is a trick that is worth trying. One may find alternatives for all of these. For example, one may find another route or a different shop to avoid crowding and irritating environment.

7. **Professional help**

Sometimes individuals who suffer badly due to extreme anger have to take help of a therapist. Therapies like rational emotive behavior therapy works well in such situations. One has to focus on attribution error. The reevaluation of assumptions and understanding all aspects of a given situation helps. Regular training in relaxation and cognitive restructuring also are recommended. The most obvious thing is to be objective and evaluate one's behavior. In 2010, Fernandez gave a new therapy called the cognitive behavioral affective therapy (CBAT) to deal effectively with feelings of anger in three phases of treatment: prevention, intervention, and postvention dealing with the onset of anger, its progression, and the residual features. There are some technics to manage physiological effects also. Heart coherence training teaches participants specific mindfulness and biofeedback techniques to shift their heart rhythm which stabilizes the autonomic nervous system. Coherence techniques also reverse the negative effects of anger on the immune system. Hence, it is very effective.

8. **Constructive change**

Anger is an emotion that can motivate constructive behaviors, such as standing up for one's rights.

Lokesh was always being harassed by some of his classmates as he was meek and weak. He was very unhappy about it. Once he was insulted in front of the whole class and became very angry. He then decided to fight back. He started going to gymnasium and discussed his problems with the college counselor. Then, he started improving his style of communicating and interacting in the group. After a month's time, he became so assertive that he could easily find an opportunity to improve his image and stand for his own rights.

One should channel anger constructively. Stress inoculation training is a way to do this. It involves the following main steps:

1. **Learning how to relax with deep relaxation techniques**—It involves progressive muscle relaxation in which one progressively tenses and relaxes muscle groups throughout the body and visualization of a special place in which you can relax such as the beach, the woods, or on top of a mountain.

2. **Developing an anger hierarchy**—This is related to an individual's perception regarding situations resulting in different levels of intensity of anger which have equal difference from each other.

3. **Producing stress-coping thoughts for anger**—Two types of thoughts are responsible for anger:

   a. *Should statements:* These indicate that someone else has done something wrong or has violated rules or norms and due to that the individual is suffering. Something wrong happens with the individual. However, it depends on the individual's understanding and attribution style. Behavior that is fair according to an individual may be unfair for the other. An individual generally does something that is good for them than what is fair.

   b. *Blaming statements:* An angry individual thinks that someone else is responsible for his or her suffering. Someone else is hurting the individual on purpose. The person has to vividly visualize the stressor. Both psychological and physical tension should result. Then, self-relaxation and other coping resources to cope should be used.

As anger is associated with aggression, harsh language, violating others' rights, and disturbed interpersonal relations, we cannot encourage any tendency to experience and express anger. In a country like India many male adults are known for their extreme anger. They also take pride in that and enjoy the way they control others. It not only affects interpersonal relations but affects individual's own heath—mental and physical. It is worth noting that most of the crimes result from extreme anger such as road rage, marital discord, dispute among friends, or murders. Hence, parents and society at large should not reinforce these wrong and detrimental emotions while socializing the child, and adults should not play a role model for anger.

15.9 FEAR

15.9.1 NATURE OF FEAR

Ranjeet was playing on the ground with his friends. Suddenly a huge snake came there and Ranjeet saw it. He screamed loudly and started running toward the college building. He was so afraid that he did not even bother to collect his sack having valuables in it.

Fear plays a very important role in human life. Actually, it is essential for the survival of all living beings. Hence, even the lower level species experience fear. Fear is omnipresent and is experienced by everyone irrespective of age, gender, education, socialization, culture, and the like. It may be a functional reaction, leading to life-saving behavior, or dysfunctional, as in experiencing a phobia. Fear is seen in all species and often looks highly similar from one animal to the next.

Epstein (2013) described fear as an "avoidance motive." The individual may fight or flee, unless there is some impediment to these actions, and the fear can be resolved.

Fear is an emotion induced by a perceived threat. It is a basic survival mechanism occurring in response to a specific danger. In short, it is the ability to recognize danger leading to an urge to confront it or flee from it. Fear is frequently related to the specific behaviors of escape and avoidance. Fear almost always relates to future. It can also be an instant reaction to something presently happening. A lot of research has been done and is being done on fear.

Deena was to present her research paper in a national conference. Everyone was praising her as her paper was accepted though she is a student. Deena, however, was very upset and worried about the presentation. She is afraid of standing in front of the audience and presenting a paper. She went to the conference but was freezed with fear and could not present her paper.

Emotionally, fear is unpleasant. Behaviorally, there may be an immediate freezing, a startle reaction, or the person may become still and quite. A startle reaction may involve jerking of body or limited response tendency. During experience of fear, the individual becomes vigilant and attends closely to the potential danger. Thus, perceptually, fear is alertly focusing attention on the object related to fear.

With age, the nature of fear changes, that is, from specific fears to general fears. A very well- known developmental psychologist Hurlock has mentioned that among older children, fears are concentrated on supernatural powers such as ghosts or remote dangers like unknown unexpected danger which will destroy the whole world as expected tsunami or earthquake; on real or imaginary creatures associated with dark; on death and injury; on storms, thunder, and lightning; and on characters recalled from fictions and television.

As children grow, they can manage reactions to sudden fear arousing stimuli. Overt fear responses are suppressed by social pressure. Shyness, embarrassment, worry, and anxiety are some fear-related emotions. Common fears even in adults are fear of failure, being ridiculed by others, and being different from others.

In day–to-day life situations, people are afraid of public speaking, swimming, flying, blood, accident, death, and many more things. The fear of death motivates religious commitment. It is proved that religious people are less afraid of dying.

There is also the fear of the unknown in future. Many people are too scared to take the path they want to because of the thought what will happen tomorrow. The fear of uncertainty also is very common. Teaching children and students as to how to manage the risk is more important than teaching them to avoid the situation leading to uncertainty.

15.9.2 Causes and Consequences of Fear

1. Fear conditioning

Anuja is a five-year-old normal girl who is afraid of cockroaches and lizards. As soon as she comes across any such stimuli she screams loudly and starts running around in agony. When Anuja was two years old and playing in a kitchen while her mother was cooking, she saw a big cockroach that was flying. Anuja's mother was terrifically afraid and she started screaming loudly and forcefully running to the other adjacent room. In the meanwhile, the cockroach came and sat on her sari. She was extremely upset and started using all her energy to get rid of the cockroach. Anuja was observing all these things and she also started screaming loudly thinking that something horrible is going to happen.

This is a simple example of classical conditioning where two stimuli are associated only because they are taking place one after the other. The individual reacts similarly to them. This may happen unconsciously or without awareness.

Most of the fears are learned. A baby who is a few months old plays with a snake without any fear. A very well-known example of research regarding how children learn fear was given by Watson (1925) approximately hundred years ago. Emotional reactions are learned by the procedure of classical conditioning.

Classical conditioning occurs when an organism associates two external stimuli and, therefore, learns to react very similarly to these two stimuli. A study conducted on little Albert (1920) demonstrated that an emotion could be conditioned in an infant. Watson and Rayner took the nine-month-old Albert who was not initially afraid of the rat and used to play with it. Next, the researchers presented Albert with a stimulus that he naturally feared—a loud noise produced with the help of a drum and presented with the white rat simultaneously. The loud noise and the rat were paired and presented to Albert several times. Albert cried during these conditioning trials. After seven pairings of the noise and rat, Albert began to cry and demonstrated other fear behaviors when only the rat was presented without noise. Albert learned the fear and after generalization of the fear he was afraid of all furry animals and men with white beard. Likewise, one can introduce fear in a child's mind or unknowingly be the cause behind the fear.

There are many parents in various communities in India who introduce some fear in the mind of a child just to control its behavior.

2. **Phobia and traumatic experience**

Phobia is intense persistent, irrational and recurrent fear of a specific object, place, or situation that results in a compelling desire to avoid the dreaded place, activity, or situation. The fear that one experiences is intenser than the stimulus can otherwise evoke. Agora phobia is the most common phobia. In this case, the individual is afraid of unfamiliar places, public places, crowded places, or any place where there is no easy escape. The individual is afraid of all these places to such an extent that he or she prefers to stay back at home and becomes overdependent on some family member.

Extreme fear or phobia can be a result of a traumatic experience, for example, the fear of heights—acrophobia; enclosed spaces—claustrophobia; or water—aquaphobia. Zoophobia or fear of animals and phobia regarding illness and medical treatments are some common types. Many more types are reported by psychologists.

Chinu is just six years old, but he has developed aquaphobia. He avoids any waterbody and hates any situation near a water reservoir. He used to go for swimming classes and enjoyed swimming. But, just on the ninth day, his foot was held up due to some gap in the stones when he was approximately under water. He was extremely afraid and could not even scream. Fortunately, he was rescued by some unknown person. He was terribly frightened and could not breathe properly. He was pretty upset and started crying loudly. He cannot forget this traumatic experience. As so now he cannot even tolerate the sight of a bucket full of water and even his bath becomes a problem for his mother.

3. **Physiological consequences**

Physiologically, fear is an activation of the sympathetic nervous system, preparing the individual to fight or flight. Heart rate, blood pressure, and respiration all increase; stress hormones are released, energy is mobilized, and a number of other changes occur in the body.

If the process of fear is considered, the thalamus collects sensory data from the senses. Sensory cortex receives data from thalamus and interprets it. Sensory cortex organizes the information for dissemination to hypothalamus, which may be fight or flight orientation, information from amygdala about fear, and memory from the hippocampus.

The brain structure that is related to fear is amygdala that is located behind the pituitary gland. In the presence of a threatening stimulus, amygdala generates secretion of hormones that influence fear and aggression. Damage to the amygdala can render an organism unable to learn new fears through conditioning.

Observing the fear in others may also lead to extreme fear. Amygdala is affected both by experiencing a threat or observing it for others.

Once response to the stimulus in the form of fear or aggression commences, amygdala may elicit the release of hormones resulting in alertness and enhance the ability and readiness to move, run, or fight.

Some of the hormones involved during the state of fight or flight include epinephrine, norepinephrine, and cortisol. Hence, increase in the heart rate, blood flow to skeletal muscles, blood sugar level, and metabolism rate results. Particular brain chemicals, such as the chemical messenger gamma-aminobutyric acid (GABA) that inhibits firing of neurons, are involved in fear.

Storing this memory leads to long-term effects and results in various disorders related to fear. While fear is generally considered unpleasant, some people seek a temporary thrill in things that are scary (e.g., roller coasters and horror movies). These things may cause some degree of fear, but people generally do not perceive them as actual threats to life or limb. Risk-taking is also associated with adrenaline balance.

Aphobia is a temporary loss of fear due to some intense wish or aspiration of achieving some more important thing; like a mother will run in the fire to save her child.

15.9.3 OVERCOMING FEAR

1. **Exposure therapy**
   Fear is more complex than just forgetting. We have to follow an active confrontation of fears over and over again. By confronting fear successfully and safely a person can suppress the fear-triggering memory. This is called exposure therapy; this practice can help cure up to 90 percent of the general fears.

2. **Systematic desensitization**
   As fears can be introduced with the help of classical conditioning, they can also be reduced with the help of classical conditioning. Systematic desensitization is a treatment for phobias. Here, people are taught through classical conditioning to associate the feared object or situation with something pleasant. After conditioning, a lack of fear will occur when the individual is exposed to a previously feared object or situation. Classical conditioning can also be used as treatments for addiction, obsessive-compulsive disorder, eating disorders, behaviors associated with autistic spectrum disorders, and other disorders.

Behavior therapy called systematic desensitization was developed by Wolpe in 1958 for treating phobias or extreme fears. This technique involves learning how to relax while gradually being exposed to a feared object or situation.

If a child is extremely afraid of snakes, and starts showing fear response even after thinking about snakes, systematic desensitization can be used:

1. First, the child is trained to relax.
2. Then, it is told to rate least feared to most feared situations including snakes.
3. Then, it is told to pair relaxation with hierarchically increasing fear situations.

With young children we can introduce some sweets or ice cream for inducing a pleasant relaxed mood.

For example, while dictating some stories about snakes a chocolate can be given to the child. Afterward, a photograph or a documentary can be shown to him or her while he or she is enjoying his or her favorite chocolate, and then finally a scary scene can be shown. Gradually, the child can be shown a snake in a cage kept in the farthest corner of a room and then the distance can be decreased by and by. The child can then be allowed to touch the snake constantly being paired with some very pleasant stimuli. Finally, the child will show no fear when he or she is to handle the snake, or when the snake is placed around his or her neck. Repeated sessions are necessary.

15.10   ANXIETY

Many researchers distinguish fear from a related emotion, that is, anxiety. Both emotions involve a perceived threat. With both, the reaction itself includes a subjective experience that is unpleasant and a physiological response. The two emotions differ in a few ways. First, fear involves a clear stimulus: something potentially threatening happens and the individual reacts with a fear response. **Anxiety is more general and diffuse. When someone is anxious, there is a dread about something that could happen or that is about to happen, or the person may not even know the source of the anxiety.** Researchers have stated that fear is associated with coping, whereas anxiety means a failure in ability to cope.

With anxiety, threat is perceived but the arousal is undirected and avoidance or defensive reactions do not clearly resolve the emotion.

Fear and anxiety have overlapping but somewhat different physiological reactions and somewhat different physiological mechanisms. The experience of fear involves an acute fear response (e.g., increased heart rate) when an eliciting stimulus is present. However, in anxiety relatively high resting sympathetic nervous system activity is seen but may react less intensely to acute stressors. Additionally, while the amygdala is clearly involved in fear, the stria terminalis, a part of the brain, may be more directly involved in anxiety.

Distinguishing between fear and anxiety is necessary for the understanding of the variety of anxiety disorders. On the basis of the behavioral and physiological responses associated with them, specific phobias—for which a clear stimulus is present (i.e., dog phobia, aquaphobia, and claustrophobia)—are fears. Generalized anxiety disorder and panic disorder more closely resemble anxiety. Posttraumatic stress disorder and social phobias have elements of both fear and anxiety.

Test anxiety is related to unhappiness and insecurity. Anxiety requires imagination and thinking about something that is not available to the senses. It develops in early school years and tends to increase during middle school years. Anxiety is related to depression, nervousness, irritability, mood swings, restless sleep, quick anger, and increased sensitivity to others' remarks and reactions. There are examples of very bright students getting extremely upset at the time of oral examination or viva. It is a specific situational anxiety. It affects physical and mental efficiencies. Examination is associated with some danger. It basically is a sort of irrational fear which depends on the examinee, examiner, and other stimuli present at the time of examination.

Relaxation technique, diary method, autosuggestion, systematic desensitization, and meditation help to overcome such fear.

If you think that anxiety is detrimental to performance and so no anxiety will lead to better performance, it is not true. For example, Salil has his final year engineering examination next month. He is very much relaxed and has not yet started studying. He is enjoying life and wasting his time. He is just not bothered about anything. Salil has no stress no anxiety.

What do you think will be his performance like? There is an inverted U-type relationship between anxiety and performance. It means that too much and too little anxiety leads to poor performance.

15.11 SUMMARY

Anger is one of the universal emotions in all human beings. Anger results from perceived unfair treatment given by others. It is useful as self-defense and emotional catharsis. There are different types of anger. Anger differs in intensity and frequency. If it is not managed properly and goes beyond limits, it is hazardous to the individual and to others.

There are many ways and means to manage anger. If managed in a conducive manner, anger is not harmful.

Fear plays an important role in human life as it saves the individual from danger. Most of the fears are learned through socialization. Learning by observation and by conditioning is the major source of learning fear. Phobias are irrational fears where fear is disproportional to actual danger. There are ways to overcome fear and phobias which are proved to be very effective. Anxiety and especially test anxiety is a major cause of emotional disturbances. However, some anxiety is necessary for optimum performance.

QUESTIONS

1. Explain the nature of anger.
2. Describe the causes of anger.
3. What are the different types of anger?
4. What are the physiological consequences of anger?
5. Discuss the emotional disturbances caused due to anger.
6. What are the ways to manage anger?
7. Explain the nature of fear. What are its functions?
8. Discuss the causes of fear.
9. Describe the physiological correlates of fear.
10. What are the ways to overcome fear?
11. What is anxiety? Explain the nature of test anxiety.

APPLICATION ORIENTATION

1. Make a list of incidences when you suffered from anger during the last month. What are the precipitating factors according to you? With whom were you interacting at that time? Discuss regarding their perspective if they are your family members or friends. Analyze the difference between your perspective and theirs.
2. Write down a diary regarding how many times you express your anger aggressively and how many times you kept quiet but were disturbed from within. What are the differences between the two types? Why there is more aggressiveness in some types of interactions.
3. Describe your mood immediately after you have experienced intense anger. Explain your bodily changes and their consequences.

4. Practice anger management techniques given in this chapter and see the difference in your intensity of anger.
5. Write down the childhood memories regarding different fears that you have experienced during that stage.
6. Give two examples of how you have learned some fears by conditioning.
7. Try different techniques of overcoming fear and find out how effective they are.

SUGGESTED READINGS

Berkowitz, L. (1969). Frustration aggression hypothesis revisited, In Berkowitz, L *Roots of Aggression*, Atherton press: New York.

Deffenbache, J. L., and Mckay, M. (2000). *Overcoming situational anger and general anger: Client Manual*. Oakland, CA: New Harbinger Pub.

Epstein, M. (2013). *The trauma of everyday life*. London: Penguin books.

Fernandez, E. (2010). The angry personality: A representation on six dimensions of anger expression. In G. J. Boyle, D. Matthews and D. Saklofske (eds), *International handbook of personality theory and testing* (vol. 2, Personality measurement and assessment, pp. 402–419). London: SAGE.

Hurlock, E. B. (1980). *Developmental psychology: A life span approach*. New York: McGraw Hill.

Kalat, J. W., and Shiota, M. N. (2007). *Emotion*. Belmont, CA: Wadsworth Publishers.

Lewis, M., Haviland-Jones, J. M., and Barrett, L. F. (eds.). (2008). *Hand-book of emotions* (3rd ed.) New York: Guilford Press.

LeDoux, J. (1996). *The emotional brain: The mysterious underpinnings of emotional life*. New York: Touchstone Books.

Saarni, C., Campos, J. J., Camras, L. A., Witherington, D., Eisenberg, N., Damon, W., and Lerner, R. M. (2006). *Social, emotional and personality development* (6th ed.). Hoboken, NJ.

Spielberger, C. D. (ed.). (1972). *Anxiety: Current trends in theory and research* (Vol. 2, pp. 291–337). New York: Academic Press.

Spielberger, C. D. (1999). Professional manual for state-trait anger expression inventory-2. Odessa, FL: Psychological Assessment Resources.

Watson, J. B. (1925). Behaviorism. New York: Norton.

Watson, J. B., and Rayner, R. (1920). Conditioned emotional reactions. *Journal of Experimental Psychology, 3*, 1–14.

Wolpe, J. (1958). *Psychotherapy by reciprocal inhibition*. Palo Alto, CA: Stanford University Press.

16 | Stress

Objectives

After reading this chapter you will be able to:

1.   Understand the nature of stress and its reasons.
2.   Explain the relation between demand and coping.
3.   Introspect about the causes responsible for stress.
4.   Learn about the effects of stress: physiological and psychological.
5.   Understand strategies to manage stress.
6.   Find out how effectively you mange time and the strategies to improve it.

16.1   NATURE OF STRESS

Chaya is appearing for the final examination of pharmacy. She is studying very hard and aspiring to get a good rank in her final year as she wants to get a job in a reputed company. Her father, however, wants her to take a final decision about marriage within a week's time. She actually is not interested in getting married till she becomes self-sufficient. The pressure from her family is increasing day by day. Her parents want her to get married before her examination. That creates a lot of stress in her mind and she cannot even sleep properly. While studying she cannot concentrate and she gets disturbed due to all this.

Why is stress so difficult to tolerate? What are its psychological and physiological effects on an individual? How to deal with stress? These are the important questions that one should be able to answer in order to lead a normal life.

Let us deal with these issues in detail.

Most of you must have experienced a lot of nervousness just before you enter the examination hall or for the viva of your practical examination. A dry mouth, stretched facial muscles, an unsteady breaking voice, tension in the neck and shoulders, sweating, a frequent need to go to washroom, and on top of it the inability to recall the lessons the lessons you have learned properly are nothing but results of stress.

As each one of us faces new challenges every now and then, stress should be considered as a natural outcome of day-to-day life. Stress is essentially an unavoidable part of human life. Hence, it is the most common fact. Stress affects all individuals irrespective of age groups, marital status, castes, creeds and communities, educational background, and gender. It is an inevitable result of interaction between the individual and the environment. Stress is tension from extraordinary demands, constraints, or opportunities. If one is experiencing a lot of stress for a substantial period of time, then the capacity of the individual to tolerate it reduces. There is a continuous change in the environment and one has to survive it successfully. So, it is an adaptive response by the body to changes in the environment. Minor stresses experienced frequently may lead to their exerting a cumulative effect. If stress is managed properly, it helps performance; however, if neglected, it may take a toll of not only efficiency but human life as well.

Generally, stress is defined in terms of an unpleasant experience. It may result from experience of too much or too little pressure, feeling frustrated or bored, being in a situation that one is not capable of handling and controlling, and various kinds of failures, bereavement, and disharmony. Actually, these cause distress. Stress also results from pleasant, exciting, stimulating, and thrilling experiences. Some people intentionally invite a challenging situation and are capable of handling the same. They enjoy interesting, stimulating tasks, and being creative, and productive. This is eustress. The experience of stress is different for everyone. What is eustress for one person may be distress for the other. For example, a parachute jump may be threatening for one college student but may be thrilling and exciting for the other. It is because of their assessment of the demands of the situation and their ability to deal with it.

Stress can be broadly defined as responses of individuals to circumstances and events called stressors that threaten them and tax their coping abilities.

Lazarus and Folkman (1984) have discussed stress as an internal state which can be caused by physical demands on the body or by environmental and social situations which are evaluated as potentially harmful, uncontrollable, or exceeding our resources for coping.

16.2 RELATION BETWEEN DEMANDS AND COPING

Stress can be defined as a stimulus or a response, or as a whole spectrum of interacting factors.

When there is a mismatch between perceived demands and perceived ability to cope, it results in stress. In day–to–day life situations when routine activities are being done, one is in the normal zone and there is no stress. Imbalance between demands and coping resources occurs in two ways:

1. Alteration in the perceived nature of demands.
2. Change in the perceived ability to cope.

When the fluctuations in demands and coping resources are within a particular range, it is the normal zone of stress. In some other situations, if demands are more than the perceived ability to cope, distress increases. When this ability to cope outweighs perceived demands, it is an eustress zone. This is a desirable situation. It gives rise to confidence, and the feeling of being in control and being able to handle the tasks, challenges, and demands. The person becomes alert and

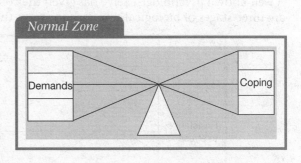

gives appropriate mental and physical responses. However, if perceived coping abilities increase further as compared to demands, boredom, frustration, and distress are experienced.

After Sunita did her degree in engineering, she got married. Due to family responsibilities, she had to stay back at home and forget about her career which she enjoyed greatly. Sunita hardly had any time for serious reading, hobbies, and any new intellectually stimulating activities. She experienced a lot of apathy, boredom, and lack of motivation. She thought she was wasting her life and that others had surpassed her. She felt helpless and perceived her self-worth to be very low.

The obvious example of educated housewives who have been doing a lot of academic work and intellectual assignments in the past, and subsequently stay back at home without substantial cognitive stimulation, will be enough to understand distress zone two. They are in charge of the household jobs which require comparatively less cognitive stimulation, and this leads to cognitive deprivation. The effects of cognitive deprivation are such that the cognitive efficiency of the person decreases and after a few years their intellectual ability decreases as well. It is reported in research that if a lady stays back at home for 10 long years, her intelligence quotient decreases by 20 points. Distress can result from experiencing too few demands and

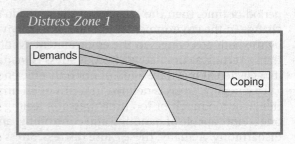

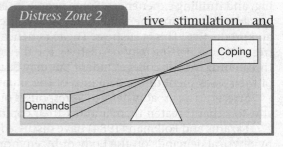

results in boredom, frustration, and poor self-esteem. This distress is equal to the distress when there are too many demands and limited time. Many people experience this type of distress when they retire. They are working full time for many years till the time they retire, and suddenly have to stay at home from the day of retirement. To understand this balance, one needs to reappraise how one perceives and interacts with his or her environment. Learning the skills to alter the balance becomes important to deal with stress. If demands are less, one may increase some demands, and if coping strategies are incapable of meeting the demands, one should learn more skills to cope with the situation.

16.3 GENERAL ADAPTATION SYNDROME

A well-known psychologist Selye has given the concept of general adaptation syndrome. There are three stages of biological reactions to stress, they are: alarm, resistance, and exhaustion.

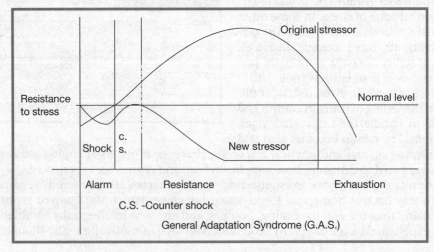

First is the alarm and mobilizing stage. It leads to a shock which results in a drop in blood pressure and depressed body temperature, and affects muscle tone. This is the stage when we are not ready for resistance. After this stage, conditions such as alertness and tension are heightened. In the second stage, which is called the resistance stage, hormonal substances and glucocorticoids or blood sugar increase. If it happens very frequently, further damage takes place. The ill effects of fighting these conditions are seen. One uses extra energy during this stage. As a consequence, in the third stage, which is an exhaustion stage, one experiences a lot of fatigue, anxiety, and depression. In extreme cases, death occurs.

A simple example is if an individual is working overtime for many months, the adrenaline levels go up. This directly leads to biophysical problems and emotional disturbances.
If after such extreme exhaustion, there is one more stress-creating situation, the person becomes too tired and fatigued to resist.

Stress is a nonspecific reaction of the body to the demands made upon it. It includes various physiological reactions. If we are confronted by an actual life-threatening situation like car out of control or someone attacking us or a snake next to us, our body gives an emergency response or an alarm reaction. It is a flight or fight response. Many doctors and researchers believe that the activation of stress responses, without physical activity for which the body is actually ready, can be potentially harmful for health. The consequences of this response are an increase in blood pressure, heart rate, and respiration rate; release of adrenaline; and increased muscle tension. It is also accompanied by decreased digestive functioning. This response is not appropriate to deal with long-term threats and demands. It requires a continual adjustment over a relatively long period of time. This is called resistance reaction. In this case, the threats are not immediate and directly life threatening but are challenges to our personal security and well-being. An example of this would be coping with a situation something like the death of a spouse or a chronic disease such as thyroid imbalance or diabetes. The whole life of the individual gets affected. Hence, the individual has to put in extra effort to adjust to the demands. These long-term demands may include maintaining one's own and one's family members' well-being, and interpersonal relations. One can interpret the situation in three ways. These are:

1. "I can cope with this situation"—Here we are in the normal zone of stress.
2. "I am not sure whether I can cope with the situation"'
3. "I can't cope with this situation"—The last two lead to distress and fight or flight or resistance response.

In a way an individual may be disturbed not by things but by views they develop regarding these things. Demands, coping, and stress responses are related to each other along with inherited factors, personality, and health on the one hand and education, experiences, beliefs, attitudes, expectations, and needs on the other.

16.4 TYPES AND CAUSES OF STRESSORS

There are five types of stressors:

1. Environmental
2. Behavioral
3. Cognitive
4. Emotional
5. Physiological

Factors involved in stress are of different types. They are illustrated in the following figure.

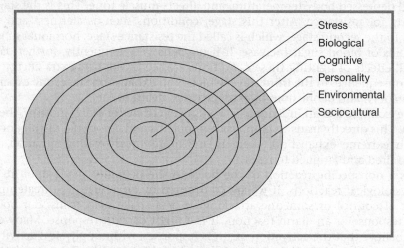

In this sense, stressors are classified in a similar way.

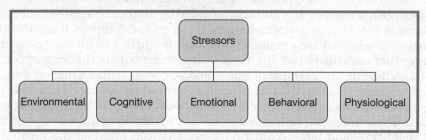

1. **Environmental**—Natural disasters such as flood, fire, earthquake, tsunami, or any phenomenon which is beyond the control of human beings and causes tremendous loss in terms of human life and material causes a huge amount of stress. Some physical stimuli such as electrical shock, extreme temperature, loud noise, extreme light, and others cause stress which is beyond tolerance. Some kinds of social change such as poverty or sudden change in social status of the family may also cause stress.
2. **Cognitive**—Personal cognitive limitations such as below-average intellectual abilities like memory, understanding capacity, or problems like learning disabilities are major cognitive sources of stress. Incongruent thoughts, confusion regarding an important decision, difficulty in justifying one's own deeds, and dissonance concerning values are some glaring examples of cognitive stressors. If an adolescent who has been taught values like honesty discovers that his father is cheating the poor and illiterate people to get extra money, he may face a lot of stress.
3. **Emotional**—Death of a family member, lack of harmonious relations with family members, transfer in employment, and quarrel with close friends are examples of emotional stressors resulting in very unpleasant feelings and emotions. Various fears, anxieties, phobias, and irrational emotional experiences result in stress.
4. **Behavioral**—The behavior of others and also of one's ownself may cause stress. A parent or a teacher who is very strict causes terror in the mind of students. If a person cannot control his or her own expressions of negative feelings, he or she may get involved in a behavior

pattern which causes various problems and stress. Addiction and abuse of alcohol or tobacco is also a serious problem leading to stress.

5. **Physiological**—Disability-causing limitations and social stigma, illness, accident, chronic disease, acute pain, frequent problems such as cold and cough, and similar other conditions are responsible for substantial stress along with problems like poor self-esteem.

In short, stress may be caused by all sorts of emergencies, illnesses, injuries, work demands, career development, intense emotional demands, and similar other experiences. Age and gender are associated to types, causes, and consequences of stress. The nature of stress depends upon the importance of stressor, duration, intensity, frequency, and uncertainty regarding the stressor. The common causes of stress are:

a. Home and work balance may be one of the basic issues resulting in stress. It includes working overtime, making repeated journeys, domestic and financial problems, and problems related to office work. Many responsibilities, poor interpersonal relations, insecure environment, and mismatched demands at home and the workplace lead to stress.

b. Some life events are crises that must be faced. Most of us face these at some time in our life. Some examples are: death of a family member, loss of job, transfer, failure in an important examination, and similar other events may cause negative stress or distress. On the other hand, promotion, new added responsibility, and the addition of a family member may cause positive stress.

```
            Life event
                Perception of stress
                    Emotional arousal
                        Physiological arousal
                            Ill effects
```

c. Poor relations with boss, teachers, colleagues, and clients at school, college, or work may lead to stress. Work overload, time pressure, a poorly defined job, poor communication, etc. can result in more stress.

d. Personal limitations such as deficiencies in social and intellectual skills, deficiencies in education and training, and sensory and motor handicaps may precipitate a lot of stress. If a particular limitation is very important for an individual, it may cause more stress. If the leg of a player or a dancer is amputated due to some accident, it will lead to extreme stress.

e. The lack of capacity in terms of economic, social, emotional powers to deal with adverse environmental events and natural disasters leads to a huge amount of stress due to other consequences related to them.

f. Minor everyday hassles such as the nonavailability of daily requirements, uncomfortable living conditions, unwanted and heavy responsibilities, problems-related travel, etc. may lead to stress.

g. Conflict over goals, for instance, uncertainty regarding what exactly should be achieved may lead to a stressful situation. Say for example, decisions regarding what course or what college should be selected, and other similar situations may cause substantial stress. If there is a mismatch between an individual's abilities and aptitude on one hand and the demands of the course or related job, the individual may face problems for his or her entire life.

h. Personality characteristics of people with type A personality include hard driving, impatient, struggling against time, competitive, and overcommitted. These personality features may lead to burnout. Such individuals want to gain control over their environment and, hence, are engaged in a constant struggle even when there is no real threat. They are called "hurry sick". A simple example is that of a man with type A personality who would like to shave with two razors simultaneously or a woman who would like to use two hairdryers to dry her hair at the same time. Type A behavior is correlated to workaholic tendencies. Working mothers generally face these problems. Personality type A people find it difficult to relax as they think that it is a waste of time.

i. Ethical dilemma- if one is asked to do things that violate the law or personal values, it creates a lot of confusion. This, in turn, results in stress. An adolescent who is involved in socially unacceptable behavior or delinquency will feel guilty and be afraid of being caught. This is a major dilemma.

16.5 EFFECTS AND INDICATORS OF STRESS

Some experts use the terms constructive stress and destructive stress for eustress and distress.

Distress may lead to headache, indigestion, frequent cold, neck and back ache, and unhappy relations. In organizations, such as educational institutes and offices, it leads to absenteeism, poor performance, accidents, and reduced creativity. Along with this generalized reaction, there are specific responses such as running away, fighting off, becoming tense and frustrated, becoming angry, and mobilizing the immune system to destroy bacteria and viruses.

16.5.1 Cognitive Symptoms of Stress

1. Memory problems
2. The inability to concentrate
3. Poor judgment
4. The impact of anxiety
5. Pessimism in thinking

16.5.2 Psychological Indicators of Stress

1. Mood swings
2. Irritation, agitation, and unhappiness
3. The inability to relax
4. Feeling overwhelmed
5. Proneness to anger
6. Hopelessness
7. A lack of confidence
8. A loss of enthusiasm
9. Aloofness and restlessness
10. Depression, loneliness, and crying
11. Difficulty in concentrating
12. Difficulty in making decisions
13. Negative thinking

16.5.3 BEHAVIORAL SYMPTOMS

1. Sleep disturbances, that is, sleeping too much or too little
2. Eating disturbances, that is, either eating too much or very less
3. Increase in drug dependence or alcohol dependence
4. Difficulty in relaxing
5. Difficulty in mixing with others
6. Lack of interest in social and close relations
7. Neglecting responsibilities
8. Nervous habits like nail biting

16.5.4 PHYSIOLOGICAL SYMPTOMS

1. Aches and pains
2. Increased blood pressure
3. Increased heat rate
4. Increased respiration rate
5. Diarrhea or constipation
6. Nausea and dizziness
7. Chest pain and rapid heartbeats
8. Loss of sex drive
9. Frequent cold
10. Irregular menstrual cycle
11. Depressed immune system
12. Tensed muscles
13. Heightened alertness

Physiological consequences are related to biochemical changes like release of adrenaline.
It is flight or fight response
Long-term effects of stress may aggravate:

1. Hypertension
2. Coronary heart disease
3. Ulcers
4. Migraine headaches
5. Tension headaches
6. Allergies
7. Asthma
8. Hay fever
9. Backaches
10. Cancer

Three general reactions to stress are:

1. Maladjustment—It is not effective and leads to other problems.
2. Adjustment
3. Competence—It is associated with creative problem solving.

Maladjustment	Adjustment	Competence
Behavior not very effective		creative problem-solving

16.6   CORRELATES OF STRESS

16.6.1   STRESS-CREATING MUSTS

Some ideas regarding perfectionism are prevalent in our mind. We expect that each and every task should be done perfectly by us. Our inability to achieve this goal or even the idea that we may not be able to achieve it creates stress.

Common stress-creating musts and ideas are:

1. I must do everything perfectly.
2. It is impossible to change one's behavior, habits, and attitudes.
3. I must always be on time.
4. Others too should always be on time.
5. I must always say "yes" when asked to do additional work.
6. I must earn a fat salary to afford a large house and an expensive car. I must get on well with everyone.
7. I must always help others.

Let us take only one example of reaching on time for meetings. It is obvious that it is desirable to be on time; but because of some unavoidable reason one cannot always be on time; then due to stress created by "must," one may experience some negative consequences like headache and may not be in a position to work properly. Therefore, instead, one should be relaxed and eager to work after expressing an apology. One should not be frustrated and upset due to these small things.

16.6.2   STRESS AND ILLNESS

It is necessary to understand that illness increases along with boredom, irritation, and frustration. There are different ways to measure stress. A very popular way is to measure stress related to life events. It gives ranges of the risk of developing stress-related illness.

The relationship between illness and stress is U shaped. When stress is too much or too little, illness prevails. When stress is moderate, the person can maintain good health.

16.6.3   STRESS AND PERFORMANCE

The relation between arousal and performance efficiency is studied by researchers. It is like an inverted U. When arousal is very low or very high, stress increases. When there is no stress, performance efficiency drops to zero. In the same way, when arousal is extreme, there is exhaustion and illness and performance drops to zero. Frustration, boredom, and under-involvement are prevalent. As arousal increases performance, alertness, creativity, and general effectiveness also increase. This increase is seen only up to a particular degree of arousal.

After that, work performance diminishes; there is mental and physical deterioration; reduced efficiency and creativity; and reduced alertness, indecision, anxiety, and confusion which lead to illness and even death. Healthy arousal leads to good performance and a balanced life style. In this case, the individual is relaxed, confident, and energetic. This is the highest performance.

If the person starts to neglect health and accepts very difficult assignments, he or she is traveling toward decline. One has to listen to one's body. For instance, if one has a headache, one generally takes some medicine and cures it. However, the actual reason for stress should be traced and attempts should be made to change the environment. If the individual is feeling exhausted, he or she should rest and take proper care. An individual's behavior is going to affect office and family.

16.6.4 PERSONALITY FACTORS RELATED TO STRESS

Reaction to stress depends on skills of stress management. Some personality factors may alter the experience of stress to a large extent. They are:

1. Hardiness
2. Type A personality

Hardiness as conceptualized by Kobasa (1979) is a group of personality characteristics that act as a resistance resource for an individual when he or she faces stressful life events. Hardiness explains why people experience variable ill effects of stress and comprises of three things—commitment, control, and challenge. Commitment is the tendency to get involved in one's activities, instead of experiencing alienation from them. Control is related to the locus of control. It is a generalized expectancy of internal and external control of reinforcement. Internal locus of control is a tendency to feel and behave as if one can substantially influence outcomes using one's imagination, skills, knowledge, and choice.

The locus of control is related to an individual's experience and reaction to stress. Challenge is the belief that change is more normal than stability. And, change is considered as a contributing factor to growth than a threat to security. Highly stressed but hardy individuals remain healthy and may not get involved in irresponsible adventures. Hence, many psychologists focus their attention on hardiness.

We have already discussed type A personality with reference to causes of stress. Type A personality pattern also explains the relation between stress and disease. It is defined as an action-emotion complex. The person is aggressively involved in constantly struggling hard to achieve more and more in less and less

> Some stress is essential for good performance.
> Reduce unnecessary stressors and daily hassles.
> Learn better coping styles and use all resources.
> Relaxation and hobbies help to enhance mental health.
> Sharing emotional problems and social support helps to decreases stress.
> Self-talk improvement is essential
> Positive thinking and hardiness reduce stress substantially
> One should try to change the environment as far as possible.

time, and if necessary, against the opposing efforts of other factors and other persons. This is called coronary-prone behavior and is associated with speed and impatience, job involvement, and competitive behavior. It also involves precision, responsibility, and effort. Due to extreme time urgency these people cannot face new challenges. They have an intense drive.

16.6.5 RELATION BETWEEN GENDER AND STRESS

A huge amount of research has been done regarding gender differences in stress.

Some glaring differences in experiences of men and women about stress are explained as follows.

The expression of experienced stress is more in case of girls and women as compared to boys and men. Men show a problem-focused coping style and women use emotion-based problem-solving when they are under stress. Women are disturbed emotionally when they have to solve some stress-producing problem. A college-going girl may start weeping if her mobile is lost, and a young mother shows similar response when her baby is not well. They have to use a lot of psychological energy to control their emotional outbursts.

Research has indicated that men experience more damaging effects of stress because they do not share their problems with others. Right from childhood they are socialized to hide their problems and pretend that they can control everything. They are not supposed to express their emotions and think logically as well as play the role of the head of the family. In India, it is even more obviously seen that a young male child even at the age of 4 or 5 is criticized heavily if he cries and weeps due to pain, injury, or insult. He is to bare all these things without overt expression of agony or helplessness. Low self-disclosure leads to a lack of empathy and as they grow older, they become more tough-minded. Gradually, the lack of insight regarding oneself and incompetence at expressing positive emotions such as love and affection are seen in males. All these things are directly related to the experience of stress. Adult male members consider themselves worthless when they do not have work and they do not earn.

Women experience stress due to unavoidable circumstance in their lives. In Indian community, women, by and large, get less importance in the family, in the society, and at workplace if at all she is working. Sexual harassment of women at workplace, pregnancy and child birth, crimes against women, and general insecurity are very common stresses producing gender-specific issues.

As aging starts, stress increases due to various uncontrollable factors. Life events such as death of a friend or a life partner, retirement and loss of status, less earnings, more physiological problems, deterioration of general health, chronic diseases, and a lack of proper social support result in more stress.

A huge amount of research has been done regarding physiological correlates of stress. Cardiovascular system, digestive system, muscles and joints, as well as the immune system are affected by stress. Many diseases such as diabetes, cancer, rheumatoid arthritis, allergies, asthma, cold and flu, skin disorders, and sleep disorders are associated with stress. Angina and heart attacks are proved to be related to stress. Such emotional problems are responsible for 25 percent of all infertility problems.

16.7 MANAGEMENT OF STRESS

Stress can be managed by preventions such as making adjustment to stress-producing factors, by promoting personal wellness, taking steps to maintain a healthy body and mind capable of better withstanding stressful situations. Some important steps of stress management have been discussed as follows.

1. **Awareness regarding the experience of stress**
   Awareness of one's experiences is essential for managing stress. For assessing one's own signs and symptoms, it is necessary to evaluate in detail the psychological and physiological changes. Physical signs that one should be able to understand are heart beats, palpitation, breathlessness, lump in the throat, dry mouth, butterflies in stomach, indigestion, nausea, acidity, muscle tension in jaw and shoulders, pains and aches, helplessness, hyperactivity, fatigue or exhaustion, sweaty palms, hot flushes, frequent desire to urinate, cold hands and feet, irritation, impatience, loneliness, and so on. However, at the mental level one should be able to understand symptoms such as being worried, upset, helpless, anxious, depressed, frustrated, bored, guilty, insecure, vulnerable, rushed, forgetfulness, silly

mistakes, accidents, unreasonable behavior, and similar other things. Signs of eustress are: being euphoric, excited, thrilled, helpful, understanding, confident, creative, rational, industrious, jolly, and happy.

2. **Attacking the causes of stress**

For attacking the causes of stress one has to:

a. **Add resources**—equipments and materials that may reduce unnecessary load and extra efforts.

b. **Reorganize for less stress**—if people are disturbing and the job is suffering, one has to decide a particular time for meeting others.

c. **Avoiding particular stressors**—avoiding unpleasant conditions, unnecessary meetings, and similar other things when they can be avoided leads to less stress.

d. **Decreasing the causes of stress**—if one has to travel a lot for going to office, then one should try to get a residential accommodation near the office premises.

e. **Change style and personality pattern**—if one has type A personality, he or she should try and relax, plan tasks comfortably, and accept jobs considering the available time and energy. People who have type B personality should decide goals, share responsibility with others, and accept their responsibility after understanding it clearly and interacting assertively.

Even otherwise, assertiveness decreases the possibility of injustice and misunderstanding.

f. **Obtain social support**—if friends, relatives, and family members are ready to share problems and feelings, it leads to stress reduction.

g. **Seek small wins**—a sense of satisfaction and that of achievement is essential for stress reduction.

h. **Getting involved in hobbies and other pleasant leisure time activities**—music, dance, and other performing arts result in the reduction of stress.

i. **Exercise, meditation, and yoga**—these may help to reduce stress. Prayers are also recommended depending on the belief system of the individual.

j. **Keeping a diary and writing**—small details of day-to-day experiences, reactions to them, coping styles, and their effectiveness if written enhance the understanding regarding all these issues. It should be maintained at least for three weeks. Ineffective uses of coping styles and repeated use of unwanted reactions can be analyzed. What changes are necessary, what type of experiences are to be avoided, and what psychological as well as physiological disturbances can be reduced become obvious because of such a written record.

3. **Changes in self**

More effective strategies to cope with various types of stress can be improved with the help of introspection.

The core psychological aspects are:

a. Accept oneself.
b. Express emotions.
c. Accept others as they are.
d. Change the environment positively as far as possible.
e. Avoid perfectionism.
f. Work out your priorities.
g. Be realistic regarding goals that are achievable.
h. Find educational and vocational branches suitable to your abilities and aptitudes.
i. Be assertive.

4. **Organizational strategies to manage stress**
   For better stress management in an organization one has to:

   a. Talk to others for emotional catharses.
   b. Increase some activity like walking.
   c. Accept things that you cannot change.
   d. Practice positive thinking.
   e. Create conducive environment as far as possible.
   f. Keep the working environment clean and tidy for example keeping the table neatly organized.
   g. If getting distracted by phone or computer, then keep them away from your table.
   h. Do not work where common utilities are placed.
   i. Plan and organize work properly.
   j. Reduce paperwork.
   k. Dispose unwanted papers.
   l. Control interruption.

   Those who have more social support suffer comparatively less. Emotional problems increase due to loneliness. Social support helps the individual to cope with illness, surgery, or unemployment. It helps even in pregnancy. There is someone to share with, emotional catharsis is possible, and there is someone to advice. Conflict resolution in proper way also increases social support.

5. **Health-promoting life style responses**
   Following are the responses that help in providing a healthy life style:

   a. Adaptive behavior response such as assertiveness and time management lead to better self-esteem, self-respect, and self-confidence.
   b. Adaptive physical responses such as nutrition, exercise, and relaxation increase resistance to diseases and improve physical health.
   c. Adaptive emotional and cognitive responses such as hardiness and cognitive restructuring result in improved mental health and resistance to future stress.

   In short, healthy balanced life style, relaxation, exercise, proper diet, and involvement in hobbies are essential for stress management.

6. **Autosuggestion**
   Experts in psychology advocate autosuggestion for effective stress management. To avoid uncontrollable physiological and psychological symptoms, an individual should engage in intrapersonal suggestions talking to self, regarding his or her calm and quite status and heart beats as being normal. It helps reducing stress and the person perceives himself or herself as being in control of all these things.

   Generally, doctors treat one's stress-related symptoms and diseases resulting from stress. These remedies reduce one's pain, help the person to sleep, improve digestion, and similar other problems. Drugs, alcohol, a variety of food, diversions such as TV, hobbies, or else withdrawal from world and living in isolation are some commonly seen strategies to deal with stress. These things distract the individual's attention away from stress; however, the individual's mind may or may not be free from it.

   Thought stopping is the only effective method for 70 percent of the persons having phobias or irrational fears and 20 percent of the cases having compulsive behavior. Thought stopping is recommended when the basic problem is cognitive rather than behavioral. When specific behavior is repeatedly experienced as being stressful leading to unpleasant emotional thoughts, thought stopping is very effective. For thought stopping, one has to:

a. **Explore and list stressful thoughts**—such as is it a sensible and reasonable thing? Is it just a habit? Is it really necessary or unnecessary? Does the person try to stop it or try very hard to stop it? The degree of interference to the thought causes should be assessed.

b. **Imagine the thoughts**—the individual should close eyes and imagine the situation due to which the stressful thoughts are emerging. A combination of normal and repetitive obsessive thinking helps. Now it is a must to stop that particular thought and continue normal thinking.

c. **Thought interruption**—one may use a time indicator, for example, an alarm clock, may be after three minutes and shout "stop" after getting the alarm. It is also recommended that one can use tricks such as raising his or her hand or standing up. During the next 30 seconds one has to keep the mind empty of the disturbing thought, and again shout stop if the thought returns. Using a tape recorder shouting stop after variable time intervals also helps.

d. **Unaided thought interruption**— Gradually the individual is supposed to practice saying "stop" to interrupt his or her thought in a normal voice, and then finally just whisper. After one finds this effective, one may try just imagining that he or she has said the word stop and use only a sub-vocal command.

e. **Thought substitution**—during that disturbing thought, one may replace it by more pleasant and assertive thoughts. If one is experiencing stress during examination, one must think of going ahead and getting a degree certificate.

Though there are many strategies to manage stress, understanding self and others, positive thinking, increasing or reducing demands or coping strategies, and time management are the most important ones. Most of them are discussed in detail in this book. Time perception is a very useful strategy which needs some more attention.

16.8   TIME MANAGEMENT AND STRESS REDUCTION

Human life is limited. Hence, time is as precious as life. Time should be managed properly so that maximum can be achieved.

Joy is studying in a junior college. He is a happy-go-lucky kind of a guy. He enjoys the company of his friends and is generally interested in spending a lot of time in having fun. Actually, he is a student of the science stream and is supposed to complete his practicals, write journals, and submit various assignments on time. Joy takes everything easily and generally submits everything late. He never gets enough time to study and so gets poor grades. Actually, his parents and teachers think that he is an intelligent person and will be able to get admission in a prestigious college for a professional course if he concentrates on his studies. However, Joy wants to postpone everything other than enjoyment. What do you think will happen to his career?

Sona works in a company as an office assistant. She is sincere and hard working. She is obedient and docile. She generally faces problems due to missing papers. Her boss usually asks for reference papers immediately which she cannot find and gets confused. Sona tries to get the papers but sometimes takes hours to locate them.

Why do you think does Sona suffer?

Human life is limited. Hence, the most important thing in human life is time. Once gone it is gone, it is gone forever. It is accepted theoretically but in day-to-day situations, it is difficult to follow. When it comes to any examination, competition, or completion of a job, all participants have equal time. The only difference is how do they utilize it? There are only two ways in which one can utilize time: appropriately and inappropriately. One cannot differentiate clearly between productive time and the time that is wasted. It is essential that sometimes the individual enjoys watching television, playing, or even social visits. This time is not wasted because it results in decreased stress, tension, boredom, and fatigue. This leads to better performance. One has to act smarter than harder while using time effectively and has to manage time in such a way that maximum goals can be achieved.

Time passes even if we do not use it properly. There are two points to keep in mind with respect to time:

1. It may be utilized adequately or inadequately.
2. It cannot be differentiated on the basis of being used in productive and nonproductive activities.

Those who are always busy and say that they do not have time actually are managing their time poorly. It is reported in research that at least six weeks in one year are wasted in finding out lost official papers in organizations. To save this time one can use the following strategies.

Strategies for effective time management:

1. **Find out how you use your time:** One has to think about all activities and the total time devoted per activity. Divide the total time available in a day and write down how one spends every 15 minutes. One should calculate how much time one is devoting for every activity like watching television, writing mails to friends, reading important matters, and so on. On the basis of this understanding, one can reorganize the schedule and use time more effectively.
2. **Use a timetable, a diary, or a calendar for planning activities:** Prepare a time table and devote a particular limited time for calling people on phone, meeting colleagues, and even for tea and lunch. However, it should not be a time-consuming activity. For example, if one does not know how to use an electronic diary, one should not use it.
3. **Find out the peak time:** One must find out when he or she is alert and more efficient, and can understand things quickly. One should plan things in such a way that this time is utilized for important activities.
4. **Mark repeated activities on the planner:** Like for example, if a departmental committee meeting takes place on the first Monday of every month, then one should mark it for the whole year, to start with.
5. **Calculate time:** One should decide some deadlines and goals to achieve in every day, week, and month. He or she must calculate time from completing the work to the present status inversely for important deadlines. He or she must also utilize time accordingly and give some rewards to self for that.
6. **Expect that unexpected problems will delay the work:** Start the work in such a way that even if some time is wasted because of some problems, it will be completed on time.
7. **Plan properly:** One must plan about the assignments to follow in advance.
8. **Do not wait for the last moment:** One should break the habit of somehow completing the tasks at the last moment.
9. **Avoid calling colleagues to discuss something:** If one has to discuss something with colleagues, one should go to their office and avoid calling them to one's own as they may take some more time than what is expected. Delegating and sharing responsibilities and avoiding trivial tasks, and assertiveness while saying no to some requests to join unwanted activities work well in saving time for more important work.

10. **One has to decide priorities:** Tasks that are essential and important, that can be done afterwards, and those that may not be done should be segregated. If something is important and some immediate action has to be taken, one should do it, if it is to be filed and used repeatedly, one should file it, and if it is not important and need not be preserved, it should be discarded immediately. If a task to too long, it is better to divide it and complete the parts one by one. FRAT formula, that is, file it, refer it, act on it, and trash it, works well to save time. One should never postpone these things and get involved in piling work. Using different files like red file for very important and urgent matters also works well. Deleting unwanted e-mails without reading also saves time. We have already discussed time management with reference to important and urgent work and and its relation to success (see page 143).

One has to act smarter than harder. If we have no time, it is obviously nothing but poor time management.

To sum up, what we can do is recognize the symptoms of stress and be aware of the psychological and physiological changes related to it. Once we accept this cause–effect relation, we can find out the ways to change the situation in such a way that increase in coping strategies and decrease in demands will help to reduce stress. An exactly opposite situation will require increase in demands. We must try to make ourselves hardy and healthy to tolerate stress. We cannot avoid it but make ourselves more ready to face it in a better way.

> Benefits of time management:
>
> 1. Discipline in work
> 2. Better achievements
> 3. Balance in life
> 4. Stress management
> 5. Mental health
> 6. Availability of time for hobbies and keeping good interpersonal relations.

16.9 SUMMARY

Stress is an essential part of life. No one is completely stress-free. Some stress is essential for leading a normal life and maintaining motivation. Different types of stress result in different effects on the individual. Evaluating demands and coping strategies are a must. There are physiological and psychological ill effects of excessive stress. Hence, stress management becomes a must. Everyone should enhance stress management abilities to maintain mental health. A simple example of which is time management. We can change our lives by these important tricks.

QUESTIONS

1. Describe the nature of the types of stress.
2. Discuss the various causes of stress.
3. What is GAS?
4. Discuss indicators and effects of stress.
5. What are the important correlates of stress?
6. What are various ways to manage stress?
7. What is the importance and ways of time management?

APPLICATION ORIENTATION

Introspect and write down the following answers. Be as objective as you can

1. Write down the various stresses you have experienced during the last three months.
2. Arrange them hierarchically.
3. Which of them were positive stresses? What was the basic difference between distress and eustress that you have experienced?
4. Enumerate the physiological disturbances you experience due to stress. How much time is generally required to overcome them?
5. Try to understand your intrapersonal communication when you are under stress.
6. Prepare a table dividing your time in short segments and mention what you accomplish during that period. Continue doing this exercise for eight days and find out when and how you waste your time.

SUGGESTED READINGS

Davis, M., Eshelman, E. R., and Mattew, M. (2008). *Relaxation and stress reduction workbook*. Oakland, CA: New Harbinger Inc.

Kobi a, S. C. (1979). Stressful life events, personality, and health-inquiry into hardiness. *Journal of Personality and Social Psychology, 37*(1), 1–11.

Lazarus, R. and Folkman, S. (1984). *Stress, appraisal and coping*. New York: Springer.

Schultz, D. P. and Schultz, S. E. (2010). *Psychology and work today*. New York: Prentice Hall.

Wade, C. and Travis, C. (2006). *Psychology*. New Delhi: Pearson Education.

Relating to Others

4

17 Empathy

Objectives

After reading this chapter, you will be able to:

1. Understand the nature of empathy.
2. Realize the importance of empathy.
3. Know the correlates of empathy.
4. Explain other relevant ideas related to empathy.
5. Learn how to enhance empathy.
6. Develop insight into applications of empathy.

Samar was selected in a very well-known government engineering college. He joined the college with great ambitions and his parents were very happy. In spite of their economic problems they supported his fees, hostel charges, and other expenses. Some of his seniors have been involved in ragging juniors and they started harassing him from the first day of college. They wanted him to serve them, please them, and used to force him to wear crazy dresses in college, insult girls, and break the rules of the college in which he was never interested. After that they started sexually exploiting him.

Samar tried to commit suicide. Fortunately, he survived but he lost his mental balance forever, and had to drop out. His parents never knew what to do.

Why were the seniors enjoying serious ragging of this sort where the individual's whole life was ruined? How is it that they never realized the consequences of these malpractices? Why did they fail to understand that he was also a student like them and had every right to peacefully complete his education?

Rekha was in a great hurry and carrying a number of books when she discovered that her shoe laces were untied on the staircase. She told Shrushty to tie the laces. She could not even realize that Shrushty will not be able to do it. Shrushty was feeling awkward and confused. She is born without fingers of the right hand. Though she is doing her graduation, she has many limitations, as for example, she cannot drive a two-wheeler, cannot get speed when she types on a computer, and cannot even button her clothes. Rekha should not have hurt Shrushty.

Was Rekha intentionally insulting or hurting Shrushty? What was missing in her communication? What should be avoided in communication with others? What is the role of understanding others in communication and interpersonal relations?

While interacting with others, people fail to understand and even remember their problems, limitations, experiences, and emotions. It results in a distorted image of the person and poor interpersonal relations.

If we consider these different interactions, we will be able to understand that there is something that is missing in all these individuals. It is a lack of empathy that results in such type of negligence of someone else's emotional problems.

17.1 NATURE OF EMPATHY

The best example of empathy is a young mother of a very young baby. When the baby is feeling uncomfortable and cries, the mother tries to understand its innermost experiences and also tries to console it. Simple routine needs of the baby are routinely fulfilled by the mother, but if the baby cries in distress, mother has to guess what the reasons could be. Then, she tries to make the baby comfortable, gives medicine, and so on. Even you must have experienced that when you are not well your mother can easily understand it.

There are various conceptualizations of empathy where the basic idea is that one has to adjust one's perception of the world according to the other person. Many a time, young ones start weeping for simple reasons such as their mother does not give them a chocolate or something like a book, or their notebook is lost. We cannot understand what is so serious about it and we start laughing or making fun of them. In this case, there is a lack of empathy and understanding regarding how the child perceives the incidence is obvious.

It was approximately 100 years ago that Adler gave significant aspects of empathy. According to him, a tendency to empathize is not natural , and must be supported by the parents and culture at large. Adler proposed that those who are competent and doing well can afford to think about others. If an individual has inferiority complex, his psychological energy will be mostly used to overcome the same and the individual will not be able to think about others. Hence, due to low social interest no empathy can be developed.

17.1.1 Definitions

Empathy has many different definitions that encompass a broad range of emotional states, from caring for other people and having a desire to help them to experiencing emotions that match another person's emotions. Empathy is knowing what the other person is thinking or feeling, blurring the line between bodily feelings and combination of beliefs and desires. The ability to imagine oneself as another person is a sophisticated imaginative process. There are various definitions of empathy where the basic idea is that one has to adjust one's perception of the world according to the other person.

> Empathy is the act of communicating to our fellow human beings in such a way that we understand how they are feeling and what makes them feel that way (Hogan, 1969).

Many definitions of empathy concentrate on understanding someone else's psychological state as clearly as the individual experiences his or her own. Empathy is communicating understanding. Oxford Dictionary of Psychology (2006) defines empathy as "the capacity to understand and enter into another person's feelings and emotions or to experience something from the other person's point of view." A pioneering researcher Titchener (1908) gave this term approximately hundred years ago. Empathy has a survival value also as if the others are suffering today, one may also suffer tomorrow. Understanding regarding human nature helps in interpreting the behavior and intentions of others. Stein (1989) defined empathy as an experience of foreign consciousness in general.

When one is convinced that others fully understand him or her without judging why he or she is feeling or reacting that way or advising him or her to feel differently, he or she experiences a sense of acceptance. Empathy involves unconditional acceptance of the individual in need of help where evaluation and judgments of feelings are never offered. Empathy means understanding another person so well that one identifies with that person and feels like he or she does.

Empathy is one's ability to recognize, perceive, and directly experientially feel the emotions of another. As the states of mind, beliefs, and desires of others are intertwined with their emotions, one with empathy for another may often be able to define another's modes of thought and mood more effectively. Empathy is often characterized as the ability to put oneself into another's shoes, or experiencing the outlook or emotions of another being within oneself, a sort of emotional resonance. Reading about a feeling and intellectually knowing about it is very different than actually experiencing it for yourself.

Empathy involves two specific skills—perception and communication.

17.1.2 Phenomenology

In phenomenology, empathy describes the experience of something from the other's viewpoint, without confusion between self and other. In the most basic sense, this is the awareness of the other's bodily experiences. Empathy is also considered to be the condition of intersubjectivity.

Answer the following question in three sentences:

If you were a person of opposite gender, how your life would have changed?

Write down your answer and show it to a friend of the opposite gender. Discuss with your friend if his or her life is like that or not. If your friend confirms that it is correct or approximately correct, then you have developed some empathy about the opposite gender. If not, you have to think again why your answer is not so accurate? Even if the same question is asked to middle-aged very well-educated male adults who are senior officers, they cannot give appropriate answers. They generally agree that they have not given a thought to it.

The basic issue is specially that the male members never think about how is the life of a female. They do not bother to understand how experiences of a female are different from their own. In mother–son, sister–brother, or even husband–wife relations people stay together for years but cannot understand each other's perspectives. They lack empathy. Male young adults, for example, cannot understand why their mother tells them again and again to be careful while driving. They get irritated and start screaming one fine morning to insult their mother.

17.2 TYPES OF EMPATHY

There are different levels at which one can experience empathy. On this basis empathy can be divided into two major components—affective and cognitive.

1. **Affective empathy, also called emotional empathy**—It is empathy regarding feelings. Here one can achieve understanding the emotional experience of the person concerned. It is the capacity to respond with an appropriate emotion to another's psychological

states. One's ability to empathize emotionally is based on emotional contagion being affected by another's emotional or arousal state.

Affective empathy can be subdivided into the following types:

a. *Empathic concern:* Sympathy and compassion for others in response to their suffering.
b. *Personal distress:* Self-centered feelings of discomfort and anxiety in response to others' sufferings.

Infants respond to the distress of others by getting distressed themselves; only when they are 2 years old do they start responding in other-oriented ways, trying to help, comfort, and share.

2. **Cognitive empathy**—It is the capacity to understand others' perspectives or mental state. Cognitive empathy can be subdivided into the following ways:

a. *Perspective taking:* The tendency to spontaneously adopt others' psychological perspectives.
b. *Fantasy:* The tendency to identify with fictional characters.

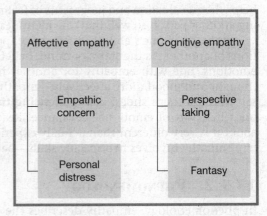

Some psychological disorders are characterized by a lack of either affective or cognitive empathy. In normal healthy individuals also the balance between affective and cognitive empathy varies. Actually, it depends on the activation of specific brain areas. Different brain areas are activated during affective–perceptual empathy and cognitive–evaluative empathy. Researchers have proved that the inferior frontal gyrus appears to be responsible for emotional empathy, and the ventromedial prefrontal gyrus seems to mediate cognitive empathy.

In counseling, the counselor has to communicate primary empathy. This is the ability to understand the major issues that the counselee has to communicate. Various verbal and non-verbal strategies are used for that, for example, leaning forward and speaking in a soft voice. In the advanced stage, advanced empathy is to be used to help the client to explore themes, issues, and emotions that are not available to his or her awareness. One more type of empathy is labeled by some researchers. That is, compassionate empathy—the intention to help. It is at the behavioral level that one is motivated to change the concerned person's life. Here, one should always remember that no one can change everything but try to change the perception of the individual, give him or her support, and reduce helplessness that he or she is experiencing.

17.2.1 METHODS OF EMPATHIZING

There are two methods of empathizing:

1. Simulate "pretend" versions of the beliefs, desires, character traits, and context of the other and see what emotional feelings this leads to.
2. Simulate the emotional feeling and then look around for a suitable reason for this to fit.

Either way, full empathetic engagement is supposed to enhance the understanding and anticipation of the behavior of the other.

According to some researchers, the modes of empathic arousal which produce an empathic reaction in a person are:

1. **Mimicry**—Which involves changing one's facial expression, posture, and tone in response to changes in the facial expression, voice, and posture of the other person. This information results in feelings in the empathizer that are similar to the feelings in the other person.
2. **Conditioning**—An individual mentally associates own emotions with the emotions of another. This may also explain the relationship between someone who is helpless and cannot communicate like an infant does with his or her mother.
3. **Direct association**—Similarity between experiences essentially is seen in such empathy. This is seen when an individual had an emotional experience and can help one to empathize with another person who is going through a similar experience.

   These three modes are related to primitive empathy. The other two forms of empathy are more sophisticated and higher order thinking. Even when the target of empathy is not present, it works.
4. **Verbally mediated association**—This basically depends on verbal information about the individual who is the focus of empathy. Whatever emotions the person is experiencing are described by the individual in person, through mail, or any other way. Here, nonverbal communication may not be available; so, it creates symbolic representations.
5. **Perspective taking**—Imagining oneself in another's place for understanding his or her emotions is also useful for developing empathy.

17.3 CORRELATES OF EMPATHY

1. **Perceived responsibility of the person who is suffering**—If the person who is suffering is perceived as being responsible for his or her condition, then there is less empathy. The perceiver will not be able to identify himself or herself with the sufferer.

   Devendra met with an accident and was injured. Some unknown passersby stopped to help him or her. Immediately, a policeman came and asked him some questions. It was obvious that Devendra did not have a license to drive a two-wheeler as he was just 15, and he was driving on a no-entry road at tremendous speed. People started moving as they understood that he is responsible for the accident and was driving against the rules. They lost the interest in helping him.
2. **Familiarity and similarity between the empathizer and sufferer**—Moreover, some research suggests that people are more able and willing to empathize with those most similar to themselves. In particular, empathy increases with similarities in culture and living conditions. We are also more likely to empathize with those with whom we interact more frequently.

   Vidya and Salama are doing their nursing course. They are very friendly with each other. Once, when they were working in the male surgery ward, a patient misbehaved with Salama. Vidya ran to her rescue and told everything to the in charge of the ward. She made Salama comfortable and shouldered her responsibility when she left the ward. These things were discussed many times with the authorities and every time Vidya went there to support Salama as she could feel with her and understood the agony behind it.
3. **Proximity**—This leads to better empathy. We cannot feel the pain and problems of people staying in some faraway country but can better understand the agony of our own countrymen. It is the general atmospheric conditions as well as social experiences, values, and attitudes of the community that are related to empathy.

4. **Prosocial behavior**—Empathy is known to increase prosocial or helping behavior. Some cultures socialize its members for individualist ideology leading to self-orientation. In these cultures empathy and prosocial behavior are not developed fully. Explaining prosocial behavior often mentions the presence of empathy in the individual as a possible variable. Empathy is the definitive factor for altruistic behavior according to Batson and Powell's (1988) empathy-altruism hypothesis. If empathy is felt, an individual will help by actions or by words, regardless of whether it is in their self-interest to do so and even if the costs outweigh potential rewards.

Even more, people can empathize with animals. As far as blue cross is concerned, empathy is thought to be a driving psychological force behind it.

> Empathy increases prosocial behavior, and altruism.

5. **Pain**—Empathy may be painful to oneself seeing the pain of others. Many a time, the problems of victims depicted by mass media disturbs the individual. It can cause temporary or permanent depression in extreme cases. Hence, the person may try to protect himself or herself from it. Without a basic emotional understanding of others, there is no basis for a relationship; therefore, a tension struggle lies in the dilemma to protect oneself from the pain of empathy or to seek to relate to other humans despite the potential risk of injury.

For example, people who were going for a religious pilgrimage to Kedarnath in June 2013 experienced traumatic flood and extreme rain. About 5,700 people were killed. The reports of this calamity shown on various news channels were also vividly depicting the horrible conditions over there. People were helpless and it was also difficult to help them. Such reports result in empathy in the viewers' minds as it is painful to think about the sufferings of the affected people. Hence, those who are afraid of that unpleasant situation, protect themselves by avoiding watching it.

6. **Aggression**—It is scientifically proved that a lack of empathy leads to aggressive tendencies. Socialization of male members does not cultivate empathy in them, and as a consequence, they are more involved in aggression. There is a negative correlation between aggression and empathy. More the empathy, less are the aggressive tendencies; less the empathy, more are aggressive tendencies.

7. **Emotional intelligence**—As there is an overlap between emotional intelligence and empathy, there is a positive relation between them. However, irrespective of the equal level of emotional intelligence, the experience of the widest range and variety of feelings is associated with the ability to empathize with the greatest number of people from all walks of life. On the other hand, when we say that someone cannot relate to other people, it is likely because he or she has not experienced, acknowledged, or accepted many feelings of his or her own.

8. **Acknowledgment**—Empathy begins with the awareness of other's feelings. It is easy to achieve it if others would simply tell us how they felt. Most people do not tell us their real feelings; we must resort to asking questions, read between the lines, guess, and try to interpret nonverbal cues.

Emotionally expressive people are easiest to read because their eyes and faces constantly let us know how they are feeling. Hence, they may generate more empathy.

9. **Sensitivity**—It is obvious that sensitivity is the basic requirement of empathy. These two are related to each other. However, sensitivity without any involvement is of no use for empathy. Such an individual will be misusing his or her sensitivity by judging, insulting, rejecting, or exploiting the individual.

10. **Compassion**—This is a correlate of empathy. It is also a prerequisite of empathy, and it precedes empathy. Understanding and compassion lead to more involvement and detailed information regarding an individual. These in turn, lead to better empathy.

11. **Conscience**— It is equally important to have conscience for empathy. A person who does not have adequate conscience will not feel guilty after exploiting and abusing others even if he or she has the understanding of their feelings. Empathy is oriented toward the welfare of the sufferer, the wish to help him or her, and going beyond selfish motives. However, there are even criminals who take undue advantage of some natural calamity and rob the victims after understanding their helplessness.

12. **Socialization**—The whole process of socialization in most of the Eastern civilized societies is to enhance empathy among the next generation. Right from the beginning, children are encouraged to think about effects of their own behavior on others. Children are appealed to understand equal rights of their playmates and develop a sense of fair play. Say if a five year old hits his or her friend, immediately the adults scold him or her and try to generate the other-oriented feeling. "Fighting hurts others" should be the lesson. There are cultures that give reinforcement to empathic understanding and behavior, so that social conformity and acceptance may generate empathy.

13. **Physiological correlates**—Researchers have reported that when children are shown video clips with situations where they see people suffering and pain, neural circuits related to pain are activated in their brain. By the age of 2 years, children normally begin to display the fundamental behaviors of empathy by having an emotional response that corresponds with another person's emotional state. Even earlier, at 1 year of age, infants understand that just like their own actions, other people's actions also have goals. Also, during the second year of life, toddlers try to make other children comfortable. In make-believe also some empathy is essential.

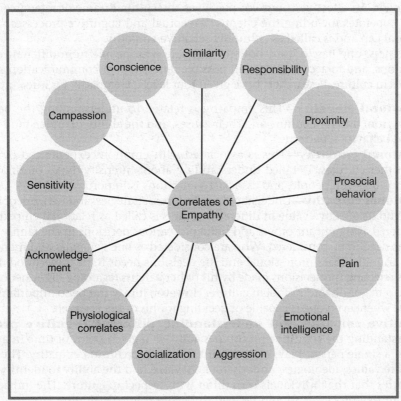

298 Life Skills for Success

The theory of mind relies on the structures of the temporal lobe and the prefrontal cortex, and presents the idea that empathy depends on the sensorimotor cortices as well as limbic and paralimbic structures. Proper empathic engagement helps an individual understand and anticipate the behavior of another. Recent research regarding mirror neurons has proved that mirror neurons are activated by observing others while doing a particular activity in the same way as when the individual does the same activity. These are found in premotor cortex, supplementary motor area, primary somatosensory cortex, and inferior parietal cortex. Deficit of such activity leads to social problems. it is also found in autism. in short, mirror neuron system is involved in empathy.

Other correlates like the individual's own experiences, general religious, as well as cultural orientation are also well documented.

17.4   OTHER RELEVANT CONCEPTS

1. **Intercultural empathy**. In every culture, there are different perceptions, conceptual understanding, rituals, and traditions. If we are not capable of understanding them, we may not be able to develop empathy for the people from different cultures. Intercultural empathy is the ability to perceive the world as it is perceived by a culture different from one's own. Cross-cultural analysis includes cultural communication differences; an example is the different conceptions of time, fun, or death. In different cultures, the same concept or behavior leads to different reactions, social acceptance and expectations, interaction, and behavior. An effective counselor perceives the cultural frame of reference from where the client operates including the client's perceptual and cognitive processes. This bridges the cultural gap and is called as culturally sensitive empathy.

   In business, one has to learn how to negotiate with people from different cultures and organizations, and to accommodate all possible differences of communication styles due to differences in culture. Researchers have given four levels of empathy for intercultural setting:

   a. **Behavioral empathy**—This empathy is related to understanding the behavior of a person from different culture and their causes, and the ability to understand reasons and related behavioral patterns.

   b. **Emotional empathy**—This is associated with emotions experienced by individuals from other cultures. Detailed understanding about intensity, types of emotional lives, relations between people, and associated emotions is important.

   c. **Relational empathy**—Understanding the types, strategies, and network of human relations and its affective value in different cultures is called as relational empathy. Who are considered as significant others and influence various decisions in the family and organizations need to be considered. Who are considered as one's enemies and friends, who can affect an individual's professional and life decisions needs to be understood. If an adolescent is rejecting the decisions made by his or her parents regarding his or her career, it may lead to a major discord in Indian culture. However, it may not be so important in Western culture where everyone is capable of deciding for his or her own self.

   d. **Cognitive empathy and understanding different cognitive prototypes**—Understanding the cognitive prototypes active at a given point of time in a certain culture in a single person plays a significant role in intercultural empathy. The beliefs that generate values, ideologies, underlying behaviors, and the ability to identify the mental structures that the individuals own differ with respect to culture. The impact of culture on cognitive processes should be well understood for developing empathy. It is worth remembering that empathy may or may not result in socially acceptable behavior. Empathy and the wish to help a person who is interested in unethical practices and illegal activities will lead to hazardous consequences.

2. **Critical empathy.** In counseling relationship, critical empathy is required for understanding the client's psychological status. As the counselor has to completely identify himself or herself with the counselee for grasping all details of feelings and thoughts, empathy is utilized to its fullest extent. However, afterward when the counselor has to objectively analyze the actions, reactions, and emotional problems of the counselee, empathy needs to be reduced and a balanced point of view is to be made. If not, then the counselor will be so driven away by the counselee's problems that he or she may not be able to interpret the information objectively and scientifically.

   The appropriate role of empathy in our dealings with others is highly dependent on the circumstances. For instance, Tania Singer claims that clinicians or caregivers must take care not to be too sensitive to the emotions of others to overinvest their own emotions at the risk of draining away their own resourcefulness.

3. **Sympathy.** Empathy is totally different from sympathy. People use sympathy more frequently than empathy. If someone is suffering, the reaction will be different in case of sympathy and empathy.

   Sympathy is based on unequal relations that mean the sympathetic person perceives the other one as having low status and looks down toward him or her. For example, if a friend's mother is a victim of terminal disease, and he or she is weeping, the expression will be like:

   The person who has sympathy will think "Oh, poor fellow, he or she is suffering," "nothing can be done about it" and say, "I can feel your pain."

   If empathy is experienced, the person will think about all emotions, pain as well as concern and affection. He will say, "I can understand your pain and have deep affection for your ill mother."

   A sympathetic person will concentrate only on sad, unpleasant experiences and feelings. However, empathy leads to equal attention to both pleasant and unpleasant feelings. There is no expression of pity in empathy but in sympathy there is. Both empathy and sympathy can be used in combination.

   Empathy is distinct from sympathy, pity, and emotional contagion. Sympathy is a concern for another, the wish to see him or her better off or happier. Pity is a feeling that another is in trouble and in need of help as he or she cannot fix the problems himself or herself, often described as "feeling sorry" for someone.

   Sympathy is, "I'm sorry for your sadness, I wish to help." Empathy is, "I feel your sadness." Apathy is, "I do not care how you feel."

4. **Gender differences.** The issue of gender differences in empathy is quite controversial. It is reported that females are more empathic than males. Most of the evidence depend on self-reports that in turn are influenced by the impact of social desirability and gender stereotypes. On an average, female subjects score higher than males on the empathy quotient. It is worth noting that the development of empathy is highlighted in the socialization of a female child.

5. **Emotions.** Empathic anger is an emotion, a form of empathic distress. It is felt in a situation where someone else is being hurt by another person or thing. It is possible to see this form of anger as a prosocial emotion.

   The relationship between empathy and anger response toward another person has also been investigated. Research studies basically found that the higher a person's perspective taking ability, the less angry he or she was in response to a provocation. Empathic concern did not, however, significantly predict anger response, and higher personal distress was associated with increased anger.

Empathic distress is feeling the perceived pain of another person. This feeling can be transformed into empathic anger, feelings of injustice, or guilt. These emotions can be perceived as prosocial, and some say they can be seen as motives for moral behavior.

6. **Ethics.** Philosophers usually present two reasons why empathy is essential for deciding right and wrong. Empathy is partly self-standing, and so provides a source of motivation that is partly within us and partly outside, as moral motivation seems to be. This allows empathy-based judgments to have a sufficiently different opinion from a personal opinion considered as moral. Empathy for others is the route to value in life, and so the means by which selfish attitude can become a moral one.

Limits and obligations of empathy and in turn morality are natural. These natural obligations include a greater empathic and moral obligation to family and friends, along with an account of temporal and physical distances. In situations of close temporal and physical distances, and with family or friends, our moral obligation seems stronger to us than with strangers at a distance naturally. Actions are wrong if and only if they reflect a deficiency of fully developed empathic concern for others on the part of the individual.

17.5 ENHANCING EMPATHY

As empathy is one of the most important emotional abilities in social life, one should try to enhance it. There are different strategies useful for increasing empathy. Some significant ones are listed as follows.

1. **Understanding self**
   It is necessary to understand one's own emotions and feelings. It is only after this that an individual is able to extend sensitivity to others. It results in good relations, emotional intimacy, and happiness. It gives a lot of psychological support.

2. **Empathic listening**
   Communicating with others is facilitated with the demonstration of empathy. Communication becomes free and open along with emotional closeness being felt by the receiver.

   Listening carefully and actively leads to a better understanding of what the individual wants to communicate. It is listening so intently and so closely that you experience the other person's situation, thoughts, and emotions. Empathic listening shows that the individual cares and has understood the exact problem. The person prefers discussing his or her real feelings and problems, and without hesitation tells what he or she thinks. There is less possibility of misunderstanding, and if at all some misunderstanding takes place, it can be corrected immediately. It directs the conversations to important emotional issues close to the individual. As acceptance is communicated satisfactorily, emotional catharsis becomes easy and the person feels safe to discuss deep-rooted emotions. Empathic listening involves listening so intently and closely that you experience the other person's situation, thoughts, and emotions. One precaution should be taken in communicating empathically: it should not be taken for granted that empathy means accepting everything as a fact. It means the person who tries to understand should not give the impression that he or she has accepted all the points of view of the other individual.

   Understanding facial expression and tone with emotions is necessary. Nonverbal communication many a time gives better indications of the emotional state of the individual.

3. **Empathic reasoning**

Apart from the automatic tendency to recognize the emotions of others, one may also deliberately engage in empathic reasoning. Two general methods have been identified here. An individual may simulate either fictitious versions of the beliefs, desires, character traits, and context of another individual to see what emotional feelings it provokes. Second way is to simulate feeling to be appropriate for that specific environment.

4. **Expression of empathy**

Without expression, empathy will be worthless. For example, a simple sign of affection such as a hug or a pat may indicate a lot of empathy. If someone is weeping, a gentle touch on the shoulder may be of great help for communicating empathy. Asking questions regarding facial expressions, tone, emotions expressed, and environmental pressures also helps.

5. **Scientific measurement related to training**

Researchers have approached the measurement of empathy from a number of perspectives. Behavioral measures normally involve raters assessing the presence or absence of both verbal and nonverbal behaviors. These behavioral patterns captured on video, an individual's comment on his or her own feelings and behaviors, or those of other people are evaluated as indirect ways of signaling their level of empathic functioning to the raters.

Physiological responses tend to be captured by elaborate electronic equipment and are also used with measuring empathy through facial and other nonverbally expressed reactions and physiological changes.

A measure of how well a person can infer the specific content of another person's thoughts and feelings has been developed by Ickes (2003). Ickes and his colleagues have developed a video-based method to measure empathic accuracy and have used this method to study the empathic inaccuracy of aggressive and abusive spouses. Systematic interpretation of facial expressions and intercultural differences, and explanations of videos helps a lot.

Another method is asking the individual to watch video scenarios either acted or actual life situations and to make written responses which are then assessed for their levels of empathy. Jefferson Scale of Physician Empathy, health professional version, to assess empathy of doctors is widely used in the field of medicine.

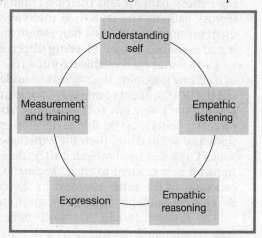

17.6 APPLICATIONS OF EMPATHY

1. **Understanding each other**

The most important application of empathy is understanding each other. Without empathy we cannot accept the other person's emotions, intentions, and behavior. It is the basic requirement for developing trust, a sense of support, and mutual acceptance. Hence, in any interaction that requires cordial relations, empathy plays an important role. In relations between mother and child, brother and sister, husband and wife, and friends, everywhere empathy is the most salient feature.

2. Developing counseling relationship and helping clients to develop empathy

Rogers in 1961 defines empathy as "a counselor's ability to enter the client's phenomenal world, to experience the client's world as if it were his own." Rogers has given a client-centered therapy where the individual's perception is of paramount importance. To make the client's ideas clear to his or her own mind, the counselor has to use reflective questions. It is to make sure that the counselee becomes aware of his or her own emotions, perceptions, and problems, and vividly differentiate between them. With the help of empathy, the counselor helps the client to enhance self-acceptance. In counseling, empathy is the ultimate thing to achieve. An adequate expression of empathy makes the relationship in counseling more meaningful and fruitful. The counselee feels comfortable and expresses every confidential matter while interacting with the counselor.

In case of some psychological and psychiatric problems, empathy for others changes the whole scenario. Think of an adolescent who is involved in alcohol or drug abuse. If he or she can understand the effects of his or her behavior on parents and can develop empathy for them, he or she will be able to have a strong wish to terminate the abuse. Developing skills of empathy is often a central theme in the recovery of different addicts and those who run away, drop out, or attempt suicide.

3. Effective teaching

A teacher may not be able to understand his or her students if he or she does not develop empathy for them, especially for those who have some problems. In teaching, it is essential to develop empathy in the mind of students.

Anjana is doing her postgraduation in social work. She has been given a project regarding leprosy patients and their psychological health. She has to visit various institutes for leprosy patients and take their interviews. Anjana, however, feels that it is some punishment given to her. She just hates them and is afraid of being with them. It is disgusting for her to even look at their bleeding fingers and distorted faces. She wants to leave her course.

One cannot even establish formal relations without some empathy. An important target of teaching is helping the student to understand the subject well. It is never complete without the development of empathy. For example, if teaching about those who are not normal, coming from very low socioeconomic strata or orphans or those who are abused and tortured, students must be able to develop empathy for them, at least think about their conditions and feelings and their life experiences as it may lead to a better understanding of the subject. It is not by choice that they are suffering but there is no way out. Students have to transmit new content to their classmates, so that they reflect continuously on the mental processes of the other students in the classroom. This way it is possible to step-by-step develop the students' feelings for group reactions.

The students should be able to have understanding regarding others, so that no one teases, calls names, or threatens others in schools and colleges. Ragging is the extreme condition where there is no empathy at all. According to Rogers (1961), in effective psychotherapy and teaching, empathy coupled with unconditional positive regard or caring for students is the basic requirement.

4. Helping professions

Having adequate knowledge and expertise is the most important requirement in helping professions like practicing medicine. However, equally important is to develop the understanding of the pain and suffering of the patient. It adds into effectiveness of interaction and treatment. If a patient is complaining about extreme weakness, and if the doctor gives advice regarding exercise, he or she does not have empathy. In this case, the patient will lose faith and may find out a better doctor.

5. **Business**

In business and management also the sense of empathy for customers and employees enhances the business and it works well. It creates workplaces that offer employees a greater sense of mission in their jobs. It is the guarantee that no violence will be communicated in interactions. Empathy is found to be the strongest predictor of ethical leadership behavior out of 22 competencies generally studied, and empathy is one of the three strongest predictors of senior executive effectiveness.

Empathy regarding customers results in very effective services and other types of businesses also. Say for example, in business regarding travels one needs to understand every need of the customers and, thus, plan accordingly. What the travelers of various ages would need if they have to travel in winter, summer, or rainy seasons; what would be the requirements if there are old individuals; and which health-related provisions should be made available are the issues depending on empathy.

17.7 SUMMARY

Empathy is the most essential experience that is a must for understanding self and others, adjusting one's perception according to others, and maintaining proper interpersonal relations. It is the link between two individuals' phenomenological experiences. No interpersonal relation becomes satisfactory without empathy. Empathy makes others' feelings, behavior, and intentions quite clear. In any interpersonal relations where trust is required for the freedom of expression and emotional catharsis, empathy plays a major role. There are different types of empathy and various levels of experiencing empathy. There are many correlates of empathy.

Though empathy is seen right from childhood, one can enhance it by various ways. Empathy is applicable in various fields including counseling, teaching, practicing medicine and business, and in almost all spheres of life. In any job where one needs to interact with others, empathy increases the possibility of better benefits.

QUESTIONS

1. Describe the nature of empathy. What are its contributions in interpersonal relations?
2. What are the types of empathy?
3. What are the ways to enhance empathy?
4. Discuss different correlates of empathy.
5. Explain the applications of empathy.
6. State the difference between empathy and sympathy.

APPLICATION ORIENTATION

1. Write down your reactions after watching a news regarding a serious natural calamity. Given a choice what would you like to do for the victims?
2. Select two individuals who can understand your emotions even when you do not tell them. They can understand your moods, pleasure and grief, and their intensities and as a

consequence, and usually you are most comfortable with them. Now describe the interaction between you and these two individuals. Compare them with others and find out the difference.

3. If you have any problem when you are in college, which teacher would you contact and why? Think about the teacher whom you would never contact. Why? Write down the difference between them.

4. Observe children who are 2–3 years old

    a. When they see other children crying

    b. When they see other children who are happily playing.

SUGGESTED READINGS

Batson, J. G. and Powell, A. L. (1988). Five Studies testing two new egoistic alternatives to the empathy altruism hypothesis. *Journal of Personality and Social Psychology, 55*(1), 52–77.

Beverly, E. (2006). *Healing your emotional self.* Avenel, NJ: John Wiley & Sons.

Hammer, W. D. (2015). *Psychology applied to modern life: Adjustment in 21st century.* Las Vegas: Cengage Learning.

Hogan, R. (1969). Development of an empathy scale. *Journal of Consulting and Clinical Psychology, 33*(3), 307–316.

Ickes, W. (2003). *Everyday mind reading: Understanding what other people think and feel.* Amherst, NY: Prometheus Books.

Reevy, G. M. (2011). *Encyclopedia of emotions.* Santa Barbara, CA: Greenwood Publishers.

Strongman, K. T. (2006). *Applying psychology to everyday life: A beginner's guide.* West Sussex: John Wiley & Sons.

Stein, E. (1989). *On the problem of empathy translated by Waltraut Stein.* Washington, DC: ICS publication.

Titchner, E. B. (1908). *Lectures on elementary psychology of feeling and attention.* New York: MacMillan.

18 Friendship

Objectives

After reading this chapter, you will be able to:

1. Learn about the nature of friendship.
2. Analyze how friendship changes with age.
3. Understand the types of friendship.
4. Know the various correlates of friendship.
5. Evaluate the benefits of friendship.

Sanil and Mihir are good friends for the last 10 years. They share everything with each other. They spend the whole day with each other, help each other, and are ready to sacrifice for each other. Eventually, as Sanil's family business flourished his family decided to shift to America forever. Sanil was extremely unhappy and denied to be with them. He neither wanted to leave Mihir and go to a foreign country nor was he interested in studying abroad. His family tried to convince him but it was all in vein. Ultimately, his parents decided to take Mihir also along with them to America.

What type of bond is this? Why was Sanil reluctant to go with his family? What are the benefits and prerequisites of friendship? What are the various types of friendship?

As friendship plays a very significant role in human life let us discuss it in detail.

18.1 NATURE OF FRIENDSHIP

Various dictionaries define friends as persons who know each well and are regarded with liking, affection, and loyalty; it is an intimate relation with emotional sharing. Friendship is characterized by mutual affection between two individuals. This relationship results in mutual support and happiness. Interest in each other's well-being is essentially seen in friendship. Some researchers have defined friendship as "a form of close relationship that involves enjoyment, acceptance, trust, intimacy, respect, mutual assistance, understanding, and spontaneity."

> Friendship is a voluntary relationship between individuals which is mutually gratifying. It lasts a long time and is characterized by mutual concern. It develops from sharing of interests and experiences, as well as feelings.

Everyone likes to spend time with friends and friendship of a person is accepted without trying to change him or her. We are sure that our friends will act in our best interest. We also assume that they understand us and make good judgments. One can share personal matters with friends in detail without fear of loss of status. We are assured that our friends will understand our point of view. One feels free to be oneself. Parlee in 1979 studied 40,000 individuals and found that many of these characteristics are considered as qualities of a best friend. Friendship is necessary for maintaining good mental health as it leads to happiness. Irrespective of age, gender, caste, creed, and community, friendship plays an important role in people's emotional lives. It is proved in research that women and men, across the large age range, express similar norms in friendship. Generally, people coming from similar backgrounds, educational and occupational types, and similar socioeconomic conditions become friends.

Researchers have proved that people across the life cycle report that they are happier when they are with friends than when they are alone or with family. Friendship provides a variety of benefits which in turn create great joy and happiness. There are three spheres of human life that are associated with friendship.

Some researchers have given the provisions of friendship in three broad categories: affective (emotional), communal, and sociable.

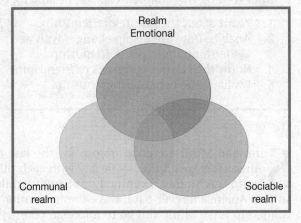

1. **Affective or emotional realm**
   In the affective realm, friends convey concern, warmth, caring, acceptance, and appreciation. In friendship, people feel free to share their innermost thoughts and feelings. This facilitates emotional catharsis. Friends also empathize, provide encouragement, and boost an individual's self-concept. As a result of these affective characteristics of friendships, trust, loyalty, and commitment exist among friends.

   Gouri was upset as her mother scolded her in the morning. When she went to college, she met Asha who could easily recognize that Gouri was disturbed. She asked Gouri about it and Gouri started weeping. Asha tried to console her. They discussed things for long and shared each other's experiences. Gouri went home with better understanding and mood.

2. **Communal realm**
   Friendship provides a feeling of communality. Friends share some similarities, helping each friend to feel connected to humanity. Friends engage in activities together and give and receive support and help in day-to-day activities.

   Sima and Rucha are close friends and are involved in each other's welfare and happiness. Sima is from a middle-class family and Rucha from a well-to-do family. Once they had to pay the fees for excursion and Sima did not have the money. Rucha paid Sima's fees and had to face problems as that extra money was given to her by her father to purchase some gifts for some guests. Rucha never mentioned that to Sima as she knew that Sima will feel awkward for that.

3. **Sociable realm**

Friends are sociable with one another. They have fun together, which includes talking, laughing, and sharing in recreational activities.

It was a great experience to go for trekking with friends and Amey enjoyed it. It was for the first time that he discovered the thrill of being with friends in a faraway place. He is now friendlier with many new members and has developed more self-confidence.

Friendship includes:

1. Affection
2. Empathy
3. Understanding
4. Nonevaluative interaction
5. Openness of expression
6. Trust
7. Enjoyment of the company of the other
8. Sympathy
9. Compassion
10. Altruism

That is why it is very pleasant. It results in many more positive consequences along with emotional support.

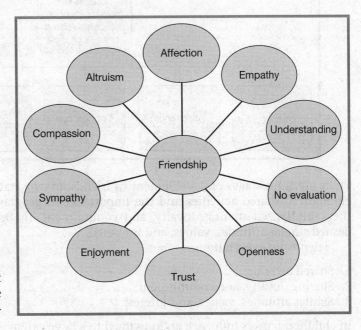

18.2 CHANGING TRENDS OF FRIENDSHIP THROUGH STAGES OF LIFE

Childhood friendships are generally temporary. In childhood it starts from sharing of toys; as the individual becomes more mature he or she understands other's points of view and develops affection and sympathy. Childhood friendship results in better social adjustment even as an adult.

The development of children's friendship follows these stages:

1. **Playmates**—They are considered as friends during the age of 3–7 years. In this stage, friends are those who play together.
2. **Assistants**—This runs from 4 to9 years of age and in this stage friends are those who help each other.
3. **Cooperators**—This runs from 6 to 12 years. Friends are supposed to cooperate, share goals and procedures, and make compromises.
4. **Intimates and mutual supporters**—This runs from 9 to 15 years. Friends in this stage share goals and values, and provide intimacy and support.

5. **Dependent but autonomous**—This runs from 12 years onwards and in this stage adult-like understanding of mutual dependence and maintaining individuality and independence are seen.

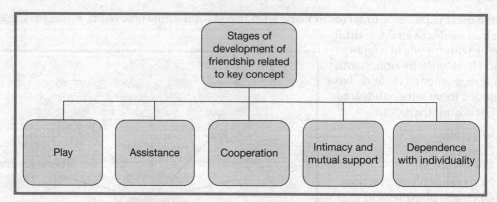

There are three stages of development in friendship expectations. In the first stage, children emphasized shared activities and the importance of geographical closeness. In the second, they emphasized sharing, loyalty, and commitment. In the final stage, they increasingly desired similar attitudes, values, and interests.

Friendship expectations:

1. Shared activities
2. Sharing, loyalty, and commitment
3. Similar attitudes, values, and interest

In childhood, peers influence an individual to a large extent. Peers are agents of socialization. They have impact on attitudes, values, behavior, emotions, and their expression. In school-days, children value their peers' opinion as more important than that of parents and teachers. Acceptance by peers is the most important issue for children. Conformity plays a major role in deciding the peer group structure.

Peer group is a group of equals. Children of the same age and sex assemble into informal peer groups. From 6 to 9 years, these groups are small, not really organized, and their membership changes frequently. Peer groups have a status hierarchy among the members. Gradually, these groups become more structured and cohesive. The members are expected to respect each other and behave according to the norms.

For conflict resolution, girls opt for cooperation while boys prefer competition.

Socialization and cultural norms are basic influences deciding the impact and interaction of the children with their peers. Personality traits are important factors in the choice of friends. Children value cheerfulness, friendliness and cooperativeness, kindness, honesty, and generosity in their friends. As they grow older, similar socioeconomic status, and racial and religious backgrounds are also considered as important issues for making friends.

Sociometry is a scientific method to measure various dimensions of interaction in groups introduced by a psychiatrist called Moreno around 1934. It is a quantitative study of interrelations between the members of a social group with the use of a sociogram. It is a chart showing the network of interrelations. Group members are requested to give their choices or rejections of one another with response to various questions. The questions are related to the choice of a person with whom the individual would like to share a desk, play material, a project, or be with him or her for a birthday party. Each individual is represented by a small circle and preferences are shown with an arrow. Some get many preferences, they are stars; those who are selected by very few are isolates. There are some cliques in which two individuals give preference only to each other.

Gottman (1977) studied 113 children and gave five distinct categories of interactions among children:

1. Sociometric stars: Those who are equally liked by all.
2. Mixers: Those who interact often with peers; may or may not be liked.
3. Negatively perceived by teacher: Teacher–student conflict.
4. Tuned out: Usually not involved in what is going on; ignored by others.
5. Sociometric rejections: Not only disliked but also actively rejected by others.

They might be rejected because they are withdrawn or socially incompetent or overly aggressive. Those who are getting many preferences have many friends and enjoy interaction with them. They are popular among the group.

18.2.1 ADOLESCENCE

Friends occupy vital importance in the life an adolescent. The developmental task in adolescence is social adjustment. As a consequence, social interaction, selection of friends, and new dimensions of social acceptance become predominant. During adolescence, friendships are the most intense relationships in the emotional life of an individual. The absence of friends can be emotionally damaging.

Friends enable adolescents to compare and evaluate opinions, abilities, and even physical changes. They want to cross-check their experiences and are involved in new identity, new roles, and new ways of conduct. Peers give information regarding that and their roles are more acceptable. In a way, friends are reference groups. Social conformity becomes a must for good social adjustment.

Adolescents are not interested in selecting friends only on the basis of availability and similar activities. On the contrary, they are interested in getting friends who have similar values and interests and who accept and understand them and make them feel secure. They need someone in whom they can confide. So, childhood friends may or may not be friends during adolescence.

Adolescents spend most of the time with their peers, and the influence of peers increases during this stage of life. Peers influence attitudes, values, interests, and behavioral patterns. A peer group becomes their real world to try out their real self and understand their role in social situations. They are evaluated by their age mates and they imbibe the views and rules laid down by the age mates. Acceptance by a peer group and dependability become most important during adolescence. It is related to self-acceptance, self-concept, confidence, and mental health in general. Many new fashions and fads are easily accepted by these individuals just for the sake of conformity with group norms. They develop their own language, verbal and nonverbal communication styles, and dress fashion. For them, the importance of family members is less than that of peer groups. If the group is oriented toward antisocial activities, the group members also get involved in the same. During teenage, groups of this sort motivate the members to behave in exiting and thrilling behavior patterns. This includes not only crimes but alcohol, tobacco, and drug abuses.

For peer acceptance, social competence is important. Social competence is the related ability to sense what is happening in social groups, and high degree of responsiveness to others. More the participation in peer groups, more is the development of social competency. An individual is oriented toward developing an adult-like behavioral pattern in a social situation with the help of friends.

The adolescents usually have two to three close friends. They are of the same sex and have similar interests and abilities. These close friends have marked influence on each other. Gradually, adolescents start showing preference toward opposite-sex friendship.

Those adolescents who do not belong to cliques get hardly any satisfaction and acceptance through social interaction. These members join a gang where the members are of the same sex and their main interest is to compensate for peer rejection through antisocial behavior.

In young adulthood, due to responsibilities of married life, time, and energy available for friends decreases. After marriage as everyone becomes more involved in various additional responsibilities, the number of friends and the intensity and frequency of interaction generally reduces. Married young individuals have each other's company. There are new roles at home and family leading to more demands. Even the unmarried individuals have to work and earn their bread and butter. Hence, they become more selective regarding friends and have fewer but more intimate friends. They have values and interests similar to the individual. The number of friends depends on the individuals' comfort in sharing personal things with others. If one wants to keep secrets, then the number of intimate friends is restricted.

In addition to a few close friends, adults also have secondary friends whom they meet infrequently. At the outer circle are many acquaintances with whom they interact occasionally.

At old age, due to more free time and reduced responsibilities, again friendship becomes important. It is the only social interaction as age increases and health problems increase. Although older adults prefer familiar and established relationships over new ones, friendship formation can continue at old age. Older adults tend to choose friends whose age, sex, race, ethnicity, and values are like their own. Fewer older people report other-sex friendships. Older women, have more secondary friends—people who are not intimates, but with whom they spend time occasionally.

Researchers have reported that sources of social contacts are affected by aging. There are three main sources of social contacts at old age. The first one is close personal friendship with members of the same sex. School or college mates are again accepted as close friends and contacts with them are made stronger. These friendships last either till the last breath or migration of one of them. Comparatively friendship cliques are lesser as after retirement their interests differ. Membership of various clubs is maintained only if they do not feel unwanted in the group. If the club is youth oriented, old individuals generally withdraw. If not, it is a good opportunity for developing new friendships and passing time.

18.3 TYPES OF FRIENDSHIP

There are different types of friendships. They differ in the intensity, activities shared, the purpose it serves, and the benefits that individuals are getting. Some important types are discussed as follows.

1. **Best friend**—This is close friendship, having strong interpersonal ties with each other. Perfect sharing of emotions, no loss of status, and intense involvement in each other's

welfare are seen in case of best friends. In close friendship, there is more mature interaction. Close friends are modest to each other, they do not lie to each other, spend great deal of time together, and have self-disclosing and emotionally supporting give and take. Generosity, sensitivity, and honesty are the basic characteristics of close friendship.

2. **Buddy**—A buddy can specifically denote a friend or partner with whom one engages in a particular activity, such as a "study buddy." They may be interested in the same hobbies, games, other extracurricular activities, or even entertainment. That is the sphere of life which is overlapping in their lives and gives an opportunity to interact with each other.

3. **Family friend**—This term can denote friend of a family member or family member of a friend. It is also used to denote an individual who is accepted as a friend by all the family members and has concern for the whole family.

4. **Agentic friend**—These are friends related to some practical purpose than being close psychologically. Here, both parties look to each other for help in achieving practical goals in their personal and professional lives. Helping each other for studies and sharing a flat are the simple examples of the intentions of such friendship. They spend time together, but only when they have time available to help each other. These relationships typically do not include the sharing of emotions.

5. **Internet friends**—Virtual friends communicate with the help of the Internet though they never meet. They can more freely share their emotions and seek for advice on personal problems. They can hide certain things if they want to and pretend as well as use fake identity. This type of friendship cannot be of substantial use in solving real-life problems or helping each other in day-to-day life difficulties.

   Previously, the concept of pen friendship was prevalent. These individuals interact through correspondence by post. There is a possibility that individuals involved in this type also may hide their identity.

6. **Communal friendship**—Here friends gather often to provide encouragement and emotional support during times of calamity or catastrophe. This type of friendship tends to last only when the involved parties fulfill expectations of support.

7. **Primary and secondary friendship**—There are intimate primary friends and less intimate secondary friends. The individual may spend leisure time with secondary friends as well.

8. **Sex-related friendship**—Another type of friendship seen in contemporary society is sex-related friendship. In friends with benefits, sexual relations exist without any formal romantic relations. Gay and lesbian friendships are sex relationships among male and female members, respectively.

   Girlfriend/boyfriend is a new concept borrowed from the Western culture and is not really accepted in Indian traditional culture. This type of friendship is related to temporary sexual relations which are not approved by the society. Due to multiple partners it leads to increased risk of other sexually transmitted diseases along with AIDS.

   Opposite-sex friendship without sexual interest is becoming rare even in countries like India. Still this type of friendship can be strong and emotionally rewarding.

9. **Frenemy**—This word has been coined to indicate a mixture of friendship and enmity. It is a friend who is also a rival, and the relation is a love–hate relation. Sometimes, the person acts as friend and sometimes like an enemy.

Though friendship is characterized by many positive things, sometimes it involves negative emotions and interactions such as dominance, conflict, and rivalry.

If there is competition between two colleagues who are friends, this may happen. If one of them gets a promotion in which the other is also interested, the relations will be strained and negative feelings like hostility may emerge.

Ritesh and Satish were involved in swimming and were interested in representing their college at the national level. They were good friends and enjoyed each other's company during two camps of selection. In the final camp, Satish was selected for the national level. Ritesh was feeling upset and thought that it was injustice. Since then, he was not happy to be with Satish and used to talk ill of him. Face-to-face interaction was as usual, but it was just superficial.

18.4 CORRELATES OF FRIENDSHIP

1. **Proximity**
   Research has proved that if one encounters a particular individual again and again, the chances that friendship will develop between them are more. As is already mentioned, the closer two people live the more is the possibility that they will be friends. They become more familiar and more comfortable. One can easily predict other's behavior. All these things are conducive to friendship. However, concern for each other and understanding as well as liking each other's personality are more important factors for friendship.

   Geographical proximity, repeated interaction and opportunity to share personal ideas and feelings result in friendship. Two college students who stay close by share a vehicle or share even their books and other resources. As a consequence, they may become friends. Two housewives staying in the same building may get an opportunity to interact every day in the lift or in the garden while morning walk, and thus, may be friendly. Two cancer patients who are attending the same group counselling meet again and again and have the same problems. They too may become good friends.

   On the contrary transfer, less time, and opportunities to interact and share feelings with each other may reduce the intensity of friendship. If one of the two individuals joins a new group, friendship may be terminated. In case of extreme disagreement, friendship may end abruptly.

2. **Popularity**
   Popularity is the focus of an individual's life especially in adolescence and depends upon friendship. Researchers have given four types of popularity along with its relation with friendship. These are:

   a. **Popular**—Popular individuals are mostly liked by others and enjoy high status. They have more close friends. They are engaged in activities with friends. They disclose and share their feeling more openly with friends. They are involved more in extracurricular activities. They are aware of their popularity and are less lonely.
   b. **Controversial**—These adolescents are liked by some and disliked by others. They enjoy all the benefits that popular adolescents get.
   c. **Rejected**—These adolescents are by and large, uniformly disliked. They have low status in the group, or in the class. They have fewer friends. As a consequence, they are less involved in social activities. They can develop very few contacts with the opposite gender. Generally, they feel lonely. Such individuals are less popular.
   d. **Neglected**—They are neither liked nor disliked but have less interaction with others and low status. They have the same status as the rejected ones. As a consequence, the social world of rejected and neglected students is less pleasant.

3. **Gender**
   It is proved in research that women and men irrespective of age express similar norms of various feelings in friendship. They are basically affection, trust, commitment, loyalty,

self-disclosure, help, tolerance, consideration, and respect in friendships. In imaginary scenarios depicting friendship situations, however, a number of sex differences emerged that indicated that women tend to expect more from their friendships than men do.

By and large, there are 3–10 friends in case of both the genders. There is no gender difference in a number of friends, but the quality of friendship is different in case of males and females. In Indian situation, it is seen that male members enjoy each other's company when they are involved in parties, fun trips, and time pass activities such as watching a cricket match on television. Most of the women are busy in looking after their families, they cannot meet frequently, but whenever they meet there is more sharing of emotions. They confide more in each other. It is reported by researchers from the Western cultures that women retain their friendships longer than men. One important point is that women's friends are from their neighborhood and men's friends are from faraway places depending on their workplace.

Gender also plays a major role in emotional disclosure which in turn is related to friendship. Gender differences are seen in same gender friendship and miscommunications between men and women in close friendship. Women are more prone to trust their friends and are involved in discussing deep thoughts with friends.

In peer relations where competition and challenges exist, male members hide weaknesses and associate self-disclosure with loss of status and control. They think that they become vulnerable if they discuss their limitations with others. Maintaining friendship at workplace is difficult as there is competition and other negative interactions. Males and females perceive self-disclosure in different ways and reveal different preferences and patterns of self-disclosure. As a consequence, the intensity of their friendship differs substantially.

Women were more critical when individuals violate friendship rules, for instance, betraying confidence, failing to stand up for a friend who is criticized in public.

Women have more close friends; they give importance to intimacy and emotional catharsis, experience more pain when they separate from their close friends, and express more intense emotional involvement.

Cross-gender friendship is welcome by male members when the lady is attractive and they expect sexual relationship to develop eventually. If this does not happen, they end it. Ladies want to have cross-gender friendship without sexual involvement and want their friends to protect them, but if a male friend expects sexual involvement, they may end the friendship. If a male does not get involved in protective role, it becomes worthless for women.

Cross-gender friendships occur less often and do not last as long as same gender friendships. Men and women disclose more to women.

Siblings may also be considered as friends. It is especially sisters who become companions in adulthood. Close sibling relationships predict good mental health.

Friendships function to offer intimacy and companionship, acceptance, a link to the larger community, and protection from physical and emotional loss. Women are more likely to have both intimate friends and secondary friends.

4. **Cross-cultural understanding**

Friendship reduces stereotypes, prejudices, and biases—if friendship takes place in a cross-cultural way that is if the friends belong to different caste, creed, and community, it helps to reduce errors in perceptions. Some things such as stereotypes, prejudices, and biases reduce as the two individuals understand the positive side of the other. They can feel with each other and develop empathy for each other. They understand the reason behind each other's behavioral patterns and limitations. This facilitates intercommunal understanding and cordial relations among them.

Sandeep invited John for Diwali vacation to his hometown. They enjoyed with Sandeep's family and then decided to go to John's hometown for Christmas. Now they have understood everything about each other's families and culture. They now accept each other in a better way.

5. **Conscientiousness**

The basic ideas in friendship are empathy for others, the wish to respect others, and not violating others' rights. These things in turn are related to conscientiousness. Conscientiousness is related to peer relations from childhood. Conscientious children are less likely to be victimized and rejected than children lower on conscientiousness. Those who are low on conscientiousness report more relation between anger and aggression. This is detrimental to friendship. Conscientiousness is associated with self-control and emotional balance. It leads to the management of emotions and mature behavior patterns.

6. **Hurt feeling proneness**

It leads to high value given to friendship, mature love, and stronger feeling to acquire a social reward. Those who are hurt easily by others can understand that they should not hurt others and they know the significance of friendship. They are more interested in getting positive feedback and avoiding negative feelings that hurt.

7. **High affiliation need**

Need for affiliation is a social form of motivation involving a need to seek out and enjoy close and cooperative relationship with other people. It also includes the desire to adhere and be loyal to a friend (Oxford Dictionary of Psychology, 2006). Psychologist Murray introduced this in 1938. High is the need for developing social contacts, more is the possibility that the individual will be involved in friendship.

Most people have a need for affiliation, an interest in establishing and maintaining relationships with other people. Individuals with a high need for affiliation project their ideas in various psychological tests that emphasize the desire to maintain or reinstate friendships and show concern over being rejected by friends.

People who have higher affiliation needs are particularly sensitive to relationships with others. They desire to be with their friends more of the time and alone less often, compared with people who are lower in the need for affiliation. However, gender is a greater determinant of how much time is actually spent with friends. Regardless of their affiliative orientation, female students spend significantly more time with their friends and less time alone than male students do.

8. **Negative correlates**

A man is known by the company he keeps. It is proved in research that if friends have bad habits and are discipline problems, there is every possibility that the individual is also oriented to these bad habits and may develop behavioral problems. In case of addiction, the impact of friendship is significant. If the friends are well behaved and getting good grades, the possibility of such negative impact decreases. We have already discussed it in the development of friendship in adolescence.

18.5   THE BENEFITS OF FRIENDSHIP

Though developing and maintaining good friendship takes time and efforts, the benefits are also significant. They help to make one's life happier and more satisfactory. Some of the important advantages of friendship are given as follows.

1. **Self-confidence**

Self-confidence is generated because of the interaction between like-minded friends. They give reassurance to each other that their opinions and views are right. Reaffirmation of personal values, attitudes, and behavior patterns result in improved self-confidence. If there is any emergency, the assurance that "friends are there to help" also leads to confidence and support.

2. **Self-esteem**

   Friendship improves self-esteem. More acceptance from others leads to better self-acceptance. Self-worth also depends on the evaluation of self by others and by self. Better relationship with friends leads to better self-worth. All these things enhance self-esteem.

3. **Health and wellbeing**

   Friendship can have a major impact on one's health and wellbeing. It enhances the possibility that the individual will be able to maintain good health.

Friendship plays an important role in people's emotional lives. People across the life cycle report that they are happier when they are with friends than when they are alone or with family. Friendships provide a variety of benefits. It results in conditions which lead to great joy and happiness. Celebrating good times and availability of support during bad times are two important benefits of friendship. They help in maintaining psychological health. Friends reduce loneliness and offer companionship. Friends can also increase an individual's sense of belonging and purpose, reduce stress, enhance happiness, improve one's self-worth, and help one to cope with traumas, failure, serious illness, job loss, or the death of a loved one.

Friends generally encourage the individual to avoid risky unhealthy life style habits, such as excessive smoking, drinking, drug dependence, or lack of exercise.

How many friends are necessary for getting the benefit in terms of happiness is difficult to decide. Friendship enhances mental health and it is not on the basis of quantity but quality of friendship. Having many friends may or may not help the individual and having only one or two may be sufficient to generate the satisfaction. It depends on the individual's personality and nature. Some people benefit from a large and diverse network of friends, while others prefer a smaller circle of friends and acquaintances. As there are different types of friendships, the individual's preferences are related to that. One may have a few close friends to turn to for deeply personal conversations, and more casual friends for entertainment activities.

As friends are usually similar in background, age, interests, and needs, there is better understanding among them. Friends offer acceptance and support during difficulty. Sharing deep feelings and needs may be more open in a friendship than even in marriage. It is especially true for women. Same-sex friendships are more intimate for women than men. Women enjoy just talking to their friends, while men choose to do some activity together, especially fun trips, parties, and sports. Men feel competitive with other men. Hence, they are resistant at revealing any vulnerability.

Good friends trust each other, feel secure with each other, and derive satisfaction from caring and nurturing and helping each other. They feel good when they help their friends and bad when they fail to do so. They help the individual to overcome anger and stress.

They are willing to forgive mistakes of the individual. They always perceive the individual from a positive perspective and try to understand and link negative aspects to some reasons. They perceive that their friendship is the best relation that they and others ever enjoy. As a consequence, they value each other and give priority to fulfill each other's needs.

Hence, friends enhance psychological and physical health of the individual concerned.

18.6 SUMMARY

Throughout various stages of human life, friendship plays a crucial role. It is a pleasant relation between two individuals which is beneficial for both of them. Though the weightage of different factors and activities vary according to age, the most common and essential thing in friendship is understanding and helping each other. There are different types of friendships and we all are involved in most of these types. A close relationship includes affection, concern, and wish to be with the other. They share all the deep emotional experiences and support each other.

The correlates of friendship are observed as increasing with enhanced friendship such as proximity, need for affiliation and consciousness. The benefits of friendship are helpful for maintaining good psychological and physiological health. There are some differences regarding the expectations and styles of men and women about friendship.

QUESTIONS

1. Discuss the nature and definition of friendship.
2. Describe the types of friendship.
3. Explain how gender affects the nature of friendship.
4. What are the correlates of friendship?
5. What are the advantages of friendship?

APPLICATION ORIENTATION

1. Write down the common characteristics of your close friends.
2. How many of your friends belong to other religion? How close are they to you? What are the general problems that you encounter while interacting with them?
3. How many of your childhood friends are still your friends? Why are the others not in your contact?
4. Describe the personality and characteristics of your best friend. Why do you consider that individual as your best friend? What type of interaction is specially seen in case of that individual?

SUGGESTED READINGS

Encyclopedia of Emotions

Feldman, R. S. (2010). *Discovering the life span*. New Delhi: Dorling Kindersley.

Gottman, J. (1977) Towards a definition of social isolation in children. *Child Development, 48,* 513–517.

Hurlock, E. B. (1975). *Developmental psychology*, 4th ed. New Delhi: McGraw-Hill.

Parlee, M. B. (1979) The Friendship Bond. *Psychology Today, 11,* 43–54.

Reevy, G. M., Y. M Ozer, and Y. Ito. (2010). *Encyclopedia of emotions*. Santa Barbara, CA: Greenwood.

19 Leadership

Objectives

After reading this chapter, you will be able to:

1. Understand the nature of leadership.
2. Know the personality pattern of a leader.
3. Find out various types and models of leadership.
4. Understand different styles of leadership.
5. Explain changing concept of an effective leader.
6. Learn more about the functions of a leader.
7. Apply the knowledge of leadership to self-improvement.
8. Develop insight into gender differences and leadership effectiveness.

19.1 NATURE OF LEADERSHIP

Netaji Subhash Chandra Bose was a leader of Azad Hind Sena where thousands of his followers had ultimate loyalty and faith in his decisions and were ready to die for his dream of independent India. He had all the powers to attract and direct them to the divine goal.

What was so special in his personality? How could he orient them to a common goal? Why could no one else do that?

As soon as we think about the concept of a leader we think about our great leaders such as Mahatma Gandhi, Lokmanya Bal Gangadhar Tilak, Pandit Jawaharlal Nehru, and many others. Their contribution as freedom fighters, in uniting the whole nation, in various social reforms cannot be underestimated at any point of time. In day-to-day life situations also our leaders are responsible for our nation's welfare, society's level of functioning, and various rules and regulations. Values such as loyalty, sincerity, honesty, and orientation toward common men are expected in a leaders' behavior.

Any organization, social activity, celebration, or interaction between people depends largely on the leader. If the leader is effective, the whole activity takes an appropriate shape. If not, the same activity may become antisocial, unpleasant, or inferior. There are many levels at which the leaders are functioning. Your class representative is a leader of that particular class; your father is the leader of your family. Group interactions, group cohesiveness, achievements of the individual as well as of the group as a whole, and atmosphere and future of any organization or group depend upon its leader. The effectiveness of a leader is a basic requirement for maintaining the performance of the members of any group.

On a highway, a biker met with an accident. It was an overcrowded road and within no time there was a big traffic jam. Everyone wanted to rush and there was chaos. Ajit called the police and an ambulance. He came out of his car and tried to direct the traffic in a better way. He was loudly telling others that the biker also needs some medical help immediately and everyone's cooperation is essential. After that, two to three other people helped him to regulate the traffic till the policemen came.

In this situation, Ajit played the role of a leader to control and manage the situation. He volunteered for that and without any gain effectively convinced others to cooperate.

Leadership has always been there since the emergence of socialized groups. Even during evolution when man stayed in groups, there used to be a leader for every group. As you can see there is a leader in lower level spices also. As a consequence, leadership is a fertile field of research in psychology, management, sociology, and many other disciplines. It is a complicated social process. It is due to dominance drive of a particular person that others get guidance and direction.

> Leadership is influencing others' behavior for accomplishment of a group goal.

Leadership can be broadly defined as influencing the behavior of others for accomplishment of the given goals of a particular group. It is influencing people to strive willingly for group objectives. The leader has to respect others and at the same time be demanding of them. Communicating effectively and persuasively is also an important function of a leader. A leader should be able to understand organizational goals and motivate the team members to accomplish the group goals.

Leadership is managing change and moving groups to new targets, getting exceptional results through others, and knowing and accepting self and others. It is influencing people to follow the achievement of a common goal. It is the ability to exert interpersonal influence by means of communication toward the achievement of a goal. It is the relation between an individual and a group around some common interest. The group members behave in a way directed and determined by the leader.

Most of the definitions of leadership assume certain points:

1. A leader must have followers.
2. A leader must be actively involved in various activities of the group.
3. Leadership includes achieving common goals. The leader should be in a position to influence the members in such a way that they willingly strive to accomplish group objectives.
4. Leadership is not based on force or coercive powers. The members follow the leader willingly.
5. Leadership is a function of the leader, followers, and the situation.
6. A leader influences not only behavior, but attitudes, opinions, thinking, and motivation of the members. They may influence the leader to some extent.
7. A leader enjoys power and influence. The leader has formal authority, knowledge and experience, personal traits, and resources.

> The leader influences not only behavior, but attitudes, opinions, thinking, and motivation of the followers.

8. Leadership is a continuous, dynamic, and complex process.

What gives a leader the capacity to influence others is a power of various sorts. Five different sources of power have been identified. Any leader may have either one or more of these powers:

1. **Reward power**
   It refers to the leader's capacity to reward the followers. The extent to which the leader can control rewards valued by subordinates, the leader's power increases. There are two types of reward powers. Rewards such as praise, attention, and recognition are included in the first type. These are actually a leader's personal powers. There are other rewards which are organizational rewards such as pay raise and promotion. The leader is capable of delivering these rewards because of his or her position in the organization.

2. **Coercive power**
   Here again, the leader is capable of using this power due to his or her both personal and organizational powers. Criticism, lack of recognition, and unpleasant and punishing interaction are personal powers. The organizational coercive power is related to demotion, firing, and withholding pay increases.

3. **Legitimate power**
   It refers to the power the leader has because of his or her position in the organization. Orders and requests by the leader are supposed to be legitimate. Norms, policies, and procedures accepted by the organization confer this power upon the leader. There is nothing personal about this power.

4. **Expert power**
   Subordinates respect and respond more positively to a leader's interaction and influence if they view that the leader is competent and has the knowledge, information, and skills necessary for effective performance. These essentially depend on his or her personal characteristics.

5. **Referent power**
   It depends upon the extent to which subordinates identify with, look up to, and wish to emulate the leader. The more the subordinates identify with the leader and admire the leader, more will be the referent power of the leader. This power depends on the leader's characteristics.

These powers are used in combination for various purposes. Expert and referent powers are more effective than the remaining three which result from the position of the leader in the organization. The followers do not respond to the powers that have nothing to do with the leader's personal characteristics.

Leadership includes many roles. The most important ones are planning, organizing, guiding, coordinating, leading, directing, and controlling.

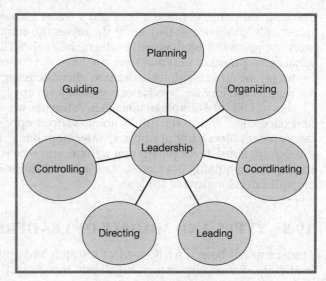

19.2 PERSONALITY OF AN EFFECTIVE LEADER

How to differentiate a leader from a follower? It can be done on the basis of personal characteristics. In a review of 124 studies, it was reported that characteristics such as intelligence, alertness to needs of others, understanding, initiative, persistence, self-confidence, and the desire to accept responsibility, dominance, and control are the most common. In recent research it was seen that personality traits such as adaptability, adjustment, assertiveness, dominance, emotional balance and control, independence, creativity, and personal independence are seen in leaders. Abilities such as judgment and decisiveness, fluency of speech, and knowledge are very common. Social skills such as cooperation, administrative abilities, popularity and prestige, interpersonal skills, tact, and diplomacy are essential for a leader.

A lot of research has been done on the personality of an effective leader. Any effective leader should have the following qualities.

1. Self-confidence
2. Decision-making ability
3. Self-respect
4. Good mental health
5. Firmness and assertiveness
6. Trust and satisfaction
7. Persistence
8. Self-knowledge
9. Enthusiasm
10. Extraversion
11. Honesty
12. Willingness to take risks
13. Willingness to accept mistakes and losses
14. Commitment
15. Consistency
16. Ability and desire for learning and self-improvement.

> A leader inspires and motivates his or her followers and is interested in their development
>
> While
>
> A boss wants only obedience. He or she may not be interested in their development.

The basic difference between a boss and a leader is that the leader inspires others while a boss wants only obedience so that he or she drives the employees. A leader is not only involved in work but wants the development of the member also. The boss may not be interested in the personal development of the employees. So, he or she wants everyone to follow his or her style. The leader, on the other hand, takes decision after discussing it with others. The leader is responsible for benefits and loss; the boss is not responsible for any loss and holds others responsible for that.

Let us take an example of a teacher. A teacher who is very strict, demands a lot of respect and obedience, and never thinks about various opportunities students should get for their development plays a role of a boss. On the other hand, a democratic teacher who is more interested in students' development and welfare, and who is friendly with students and encourages independent thinking is a leader. Such a leader in the classroom is capable of enhancing the cognitive development of students.

19.3 TYPES AND MODELS OF LEADERSHIP

Leadership has been a fertile field of research and application. There are various theories of leadership. Personality theory highlights inborn qualities, trait theory highlights stress-acquired traits, behavior theories concentrate on concern shown for production and for people, and situational theories consider ideas like leadership continuum.

19.3.1 TYPES OF LEADERSHIP

There are different types of leadership. Some leaders are formal leaders and some others are informal. Your teachers and principal are formal leaders and your friend who leads your informal group of classmates is an informal leader. Behavioral theories of leadership focus on the personal characteristics of a leader. However, they are also criticized because the effectiveness of the leader depends not only on the characteristics of an individual leader but on the situation also. Some important types of leadership are discussed as follows.

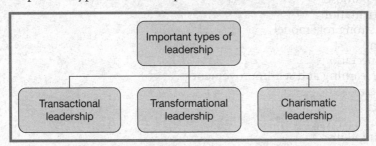

1. **Transactional leadership**
   Every leader expects a particular level of performance from his or her followers. In this type of leadership, the leader uses rewards and punishments for compliance promotion. The leader uses rewards to enhance good work and punishment for bad work. The leader is not interested in changes but wants to keep things as they are. It is because he or she accepts goals, the structure, and the culture of the organization as they are. Such leaders are willing to work in the same system. They do not go out of the way to solve any problem. Such leaders give directions and are action oriented. It is considered as one of the most effective leadership in emergency and during crisis. Here, the leader concentrates on the lowest level of need hierarchy given by Maslow. Such a leader is an extrinsic motivator who brings minimal compliance from followers. The essential characteristics for this type of leadership are:

   a. Directive and action oriented.
   b. Acceptance of goals, structure, and culture of organization.
   c. Thinking inside the box for solving problems.
   d. Passive leadership.
   e. Maintenance of status quo.
   f. Interested in improving performance of others.
   g. Responsive leadership.

2. **Transformational leadership**
   It involves anticipating future trends and inspiring others. It occurs when a leader broadens and elevates followers' interest and stirs followers to look beyond their own interest for the benefit of others. There are four dimensions in it:

   a. **Charisma**—It provides vision and sense of mission.
   b. **Inspiration**— It includes motivating subordinates for better performance and for group goals, and is essentially seen in transformational leadership.
   c. **Intellectual stimulation**—It promotes intelligence, rationality, and creative problem-solving. Giving appropriate intellectual stimulation to the followers, supervising their decisions for rational and logical orientation, and giving freedom of expression for enhancing creativity are essential features of this dimension.

d. **Individualized consideration**—It provides personal attention and treats each subordinate individually. Coaching and giving advice are also important in this style. Here, the leader makes some remarks regarding the worth of the follower as a person.

To be successful as a leader, one needs both transactional and transformational leadership qualities. Special characteristics necessary for transformational leadership are:

a. Simplicity and clarity of expression
b. Sense of purpose
c. Value orientation
d. Being a strong role model
e. Persistent
f. High expectations
g. Lifelong learning and self-improvement
h. Enthusiasm
i. Courage
j. Vision
k. Mentoring skills
l. Ability to deal with complexity

3. **Charismatic leadership**

By the force of their personal abilities, such type of leaders are capable of having profound and extraordinary effects on the followers. People get identified with the leader and follow him or her willingly. Charisma provides vision and sense of mission. Vision and ability to articulate it, willingness to take personal risk, and sensitivity to personal needs are the most important requirements of charismatic leadership.

Charismatic leadership is like magic. The followers follow the leader without any question. In such type of leadership, appealing to emotions at a deep level is seen. It includes a common bond between the leader and followers, promotes shared identity, and exhibits desired behavior. The leader develops an impression of self-confidence, social and physical courage, determination, optimism, and innovation. It involves motivating and directing by developing in followers a strong emotional commitment to vision and values.

Such charisma would add enormously in transformational leadership's effectiveness. It may be used for some antisocial things also. If the vision is unrealistic and inaccurate, the whole group will suffer. Hitler was a leader whose goals directed people to evil.

If we compare transformational leadership and charismatic leadership, two things become obvious:

a. **Transformational leadership originates with vision of change.** It motivates followers to pursue it, incorporates change in the organization, for example, Martin Luther King.
b. **Charismatic leadership originates when a person elicits trust and acceptance** of his or her values and goals by force of presence and personality. Relation with this leader and identification with his or her mission enhances followers' self-esteem, for example, John Kennedy.

19.3.2 Some Models of Leadership

Models of leadership are of various sorts. Traditional leadership models include basic models such as traits model and behavioral model of leadership. Trait model is based on the characteristics of many leaders—successful and unsuccessful. On the basis of this knowledge one can predict the effectiveness of a particular person as a leader.

It generally includes intelligence, maturity, wide range of interest, honesty, and achievement motivation or drive. The behavioral model depends on the actual behavior of a leader. How does a leader accomplish his or her duties regarding task is the focus. The way in which such a leader develops task-centered relations with the followers that focus on the quality and quantity of work is considered in this model. They are considerate and supportive.

Contingency theory and model was given by Fiedler (1967). Here, the classification of leaders and interaction between situation and type of leaders are given. Leaders are basically task and relationship oriented. Relationship-oriented leaders are interested in developing good interpersonal relations with subordinates, socializing with them, are considerate and kind as well as supportive. Here, primary motivation is affiliation. Task accomplishment is only secondary to them. Task-oriented leaders are oriented toward task accomplishment. They maintain good relations with employees only when the work is done properly.

If leader–members relations are good, they are loyal to the leader and support the leader. Here, the leader's control and influence are high. Poor leader–members relationship results in poor control of the leader.

19.4 LEADERSHIP STYLES

A lot of research has been done on different leadership styles. It is the strategy used by the leader to influence the members of his or her group. There are three broad categories of leadership based on behavioral patterns of leaders. These are:

1. **Autocratic leadership**
   In this type of leadership, the power is centered and the leader is the only person who takes every decision for the group. He or she is interested in complete control over the members. Such a type of leader uses power as coercive device and dominates all the members. He or she loves power to such an extent that he or she never shares any with anyone. He or she orders the subordinates and expects complete obedience. He or she uses rewards and punishments to accomplish things in his or her own way. The only advantage of this style is quick and firm decisions, and a satisfied leader. However, it obviously leads to frustration, low morale, and conflicts among members. Their potentials and creativity are not used to the fullest extent. There is no opportunity and development of the followers. They cannot function effectively without the leader. The members do not show any initiative and any interest in responsibility as they understand that it is of no use.

   However, when the members are uneducated or semi-educated, unskilled, and do not have enough understanding to take any decision, autocratic leadership works very well. When accuracy and precision are needed for final decision and no other than the leader has that much of understanding, to keep productivity high, this type of leadership is essential.

2. **Consultative or participative style**
   This leader takes decisions after consulting the staff or group members. It is the majority opinion that the leader follows. Such a leader gives all relevant information to members and discusses with them. There is a freedom of thinking and expression in the group as the leader listens to their opinions and problems. Here, the creativity of the members gets due recognition. The members can contribute and develop their abilities. They help the leader to take appropriate decisions. The members get better job satisfaction. Members are in a better position to accept change as they can understand the advantages and necessity of change. However, this style is time consuming. It depends on the maturity and educational level of the members. When the members accept organizational goals, it becomes easy to opt for the participative style.

3. **Free-rein or Laissez-faire leadership**

In this case, complete authority to take decisions is given to the subordinates. The leader only helps by giving extra information and proving resources. The best part of such leadership is the utilization of potentials of subordinates and job satisfaction. This leadership becomes effective when the members are well qualified, motivated, and responsible. If not, they may work in a different direction.

One more type of leadership is paternalistic leadership. A paternalistic leader is like a father in the family who looks after needs of every member. If the members achieve their goals, he or she gives them rewards. He or she is interested in both work and individual's welfare. However, it is criticized due to the nonavailability of opportunity for self-actualization of the members.

Which type of leadership will be effective depends on the characteristics of members, situation, and interaction between the leader and the members. No one style is always the best. Managers must understand the importance of all these dynamic aspects of leadership as they are the leaders in their organization. They should master the skills and see to it that their subordinates perform their duties properly. Managers should be given opportunities to try different roles and shoulder responsibilities of various sorts. Along with challenging realistic goals, they must be given proper training to deal with people.

According to some other researchers there are four basic leadership styles. They are shown in the following data:

```
DIRECTION

Low direction -------------------------------------------------------------------------- High direction
high
C                                                                                              C
O              supporting              coaching                                               O
M                                                                                              M
M                                                                                              M
U                                                                                              U
N                                                                                              N
I                                                                                              I
C                                                                                              C
A              delegating              directing                                              A
T                                                                                              T
I                                                                                              I
O                                                                                              O
N                                                                                              N
Low --------------------------------------- DIRECTION -------------------------------------------
```

When communication and direction both are low, it is delegating. When communication between the leader and followers is high and direction is low, it is supporting leadership. If communication between the leader and followers, as well as direction giving also is high, the leadership is called as coaching. When communication is low and direction is high, directing is the style of that leader.

There are four types of styles that can be used depending on the three issues enumerated just now. They are telling, selling, participating, and delegating.

1. **Telling**—When the followers are immature, the task-oriented leader is more effective. What is to be done and how it is to be done is told by the leader. The leader need not waste time on maintaining interpersonal relations. Everyone has to complete his or her work, no special cooperation is necessary in this case.

2. **Selling**—If the group is comparatively better and has moderate maturity, the leader is capable of effectively supervising work and maintaining good interpersonal relations. The need for the structure of work and dependence on cooperation are seen in such cases. If the members are more mature, it becomes a must that the leader should listen to their ideas as to how to do the job and then convince them regarding how to do it.

3. **Participating**—Somewhat more mature group expects the leader who will give importance to interpersonal relations. The members are mature enough to understand goals, responsibilities, and initiatives necessary for completing the task. They require a leader who will be able to collaborate all the activities and share the work with them.

4. **Delegating**—Most mature followers expect that the leader should just delegate the work to them. They have enough knowledge and skills to complete the task and simultaneously to maintain good human relations.

Similar styles are given in the following figure:

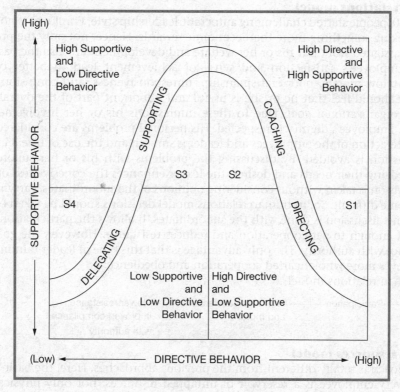

19.5 CHANGES IN THE CONCEPT OF EFFECTIVE LEADERSHIP

The idea of effective leadership is changing in contemporary organizational climate. Previously, a leader was the sole in charge of deciding what the individual was doing and getting in an organization. Obedience was considered the most important characteristic of a follower. However, today we think of using all the human potentials for the benefits of the organization and want the followers to be as active as the leader is.

Traditional leadership is based on aggressiveness. The leader in a traditional role forces others to obey his or her orders by threatening, closely supervising, and unnecessarily hurting the subordinates. Exploiting others by overutilizing power and proving his or her superiority are the behavioral patterns of such a leader. The message is, "I am always ok, you cannot be ok, nobody else can be ok." Such a leader is always interested in finding faults of the subordinates. This type of leadership results in accurate and timely completion of work. Fear motivates the subordinates to accomplish the task. However, there is tremendous loss of interpersonal relations. In long term, the subordinates' morale goes down. The quality of work goes down and the defensiveness of the subordinates increases. This increases the operative cost and the cost of training. This style of leadership is based on theory X regarding subordinates. It is called as negative style of leadership. Now no one accepts the idea of authoritarian leadership. Presently, the participatory approach is more accepted. There are two types of models regarding the participatory style. These are:

1. **Human relations model**
   From 1920, people started challenging autocratic leadership style. Employee is not a machine and is seeking something more than economic rewards. Hence, not only the production of goods or assigned work but his or her welfare and development are also the basic expected results. Employee's satisfaction and sense of achievement lead to better cooperation. Otherwise, low morale, poor craftsmanship, unresponsiveness, and confusion result. The employee should feel that he or she is useful and important part of the overall efforts for fulfilling organizational goal. Due to these impressions his or her involvement in work increases. Employee's dignity is respected. His personal problems are considered with sympathy. Interaction of the employees and leader is smooth and the use of threat and unpleasant aggression is avoided. By discussing the problems with his or her subordinates and acknowledging their needs and desires, the leader enhances the cohesiveness of the group. If any decision is taken without considering opinions of the subordinates, carrying them out may become difficult. So, in human relations model decisions should be taken only after an appropriate discussion is done with the subordinates. It allows the participation of subordinates just enough to get cooperation and reduces resistance. However, the goal is same—compliance with authority. The only advantage is that this type of leader minimizes friction and achieves more wholehearted cooperation and obedience:

   Human relations model:

   ----------Participation----------improved satisfaction----------lower resistance,
                          and moral   improved compliance
                                          with authority

2. **Human resources model**
   This approach is totally different from the previous approaches. Here, the basic assumption is that every employee is a reservoir of untapped resources, not only physical skills and energy. The organization should try to utilize these resources for a better quality of work. The simplest examples are creativity, capacity to shoulder various types of responsibility, and so on. Their participation improves the decisions and total performance efficiency. Self-direction and self-control are important characteristics of this model. It is through this achievement and opportunities of using own capacities that employees get satisfaction and that their moral is improved. It is necessary to create conducive environment in the organization for utilizing the untapped resources of the employees. Here, the goal and purpose of

participation are completely different. The improvement of decision-making and performance efficiency of an organization are the primary goals. Those who are involved directly in implementation make all important decisions and are in a better position to understand why these decisions are made this way. Here, the idea is that improvement in moral not only leads to increased participation but creates an atmosphere which supports creative problem-solving. Subordinates' satisfaction increases as a by-product of improved performance and opportunity to contribute creatively to this improvement.

Research has proved and it is seen in day-to-day life situations that leaders like to exercise the human relations model while dealing with their subordinates and want their superiors to exercise the human resources model. They rate their subordinates lower than themselves in all important qualities. In a way, they are not ready to accept that their subordinates have intellectual powers to contribute substantially to decision-making, but they expect that superiors should accept that they themselves have all these powers. This lack of confidence in others is a great hindrance in implementation of the human resources model. The basic assumption of this model is that members should have the desire and ability to meet the challenges.

Human resources model:

----------Participation----------improved decision making----------improved satisfaction
and control   and moral

What the leader thinks about the followers is also one important issue. There are three theories about it:

1. **Theory X:** The basic assumption of this theory is that common man is reluctant to work, dislikes work, and wants to avoid work as far as possible. It is necessary to control, punish, and threaten them. They do not want to shoulder responsibilities and like to do as directed. They do not have high aspirations. They only need the security of membership.
2. **Theory Y:** It assumes that to work is essentially a natural urge. As we rest, we work. In a conducive environment, common man learns to shoulder new responsibilities. It is not necessary for the leader to supervise them closely. Creativity and new thoughts are distributed equally among all individuals.
3. **Theory Z:** People do not dislike work. If leader–follower relation is capable of generating cooperation and trust, followers try to achieve the best. It should be made clear that the leader and the organization values the followers' contribution.

These three types of theoretical understanding result in different types of interaction of the leader with others.

Sometimes an individual is selected or elected as a formal leader. Otherwise, the leader is automatically working, for example a teacher, parent, or elder sibling.

While playing a role of a leader, the individual is to assess the following things objectively:

1. How much efforts is he or she doing for maintaining good interpersonal relations?
2. To what extent is he or she capable of organizing the structure of work?
3. While considering the exact time and efforts necessary to maintain interpersonal relations, structure, and necessary direction, is he taking into account the followers' abilities, skills, and initiative?

19.6 FUNCTIONS OF A LEADER

Many functions of a formal leader are assigned to the leaders by their organization. Informal leaders are comparatively free from a fixed set of functions and can enjoy more flexibility regarding their functions. It is a combination of the leaders' personal characteristics and authorities given to them with which the leaders can accomplish their task.

Even in defense where the leadership is very strict and obedience is a must, there are examples of complete failure of the leaders to influence their subordinates and the subordinates reject leaders' orders. The troops do not follow their leader.

Formal leadership includes authority, responsibility, and accountability. Authority flows downward and accountability flows upward. Following are a few functions of a leader:

1. **Motivating members of the group:** Motivating members to work for group achievement is the basic function of a leader. He or she generates loyalty, commitment, and the will to work for the group. The leader creates a conducive atmosphere in the group. Goal setting also is a part and parcel of activities. Group objectives and individual goals are used for motivating the group and its members.
2. **Decision-making and goal setting:** Defining the exact objectives of the group is an important function of the leader. This is essential for understanding the exact role of each member and outlining various operations. Making just and fair decisions is the most important job of a leader.
3. **Coordination:** Coordination of all activities of a group is essential for generating a sense of mutual understanding in the members. Only an effective leader can develop the moral of the group. He or she directs the attitude of the group members and maintains discipline. He or she keeps good human relations and maintains voluntary cooperation.
4. **Creating confidence:** Enhancing confidence of the group members is achieved by a good leader. He or she provides guidance and advice when the staff members are in difficulty and provides security to them. He or she encourages them to recognize their own potentialities

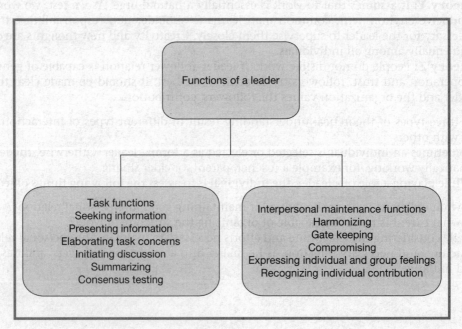

and utilize them in a proper way. By identifying with him or her, the members feel that they are more capable.

5. **Facilitating change:** It is necessary to encourage the group for change in the work environment. An effective leader is capable of increasing the acceptance of change and decreasing resistance to it. For every improvement such as use of creativity, and accepting and generating change, this is a must.

6. **Representing the group:** When it comes to protecting group welfare, the effective leader becomes involved in that. He or she represents the members and defends the integrity of the group.

Thus, an effective leader is expected to generate a conducive environment and maintain high standards in the group as well as keep achievement of the group optimum. He or she should not only think about a good product but also enhance the development of the group members.

Leadership fails because of some issues related to the individual and related to task. These are the pressure of power, detachment and feeing of superiority, false sense of greatness, isolation, out of control ego, inability to continue learning, distorted perception about people and their problems, misuse of power, lack of creativity, and poor values ethics and standards.

19.7 ENHANCING LEADERSHIP QUALITIES OF SELF

There is leadership in every job in the organization and every role in family and community. The only thing is that the degree varies. However, if leadership qualities are enhanced, the possibility of getting better opportunities increases.

How to become an effective leader? Some tips for it are given as follows:

1. Knowledge, experience, self-understanding, and continuous self-improvement are the basic things required for becoming a good leader.

2. One has to avoid the use of power which depends on punishment. That type of coercive power results in many problems. It starts a self-defeating game. Even when the teacher uses coercive power, it affects the students adversely. They can't even study properly. They avoid confrontation and communication with the teacher and prefer sitting quietly in the class. Other powers of the leader are better than coercive power.

3. One should manage change and move groups to new targets. Change is essentially a natural rule especially in an organization. Many a time, people are reluctant to accept the change as their day-to-day life and duties depend on new expectations. Skills for motivating others to acquire new knowledge and skills play an important role in leadership.

4. Develop a vision and strategies necessary for accomplishing the same.

5. Working in teams where the leader's own powers are to be kept aside and he or she has to participate only as a member.

6. Reexamine the things that you have taken for granted about your group members. Be sensitive to it as it may result in some problems. If you accept the X theory and if the group is mature, then the group will resist as it may not require much control. Consider the maturity level of the members to select the leadership style which will be appropriate for them.

7. Practice all important task functions and relation maintenance functions carefully. An appropriate balance between the two works well.

8. Match your own maturity level with the maturity level of the followers.

9. Try to increase the maturity of the members by working with them.

10. Respect others but be demanding of them.
11. Be open to ideas and effective listening of others' views.
12. Acquire knowledge regarding how to inspire others and empower them for the tasks.

19.8 GENDER AND LEADERSHIP

In India, as far as gender and power or leadership are concerned, it is a must to understand the way in which women are socialized right from the beginning. The child-rearing goals in case of an Indian girl child are virtue and social acceptance. They are to inculcate qualities associated with stereotypical sex roles. As an adult she is supposed to become a meek, docile, subjugated, serving, and sacrificing type of individual. A female is supposed to be considerate as well as conservative. The society expects the female to be submissive and to work for others, means for the family for the whole of her life. It is obvious that an Indian girl is not encouraged to have the skills necessary to gain power and respect. No opportunities are given to her for developing self-confidence. In social situations and formal organizational roles also, they are expected to be more cooperative, supportive, understanding, gentle, and involved in providing service to others.

In the Indian culture, a male child is socialized in such a way that he is supposed to develop qualities such as leadership, assertiveness, self-reliance, independence, and self-confidence. A lot of opportunities are given to them to enhance competence and effective use of power. More social exposure to various types of group interactions is made available to male children right from childhood. Men are supposed to be competitive, tough, decisive, and controlling.

As a consequence of social expectations, women cannot occupy higher positions in organizations nor become leaders in informal situations as well. They feel more comfortable as followers within the family or out of it. Very few women can really develop the skills and confidence necessary for leadership. Even in advanced countries, the percentage of women leaders is very low. In India, invariably, a woman is to shoulder the responsibility of household jobs and take care of children, and aged and ill persons in the family. As a consequence, women get less time to devote in any organizational or social activities which is a must to become a leader.

In politics also, women are still seen only as exceptions. The first Indian parliament had 4.4 percent women members, and after more than 65 years of freedom, today it is only 9 percent. In a research done regarding women in politics, women working in politics for more than 10 years were interviewed. Sixty-seven percent of the ladies told that they were afraid of character assassination if they can achieve something that their male colleagues are interested in achieving. It is worth remembering that Madame Marie Curie also had to face character assassination after the death of her husband. She is the only person who could receive two Noble Prizes.

All over the world the scenario is similar. Among the Nobel Prize winners only 1 of 16 are women.

If we consider social and cultural contribution or social leadership, the percentage of women is approximately only 5 percent in India. Even if you try to make a list of individuals who have contributed substantially in any field, you will be able to realize the same.

In India there was no female judge in the Supreme Court as reported in 2010; only 11.9 percent IAS and 4.6 percent IPS officers are ladies. There are approximately 10 percent landholder women in India.

The percentage of senior management roles occupied by women in various countries has been and is always less than 50. The global average is approximately 22 percent. In many countries such as Japan, Germany, India, Turkey, Britain, France, Sweden, and even in the USA, the percentages are less than 20. Philippines is the only country that has more than 50 percent of women in senior management roles. India has the least percentage of women working in the corporate world. A research done in 2010 states that in India fewer than 35 percent women are doing paid jobs, and the remaining are totally dependent on their families.

> Due to general low status of women in the society, and due to fear of character assassination, fear of failure, and low efficacy, women are not comfortable in a leader's role.

Four in ten business organizations worldwide have no women in the senior management.

As a consequence, even when women get power they cannot use it optimally. Due to general low status of women in the society, and due to fear of character assassination, failure, and low efficacy, they are not comfortable in a leader's role. There are extreme examples of how a woman is punished by her subordinates for using her legitimate power as a leader. A real life incident is worth recalling here. A nurse called Aruna Shanbagh from KEM Hospital Bombay was raped and hurt to such an extent by a ward boy that she was in coma for more than 42 years till she died recently in 2015. She was just trying to arrest the malpractices of that ward boy as it was her duty to do that.

There are substantial gender differences in leadership style. As we have discussed earlier, communication style of women is different than that of men. They are soft spoken, give suggestions than orders to their subordinates, and explain the correction necessary along with its causes. As far as possible, they try to maintain good human relations with colleagues. By and large, women leaders do not insult or hurt anyone in front of others. When the work is done properly, women give positive feedback to subordinates. Women leaders treat their subordinates as equals. Though there are some exceptions, most of them behave in this way. Some important characteristics of female leaders are that they:

1. Use consensus decision-making
2. View power in relational term as something to be shared
3. Encourage productive approach to conflict
4. Build supportive working environment
5. Promote diversity at workplace
6. Have a more adaptive, interactive, and transformational style

It is proved in research that men leaders generally give feedback only when there is some error. It means that they give only negative feedback and do not mention when the work is done properly. Men enjoy power and do not want to share it with others. Most of them are harsh and in Indian situation it is observed that even today they are authoritarian and want to use coercive power.

All over the world, people perceive that male members are more effective leaders.

19.9 DECISION-MAKING

To understand the depth of various functions of a leader, let us take an example of decision-making.

A leader has to make many decisions. Very simple to very complex decisions are essentially to be made as per the demands of the situation.

There are nine steps of decision-making. These are:

1. **Problem recognition**—Before the problem becomes difficult to solve, the leader should become aware of the problem. Otherwise, both problem-solving and decision-making take time, and more energy of the whole group is wasted.
2. **Problem definition**—A well-defined problem is a problem half solved. Objective and critical evaluation of various aspects of the problem need to be understood before thinking about any solution. If the leader has his or her subjective perspective, it may complicate the situation.

   If problem-solving efforts depend on half-truths and distorted perceptions of the leader, solution will never be effective. Neglecting or avoiding facts is detrimental to decision-making.
3. **Setting objectives**—Exactly what the leader wants to achieve should be decided before decision-making.
4. **Group identification**—In any organization, a decision may affect a group of employees or other type of group members. Expected effects of a particular decision on one's own group also should be considered before making any decision.
5. **Generation of options**—There are always more solutions than problems. With some efforts, the leader can implement impossible things and get good results.
6. **Effects of the decision on the organization**—What are the expected effects of a particular decision—short and long term—must be well understood before thinking about its solution. All side effects of economic, social, and similar other effects should be considered by the leader.
7. **Evaluation**—The evaluation of different alternatives is the next step.
8. **Selection of one alternative**—One has to select the best solution. However, if any change becomes necessary, it should be done.
9. **Evaluation of alternative**—The effectiveness of the option selected leads to better understanding about the changes required to make it more effective.

No effective decision can be made only on the basis of emotional reactions. Decisions should be made on the basis of logical thinking and objective understanding. Sometimes not making any decision is the best decision. If one has to change the decision repeatedly, one must find out reasons behind that. Generally, people are not interested in calculating the cost of a rare decision. If a particular decision is not made at appropriate time, it will disturb the whole group's or individuals' mental state and performance level will deteriorate.

If a decision has to be made again and again, then one gets the benefit of experience. Many a time, it is difficult to understand why someone else must have made a decision and thinks that it is logical. This failure is due to a lack of understanding regarding which aspects of the environment are important for the other person.

Decisions are of different sorts. Eight types of decisions have been described as follows:

1. **Politically popular decision**—This decision is easily accepted by most of the members though it may not be the most effective decision in the given situation.
2. **Individual-oriented decision**—Here, the individual gets all the benefits of a particular decision.
3. **Superior's political decision**—In this case, the boss gets all benefits of the decision made.
4. **Politically rewarding decision**—If someone has helped in past, he or she will get the benefit because of the decision.

5. **Politically punishing decision**—Just to punish some types of people, this type of decision is taken.

6. **Temporal decision**—A decision that has to be made at a given time immediately because of some emergency is called as temporal decision.

   a. During some calamity or catastrophe, urgent decision must be taken. However, due to great hurry, these decisions are not adequately made.

   b. Quick temporary decisions are to be made even when there is no emergency; it is due to some pressure that decisions are made quickly.

   c. Assuming that problems will be solved or reduced after passage of time, some decisions are postponed. These are called delayed decisions. If this type of delay is seen in problems related to any individual, he or she must insist that decision should be made in due course of time.

   d. Barrier decisions are made when there are barriers that are introduced every time just to avoid the decision.

   e. Underestimating the issue and not making any decision is also one strategy to deal with a given problem. This is called no decision. Even when the individual insists, it is of no use.

7. **Emotional decision**—These decisions are made only on the basis of emotional outbursts; obviously these decisions are inappropriate and result in a negative impact on the concerned party. When there is a sense of favoritism, it is beneficial for that particular individual, but unfair for others.

8. **Economic decisions**—Generally these are to be accepted as a policy decision, for example, to run the office in minimum expenditure.

9. **Risk-based decisions**—These decisions are related to a possibility of some risk, loss, and accidents. These are:

   a. High-risk decisions
   b. Low-risk decisions.

High-risk decisions indicate that the authority persons want to blame a particular individual.

10. **Conflict-based decisions**—Some decisions are made just to avoid conflicts. If no one wants to do a particular task, it is given to a person who will not be able to say no to it.

    There are people who are either temporary employees, or extremely submissive and they do not have enough assertiveness to say no to any task. So, they are easily targeted.

    Some decisions are made to increase conflict and to corner a particular individual. Its intention is negative and obviously the outcome has to be negative.

11. **Buck-passing decisions**—A decision which is unpopular is passed to unwanted people and they are held responsible for its unpleasant consequences.

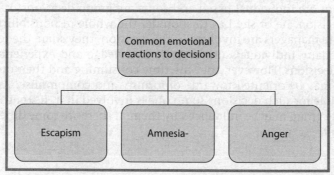

Whatever are the decisions, everyone in the organization has to adjust with them. If the effects of these decisions are positive or insignificant, they can be dealt with easily. Most of the decisions cannot be changed, and hence, even if the consequences are negative, they should be tolerated. Some common emotional reactions to decisions are:

1. **Escapism**—If some unwanted decision is made by the leader and its consequences are negative, one wants to escape from the situation. Members would like to leave the job, and hunt for other, remain absent, try for transfer, and so on.
2. **Amnesia**—Whatever is the decision, one may forget about it and stop talking and thinking about it. Underevaluating and neglecting the decision and showing that it is not an important matter is another way of dealing with unwanted decisions. If one's emotional reaction is of no consequence, then why to have that and why to waste time and psychological energy for that should be the perspective behind it.
3. **Anger**—The expression of anger as a reaction to some unwanted decision is also a very common response to it. If anger is temporary and not really troublesome, it is better to tolerate. However, if it is permanent and has detrimental effects on an individual's health, it is difficult to deal with.

19.9.1 Decision-making Skills

Decision-making is related to selecting a particular course of action out of several alternatives available. Leaders and managers have to make various decisions in different environments. In case of problem situations, one has to make a decision in such a way that all available opportunities are utilized. One has to reduce gap between what the existing and desired states of affairs are.

Decisions are made to achieve certain goal. It is a process of selecting something. It is a continuous process. It has to be done systematically. It is essentially a cognitive process which involves imagination, reasoning, and judgment. A decision depends on situational factors.

Managerial functions include various types of decisions such as selection, planning, organizing, directing, controlling, evaluating, and so on. Some are programmed decisions some others are nonprogrammed. Programmed decisions are routine decisions which are made again and again. Here, all information that is necessary is easily available. The alternative options are comparatively limited. There are well-known rules and procedures. These decisions can be made by lower level managers.

Nonprogrammed decisions are made in a new situation which may not be even known to leaders. The conditions are not predictable. There are various options available and necessary information is not available. Hence, the problem is unique and requires new solutions. Creativity is essential for solving these problems. As such decisions are difficult to make and require appropriate judgment, these are left to higher level managers.

Some decisions are individual based and some are group decisions. When an individual has to make a decision, he or she has to shoulder the whole responsibility of that decision. When two or more managers are involved in the decision, they share the responsibility. As in group decisions many individuals utilize their knowledge and experience, they are better than individual decisions. However, they are time consuming and their quality may deteriorate as members may be oriented toward conformity and compromise. Any one member is not held responsible for such decisions so no one is involved in it. If some members are dominating, the whole group may be influenced by them. If there are some differences of opinion, conflict may result.

Some decisions are strategic and some others are tactical decisions. Strategic policy decisions are about long-term commitments. They are important for the survival of the organization. They are vital decisions where the top level authorities are involved. Tactical decisions are many small decisions made for the implementation of strategic decisions. The aim is to maximize the output of the current activities. They are more specific and functional. As they require less maturity and expertise, these decisions are made by middle- and low-level managers. For example, if the top-level people have decided to relocate the factory in some suburban area, decisions regarding providing residence, buses for commuting, etc. are included in this category.

19.10 SUMMARY

A leader is very important for any type of group or organization. All achievements, interactions, and integrity of a group depend on its leader. Leadership requires various positive characteristics and social skills. The effectiveness of leadership depends on the situation and characteristics of the followers.

A leader has different powers. Some of them are available to him or her as they are given by the organization and some depend on his or her own characteristics. The functions of a leader are related to the overall development of the group and its members.

Gender differences in opportunities and socialization practices result in differences in percentages of male and female leaders. Women cannot use their powers even when they have developed essential skills, due to social pressure.

Decision-making is also inherent and a very significant activity in any organization which requires a lot of systematic efforts. There are different types of decisions depending on the situation, group, and leader. A carefully made appropriate decision essentially leads to the development of the organization and the welfare of group members simultaneously.

QUESTIONS

1. Explain the concept of leadership and types of leadership.
2. Which personality characteristics result in effective leadership?
3. Critically evaluate the changes in the role of an effective leader.
4. Discuss the functions of a leader.
5. How would you enhance leadership qualities in yourself?
6. Critically comment on how gender affects leadership.
7. What are the various types and stages of decision-making?

APPLICATION ORIENTATION

1. If you are a leader of your class, which type of power would you use to control your group? Why? Do you like to lead? Why?
2. Collect data on three best leaders, about their personality, characteristics, general decision-making, and popularity.
3. Interview five educated ladies regarding their views about opportunities for women as political leaders.

4. Take any important decision in your life and systematically go step by step in information processing. Write down the appropriate solution according to you.

SUGGESTED READINGS

Fielder, F. E. (1967). *A theory of leadership effectiveness*. New York: McGraw-Hill.

McKenna, E. (2012). *Business psychology and organizational behavior* (5th ed.) New York: Taylor & Francis.

McManus, J. (2006). *Leadership*. New Delhi: Butterworth Heinemann.

Subba Rao, P. (2011). *Personnel and human resource management*. Mumbai: Himalaya Publication House.

20 Transactional Analysis, First Impression, and Presentation Skills

Objectives

After reading this chapter, you will be able to:

1. Know that transactional analysis helps interpersonal relations.
2. Understand the impact of childhood experience on interpersonal relations.
3. Learn the importance and strategies to create positive first impression.
4. Analyze various dimensions of presentation skills.
5. Apply this understanding to improve communication skills in daily life.

20.1 TRANSACTIONAL ANALYSIS

Ashok is the only child of a well-to-do family. He gets all comforts and all his needs are taken care of. Still he is unhappy as he cannot tolerate any interaction with his father. As far as possible, he wants to avoid his father who is very strict and always scolds him. Whatever is done by his father is interpreted as a favor and he expects Ashok to be under tension to make the most of it. He always criticizes, uses horrible nonverbal expressions to declare his authority, and sometimes gives physical punishment.

What is wrong in this interaction? Why is Ashok's father always in the same state? What are the long-term effects of such behavior on children?

A very well-known strategy for understanding the details of interpersonal relations and maintaining good interpersonal relations is transactional analysis.

The ability to communicate in a socially acceptable way is generally taken for granted in any interaction; this is called communication competence. Normal functioning of intellectual powers and senses and proper socialization are essential for that. Conversation is essential to maintain interpersonal relations. It is informal and day-to-day verbal interaction. Generally, conversations have a similar process of opening, built-up, substance, feedback, and closing. These are the five stages of conversation. Conversational turns are essentially inherent in any conversation. Sending and receiving messages are the two things that both the parties are involved in. Conversations can exist in both direct and mediated settings. Speech can be formal and informal. It is defined as an intentional verbal exchange for sending a particular message.

20.1.1 BASIC CONCEPTS

Transactional analysis focuses on interpersonal transactions. It is a theory of communication. It is a theory about how people are structured psychologically and how they express themselves and function in day-to-day life situations.

A psychoanalytic theory called transactional analysis was given by Eric Berne around 1950. It presents a picture of how childhood experiences affect human beings even in adulthood.

Transactional analysis is a very useful tool for maintaining good interpersonal relations. People from different stages of life get the benefits. If we are capable of understanding the exact ego state of the individual who is communicating with us, we are capable of managing our own ego state and reciprocating some emotions or trying to balance the interaction.

> Transaction means any exchange of attention between people from eye contact to stroke. It is the fundamental unit of social interaction. It helps to understand how people function and express themselves in behavior.

When two individuals meet, someone starts communication. That is transactional stimulus. It can be verbal or nonverbal. The other person responds; this is transactional response. The goal of transactional analysis is personal growth and changes. Achieving autonomy by updating strategies for dealing with life that we had decided in childhood is the goal. How do I get along in life? What type of person am I? What matters most for me? Such type of life script is proved to be right though it is painful and self-defeating.

20.1.1.1 Ego States as Phenomenological Realities

There are three ego states in human interaction, according to this theory. Ego state is the sum total of feelings and experiences directly related to a corresponding consistent pattern of behavior. The ego state decides which emotions would arise at that particular time. There are three ego states—parent, child, and adult. These ego states are not indicating relation between individuals who are interacting but their state of mind.

Parent state →

Adult state →

Child state →

The parent state is unconscious mimicking of how parents acted and how the individual interpreted parents' actions. It is a collection of recording in the brain, during first five years, the actions of parents and parent substitutes. It is accompanied by patronizing gestures and critical words. In childhood, parents tell us never talk to strangers, do not do this, always do that, and so on. These things are recorded without questioning or analysis.

The child state is behaving, feeling, and thinking as a child. It is regression. It is a recording in the brain during first five years of emotional interactions associated with external events as the child perceives.

Adult state is interested in finding why, what, how much, how, in what way, and so on. It is attentive, interested, and straightforward. It is non-threatening and nonthreatened.

Adult state is here and now, using all resources, and interpreting information objectively. In the first year of life the individual becomes aware that he can change and control the environment and others' behavior. Transactional analysis is language within language. True meaning of language can be understood by this.

Identification of ego state is essential for further understanding.

20.1.2 Types of Transactions

There are three types of interactions are:

1. **Complimentary transactions**

   The most appropriate interaction is adult to adult. In this type of interaction both the individuals are mature, want to respect each other, and there is no emotional loading which may disturb the interaction.

   If a colleague asks, "When is the meeting of departmental committee?" The person in adult state will answer, "At three o'clock."

   There are some other complimentary interactions as well. In complimentary interaction response must go back from receiving ego state. Others are child–parent and parent–child. If say someone who has high fever asks for water, he or she is in child state. The response that is given, say for example, giving water, is from parent state. This is complimentary. If interaction is not complimentary, both of them become upset. This ineffective interaction continues till the time their interaction becomes complimentary.

2. **Crossed transactions**

   If the interaction is not complimentary, it is crossed. Here, ego state different from one that is receiving, responds.

   For example, the wife asks, "Where is my mobile?" This is an adult-to-adult message. However, the husband replies, "You always blame me for everything." This is sent from child ego state. Actually, the wife did not say anything to hold the husband responsible or to insult him, but he interpreted it that way, got annoyed, and tried to retaliate. His response was emotionally loaded and indicated that he is upset. If it would have been adult ego state, the response would have been, "Wait I shall give you a miss call so that you will get to know where your mobile is."

   Nonverbal communication plays an important role in expressing and identifying ego state.

3. **Covert transaction**

   This is the most complex type of transaction. Here, overtly the individual is saying something else and suggesting something else. You may see an old boss saying to a young lady that she is just like his daughter when he is standing close to her and touching her shoulder. The lady will be able to understand the real message if it is the same as he says or something else. It may be something like sexual harassment.

20.1.3 Other Related Issues

The following assumptions of transactional analysis are examples of some related issues:

1. People are okay. Each individual has a worth, value, and dignity as a human being and deserves to be treated accordingly.
2. Everyone has the capacity to think.
3. People decide their own destiny in making early script decisions. These decisions can be changed.

There are two basic principle uses of open communication—to exchange information and use of contracts to provide mutual collaboration and joint responsibility of communication.

20.1.4 Life Scripts

It is a story of how one perceives one's own life. What kind of person am I, what is most important for me, and how do I get along in my life are the things included in life story. It is used to prove that one is always right. Even when childhood memories are self-defeating and painful one continues to replay them.

> Life script is a story of one's life depending on subconscious impression of childhood experiences.

20.1.5 Applications

Applications of transactional analysis are seen in every field such as psychotherapy, counseling, education, and organizational climate.

20.1.5.1 Educational Applications

It is a creative approach to understand how people function and to connect human behavior with learning and education as a whole. This approach enhances the effective methods of interactions and mutual recognition. Teachers and learners should stay in clear communication and avoid unproductive confrontation. Teachers can extend empathic acceptance to students. Cooperative good will helps solving educational problems. It is useful for motivating students, improving institutional climate, culture development, staff morale, and wellbeing. In organizational development it improves relations, organizational efficiency, and problem-solving.

Counselor uses it for establishing an egalitarian and pleasant relationship.

20.1.6 Contamination of Ego States

Contamination of parent by child or adult by parent is seen very commonly. Taking a belief as fact is an example. If it is told by parents that people coming from a particular caste are aggressive, the child accepts it even in adulthood. Such type of contamination can occur both ways and there is double contamination.

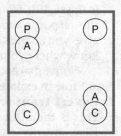

20.1.7 Strokes and Injunctions

20.1.7.1 Strokes

Stroke is human recognition, and exchange of attention or affection. They may be verbal or nonverbal. Touch is a very effective way to give recognition. When your teacher pats while saying well done, it is a strong motivating activity. Touch is essential for survival and growth of babies. In Indian culture, it is customary that the baby gets maximum warmth by being in contact with mother. It gives a sense of security. Strokes are positive or negative, conditional or unconditional. Conditional are like, "I like you when you work hard." Unconditional stoke is like, "I am always with you. When you fail or you succeed."

Scarcity of love and affection by imposing a set of social rules that govern interpersonal communication creates emotional problems. Due to the rules, we accept some strokes and reject some others. At times, we may not accept or not give the strokes that we want to accept or give, do not reject the ones that we want to reject, and do not give strokes to self. If people do not get appropriate stokes, they may even use self-damaging methods to get some. Complete lack of strokes is more harmful than getting only negative ones. In negative stokes also there is a hidden concern which helps the individual to maintain self-worth. No stroke leads to loneliness and cynicism. It further reduces the capacity to give and receive positive stokes. Transactional analysis aims at helping people to recover the capacity to accept and love self and others. Defeating stroke economy leads to better mental health. Encouraging people to give stokes they want to give, accept stokes they want, reject stokes they do not want, and give stokes to self are the aims.

Sunil actually is a good student who got involved in bad company recently. His teacher can easily understand the change in his behavior and a lack of involvement in studies. If the teacher says, "Sunil, I know that you are an intelligent and motivated student, I was not expecting such low grades from you. What is the matter?" Such a stroke is definitely going to help Sunil to introspect and rethink about his recent performance. This may lead to some improvement in his habits and behavior.

One has to analyze childhood experiences, be messages given by parents in childhood, his or her own perception regarding what type of a person he or she is, the ego state he or she uses generally to send messages to others, and so on.

20.1.7.2 Injunctions

There are many injunctions emerging from experiences in childhood. They have their impact in adulthood. Some of them are:

1. Do not be a child.
2. Do not be a grown up.
3. Do not be well.
4. Do not be independent.
5. Do not be close.
6. Do not think.
7. Do not feel.

Dos are called as drivers. They are:

1. Be perfect
2. Try hard
3. Be careful
4. Be strong
5. Hurry up
6. Please others

These are interpreted as, "it is okay for me to live so long as I try hard or...." When these people relax they become restless and feel better only when they start working again. You have the right to live only when you work hard type of pressure makes them uneasy. When they start working, they think their life is justified.

There is a phenomenon life position that colors every transaction. One is "I am okay, you are okay." Second, "I am not okay, you are not okay." Third, "I am okay, you are not." Fourth, "I am not okay, you are okay."

20.1.8 GAMES

We all are interested in playing some games and transactional analysis explains them. In that we want to create fictitious impressions. Types of games:

1. Why does this always happen to me?
2. If it weren't for you?
3. See what you made me do?
4. You got me into it.
5. Look how hard I have tried.
6. Now I have got you.
7. Why don't you, yes but.

Let us take an example of the last one. Seema is a middle-class working married lady and has been obese for many years. Now at the age of 45 she is suffering from other painful consequences of obesity. In the following conversation, she is discussing this with her colleague Meena.

> **Seema**: I want to reduce my weight.
> **Meena**: Why don't you go to the gym?
> **Seema**: I cannot afford the fees.
> **Meena**: Then you should walk for an hour every day.
> **Seema**: The only time that I can get is in the evening, but I am afraid of going alone.
> **Meena**: Why don't you avoid using lift? Better use the staircase.
> **Seema**: No no, I can't as my knees pain a lot.
> **Meena**: Then the only option is to change your diet and manage your weight.
> **Seema**: That is beyond imagination as my stomach will not be able to tolerate any change.
> **Meena**: I know how difficult it is to reduce your weight.

Meena is trying to help Seema. She tried her level best to understand Seema's problems. Now she has given up and that is what Seema wanted to achieve.

Transactional analysis has attracted attention of many researchers not only from psychology but also from sociology, education, and management. The model is being revised even now and an example of such revision is shown further.

Here, you can see that the parent ego state is divided into two parts—one is positive and the other is negative. Again in both there are two divisions. In positive, there are nurturing and structuring, and in negative, spoiling and critical parent are included. Likewise, even the child stage is also divided into positive and negative. There are many such advances in the model.

What we should remember is:

It is necessary to monitor our ego state while interacting with others. It is essential to understand the ego state of others while interacting with them. For improving interpersonal relations take into consideration nonverbal communication as well as verbal communication.

As far as possible, transaction should be done from the adult ego state. In formal as well as informal interactions, adult ego state should be maintained. Complimentary ego state transaction is the best.

20.2 FIRST IMPRESSION

Venuri is very intelligent and is always engrossed in some thoughts about studies. She is about to complete her engineering and is interested in doing some basic research. She is least interested in social interactions and saves her time by being alone. Though she gets first rank, she is not capable of getting a good placement. She generally wears ordinary dresses without ironing them, her hair are always unkept, facial expressions declare her detachment from the surrounding, and lack of proper eye contact leads to poor first impression. She cannot impress the interviewers.

The first impression is one of the most important applications of principles of communication, especially of nonverbal communication.

It is always beneficial to create positive impression in daily life while dealing with others—on the job and off the job. This image helps to use one's potentialities. Professional success is a dynamic blend of poise, self-confidence, control, and style that empower the person to command respect. Even during first impression one can be judged as self-assured and thoroughly competent. It allows one to rise above. It is a valuable skill.

There are four stages of developing interpersonal relations. First stage is the first impression, second is developing mutual expectations, third is honoring psychological contracts, and the last one is developing trust and influence. First impressions, though not accurate, are relatively lasting because they influence the way in which people see subsequent data about the perceived object or person. When people are mutually impressed, they are more likely to enter into a long-term relationship. When this happens, they develop certain expectations about each other. An effective relation is developed and maintained only when participants are willing to honor their psychological contracts. This leads to an increased level of trust and influence. When mutual expectations are met, favorable sentiments result. Even after creating a good first impression, one has to maintain that for smooth social interaction.

First impression is like primacy effect. It is a framework within which anybody is viewed. If the first impression is negative, it takes time to overcome it. When two people meet, first few minutes decide the future of interaction. The feelings of boredom or feelings of being offended depend on these first minutes.

Research has proved that first four minutes are especially important. Not only for the first time but always when an individual meets someone, first four minutes are useful for establishment and reconfirmation of relationship. Researchers say that it is only during these four minutes that we decide whether to continue a conversation or to separate. If a positive impression is created in these four minutes, one is perceived as positive.

In a work situation sometimes the time of first impression is reduced to seconds. For example, a customer who is in a great hurry will leave the shop within a few seconds if not attended to.

First impression is influenced by many things. It may be affected by biases, prejudices, and stereotypical impressions of various communities. Assumptions play an important role in first impression. Assumptions, in turn, depend upon socialization and cultural background.

The image that one projects is how others feel about that individual. Image is a tool of communication for revealing one's inherent qualities. In a way, it is a reflection of qualities. It is not a tool for the manipulation of impression.

20.2.1 DIMENSIONS

Major factors that are responsible for an image are related to three things.

1. Appearance
2. Behavior
3. Communication.

In appearance, general neatness, grooming, and appropriate dress are basically considered. Anyone who does not have appropriate verbal and nonverbal communication styles will never be able to create a good impression in the first meeting. Smile wins good will and leads to pleasant interaction. Other aspects of communication are also equally applicable to the first impression. Though these are the basic issues, some specific components have been given by researchers. They are shown in the following figure.

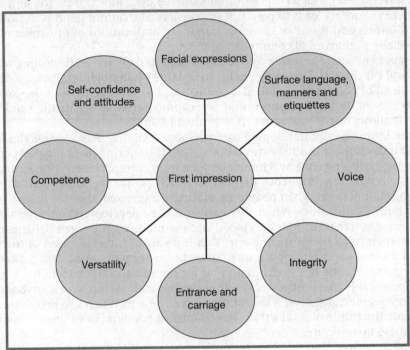

Some important components need further explanation:

1. Surface language is the pattern of immediate impressions conveyed by appearance. The clothes one wears, the hair style, fragrance, and the jewelry one uses all tell us about the person. General grooming also plays an important role in first impression. Clothing is particularly important and it should be appropriate for the occasion. It may be formal, semi-formal, or casual. What one wears decides one's perceived credibility and likeability. It is also a fact that people judge one's appearance much before they judge one's talents. If one underestimates his or her dress fashion especially in organizations, it will be a mistake. The scent used should be mild and acceptable.

2. Facial expressions declare an individual's personality, mood, interest in communication, and enthusiasm in general. As it is most visible and obvious, people depend on that. People's reaction to each other as well as first impression depends upon facial expressions. One has to express positive attitude through facial expression. A pleasant smile is the easiest way to achieve that. Entrance in a room and the way in which one carries oneself also are closely associated with first impression. It declares one's style, self-worth, and confidence.

3. Tone, speed, and volume of speech are important for face-to-face situations and also on phone. Tone is essentially an expression of positive things such as enthusiasm, sincerity,

and eagerness, and negative things such as carelessness, arrogance, and boredom. Hence, one has to be careful about it and guard against the expression of aggressiveness, overconfidence, or being disrespectful.

A relaxed tone of voice and smile indicate warmth; on the other hand, harsh tone indicates hostility. Speaking loudly, quickly, and all the time without allowing others to express declares will to control or dominance. Here, neglecting others' response, interrupting when others are expressing and using controlling tone are obviously seen. Submissiveness is signified by speaking quietly and saying little, allowing interruption and using a meek tone.

4. Various aspects of behavior may contribute to first impression. In that the following things are especially important:

   a. **General punctuality**—This declares that the individual respects others and understands the value their time; hence, it matters a lot. If a client, for example, has to wait for the dealer and the meeting is postponed, it affects first impression negatively.

   b. **Greeting**—Greeting a person in a culturally appropriate way becomes essential before one starts talking about business. The best welcome is a warm smile which makes the other person at ease and willing to communicate freely. This is the time where one can exchange good wishes and win the other person's confidence. Irrespective of gender, educational level, caste, creed, and community of the other person one must express welcome greetings as "good morning" along with appropriate facial expressions and gestures to express it more effectively.

   c. **Expression of attitudes**—While interacting one should be demonstrating that he or she values the views and opinions of the other person. For that, attentive listening has proved to be the best policy. Use of mild and polite words while indicating differences of opinions also counts a lot. Any negative expression through bodily gestures and facial expression may damage first impression. Something such as showing disinterest, being rude, or taking things casually has proved to be detrimental to first impression. Hence, one has to wholeheartedly express interest and enthusiasm.

   d. **Entering in the room**—Impressive gait and strait position of shoulders and neck lead to better self-confidence and good impression. Avoiding confused gestures and too submissive or inferior facial expression result in low self-esteem and poor impression.

One should sit comfortably but not too relaxed. One should be attentive and alert. One should shake hands only if the other person wishes to do so. While this first meeting is going on, one should not use any nervous movements, should not fold hand and tightly hold them, or move legs unnecessarily.

20.2.3 CREATING POSITIVE FIRST IMPRESSION

Strategies for creating positive first impression and its dimensions are different in different situations. The weightage given to various aspects of first impression is dependent on many things. Some important variables are:

1. **Purpose of the meeting**—This decides importance given to many dimensions of first impression and tricks to create one. One can take, for example, an interview, business deal, meeting new colleagues, informal meeting with age mates, and so on.

2. **Duration of future relationship**—It is worth noting that if a relationship is going to continue for long, one has to take things seriously and manage first impression appropriately. If it is a casual conversation with a person standing in a queue next to the speaker, first impression will not be of any consequence. However, if it is a long-lasting relation like meeting the teachers for the first time, one should take every precaution to balance important aspects such as grooming, politeness, enthusiasm, status symbols, modesty, and faithfulness.

3. **Expectations of the other party**—The purpose of meeting and expectations of the other party go hand in hand. If the owner of a factory wants to employ an accountant, he or she expects not only knowledge of dealing with calculations, but honesty and sincerity. He will try to judge the same during the first meeting.

4. **Characteristics of the individual**—Age, education and gender. Individual differences such as age decide everything that is related to first impression. A youngster appearing for an interview for the first time and a senior director going for career advancement are not expected to have the same style and strategies during the first interaction with the selection board. Education directly affects the way in which an individual greets, carries oneself, and expresses self-confidence. Gender differences affect the grooming style, greeting fashion, and so many other things like the expectations of the employer.

The first step to create a positive first impression is to enhance self-awareness. One should recognize all positive and negative aspects of one's behavior, abilities, and personality. Accepting oneself as one is, becomes the next step. Once acceptance is achieved, one becomes objective about what impact he or she can make on others while interacting. The drawbacks are to be compensated and plus points to be exploited to the fullest extent. While using communication strategies also one must first take feedback from friends, family members, and others about one's positive and negative points. These should be objectively and critically evaluated. On the basis of that one can improve verbal and nonverbal communication.

In developing a positive first impression, competence can be achieved by feedback and self-disclosure. It is the integrity of an individual's personality that is evaluated during first impression. Any fake confidence or creating a distorted image may not last longer and the individual may face serious consequences.

It is proved scientifically that first impression is not accurate and many a time it is exactly the opposite of what others perceive afterward. A very smart-looking individual may not have enough knowledge and confidence to discuss important matter with the evaluator or vice a versa. Though the first impression is not the ultimate impression, it plays an important role in human life.

Creating a positive first impression is not the ultimate goal as one has to maintain that impression in further interactions and prove that one has all the expected potentialities to fulfill the expectations.

20.3 PRESENTATION SKILLS

20.3.1 NATURE AND SIGNIFICANCE OF PRESENTATION SKILLS

Mayuresh wanted to go abroad for further studies and had applied to an NGO for financial support. He was shortlisted and was called for an interview and presentation. Mayuresh knew that his family was not capable of supporting him and he was depending on this NGO. Due to extreme stress and nervousness, his presentation failed and he was rejected.

Presentation skills are among the essential skills in achieving any higher qualifications and job-related activities. It is a part and parcel of the duties of various jobs to present the status of a particular activity, project, scheme, or target that the company wants to achieve.

A successful speech is a shared experience. A public speech can be intimately shared. There is a connection between the speaker and the listeners. The speaker has to create and maintain this connection. For that, the speaker has to use all possible tools regarding speaking. There is a possibility of a two-way communication but responsibility of keeping the channels open has to be shouldered by the speaker. The speaker must give of himself his beliefs, knowledge, insight, energy, language skills, and sensitivity to and regard for others, and the listeners give their attention, interest, and generosity of response. For effective speaking confidence, modesty, sincerity, enthusiasm, a pleasant appearance, beautiful language, clarity of thoughts, and effective delivery are all essential. It is a prepared speech presented with the aid of audiovisuals and handouts. It may take any form such as a research proposal, the solution of a problem, or some perspective. Presentation skills are essential for delivering a lecture, participating in a group discussion, or in any type of participatory assignment like brain storming.

Everything such as intelligence, knowledge, and wit are reflected in an effective speech. Since speech reflects all aspects of personality, all good qualities of an individual are seen through speech. There are no specific traits to which the audience reacts positively. Whatever positive things one has, one should bring them to the audience. The speaker is not totally different from the audience and this similarity along with a unique combination of positive traits is useful for winning them. So, the greatest appeal lies in what the speaker is. The speaker is exactly what he or she thinks he or she is and not what he or she wants to believe he or she is. He or she is what he or she honestly thinks he or she is, and his or her honesty is reflected in what he or she says, the way in which he or she says it, and how he or she looks, moves, and sounds. It is related to the intangible feeling that he or she transmits to the audience. He or she must use his or her natural endowment to the fullest extent. He or she must make maximum efforts and should care to make most of every mean of reaching a particular audience. Though one is interacting with crowd, one has to reach out to every individual of the crowd. Avoiding spreading the audience is beneficial. Asking the audience to join the speaker works very well. It is necessary that the audience feels welcome and wanted. As a consequence, they will also be interested in pleasing the speaker.

In short, one has to be very particular about:

1. Attention—one has to capture their attention
2. Benefits—one has to tell them what they will gain from listening
3. Credentials—one has to give them one's credentials for speaking
4. Direction and destination—one has to tell them the structure.

20.3.2   Types of Presentation Skills—Verbal and Nonverbal

In nonverbal skills the expression of enthusiasm, vitality, and sincerity are essential for being impressive. Even before the speaker says anything, the audience makes several assumptions and starts judging the speaker. Listeners have their own prior experiences and expectations. It may include some biases and prejudices. The speaker never gets a second opportunity to make a first impression. One has to remember that the audience is judging the speaker when they see the speaker for the first time. Smiling at the audience becomes essential to communicate to the audience, "I am happy to be here and I am glad that you are here too."

Walking confidently to the stage or podium gives the message to the audience that here is a worthwhile and interesting person. Once settled, then it is essential to relax and take deep breath. Concentrating on environmental information and being optimistic about good performance makes the task easy. At this stage, looking relaxed, cool, calm, confident, and natural becomes a major achievement.

Eye contact declares authority. It is proved scientifically that more confident people are more involved in eye contacts. It is not advisable to select some friendly and sensitive faces in the audience and talk only to them. It becomes boring to the others as they are not involved in the interaction and feel excluded. It is not only redundant but detrimental to look elsewhere, for example, looking out of the window. Here, a lack of interest on the part of the audience may be the obvious output. They feel that whether they listen or not, the speaker does not bother. In a way, if the speaker does not pay attention, he or she should not expect the audience to pay attention. To check one's ability to maintain eye contact, one should try to remember the color of the eyes of the people in the audience.

To improve the ability to establish and maintain eye contact, the speaker should register the details of faces in the audience. One may imagine that he or she is looking through a one-way screen and individuals from the audience are not capable of looking at him or her. This may enhance confidence to look freely at the audience. Eye contact in larger groups should be maintained in such a way that speaker should be looking everywhere in the room. It is something like an M or W type of movement of eyes. Many a time, the lighting arrangements are such that the audience is in darkness and the speakers are in brightly illuminated area. Still, the speaker must try to look at the audience for eye contact. Experts in this field have recommended that the time devoted to each person in the audience should be 2–3 seconds.

All the points explained in Chapter 6 (Communication) are applicable here because presentation is essentially communication. In the remaining things, hands play an important role. Hands may declare many emotional aspects of the speaker. If he or she is apprehensive, the movements of hands can easily express that. It is necessary to avoid certain things such as fiddling with the ring, watch, cuff links, buttons, rubber bands, paper clips, or anything such as a pointer or chalk. One more thing that needs to be avoided is touching and patting face, hair, pockets, table or alike. Clutching back of chair is also seen in case of nervous speakers. Scratching any part of body, hiding hands in the pockets or behind back, constantly folding and not moving the hands at all, and rubbing hands should also be avoided. The speaker should keep them empty and still. While using arm gestures the use of complete arm is a must. Making tiny movements only of hands indicates awkwardness. The gestures coincide with what one is saying only when one does not experience undue stress. Meaningless and repetitive movements of hands are detrimental to the effectiveness of the presentation. It distracts attention of the audience.

The speaker should not try to hide somewhere like behind the podium or table. He or she should learn to stand in front of the audience without any barrier. If the audience can see only the head of the speaker who is standing behind the podium, it becomes difficult to use as well as see gestures. Even when the speaker is tall he or she should stand by the side of podium. It is easy to move about and use gestures more naturally. If a microphone is fixed, it is a must to stand constantly near it. Hence, collar microphone should be used, if available.

For effective presentation, standing is always better than sitting. It declares authority and helps in proper breathing and maintaining appropriate eye contacts. Voice projection is also better in standing than in sitting positions. As the speaker is more visible to the audience, maintaining attention of the audience becomes easy. Posture in standing also should be such that it should express the speaker's confidence. Shoulders should be optimally pulled backward and neck as well as head should be in upright position.

Even when the speaker is standing, it becomes necessary to avoid certain things. Due to nervousness one may get involved in rocking to and fro, standing on one leg, repetitively taking few steps forward and backward, flexing at the knees, raising toes, and similar other redundant activities. Theses should be consciously avoided. One should stand upright giving equal weight on both the feet. Placing feet few inches apart and balancing the whole body optimally creates a better impression of a calm and confident state of mind.

Coping with nervousness is a very important issue in any presentation. Even when the speaker is well prepared and has had enough practice, if he or she cannot control his or her negative feelings, the presentation will fail. There are slightly different reasons for everyone to get upset. The influence of environmental factors also varies from individual to individual. Researchers have reported that the rating in terms of fear in case of public speaking is very high even in advanced countries. The general symptoms of such fear are:

1. Blank mind, that is, the inability to remember and focus attention on subject matter;
2. Tight throat, dry mouth, inability to swallow or even smile;
3. Wet palms, feeling very hot and cold;
4. Palpitation and churning stomach;
5. Shaking hands and legs;
6. Stuttering and shortness of breath;
7. Nervous smile and all sorts of facial expressions declaring nervousness.

It is necessary to understand the self-talk before one gets nervous. By introspection, the speaker has to understand what makes the speaker nervous. One has to list all the fears one has while talking in public. It may be the fear of forgetting, not making sense, or creating a bad impression regarding one's capabilities. One feels humiliated and ashamed. It is due to one's self-talk and imagination that one starts feeling afraid. One starts imagining that he or she has failed completely and everyone is making fun of him or her. Then when the individual actually starts speaking on the stage, these negative thoughts and imaginations attack him or her and as a consequence, his or her performance starts deteriorating.

20.3.3 DEVELOPING MATTER FOR PREPARATION

"Fail to prepare; prepare to fail" is generally accepted in case of any achievement. The same is true in case of delivering a speech.

In every respect, opening words are most important. At this stage, the audience decides as to how much of their mental energy one deserves. Actually, one has already made the first impression even before one says even a single word and when they hear one's voice. This is the first evaluation. They will decide whether the speaker is interesting and worth listening to. Does he have enthusiasm, sincerity, and vitality? Hence, the opening words must be stimulating, imaginative, and, above all, attention gaining. Similarly, the last words including the summary also become important. You have to say "to sum up" or "in summary" to indicate that you are about to finish. After these, one needs to make sure that he or she terminates the presentation. During the summary, one has to ask for action—what the speaker expects the audience to actually do? One may use a quotation once again to provide an ending that is humorous or profound depending on the mood that one wants to create.

Who can become a good speaker? Anybody, who really wants to be.

All speakers must prepare. The spine of a speech is its purpose, objective, and introduction of the subject. Conclusion emerges out of them. Authentic information should be acquired through various sources. Recent books which are written by using scientific method to explain scientific facts, scientific journals, different reports, surveys, the information given by government and nongovernment organizations, and the information available on the web should be collected.

After gathering sufficient information, it should be organized logically and hierarchically to suit the demand of the subject. While preparing the presentation, it is a must to adjust it with the level of understanding of the audience and the purpose of the presentation. One has to consider the level of expertise of the audience. Start with general objectives such as to inform, teach, or train; to stimulate, motivate, or inspire; to persuade, convince, or sell; to explore, debate, or negotiate; or to amuse or entertain.

Factual information along with charts, graphical presentation, and various types of pictures can add into the attractiveness of presentation. Facts that are otherwise dull can be translated in visual word picture. Explaining the applications of the information than just telling them about things, like policy, helps. In some other cases, giving facts and effects of facts along with benefits to the listener is more beneficial. Sometimes personal stories, personal limitations and weaknesses, or self-revealing statements are also useful to maintain the attraction of the audience.

The use of relevant illustrations also helps the speaker to make his or her point more understandable. Telling a story of how a company respected creative idea of an ordinary worker and could get more benefit may reveal the importance of creativity in the industrial world.

Avoiding jargons is, however, a must as it may make the speech difficult to understand and may result in a feeling of being detached from the audience.

The speaker has to plan which visual aid he or she has to use during a presentation. If he or she is using PowerPoint or even overhead projector, he or she has to prepare these PPTs or slides in advance. If he or she is planning to use flip board, he or she can prepare flip charts in advance and keep the markers ready. Flip board should be of adjustable height. One should never speak and write simultaneously. Making presentation more attractive is possible if one uses visuals, figures, and graphs in visual aids. Humor is useful to attract attention; however, it should be only in the form of chuckles and not laughs.

20.3.4 DELIVERY METHODS AND SYSTEMS

There are different delivery methods requiring different preparation and resulting in various advantages and disadvantages. Four important and commonly used methods are—reading, memorizing, speaking extemporaneously, and impromptu speaking.

1. **Reading**—This is the worst method and the speaker should never think of using it. Irrespective of the size, age, maturity, and prior knowledge of one's audience, there are many disadvantages. It is impossible to express sincerity, enthusiasm, and vitality if the speaker is reading. Some specific disadvantages are—one cannot keep good eye contact, one's body language is restricted, one may sound unnatural and, hence, insincere, and it declares and enhances the lack of self-confidence.

2. **Memorizing**—If the complete talk is thoroughly memorized, it may lead to inwardly oriented energy and mechanical delivery. This may lead to a lack of expression of spontaneity, enthusiasm, and warmth. If because of emotional pressure the speaker forgets a point, he or she will not be able to regain his or her place in the script which may lead to poor

impression. The speaker may memorize by heart the important points, passages, and quotations, but should never rely completely on memory for the whole lecture.

3. **Speaking extemporaneously**—This is the most effective style as it has all the benefits of impromptu speaking and none of the drawbacks of reading. Here, the preparation is done carefully, it is rehearsed properly, and the speaker uses the outline notes. Here, even if the speaker forgets something, there is a safety net to support him or her. The speaker should put all possible facts and details of the subject on the ideas' map and then should select some important ones. A second map can be drawn out of it which gives a logical sequence of these ideas. This method has the advantage of being visual and displaying the entire talk to the speaker. It provides prompts to the speaker to be used only if the memory fails, mind goes blank, or the exact sequence of points is not available to the speaker.

If one wants to use the entire script as a safety net, it does not mean reading every word. However,

1. One should use a colored pen to underline the important points.
2. Link important ideas to each other during rehearsal.
3. Use the script only to glance from time to time.

One can also use confidence cards as a safety net. Cards of 3×5 inches should be used to jot down only important points and key words. They are less distracting than papers, one can hold them in hand, and one looks more professional. If the speaker's hands are trembling, cards would not reveal that as vividly as a paper would do. One may also write instructions for oneself as smile, use visuals, and so on. Only the starting and the end statements should be written on that along with some important quotation. As one has to keep them detached, it is necessary to number them. Using confidence cards helps to:

1. Be natural as the speaker has to use his or her own language he or she sounds natural.
2. Be confident as one has a safety net even when memory fails.
3. Look at the audience as one would not need to read from the script.
4. Use expressive body language as one will be free to move.
5. Show sincerity, enthusiasm, and vitality.

The speaker should avoid the following things about the cards:

1. Should not shuffle the cards.
2. Should not keep looking at them and avoid looking at the audience.
3. While finding out the next point from the cards, the speaker should not use fillers such as eh, umm, you know, etc. One has to remember the power of a silent pause.

If the speaker forgets something, he or she need not worry about it as nobody knows that some more points were originally included in the presentation.

If the speaker wants to use visual aid as a safety net:

1. A few key words should be sufficient to provide a structure.
2. Only minimum words should be written on the visual.
3. Creative visuals should be intermittently used for attracting attention.
4. Impromptu speaking should be practiced. Good impromptu speech is to be used with no preparation time. It is obvious that planning is essential for that. Becoming over conscious may lead to poor expression. One common idea is to learn by heart some quotations or lines of well-known poems that can be used spontaneously at the spur of moment.

If one has to speak unexpectedly, one should use the following techniques to build up one's talk: building on previous speaker's comments, summarizing what has been said previously, restating the problem, adding one's views, and using mental prompts, such as, Why? How? Which? When? What? Who?.

Sometimes one has to prepare for radio or television presentation. Specific technical problems arise for radio speaking. One must adjust to the microphone and its sensitivity to the sounds of speech. Even slightly heavy breathing, slurring, too explosive plosives, turning papers, and similar other things are intensified. Clear and clean speech is necessary. Gestures and facial expressions are of no use in radio presentation. One should assure communication by imagining that there is an audience in front of you. Specially while delivering on television, eye contact with the unseen audience is essential. Overuse of gestures and facial expressions should be avoided on television.

20.3.4 Handling Question–Answer Sessions

In many presentations, the last question–answer session is quite challenging. The audience may ask any question related to the subject of presentation and the speaker should be able to give relevant answers. For this, knowing the subject thoroughly is essential. It is a common experience that participants may ask something that is not directly related to the subject but indirectly associated with the issue. Some suggestions for handling question–answer session are:

1. It is necessary to be calm and maintain pleasant atmosphere while interacting with the audience. Looking relaxed enhances optimum interaction. Whatever may the contents and style of question, the speaker has to remain polite. Expressing any type of negative feelings such as anger and hostility verbally or nonverbally may create poor impression.
2. While studying for the presentation, the speaker has to carefully think about expected questions and doubts. The speaker should know the correct answer and have enough information regarding the same. Many interrelated ideas may emerge during this session.
3. During interaction with the audience in a question–answer session one has to use a lot of creativity and presence of mind. There are some unexpected questions which may not be taken care of by the speaker. Hence, the speaker should be flexible enough for relating the question to what he or she knows and guessing the correct answer. He or she may mention that he or she does not have the details right now, but if one wants to have that information, it will be provided later. The speaker may give his or her e-mail address and ask the audience to contact for any further information that they need.
4. After delivering effectively the subject matter, the speaker may also express his or her expectations about questions like they should be of scientific nature and not restricted to individual's personal experience. They should be brief to save time. The expression that questions are welcome and the speaker is competent enough to answer them creates good impression about the speaker. While members of audience ask any question, one must see to it that the audience is not distracted. The speaker should also listen to the question carefully and enthusiastically. If the question is not clear, the speaker should ask for clarification and should not start answering it in a great hurry.
5. Even if a person asks something that is already covered in the presentation, the speaker should not get irritated and explain it in brief reminding that it was already discussed. No sign of under estimating the person should be expressed.

6. Emotional maturity and emotional intelligence both play an important role while interacting directly with the audience. Having empathy for understanding what the question is and avoiding unpleasant tone while giving a negative feedback are products of the same.
7. If someone from the audience is constantly trying to ask irrelevant questions requesting him or her politely to discuss these issues after the session is over is the only way out.
8. Substantial presence of mind is essential for handling question–answer sessions and the demand increases with increasing maturity and inquisitiveness of the audience.

20.3.5 PRACTICE

The listener cannot vary the speed of delivery even if he or she cannot understand the message. Hence, extra care should be taken by the speaker to attract attention of the audience and help them maintain a flow of incoming information. One has to utilize the flexibility available to the speaker for making the presentation as meaningful as possible.

There are many things that one should practice for improving the performance of presentation and public speaking. Some important things are:

1. **Concentration**—Concentrating attention on the subject matter and selection of already-known techniques are essential for effective performance.
2. **Relaxation**—Relaxation should be combined with concentration which may lead to the best output. The capacity of any individual to use the knowledge and skills depends upon this combination of relaxation and concentration. Relaxation and concentration help each other to progress. For higher order cognitive skills, it is necessary to concentrate on the task and forget about tension which may interfere with the task performance. In this way, one can use all the abilities for the same task.
3. **Imagination**—The speaker has to imagine various situations and their consequences. This helps in enhancing creativity and curiosity along with interest in the subject.
4. **Language**—Proper pronunciation, grammatical accuracy, and adjustment of voice as well as pitch according to meaning are the factors that are helpful in increasing the effectiveness of the presentation.
5. **Action**—Whatever the speaker is doing he or she should try to associate different reasons for his or her activities. This may make the activities more meaningful and more accurate. It is necessary to pay attention in detail. This may help to make it more accurate.
6. **Evaluation**—The speaker himself or herself should be aware of the fact that evaluation of own performance and readjusting leading to improvement in speaking is essential. One has to learn and evaluate. One has to be the learner and the teacher. Self-criticism is the best strategy as there is no loss of status.
7. **Improvement**—Improvement is the outcome that is essentially important after one critically evaluates the efforts for presentation. Though improvement may not take place suddenly, gradual improvement also may be useful for further improvement.

Rehearsing helps the speaker to become familiar with material, conquer blank mind syndrome, feel more confident, control negative moods such as nervousness, developing an effective speaking voice, and using positive and appropriate body language. Practice, rehearsal, and dress rehearsal are the three stages. Practicing is done by self, rehearsal is done in front of others, and dress rehearsal is done on site with props. While practice, speaker adds some more examples and anecdotes. Mind becomes more creative while practice. One may replace some ideas or make some others easy to understand. Using a full length mirror along with a tape recorder or using video shooting helps in improving nonverbal communication in terms of facial expressions and gestures. Critical evaluation of own performance leads to understanding more about the ways to improve it. If one has to see whether the audience can really hear what he or she says, it is necessary to keep a tape recorder in the far side or on the last chair of the classroom. In rehearsal it becomes important to openly and objectively accept comments of colleagues and friends who are playing the role of an audience. One can prepare a checklist for evaluating the important points and skills essential for presentation and give it to them. One can keep a record and analyze it again and again for repeated rehearsals. For dress rehearsal, the speaker should try to present without cards.

The attitude of the speaker is of prime importance. It will determine the attitude of the audience toward the speaker. Even if one has prepared the speech properly, it is essential that one should be able to demonstrate that in front of the audience. One has to be sensitive to the audience's needs. If the speaker's attention rests somewhere else even for a moment, the audience also assumes that they have the same privilege. It is the speaker's responsibility to bring them with him or her.

The kind of sound one makes affects the audience and it affects the speaker also. If one is not happy with the quality of voice, it will lead to dissatisfaction about inadequate involvement. The speaker's awareness of shortcoming will add a note of insecurity and may interfere with one's concentration which might adversely affect the content of one's speech. Besides, inaudibility, indistinct speech, and evident voice strain are detrimental to communication. Same is true in case of language skills.

Knowing what one is talking about, what one is making clear to oneself, and satisfaction regarding the words and syntax one selects are adequate to express what one wants to express, add to one's relaxation, and frees the vocal instrument to produce the best sound it can produce.

For becoming an effective speaker, one must understand how people listen. Which type of language, strategies, and nonverbal communication will be most appreciated by a particular type of audience has to be guessed exactly. Otherwise, the presentation will not be well received.

Most people respond favorably to a pleasant voice and good speech. The choice of language has far-reaching effects. Too flowery or too plain language should be avoided as it decreases the effectiveness of the speech. The speaker should devote himself or herself to making his or her thoughts, language, and delivery to communicate the overriding ideas of his or her speech to the audience. Most listeners are continuously assessing, accepting or rejecting, digesting, or neglecting the contents of the presentation. They have their own criteria based on their past experiences and their expectations. In a way, they are judging the speaker. They have their own prejudices also. They constantly ask various questions regarding the speaker and the presentation to themselves. Is it credible? Is it factual? Is it biased? Is it applicable? Is it some new perspective? Is it something that I would like to accept? Why is the speaker saying that? Many such questions are constantly processed by the audience.

Listening is difficult as there is substantial difference between the speed with which human beings think and the speed with which they speak. The audience gets distracted easily as:

1. The people from audience start anticipating what the speaker would say. The speaker must make it clear as to what to expect. Like he or she may say, "There are three broad areas of the issue that will be discussed." The speaker may also intermittently tell them to what extent he or she has covered the subject matter.

2. They start planning what to say when it is their turn.
3. If it is too difficult to understand, they are tired.
4. The speaker may sound monotonous to them if the presentation is too simple and basic.
5. If the speaker lacks credibility and tact to attract their attention.
6. If there are environmental distractions like too much of sound from outside, too warm or cold atmosphere or uncomfortable seating arrangement.

The speaker must be selfless but completely self-aware. It should a blend of dedication, knowledge, and responsibility of power. An involvement with listeners should be so complete and reciprocal that the connection between them becomes unconscious because of the great involvement of both in the idea. This is final integration.

20.3.6 The Obstacles to Overcome

1. **Stage fright**
   The first thing to remember about stage fright is it is not uncommon and not abnormal. It is worth remembering that even if it is present at the onset of the presentation, the whole presentation gets spoiled. There are various indicators verbal as well as nonverbal of the tension that the person feels while experiencing stage fright. Actually, it results from the true regard about self and about the audience. A nervous speaker before he or she enters is concerned about doing a good job, about appearing in good light, and about pleasing people. Extreme expectations of ultimate performance may lead to undue stress. The most important thing is these concerns only are responsible for poor performance of the individual. They create a barrier between the individual speaker and the audience. Excessive self-consciousness mixed with nervousness deflects the attention of both the speaker and the audience from the important content of the speech. It blocks communication both in private and public speaking. The preperformance worries and anxieties should be limited to preperformance stage only. As soon as the speaker steps in the room or on the stage he or she should be able to be free of these worries as they are detrimental to communication. Actually, one can use these worries for betterment of the performance. These concerns motivate the speaker to prepare properly, think and rethink about the language and actual expression to be used, and prepare handouts, PowerPoint presentations, and even preplan about the dress. The person will perceive himself or herself as being ready and that itself will decrease his or her anxiety and increase confidence.
   Many individuals are reluctant to accept that there are some inadequacies that exist in their performance prior to any experience of public speaking. The person himself or herself may be aware of these shortcomings and would not want to correct them. As far as gaps in training and information are concerned, they can be corrected at any time irrespective of age. Awkwardness and unnecessary movements can be controlled with practice. Recognition of interfering habits becomes essential for effective speaking. Habitual emotional upsets are also responsible for inhibiting learning new skills. The fear of success and feeling that one does not deserve praise are hidden blocks which arrest the progress of individual. Mental and emotional habits may lead to prejudice that may defeat all efforts.
   As a speaker, one has to visualize one's success. Imagine that the audience is stimulated and pleased with the presentation, clapping enthusiastically after presentation is over, experts agree, and subordinates are motivated. The speaker should remember his or her prior success and get involved in positive self-talk. This helps a lot.
   Overcoming physical symptoms is also equally important. Those who sweat should wear light cotton and must carry a handkerchief. Those who suffer from dry mouth should

not drink excess water. Instead, they should place their tongue across teeth and gently bite it. Imagining that one is exposed lime juice also helps to increase saliva. One may also try similar other tricks. If hands tremble, using cards is better. If throat tightens up and voice becomes restricted, yawning may be of some help to relax. Taking deep breath helps in case of breathlessness. One must always remember that overt physical symptoms emerge from psychological disturbances. Hence, controlling psychological disturbances is the basic issue.

2. **Interfering tensions**

   There are some other tensions apart from those related to public speaking that are detrimental to speech. These are common tensions which always exist in an individual's mind. Nobody is completely free from tensions in day-to-day life. One has to recognize these tensions and manage them.

   Such tensions affect the performance of the speaker to a large extent in every aspect of speech. People who are, for example, tied up emotionally cannot use their vocal techniques effectively. The inability to speak in front of others is not really related to voice or speech difficulties in case of a normal individual. The problem of poise goes considerably deeper than is generally expected. The roots of such difficulties lie in personal psychological factors. Constructive dos are recommended by researchers.

3. **Misdirected attention**

   If there is real lack of confidence regarding public speaking, it generates a lot of insecurity. In this case, instead of reaching people with effective communication strategies, one may be more worried about making a good personal impression. This in turn results from self-doubt. The individual may display his or her lack of confidence to himself or herself and to the audience. This causes discomfort for both. Selecting proper perspective is essential to communicate appropriately to the audience.

   One more thought associated with public speech is what is new in that. The speaker may get nervous thinking that there is nothing new in his or her speech. Though many things are already delivered by others, one's particular style makes it new.

4. **Use of wrong techniques of memory improvement**

   A feeling that an individual has poor memory leads to wrong practice like rote learning. One thing that is obvious is that no speaker is supposed to deliver a lecture exactly word by word as it is written. Rote learning is the most inefficient technique of remembering as it is mechanical and there is no depth of processing in that. For better memory in less effort, the interpretation of material and in-depth processing such as finding out relations, linking it with other facts, and chunking and making things as meaningful as possible work very well. Knowing what one wants to say and why one wants to say that are two important things. It is a combination of interest, motivation, and enthusiasm that works very well. When a learner is relaxed, he or she can learn better. So, when the speaker has no other anxiety and distractions, he or she will learn better and remember by putting in less effort. There are many techniques suggested by researchers, such as reading the material with rehearsal, studying it just before sleep, linking it with the material already known, and using different mnemonics, as the best ways to improve memory. Using all senses for leaning is also one trick to improve memory.

   Many a time, the speaker overlearns the beginning part of the lecture and neglects or poorly learns the second half of it. This needs to be avoided.

5. **Gimmicks**
   Various tricks are used to add in the attractiveness of the lecture. However, due care should be taken to see that it is not detrimental to the effectiveness of the presentation. Irrelevant and tasteless jokes leading to embarrassment result in difficulty in regaining the appropriate atmosphere again.

6. **Inappropriate mannerisms**
   Unattractive mannerisms which distract the attention of the audience from the material of presentation need to be avoided. Habitual nervous gestures and announcement of excessive self are the ones that hamper the effectiveness of a presentation.

7. **Inappropriate attitude**
   Inappropriate attitude toward the audience and toward oneself in front of audience leads to nonverbal communication, for example, "excuse me or ignore me" or "not worth listening to" type of state. Some hidden hostility or feeling of being unwanted or rejection may emerge without the awareness of the person. This is responsible for a sort of detachment from the audience. Generosity, feeling that people are eager to listen to the speaker, and similar other positive thoughts along with good manners and respect may win the audience.

8. **Overconfidence**
   Overconfidence is always detrimental to the performance of the speaker. The speaker who is overconfident may not prepare properly and think that he or she will be able to perform fantastically. This eliminates the motivation to improve and blinds the person to existing shortcomings. It can betray the speaker even when one becomes proficient in using various tools. Overconfidence makes the person more careless. One depends on the ease in front of the audience to carry one through. In a way, this is a delusion. It must be remembered that every speech needs optimum preparation, carries its own demands, and that these demands must be met. If one has to deliver lectures on the same subject for more than once, he or she may just mechanically repeat the whole thing. This may result in an unsatisfied audience, stale performance, and an unhappy speaker. Every audience is different and the same efforts, same enthusiasm, and same confidence are needed to win them. **More or less confidence, both are detrimental to a performance in public presentation.** One has to create live and shared experiences for oneself and the audience simultaneously.

9. **Unexpected difficulties**
   Sometimes unexpected difficulties are responsible for poor performance. One should be prepared for unexpected difficulties. In a country like India, difficulties may have a wide range. Simple things like power failure may lead to unexpected problems regarding presentation like the inability to use overhead projector or LCD projector. In such case, the speaker should be prepared to deal with the situation. Alternative ideas for making the presentation equally effective should be readily available. Without the visual aids of presentation the speaker should not get confused and be confident.

   To sum up, one should always be interested in critically evaluating self-performance and self-improvement. There is always some scope for improvement.

   As a speaker, one should always remember that three things, that is, enthusiasm, sincerity, and vitality are the most important to make any presentation effective.

20.4 SUMMARY

Three important applications of communication have been discussed in this chapter. Transactional analysis is a full-fledged theory whose applications are obvious in every interpersonal relation. Understanding ego state of self and the other person enhances the possibility of maintaining better interpersonal relations. Other uses are reducing contaminations, miscommunications, and games, and improving understanding regarding conjunctions.

Creating good first impression is essential for everyone, especially for students and those who want to get an appropriate job. Various dimensions of first impression should be considered and practiced to achieve this goal.

Presentation skills are the third issue discussed in this chapter. Everyone will be able to speak effectively in front of audience if one decides to do so. There are some cognitive and some emotional aspects that need consideration. It cannot be denied that there are some factors that cannot be altered by the speaker. However, if the individual tries his or her level to the best his or her performance will be far better than before.

As skills of presentation are important in the corporate world, every person who is aspiring for a higher position should carefully study and master these skills.

QUESTIONS

1. Discuss the different types of ego states and their indicators.
2. What are the injunctions and what are their effects?
3. Describe various games that people play with each other.
4. Which types of transactions are the best and why?
5. Discuss various dimensions of first impression.
6. How can one create good first impression?
7. Discuss the effective strategies to prepare for a presentation.
8. What precautions should be taken while interacting with the audience in question–answer session?
9. Discuss the importance and strategies of nonverbal communication necessary for effective presentation.
10. Which obstacles should be overcome for making presentation effective? How to overcome them?

APPLICATION ORIENTATION

1. Identify two individuals each who are always in child state, parent state, and adult state. Write down their styles of interacting with others in terms of verbal and nonverbal communication. Describe your relations with all of them with reference to pleasantness and unpleasantness.
2. Describe the most important injunctions in your life. What are its effects on your behavior, thoughts, and feelings?
3. Describe the first impression of your new acquaintances. Differentiate between good and bad impressions along with their reasons. Discuss your first impression with your friends. What improvements are necessary in it?
4. What are the problems that you experience while making a presentation in front of the class? Improve one thing at a time and see the difference. Finally, combine all of them. Ask your friends to evaluate your performance.

21 | Team Building

Objectives

After reading this chapter, you will be able to:

1. Understand the importance of team building.
2. Know the exact nature of team building.
3. Differentiate between various types of teams, and between team and staff.
4. Learn more about the criteria of effective team building.
5. Discuss reasons behind resistance to team building.
6. Know the agenda for team building.
7. Motivate yourself to develop teams for various purposes.

Sonu is very popular in his class and is a class representative. He has almost half of the classmates in his group. He is intelligent, smart, and comes from a rich family. In his group, he decides which game to play, how to spend time during lunch breaks, and where to go for a picnic. Those who accept his ideas only can join his group. He generally hides the mistakes and misbehavior of students from his group from the teacher. However, if not, then Sonu manipulates things and makes sure that the student gets punishment. Sonu shares important information regarding studies only with his group.

Ajay is also very popular in the same class who is another class representative. He is very cooperative and never manipulates anything. He is honest and is mature enough to keep good relations with all the classmates. In his group, every one suggests ideas and opinions about what to play and where to go. They also wholeheartedly help each other in studies. They share their resources such as books, new information, and strategies to remember better. There is no hostility in that group.

Which type of group would you like to join? First or second? Why? What is the difference between the two groups? Why?

Team is a group of individuals with complementary skills who work together for accomplishing a common purpose, common performance goals, and an approach for which they hold themselves mutually accountable. Team building enhances synergy between the team members which results in efficient outcomes. In simple language, it is expressed as, "I am because you are and you are because we are."

You must have enjoyed a circus show in childhood. Tricks are performed one after the other and one is totally enchanted due to wonderful atmosphere, risky games, and horror-generating plays with wild animals. There is no time when you feel bored. Not a single moment is wasted. Even when there is a tremendous change required in the setting, like arranging cages for lions, it is done in minimum possible time and with perfection. That is because many people are working for the same thing and they are doing their jobs flawlessly. There is no confusion, no disagreement, and no hesitation while completing the job. This is possible only because of perfect team building.

We generally use the term team to describe a cricket team, volleyball team, or tennis team. We understand and appreciate that the performance of the team is important and everyone has to contribute wholeheartedly to that.

One more example is that of a complicated surgery. There the chief doctor, other assistant doctors, nurses, and even the ward boys need to work in complete coordination. If the nurse gives scalpel instead of scissors, time will be unnecessarily wasted and may result in medical emergency. During war, if a tank is to be used, every one boarding the tank is assigned a particular duty and they are also assigned one additional duty to be performed in case of death of a war veteran working at the adjacent position. There lies a perfect team work on the tank.

As we have discussed in detail, effective leadership is essential for achieving optimum work by a group of people. However, there are other possibilities where the individuals work on their own and perform well. That is called as team building.

21.1 SIGNIFICANCE AND NATURE OF TEAM BUILDING

Scientifically, it is proved that team building results in increased productivity. Team is not equal to a group. Team is two or more people working together in unison for achieving common goals. In day-to-day life, team building does not emerge naturally. Intentional efforts are necessary for that; otherwise, people's differences of opinions, personalities, their biases and prejudices, hostility, and cut-throat competition never allow any real cooperation and best efforts. A lack of open and free communication and trust leads to a lack of coordination. Team building refers to the various activities undertaken to motivate the members and increase the overall performance of the team. One has to give positive reinforcement for novel ideas but if the person fails, the leader is not to demotivate and criticize him or her. Teams are very effective for the development of a new product, reengineering, improving customer relations, developing continuous improvement method, and total quality improvement.

Teams are capable of enhancing motivation, communication, and involvement, and result in greater sense of belongingness.

Uses of teams are varied and are reported unanimously. Teams are formed for the following reasons:

1. Quality improvement
2. Continuous improvement
3. Considering special issues such as cross-functional problems or strategic planning

The team-building cycle is as follows:

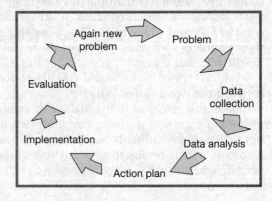

There is a circular action which goes on for solving various problems in an organization. After a particular problem is settled, that team may be terminated and a second team may start working for the next issue.

In day-to-day life situations, there is a leader and the subordinates are just supposed to follow what the leader wants them to do. All the members do not contribute their ideas and views regarding decisions to be made. Overtly, it creates an impression that it works, but there are some limitations to this general procedure. Hence, let us discuss various problems and indicators which suggest that team building is necessary.

The distinct features of a team are listed as follows. They make the meaning of a team clearer:

1. Teams are empowered to share various management and leadership functions.
2. They plan, control, and improve their own work processes.
3. They set their own goals and inspect their own work progress.
4. They prepare their own budget and coordinate with other departments.
5. They take their own decisions about purchase, training, and hiring.
6. They shoulder the responsibility of the quality of their products.

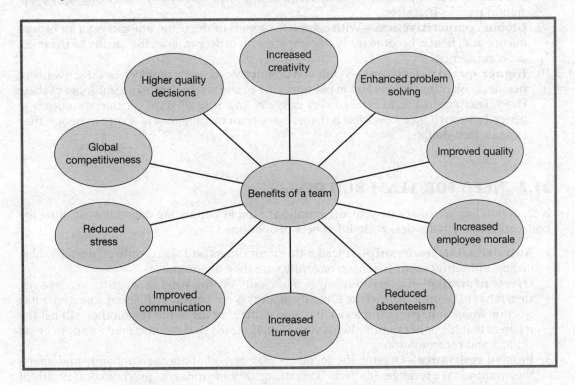

There are many benefits of a team. Some important advantages are listed as follows and also shown in the figure:

1. **Creativity**—The atmosphere within a team is open and nonthreatening. Each member can participate freely and express creative ideas for group goals.

2. **Enhanced problem-solving**—If every member utilizes his or her abilities and skills for the team goal, problem-solving improves.
3. **Improved quality**—The members contribute to the work wholeheartedly, and hence, the quality of output is better than any other type of work conditions.
4. **Increased moral of the members**—The right to participate in every important decision and equal status within the team results in improved moral of the members.
5. **Reduced absenteeism**—When team members get every opportunity to think and act independently, they get involved in the team work. This is how absenteeism and dodging work reduces.
6. **Increased turnover**—In an organizational setup, team building is reported to have an extra advantage of increased production and enhanced profit.
7. **Improved communication**—As each member tries to understand the others' point of view and actively listens and expresses respect for each other, communication has to improve.
8. **Reduced stress**—Many a time, organizational stress precipitates due to hostility and disturbed interpersonal relations with colleagues. Ambiguities about work and about one's role lead to stress. Open atmosphere in a team and clear division of work along with cooperation reduces that stress.
9. **Global competitiveness**—With complete support of the team, one can get a lot of confidence and, hence, become ready to compete with others as far as the quality of the product is concerned.
10. **Higher quality decisions**—While making decisions, each member can discuss his or her ideas, ask others' views and explain why he or she is reluctant to accept some of these views. Decision in a team is taken very carefully. In a way all-sided consideration leads to better decisions. Once a decision is made, every team member has to accept it; hence, they clear all their doubts.

21.2 NEED FOR TEAM BUILDING

Is team building necessary in your organization? Simple criteria are depending on how the leader and subordinates deal with differences of opinion.

1. **Authoritarian leadership**—If leader threatens others and wants only conformity, obedience, unhealthy submissiveness, or conflict are the only outputs.
2. **Overconformity**—If every decision is made only on the basis of what the leader says, then it has to be unhealthy as the diversity of ideas is not considered. This is something like reaction formation. For example, a child who is afraid of his or her stepmother will tell the relatives that his or her stepmother is very kind. It means that members only want to avoid conflict and confrontation.
3. **Passive resistance**—Overtly, the members may agree but are very unhappy and angry, they want to take revenge. It affects both the quality of work and psychological health of the individuals. They work only for the sake of somehow completing the job.
4. **Quarrels**—Unpleasant expressions of differences of opinions direct or indirect during meetings indicate that conflict needs to be managed properly.
5. **Complaints and discord**—Differences regarding values, personalities, and views become intolerable. Then things are taken to the leader. Reluctance to talk to each other, dodging work, and not sharing important information are the clear consequences.

How much team building is necessary in a particular organization depends on various things. For example, team building in a university's academic department is comparatively less than the accounting department. In finance, everyone's work depends on someone else's work. Even if a single person makes some minor mistake, all the others will suffer. When there are stages of work, more team building is necessary.

Team building is a procedure, it is not an event. It is continuous. If it is just temporary, it is of no use.

Amita was interested in helping the differently able people. She started a self-help group for them and a core team to manage the whole thing. For first few meetings all the members of the core team were present, but then they started taking things for granted, dodging the responsibility, and taking things casually. As the work was nonremunerative, few members were not involved in it. The members of self-help group also did not contribute anything and expected Amita to do everything for them. Gradually, the group was dissolved and the team also vanished.

Team building is based on the idea of intermittent evaluation of work done and finding a way to success through improvement.

Teams are formed for improving the quality of work.

Guidelines for team building:

1. Everyone should express the best thought wholeheartedly.
2. Even if the thought may not be acceptable to others, it must be freely expressed.
3. Everyone should be trained to follow the golden rule of communication. If one wants others to listen, one should first listen to what they say.
4. It is a must to consider every member's opinion before finally deciding anything.
5. Everyone should respect others.
6. Controversies should be discussed openly and constructively.
7. Objective evaluation of team's performance should be done.

21.3   DIFFERENCE BETWEEN A TEAM AND A STAFF

Not all groups in any organization are a team, but all teams are groups. A team is essentially interdependent for achieving common goals.

Some leaders use the term team to indicate staff. They consider that both team and staff mean the same. However, there is a substantial difference between a team and a staff. Most of these differences are related to the leader and the followers' interactions with each other. Staff is treated as subordinates and team members are treated as equals.

Some basic differences between staff and team are discussed as follows:

1. When it comes to a staff, decisions are made and work is distributed by the boss. In a team, decisions are made by the whole team and work and responsibilities are divided by the team.
2. In a staff communication is one way, from the boss to the subordinates, and in a team it is free among all members. In fact, that is one major prerequisite in forming a team.
3. In a staff, subordinates are supposed to work only as per the instructions given by the authority. In a team, however, everyone has to take an initiative and help even in planning.
4. In a staff, loyalty is of utmost value. Those who are loyal to the leader get rewards and benefits. On the contrary, in a team, trust and creativity are valued. Here, personal relations with the leader are kept aside.

5. In a staff, people become defensive when an objective evaluation of their work is done. However, in a team, it is well understood that such evaluation is essential for improvement in performance. It is also quite clear to everyone that one's contribution to the performance of team is essentially important.

6. In a staff, controversial issues and disputes are suppressed, but in a team, they are managed properly. These issues are discussed openly and appropriate feedback is given to everyone. The goal is self-improvement and improvement of the atmosphere in the team.

7. In a team, members shoulder responsibility of the task as a whole and each other's task also. They work for making each other's work better and easy. However, in a staff, they are responsible only for their own work. If someone's work is not up to the mark, others' will only criticize and make the person feel inadequate.

8. In a staff, the boss is interested in getting the work done where the work is only organizational goals. an individual's welfare and achievements are neglected. In a team, the boss is involved in work and progress of the members simultaneously.

21.4 STAGES OF TEAM BUILDING

A team development model says that when the team starts working, the leader's power is comparatively more than a group power. When it reaches a mature stage, group power is more than the power of the leader.

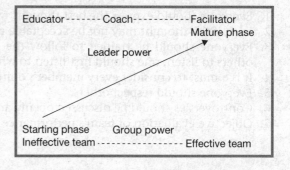

Team leaders are supposed to play a role of an educator and need to have enough knowledge, training, and presentation skills for that. As the team members become more mature, there is more decentralization of power and members share their views more openly and fearlessly. The leader should tactfully enhance open communication in the team. Enthusiastically, he or she should request the members to share their real feelings and views. Sometimes games help to achieve this goal. There are many types of games which are interesting and useful for facilitating interactions between adults. Feedback should be given in such a way that it can be used positively. It should not be only negative and harsh. After every meeting feedback regarding how the time was used should be given and improvement should be planned for next meetings.

When a leader becomes a coach he or she is expected to be more ready to share power with members. He or she may stop the work of the team and give feedback to point out some problems. While doing so, there is every possibility that he or she may start using his or her traditional power. Hence, it is a must to make sure that the leader and the members do understand their role and power sharing.

When the team members become more mature, the leader plays a role of a facilitator. "Let us participate wholeheartedly and reach our goal in a better way" is the message.

In a team, the general goal is productivity, results, and output, but even the members' needs are considered—workers are happy and their morale is high.

Five stages of team building are listed as follows. Time and energy devoted to each stage depends on the maturity and experience of the leader as well as the team members.

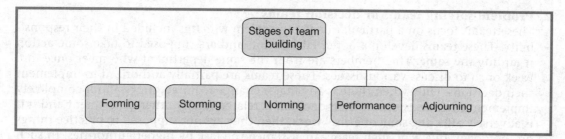

1. **Forming stage**—Developing and understanding goals and developing procedures for performing tasks are the initial tasks of every team. During the forming stage, understanding each member's role as well as the nature of leadership, attitudes, and tendencies of the members to depend on the leader need to be understood. If not, then a lot of confusion regarding what is expected of the members may be generated.

2. **Storming stage**—Conflicts over work behavior, priorities regarding goals, division of labor, and distribution of responsibilities are seen during this stage. Some members may withdraw completely or partially, directly or indirectly during this stage. Some may feel isolated and become emotionally detached. Effective management of conflict is a must. Suppressing conflict will resolve in bitterness and resentment. Withdrawal may cause failure of the team to perform effectively.

3. **Norming stage**—Sharing of important information, accepting different options, positive attempt to make decisions for compromise, and setting rules are important features of the norming stage. Empathy, concern, enhancement of cohesion, cooperation, and shared responsibility are seen in this stage.

4. **Performance stage**—This is the stage when the team shows its ultimate performance. Individual members accept their role and responsibility. They learn how to work independently and simultaneously help each other. The ultimate performance depends upon the effectiveness of leadership, the development of proper norms, and a conducive environment in the team.

5. **Adjourning stage**—Some teams are oriented toward a short-term goal, while others can continue working for long duration. Adjourning of the term depends even on decisions made by the top management. Sometimes resignation of one or more members may lead to changes in a team.

Most of the teams go through these five stages.

21.5 TYPES OF TEAMS

There are many types of teams. Let us consider the basic five types:

1. **Functional teams**

   A functional team includes individuals who work together daily on similar tasks. Such teams are seen in functional departments such as marketing, production, and finance. More than one team may be working in the same department for performing subtasks. Similar is the concept of task teams. Here, decisions affect team effectiveness and if decisions are made without considering everyone's opinion, people are reluctant to implement them.

2. **Problem-solving teams or decision teams**

   These teams focus on a particular issue or problem which is included in their responsibility. These teams develop a potential solution and are supposed to take some action regarding the same. The members are from the same department who meet once in a week or so to discuss various issues. These teams are partially authorized to implement their decisions. Only when there is any major change required, they cannot completely implement their decisions. If their decision is related to any other department and if it is adversely affecting someone else' work, then they are not supposed to practice things on their own. In a way, such teams are assigned the task by higher authorities. In such teams, problem-solving is much more effective as compared to individual problem-solving. Individual problem-solving leads to poor coordination, lower creativity, and more errors. Greater diversity of experience, knowledge, and different approaches to the same problem make problem-solving more effective in a team. In short, wholehearted participation and demonstration of respect for each other are the crucial characteristics of such teams which lead to a conducive environment where the team members rely on each other for performing their job. Generally, these teams set goals, plan strategies, give assignments, reallocate resources, prepare schedules and deadlines, achieve goals, and evaluate.

3. **Cross-functional teams**

   Cross-functional teams bring together people from various work areas to identify and solve mutual problems. Such teams are capable of cutting across departmental and functional line for achieving goals. This type of team may work for long period or may be dissolved after the problem is solved. It leads to quality improvement and linking various functions to increase innovations.

4. **Self-managed teams**

   Self-managed teams are always more effective than other types of teams. Here, leadership is shouldered by the whole team. The leader is supposed to completely sacrifice the traditional powers of a leader. He or she is just a facilitator. There is no special privilege to the leader. He or she has the most useful device, but there is no ego satisfying use of authority for him or her. Self-managed teams comprise of members who work together for manufacturing the entire product. As the members are performing a particular job, decisions regarding these jobs are to be made by the team. For example, if a decision is to be made regarding the uniform of a policeman, then it should be discussed with policemen. Those who stand in the sun and rain for more than 12 hours a day know more about their exact problems. In these teams, the members perceive the team as being effective, performing important and valuable tasks, and enjoying autonomy. As a consequence, they experience a sense of importance. Generally, the tasks of such a team are setting goals, hiring, and evaluating each other's performances.

   There are two types of self-managed teams:

   a. Autonomous
   b. Semiautonomous

Autonomous teams can work without a leader, or there is a rotation of leadership, or members can select their own leader. An autonomous team can make every decision about the plan, schedule, pay raise, vacation, training needs, etc.

In a semiautonomous teams there is a designated leader. The team can function independently and can make own decisions. The leader is like a facilitator or a consultant.

5. **Virtual teams**

Virtual teams operate from distance with the help of advances in computers and telecommunication technologies, as the members cannot meet each other in person. It also can work across time and across organizations. Clear, precise, and mutually agreed goals are accepted by the members. Every member in this team is autonomous and self-reliant. Each one is working collaboratively with others. They use either desktop video conferencing system, collaborative software system, or the Internet/Intranet systems.

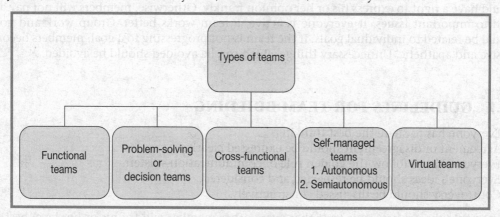

Some researchers have given one more type of team which is called perceived membership teams. These are teams indirectly working together. For example, individuals who are donating money for some social work or for people suffering due to some calamity.

In short, various types of teams work for slightly different goals and they use different strategies to achieve these goals.

The need for team work is dependent on the exact nature of the organization and the work done.

The number of members in a team is not fixed. Any effective team may be of two, four, or ten members. Otherwise, the whole institute or organization can work together.

21.6 EFFECTIVENESS OF TEAM BUILDING

Individuals in a team, culture of the team, and the system play an important role in the performance of any team. Culture gives an understanding of what is right and wrong, when will one land into trouble, what is corporate world, etc. It is imbibed from culture. System is a method which is taken for granted. System and culture should be in congruence with each other. System includes social, technical, and administrative systems. A social system includes emotional climate, role relations, and decision climate. A technical system includes the arrangement of equipment, materials, space, and work flow. An administrative system means standards, rules, regulations, salary, hiring and firing practices, etc. Individuals should have appropriate strategies and expectations. If a particular type of thing is taught in training programs, same things should be encouraged in daily work environment. Members, their family problems, other opportunities, and social value system should be taken care of. Many a time, team building is done and then team becomes less effective due to inappropriate handling. Half of the teams dissolve due to poor leadership and a lack of proper attitude of the members. Team meetings require place, clerical support, and reduction of work load during that period. The members should have knowledge and skills for team work. They should be able to work with others, communicate properly, and have social skills such as the ability to persuade, manage conflict, negotiate, compromise, as well as make others feel important. The nature and importance of group processes and principles of group decisions should be well understood by the members. Social skills such as conflict management and assertiveness are essential for an effective group work. In any group, it should be always remembered that each and every member should have a right to express his or her opinion frankly. Otherwise, members will not pay any heed to important issues. If everyone is active, a team works better. Group work and goals should be related to individual goals. If the team is not progressing to a goal, members become passive and apathetic. Unnecessary things which can be avoided should be avoided.

21.7 GUIDELINES FOR TEAM BUILDING

1. Everyone has to share the best thinking.
2. Agreement or disagreement should be expressed clearly.
3. Everyone has to follow the golden rule of communication—listen.
4. Everyone's ideas should be respected and considered.
5. Controversy should be discussed constructively.

All members should have this trust that every other member will try his or her level best for achieving team goals, will help each other, and share all relevant information with the team. This impression leads to a better interaction between the members. If it is lacking, open and clear discussions regarding each other's behavior that produce doubt, listening to explanation, accepting one's own faults make conflict resolution easy. One should concentrate on the present and the future than on the past of interpersonal relations. Self-defense should not be the goal. Management of diversity is essential for the effectiveness of team work. Otherwise, diversity may lead to bitterness, hostility, and controversies. Constructive controversy is the ultimate style.

There are some factors influencing the effectiveness of any team. Researchers have reported several of this sort. They are somewhat overlapping.

1. **Size**
   Normal size which is effective ranges from 2 to 16 members. Hence, a team can be of two people, four people, or ten people; for example, a team of table tennis, or that of *hututu* (an Indian game). It is reported that 12 is the largest limit where the members can interact properly with each other in face-to-face interaction. Such larger groups can have structured and interdependent relations. As the team becomes larger, the emotional identification and commitment decreases. Of course, in virtual teams more members can be accommodated effectively.

2. **Team members—roles and diversity**
   In any job, people coming from different caste, creed, religion, educational background, age, gender, culture, lifestyle, and ethnicity work together. All of them should try and understand each other and avoid stereotypical ideas and biases regarding each other. Respecting and accepting people coming from different backgrounds are

> It is recommended that team members should come from various types of education, training, experience, cultural background, age, and both genders.

essential for positive multiculturalism. A team gives an opportunity to develop good working relations with others and to understand their views regarding various issues. The effectiveness of a team essentially depends on its diversity.

So, one major consideration is about how to select team members? Should we select all our friends as our team members? It is tempting to do that. However, for effective functioning of a team, it is recommended that members should come from various types of training, experience, and cultural backgrounds. They should not be good friends to start with. If they are friends, they will try to please each other, and will not critically evaluate and criticize ideas expressed by each other. This may deteriorate the decisions. Though team members may not appreciate each other's views and values, philosophy and behavioral patterns, essentially, they should have trust.

If the members come from different background, age groups, and have varied experiences, teams are capable of producing more innovative and creative ideas and they are more stimulating to the members. As is mentioned earlier, it is not necessary to select members who are very friendly with each other. On the contrary, if they are very friendly, they will make some decisions only because they never want to hurt others. Maintaining good relations with each other may decrease their effectiveness. However, if proper training is not given problems such as conflict, low attendance apathy, and jealousy cannot be handled properly

There are basically three types of roles—task oriented, relation oriented, and self-oriented. In work-related roles, the member facilitates and coordinates work-related decision-making. Suggesting different options to solve the problems of the team, seeking new information, coordinating ideas and activities of the team members and evaluating team effectiveness are the important responsibilities in this role. Relation-oriented roles include facilitating team interactions and enhancing team-centered feelings. Expressing warmth and solidarity, encouraging participation of the members, and managing conflict are the most important things in these roles. Self-oriented roles are self-centered behavioral patterns. Such an individual becomes stubborn, negative, and resistant so that the progress of the team is blocked. Being aggressive, seeking recognition, boasting, dominating or avoiding responsibility, and similar other things are self-oriented. They place self before the team goals and self-goals are perceived as more important by them. Some others are not interested in any interaction and not involved in any team-related issue. Such team members make the team weak.

3. **Norms**

Team norms are formal or informal, temporary or permanent. Norms are indicators of social atmosphere in the team. They directly and indirectly affect the behavior of the members. They can change the attitudes of members toward others. Every member should know the norms and should be able to understand and accept them. Amendment in norms also should be practiced as per requirement.

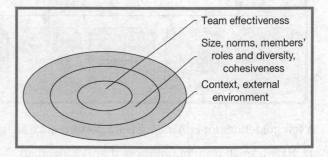

4. **Goals**

Team goals are desired by the team as a whole and may be different from individual goals. Compatible and conflicting goals may coexist in any team.

A balance between task orientation and relation orientation also is essential for proper development of goals. Otherwise, conflict and poor performance will deteriorate goal orientation of the team. The compatibility of an individual, a group, and organizational goals is also an important issue.

Effective team building is essentially related to some conditions. These are:

1. Goals and values should be clear to every member.
2. Everyone should understand his or her role and how important it is. Overlapping authorities should be avoided.
3. Climate should be conducive, which means there should be mutual trust and willingness to support each other.
4. Communication should be free and clear. Every member should be able to communicate all relevant facts freely.
5. While taking any decision, each and every member should get an opportunity to participate.
6. Everyone should respect the decisions made and do accordingly.
7. Along with high standards, the leader should be able to support the members. He or she should not miss any opportunity to empower the members.
8. Differences of opinions should be recognized and managed properly than neglecting them.
9. There should be enough flexibility in structure and in the procedure of team according to task, goals, and individuals in the team.
10. If there is any dispute in two members of the team, that should be solved outside the team meeting.
11. If necessary, external facilitator should be made available for helping in case of a major dispute in the team.

Trust in teams is related to seven important things. They are shown in the following flowchart:

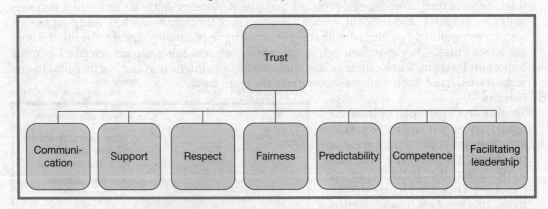

A few guidelines for enhancing team performance are given by researchers. These are:

1. Have a small team of not more than 12 members.
2. Members should have problem-solving skills and interpersonal skills.
3. A team should have a specific goal and should develop commitment for achieving that.
4. A team should have a proper leader.
5. A team should have an objective performance evaluation and reinforcement system.
6. A team should have clear rules of conduct.
7. A team should have a clear standard of performance.

21.8 FACTORS RESPONSIBLE FOR RESISTANCE TO TEAM BUILDING

Generally, leaders with traditional ideology keep on creating an impression that they can manage the staff optimally, they are the ultimate leaders and can give the maximum results, and they can control the problems in their office. Actually, there is pretended agreement than constructive controversy.

Many a time, though there is no proper agreement, people pretend that there is complete agreement. The question is how to identify this position? Resistance to team building decreases if the members accept the following things:

1. There is an open conflict, pain, frustration, and feeling of waste of time.
2. Members discuss problems with each other privately.
3. Everyone blames the other person.
4. Small groups gather to discuss complaints, ideas, and strategies to be used.
5. People hide real feelings and give exactly opposite impressions.
6. Information is not shared.
7. Anger, irritation, and dissatisfaction are seen among members as decisions are taken exactly opposite of what they expect.
8. When members are out of the team, they are more comfortable, and keep better relations with others who are not team members.

Team members also can judge that there is something wrong about the effectiveness of the team if they observe the following things:

1. If they feel that it is impossible to solve organizational problems. They also feel that they are not competent enough and are helpless.
2. If they are discussing important questions related to team in private with some of the team members.
3. If they hold their superiors responsible for their problems.
4. If they are not ready to express their ideas about strategies they think are the best to solve problems.
5. If they think that attempt to solve the problems may even worsen them.
6. If they try to avoid team meetings when important questions are to be discussed.

Why is team building not done? Even when members can understand all these things, there is no possibility that they will try team building.

1. People do not know how to do it.
2. They do not understand the benefits.
3. They think that that it is not rewarded in their organization.
4. They feel they do not need it.
5. They feel it takes too much of time.
6. They think that they will not have support from their boss for this activity.

That is why the authority persons should insist that team building should be done.

21.9 AGENDA FOR TEAM BUILDING

General agenda for team building should concentrate on the following points:

1. **Discussion regarding goal**—Goal setting is essential so that every member must know the exact goals set for a month, six months, and for a year.

2. **Strategic planning**—Where the group has to reach within six months and what all is to be done for that should be discussed with all members.
3. **Expectations from others should be made clear to each other**—When working, what type of cooperation is expected from others also should be specifically communicated. The leader should also make it clear what he or she expects from the members.
4. **Decision procedure**—What all decisions are being made and whether all members who will be affected are involved in it is the major issue.
5. **Coordination**—Each member should be told about the nature of his or her job and its relation with what others are doing. This adds in to the effectiveness of the work done.
6. **Morale**—The status of morale in the team should be understood properly by the leader. If necessary, it should be improved.
7. **Relationship between various departments**—This also should be considered and attempts should be done to improve the relations.
8. **Communication**—All important aspects of the task should be known to every member so that the team can function effectively.

21.10 SUMMARY

This chapter covered the nature and functions of a team. There is a need for team building in most of the organizations and groups. Due to unequal distribution and misuse of power, people are reluctant to share their real thoughts and ideas. As a consequence, human resources are wasted. Creative problem-solving cannot be achieved without every one's wholehearted contribution to group decisions. Various types of team-building strategies and types of teams are discussed. Ways to identify problems in any group and the reasons regarding why people do not opt for team building have also been discussed.

QUESTIONS

1. Explain the significance and need for team building.
2. Discuss various stages of team building.
3. Compare and contrast a staff and a team.
4. What are different types of teams? Give one example each.
5. What are factors related to the effectiveness of team building?
6. Why are people reluctant to build a team?

APPLICATION ORIENTATION

1. Enumerate the various types of teams that you have seen in various organizations. Evaluate their functioning and describe their communication patterns.
2. Imagine that for doing some work in your college like looking after seating arrangement for social gathering, you have to prepare a team and work exactly according to the principles of effective team work. Write down the exact work and distribution as well as the interaction within the team.

3. In a group of your friends, if you realize that there are negative emotions among the members such as hostility and anger, then describe the ways to improve atmosphere. Suggest some strategies for that.

SUGGESTED READINGS

McManus, J. (2006). *Leadership*. New Delhi: Butterworth–Heinemann.
McKenna, E. (2000). *Business psychology and organizational behavior*, 3rd ed. Philadelphia, PA: Taylor and Francis.
Subba Rao, P. (2011). *Personnel and human resource management*. Mumbai: Himalaya Publication House.

22 | Interpersonal Relationships

Objectives

After reading this chapter, you will be able to:

1. Know various types of important human relations.
2. Understand the factors affecting interpersonal relations.
3. Learn about difficulties in interpersonal relationship.
4. Know the various barriers of effective communication.
5. Find out ways to maintain good interpersonal relations.
6. Know the dimensions of relating to others in the virtual world.
7. Utilize this knowledge for improving one's relations.

22.1 INTERPERSONAL RELATIONS

Sonu is an 18-year-old student who thinks that he is very close to his mother and cannot maintain good relations with his father. He shares everything with his mother. He talks for hours with her and expects her advice regarding all important decisions. Sonu generally avoids his father. He hides his concerns from him and gives minimum information even when his father asks something. He thinks that his daddy is not interested in his world and too busy in his own world. His father never spends time with him and never listens carefully to what he says. If Sonu wants some permission like for going to educational tour, he asks his mother to get daddy's permission.

Why such substantial difference exists in relationships in the same family? May be Sonu's mother is kinder, considerate, less evaluative, more soft spoken, and listens more effectively. She is interested in what Sonu wants to express, devotes more time and energy in communication, remembers what Sonu says, and so on. On the other hand his daddy may be too busy and pre-occupied while communicating, gives less importance to the communication and Sonu's emotions, evaluates everything negatively, and never praises Sonu for his behavior or achievements.

As we have seen in Chapter 6, interpersonal relations are extremely important in human life. An individual's satisfaction and happiness depends on his or her interpersonal relations. Even in organizations, people consider interpersonal relations while hiring, promoting, and firing people. As we have seen in Chapter 13, success and social acceptance depend on interpersonal relations.

The significance of interpersonal relations in every sphere of life is ultimate.

22.1.1 NATURE OF INTERPERSONAL RELATIONS

Human relations are immensely important not only from a social perspective but a psychological perspective also. Interpersonal relations decide most of the positive and negative emotions. Any relationship is an association between two or more individuals. It may be brief or long term and may be based on kinship, love or liking, business, or social commitment. There are many types of interpersonal relationships, including mother–child relations in family, in-laws in a marriage, student–teacher and classmates' relations at college and school, friends, and other acquaintances like neighbors. These relations differ in intensity and functions also. Relationships influence both the parties. It is sharing thoughts, feelings, and helping each other and participating in each other's family functions and rituals. Interdependence is essentially the basic issue in relations. Relations are related to temperament, family background, culture, gender, and role expectations of each member.

Emotions play an immensely important role in relations. The experience of emotions guides behavior and emotional expression, and facilitates social communication, relations, and interactions. Selfish emotions, which are called hard emotions, focus on self-preservation, conflict, competition, and fighting. On the other hand, soft emotions are prosocial emotions that focus on interpersonal relationships, cooperation, and attachment. Hard emotions are associated with negative outcomes such as hostility, aggression, and anger. Give and take of hard emotions leads to disturbances in a relationship and is detrimental to any relationship. It enhances conflict. Soft emotions indicate a need for support, or readiness to give support, help, or comfort behaviors, and enhance conflict resolution. Hard emotions are predictive of increased negative communication, decreased positive communication and less relationship satisfaction.

Features of some mental health disorders include difficulties with interpersonal relations. Culture also plays a significant role in interpersonal relations. It decides the nature, interpretation, and importance given by an individual to a particular relation. For example, Western culture focuses on independence and individual autonomy, while Eastern culture is oriented to interdependence of family members and responsibility to the family. Hence, family relations are more important in Eastern culture. Culture influences relationships. Expectations and strategies for expressing emotions and which emotions are essentially to be expressed for maintaining good interpersonal relations are the things taught during socialization. When a relationship is new, people generally think of creating good impression and express positive emotions as well as emotions that produce harmony. More negative expressions are tolerated with more interactions and more time spent with each other.

If there are major problems regarding interpersonal relations, they are indicative of mental health problems of the individual concerned. Keeping good interpersonal relations is related to the mental health of the individual. Both depend on each other.

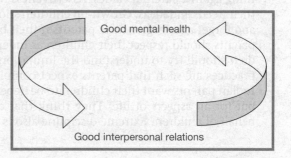

Good mental health

Good interpersonal relations

Pepinsky and Pepinsky (1954) defined relationship as "a hypothetical construct to designate the inferred character of the observable interaction between two individuals." A lot of research has been done on helping relationship that is defined as "the relationship in which at least one of the parties has the intent of promoting growth, development, maturity, and functioning, and of coping with the lives of others" (Rogers 1961).

Intrapersonal relations are relations of the individual with oneself. It is also a significant aspect of self-worth and self-awareness. Self-acceptance, self-discipline, self-management as well as self-direction depend upon intrapersonal relations. We have already discussed this in Chapter 1. Whatever we communicate with self is of immense importance to either increase or decrease satisfaction regarding self. Objective evaluation of self helps individual to develop good contact with reality and can improve things which are lagging behind.

22.2 FORMAL AND INFORMAL RELATIONS: AN INDIAN PERSPECTIVE

There are different ways in which human relations are classified. The basic classification is formal and informal relations. In informal relations, the most important ones are family relations which have tremendous impact on human mind and personality. We are going to discuss most of them in nutshell.

1. Parent–child relations

In informal relations, parent–child relations, relation of the individual with other family members, and relation of the child with significant adults are generally taken into account. Parent–child relations are the relations that influence the whole human life. Acceptance–rejection and authoritarian–democratic practices are the two continuums generally studied by researchers. Psychological and physical welfare as well as all sorts of development of children depend on parent–child relations, that is, social, emotional, moral, cognitive, and educational development. Self-esteem, self-acceptance, and whole personality of a child depend on parent–child relations. Unconditional love and wholehearted acceptance of the child by the parents result in psychological security in a child's mind. The expression of warmth and affection is essential along with value orientation and discipline. A balance between positive reinforcement and enhancement of internalization of values is the most important achievement in this relationship. Trust plays an important role in any interpersonal relations, specially, in parent–child relations. Parents should create nonthreatening atmosphere leading to nonpossessive warmth. Empathic understanding on the part of parents makes the child feel free to discuss emotional disturbances, fears, and anxieties. Children should be encouraged to unconditionally respect their parents, not to get involved in telling lies, giving fake impressions, hiding some information, as well as doing something against parental values. Assertiveness needs to be enhanced while they communicate their needs and ideas. Grown-up children should try to understand parents as human being and forget and forgive their parents if their behavior is not just and fair. On the one hand, parents should respect their children as independent human beings and on the other children should try to understand the limitations of parents. Indian culture and child-rearing practices are such that parents expect complete submission and obedience from children. Indian parents want their children to be dependent on them for not only economic matters but for all aspects of life. They think that decision-making is to be done by parents on behalf of children. Extreme discipline also is considered as an indicator of good parenting.

Considering all these issues parents should reevaluate some of their practices and children should be given enough opportunity for self-actualization and optimum utilization of potentials as far as possible.

Other significant adults from children's perspective are siblings, grandparents, uncles and aunties, cousins, other relatives, and family friends. Interaction with them is essentially important from the point of view of development of the child's self-esteem, general social adjustment, and emotional maturity.

2. **Husband–wife relations**

Indian families are very stable and obviously useful for enhancing the psychological health of the next generation. However, division of labor and power in traditional families is such that women get a subordinate status. It is reported by psychologists that wives do not get equal status in the family and equal opportunities to develop their potentials. Even today, in most of the communities wives are supposed to be full-time housewives and dependent economically on their husbands. As a consequence, they are treated as domestic caretakers and are deprived of emotional warmth as well as security. Effective interpersonal relations between husbands and wives expect equal status and power. Exploitation of women is the easiest way to maintain family in Indian society, as women are not really aware of it and as men take it for granted.

3. **In-laws**

In traditional Indian families, in-laws are the final authorities to decide the destiny of a woman. She is supposed to obey their orders, please them, serve them, and accept their advice in every matter. An ideal daughter-in-law is docile, subjugated, soft spoken, and humble. Though the scenario is changing gradually, by and large, the daughter-in-law is conditioned to take care of household jobs and of all family members. It is taken for granted that she should devote her whole life for the family. There is no special consideration of her self-actualization. This interpersonal interaction needs reconsideration. Women should be given some opportunity to enhance their cognitive functioning and to pursue their hobbies. Otherwise, cognitive deprivation emerging from only repetitive tasks may result in boredom and frustration. A lack of opportunities to utilize cognitive abilities result in deterioration of the same and the intelligence quotient decreases by 20 points in 10 years. It is proved by researchers that specially educated housewives face more emotional problems. It is a sheer wastage of human resources if they are deprived of work appropriate to their cognitive functioning and knowledge.

4. **Social relations**

Sociocultural background, individual's status, and family's status in the community decides social relations. Individuals who have more recognition in the society due to their wealth, wisdom, or power enjoy a lot of social appreciation. Those who are involved in some social work or charity and who maintain huge social interactions also are respected by the community. In general, a common man keeps social-conformity-oriented behavior which leads to the maintenance of good interpersonal relations.

5. **Peers and classmates**

Right from the beginning, a child interacts with peers and classmates for substantial time every day. This interaction gives an opportunity to the child to explore more about social interactions, ways to deal with a variety of problems, and understand his or her own status in a group. The real meanings of cooperation, competition, compassion, and hostility are understood in this group. It gives the child tremendous pleasure such as playing together, studying together, and sharing emotional experiences. If the child is accepted in the group, his or her self-worth and self-confidence increases. If not, then he or she becomes withdrawn and apathetic. His or her self-worth and self-image deteriorate.

Formal relations also play an important role in human life. Some prominent ones are discussed as follows:

1. **A teacher–student relationship**
   This is one of the most salient social interactions as it is associated with not only motivation and academic achievement of the student, but his or her aspirations, future plans, confidence, and self-worth also. A teacher who accepts the students unconditionally as they are, tries to maintain free democratic atmosphere in the class, never threatens the students, and maintains good interpersonal relations with the students creates a conducive environment for students' development. If a child is not capable of developing good interpersonal relations with a teacher, the child will avoid the teacher, dislike the subject, and feel inferior.

2. **Colleagues**
   In adulthood, any individual spends maximum time with colleagues. If the relationship is pleasant, it helps the individual to be comfortable in the organization and work peacefully. If there are problems like cut throat competition, hostility, gossiping, and sexual harassment, the workplace becomes unpleasant due to the atmosphere. Helping each other, keeping good working relations, sharing knowledge, respecting each other, and avoiding exploiting others enhance the sense of security and satisfaction. Excessive use of power, as well as aggressiveness, is always detrimental to human relations.

22.3 FACTORS AFFECTING INTERPERSONAL COMMUNICATION AND RELATIONS

Interpersonal communication and relations basically depend on various factors. Some of these factors are interrelated and overlapping. Let us take for example, Pranav's interaction with his grandmother.

Pranav is a 15-year-old student and is the only offspring of his parents. He goes to school early in the morning and comes back by 2 in the afternoon. As both the parents are serving, Pranav has to stay with his grandmother till the parents come back, that is, till late evening. He finds this duration very boring and unpleasant. His granny is pretty old and has substantial hearing loss which is not curable. His granny talks very loudly, asks many questions, and cannot understand what he says. He has to shout loudly again and again and still she misinterprets everything. Then, she pretends that she has understood it and starts talking something which is redundant and irritating. Pranav cannot study properly, rest, or go to his friend's house. He can neither enjoy television programs as she wants to watch something else and wants to control Pranav's behavior. He thinks that it was better when he used to stay alone.

The purpose of communication and interpersonal relations are interdependent. The number of communicators involved, the physical proximity of the communicators in relation to each other, the immediacy of the exchange, whether it is taking place as live or on a delayed basis decide the level of communication. The number of sensory channels including visual, auditory, and tactile is an important issue in deciding interpersonal communication and relations. The context of communication that means whether face-to-face or mediated, formal or informal, or personal or impersonal also affects interpersonal communication.

Let us discuss the important factors affecting interpersonal relations:

1. **Physical factors**
   Psychophysical factors like normal cognitive, sensory, or motor functioning are essential in communication and interpersonal relations. A person having visual impairment is not able

to interpret facial expressions and one having aural handicap is not able to receive fine cues regarding tone indicating different meanings. If a person has Bell's palsy or facial paralysis, or laryngeal cancer, he or she will not be able to articulate words properly. Some other diseases such as Alzheimer's or stroke also interfere with interpersonal relations. Certain mental disorders such as depression, extreme anxiety, as well as the medicines given for these mental disorders are detrimental to interpersonal relations. Delusions and hallucinations are clear examples of it. If a person's contact with reality is inappropriate, he or she will unnecessarily claim certain things and it will become difficult for others to deal with him or her. Some other personality disorders are equally detrimental to human relations. Think of a husband who blames his wife and claims that she has an extramarital relationship with someone even if there is no evidence and the wife is not at all involved in any such things.

2. **Emotional and social factors**

Emotional factors include an individual's normal emotional development and proper socialization regarding emotional expression. Individual's capacity to understand and interpret others' emotions is the most important factor affecting interpersonal relations. Experience of various types of social interactions decides the accuracy of understanding and skills of adjusting with people coming from different backgrounds.

3. **Age**

Age is also a decisive factor affecting interpersonal relations. Young children are unable to understand different verbal as well as nonverbal communication styles completely and the impact of emotions is more in case of children. Hence, it affects interpersonal relations.

A sweet little girl Tulip goes to nursery school. Everyone adores her and even the teachers like her the most. Since last few days she is looking upset, disturbed, and weeps very often in school and even at home. Her parents asked her many a time as to what is the problem. However, she says something ambiguous and complains vague pain all over her body. She does not eat properly and sleep calmly. When she was taken to the doctor, she did not answer the questions adequately and started crying. When the school psychologist discussed things with parents, teachers, and classmates, she started observing Tulip systematically. Ultimately, they discovered that it was a case of child abuse. As Tulip never knew appropriate language to express her experiences, communication was severely hampered.

A very old individual also may suffer due to his or her sensory and memory problems. Though age is an objective chronological measure, the perception of age also differs with education, socioeconomic status, and roles that the individual plays in the social world. Like for example, a very well-educated urban lady serving in a multinational company will think about her marriage at the age of 32 and will consider herself as young. At the same time, in a rural area an illiterate lady of the same age married at the age of 14 will think about her daughter's marriage and will consider herself as a middle-aged lady. So, the concept of age depends on responsibilities.

4. **Sociocultural factors in the family**

In a developing country like India, lower social strata consist of illiterate parents. This fact itself affects communication and interpersonal relations. Education affects general understanding, objective assessment of environment, and interpretation of each other's behavior. It is reported in research that instead of explaining the cause–effect relations or danger involved in a particular activity, an uneducated mother will use physical punishment to control the child's behavior.

These factors also affect interpersonal relations. Europeans are more open when they discuss private family matters, while Asians are reluctant to discuss personal and family matters. Self-expression and understanding fine meaning in spontaneous communication depend on the knowledge of language.

5. **Gender**

Researchers have reported that there is a substantial difference between communication styles and strategies of males and females. For maintaining good interpersonal relations—formal as well as informal—we should be able to differentiate between the genders from this perspective. Males communicate to achieve goals, establish individual status and authority, and compete for attention and power. They discuss topics where personal feelings are not involved. Their communication is direct for giving orders and criticizing others. They use banter, teasing, and put down; men usually want others to know about their accomplishments.

Women, on the other hand, communicate to establish and maintain human relations, to express emotions, to cooperate, show interest, to support others. They discuss personal matters and feelings. They underestimate their own achievements. They speak indirectly and give orders softly. They do not hurt others while giving negative feedback.

For maintaining decent relations with the other gender, we must understand these specific styles along with cultural and societal expectations and norms. This is an important issue as is discussed in the subsection of sexual harassment.

Communication may get colored because of gender differences. Experts have given warning regarding gender differences in communicating and receiving various messages neglecting which may lead to misunderstanding not only at home but at workplace also. Men are more task-oriented, not interested in human relation maintenance, more harsh at workplace. They are in the world of hierarchy. They give negative feedback when something goes wrong. They give direction and take things literally, and solve their own problems than asking for help.

On the other hand, women are more soft-spoken, they suggest than giving orders, are interested in interpersonal relations, and discussing personal problems. They give feedback when performance is excellent. Women use more closed words. They are overwhelmed when there is some stress and immediately ask for help if there is any problem. Women are better motivated and their performance is better when they are respected and cared for. Their language is indirect and suggestive.

Research regarding whether men or women talk more is controversial. Some studies have shown that men talk more, some others have indicated that women talk more, and some more studies have resulted in no gender differences in talking. However, further studies of details have shown that men talk more in structured or formal settings. When the setting is informal and there is more socioemotional conversation, men talk less. In addition, it has been proved that men refer to quantity more frequently in speech, use directives, and make more reference to their own selves. They, on an average, talk more about money, sports and business.

Women are more likely to use intensive adverbs, refer to emotions, use longer sentences, ask more questions, and use hedges such as sort of, may be, or kind of (Mulac,1998).

Women and men are shown to have different emphasis on relationships. Women talk to maintain relationships, encourage others to talk more by asking questions and making encouraging responses such as uh uh, ok, or nodding response. Women listen more carefully, give more positive feedback, and use vocal indicators to encourage the communicator. They talk more about interpersonal relations and emotional experiences.

Men's language is less facilitative of relationships. They interrupt, ignore, challenge, and may give delayed responses. They are more interested in declaring facts and opinions.

The lack of assertiveness is also obviously seen in women's communication. They use more disclaimers like "I may be wrong, or this idea may not work, but I think ...." or qualifiers like "generally I come on time unless there is some emergency."

In short, it is proved that men's language is direct and women's language is indirect. Women's language is more elaborative as compared to men. Their language is more affective and men's is instrumental.

The intention of interruption in verbal communication is also different among men and women. Men interrupt to assert themselves and to show authority in formal as well as informal settings. Women talk at the same time when the other person is talking, and complete each other's sentences to express enthusiasm and involvement.

Sex differences in language are also related to the subjects of communication. Men and women talk regarding different subjects. Males talk about sports, women, about enjoyment like drinking. Women are more interested in families, relations, and emotions. They can express and interpret emotions in a better way.

Around 2,000 meta-analytic studies were done regarding nonverbal communication with reference to genders. It is reported that women smile and establish better eye contacts than males. Most smiling is observed among two women and least among two men. Two females stand closest to each other, two men stand farthest, and the mixed groups fall somewhere in between. Females stand closer to others and face others more directly. Body movements are also different. Males have more expansive body movements than females.

All reported gender differences depend on whether the interaction is with the same or opposite gender. Women use more disclaimer and more question tags while talking to men than while interacting with women. Men interrupt very often than women, but in interaction with the same gender there are no differences.

As there is a substantial difference between communication of men and women, it is said that "the challenge for men is to understand women when they talk, and it is a challenge for women to understand men when they do not talk."

6. **Stereotypes, prejudices, conformity, and obedience**

These essentially affect interpersonal relations. If the understanding and perceptions are distorted, these influence interpersonal interaction, behavior, and feelings regarding the individual. Hence, they can enhance or hinder communication and relationships as they can be positive or negative.

Stereotypes, for example, contain ambivalent beliefs about relationships between groups. They heighten the perceptions of negative and extreme behavior. They maintain divisions between in-groups and out-groups. They make it difficult to correctly interpret information that we see and hear, and lead us to presume the worst in others. This is an example of communication breakdown, where a normal process of communication is thwarted because inappropriate and erroneous interpretations are given to incoming information. In everyday life, we make judgments about people which are distorted due to all these. For example, in personal, family, and social contexts, stereotypes play a role in parents' decisions about their children's friends as well as people's business relationships, or even relations between nations.

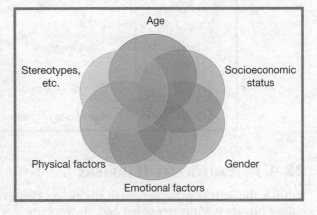

In the figure above are the determinants of interpersonal relations which are interdependent and influence each other:

22.4 BARRIERS TO EFFECTIVE COMMUNICATION

Amita was upset and told Farida "I will have to go to Himalaya now and I will definitely go in near future." After reading this what have you understood? You must have interpreted that Amita will be going to Himalaya the great mountain. However, this is not the correct interpretation of the statement. Amita is not getting some cosmetics that she wanted and these are available only at the Himalaya store.

As communication is a two-way process, both the receiver and the sender are responsible for the production of meaning. Meaning also depends upon contents, intention behind it, and significance attached to it. Hence, the sender or the receiver should not take it for granted that the message sent is equal to the message received. The message may be interpreted in a different way. Researchers have given such warning that if there is any possibility of misinterpreting the message, it will be misinterpreted.

The process of communication is very complex. It depends on context, characteristics of participants, actual message, channels used, noise or hindrance, and feedback. If any of these aspects is not taken into consideration, communication suffers. There are cognitive, physical, social and emotional, as well as semantic barriers to communication. Status effect, perceptual distortions, cultural differences, poor choice of communication channels, and lack of proper feedback also are responsible for reducing the effectiveness of communication. One has to check at every stage that means while sending, receiving, understanding, and accepting the message if there is any problem that can hamper the communication.

Breaking communication barriers becomes a must even in formal or official communication. One has to encourage communication with colleagues irrespective of their position or designation. Specially, the authority persons should have an open door policy. Using face-to-face communication and being sensitive for the needs and feelings of others help. Avoiding credibility gaps and watching proper timing for a particular type of communication become essential. Conflict is inherent in almost all types of relations; hence, identifying and managing conflict is also necessary.

As there are many barriers to effective communication, it is necessary to avoid them and be careful about their ill effects.

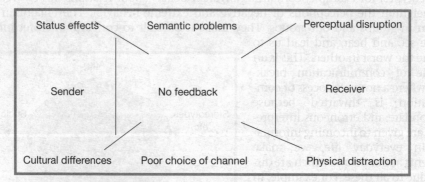

22.4.1 EMOTIONAL BARRIERS

Rahul is the least popular person in his group. He never enjoys anyone's company and no one enjoys his. He is short-tempered and always criticizes everyone. He talks with a frowning face and reluctant voice. He is an introvert and never initiates any interaction. He keeps quite if someone wants his help. Rahul is now excluded from most of the activities of his group and is isolated. He is unhappy due to that.

Human relations play a decisive role in human happiness and welfare. Though human relations vary in their weightage and importance in human life, most of them have no options. One cannot choose one's biological parents, siblings, and other relatives. A pupil or a student cannot select his or her teacher, classmates, coach, and colleagues at the workplace. There are very few relations that we can opt for on our own like friends. Obviously, we have to deal with the persons who are already there around us. If we can maintain good relations with them, it is beneficial not only for our psychological adjustment but for future achievements also.

In emotional barriers the important ones are:

1. **Lack of self-understanding and self-acceptance:** If an individual does not have objective understanding of the self, he or she will misinterpret the message. Simple things which are observable and easily evaluated are also not accepted by most of the individuals. A student who is selected as a volunteer for social gathering may misinterpret it as because he or she is not good for anything else so he or she is selected for such a generalized activity. Actually, it may be because of his or her smartness and leadership qualities that he or she is selected for it.

   When we are talking to someone, we are actually communicating to ourselves. In a way, the sender is communicating to his or her image of the receiver. It may be different from reality. It becomes a must to develop appropriate understanding of self and of the other person and the environmental clues to avoid distortions in communication.

2. **Lack of understanding others' points of view:** What exactly is the other person's perception should be well understood. Varun's father told him that he should cut down some of his extracurricular activities at least for a month or two till his examinations are over. Varun was very upset and thought that his father intentionally wants to decrease his popularity in his group.

3. **Inappropriate coping with self and others:** If the person has ambivalent feelings and attitudes while making communication meaningful, he or she will not be able to cope appropriately with self as well as with others. If a mother loves her child and also hates the child, her relations with the child will be poor.

4. **Lack of empathy and insight:** If someone is facing a problem, without having empathy nobody will get the real message. "I am not coming to your college to watch your solo dance," if the mother says so, the daughter who cannot understand empathically that her mother is feeling very weak due to high fever may distort the message.

5. **Insufficient desire to relate to others:** If two individuals do not have or any one of them does not have the wish to relate to the other, they may not take any interest in the message sent by each other. Many a time, when we are travelling or standing on the bus stop, we may observe such type of interaction. If such interaction is taking place in a family or a close group, it is harmful. A daughter-in-law who does not want to relate to the mother-in-law will not focus on the messages sent by her.

6. **Uncontrolled emotions:** Loss of control of emotional expressions results in the loss of respect by others. It is necessary to maintain a calm and positive emotional state for effective communication. As is discussed in Chapter 15, one loses his or her capacity to process any information objectively when extreme emotions are experienced.

7. **Lack of readiness to respond to the needs of others:** Shaila was staying with her aunty just for a few days but was fed up as her aunt was suffering from Parkinson's disease. Every now and then she expected Shaila to serve her. During night, Shaila used to sleep comfortably in spite of the fact that her aunt needed her help.

8. **Excessive use of ego defense mechanisms:** One more important but generally neglected thing is the tendency of any individual to use various ego defense mechanisms.

Ego defense mechanisms are techniques that one uses consciously or unconsciously for maintaining the balance of mind and for reducing maladjustment. Following are a few examples: rationalization, regression, repression, reaction formation, projection, denial of reality, compensation sublimation, and so on. These are tricks to deceive oneself and others and affect communication adversely.

Any message may be distorted by defense mechanisms. Abhinandan's father is so strict that he is extremely afraid of his father even at the age of 20. He never talks against his father and tells everyone that he loves his father very much. He interprets every message in a particular way which is not accurate.

9. **Projecting one's ideas:** If relations between any two individuals are influenced by the projection of any one's ideas, the interpretation of communication between the two will be distorted substantially. Pravin was angry when he saw that his father had purchased a new bicycle for his sister and nothing for him. He started quarrelling and saying that his father likes his sister more than him and always overpampers her. However, actually, his father wanted to buy a motorcycle for him within a few months.

10. **Personality problems:** Personality disorders may lead to problems such as narcissistic personality, excess love for self, paranoid personality disorder, or extreme suspicion. In antisocial personality, the person can convince others and simultaneously be involved in lying and cheating.

11. **Impact of specific interests, needs, expectations and sets:** The meaning of any communication is influenced by all these. Let us take the example of a set. In a simple experiment, if we present some names of birds and then give the stimulus "bat," it will be interpreted as a bird. If, however, names of materials necessary for playing cricket are shown such as ball and stump, and then the same stimulus "bat" is given, it will be interpreted as a bat to play with. This is the impact of set.

    Interest also results in altered interpretation of physical stimulus. A student of health sciences will be interested in making an article on new treatment for a disease more meaningful and remembering it in detail. The same will not be true of students of other faculties.

12. **Historical context with reference to past communication with that person and past events in general:** Past interactions of the individuals may lead to positive or negative emotional backgrounds. That itself may color the interaction and communication. If one hates a classmate who has insulted him or her in the last year, further communication will be affected by these old memories.

13. **Attitudes and values:** Attitudes regarding a particular caste, creed, and community as well as specific value system may distort the message communicated.

14. **Cognitive barriers:** As far as cognitive barriers are concerned, they change the whole interaction and its meaning. Some important cognitive barriers are listed as follows:

    a. **Thought–speech speed.** Humans think very fast, that is, 600–1,000 words per minute; however, they can speak only 125–150 words per minute. If the thoughts of the receiver are not related to the subject of communication they are detrimental to the process of communication.

    b. **Colored perceptions.** Due to past experiences, mood, or attitudes, perceptions of two individuals may be totally different. That is why feedback becomes essential.

    c. **Message not within the range of sensory organs.** Too loud or too weak stimuli may not be interpreted by human sense organs. It directly affects communication.

    d. **Inappropriate attention.** If one does not focus one's attention on the stimulus, it will be vanished without interpretation.

e. **Insufficient processing including encoding and decoding.** If the meaning of any message is not processed in depth, the original message will be deteriorated within no time.

f. **Inadequate retrieval from memory.** For making any new message meaningful, it is necessary to retrieve back information from long-term memory. If it cannot be retrieved completely, communication suffers.

15. **Ambiguity in verbal communication:** As far as verbal message is concerned, words are verbal symbols. It is very difficult to have completely common language with anybody. It is rare to acquire a complete knowledge of the dictionary meaning of all the words included in any dictionary. For example, regular English into Hindi or any other regional language dictionary may contain six lakh of words. Very few people can remember all of them along with the exact meaning. Any dictionary may give many different meanings of a particular word. On the top of it, words are used to indicate a different meaning than the dictionary meaning. Intentional and deliberate use of doublespeak leads to more ambiguity. It is obvious that sometimes words suggest something else. No dictionary provides the information of such ever changing meanings as it changes from person to person and context to context, and is related to nonverbal cues. Any dictionary actually gives the general meaning of any term which was in vogue during that particular era. It is seen that some words are used to indicate different things by different generations or different groups of different age, gender, and education as well as cultural background. Some words have changed their meaning completely. Approximately 30 years ago the word "hot" was used only to indicate its dictionary meaning as warm; however, today the young Indian generation will take it to mean something else such as sexually stimulating and attractive. Same is the case of the word "gay," which previously meant only happy now is interpreted as homosexual.

In addition to that, there are many words which are used in daily conversation but are not found in any dictionary. The dictionary meanings of "net, web, and tablet" may be something else; however, they are used to indicate some technological advances. A word may indicate different ideas in different cultures and different languages. For example, gift means poison in German. A particular type of abusive language is very popular and is commonly used without any negative meaning or consequence in a particular area and subculture; but the same may be interpreted as some serious insult in other subculture. This difference is seen in different subcultures which are just 50 km away from each other, say in Maharashtra. Similar examples are very popular where a sentence in Portuguese means "you have embarrassed me" and in Spanish it means "you have made me pregnant."

Different meanings of words:
"They call you wise when they think that you are otherwise" obviously means that the words have different meanings and are used in various ways to express something else than they obviously suggest. Even when the same meaning emerges it may have different dimensions. The meaning of a good student is different for every professor as they give more weightage to different traits and behaviors of the individual student. The characteristics that are essential in a good student are exactly opposite in India and Germany. In India, a submissive student is perceived as the best and in Germany good student is the one who can think independently.

The same word is also interpreted differently by individuals coming from the same cast, creed, community, and culture. For example, if the message is "xyz is a good leader." The meaning of such a sentence may become ambiguous due to difference in encoding and decoding. The sender may think that particular traits are essentially important and essential to be a good leader. Intelligence, empathy, and hardiness may be perceived as qualities of a good leader. The receiver may perceive some other qualities as honesty or sincerity as the basic requirement of a good leader. So, both will not be able to understand that there is any difference between the sent and the received messages, but it will always be there.

Hence, it can be summarized as:

a. Words may indicate different meanings.
b. New meanings of the old words may immerge.
c. Regional or cultural differences may affect the meaning of any word.
d. Doublespeak may make understanding a word more difficult.
e. New words may be added in any language.
f. Non-verbal communication and context may change the meaning of any word.

16. **Inability to create and translate message:** There are many reasons for inability of creating and translating the message. Not knowing the language well results in such inability. If without knowing Japanese language we go to Japan, we will not be able to communicate even for simple messages. There are some physiological disorders and conditions resulting in such inability. For example, brain damage resulting in damage to Broca's area and Wernicke's area may result in such inability.

17. **Lack of familiarity with meanings and symbols and experience:** Specific meanings emerge in a particular environment. A lack of familiarity leads to confusing interpretations. Communication depends upon familiarity not only with the person but his or her culture, general communication style, personality, and so on. A new acquaintance cannot interpret a hidden message given by a person.

18. **Inappropriate exposure to communication:** If enough time is not devoted to communication, it will fail.

19. **Masking various semantic disturbances:** If there are two meanings of the same communication—one, the simple meaning or dictionary meaning and the other the suggested meaning—inappropriate meaning selected by the individual may lead to complete misunderstanding the message. The word "chair" may be interpreted as a concrete chair such as wooden or steel chair, but the suggested meaning is the power or authority. We may pretend that we have understood the message when the real meaning is not clear.

20. **Lack of nonverbal cues due to faulty seating arrangement:** If we cannot see the facial expressions and gestures of the speaker, we will not understand the message as 55 percent of the message is communicated nonverbally.

21. **Wrong organization of information:** Organization of information leads to better interpretation of the message. If not, then confusing impressions are formed.

22. **Thought disorders:** Hallucinations, that is, perceptions of things which do not exist or distorted perceptions, and delusions are false beliefs. Both are generally seen in mental illness. Here, the individual may perceive a snake gourd as a real snake. Delusion leads to distorted thoughts resulting in misunderstanding regarding the other person's intention. Even if someone gives food with a good intention, the receiver may think that there is poison in it and the giver wants to kill him or her.

23. **Message overload:** If too many messages are to be received and interpreted, communication suffers. If the messages are delivered with tremendous speed so that the individual does not get time to process the information properly, communication may be hampered.

24. **Inappropriate listening:** Surendra was in great hurry and told his mother that he will be late in the evening. His mother was shocked to see that, as she had told him yesterday that she wanted him to accompany her to the hospital. His mother wanted to see Surendra's

aunty who was admitted to the hospital close to his college. Surendra was surprised to see that as he thought he has never been told about it.

Surendra was watching a match on television while chatting on WhatsApp with his friend yesterday when his mother told him this. She was worried about his aunty and was almost in tears when she narrated the health condition of her sister. He was intermittently looking at her and pretending that he has understood the message. However, he could not even partially remember it.

As was indicated in the Chapter 6 only 7 percent message is verbal. Hence, for maximum understanding of any message it is essential to focus on the nonverbal message which indicates 55 percent of the message and tone which carries 38 percent. Listening is the most basic and essential skill in communication.

Many difficulties in communication emerge only because of not listening properly and carefully. It is one of the most important aspects of communication which decides its effectiveness. The golden rule of communication is listening carefully what the other person wants to communicate. Poor listening can hurt the sender and may result in numerous errors of understanding in every field.

Any normal individual who does not have hearing loss can hear. However, listening is a skill that requires training, concentration, and commitment. Listening is hearing with purpose. The process of effective listing is focused, active, and selective. Hearing is detrimental to communication if it is not clubbed with listening.

Hearing	Listening
Pure physical function	Mental and emotional experience involving feelings
Activity of central nervous system	Requires interpretation, analysis, and evaluation
Automatic and effortless	Attention and concentration are needed
Unintentional, easy, and relaxing	Intentional, tiring, and require cognitive processing

There is a basic difference between listening and hearing. Hearing is a physiological process and listening is a psychological process. That is why for listening it is essential to get some training. If we don't listen carefully, we tend to take things for granted.

Indicators of poor listening are:

1. Thinking of something else while waiting for next words of the speaker.
2. Listening only for facts and not for ideas.
3. In case it is difficult to understand, just neglect it.
4. Thinking that the individual will not discuss anything interesting only on the basis of his or her appearance.
5. Attending to other stimuli in the environment.
6. Not devoting complete attention and eye contact.

Good listening is essential for effective relations. The best relation in the world is based on empathic listening. The person who listens carefully and takes interest in what one says is the most intimate relation.

Right from childhood, everyone prefers the person who listens carefully and with interest and enthusiasm. Mother, for example, can establish the closest relation with child as she is the one who devotes a lot of time for only listening to what the child wants to communicate. She shows interest in every detail of that. Likewise, close friends, life partners, and other close relatives are dear to any individual only and if only they are listening wholeheartedly. Empathic listening is related to emotional catharsis. With the help of emotional catharsis, the individual gets a lot of emotional support. Many a time, the individual is not interested in anything else like advice, but only wants to share his or her emotional problems. For developing skills of empathic listening one should:

1. Avoid being judgmental. No evaluative remarks should be passed. It is necessary to be objective and detached.
2. Accept what is said. It is not necessary to agree with the message, but it is a must to understand it completely.
3. Be patient. One cannot think of empathic listening in a great hurry. As it takes time, all the other assignments should be kept aside.

Effective listening reduces misunderstanding, rumors, accidents, and other errors in all sorts of organizations. In organizations, it has been proved that people perform better when they think that seniors listen to them.

A lot of research has been done about listening and its importance in communication. This is nonverbal communication which is extremely essential to encourage the speaker and generate a sense that the listener is interested in the message. These responses are given quietly and briefly so that the speaker is not disturbed. It means that the listener is interested and wants to continue. Generally, these responses are given when the speaker takes a pause. There are five common types of such responses:

1. Nod
2. Pause—waiting for a next word
3. Saying something—such as I see, uh-huh, is that so, etc.
4. Echo—repeating the last words
5. Reflecting ideas.

For effective listening in organizations, one has to:

1. Show interest
2. Express empathy
3. Be silent when silence is needed
4. Eliminate distractions
5. Allow adequate time for discussion
6. Take note of nonverbal cues
7. Restate what is heard
8. Ask simple questions to get information

There are certain things that one should avoid in organizational settings as they are detrimental to effective listing. One should not:

1. Argue
2. Interrupt
3. Engage in other activity
4. Jump to a conclusion
5. Let other person's emotions act directly.

Listening results in rapport establishment which leads to more sharing of confidential information by the individual. It reduces tension and anger.

Obstacles to listening: Physical setting, feelings about the client, and various biases and conditions of the communicator such as lack of sleep, ill health, or drug addiction are various obstacles to effective communication.

22.4.2 GENERAL PSYCHOSOCIAL BARRIERS

Some more psychosocial barriers to effective communication are as follows:

1. **Over eagerness to respond:** The interruption of the message given by others means that the receiver is not interested, it is not important, or it is already known.
2. **Judging:** A general statement regarding evaluation leads to no exact message as to what is wrong.
3. **Lying:** Deliberate deception for one's benefit or other's detriment is the worst thing for communication. Identifying that the person is lying on the basis of facial expressions and some physiological indicators is possible.
4. **Snap judgment:** Jumping to a conclusion without proper information is detrimental to communication.
5. **Closed words:** Gross generalization like "the whole department is useless" creates a lot of negative feelings and negative attitudes in the receivers.
6. **Attacking the individual:** Criticizing the person and pointing out something that the person cannot change leads to offending the individual. Instead of that the exact behavior of the individual that needs modification according to the communicator should be communicated.
7. **Rank:** People generally avoid going to their boss as they think that it will be equivalent to inviting trouble. Both should be more open and should try to communicate calmly and freely.
8. **Credibility gap:** If a person only says something that he or she is not doing, others will not trust him or her. One has to respect what one says and behave accordingly.
9. **Gatekeeper:** Sometimes secretaries and assistants may screen the information and decide on their own as to what should be passed on to their boss. This may lead to a lot of misunderstanding. It becomes essential to keep good relations with them and find out other ways of communication like an e-mail.
10. **Interference:** It is anything that distorts the information transmitted to the receiver or distracts him or her from receiving it. There are two types of interferences commonly seen. These are:

    a. **Technical interference.** It is related to the transmission of sound like one may not hear what his or her friend says because of loud stereo sound.
    b. **Semantic interference.** Here the receiver does not attribute the same meaning to the message that the sender wants to communicate. No two people attribute exactly same meaning to the message.

11. **Verbal cocoon:** If the receiver is intentionally ignoring some relevant information, it obviously leads to poor communication.

22.5 ROLE OF FEEDBACK IN INTERPERSONAL COMMUNICATION

Feedback enhances meaning in communication. It sustains the communication process. It is useful to decide the changes in further communication and action. It is the mutual exchange of understanding between the speaker and the receiver.

Feedback is a response to an action, communication, or situation. It is a part of communication and every effective communication requires feedback. Feedback eliminates misunderstanding and ensures that the message sent is correctly interpreted. It by and large is initiated by the receiver but even the sender may initiate it. Here, it is the receiver's interpretation that is verified with the sender. In public speaking, feedback is audience's response that enables the speaker to evaluate the effectiveness of his or her message.

A lack of feedback leads to distorted communication, frustrated colleagues, unmotivated receivers, and generation of negative feelings and atmosphere. Feedback is very useful to create healthy relationship with others in informal groups and in world of work.

Strategies to give proper feedback:

1. Feedback should be specific and related to a particular task. It should not be used to flatter someone or criticize anyone's opinions.
2. The timing to give feedback should be right. It is essential to devote appropriate time for feedback.
3. One has to select proper words. Specially to start with, one must not criticize the person as a whole but the behavior that needs to be changed. Even if you are the authority person, you should not say "you must do it." Instead of that saying "I noticed that" or "I understand that" is better. The receiver becomes defensive if you start evaluating or blaming.
4. One should start with positive feedback. It is necessary to acknowledge good performance and contribution of the individual. Here, giving specific examples is better than just giving a general remark. In organizations or informal groups also, the individuals should be given the information regarding how their actions are being positively appreciated by others and what are their impacts on others.
5. Be descriptive and discuss the facts. It is not necessary to discuss the feelings but one should focus on the facts as objectively as possible. Giving reason why it is an issue to be discussed and its impact on others also enhances effectiveness of feedback.
6. Let the individual collaborate by contributing ideas for improving performance. One can always give suggestions, but such contributions lead to better involvement of the individual also.

   Consider, for example, Ramesh helps his grandfather on time for daily activities and also gives him medicine. However, his mother has observed that Ramesh is being rude and his nonverbal and verbal communication indicates that he dislikes his grandfather. His mother should give him the following feedback.

   > Ramesh, I really appreciate that you are assisting your grandfather and also keep the exact time in mind. He is very happy about it and appreciates your involvement. However, if you could improve your words and facial expressions a bit, it will generate much more positive interaction and good will.... What should we do to change that?

   Ramesh may understand the exact problem and how to solve it. Ramesh may put forth the idea that he can at least pretend that and discuss his emotional problems with his mother in detail. May be after catharsis, he will be in a better position to deal with the situation.
7. One should keep feedback impersonal. Instead of blaming the individual, one has to focus on the behavior or change in performance that is required.
8. Feedback should be goal oriented and should have a specific achievable goal.
   Specific issues that the recipient will be able to change should be highlighted. Otherwise feedback will be frustrating. It may lead to hopelessness.
9. Make sure that the feedback is understood. Using jargons and difficult to understand language makes the feedback less effective. Otherwise, feedback of the feedback becomes a must.

For receiving effective feedback:

1. One should avoid becoming reactive or defensive to the feedback. Be calm and think coolly. A defensive individual cannot properly analyze the information. His or her perception may be colored and he or she may lose emotional balance.
2. Ask questions to clarify the issue. Probing questions also help to understand the other person's perspective.
3. Accept the feedback and reflect on it peacefully.
4. One has to find out the way in which he or she can improve his or her behavior and performance on the basis of the feedback.
5. One should be thankful to the individual for giving the feedback.

22.6 CONFLICT MANAGEMENT

Conflict is natural part of human interaction. Whenever two people interact, there is a potential for conflict. Conflict may be advantageous when it is handled properly in an assertive and a responsive way. It is an interactive process manifested in incompatibility, disagreement, or dissonance within or between social entities. It is the perceived difference that the individuals evaluate as negative, resulting in negative emotional states and behavior. Conflict can be disagreement, presence of tension, or some other difficulty in two or more individuals. It may be between individuals, groups, or organizations or even nations. It is generally related to opposition or interference between the parties. Both individuals or parties involved perceive the other party as one that frustrates their needs and goals. If a continuum of interaction is from competition to cooperation, conflict occupies a middle position.

> If in any informal or formal group or organization, people acknowledge its existence, and think about problem-solving using different strategies, conflict may result in positive outcome.

Conflict is neither good nor bad.

An attempt to prevent it may result in positive or negative things. There are two types of conflicts:

1. **Cold conflict:** It is cognitive conflict. It involves seeking information, examining alternatives, evaluating options, and deciding between alternatives. Hence, it is less emotional. Here, individuals involved are considerate, calculated, and well intentioned.
2. **Hot conflict:** It is a mixture of emotional and cognitive issues. It may occur within and between persons that can result in harmful behavior. These people become angry, frustrated, sad, and have the tendency to attack the other person. They are involved in excluding, insulting, and hurting others. So, this results in negative things.

Cushnie in 1988 has given four categories of conflict intensifying the degree of difficulty from first to last.

1. **Conflict regarding facts:** It arises from differences in available data and if more information is made available from reliable source, conflict may be resolved.
2. **Conflicts regarding method:** When there is no specific standard procedure that is well accepted by both the parties, such conflict can occur. If both the individuals decide a particular criterion, then selection of procedure becomes easy.

3. **Conflict regarding goals:** If there is difference between desired outcomes, then such conflict occurs.
4. **Conflict regarding values:** Most common conflict. High motivation is necessary to resolve it. Instead of classifying goals as right and wrong, compatible goals should be accepted.

Several forms of conflict are seen:

1. Intrapersonal
2. Interpersonal
3. Intragroup
4. Intergroup

Antecedent conditions are the causes of conflict like aggression shown by one party. It can be overt or subtle. Perceived conflict emerges from the impression that the parties are threatened in some way. If the disadvantage caused by one party is not perceived by the other as threat, then there will be no conflict. When people perceive actual or potential disagreement, it leads to increase in frustration, fear, anger, or anxiety. Perceived trustworthiness decreases. They feel that they are unfairly treated and worry about their ability to cope with the situation.

Manifest conflict is a reaction to the perceived conflict. It includes arguments, appeal for goodwill, aggression, or constructive problem-solving. The next is conflict resolution or suppression. In resolution, parties agree upon how to solve a problem. If one party defeats another, conflict may be solved. When parties avoid strong reactions or try to ignore each other, suppression takes place.

Conflict aftermath includes the feelings that remain after the conflict is resolved or suppressed. If it is resolved positively, good feelings and harmony may result. If not, then hard feelings and resentment persist which may generate a new conflict.

Conflict depends on perception than reality. According to Rubin et al. (1993), there are three stages of conflict. These are:

1. **Escalation:** One party wants to prevail and makes the other to submit. It has a negative tone. One wants to do better than others.
2. **Stalemate:** This is the stage when there is stagnation. There is no energy left to prevail. It is seen when an individual loses the hope of beating the other.
3. **De-escalation:** Here, the relationship again turns to cooperation. Again there are common goals that are accepted.

One view about conflict is that it is preventable. If the concerned individuals change their attitudes and behavior, cooperation can emerge. If new policies and plans are developed to ensure mutual efforts for common goals, conflict may reduce. According to another view, conflict is inevitable and it cannot be eliminated entirely. Sometimes, various individuals or departments in the same organization work for exactly opposite goals. Hence, it is essential to accept some conflict. Training to face disagreement and keeping conflict within tolerable limits helps.

A third point of view is that some conflicts are healthy for the effectiveness of various formal and informal groups, departments, and the organization as a whole. If there is absolutely no conflict, it means that there is no involvement and individuals concerned are not bothered about important issues. In organizations no conflict means people are not involved in their work such as quality control, sales targets, etc. Hence, relation between conflict and effectiveness is like an inverted U. That means very low or very high conflict is detrimental to organizational effectiveness but medium conflict leads to maximum organizational effectiveness. At the optimum level, each person and unit perform at the highest level and there are active attempts to improve quality. People welcome changes that are useful to make the organization more competitive and effective. Employees are stimulated to work, and new understanding and insight may emerge. Tensions and frustrations are channeled in a positive and productive way.

When the conflict is within groups, the group members are motivated to work harder for the protection of group identity. Intergroup conflict makes the groups more cohesive and coordinated. If autocratic leadership helps, members are more willing to accept it in case of intergroup conflicts. Thus, the alertness of the members to the group actions increases. There are some negative consequences also. Distorted perceptions, stereotyping, hostility, and similar other things may emerge.

The management of the causes of conflict becomes essential to resolve it. There are three categories of causes of conflict:

1. **Characteristics of individuals**—such as values, attitudes, beliefs, needs, perceptions, and judgments.
2. **Situational conditions**—such as the degree of interaction, the need for consensus, communication, and ambiguous responsibility.
3. **Structure of organization**—such as specialization, differentiation, task interdependence, goals, scarce resources, multiple authorities, policies, procedures, rules, and rewards.

Forcing, withdrawing, smoothing, compromising, and problem-solving are the different ways of dealing with conflicting situation. Problem-solving is the best integrative approach.

There are different styles to deal with a conflict. Five important styles are avoiding, accommodating, competing, compromising, and collaborating. Concern for one's own interest and concern for the other party are the dimensions considered in this case. High concern for others reflects cooperativeness and the desire to maintain a relationship. People who are low on this dimension are not bothered about other party's concern and relations with them. This is an uncooperative attitude. The other dimension is the extent to which the individual is concerned about his or her own needs and goals. People high on this dimension are assertive and want to achieve their own goals. Low concern reflects unassertiveness and willingness to sacrifice one's own needs and goals. The different styles have been discussed as follows:

1. The avoiding style is associated with emotional upset because of tensions and frustrations of a conflict. This is based on the belief that conflict is evil, undignified, and unnecessary. When the issue is insignificant and the cost of conflict is more than the actual benefits, the best policy is to avoid it.
2. Accommodating means giving into the wishes of another person. Such a person is focused on relationships and wants to protect relations. This style reflects generosity and obedience.
3. Competing is a style where the person wants to pursue his or her own wishes at the expense of the other party. A conflict is viewed as a game to be won. Assertiveness and uncooperativeness are the basic traits of these individuals. If the other party takes undue advantage, the best way is to protect self.
4. Compromising is a give and take policy based on the principle that people cannot always have their way. When both the parties have equal power, this is the best policy.
5. Collaborating is the willingness to accept other party's needs while asserting one's own. Here both the parties can be satisfied. When both the parties are strongly committed to different goals and when compromise is very costly, this is the best method. This safeguards relationships. Openness, trust, creativity, and hard work are essential for such a strategy.

One cannot avoid conflict. What one can achieve is feeling uncomfortable when we encounter conflict. There are three ways of conflict resolution:

1. Win-win strategies are positive approaches to resolve a conflict in which each side gains something, though perhaps not everything sought. Here, goodwill and creativity both are essential.
2. Lose-win strategies are used when one decides that the other person's needs and problems are more pressing, and one allows the other person to win.
3. Win-lose strategies are negative approaches to a conflict in which one side emerges as a clear winner and the other as a clear loser. The individual may satisfy himself or herself at the cost of the other.

Organizational climate as well as stability and the nature of the relationship depend on which strategy is used to solve the conflict. Leaders should be ready and trained to use these strategies in combination as per the environmental demands. They should be flexible enough to mix these ways of conflict resolution.

22.7 STRATEGIES FOR MAINTAINING GOOD INTERPERSONAL RELATIONS

For developing and maintaining good interpersonal relations, we should use some strategies and be careful so that we should not do anything that is detrimental to the relations. For example:

1. **Listen effectively and have empathy**—We have covered importance and strategies for effective listening. The ultimate relation with a person develops only when the person listens carefully and effectively. If at all you want to develop true friendship with someone, or be close to your siblings, start listening effectively. Listening carefully and understanding empathically are extremely important strategies for building good interpersonal relations.

   Listening respectfully and generously enhances interpersonal relations. Listening respectfully means paying attention and truly allowing people to finish their thinking and speaking. Listening generously means allowing people to express ideas and views different than our own without resisting their speaking either verbally or nonverbally.
2. **Being authentic and candid helps**—This means speaking honestly in a way that forwards the conversation. It means speaking as friends and straight—saying what is so important for us. It means not leaving a conversation with something still unsaid that needs to be said.
3. **One has to avoid evaluation**—Nilima is fond of fashionable and stylish clothes. Every day when she gets ready, her grandmother starts criticizing her dress fashion and she gets irritated. She wants to avoid her grandmother and plays various tricks for that. Right from the beginning what she remembers about her grandmother is that she has been very evaluative and critical about every performance of Nilima.

   Do not be judgmental regarding what the other person is communicating. If it is good or bad, right or wrong should not be the conclusion. On the contrary, we should try to be with the individual and try and adjust our perception with him or her. Sometimes, we cannot understand why the individual is behaving in a particular way. It is because we cannot understand his or her perspective. Hence, being judgmental indicates that you want to prove that you are superior and the other person cannot deal with the environment as effectively as you can.

4. **No projection of own ideas should be done.** Projection means attributing one's own unacceptable ideas and impulses to another individual. We make others' communication meaningful by utilizing our own views, perspective, experiences and understanding regarding life. In a way, we are projecting our own ideas on someone else. This is detrimental to maintaining good interpersonal relations as we interpret everything as per our convenience. So, there is every possibility that things will be misunderstood.

Sumit used to get a number of good books as his brother teaches in a college. But he never even used to tell his friends about which of them are good. He used to hide every information and the books as well. Once Sumit had requested Arman to give his book only for two days as it was not easily available. Arman, however, had forgotten to get it for Sumit. Sumit immediately came to the conclusion that Arman is not interested in helping and wants to deprive him of the book. Because he is doing it regularly, that is the first interpretation which comes to his mind.

5. **Avoid other ego defense mechanisms.** Ego defense mechanisms are patterns of feelings, thoughts, and behavior arising in response to a perception of psychic danger, enabling the person to avoid conscious awareness of conflicts or anxiety arousing ideas (Oxford Dictionary of Psychology, 2006). In such a situation, the individual either tries to forget, or distort the information, merge it with other bits of information or reduce its importance. It is an unconscious function of ego. Ego defense mechanisms such as identification, regression, repression, reaction formation, displacement, rationalization, dissociation, withdrawal, sublimation, suppression, and denial of reality create a distorted perception of the individual. All of us use defense mechanisms in day-to-day life situations, but excess use of these things leads to problems in human relations. Like in denial, one disregards the truth. In identification, one takes the feeling or behavior of someone else as one's own. In regression, due to stress the individual starts functioning at a previous level of maturity. If such types of exaggerated ideas are used, interpersonal relations can easily get spoiled.

6. **One should not take things for granted.** While communicating if we take things for granted and expect that the other person is communicating a particular thing and give reaction accordingly, not only communication but interpersonal relations also are affected negatively.

Pinki was out of station for complete two months as she was representing her state in interstate tournaments. During that period, the application form for final examination was to be submitted to the university. Pinki took it for granted that some of her friends or the college office will inform her as everyone knew that she was out. After coming back she discovered that the last date even with the payment of fine was over, and she was shocked. Pinki had never discussed it with anyone before she left and just assumed that others will do the needful. She had fought with all her friends and was very unhappy.

We generally take it for granted that our mother will keep the food ready, keep the house clean, and will always be ready to help us whenever we need anything. We never consider that she is a human being and may need some rest or appreciation.

7. **One should not assume that he or she knows everything about the individual.** Parents and teachers assume that they can understand everything about children. Even internal experiences such as pain and uneasiness are treated as well understood. This spoils the relationship and trust that the child can maintain for these adults. A child who is five years old and telling that he or she does not want to eat as he or she has stomach ache or an adolescent who dislikes a particular professional course are equally suffering, especially in the Indian scenario, only because parents do not trust them. Parents think that they have understood everything that happens with the child.

8. **Cutting others' communication should not be practiced.** Over eagerness to respond and not allowing the other person to fully express his or her feelings, emotions, and ideas is detrimental to human relations. Here, the student, offspring, or junior will stop freely expressing his or her own ideas and emotions. As a consequence, communication and interpersonal relations deteriorate.

9. **One should not hurt anyone unnecessarily.** Aggression and insulting anyone is detrimental to human relations. At home, school, college, or office, one should try to avoid insulting anyone. If one is assertive, one would also be able to give orders appropriately without insulting anybody. This increases the opportunity to develop good interpersonal relations.

10. **One should take care not to disclose someone else's secretes to others.** This results in complete loss of trust and dependability. The person is hurt and feels insulting and awkward when he or she understands that his or her secret is made public.

11. **One should not use "if I were u" sentences.** When we use such language, it is derogatory to self-esteem of the other person. It obviously means that the other individual is not capable of solving his or her problems and you are wiser to understand what should be done. It is indirectly insulting the person. Avoiding such statements is better.

12. **No unnecessary expression of superiority or inferiority complex should be depicted.** Inferiority or superiority complex will alter an individual's communication as well as interpersonal relations. Do not pretend things, show off, or unnecessarily underestimate others. At the same time, if a person always devaluates one self and underestimates self, or feels inferior, there will be no open discussion as there will be many things to hide.

13. **Recognition seeking needs to be avoided.** If an individual is interested in talking about self and own achievements, and not interested in anything about the other person, communication will be ineffective and interpersonal relations will be so unpleasant that the other person may avoid the communicator. In Chapter 6, we discussed this in detail. Recognition seeking results from the fear that others will underestimate that individual. Such an individual keeps telling about his or her significant and insignificant achievements where it is redundant to do so.

 Deena came to see her friend Uma as she was not well and was admitted to the hospital. Immediately after entering the room, Deena started talking about her visit to America and her future plans regarding going abroad for higher education. It was overwhelming for her and she described it in detail. After half an hour when she got up and was about to leave, she casually asked Uma as to why was she admitted to the hospital and remarked that she had forgotten to ask more about it since she came. Then she left the room after five minutes.

14. **No emotional abuse should be practiced.** Emotional abuse and taking undue advantages of others' emotional state may spoil interpersonal relations. Chotu was just 8 years old when he was threatened by his mother that if he does not study hard, she will set herself on fire. Once when he was studying and she was threatening as usual, her sari actually caught fire. She died in the accident. This is a true story of a child's emotional abuse.

 Sheela was emotionally upset as she lost her mother. She used to weep a lot and was apathetic. Rahul was supporting her and helping her in daily activities. He used to tell her important information about various submissions and other activities. Sheela was a student representative and was invited by university authorities for some meeting. Rahul told the authorities that Sheela will not be attending it even without consulting her. This is a clear example of taking undue advantage of others' emotional state.

"I will not eat if you do not come to meet me" type of conversation is beyond the limit of maintaining good interpersonal relations.

15. **Holding others responsible for our own problems is a similar malpractice.** Whatever we do, we have to face the consequences. While making a decision, we have to be more focused and think coolly. Afterward, even if we blame others we are not capable of going back and change the past. It only disturbs our relations with that individual.

16. **One should avoid gossiping.** Discussing half-truths and wishful thinking along with some unpleasant expectations is very unfair. It is a very effective way of spreading some unfair information about an individual. However, it should be remembered that the speaker also damages his or her own image in that type of communication though he or she wants to spoil someone else's. There is every probability that the person concerned may come to know about it and the consequences are detrimental to the relations. If you do not know something, do not discuss it with others.

17. **One should not criticize anyone without offering a solution.** If you cannot help an individual, you should not criticize him or her. It is very easy to use derogatory remarks about others without thinking properly about the options they have.

Pandit stays with his mother who is ill. He locks the door and keeps her alone inside and goes for his office and college. Anyone will feel pity for her and start criticizing Pandit. However, no one thinks about how to solve the problem. He has no relatives to support him neither is he earning enough money to pay for an attendant. He has to earn and attend college. There is no way out.

18. **Do not expect others to do as per your expectations.** If we keep on insisting that others should accept every advice given by you without considering the consequences, it is taxing for them. If this happens repeatedly, it will introduce disturbances in relations and may negatively affect it forever.

Leena has completed her graduation in health sciences. Due to some health problems she is suffering from anemia. As she has intolerance to iron intake, she cannot consume anything having direct source of iron like some specific vegetables, dates, food cooked in an iron container, or medicines having iron. Her father who is a lawyer insists that she should consume some medicines which he recommends. Once when she denied, he was irritated and stopped enquiring about her health since then, even when she faces different problems and needs his help. His argument is always the same that she is not obeying him and not going according to his advice.

If it is only due to age or status that one expects others to follow his or her directions, then that is not going to help. As in the above example, Leena knows better than her father.

19. **Accept that you cannot change others' behavior but reaction to it.** There is no way to change others' behavior. However, we can change our reaction to it. If a person is insensitive to our psychological needs, we say that he or she is self-oriented, rude, and so on; we should not over react to it but keep cool and forget it. If it is his or her regular style of interacting with you, then you should be prepared to bear that and should not get disturbed. If a boss has the habit of screaming loudly and irritating the staff, the subordinates should learn how to be calm. Otherwise a lot of mental energy will be wasted.

20. **Accept reality.** In interpersonal relations, one has to accept the reality as it is. If an individual has Asperger's disease, he or she will not be bothered about others' emotions and may not be able to develop empathy. If this is so, then all the related people should accept and remember his or her limitations. While interacting with him or her they should not expect something that is difficult to accomplish.

21. **Be honest.** Trust depends on honesty. In any interpersonal relation, honesty plays a crucial role. Sincere expressions of honest feelings enhance dependability and prediction of support.

22. **Praise occasionally.** Deepak got first class in his final year engineering. He was very happy and excited. He called his father to communicate the results, and his father did not even congratulate him. He immediately started talking about some other work that Deepak was supposed to do for him.

    Praise increases intimacy and guarantees that the other person accepts and appreciates us. This in turn, increases pleasantness and comfort in any relation.

23. **Accept your mistakes.** Jaya told Amita that she is getting engaged and requested that it should be a secret. Out of excitement, Amita told it to other friends and Jaya was upset. Amita realized it and immediately expressed an apology. If we accept our mistakes, it helps maintaining good relations.

24. **Meta communication.** This has also been reported by researchers to be very effective for improving communication. It is communication about communication. Like for example, "your style of talking is declaring that you are very much stressed," or "when I talked about the issue, I was angry," or something like that is very effective to improve communication. Meta communication occurs when people communicate about their communication. Like they give verbal or nonverbal instructions about how their message should be understood. Such remarks like "I was only kidding" or "it makes me uncomfortable to talk about that" are signals as to how to interpret the message. It may or may not be explicit. The ability to use meta communication is beneficial for resolving a conflict and increasing awareness about the effectiveness of own communication. If feedback is given in a polite way, it may improve the communication of the sender.

25. **Initiating a difficult conversation.** If interpersonal relations are strained, due care should be taken to initiate a conversation. Some guidelines are given by experts for initiating a difficult conversation. One has to respect the individual as he or she is. Treat him or her as a worthy individual. Being gentle and kind and using soft language helps in such a situation. Take into consideration the person's age and the ability to understand.

If one is communicating threat verbally and nonverbally, the communication will result in an unpleasant situation. It is necessary to avoid a confrontational style.

When the other person is extremely upset, one should avoid talking to the person. One should not communicate when the individual is under the influence of a substance or alcohol. One should communicate directly and briefly. Labelling must be avoided since it hurts the individual and is associated with social stigma.

You may need to discuss the issue in several sessions gradually leading to an appropriate direction. One has to be consistent and patient in expressing concern without exerting undue pressure. Explaining the exact point to be discussed becomes essential. Instead of blaming the individual, we should talk about our own feelings.

In a group situation, one should try to understand each person who speaks. One should listen carefully. Let others finish without interruption. Be patient. Acknowledge that you have understood what others have said. Reflect and paraphrase if appropriate.

We should try to understand what is being said. We should not evaluate it. Without expecting any explanation, justification, or expressing disagreement, focusing on its meaning helps. One should decide what exactly one wants to express and one should have the courage to say that.

To sum up, it can be said that criticism and evaluation, contempt and hostility, defensiveness, stonewalling, unresolved complaints, lack of appreciation, lack of responsibility, and emotional disconnection are also major problems in maintaining good interpersonal relations. It is essential to accept and respect, maintain reciprocity-relationship enhancement, persistence, and continuity for enhancing relationships.

Lack of these things affects negatively verbal and nonverbal skills, negotiation skills, problem-solving, assertiveness, decision-making and last but not the least mental health.

It may also results in family violence, abuse—emotional, physical, and sexual—aversion regarding sex or relations, apathy contempt, hostility, underachievement, and various adjustment problems.

22.8   RELATING TO OTHERS IN VIRTUAL WORLD

The explosion of knowledge has affected human life tremendously. Mobile phones and smartphones have affected human relations to a substantial extent. Due to the advancement of science and technology, most of the educated adults and adolescents are interacting with people without meeting them in person only with the help of various gadgets. All of us are indirectly related to the world by watching electronic media like television. Though the benefits are obvious, ill effects are neglected. Hence, let us discuss some important issues and research findings regarding it.

22.8.1   MODERN WAYS OF COMMUNICATION

In the present era of technological advancement, new ways of communication are becoming more popular. They are:

1. Oral communication on mobile phones
2. Writing electronic mails
3. Video chatting
4. Writing messages on mobile phones
5. Updates from social websites
6. WhatsApp, Wechat, Viber, Skype, and similar other messengers for sending written and oral messages, pictures, and photographs, and for video conferencing.

Mobile phones are capable of providing many more facilities like one can see the phone number and the picture of the receiver, can record the name, easily record the whole conversation, can change the voice of the individual, can insert some sounds to create an impression that the speaker is in a hotel, at college, on the road, and so on. One can transfer the phone from one number to another, can have conferencing, send and receive SMS, MMS. With the help of net connection on phone, one can buy things and send gifts; banking services also can be availed with it. One can get free books, journals, and encyclopedias on smartphones.

These communication strategies have their own style, advantages and disadvantages, as well as new expressions that have emerged in due course of time. The simplest example is the smileys used in SMS, mails, and chats to communicate many things with the help of small faces, human figures, and gestures. Voice smiles are also used to express various different ideas and hints. Smileys that one is feeling happy or unhappy, those indicating that one has to terminate the conversation, that is, saying "bye bye" are very common. Group messages can be sent and it may save time and energy. Pictures can be sent to the receiver which may be very effective in explaining the message.

Writing e-mail is a very popular method of formal and informal messages. As it is very quick, it becomes beneficial. One can write and receive mails from all over the world.

Video chatting also has all the advantages of face–to-face communication and one is capable of getting all nonverbal cues.

An SMS is generally written in very brief and, hence, there are many shortcuts which are becoming universal. The simple example is, "t.c.," "g.m.," and "g.n." which mean take care, good morning, and good night, respectively.

Social websites like Facebook, Twitter, and Orkut are one-way or two-way communications. If one is just reading the updates, it becomes a one-way communication, and if one is interested in writing something, in response to, it becomes a two-way communication.

The possibility of anonymity or fake identity is one of the major problems of Internet communication. Anyone can tell lies and establish a specific relationship with the other. Greater anonymity, more time for creating and editing verbal message, more control over self-expression, and impression management are the basic characteristics of this interaction.

As adolescents and young adults are more involved in Internet activities, their lives and psychological health is affected due to it. Many researchers, parents, teachers, educationists, and psychologist are concerned about it. Internet addiction is considered as a clinical disorder or disease. China is the first country to recognize this addiction as a disorder. Addiction is masked and overtly justifiable due to many uses of the Internet.

Though a lot of research has been done in advanced countries, comparatively less research has been done in India. It is reported by researchers that more Internet use is seen in younger population from 12 to 18 years of age. On an average, 5–15 hours Internet use is seen among these youngsters. Male members are more addicted to Internet use. The correlates of excess Internet use are all detrimental to the individual in the long run. These are:

1. **Antisocial behavior—**In India, it is reported that various types of antisocial behaviors are related to excess Internet use. Cybercrimes, fake identity, illegal marriages, circulating pornographic information, as well as sexually exploiting ladies are included in that. Such type of antisocial behavior is tremendously increasing in recent years.

2. **Poor contact with reality and pseudo coping mechanisms—**Continuously getting involved in the virtual world and with people in the virtual world reduces interaction with immediate environment and stimuli around the individual. As a consequence, contact with reality reduces and that is detrimental to one's mental health. To combat stress one needs to tackle with the problems as they are in reality. However, in case of these individuals fake or pseudocoping mechanisms are used and it leads to poor coping.

3. **Low self-esteem—**Internet addiction leads to low self-esteem, decreased confidence, and poor self-awareness. Distorted self-identity emerges which leads to more psychological problems.

4. **Poor interpersonal communication—**The time and energy utilized for developing and maintaining interpersonal communication with the real world reduces tremendously due to Internet addiction.

   Lack of social skills, loneliness, and social anxiety leads to serious personality disorders. As a consequence, decreased communication with family members and friends results and the social circle reduces. Social isolation also results in extreme cases.

   Asad was busy chatting with his friend when his mother called him and told him that his grandmother was not feeling well and some medicines were needed immediately. She requested him to go and get these medicines as soon as possible. Asad only overheard the message and even without any eye contacts with his mother he nodded his head. He continued chatting and gradually forgot that he has to go somewhere. After 10 minutes when mother came again she was shocked to see that he was still there.

5. **Compulsive behavior is otherwise seen in abnormal individuals**—In case of Internet addicts, it is seen that they very often open their message boxes and expect that someone must have written a message to them.

Madhuri generally devotes at least one hour to messaging immediately after she gets up in the morning and before she goes to bed at late night. Still, Madhuri opens her WhatsApp every 10 minutes even when she is in the lecture room and the lecturer is teaching, she is studying, or she is with her friends. She just cannot resist that temptation though she knows that no one will be sending messages every now and then.

6. **Vulnerability**—A lack of satisfaction and loss of hope are the possible outcomes of excessive Internet use. Ill health, unemployment, and academic instability are the correlates, and temporary escape is achieved again by excess Internet use.

7. **Depression**—In case of Internet addiction, the individual is totally detached with the family and community and may experience depression. If the person cannot use the Internet, anxiety and depression are the more common outcomes.

8. **Sexual addiction**—Anonymous sex chat and pornography leads to sexual addiction with the help of Internet. This may lead to various sex-related crimes and maladjustment in general. Online sex increases the possibility of having pervert behavior.

More ill effects are associated with meeting people online, form relationship seeking emotional support, chat rooms, interactive games, and so on. Abstinence reaction is a syndrome when use of net is stopped. It includes dysphoria, insomnia, emotional instability, and irritability. They even neglect their health.

Psychotherapy such as cognitive behavior therapy, life style changes, and more psychological support from the family help these addicts.

22.8.2 Effects of Television on Children and Adolescents

Television has been the most pervasive medium of mass communication all over the world. Its influence cannot be underestimated for individuals at any stage of life. Psychologists are considering television as one of the six important socialization agents—parents, siblings, friends, school, personal experiences, and television since 1990.

It has been reported that in childhood, time spent in watching television ranged from 20 to 77 hours a week. It is equivalent to 5 years in first 20 years. Approximately 75 percent children watch television during evening and 35 percent also watch at late night. The estimate of time spent in watching television varies greatly with age, gender, socioeconomic status, intelligence, and many other factors. In general, it is well accepted today that children devote more time on television as compared to school and related activities. In research, it is seen that 84 percent of children mention television watching as their favorite activity. They watch television with full devotion. From age 3 to 9, 14to 96 percent children watch television regularly. Researchers have reported that children's preference is to watch adult programs and advertisements and the purpose of watching is entertainment and relaxation.

Heavy television viewing affects the whole nervous system, diminishing efficiency of brain, sense organs, and general vigor and energy. In the long run, it may lead to many health problems. In psychological research, 80 percent of research has been done on violence. It indicates statistically significant positive correlation of human aggression and heavy television viewing. Researchers have classified various uses of television into four fold categories, that is, cognition, diversion, social utility, and withdrawal. Cognition includes the knowledge of current events, and general information. In diversion, stimulation, relaxation, and emotional release are important. Providing conversational currency and maintaining parasocial relationships are the basic social utilities. Avoiding people and work, and isolating people from each other are the advantages in withdrawal. By and large, girls and women like to watch stories regarding human relations and families, or stories related to women's lives. However, men and boys like to watch action, sports, and violence. Young children like watching cartoon films and action dramas.

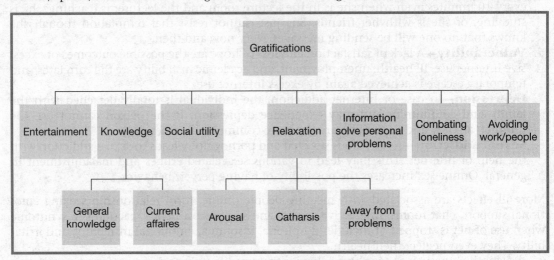

Effects of television are overlapping and interdependent. Inherent effects are common effects of watching TV irrespective of program contents, and program-specific effects are related to the contents of the program. Some effects are psychological and some are physical. Some are direct and some are indirect. Effects are also classified as immediate effects and long-term effects. In physical effects, general arousal results in excitement among viewers which may lead to a socially inappropriate behavior. Watching television results in simple, constant, repetitive, and ambiguous visual stimuli which reduces alertness and the capacity of higher cognitive process. Creativity is hampered due to heavy television watching. Researchers have reported that immediately after one starts watching television, brain waves change from more alert beta waves to alpha waves. It decreases the efficiency of left brain regarding logical thinking, analysis, reasoning, and similar higher order processes. These effects are similar to the effects of sensory deprivation for many hours. Right brain deals with noncritical lower order processing such as color, image, music, and emotions. Long-term effects include lack of sleep, fatigue, lack of concentration, inaccurate perception, low confidence, obesity, and general ill health. Substantial research has been and is being done on psychological effects of television viewing. It directly affects attitudes, values, social interactions, and expectations regarding life as well as regarding interpersonal relations. Heavy television viewing is related to violence and aggression, academic underachievement, distorted perceptions, and poor interpersonal relations. The individual neglects even significant others and communication gets hampered. To sum up, excessive involvement in virtual communication and relations are detrimental to real-world relations. It affects mental health of the individual. One should find out a balance point where one should get all the benefits of advancement of science and technology, but should be able to protect one's homeostasis.

22.9 SUMMARY

This chapter discusses in detail the important interpersonal relations in human life. In brief, it tries to encompass the nature of interpersonal relations and depicts their importance in human life. Whole life of the individual, satisfaction, happiness as well as mental health depend on interpersonal relations. Indian culture gives utmost importance to interpersonal relations in family. Hence, it needs to be understood properly. Various factors that affect interpersonal relations are considered for developing and maintaining good interpersonal relations.

In day-to-day life situations, we take things for granted and communicate and behave in such way that may be detrimental to interpersonal relations. Strategies for maintaining good interpersonal relations are to be learnt and followed to enhance them.

In contemporary world, virtual relations are influencing human life substantially, both positively and negatively. A balance point needs to be found out.

QUESTIONS

1. Discuss the nature of interpersonal relationships and its importance in human life.
2. Describe the different types of interpersonal relations and their dimensions.
3. Explain the factors affecting interpersonal relations.
4. What are the strategies to maintain good interpersonal relations?
5. What are the advantages and disadvantages of relating to others in the virtual world?

APPLICATION ORIENTATION

1. Draw a diagram depicting your relations defined in terms psychological support and unconditional acceptance from maximum to minimum. It should not consider how they should be, or what should it be as per the social expectations.
2. Select any two factors affecting interpersonal relations, for example, age. Select two individuals from extreme ends of the continuum and jot down the difference between your interactions with them.
3. Introspect and enlist the errors that you generally make while interacting with others, intentionally or unintentionally. How would you correct these errors?
4. Record how often you are interested in giving and receiving a feedback? What are your general emotional reactions to any negative feedback given to you? Can you improve your style?
5. How much time do you spend in watching television and on web? If you do not do that, what activities do you do?

SUGGESTED READINGS

Beverly, E. (2006). *Healing your emotional self*. NJ: John Wiley & Sons.

Cushnie, P. (1988). Conflict: developing resolution skills. *AORN Journal, 3*, 734–745.

Brown, R., and Gaertner, S. (ed.). (2001). *Intergroup processes*. Oxford: Blackwell Publishers.

Knapp, M. L. (1984). *Interpersonal communication and human relationships*. Boston, MA: Allyn & Bacon.

Mulac, A. (1998). Gender linked language effect. In D. J. Canary and K. Dindia (eds), *Sex differences and similarities in communication*. Mahwah, NJ: Erlbaum.

Operrario, D., and Fiske, S. (2001). Stereotypes: Content, structures, processes, and context. In R. Brown and S. Gaertner (eds.). *Intergroup processes*. Oxford: Blackwell Publishers.

Pepinsky, H. B. and and Pepinsky, P. N. (1954). *Counselling theory and practice*. New York: Ronald Press.

Rubin, H. R., Chen, X., and Hymel, S. (1993). Socioemotional Characteristics of withdrawn and aggressive children. *Merrill-Palmer Quarterly, 39*(4), 518–534.

Trenhold, S., and Jensen, A. (2000). *Interpersonal communication*, 4th ed. Belmont, CA: Wadsworth.

BIBLIOGRAPHY

Allport, G. (1979). *The Nature of Prejudices*. New York: Perseus Books.

Baron, R. A., Byrne, D., & Branscombe, N.R. (2008). *Social Psychology*. New Delhi: Pearson Education.

Berk, L. E. (2006). *Child Development* (7th ed.). New Delhi: Pearson education.

Beverly, E. (2006). *Healing Your Emotional Self*. St Hoboken, NJ: John Wiley and sons.

Bishop, S. (2010). *Develop your Assertiveness*, New Delhi: Kogan Page.

Black A. and C. (2009). *Assert Yourself: How to Find Your Voice and Make Your Mark*. London: A& C Black [E book].

Boniwell, I. (2012). *Positive Psychology in a Nutshell*. New York: Open University Press; McGraw-Hills.

Bowden, T. B. (2007). *50 Psychology Classics*. London: Nicholas Brealey publishing.

Brown, R., & Gaertner, S. (eds). (2001). *Intergroup Processes*. Oxford: Blackwell.

Burns, R. B. (1989). *The Self Concept in Theory, Measurement and Behavior*. London: Longman.

Caruso, D. R., & Salovey , P.(2004). *The Emotionally Intelligent Manager:How to Develop and Use the Four Key Emotional Skills of Leadership*. San Francisco, CA: Jossey Bass; John Wiley and sons.

Covey, S. R. (1997). *The 7 habits of Highly Effective People*. London: Franklin Covey Pocket Books.

Davis, M. (2000). *Relaxation and Stress Reduction Workbook* (6th ed.). Oakland: New Harbinger.

Dovidio, J. F., & Gaertner, S. L. (2010). "Intergroup Bias". In S.T. Gilbert and G. Lindzey (eds), *The Handbook of Social Psychology* (5th ed., vol. 2). New York: Wiley.

Drafke, M. W., & Kossen, S. (1998). *The Human Side of Organization* (7th ed.). Boston, MA: Addison-Wesley.

Elliot, S. N., Kratochwill, T. R., Cook, J. L., & Travers, J. F. (2000). *Educational Psychology: Effective Teaching, Effective Learning* (3rd ed.). New Delhi: McGraw-Hills.

Eugene, M. (2000). *Business Psychology and Organizational Behavior* (3rd ed.). Sussex: Psychology Press Limited.

Eysenck, H. J, Arnold, W. J., & Meili, R. (1975). *Encyclopedia of Psychology* (3rd ed.). Fontana: Collins.

Feldman, R. S. (2008). *Essentials of Understanding Psychology*. New Delhi: Tata McGraw-Hills.

———. (2010a). *The Life Span Development*. New Delhi: Pearson Education.

———. (2010b). *Discovering the Life Span*. New Delhi: Dorling Kindersley Publications.

———. (2011). *Understanding Psychology* (10th ed.). New York: McGraw-Hills.

Franzoi, S. (2003). *Social Psychology*. Boston, MA: McGraw-Hill.

Galotti, K. M. (2014). *Cognitive Psychology: In and Out of the Laboratory* (5th ed.). Minnesota: SAGE.

Halonen, J.S, & Santrock, J. W. (1999). *Psychology: Context and Application*. New York: McGraw-Hills College.

Hammer, W. D. (2015). *Psychology Applied to Modern Life: Adjustment in 21st Century* (11th ed.). Stamford, CT: Cengage Learning.

Helgeson,V. S. (2006). *Psychology of Gender* (2nd ed.). New Delhi: Pearson-Education.

Hunt, R. R., & Ellis, H. C. (2006). *Fundamentals of Cognitive Psychology*. New Delhi: Tata McGraw-Hills.

Hurlock, E. B. (1979). *Developmental Psychology* (4th ed.). New Delhi: Tata McGraw-Hills.

Janasz, S.D., Karen, D., & Schneider, B. (2006). *Interpersonal Skills in Organizations* (2nd ed.). New Delhi: McGraw-Hills.

Kalat, J. W., & Shiota, M. N. (2007). *Emotion*. Belmont, CA: Thomson Wadsworth.

Knapp, M. L. (1984). *Interpersonal Communication and Human Relationships*. Boston, MA: Allyn & Bacon.

LeDoux, J. (1996). *The Emotional Brain: The Mysterious Underpinnings of Emotional Life*. New York: Touch-stone.

Lewis, J. M., Haviland, J., & Barrett, L. F. (eds). (2008). *Handbook of Emotions* (3rd ed.). New York: Guilford.

Mangal, S. K. (2002). *Advanced Educational Psychology*. New Delhi: Prentice Hall of India.

Maslow, A. H. (1970). *Motivation and Personality* (2nd ed.). New York: Harper and Row.

Mcentarffer, R., & Weseley, A. (2012). *J. Barron's AP Psychology* (5th ed.). Barron's Educational Series. First E book.

McKenna, E. (2000). *Business Psychology and Organizational Behaviour* (3rd ed.). New York, PA: Taylor and Francis.

McManus, J. (2006). *Leadership*. New Delhi: Butterworth Heinemann.

Morgan, C. T., King, R. A., Weis, J. R., & Scooper, J. (1993). *Introduction to Psychology*. New Delhi: Tata Mc-Graw Hills.

Operrario, D., & Fiske, S. (2001). "Stereotypes: Content, Structures, Processes, and Context." In R. Brown & S. Gaertner (eds), *Intergroup Processes*. Oxford : Blackwell.

Peale, N. V. (2006). *Power of Positive Thinking*. The Quality Book Club. E book.

Prior, V., & Glaser, D. (2006). *Understanding Attachment and Attachment Disorders: Theory, Evidence and Practice*. Child and Adolescent Mental Health. London: RCPRTU.

Pruitt, D. M. D. (2000). *Your Adolescent: Emotional, Behavioral and Cognitive Development from Early Adolescence Through the Teen Years*. New York: Imprint Harper paper backs.

Quillam, S. (2008). *Positive Thinking*. New Delhi: DK Publishers.

Reed, S. K. (2010). *Cognition: Theories and Applications*. London: Cengage.

Reevy, G. M. (2011). *Encyclopedia of Emotions*. California: Greenwood.

Schultz, D. P., & Schultz, S. E. (2010). *Psychology and Work Today* (10TH ed.). New York: Prentice Hall.

Solso, R. L. (2006). *Cognitive Psychology*. New Delhi: Pearson Education.

Spielberger,C. D. (ed.). (1972). *Anxiety: Current Trends in Theory and Research* (vol. 2, pp. 291–337). New York: Academic Press.

Sqilliam, S. (2008). *Positive Thinking*. New Delhi: DK Publishers.

Strongman, K. T. (2006). *Applying Psychology to Everyday Life: A Beginner's Guide*. New Zealand: John Wiley and Sons.

Sternberg, R. J. (2009). *Applied Cognitive Psychology: Perceiving, Learning, and Remembering*. London: Cengage.

Sternberg, R. J., & Lubart, T. I. (1999). "The Concept of Creativity: Prospects and Paradigms." In R.J. Sternberg (ed.). *Handbook of Creativity*. London: Cambridge University Press.

Sternberg, R. J. (2006). "The Nature of Creativity." *Creativity Research Journal, 18*(1), 87–98.

Subba Rao, P. (2011). *Personnel and Human Resource Management*. Mumbai: Himalaya Publishing House.

Taifel, H. (1982). *Social Identity and Intergroup Relations*. Cambridge: Cambridge University Press.

Trenhold, S., & Jensen, A. (2000). *Interpersonal Communication* (4th ed.). Belmont, CA: Wadsworth.

Wade, C., & Travis, C. (2006). *Psychology*. New Delhi: Pearson Education.

INDEX